Unified Theories of Cognition

The William James Lectures, 1987

Unified Theories of Cognition

Allen Newell

Harvard University Press
Cambridge, Massachusetts
London, England

First Harvard University Press paperback edition, 1994

Library of Congress Cataloging in Publication Data

Newell, Allen.
Unified theories of cognition / Allen Newell.
p. cm. — (The William James lectures ; 1987)
Includes bibliographical references.
ISBN 0-674-92099-6 (alk. paper) (cloth)
ISBN 0-674-92101-1 (pbk.)
1. Cognition.   2. Cognitive psychology—Philosophy.   3. Cognitive
science—Philosophy.   I. Title. II. Series.
BF311.N496   1990   90-33423
153—dc20   CIP

For Noël

Special Acknowledgments

John Laird

Paul Rosenbloom

Kathleen Carley

Bonnie John

Rex Flynn

Thad Polk

Olin Shivers

David Steier

Gregg Yost

Preface

During the spring of 1987 I delivered the William James Lectures at Harvard University. This book is the record of the lectures. It puts forward a thesis—that psychology is ready for unified theories of cognition—and bends all the lectures to the end of supporting that thesis.

It was indeed an honor to be asked to deliver the William James Lectures. I was actually awed by the number of people who came to the initial lecture—the large auditorium was filled to overflowing. It put me in mind of the great physiologist Charles Sherrington, who gave "The Integrative Action of the Nervous System" as the Silliman Lectures at Yale in 1904. It is reported that his first lecture attracted a large and enthusiastic crowd, but by the last lecture there was an audience of just four people hanging on. This gave me pause, but it also helped me to set my own goals for having at least five people at the end of my lectures. What's more, Sherrington's lectures were the basis for one of the great classics in neurophysiology (Sherrington, 1906), so I assuaged my anxieties with the thought that I would have a second chance, no matter how the lectures themselves turned out. It did not occur to me then that a second chance implies, as the day the night, a second round of anxieties. It occurs to me now, as I ship this book out to the world.

There is, of course, no typical William James Lecturer—it even seems somewhat odd to entertain the thought. However odd, I am certainly not it. My basic education is in physics and mathematics. My graduate education is in industrial administration. Part of me is grounded in applications and engineering. I've lived all my academic life in a computer science department, and before that I was immersed in the original think tank (the RAND Corporation). These are not quite your average specs for a William James Lecturer.

Averages don't count for much in lectureships, though. So it is fitting that, while being untypically odd, I am simultaneously untypically close to another William James Lecturer. I speak, of course, of my once and forever colleague, Herb Simon, distinguished predecessor in giving the William James Lectures in 1963. I am not so different from him, despite the fact that his demographics differ from mine on almost every point. In something of a panic, I acquired from him his lecture notes and looked them over. Was there anything new and different for me to say? I believe there is, and Herb himself has played a large part in making it so (Newell, 1989). It is not often that two colleagues get to deliver a major lectureship on the same topic. It adds both to the honor and the obligation.

Prime issues to be faced in writing up a series of lectures are depth and completeness. In prospect, eight lectures seemed an eternity of opportunity to lay out in detail a coherent thesis, in my case on unified theories of cognition. But, in the giving, it became all too apparent that I rushed from topic to topic, like the Mad Hatter of *Alice*. Almost from the start, I entertained the fantasy of turning the lectures into a treatise, in which I would hammer home each point in infinite detail to construct a solid . . . (my imagery failed me here, but it was certainly going to be a solid something). But reality prevails. Such a project would stretch out into the future in a great forward recursion, each new result from the research of my colleagues and myself inducing yet one more expansion of the book.

Noël, my wife, also has a fantasy. Long ago, I promised her that I would dedicate to her alone my first single-authored book. Her fantasy is that she will never get her dedication, because I will never get such a book finished. I need coauthors to curb my picky penchant for perfection. Indeed, my promise was made to her on the occasion (if such it can be called) of not finishing an earlier book.

The resolution of this issue, completely obvious all along to everyone but myself, was to cleave as closely as I could tolerate to the form in which the lectures were given. This is what I have done. There has been a certain amount of tuning up of some of the topics, where a little more scholarship and a little more care helps the argument. After all, in the hurly-burly of the lectorial moment, a certain amount of violence occurs to the fine structure of truth. But the chapters here follow exactly the lectures, and I worked from transcripts of them. (Videotapes are available from the Department of Psychology, William James Hall, Harvard University.) Where there has been a direct advance in research on the examples used in the lectures, however, I have incorporated the new systems and results to keep up with the state of the art. I could certainly do no less, though I could feel myself slipping into the great forward recursion.

As will become apparent, the vehicle for the thesis of these lectures is a system called Soar. Behind that system is a group of colleagues, situated principally at three universities, Carnegie Mellon University, the University of Michigan, and the Information Science Institute of the University of Southern California. These are indeed the friends who have provided that "little help," made famous by the Beatles, that allowed me to get by. They made the lectures possible. Debarred by my deeply felt obligation to dedicate this book to Noël from acquiring either coauthors or a full collection of dedications, I have chosen to list them separately on an acknowledgment page facing this preface. But I need also to tell the story of that "little help" and just how much it mattered.

Soar has its roots in thirty years of research on the nature of artificial intelligence (AI) and human cognition. A number of basic concepts have been explored along the way, prominent among them being problem spaces, goal-subgoal hierarchies, weak methods for problem solving, and production systems. These concepts and their operational counterparts have become staples of both cognitive psychology and AI. Soar was created in the early 1980s by John Laird, Paul Rosenbloom, and myself as another try at putting together a complete system that integrated all these elements and learning too, as it turned out. (See the preface of Laird, Rosenbloom, and Newell, 1988, for more detail on Soar's genesis and the roles of the various participants.) It was natural—even necessary—that we focus the initial efforts on strictly functional aspects, which is to say, the AI aspects. But the need to cast Soar as a theory of human cognition was always on our future agenda. However much Soar was described as an AI system, it was compounded of mechanisms that had strong, established validity as elements of psychological theory.

The invitation to give the William James Lectures provided the opportunity to pursue the conversion of Soar to a full-bodied psychological theory. As the chapters of this book reveal, it was also the occasion to rethink more generally the current status of cognitive science and where it should be going. What emerged was the general thesis about unified theories of cognition, with Soar playing the role of exemplar rather than a theory ready to compete on an even footing with other theories. But the effort internally (at home, so to speak) was to convert Soar to a cognitive theory. That is where my friends came in.

To "convert" an existing AI system to a cognitive theory seems perhaps a rather strange operation. In the event, there turned out to be two activities. The first can only be described as contemplation—contemplate Soar in the light of everything I knew about human cognition, to see what fits and what doesn't, how the mechanisms fare, and what role they play in explaining psychological phenomena. Though Soar presented itself as a fixed set of mechanisms, these were open to adaptation under the press of becoming a theory of human cognition. This act of contemplation was my principal occupation during much of 1986, whatever might have seemed to be the case from my daily appearance. The second activity was to attempt to use Soar as a theory of cognition to model and explain in detail specific psychological phenomena and data in a wide range of domains: in short, to exercise Soar. That was also to be my task. Alas, the act of contemplation took hold of me and late fall of 1986 arrived with no exercising accomplished, but with the first lecture scheduled for the coming February, only a few months away.

I did then what I had long promised myself never to do. I mobilized my graduate students, sidetracking them from their other research on Soar, each to take some domain of cognitive phenomena and help me apply Soar to that domain in an interesting way. Let me go the rounds of what was done, to give credit to each of these friends. Bonnie John and I mapped the stimulus-response compatibility results of her ongoing research into Soar and also the work on transcription typing (in Chapter 5). Olin Shivers and I produced a detailed Soar simulation of the early cryptarithmetic studies of Newell and Simon (1972) (in Chapter 7). Thad Polk and I initiated research on syllogistic reasoning and developed detailed simulation models of that phenomena (in Chapter 7). Gregg Yost and I developed an approach to natural-language comprehension in Soar so we could model the sentence verification studies of Clark and Chase (1972); and we extended this Soar system to taking instructions (in Chapter 7). Rex Flynn and I explored the issue of transition mechanisms in development and developed a Soar system that exhibited such transitions for the balance-beam task (in Chapter 8). Finally, Gregg Yost and I again extended the natural-language system so it did a little bit of language learning (in Chapter 8).

In each case an absolute deadline was given by the lecture on that particular topic. Results had to be in hand and integrated into the lecture by then. In each case, there could have been failure. The effort could have come up empty—either the Soar system would fail to work in time or, even more deadly, the psychology exhibited would be just plain wrong. In fact, each deadline was made, each piece of research succeeded (though often with only days and sometimes hours to spare). This was what I call real-time science. It is the "little help" I received from my friends. I owe my scientific life to them.

Other friends in the Soar community helped me understand Soar and its potential as a psychological theory. I have made explicit use of David Steier's work on algorithm design (in Chapter 4), of John Laird's examples of the blocks world (in Chapter 4), of Paul Rosenbloom and John Laird's work on data chunking (in Chapter 6), and of explorations with Kathleen Carley on applying Soar at the social level (Chapter 8). Finally, my obligation to John Laird and Paul Rosenbloom, my co-creators of Soar, for every chapter of this book should by now be apparent.

In 1986, the year of preparation, research on Soar was organized as a project distributed among three sites. Since then the Soar effort has grown into a substantial, but loosely organized, community of researchers with individuals and small groups at a number of additional institutions, including notably the University of Groningen in the Netherlands, with John Michon, and the Medical Research Council's Applied Psychology Unit in Cambridge, England, with Richard Young. These friends of course had only a little chance to help me in 1986, but they have been a source of sustenance since then, while the book has been in preparation.

And as we go the round of friends, we come back to Herb Simon. It is not enough to acknowledge him as my William James predecessor. Our many joint publications, starting in 1956, trace the degree to which Soar as a unified theory of cognition builds on Herb's ideas and research. As the years have progressed, each of us has worked increasingly with colleagues close to hand and our explicit collaborations have become less frequent. That has had no effect on our implicit collaboration on the nature of cognitive science and how it should progress. But, in fact, Herb has his reservations about Soar, which reflect a general skepticism about the fruitfulness of research into cognitive architectures—not that they aren't there, but that the scientific yield from discovering their nature isn't where the major scientific action is. That's fine with me; Herb still must share in the responsibility for a large number of the scientific ideas that are welded into Soar.

Soar is a creature of the CMU environment in cognitive science, or better said, in psychology, AI, and computer science. I do not normally like to think of science in terms of institutions—the "MIT school of AI" or the "CMU school of cognitive psychology." I hear these phrases and inwardly cringe. We all do science as best we know how, building on and relating it to the relevant science being done elsewhere, wherever elsewhere might be. But that does not keep me from recognizing and appreciating the rich interdisciplinary environment that has built up here at CMU, with its broadband connection between psychology and computer science. John Anderson, Pat Carpenter, Marcel Just, David Klahr, Jill Larkin, and Bob Siegler on the psychology side, Hans Berliner, Jaime Carbonell, Tom Mitchell, and Raj Reddy on the computer science side, and Kurt Van Lehn evenly between the two have all had their influence on my research and on Soar. I felt strongly enough about this community so that I repeated the William James Lectures at CMU in the fall of 1987. My friends there seemed to me an audience that was especially able both to appreciate and to react critically to the message of the lectures.

During the spring of 1987 I traveled back and forth to Harvard each week to give the lectures. As noted above, it was a good thing I stayed at home during the week, for there was much to do. My hosts at Harvard, Shep White and Bill Estes, along with Steve Kosslyn, Duncan Luce, and Phil Stone, made me feel welcome on each and every trip. Especially do I remember Pamela Murray, who made all the arrangements seem easy.

I owe a special note of thanks to the Information Science and Technology Office (ISTO) of DARPA, the Advanced Research Projects Agency of the Department of Defense. DARPA's special role in bringing computer science into existence during the 1960s and 70s is well known. ISTO has been the backbone of my own research support since 1962, almost thirty years. Its administrators have been extremely farsighted in their support, permitting me (and many others) to push the development of the field as we saw fit— just as long as we made things happen scientifically. Although they have never supported work in cognitive psychology programmatically, they have always understood it to be part of my research strategy. During the last five years the work on Soar as a unified theory has had additional support from the Office of Naval Research under the University Research Initiative of the Department of Defense. Thus, the development of this very basic psychological theory must be credited to the research funding of the Department of Defense, confounding a little, perhaps, the simplistic assignment of all defense-supported research exclusively to defense-related results.

Despite my best efforts, it has taken a while for the book to emerge from the lectures. During the interval various drafts have circulated among my friends and colleagues, well beyond the Soar community. I am grateful to all these people for the many comments offered along the way.

Both lectures and books require preparation, as every author knows, and for this project the two ran seamlessly into one another. I thank Betsy Herk, my secretary, for all the many ways she helped. I thank Kim Faught for doing the figures for my lecture transparencies and Clare Macdonald for reworking these figures for the book. Also thanks to Kate Schmit, a lady whom I've never met, but with whom I've traveled the full length of this manuscript. It was a very pleasant trip, despite all the crises I managed to create along the way. Kate was unflappable.

And last, to my wife, Noël. Here it is, the book dedicated to you. I cannot even conceive of what the last forty-six years of my life would have been like without you, much less the last four years giving birth to this book.

Contents

Unified Theories of Cognition

Introduction

$$\boxed{1}$$

If one is given the William James Lectures, one must do something with them. Not just summarize a past of research, not just reflect on the interconnections of things, but *do* something. I am going to urge on psychology unified theories of cognition. Stated in full:

> Psychology has arrived at the possibility of unified theories of cognition—theories that gain their power by positing a single system of mechanisms that operate together to produce the full range of human cognition.

> I do not say they are here. But they are within reach and we should strive to attain them.

This is the theme I wish to address. This is what I wished to do with my William James Lectures and what I intend to do in this book based on the lectures.

To provide some context, let me start with a bit of personal history. Almost twenty years ago I gave some comments on the papers at a Carnegie Symposium on Cognition on the topic of visual information processing, and my remarks were published as "You can't play 20 questions with nature and win" (Newell, 1973a). That paper has had a certain amount of play over the years. Many people have picked it up, each in a distinctive way. It expresses an important part of the attitudes that lie behind this current effort.

Let me recreate that situation. In 1972, it seemed to me that there had been a great accumulation of superb data in psychology, most but not all of it chronometric. It seemed to me, also, that the cognitive revolution was already well in hand and established. Yet, I found myself concerned about the theory psychology was developing. The scientists I was discussing at that conference included Bill Chase, Herb Clark, Lynne Cooper, Mike Posner, and Roger

Shepard—people I believed did the finest experimental work and thought most deeply about the results. Still, I was concerned about theory. I tried to make that point by noting that what psychologists mostly did for theory was to go from dichotomy to dichotomy. They would worry about whether the processing was serial or parallel, or whether practice was massed or distributed, and so on. Theoretical life in psychology seemed just a forever-long sequence of dichotomies. What's more, there never seemed to be any real resolution. That wasn't my notion of how psychology would get to a real theory even in the long term.

This paper has attained a mild notoriety (Allport, 1975; Baddeley, 1978; Fiske, 1986; Johnson-Laird, 1988a; Neisser, 1974; Wickens & Flach, 1988). Almost everyone who picked up on this paper has used it to signify that cognitive psychology was in trouble—to accentuate the negative message. I certainly wanted to capture the attention of my colleagues, but, as I said in the opening line of that paper, "I am a man who is half and half—half of me is quite content and half of me is half concerned." That is only one-quarter negative at worst.

I had something more in mind than just to complain. I described three ways that might move us toward the sort of theory I felt psychology needed. First, psychology could construct complete processing models. Second, it could take particular tasks and analyze all of the psychological phenomena involved in them. Third, it could apply a model of a single phenomenon to lots of diverse situations where that phenomenon arose. These suggestions were all ways of forcing ourselves away from general polar comparisons and toward theories that could deal with complex psychological situations.

I went further than just making general methodological suggestions. In the second half of my comments, published as a separate paper in the proceedings (Newell, 1973b), I laid out production systems as detailed models of the human control structure. Production systems had just emerged as an interesting program formalism for describing human problem-solving behavior (Newell & Simon, 1972, chap. 14). But control structures for detailed chronometric behavior were unexplored territory. Some theory of control was a necessary ingredient for detailed theories of cognitive mechanisms, and one which I took as an important move beyond the game of "twenty questions."

The William James Lectures, and this book, can be taken as

another installment of my response to my own earlier commentary. This is my attempt, at this particular historical moment, to help put psychological theory together. It is offered in a positive spirit. For me, it is the same spirit I had in the twenty-questions paper. But much has happened in the years since I gave that talk. Then, indeed, I *was* half and half. Now, though hardly yet completely content, I am convinced that psychology has matured to where another big forward step is possible.

That said, I can now lay out the plan for this introductory chapter. Since there is an entire book in the offing, its task is simply to describe the enterprise. I will first discuss briefly the nature of theories, so we have some kind of common ground. Then I will move on to what I mean by "unified theories of cognition." That will lead naturally into whether psychology is ready for unified theories. Finally, we will come to the task of the book in its entirety.

1.1. The Nature of Theories

Let's begin by examining some simple examples of theories that are already part of psychology. Each of these will show us something about the nature of psychological theory, which will lead us to a general view sufficient for our purposes.

1.1.1. Fitts' Law

Figure 1-1 shows some data that illustrate *Fitts' law* (Fitts, 1954). If a person moves a finger or pointer from one place to another, how long does it take? It turns out that the time varies as the logarithm of the ratio of the distance moved (D) to the size of the target region (S) to which the move must be made. As the figure shows, the data fit the law (the straight line) fairly well.

Fitts' law is extremely robust (Keele, 1986). It holds whether the movement is repeatedly made back and forth, which is the experiment that Fitts did, or a single movement from one place to another. It holds for finger or hand movements or for using a mouse to point to a CRT display. It holds for moving a leg or a foot, for guiding a pointer held in the teeth, and even for a person who is underwater or looking through a microscope and using a micromanipulator. Indeed, it is so neat, it is surprising that it doesn't show up in every first-year textbook as a paradigm example of a psychological quantitative law. After all, psychology doesn't have

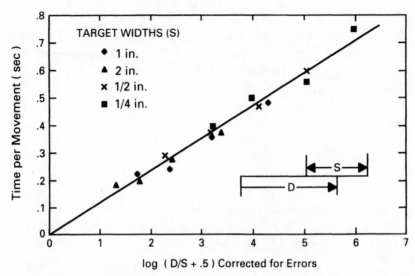

Figure 1-1. Fitts' law with typical data.

all that many great laws. But the law is almost never mentioned, and many psychologists hardly know of it at all.

A theory has been proposed to explain Fitts' law (Crossman & Goodeve, 1963; Keele, 1968). In a nutshell, the motor system has only limited accuracy when operating open loop, so that a sequence of visually based corrections are required to bring the movement within the target area. The system thus operates by simple feedback control. Consider being a distance X from a target of size S. X will initially be the distance D in the figure, but we need to consider the movement at any point along the way. Let the basic accuracy of the motor system be ε. Thus, the initial aim is only accurate enough to hit within a target of size εX. At some point during the flight, say X_1, the system can be re-aimed at the target to correct for any errors. At that point, the system can get within εX_1. This may still not be sufficient, so that at some X_2 a second correction can be made. This can continue until the pointer can be brought within the target region. We thus get a sequence of corrections:

$$X_0 = D$$

$$X_{n+1} = \varepsilon X_n$$

Stop when $X_n \leq S/2$

We can solve this simple recursion to find out how many corrections are required:

$$X_n = \varepsilon^n X_0$$

$$\varepsilon^n D \le S/2$$

Since the system stops as soon as it can, the inequality can be replaced by equality, and we can solve for n, the number of iterations:

$$n = - \frac{\log(2D/S)}{\log(\varepsilon)}$$

The number of iterations determines the *movement time* (*MT*) if we assume that the system makes corrections as quickly as it can, but that there is a certain delay, δ, to get around the loop of perceiving an error and making a correction:

$$MT = \delta n = - \frac{\delta\log(2D/S)}{\log(\varepsilon)}$$

This is essentially the equation that is plotted in Figure 1-1, and it gives a good fit. The fitted parameters correspond to an accuracy of about 10 percent and a delay about 200 milliseconds, both of them reasonable values.

So here we have a theory of a psychological phenomenon. I want to make three points about it. First, it is just a microtheory. It is a theory of just this one phenomenon. Second, you can really make predictions with it. You can calculate about how long it takes to make actual movements—and movements under field conditions as well (Card, English, & Burr, 1978). Third, it is an approximate theory. It is approximate in accuracy. Actually, Figure 1-1 shows one of the better fits; there is often a little more scatter. But it is also approximate in mechanism as well. It's rather easy to show that the particular theory can't be completely right. If actual trajectories are recorded, a correction is sometimes found, but never a series of converging corrections, one after another, as demanded by the theory. The microscopic structure of the derivation argument can't be quite right either. The observation of error must wait until the error develops, which takes some time and occurs only after the pointer is down course a ways; but by the time the correction is made the pointer is further along. Despite all this, the theory provides a useful way to think about the phenomena. For instance, it does reflect that the issue is not one of physical distance, but one of control; and it correctly predicts that if the movement has to occur without vision (blindfolding the person), then it will be much less accurate. The theory will remain useful, until it is replaced by a better one.

1.1.2. The Power Law of Practice

Here is a second example of a theory. Figure 1-2 shows another body of very well known data, taken from Seibel (1963). This is a *1,023-choice reaction time* task. A person is faced with ten lights above ten buttons for the ten fingers, one below each light. At a trial, a pattern of lights comes up and the person presses the corresponding set of buttons—striking the corresponding chord. The figure shows how long it takes to press the buttons as a function of the number of times the task was done—that is, as a function of practice. There are ten lights, hence $2^{10} - 1$ or 1,023 different patterns (ignoring the pattern for no lights turning on).

As the figure shows, when a person first starts to do the task, it takes about a second and a half (1,500 milliseconds) to respond. But with practice the reaction time speeds up. This person (the graph plots the performance of a single individual) was induced to practice the task a little over 70,000 times (70 times through the entire 1,023 patterns). Reaction time comes down to about 450 milliseconds. This still takes longer than the time to react in the simple task of just pushing a button when a light goes on, which can be under 200 milliseconds. But it has still improved a lot. Furthermore, and the important feature for us, learning obeys a simple quantitative law. If (as in the figure) the logarithm of the reaction time (T) is plotted against the logarithm of the number of practice trials (N), the result is a downward-sloping straight line. The figure actually plots the logarithm of T minus an estimated asymptote (A) versus the logarithm of the number of trials plus an estimated number (E) of trials that occurred prior to the particular experiment. This straightens the curve out somewhat.

The important point is that there is a regular law. The law has been known for a long time, having been first described by Snoddy (1926) in connection with learning to trace geometric figures in a

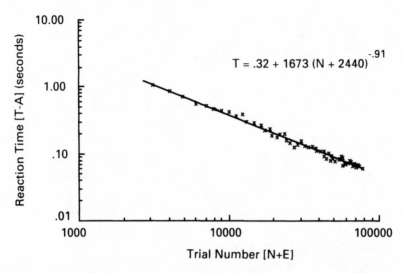

$$T = .32 + 1673 (N + 2440)^{-.91}$$

Figure 1-2. Choice reaction task (adapted from Seibel, 1963).

mirror. Just like Fitts' law, it is extremely robust. It holds not only for immediate motor-perceptual tasks, like reaction-time tests and mirror tracing, but also for recalling facts, editing with text editors, and on through cognitive tasks such as checking proofs or playing solitaire (Newell & Rosenbloom, 1981). Thus, there is a ubiquitous quantitative law of practice, which has come to be called the *power law of practice*. (Taking logs of both sides of a power law, $T = BN^{-\alpha}$, yields the linear curve, $\log(T) = \log(B) - \alpha\log(N)$.) Again, you would think it would appear in all our elementary psychology textbooks, but it doesn't.

A few years ago, Paul Rosenbloom and I developed a general theory for this power law of practice, based on the notion of *chunking* (Newell & Rosenbloom, 1981). Chunking has a long history in psychology. The term was coined by George Miller in his classical review of short-term memory limits (Miller, 1956; Bower & Winzenz, 1969). A chunk is a unit of memory organization, formed by bringing together a set of already formed chunks in memory and welding them together into a larger unit. Chunking implies the ability to build up such structures recursively, thus leading to a hierarchical organization of memory. Chunking appears to be a ubiquitous feature of human memory. Conceivably, it could form the basis for an equally ubiquitous law of practice.

This theory of practice is summarized in three general propositions. First, people chunk continuously at a constant rate. Every time they get more experience, they build additional chunks. Second, performance of the task is faster, the more chunks that have been built that are relevant to the task—that is, where the experience that has been chunked has to do with the task. This contrasts with the way subroutines behave in computers. In terms of memory organization, subroutines behave like chunks. Once a subroutine is built it can be evoked in some other subroutine simply by calling its name—producing exactly the expected hierarchical structure. But when the computer executes a subroutine, it runs all the way down to the bottom every time and executes the ultimately primitive machine instructions. In fact it actually runs a little slower because of the processing overhead of passing parameters and jumping back and forth. The theory of practice, in contrast, assumes that somehow the system works more directly and faster once relevant chunks are in place. Third, the structure of the environment implies that higher-level chunks recur more rarely. A chunk is essentially a pattern that describes an environmental situation. The higher the chunk in the hierarchy, the more subpatterns it has; and the more subpatterns, the less chance there is of it being true of the current situation. If one chunk is a man with a hat and cigar, and another chunk is a man with an overcoat and spats, then one will see each of these situations more frequently than a man with a hat, cigar, overcoat, and spats.

These three assumptions, suitably quantified, provide an explanation for the power law of practice. Even without the mathematics, it should be evident that there is a practice effect—as chunks build up, the human speeds up. The constant chunking rate and a reasonable assumption about speedup with chunking yields exponential learning. But as higher-level chunks build up, they become less and less useful, because the situations in which they would help do not recur. Thus, the learning slows down, being drawn out from an exponential toward a power law. Actually, the law isn't a power law in mathematical form, but it turns out to be fairly indistinguishable from it.

Again, we have a theory to explain a regularity in human behavior. The ubiquity of chunking is what underlies the ubiquity of the power law of practice. Although the form of its assumptions is plausible overall, the question of how the speedup actually occurs with additional chunks remains unexplained. It was just posited

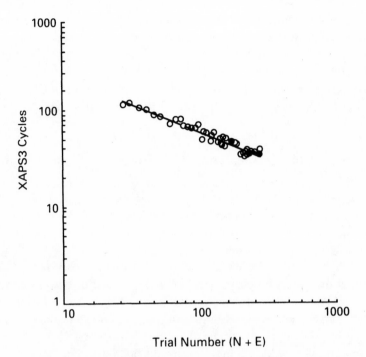

Figure 1-3. Simulated practice curve for Seibel's task,
using Xaps3 production system.

that the speedup occurred and obeyed a simple plausible law.
Rosenbloom and I (1986) then took the next step, which was to
create an experimental system architecture that actually learned by
chunking, producing a speedup in the Seibel task and reproducing
the power law of practice, again empirically, but not of the exact
mathematical form of the power law. This architecture used productions, and chunking consisted of the growth of additional productions. Figure 1-3 shows the simulated practice curve for Seibel's
task.

Again, I want to make three points about this example. First, like
Fitts' law, it is also a microtheory. Unlike that law, however, it
deals with a phenomenon, practice, that occurs over a long time
span and that occurs in a wide variety of contexts. Second, also like
Fitts' law, the explanation is cast in terms of mechanisms. Several
mechanisms combine to yield the result we see in behavior. Third,
the content of this theory does not reside just in the general assumptions, but also in the details of the architecture. The simulation is

not just a computation of what is fully specified by the theory. The architecture adds assumptions about the details of processing—the general specifications for productions, the details of their condition and actions, how tasks are represented, and so on. Thus, the total theory is an amalgamation of information spread over both theoretical media, the general principles and the simulation details.

1.1.3. Search in Problem Solving

Consider a final example. Figure 1-4 shows a little bit of behavior of a person playing chess (Newell & Simon, 1972). This display is called the *problem-behavior graph*. It is constructed from a protocol of the person talking aloud, mentioning moves considered and aspects of the situation. The time moves from left to right and down the figure. Thus, the first four moves are B × N'/5, P' × B, B' × B, N × B', where the prime indicates the black pieces. The graph shows that the person searches in a space of chess positions with moves and countermoves as the steps in the search. The search can be seen to have a definite pattern, it does not just wander at random or jump around. The pattern is called *progressive deepening:* search down in a depth-first fashion; then return all the way back to the initial situation; then search back down again, following an old path for a while, before either going deeper or branching out to the side. In the figure the single lines show the search into new territory; the double lines show where the search repeats prior paths; the initial position is over at the far left, repeated at the beginning of each of the episodes (E2, E3, . . .).

Here is a general qualitative theory of this behavior. First, problems are solved by searching in a *problem space*, whose states include the initial situation (the beginning board position) and potential desired situations (winning positions), all as envisioned by the problem solver. The search in that space is conducted by means of operators that reflect the task (here, legal chess moves). These operators have the property that they may be freely applied, and if a desired state is ever encountered, then the task will be attained. (Variations of this condition apply in chess, since the opponent is a source of uncontrolled change in the situation.) This assumption implies coherent searches in the problem space. Second, attention is focused on locally experienced difficulties. The problem solver, in doing something, runs across a new aspect that is not understood or that offers an opportunity or causes trouble; then he spends

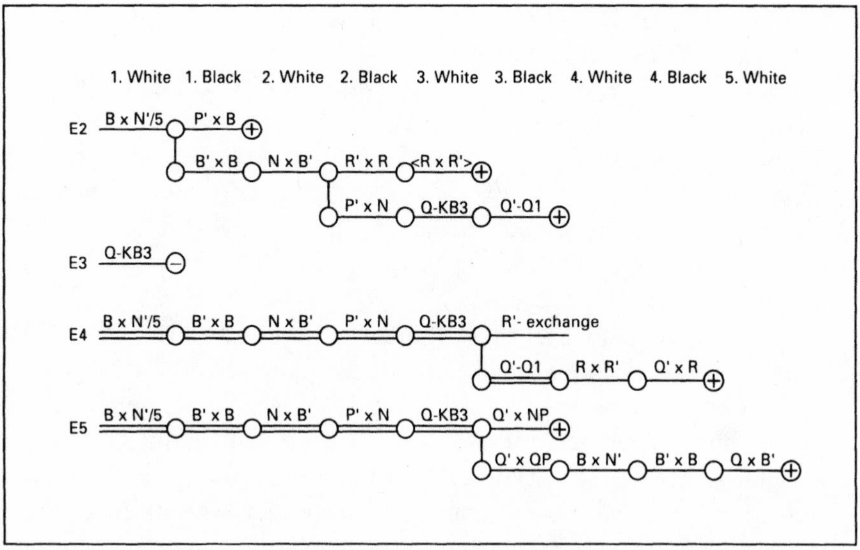

1. White 1. Black 2. White 2. Black 3. White 3. Black 4. White 4. Black 5. White

Figure 1-4. Problem solving in playing chess (adapted from
Newell & Simon, 1972, figure 12.4).

additional effort on that aspect. Such local focusing leads to a
depth-first search, rather than other types of searches that save
many states (as on an agenda) and select globally at each moment
which state to work on. Third, short-term memory is limited to
holding a single temporary state. This limitation might stem from
interference effects if successive states were highly similar, or from
capacity limitation, if multiple states required lots of memory.
Whatever the cause, holding only a single dynamic state makes a
number of search strategies difficult to carry through successfully.
In particular, the general depth-first strategy, which exhausts the
explorations of each state and then backs up to the immediately
prior state, is not possible because the stack of prior states along
the search path cannot be kept in mind. Progressive deepening,
however, is a search strategy precisely adapted to this demand.

As one last wrinkle to the theory, an examination of Figure 1-4
reveals that the search is not pure progressive deepening; one-step
look-ahead occurs quite often, as in the P′ × B and B′ × B moves
early in E2, where search does not return to the base position. This
modified progressive deepening, as it is called, arises from the way
operators are generated. Analysis of a chess position yields the
functions that must be performed—defend the bishop—not the ac-

tual moves—Q-KB3 to defend the bishop by checking the king, or whatever. These actual moves must be generated by further analysis of the details and structure of the whole position. There may be several such moves and they must each be considered at least briefly. Indeed, all of the little tufts of one-move searches in the figure constitute the clusters of moves that satisfy some function (which is often enunciated in the protocol). Thus, the pattern of search behavior is explained by the theory, even to the modification of pure progressive deepening.

It is easy to show that this behavior pattern is not necessary for playing chess. In computer chess programs, the constraint on short-term memory does not exist. Progressive deepening is never used there, but always general depth-first search. Furthermore, chess programs mostly look at all legal moves and do not generate them selectively as a function of analysis. Hence there is nothing corresponding to the two-level generator of functions followed by actual moves that characterizes Figure 1-4. Rather, a simple enumeration of all legal moves occurs and these are then ordered according to threat value—a very different pattern.[1] Thus, the theory of problem solving that explains the observed human search pattern is explicitly based on the characteristics of the human information-processing system.

The points I wish to make about this example involve the other examples as well. First, the explanation is in terms of processing mechanisms, just as with the other two. Second, the examples come from different areas of human behavior varying widely in time scale—motor control, taking seconds; skill learning, taking hours; and problem solving, taking minutes. Finally, all the examples derive from seeing the human as an information-processing system. This is obvious in the practice and problem-solving examples. If it does not seem equally so in the case of Fitts' law, it is only because we have allowed usage to narrow inappropriately. Continuous control systems (here actually a sampled data system) pick up information from the environment and process it to select or determine actions in the world. This is information processing, perfectly well.

---

1. Actually, matters are a little more complicated. A search strategy called *iterative deepening* is now commonly used, comprising successive depth-first searches to gradually increasing depth. But the pattern is still very different.

1.1.4. What Is a Theory?

The points brought out by these three examples make evident what I mean by a theory, generally speaking. This view of theory, by the way, I take to be unexceptional—even old-fashioned. It is just the notion developed by any working scientist who uses successful scientific theory—in chemistry, physics, biology, geology, meteorology. There are a lot of such people around, and they learn and use a lot of theory every day. That's why I call it old-fashioned. There are no surprises or new wrinkles due to the theory being about human behavior—no notion that, because we are dealing with human behavior, or ourselves, or thinking beings, or whatever, that somehow there should be something special about what a theory means or does.

To state it positively and in general, let there be some body of explicit knowledge, from which answers can be obtained to questions by inquiries. Some answers might be predictions, some might be explanations, some might be prescriptions for control. If this body of knowledge yields answers to those questions for you, you can call it a theory. There is little sense worrying that one body of knowledge is "just a collection of facts" (such as a data base of people's heights and ages) and another is "the fundamental axioms of a subject matter" (such as Newton's three laws plus supporting explication). The difference, of course, is important. But it is clear what is going on—they answer different sorts of questions and have different scope and have different potential for further development. That is, they are indeed different bodies of knowledge. But both play a role in providing needed answers, and neither substitutes for the other, except in special cases.

The theory gives the answers, not the theorist. That is important, because humans also embody knowledge and can answer questions. Humans (as question answerers) and theories have different properties. People often can't provide much additional knowledge about why their answers are right or to what approximation. They also tend to argue a lot about their answers and tend to serve their own goals in giving answers—all of which complicates matters. In contrast, a theory is an *explicit* body of knowledge, from which answers can be obtained by anyone skilled in the art. What questions can be answered by a theory may well depend on the skill of the theorist, but the answer itself, if obtained, does not—it depends on the theory, not the theorist. Thus, theories tend to be cast in terms of calculi, proof schemes, simulations—all things that tend to objectify the body of knowledge and make the answering of questions routine, dependent only upon acquiring the skill of application.

Theories are approximate. Of course, we all know that technically they are approximate; the world can't be known with absolute certainty. But I mean more than that. Theories are also deliberately approximate. Usefulness is often traded off against truth. Theories that are known to be wrong continue to be used, because they are the best available. Fitts' law is like that. How a theory is wrong is carried along as part of the theory itself. Grossly approximate theories are continuous launching pads for better attempts. Fitts' law is like that too. The scientist does the best he can with what he's got—and the engineer, who has to have answers, even more so.

Theories cumulate. They are refined and reformulated, corrected and expanded. Thus, we are not living in the world of Popper (Popper, 1959), as far as I'm concerned, we are living in the world of Lakatos (Lakatos, 1970). Working with theories is not like skeet shooting—where theories are lofted up and *bang,* they are shot down with a falsification bullet, and that's the end of that theory. Theories are more like graduate students—once admitted you try hard to avoid flunking them out, it being much better for them and for the world if they can become long-term contributors to society.

Theories are things to be nurtured and changed and built up. One is happy to change them to make them more useful. Almost any body of knowledge, structured in almost any sort of way, can enter into a theory if it works. An especially powerful form for theory is a body of underlying mechanisms, whose interactions and compositions provide the answers to all the questions we have—predictions, explanations, designs, controls. Such forms have been at the bottom of all my examples. But, it is worth emphasizing, that is because mechanisms are just what works. There is an overwhelming amount of evidence that the world is put together this way, so that theories described as systems of mechanisms give us good answers. But mechanistic explanations have no special a priori methodological or prescriptive status. Teleological principles are also just fine when they work, as in the *principle of the shortest path (Fermat's principle)* in geometrical optics.

In sum, when I talk about a unified theory of cognition, I'm

Problem solving, decision making, routine action
Memory, learning, skill
Perception, motor behavior
Language
Motivation, emotion
Imagining, dreaming, daydreaming, . . .

Figure 1-5. Areas to be covered by a unified theory of cognition.

talking about a thing that is all of the above—and the more the better.

1.2. What Are Unified Theories of Cognition?

Having indicated what I mean by a theory, let me now say what I mean by a unified theory of cognition, the theme of this book. I mean a single set of mechanisms for all of cognitive behavior. What should that cover? Figure 1-5 presents a list.

Problem solving, decision making, and routine action? These are at the center of cognitive behavior. Memory, learning, and skill? These equally belong at the center. Skill might not have been so obvious a decade ago, but since then the study of cognitive skill on the one hand and automatic behavior on the other now makes its inclusion obvious.

Perception and motor behavior? Matters now get interesting, because they are often excluded. Indeed, the term *cognition* emerged in part to indicate the central processes that were ignored by peripheral perception and motor behavior. Yet one problem with psychology's attempt at cognitive theory has been our persistence in thinking about cognition without bringing in perceptual and motor processes. Given all that we now understand about human information processing, and especially how it must have evolved from creatures who had well-developed perceptual and motor capabilities, the distinction is clearly one of analysis and not one of nature. Perception and motor behavior must be included.

Language? Now matters get convoluted—at least for me. There is no question that language should be included. Many people would start with language, and not with problem solving, decision making, and routine action, as I did. Even if one were to classify language under perception and motor behavior—and an interesting case can be made for that—these peripheral processes have been unhesitatingly included. So should language. Yet I demur from simply adding it to the list in its proper station, so to speak. Too much is known about language, especially from nonpsychological sources: phonology, syntax, semantics, and discourse (actually somewhat less about the latter). Language should be approached with caution and circumspection. A unified theory of cognition must deal with it, but I will take it as something to be approached later rather than sooner.

Motivation and emotion? And there are other things as well, such as imagining, dreaming, daydreaming, hallucinating . . . I could not bring myself to add to the list: development, social behavior, personality structure, and on through the rest of psychology's standard chapters. By this time, it's clear that we are discussing a fantasy. Clearly, I can't mean a theory of all that! A unified theory of cognition is just a fantasy.

What to do? Perhaps a retreat to clichés is in order: *The best is the enemy of the good.* (Though if one must resort to cliché, Voltaire is not a bad choice for a source.) We cannot face the entire list all at once. So let us consider it to be a priority list, and work our way down from the top. What I will mean by a unified theory of cognition is a cognitive theory that gets significantly further down the list cumulatively than we have ever done before. If someone keeps asking how the unified theory explains dreaming or how it describes personality, I will simply point back to this list. It is right to ask, but wrong to insist.

A unified theory of cognition does not mean a high-level theory that gains its unification because it backs off to vagueness and platitudes. Calculations and simulations count. The examples given earlier in the chapter are meant seriously, although they each touch only a single aspect of human behavior and are not yet unified. We don't want a contemporary version of what has come to be called "the grand theories of the 1930s."

A unified theory will unify our existing understanding of cognition. It will not be a brand-new theory that replaces current work at every turn. Rather, it will put together and synthesize what we know. On the other hand, it can't be just a pastiche, in which disparate formulations are strung together with some sort of conceptual baling wire. Its parts must work together. Nor can it be what have come to be called *frameworks*, which are conceptual structures (often computer systems) that are reputed to be relatively content free but that permit specific cognitive theories to be inserted in them in some fashion.

The book is titled *Unified Theories of Cognition*. It is not titled *The Unified Theory of Cognition*. This is an important point. I am not asserting that there is a unique unified theory and we should all get together on it. In the current state of the art, multiple theories are the best that we can do. The task at hand is to try to get *some* candidate theories that have a large enough scope in order to get the gains inherent in such unification, and to show us all that they are real. The task is somehow to cajole ourselves into putting it all together, even though we don't know many of the mechanisms that are operating. The long run can be entrusted to take care of the eventual emergence of a single unified theory and how that convergence or selection will take place.

Thus, there will be multiple unified theories for quite a while—if we can just get a few started, to show the way. My concern is that each one, itself, should be unified. We should be comparing one unified theory with another. From what has already been said it should be understood that any such theory will be inadequate and so it will change and grow. What I want is for psychology to begin working with much more integrated theories. This is what I want to make plausible and attractive in this book.

1.2.1. Why Strive for Unified Theories?
As members of a scientific community, we all understand automatically that unification is a good thing. It is an "apple pie" of science. I clearly have more than this in mind in urging unified theories on psychology at this particular time. Figure 1-6 gives my list of reasons.

Most important, beyond the apple-pie reason, is that a single system (mind) produces all aspects of behavior. It is one mind that minds them all. Even if the mind has parts, modules, components, or whatever, they all mesh together to produce behavior. Any bit of behavior has causal tendrils that extend back through large parts of the total cognitive system before grounding in the environmental situation of some earlier times. If a theory covers only one part or component, it flirts with trouble from the start. It goes without saying that there are dissociations, independencies, impenetrabilities, and modularities. These all help to break the web of each bit of behavior being shaped by an unlimited set of antecedents. So

1. Unification is always an aim of science
2. Bringing all parts to bear on a behavior
3. Bringing multiple constraints to bear
4. Increased rate of cumulation
5. Increased identifiability
6. Amortization of theoretical constructs
7. Open the way to applications
8. Change from discriminative to approximative style
9. Solve the irrelevant-specification problem

Figure 1-6. Why unified theories of cognition?

they are important to understand and help to make that theory simple enough to use. But they don't remove the necessity of a theory that provides the total picture and explains the role of the parts and why they exist.

Next, the mind is shaped by multiple constraints. It requires a unified theory of cognition to bring these constraints to bear, to discover how they jointly affect and determine the structure of mind. This point may seem somewhat indirect, so let us step aside to consider it in a little more detail. Figure 1-7 gives a slight reworking of a list of constraints from an earlier discussion on the nature of physical symbol systems (Newell, 1980a). Mind, which can be taken as a word to express the human's ability to deal with the world, has been built up in response to many different requirements.

(1) Behavior must be flexible as a function of the environment. If a system cannot make itself respond in whatever way is needed, it hardly can be mind-like. (2) Flexibility by itself is only a means—it must be in the service of goals and rationally related to obtaining the things and conditions that let the organism survive and propagate. (3) Mind must operate in real time. That is a very important demand from the environment in which we find ourselves situated. (4) The structure of this environment has its own impact. For humans, the environment is full of richness and detail, changing rapidly and simultaneously on many fronts. This overall constraint shows up in many ways. There must be multiple perceptual systems, they must all operate concurrently and dynamically, and some must have high bandwidth. There must be very large memories, because the environment provides the opportunity to

1. Behave flexibly as a function of the environment
2. Exhibit adaptive (rational, goal-oriented) behavior
3. Operate in real time
4. Operate in a rich, complex, detailed environment
   • Perceive an immense amount of changing detail
   • Use vast amounts of knowledge
   • Control a motor system of many degrees of freedom
5. Use symbols and abstractions
6. Use language, both natural and artificial
7. Learn from the environment and from experience
8. Acquire capabilities through development
9. Operate autonomously, but within a social community
10. Be self-aware and have a sense of self
11. Be realizable as a neural system
12. Be constructable by an embryological growth process
13. Arise through evolution

Figure 1-7. The multiple constraints that shape mind.

know so many relevant things—and opportunity implies obligation in an evolutionary, hence competitive, world. The motor system to get around in a complex world requires many degrees of freedom, which are actually degrees of freedom per second, because the environment keeps changing. Actually, the number of degrees of freedom for humans is only moderately large—hundreds of degrees of freedom. It is not very large—thousands or tens of thousands of degrees of freedom. It is not clear why the number is so small.

(5) Mind is able to use symbols and abstractions. We know that just from observing ourselves. (6) It is also able to use language, both natural and artificial. These two constraints, symbols and language, might amount to the same thing or they might impose somewhat distinct requirements. Opinions vary with scientific persuasion; which way it turns out is not important for this list as long as there is coverage. Indeed, either or both of these could be effectively equivalent to the constraint of flexibility or vice versa. They all have to be there.

(7) We must be able to learn from the environment, not occasionally but continuously, and not about a few specifics but everything and every way under the sun. (8) We must acquire capabilities through development. When the neonate first arrives it is surely

without many capabilities and, therefore, does not seem to have the mental equipment to develop them. In fact, of course, it does develop over time—so the difficulty is with our scientific understanding, not with the infant's capability. Nevertheless, this is a strong constraint. As with some of the other items, the relationship between the learning constraint and the development constraint is unclear. No consensus exists within developmental psychology whether development is a species of cognitive learning or is supported by other biological processes. Again, coverage is what counts.

(9) Humans must live autonomously within a social community. This constraint is a little odd, because it is bimodal. One aspect of autonomy is greater capability to be free of dependencies on the environment. When we consider how far from autonomy our current computers and robots are, the constraint seems to speak in a major way to increased capabilities. But, conversely, much that we have learned from ethology and social theory speaks to the dependence of individuals upon the communities in which they are raised and reside. The additional capabilities for low-level autonomy do not negate the extent to which socialization and embedding in a supportive social structure are necessary. If you take us out of our communities, we become inept and dysfunctional in many ways. (10) The constraint of self-awareness is again somewhat anomalous. We surely have a sense of self, but it is not evident what functional role self-awareness plays in the total scheme of mind. To be a little more precise, it is clear that considering the self and its capabilities in relation to the environment—what psychologists call metacognition—is important. But the link from that to the full notion of a sense of self remains obscure.

All the items so far reflect requirements of performance. Other types of constraints arise from our construction. (11) The mind is built out of the technology of neural systems; (12) the construction process is by embryological growth; and (13) the whole apparatus, both product and process, was constructed by the technology of evolution. All these technologies have myriad consequences.

The mind can be viewed as a solution to all of these constraints, worked out through eons. It reflects them all and, given the view of evolution as a tinkerer (Jacob, 1982), they are woven together in a tapestry that renders their individual contributions only obscurely. Taken all together, the constraints are daunting. No individual scientist can deal with very many of these constraints. Perforce, to look at some implies that others must be abandoned. Like-minded investigators cluster together to make subfields, and these tend to differentiate along exactly such lines. I am no different from others—I ignore many of the constraints because I have no way of taking them into account. I demote linguistics in Figure 1-5 not because linguistics is unimportant but because I am not a linguist. It is even rumored that some linguists do the same with cognition.

Developing a unified theory of cognition is a move in the direction of taking more constraints into account. From one point of view, that will no doubt increase the difficulty and the puzzlement. From the point of view of constructing a theory, however, what is needed is more constraint rather than less. The issue is how to discover where each of the constraints in the figure has an impact on the nature of mind. With more aspects of cognition within the pale, there is more opportunity to find those points of impact and then to propagate the constraint from the place where its bite is clear to other places where its role has not been heretofore suspected or calculated.

We have not yet completed the list of advantages for unified theories of cognition (Figure 1-6). Each theory will increase the rate of cumulation. A unified theory becomes a repository of knowledge that fits together. Even if the unified theory is highly approximate, it plays a mnemonic role, helping us to remember all the empirical results and the low-level regularities. Once the empirical results are poured into a common theoretical scheme, comparison is forced and the data get sorted out. Anomalies don't go away, of course, but they do get identified and clarified.

A unified theory would result in great increases in identifiability. There exists within psychology a minor research theme that focuses on establishing what can be ignored because it is beyond the pale of determination. It is not possible to tell whether a process is serial or parallel (Townsend, 1974). It is not possible to tell what kind of a representation people are using (Anderson, 1978). Showing that a theory implies universal computation destroys its usefulness, because that makes anything possible (Peters & Ritchie, 1973). John Anderson has gone so far as to believe that difficulties of identifiability make all models of cognitive mechanisms merely notations (Anderson, 1989). It is useful to have the technical results behind these statements, for the analyses are often quite penetrating, but by and large this nonidentifiability enterprise seems to me misplaced. It arises from a narrow focus on the data admitted to identify a theory. The way to solve the identifiability problem is by bringing to bear large, diverse collections of quasi-independent sources of knowledge—structural, behavioral, functional—that finally allow the system to be pinned down. The more unified the theory, the better the chances of identifiability, because then the chance of being able to bring diverse sources of knowledge to bear is greater.

Related to identifiability is the amortization of theoretical constructs. If a microtheory is proposed, such as the ones early in this chapter, the data must bear the full weight of establishing all the theoretical propositions and constructs. There can be too many degrees of qualitative freedom in specifying the structure of a theory, just as truly as there can be too many free parameters to be determined by the available data. When a theory stands in isolation, this almost always occurs, though often it is passed over in silence. On the other hand, if the basic propositions about the nature of problem spaces or the nature of control structures were part of a common theory, then any particular local use of the theory would not burden the data with justifying these aspects of the theory. The data can be used, properly, to deal with the new theoretical wrinkle, or to estimate parameters, or whatever.

Unified theories open the way for application. It is not that psychology does not have applied areas already; it certainly does. But in many areas of application a wide variety of aspects enter into each applied problem. What is required is not just an aptitude or selection test. Rather, memory, perception, motor behavior, problem solving, skill acquisition—all are involved in a single attempt to use psychology to solve an applied problem. In an area in which I have done some work, humans interacting with computers, the situation is certainly this way. Without a theory that puts it all together, application is limited to empirical techniques.

The final two items in the list may seem a little special. Changing psychological theorizing from a discriminating to an approximating style is a benefit I believe attends unified theories. This is a distinction that is rarely the subject of attention. In psychology, a theory is treated primarily as something to be shown right or wrong. One searches for the experimental test—the so-called crucial experiment. Whatever aspect presents itself, however arcane, will do.

This activity retains a decided Popperian flavor that falsifiability is next to godliness. Theories are not to be treated as a tool to be used for some externally given purpose, where happiness is an answer sufficient unto the day thereof. Thus theories become objects of discrimination. The alternative is to treat theories as objects of approximation. Approximation is the natural state for a unified theory, because the pressure is to fit in the best story that science can tell at the present moment. One therefore approximates, and tags on notes about anomalies, conclusions that should follow instead, and so on. Shifting from discriminating to approximating would be a beneficial change for the development of pure psychological theory.

Finally, a unified theory solves a rather specific methodological problem about simulations—the *irrelevant-specification problem*. It has long been a complaint about computer simulations of cognitive processes that they force the stipulation of large numbers of assumptions, "just to make the simulation run" (Reitman, 1965). What aspects of a program actually make psychological claims? The difficulty of separating the psychologically relevant from the adventitious has become a stock form of criticism of simulation results. But if one has a truly unified theory, which lays out the entire structure of human cognition, this complaint goes away. The theory comes closer to specifying all of the details of the simulation, which is to say, all that is needed to make the simulation run. There is no large collection of psychologically unmotivated programs and data structures.

To summarize, the items listed in Figure 1-6 are the sorts of benefits I would hope for—indeed, expect—from a unified theory of cognition. It is a sizable budget of benefits and, of course, psychology will get only what it pays for. Which is to say that unified theories, as all science, require a lot of work and will not happen just by wishing for them—or writing books in praise of them.

1.3. Is Psychology Ready for Unified Theories?

It is relevant to ask "why now?" Why should psychology strive for unified theories of cognition in the 1990s, rather than the early 1970s or the beginning of the new century, a comfortable decade away?

One relevant observation is the rise of cognitive science. The cognitive revolution is now into its fourth decade—it is over thirty years old. At some point we must stop talking about it like it was a young child. It has been around for a while. To pick a not-so-random comparison, John Watson wrote his *Manifesto for Behaviorism* in 1913 and Clark Hull wrote his *Principles of Behavior* in 1943. That is again thirty years—from the beginnings of behaviorism to its high point. So it is high time that we move forward. We cannot claim we are a kid—a young science—forever. In fact, we even had a name change almost a decade ago, to *cognitive science,* the umbrella term that we now use to indicate the breadth of our field.

I do not raise this question of the maturity of cognitive science to cast aspersions—to mutter about all these years with no results. On the contrary, my view is that there has been immense progress in all parts of cognitive science—in artificial intelligence, linguistics, education, and, especially, psychology. Such an assertion is contentious. For instance, Fodor, in his *Modularity of Mind,* claims that essentially nothing is known about central cognition (Fodor, 1983, pp. 126–129). Perhaps it is mere rhetoric, but he certainly seems to be in earnest. Perhaps Fodor simply lives in a different world than I do. Perhaps we are both staring at the same glass, but it is half full for me and half empty for him. I really cannot imagine. In any event, progress seems very real to me.

For instance, it is clear that cognition has established a new paradigm, even with all the defocusing of that concept that has occurred since Kuhn introduced it (Kuhn, 1962). One amusing sign that this has happened is that calls have begun for a new paradigm to replace it. A few years ago, for instance, there began the cry for ecological realism, flowing from the position of Jimmy Gibson (1979). "Information processing has done its thing," went the call in effect, "it's time for the next paradigm to come along and we're it" (for example, Shaw & Bransford, 1977). The critics are prepared to recognize the old paradigm at the point when they wish to argue for its replacement. At the current time, a similar set of calls are coming from the connectionists, who believe they are the next revolution (Rumelhart, McClelland, & the PDP Research Group, 1986; McClelland, Rumelhart, & the PDP Research Group, 1986). Critics need to identify the reigning paradigm, and they are pretty clear that it is symbolic cognitive psychology. They certainly do not rail against behaviorism anymore, and I know no one who thinks that ecological realism is in the saddle and needs to be overthrown.

There are, of course, less social indices of progress. For me, the important one is the massive body of beautiful, detailed data that experimental cognitive psychology has accumulated. I was impressed with it in 1972, when I wrote the twenty-questions paper (Newell, 1973a); it has only continued to grow in both volume and quality. It is mostly about immediate-response behavior—down where the mind's work shows through. This is exactly what is needed to understand how mind is constructed. What has grown up is not just data, but large numbers of regularities, many parametric and robust, plus quite a lot of theory, most of it local to some small body of data. An indicator of current progress is the recently published *Handbook on Human Perception and Performance* (Boff, Kaufman, & Thomas, 1986) in two large volumes. I recommend it as a survey of what is now known and of the extent to which this knowledge can be systematized. It begins to approximate the classical ideal of a scientific handbook set by the great *Handbuch der Physik*. It is still short on global theory, but the amount of local theory is impressive.

The extent and elegance of the growing body of data has not erased the concerns of the twenty-questions paper (Newell, 1973a). If anything, my concerns are doubled by the addition of a new one. Will the body of important, regular data and first-order regularities become so large that the task of theoretical integration becomes overwhelming? This is not an idle question. Prior to scientific integration, a body of scientific data always presents a collection of dissonances and apparent contradictions—if it were not so, the integration would already have occurred. As theoretical activity confronts the data and the regularities, it senses these dissonances. The puzzle solving required of the theorist is to use the clashes and gaps to evoke the right insight. It is thus that the more constraint the better. The theoretician faces a bigger puzzle, but there are more signposts to guide him, if only he can decode the signs. It is one thing if there are three or four of these clashes, another if thirty or forty, and yet another if there are three or four hundred inconsistencies. Then every turn can seem blocked—every signpost has two others pointing a different way. In my view, it is time to get going on producing unified theories of cognition—before the data base doubles again and the number of visible clashes increases by the square or cube.

1.3.1. Harbingers of Unified Theories

So far we have been engaged in stating the need and the benefits of starting on the enterprise of developing unified theories of cognition. It is important also to assess cognitive science's readiness to produce such unifications. Science, even more profoundly than politics, is the art of the possible. It does only what can be done next. In fact, I see a number of harbingers that suggest that we are ready to tackle this project.

The first one is Act*. This is the cumulation of a long development by John Anderson, starting with HAM, his thesis with Gordon Bower on a semantic-memory model of memory organization (Anderson & Bower, 1973), through ActE, which added a production system model of procedures (Anderson, 1976), to Act* itself, which added skill acquisition (Anderson, 1983). More recently Anderson has moved on to PUPS (Anderson & Thompson, 1989), which is a learning production system that embodies the analogical schemes central to the skill acquisition theory of Act*.[2]

Act* is a theory of the human cognitive architecture. It specifies the memory and processing structures that underlie human performance in all tasks. Figure 1-8 gives the block diagram of the Act* architecture. There is a long-term declarative memory in the form of a semantic net. It has multiple basic data types—for sequences, for images, and for propositions—linked together by associations. There is a long-term procedural memory in the form of productions. Each production has a set of conditions on the declarative memory and a set of actions that create new nodes or associations in the declarative memory. The architecture is activation based. The nodes of the long-term declarative memory each have a degree of activation, and the working memory is that part of the long-term memory that is highly activated. Activation spreads through the semantic net automatically. Activation also determines how fast the matching of productions proceeds.

All the above relates to performance. Act* also embodies a theory of learning. First, the new nodes and associations created by productions have high activation but are temporary. However, there is a probability that they will become permanent. This is a form of direct declarative learning. Second, new productions can be

---

2. Even more recently Anderson appears to have moved away from architectures to analysis (Anderson, 1989), but this does not affect the picture drawn here.

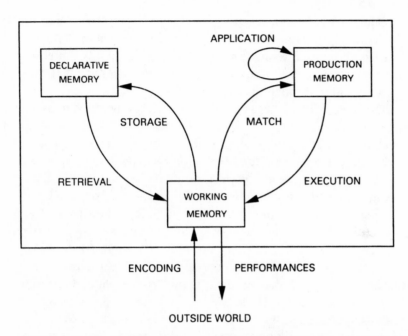

APPLICATION

DECLARATIVE
MEMORY

PRODUCTION
MEMORY

STORAGE   MATCH

RETRIEVAL   EXECUTION

WORKING
MEMORY

ENCODING   PERFORMANCES

OUTSIDE WORLD

Figure 1-8. The Act* cognitive architecture (after Anderson, 1983).

created. This happens automatically by the composition (or chaining) of the productions that execute in sequence. The new production thus moves directly from the initial situation to the final result.
Third, productions have an associated strength, which determines
the likelihood that they will fire, given that their conditions are
satisfied. These strengths increase with use and decrease with dis-
use, so there is a continuous tuning effect. These last two learning
mechanisms provide a theory of cognitive skill acquisition.

Act* is specified as a set of rules about its structure and the ways
actions occur, plus a set of equations for the flow of activation and
the fluctuations in production strength. The theory is too complicated for any but the simplest explicit calculations, but some
simulations have been run to show the effect of the whole model;
and there is a production system called Grapes (Sauers & Farrell,
1982) that embodies the basic production action and automatic creation mechanisms.

The scope of Act* is very large. At the immediate-response level
it covers a lot of regularities about priming, fact retrieval, and memory effects; there is even an explanation of how mental rotation
would go (Shepard & Metzler, 1971). At the cognitive-skill level it

explains how children learn to check geometry proofs and to do elementary programming. There is language learning, with extensive simulations. Explanations of all these essentially come out of the same theory. Act* is an integrated theory that can be applied to a wide domain of phenomena.

Of course, when Act* is examined closely, the explanations are not totally integrated or always convincing. Given a complex mechanism, not every part enters into every prediction. In fact, the processing of activation tends to enter the immediate-response predictions and production composition tends to enter into skill acquisition. However, in more subtle ways each of these aspects does provide constraints and structure for the other. For instance, how the activation flows, providing activation-based priming, is defined by a set of productions. There are also limitations to the range of mechanisms in Act*. The perceptual and motor systems are essentially undefined, so that perceptual and motor phenomena simply cannot be dealt with. Thus, the Act* explanations of some tasks, such as mental rotation, are hard to evaluate, because the explanations that Act* would offer to related phenomena, such as watching stroboscopic images, are not defined.

Often, as well, when Act* predictions are examined closely, much of the prediction depends on aspects of the Act* program rather than on the Act* architecture itself. This difficulty has already surfaced—it is the numbers of degrees of freedom required to specify a theory. It is real for Act*, but it is real, as well, for any theory of cognition.

A different sort of criticism is that Act* does not exist as a coherent operational computer system. That may seem an odd sort of criticism, given its advanced state along the computer-simulation dimension relative to most of psychology. However, I believe it rather important. The issue is not simulation versus no simulation; rather, the issue is whether it is easy to work with the theory to produce explanations. Techniques other than simulation might be used, of course, but Act* is much too complex to be mathematically tractable, except in simple cases. There is a simulation language called Grapes, but it embodies only partial aspects of Act* and has remained a somewhat difficult vehicle. There is no way to build systems that behave like Act* and do substantial tasks, rather than just little slivers of behavior here and there. Finally, on a more substantive note, Act* is missing any higher levels of organization above that of the production. All activity takes place in a single problem space, with productions as operators. This reflects in part the relatively short duration of the behavior Act* is aimed at, but genuine extension is still required for Act* to cope with behavior above a minute or two in duration.

In an important sense, all these criticisms are beside the point. Act*, in my opinion, is the first unified theory of cognition. It has pride of place. It has joined together enough coverage of cognitive phenomena with enough precision as a theory. It provides a threshold of success which all other candidates for being a unified theory of cognition must exceed.

Act* is not the only harbinger, though. The recent book on *Induction* (Holland, Holyoak, Nisbett, & Thagard, 1987) is another. It is a strongly interdisciplinary effort, the four authors spanning computer science, cognitive psychology, social psychology, and philosophy, but it is much less integrated than Act*. In fact, it does not represent a really integrated system, but rather an attempt to show the central role of inductive processes. Different system vehicles are allowed to carry the story at different points, such as Holland's classifier systems and then more classical problem-solving systems. But the conviction behind this book clearly shows that it is appropriate in the current era to attempt more integrated treatments.

A harbinger of a somewhat different flavor is the *Model Human Processor (MHP)*, which is the result of work by Stu Card and Tom Moran, at Xerox PARC, and myself (Card, Moran, & Newell, 1983). Our concern was not all of psychology but the application of psychology to the emerging area of human-computer interaction. We had in mind the need for a theory for designers of interfaces. The design of the interface is the leverage point in human-computer interaction. The classical emphasis of human factors and man-machine psychology on experimental analysis requires that the system or a suitable mockup be available for experimentation, but by the time such a concrete system exists, most of the important degrees of freedom in the interface have been bound. What is needed are tools for thought for the designer—so at design time the properties and constraints of the user can be brought to bear in making the important choices. The situation is essentially the same as in any other design-oriented area of engineering.

Our objective was to develop an engineering-style theory of the user that permitted approximate, back-of-the-envelope calculations of how the user would interact with the computer when operating at a terminal. From our point of view in the book, the focus was on a fairly narrow range of tasks, such as text editing and using command languages. We were concerned with being able to make zero-parameter predictions, that is, a priori predictions, where no parameters at all are to be set from the data on the situation to be predicted. The need for this emphasis, which does not arise in the experimental laboratory, follows directly from the context of design, where the situations being designed do not yet exist, so that perforce parameters cannot be estimated from observing them.

Figure 1-9, from our book, shows the memories and processors of the MHP. There is a long-term memory, a working memory, and sensory buffers for vision and audition. There are independently operating processors for perception, cognition, and motor behavior. There is only one cognitive processor, but there are distinct processors for distinct perceptual modes and distinct muscle systems. Associated with each memory is a type of code, a capacity, and a decay rate. Associated with each processor is a cycle time, which is the time for it to do a single primitive operation.

Figure 1-9 is a version of the familiar information-processing block diagram, whose roots go back to Broadbent (1958) and which has become standard in cognition-oriented textbooks (Haber & Hershenson, 1973; Lachman, Lachman, & Butterfield, 1979). Its form accords modestly well with the current fashion—the short-term memories are parts of long-term memory, not separate memories requiring transfers; and the system exhibits strong but limited parallel-processing capabilities.

In addition to the block diagram, there is a series of principles of operation for the system. These are listed briefly in Figure 1-10. The principles are all familiar and robust generalizations from the current understanding of cognition. Indeed, the three examples of simple theories earlier in the chapter show up here—Fitts' law, the power law of practice, and problem spaces. The basic view of control in the human—the recognize-act cycle—is simply a generalized form of production systems and thus is consonant with Act*. This same recognition characteristic implies that memory retrieval must work from the clues that are available in working memory, which is the central notion behind the encoding specificity principle (Tulving, 1983). That behavior always slows down as the task situation

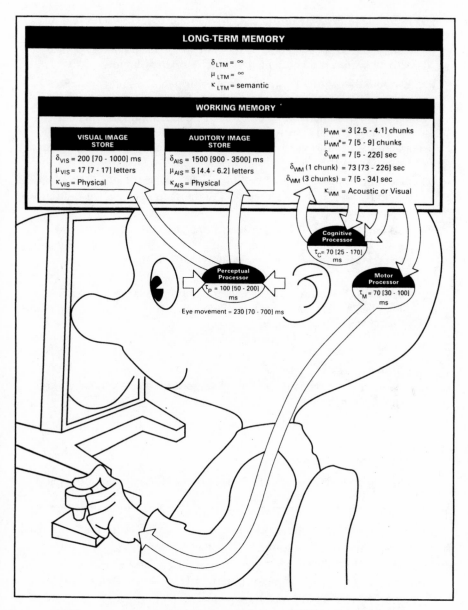

Figure 1-9. The Model Human Processor (MHP) block diagram (adapted from Card, Moran, & Newell, 1983).

P0. Recognize-Act Cycle of the Cognitive Processor. On each cycle of the Cognitive Processor, the contents of Working Memory initiate actions associatively linked to them in Long-Term Memory; these actions in turn modify the contents of Working Memory.

P1. Variable Perceptual Processor Rate Principle. The Perceptual Processor cycle time τ_p varies inversely with stimulus intensity.

P2. Encoding Specificity Principle. Specific encoding operations performed on what is perceived determine what is stored, and what is stored determines what retrieval cues are effective in providing access to what is stored.

P3. Discrimination Principle. The difficulty of memory retrieval is determined by the candidates that exist in the memory, relative to the retrieval clues.

P4. Variable Cognitive Processor Rate Principle. The Cognitive Processor cycle time τ_c is shorter when greater effort is induced by increased task demands or information loads; it also diminishes with practice.

P5. Fitts' Law. The time T_{pos} to move the hand to a target of size S which lies a distance D away is given by:

$$T_{pos} = I_M \log_2(D/S + .5),$$

where $I_M = 100\ [70-120]$ ms/bit.

P6. Power Law of Practice. The time T to perform a task on the nth trial follows a power law:

$$T_n = T_1 n^{-\alpha},$$

where $\alpha = .4\ [.2-.6]$.

Figure 1-10. The Model Human Processor (MHP) operating principles.

---

becomes more uncertain, at least at the level of immediate responses, is not usually stated as a general principle (as are some of the others); but there is a very wide range of experimental situations that exhibit the property, such as Hick's law (Hick, 1952).

The MHP was an attempt to synthesize, from the state of psychological understanding circa 1980, a model of the human that was relevant to interaction at the computer terminal or workstation. We attempted to refine and make quantitative the standard information-processing block diagram, so that it would be possible both to think about what the human was doing when operating at the interface and to do simple computations to predict whether one task would

P7. Uncertainty Principle. Decision time T increases with uncertainty about the judgment or decision to be made:

$$T = I_c H,$$

where H is the information-theoretic entropy of the decision and I_c = 150 [0–157] ms/bit. For n equally probable alternatives (called Hick's Law),

$$H = \log_2 (n + 1).$$

For n alternatives with different probabilities p_i of occurrence,

$$H = \Sigma_i p_i \log_2 (1/p_i + 1).$$

P8. Rationality Principle. A person acts so as to attain his goals through rational action, given the structure of the task and his inputs of information and bounded by limitations on his knowledge and processing ability:

Goals + Task + Operators + Inputs
+ Knowledge + Process-limits → Behavior

P9. Problem Space Principle. The rational activity in which people engage to solve a problem can be described in terms of (1) a set of states of knowledge, (2) operators for changing one state into another, (3) constraints on applying operators, and (4) control knowledge for deciding which operator to apply next.

Figure 1-10 (continued).

---

take longer than another, or how many seconds it would take to perform a given editing task. Indeed, we wrote chapter 2 of the book, which introduced the MHP, in the image of a physics textbook—as a series of little problems for which it was possible to calculate the answers.

The MHP is certainly an attempt at a unified theory of cognition, within the range of behavior elicited by the computer-interaction situation. In some ways that situation is quite narrow, but in other ways it is extremely broad, with elements of perception, memory, decision making, problem solving, motor behavior, and cognitive skill all occurring in the same task. The MHP is much looser than

Act* and much less complete. It was committed to being more synthetic, trying to incorporate what has wide acceptance.

Another harbinger comes from the area of reading and discourse. Marcel Just and Pat Carpenter have recently published a textbook on *The Psychology of Reading and Language Comprehension* (1987) that makes the point well. The book is built around a production-system model (CAPS), which provides a vertical integration of what goes on in reading: starting from eye movements, word encoding, lexical access, syntax, semantics, text schemas, and referential processes. The authors make use of this theory in all their theorizing, and they derive from CAPS a regression model for how long it takes to read a text. Most of the variance comes from word-length and word-frequency effects, but other effects, such as end of sentence processing, can be identified. Besides providing an assessment of what enters into reading speed, this same scheme also provides the basis for understanding issues such as the difference between Chinese and English, and characteristics of dyslexia, and to what extent speed reading is possible.

The work by Just and Carpenter does not stand alone. Reading has been intensely investigated for many years. A small collection of investigators, maybe twenty in all (Britton & Black, 1985; Kieras & Just, 1984), have produced a set of slightly variant theories of reading and used slightly different experimental paradigms. (For example, Carpenter and Just use free reading with recorded eye movements; others use discrete reading where each next word is called for.) Some theories concentrate at the higher levels, for instance the discourse model of van Dijk and Kintsch (1983). An interesting aspect of this latter effort is that, having been developed over several years, it is being used as part of a model of how young children read and perform simple word problems in arithmetic (Kintsch & Greeno, 1982). Other theories concentrate at lower levels.

CAPS is a harbinger because it provides a significantly integrated treatment of its domain. The integration is vertical and not horizontal, but the integration is nonetheless real. CAPS itself is far from complete. Thus, within their textbook Just and Carpenter treat many aspects of the area that do not yet fall within CAPS in any strict way. But these other phenomena—which they are called upon to include in a textbook—are consonant enough with CAPS, so that CAPS provides the conceptual backbone of the whole textbook. This seems to me part of its significance as a harbinger.

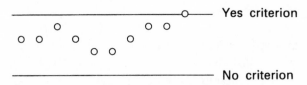

Figure 1-11. Random-walk mechanism for perceptual decisions.

Let me provide one final harbinger, from the work on the way perceptual decisions are made in the cognitive system, such as deciding that an expected signal has occurred in the environment, deciding whether two perceived items are the same, or recognizing a presented item or scene that has been seen before. This is a harbinger not because the theory is of wide scope, but because psychology seems able to attain some agreement on basic types of mechanisms.

Figure 1-11 gives the central idea, which is quite simple. The evidence for a decision yes or no arrives over time. The decision mechanism accumulates this evidence bit by bit and moves toward a criterial state where it will commit to yes or no. The evidence is noisy, however; a random walk ensues and the decision drifts first toward one boundary and then the other, until with enough time the decision is made.

There are many variations of this scheme, variously called run models, random-walk models, sequential sampling models, diffusion models, and counter models (see Ratcliff, 1985, for some examples). They all have the properties of being fundamentally stochastic evidence-accumulating mechanisms. They all have a built-in speed-accuracy trade-off, controlled by setting cutoffs. They all are able to terminate the process at any time, with a viable decision, but with decreased probability of error the longer they wait. All of these features are characteristic qualitatively of human immediate decision making.

Each type of theory seems able to do about equally well in fitting the quantitative data. Each fits about the same collection of data and does it quite well. The odd thing is that we cannot yet (circa 1989) extract the core mechanisms in a formal way, but must be content with the family resemblance indicated by the figure.

The multiple theories of this decision process—almost as many as there are theorists, as the saying goes—may make this seem like a typical divergent area of experimental psychology with micro-models. They might be taken to indicate the nonunified nature of current cognitive theories. But the conclusion to be drawn is quite a different one, namely, one consistent with random-walk models being a harbinger for unified theories. The details of the models are not critically important, though an appropriate set of details is necessary to get out detailed predictions. Any mechanism with the common properties epitomized in Figure 1-11 will do all right. This means that we may be able to settle on an important schematic characterization of an elementary mechanism of the mind. And we can trust the incorporation of this mechanism into unified theories of cognition that may appear to have quite different structure.

To sum up this whole section, I see a number of harbingers of unified cognitive theories. None spans the whole of cognition, though Act* comes close, but each covers an important aspect of what a unified theory requires. And what is more important, these harbingers all announce fundamentally the same theory. Of course, they differ in detail and each has the stamp of the individual theorists. But where they address the same issues they yield approximately the same answers and use variants of the same mechanisms. And there are other examples as well that I have not taken the space to mention (MacKay, 1987). It is time to attempt to push this idea forward.

1.4. The Task of the Book

My goal for this book is to convince you that unified theories of cognition are really worth striving for—now, as we move into the 1990s. The way not to do this is to talk about it, although I have been doing exactiy that in this initial chapter. The only way I know how to make the case is to put forth a candidate, so that we can see what a unified theory of cognition means and why it is a plausible goal for cognitive science. Thus, throughout the rest of the book I will focus on a single candidate.

1.4.1. The Risks

Presenting a single candidate is not without serious risks, though it seems to me the only way to proceed. Let me spin out some of the risks that will bedevil the enterprise.

First, there is what can be called *the Popperian damnation*. The reader at some point spots a particular prediction of the theory, and recalls that in (say) 1965 someone published an article that shows that the prediction is wrong. Since the aim of scientific endeavor, according to Popper, is to prove that theories are false, once the candidate theory is shown to be false it can be dispensed with. The book can be safely closed and discarded, to await the next candidate unified theory, perhaps in some future William James Lectures.

The second risk can be called the *bugaboos of psychology*. We are acutely sensitive, in psychology, about having theories—as if they are too grand a thing for psychology in its nascent state to have. Indeed, it was so bad at one time that, in order to avoid having to talk about having a theory, we talked about *pretheoretical orientations* (Kendler, 1961). We have perhaps gotten back to where we can talk about theories. But if someone begins to talk about *unified theories*, this sense of modesty can be expected to return. Unified theories are too grand a conception to entertain. Psychology needs to wait until—well, until some indefinite future— before entertaining such a thing.

The next risk is to be found guilty of the *sin of presumption*. Who am I, Allen Newell, to propose a unified theory of cognition? We have never had one of these before (though I have already said that John Anderson really has one). Psychology must wait for its Newton. And we all know that only two people could possibly replace Newton—they are Archimedes and Einstein, both of whom are already dead.

Next is the *necessity of selection*. Developing a unified theory, as will become apparent, is a synthetic enterprise. It is not an enterprise of showing that what psychology has already discovered is wrong. Rather, it is an attempt to synthesize the existing understanding into one unified whole, so we can go forward with the task of fashioning it into a better whole. Alas, selections must still be made, because many of the constructs in psychology are genuinely alternative conceptions, even though there is usually some truth on both sides.[3] For instance, if one has productions and semantic nets but not frames or schemas, then that half of the cognitive psychologists who think schemas are grand will be convinced that the enterprise is really not a synthesis at all, but a competitive device to

3. Richman and Simon (1989) have made the point that the same common mechanisms may explain the same phenomenon even when two theories are as different in surface form as symbolic and connectionist theories. This point is related to the discussion above of the random-walk models of decision making.

replace schemas with another construct. There is, of course, a kernel of truth in what they say. Even so, the enterprise loses way.

Another risk is the *half-empty–half-full reaction*. I keep saying, "Look at how much this formulation explains," and the echo keeps coming back, "Look at how much this formulation fails to explain." To one the glass is half full, to another the glass is half empty. No matter how much one tries to show a unified theory and our progress toward it, there will be huge domains in which unification hasn't made significant progress.

The final risk is the *rising tide of connectionism*, which is showing signs of sweeping over all of cognitive science at the moment. The excitement is palpable—we are all hot on the trail of whether neuroscience and the cognitive world can finally be brought together. That is indeed an exciting prospect. But my message relates to symbolic architectures and all the other good things that connectionism sees as the conceptual frame to overthrow. So the final risk is that my timing is terrible. John Anderson had it right when he wrote his book on the architecture of human cognition for publication in 1983. It is too late now.

Believe me, I feel these risks in making the case for unified theories of cognition by putting forward a single candidate and riding that candidate for seven chapters. Iterating through the list of conceivable types of risks at the outset is clearly an attempt on my part to disarm the critics in advance. But having made my magic incantations, it is now time to get on with the business at hand. I do have one last verbal amulet. The late Warren McCulloch, one of the world's great cyberneticists, when attacked sharply at talks, often used to respond with "Don't bite my finger, look where I'm pointing" (McCulloch, 1965, p. iv). Indeed, I will appropriate this epigram as my motto here. I am sure Warren would not mind.

1.4.2. The Vehicle: Soar

There are still two more preliminaries. First, there needs to be the vehicle. I will propose a system called *Soar* as a candidate unified theory. Soar is an architecture for general intelligence, developed by John Laird, at the University of Michigan, Paul Rosenbloom, at the Information Sciences Institute of the University of Southern California, and myself. Soar was first realized as a computer program in 1983 (Laird, Rosenbloom, & Newell, 1986), and there is a current operational version, Soar4.4 (Laird, Newell, & Rosenbloom, 1987). Soar was raised as an AI system, so to speak. It has solved problems and learned on many different tasks, several of which will appear in the following pages. So it is a real system with real properties. As is standard practice in AI, however, a new version (Soar5) is on the way. (Indeed, it is being phased in as this book goes to press.) Thus it will sometimes be a little difficult to know what is fully operational and what is not. But in the main, Soar may be taken as an operational system.

Soar already has the major mechanisms of a cognitive system, as that notion has developed over the last decade in cognitive science. It is largely consonant with the several harbingers above. It has a symbol system and a goal hierarchy. It uses a production system as the foundation of the architecture, thus being a kind of recognize-act system. It uses problem spaces everywhere to do all of its business, that is, to formulate all its tasks. It has a chunking mechanism as part of its architecture, and it learns by chunking on everything it does. In the Soar project we are currently busy moving it toward becoming a unified theory of cognition in detail, in ways that this book will describe.[4]

Though in general Soar fits into the community of symbolic systems being used in cognitive science, it does have a few highly contentious features. The biggest one, as we shall see, is that its memory seems to be entirely procedural—that is, it is made up entirely of productions. Although it is useful, interesting, and fun to explore such unique assumptions, it may detract a little from using Soar simply as an exemplar for a unified theory of cognition, where the emphasis is on being synthetic and noncontentious. It is perhaps not quite vanilla-flavored enough.

1.4.3. The Role of Artificial Intelligence

It is worth being explicit about the role of artificial intelligence (AI) in this enterprise, since AI is often seen as contrasting with cognitive science—pure (engineering) AI versus mechanisms of human intelligence—as if these were different subject matters. Soar itself

---

4. In part, this is why Act* is not the vehicle of choice for this book. To work on a cognitive architecture one must be able to control it and change it. So one must have one's own variant architecture. But also, much has been learned since the specification of Act* in relatively mature form in 1983, from Act* itself and from elsewhere. Soar has important properties and capabilities that make it a worthwhile exploration in its own right.

already provides a clue. As far as I am concerned, AI is the study of the mechanisms of intelligence and all supporting technologies, extending to perception and motion, namely robotics. AI is itself part of computer science, which is the study of information and its processing in all its variety.

AI provides the theoretical infrastructure for the study of human cognition. It has already provided much of our knowledge of what intelligence is all about and how it is to be realized in information-processing mechanisms. Being an infrastructure, AI fills an entire spectrum of specific roles (Newell, 1970)—from enforcing operational thinking about processes, to a theoretically neutral language of processing, to metaphors about the kinds of processings that might occur in the mind. Various of these specific roles are sometimes taken as the primary way AI relates to psychology. In fact, it plays them all.

AI has one additional critical contribution to make to understanding the mind. What's most important in understanding intelligence is how it functions. The first question to ask about any theory of the nature of intelligent action, whether in humans or machines, is whether it in fact produces intelligent action—effective problem solving, perception, learning, movement, or whatever. Though the issue of functionality might not be central in some areas of psychology, it is critical for perception, cognition, and action. Thus the basic theory of the mechanisms of intelligence is central to human cognition.

I will draw on AI in all these ways throughout the book, without further special comment or acknowledgment.

1.4.4. Preview of the Chapters

This brings us, at last, to a foreshadowing of the chapters themselves. Chapter 2 will introduce the foundations of cognitive systems. What do the terms mean that we all use—knowledge, representation, computation, symbols, architecture, intelligence, search. This will take us back over familiar territory, but it is useful. It gets us started in the right way and prepares the ground. As a minor benefit, it will provide for those readers who feel a need for definitions.

Chapter 3 moves to basic aspects of the human cognitive architecture. We inquire into what general conditions shape the human architecture. Given that the human is constructed out of neural technology, on the one hand, but is capable of intelligent action, on the other—does this provide constraints on a theory of human cognition? It turns out that it does.

Chapter 4 contains the full detail of the architecture that will be our candidate cognitive architecture, namely Soar. This architecture will, naturally enough, abide by the constraints revealed in Chapter 3. The chapter will focus on the structure of that architecture and how it manages intelligent action. The chapter ends by showing how Soar maps into human cognition.

The next three chapters will range over different domains of cognition, showing how Soar provides a unified treatment. Chapter 5 will start with immediate behavior—tasks that go from presentation to completion in just a second or two. Chapter 6 covers learning, memory, and skill acquisition—behavior that cuts across the time dimension. Chapter 7 moves up to tasks that take long enough so the system can attain modest degrees of rationality, namely tasks of the order of minutes and more.

Finally, Chapter 8 explores the frontier that separates what Soar can currently treat, in at least modestly concrete terms, and what is still pure speculation. A unified theory of cognition must indeed be able to address the full range of cognition, even if the actual investigation is still to be done. It is important at least to ask what approach would be indicated for such areas as language and development, and what the relation could be to the bordering system layers, neurophysiology below and social systems above. Then, having made these few probes of the frontier, we bring the case to a close.

Foundations of
Cognitive Science

2

We start with the foundational issues of how to describe the basic structure of cognitive systems. We need some common ground as we go forward, so that we don't become distracted, say, about the nature of knowledge or representation. We will be covering familiar territory, for much attention has been paid to these notions. Some of them have a classical philosophical literature, and all of them have attracted continuing consideration in cognitive science in the last decade, especially as philosophers have finally come to take an interest in the subject. Still, it is worthwhile reworking the familiar. It must be recognized, though, that there is never much agreement on foundations—they are always less secure intellectually than what they support.

Despite the disclaimer, I do have something I am attempting to achieve while reviewing these notions. I want to tie them closer to the physical world than is usually the case. Rather than emphasize the abstract character of the various types of systems we will deal with, I will emphasize how they are grounded in humans as physical systems in a dynamic world. Theories of human cognition are ultimately theories of physical, biological systems. Our ability to describe human cognition in one way rather than another rests ultimately on the physical and biological nature of human beings. Furthermore, the fact that human beings are grounded in the world implies additional constraints that must be taken into account in constructing our theories.

For convenience' sake we will take up, in turn, the major terms that will come up again and again, starting with the notion of a behaving system, which is just a necessary preliminary. After that we will cover knowledge, representation, computational systems, symbols and symbol systems, architecture, intelligence, search and problem spaces, and preparation and deliberation.[1]

2.1. Behaving Systems

I want to take *mind* to be the control system that guides the behaving organism in its complex interactions with the dynamic real world. So, Figure 2-1 shows the environment behaving through time and the organism behaving through time, with a series of interactions between the two. Although single transactions can be isolated analytically—where the environment presents and the organism responds, or vice versa—these transactions are embedded in a sequence such that each becomes part of the context within which further actions follow. The mind then is simply the name we give to the control system that has evolved within the organism to carry out the interactions to the benefit of that organism or, ultimately, for the survival of its species.

Whatever higher point of view might also be valid, mind can be seen to provide *response functions*. That is, the organism takes actions as a function (in the mathematical sense) of the environment. If the environment is different, the organism can behave differently, even with the same response function. That is what it means to be in interaction. However, many different response functions occur as the organism goes through time. During the period labeled A in the figure the organism behaves with one response function, during B with another, during C with yet another. There are different response functions in different kinds of situations.

Imagine yourself going through a day. There is one response function when you get yourself out of bed, one when you reach for your clothes, one when you face yourself in the mirror, another when you go to breakfast and talk to your spouse, another when you get in your car and drive to work. Each of those situations is radically different and each calls for a quite different function about how to respond with respect to the environment. One involves beds, floors, and covers; another involves mirrors and faucets; an-

1. In the original lectures, purely for reasons of time, the last two topics—search and problem spaces, and preparation and deliberation—formed the initial segment of lecture 3. Here, all the foundational material is pulled into one chapter.

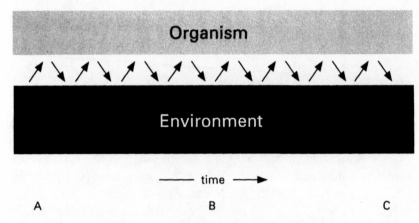

Figure 2-1. Abstract view of mind as a controller of a behaving system.

other yet something entirely different. When you come back to the same situation you may have a different response function. You climb into the car and something happened differently and you can't remember where the key is and now you do something different. The world is divided up into microepics, which are sufficiently distinct and independent so that the control system (that is, the mind) produces different response functions, one after the other.

It is certainly possible to step back and treat the mind as one big monster response function; that is, treat the mind as a single function from the total environment over the total past of the organism to future actions (under the constraint that output at a given time never depends on future input). Describing behavior as multiple response functions implies some sort of decomposition within the organism. In effect the organism treats the environment as different enough from time to time, so that the aspects that enter into the function (that the behavior is made a function of) have little in common. Thus it is possible to describe the organism as using separate functions, one for each situation. This phrase, *response function,* will occur over and over again throughout the book, so remember it.

2.2. Knowledge Systems

How then should we describe systems? How should we describe their response functions? To speak of mind as a controller suggests immediately the language of control systems—of feedback, gain, oscillation, damping, and so on. It is a language that allows us to describe systems as *purposive* (Rosenbleuth, Weiner, & Bigelow, 1943). But we are interested in the full range of human behavior and response—not only walking down a road or tracking a flying bird, but reading bird books, planning the walk, taking instructions to get to the place, identifying distinct species, counting the new additions to the life list of birds seen, and holding conversations about it all afterward. When the scope of behavior extends this broadly, it becomes evident that the language of control systems is really locked to a specific environment and class of tasks—to continuous motor movement with the aim of pointing or following. For the rest it becomes metaphorical.

A way to describe the behavior of systems with wide-ranging capability is in terms of their having *knowledge* and behaving in light of it. Let us first see what that means, before we see how we do it. Figure 2-2 shows a simple situation, the *blocks world,* which is suitably paradigmatic for systems characterized as having knowledge. There is a table, on which sit three blocks, *A*, *B*, and *C*, with block *A* on top of block *B*. Some agent *X* observes the situation, so that we can say that *X* knows that *A* is on top of *B*. Another agent, *Y*, who does not observe the situation, asks *X* whether *B* is clear on top. We say, almost without thinking, that *X* will tell *Y* that *B* is not clear. We have actually made a prediction of *X*'s response. Let us say that is exactly what happens (it is certainly plausible, is it not?). What is behind our being able to predict *X*'s behavior?

A straightforward analysis runs as follows. We assume that *X* has a goal to answer *Y* truthfully. There must be a goal involved. If we can't assume any goals for this agent, then no basis exists for predicting that *X* will answer the question, rather than walking out of the room or doing any other thing. The agent's goal (in this case) is something like this: if someone asks a simple question, answer truthfully. We take it that if *X* knows something, *X* can use that knowledge for whatever purposes it chooses. Thus, we calculate: *X* knows that block *A* is on top of block *B*; *X* wants to answer the question truthfully; *X* has the ability to answer (*X* can communicate); consequently, *X* will tell *Y* that block *B* is not clear on top. Thus, we can predict what *X* will do. The prediction need not always be right—we may be wrong about *X*'s goals, or about what

Let X observe a table of stacked blocks
We say "X knows that A is on top of B"
A nonobserver Y asks X whether B is clear on top
We say (predict) "X will tell Y that B is not clear"

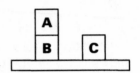

Figure 2-2. The simple blocks world.

X knows, or some other aspect of the situation that could prevent the action. Still, this is a useful scheme to predict a system's behavior.

The analysis of knowledge has a long philosophical history, and indeed constitutes the standard subarea of epistemology. It has a continuation within cognitive science (Goldman, 1986). That analysis takes knowledge as something sui generis—something special with special issues about what it means for a system to have knowledge and especially what it means for knowledge to be certain. What I claim cognitive science needs, instead, is a concept of knowledge that is used simply to describe and predict the response functions of a system. There can be, of course, a different response function for every goal and every body of knowledge, but the little situation with the blocks is entirely paradigmatic of our use of the concept. It is a way of characterizing a system such that we can predict (with varying degrees of success) the behavior of the system.

Thus, to treat something as having knowledge is to treat it as a system of a certain kind. We always describe systems in some way, if we are to deal with them at all. Some systems we describe in one way, some in another. Often we describe the same system in multiple ways. To describe a system as a *knowledge system* is just one of the alternatives that is available. The choice of what description to use is a pragmatic one, depending on our purposes and our own knowledge of the system and its character.[2]

2. The use of the phrase "our purposes and our own knowledge" in order to describe the nature of knowledge is benign and does not indicate any vicious circle. To discuss when an agent uses a given type of description, we must describe that agent. In this instance, the appropriate description for the agent, which is us, is as a knowledge system.

Knowledge-level systems
Medium: Knowledge
  Laws: Principle of rationality

Program-level systems
Medium: Data structures, programs
  Laws: Sequential interpretation of programs

Register-transfer systems
Medium: Bit vectors
  Laws: Parallel logic

Logic circuits
Medium: Bits
  Laws: Boolean algebra

Electrical circuits
Medium: Voltage/current
  Laws: Ohm's law, Kirchhoff's law

Electronic devices
Medium: Electrons
  Laws: Electron physics

Figure 2-3. The hierarchy of computer systems.

Consider the familiar computer-systems hierarchy, shown in Figure 2-3, which we will encounter repeatedly in the course of this book. A computer system can be described in many ways. It can be described as a system of electronic devices, or as an electrical circuit, or as a logic circuit, or as a register-transfer system, or as a programming system. There are other ways as well, ways that are not related to its primary function, such as an item of cost in a budget, a contributor to floor loading, or an emblem of being high-tech. All the descriptions based on the computer as a behaving system are types of *machines*. In each case there is some kind of *medium* that is processed. Working up from the bottom, the media are electrons, current, bits, bit vectors, and data structures. At any moment, the *state* of the system consists of some configuration of its medium. There are *behavior laws* that can be used to predict the behavior of the system. Electrons are particles that move under impressed electromagnetic forces; electrical circuits obey Ohm's law and Kirchhoff's law; logic circuits obey Boolean algebra; the processing in programs obeys the stipulated programming language. In each case, if we know the state of the system and the laws of its behavior, we can obtain the state of the system at some point in the future. Each of these descriptions provides a different way to make predictions about system behavior.

A clarification is in order. All along, I keep referring to predictions. This is simply shorthand for all the various uses of descriptions, such as explaining behavior, controlling behavior, or constructing something that behaves to specifications. Although there are differences in these activities and some descriptions are more suited to one than the other, it becomes tiresome to have to be explicit each and every time. "Prediction" will cover them all.

The descriptions of computer systems form a hierarchy of *levels,* because each higher-level description is both an abstraction and a specialization of the one below it. Consider the level of electrical circuits. Its medium, current, is the flow of electrons. Its laws, Ohm's and Kirchhoff's, can be derived from electromagnetic theory, specialized to networks of conductors. Or consider the program level. Data structures are sets of bit vectors, to be interpreted in fixed ways by various operations. The operations can be described as the outcomes of specific register-transfer systems, as can the interpretation of a program data structure that determines which operations are executed. Each level abstracts from many details of the level below.

Systems become more specialized as the hierarchy is ascended. Not every system describable as an electrical circuit is also describable as a logic circuit. Not every system describable as a register-transfer system is a programmable system. The relationships between the levels are sometimes quite transparent, as is the simple aggregation that connects the logic level to the register-transfer level, where bits are simply organized into vectors of fixed length and handled in a uniform way, except for a few special operations (such as addition and multiplication, with their carries). Sometimes the relationships are less obvious. Inventing electrical circuits that behaved discretely according to the laws of Boolean logic required a rather substantial evolution, mediated by the work on pulse systems for radar.

Knowledge systems are just another level within this same hierarchy, another way to describe a system. As a level in the hierarchy, knowledge is above the program level in Figure 2-3. The knowledge level abstracts completely from the internal processing and the internal representation. Thus, all that is left is the content of the representations and the goals toward which that content will be used. As a level, it has a medium, namely, knowledge. It has a law of behavior, namely, if the system wants to attain goal G and knows that to do act A will lead to attaining G, then it will do A. This law is a simple form of rationality—that an agent will operate in its own best interests according to what it knows.

As just another level in the hierarchy of Figure 2-3, there is nothing special about the knowledge level, in any foundational or philosophical sense. Of course, the knowledge level is certainly different from all the other levels. It has its own medium and its own laws and these have their own peculiarities. But, equally, each of the other levels is different from all the others, each with its own peculiarities. The levels can, of course, also be classified in various ways, such as discrete versus continuous, or sequential versus parallel. But the classification is not very important, compared with the individual particularity of each level, in how it describes a system and what are the characteristic modes of analysis and synthesis that go with it so that it can be used effectively.

Descriptive schemes like the one put forth in Figure 2-3 do not carry with them obvious scientific claims. They seem to be simply ways of describing parts of nature. However, they are far from theoretically neutral. Scientific claims arise when we discover (or assert) that such a descriptive scheme can actually be used successfully, or with such and such a degree of approximation, for a given real system or type of system. The criterion for success is that the system is operationally complete—its behavior is determined by the behavior laws, as formulated for that level, applying to its state, as described at that level. The claim is that abstraction to the particular level involved still preserves all that is relevant for future behavior described at that level of abstraction. The force of such claims can be appreciated easily enough by imagining someone handing you a small closed box and asserting, "There is a programmable computer inside." This means you will find something inside that can be successfully described as a programmable computer, so that you may treat it so, expecting to be able to program it, execute it with a loaded program, and so on. Taking the abstraction as given and acting on your expectations, you would be in for one successful prediction after another (or failure thereof) about a region of the world you hitherto had not known.

Thus, to claim that humans can be described at the knowledge level is to claim there is a way of formulating them as agents that have knowledge and goals, such that their behavior is successfully predicted by the law that says: all the person's knowledge is always used to attain the goals of the person. The claim, of course, need not be for completely successful prediction, but only to some approximation.

It is easy to see why describing a system at the knowledge level is useful. The essential feature is that no details of the actual internal processing are required. The behavior of an existing system can be calculated if you know the system's goals and what the system knows about its environment. Both can often be determined by direct observation—of the environment, on the one hand, and of the system's prior behavior, on the other. The knowledge level is also useful for designing systems whose internal workings are yet to be determined. The knowledge level provides a way of stating something about the desired behavior of the system and about what it must incorporate (namely, the requisite knowledge and goals). Specifications for systems are often given at the knowledge level. Every level, of course, can and does serve as a specification for the level below it. The special feature of the knowledge level is that it can be given before anything about the internal workings of the system is determined.

Let us summarize by restating rather carefully what a knowledge-level system is (Figure 2-4). A knowledge system is embedded in an external environment, with which it interacts by a set of possible actions. The behavior of the system is the sequence of actions taken in the environment over time. The system has goals about how the environment should be. Internally, the system processes a medium, called knowledge. Its body of knowledge is about its environment, its goals, its actions, and the relations between them. It has a single law of behavior: the system takes actions to attain its goals, using all the knowledge that it has. This law describes the results of how the knowledge is processed. The system can obtain new knowledge from external knowledge sources via some of its actions (which can be called perceptual actions). Once knowledge is acquired it is available forever after. The system is a single homogeneous body of knowledge, all of which is brought to bear on the determination of its actions. There is no loss of knowledge over time, though of course knowledge can be communicated to other systems.

Characterizing knowledge as the medium of a system level, which is just one system level among many, constitutes a particular

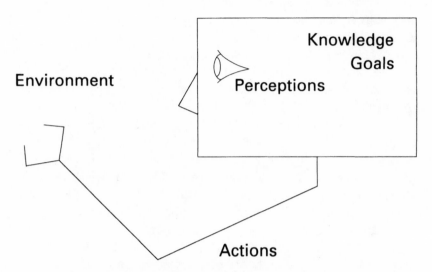

Figure 2-4. The knowledge-level system.

theory about the nature of knowledge. The existing extensive philosophic literature about knowledge does not describe knowledge in these terms. In general it does not describe knowledge in terms of a system at all, but simply proceeds to inquire after its validity and certainty. Daniel Dennett's (1978, 1988a) notion of an *intentional system,* however, is substantially the same as a knowledge-level system. Actually, the key concept for Dennett is that of the *intentional stance,* which is the way the observer chooses to view or conceptualize the agent.[3]

Although this knowledge-level systems theory is indeed a theory of knowledge, it is not in fact anybody's theory. It certainly is not *my* theory. I am not putting forth something that I have discovered or invented. Rather, this way of using knowledge systems is the actual standard practice in computer science and artificial intelligence. All that I have done is to observe the way we use this concept of knowledge and make it explicit.

It is useful to note that this theory of knowledge arose without specific authorship—without a specific inventor or discoverer. It

---

3. Dennett thus puts the emphasis on the nature of the observer rather than on the nature of what is observed. The reader interested in following up the way philosophers treat these matters and the relation of the intentional stance to the knowledge level can consult Dennett (1988b) and Newell (1988).

will help to sort out the various notions of knowledge that are around. The sociological structure of science, and scholarship more broadly, incorporates a view that ideas are authored by individuals of note, who are thereby to be honored and rewarded for producing and disseminating these ideas. Whatever view might be held about the ideas themselves, whether actually invented or merely discov-ered, they do not become part of science and society without the agency of particular men and women. There may be difficulties of determining who first discovered this or that idea. There may be genuine cases of simultaneous discovery (Merton, 1973), but some specific set of scientists or scholars still gets the credit. The case in hand doesn't fit this frame, however, nor do others coming later in the chapter, namely, symbols and architecture.

Computer scientists and engineers *as a group* developed what I argue is the appropriate theory of knowledge. They did so without any particular author laying out the theory. Lots of words, cer-tainly, were written about computers and how to deal with them—from highly technical and creative efforts to general musings and on to popularizations and advertising copy. And some of these words have put forth novel ideas that can be said to have been authored, in perfect accordance with the standard view of science. John von Neumann is generally credited with *the stored-program concept* (though there is a modicum of dispute about it because of the events surrounding Eniac, Eckert and Mauchly, and the Moore School). But the stored-program concept (or any of the other ideas that were articulated) is not the notion of knowledge-level systems.

I do not know of any clear articulation of the idea of the knowl-edge level in computer science prior to my 1980 AAAI presidential address (Newell, 1982).[4] But that was almost twenty years after its use was common—after computer scientists were talking techni-cally and usefully about what their programs knew and what they should know. All my paper did was give voice to the practice (and it was so represented in the paper). I have been, of course, a partici-pant in the developing use of this notion, having been involved in both computer science and AI since the mid-1950s. And I have certainly done my share of writing scientific articles, putting forth

4. Dennett's writings on the intentional stance go back to the late 1960s but do not seem to owe much to computer science, on this score at least; see references in Dennett (1988a).

theories and concepts. But I was simply part of the community in how I learned to use such notions as knowledge. Here is a sentence and its explanatory footnote taken from an early paper (Newell, 1962, p. 403):

> For anything to happen in a machine some process must know* enough to make it happen.
>
> *We talk about routines "knowing". This is a paraphrase of "In this routine it can be assumed that such and such is the case." Its appropriateness stems from the way a programmer codes—setting down successive instructions in terms of what he (the programmer) knows at the time. What the programmer knows at a particular point in a routine is what the routine knows. The following dialogue gives the flavor. (Programmer A looking over the shoulder of B, who is coding up a routine.) "How come you just added Z5 to the accumulator?" "Because I want . . ." "No, I mean how do you know it's a number?" "All the Z's are numbers, that's the way I set it up." (B now puts down another instruction.) "How can you do *that*?" "Because I cleared the cell to zero here at the start of the routine." "But the program can branch back to this point in front of you!" "Oh, you're right; I don't know it's cleared to zero at this point."

The philosophers, of course, have had their own technical development of the concept of knowledge, which did not contribute to the computer science and AI concept, as far as I can tell. Certainly they are distinct concepts. One difference is clearly evident in what is here called *knowledge* is called *belief* by the philosophers, who reserve *knowledge* for something akin to *justified true belief*. Peculiar problems of scholarship are raised when technical communities acquire important new concepts by their practice. For instance, the philosophers have a notion (perhaps even a conceit) called *folk psychology*. It distinguishes the psychology of the folk—of the untutored masses, so to speak—from the psychology as given by science. Is, then, the use of *knowledge* by computer scientists part of *folk philosophy*? It is certainly not what the computer scientists write that counts, but how they use it in their practice. One might equally entertain the notion that the philosopher's use of *knowledge* was *folk computer science*. Except that philosophy got there first, even if by a different route. Now that philosophy has a pseudopod into cognitive science, these two views of knowledge are brought together, mixing in some odd ways.

2.3. Representation

Knowledge abstracts from representation, yet knowledge must be represented in some fashion in order to be used, told, or thought. This may seem like a special philosophical statement, justified by some particular argument. But it is not. It is simply the proposition that knowledge-level systems are simultaneously describable at lower levels and that systems that exist in the physical world have physical descriptions. Thus, to use Figure 2-3 as a guide, a knowledge-level system that exists in the physical world also can be described as a programmed system, a register-transfer system, a logic system, an electrical circuit, and an electronic device. Of course, the hierarchy of that figure is not necessarily the only hierarchy that can have knowledge systems at the top. The figure exhibits one hierarchy that we know of that does include knowledge systems. Other hierarchies might well exist. Indeed, in the case of humans, who are describable as knowledge-level systems better than any of the computer systems we have around, the hierarchy must be quite different as it makes its way down to the biological substrate. Establishing the existence of alternative hierarchies that support a knowledge level is a scientific task or an engineering task, depending on whether we discover the hierarchy by the analysis of existing systems or invent it by the design and construction of hitherto nonexistent systems.

Let us turn, then, to the nature of representation, which is another fundamental concept in cognitive science. Let us start by being specific. A standard way of representing knowledge is with a logic. Figure 2-5 provides such a representation for the blocks world. The representation consists of the expressions in the figure. There is a predicate, *block,* that can be used to assert that A is a block, B is a block, C is a block, and the table T is not a block. Another predicate, *on,* can be used to assert that B is on the table T, A is on B, and C is on T. Another predicate, *clear,* is defined in terms of *block* and *on: x* is clear if and only if x is a block and, if y is any block, then it is not on x. From this information it can be inferred that block B is not clear. Thus if expressions 1–3 in Figure 2-5 represent what X knows, then X also knows that B is not clear. And if we couple this with knowledge of X's goal, Y's request, and X's ability to communicate, then we can predict that X will tell Y that B is not clear.

Posit
1. (block A), (block B), (block C), not(block T)
2. (on B T), (on A B), (on C T)
3. (clear x) iff (block x) and (y) (block y) implies not(on y x)

Infer
4. not(clear B)

Figure 2-5. The blocks world in logic.

One might be tempted to object that X knows not(clear B) directly from observation, not indirectly via some inference. But this confuses the knowledge that X has with the representation that X has of that knowledge. Certainly, X has some representation of this knowledge. But we do not know that it is the logic representation of Figure 2-5. In fact, if X is a person and you are a psychologist, you'll bet that it isn't. All we assert is that this logic representation tells us the knowledge that X has. Nothing is said about the form of that representation, certainly not that the individual expressions in Figure 2-5 correspond to anything particular in X's representation.

It is important to be clear that a logic is just a way of representing knowledge. It is not the knowledge itself. To see this, let $K(1)$ be the knowledge represented by expression 1 in the figure. Thus, by writing down expressions 1, 2, and 3 as the knowledge that X has, we certainly mean that X has knowledge $K(1)$ and $K(2)$ and $K(3)$. One might think that it makes no difference whether we talk about the expressions or the knowledge—they are in one-to-one correspondence. But that is not the only knowledge X has. X also has $K(4)$. $K(4)$ certainly does not correspond to any expression that we originally wrote down (namely, 1, 2, and 3). X has $K(4)$ because expression 4 can be inferred from expressions 1, 2, and 3 (and the rules of the logic).

The general situation for logic can be stated easily. If X has the knowledge represented by a conjunction of expressions $K(1, 2, \ldots, M)$, and expression N follows from $1, 2, \ldots, M$, then X has the $K(N)$, the knowledge of expression N. Since, in general, there are an unlimited number of expressions that follow from a conjunction of expressions, X's knowledge is correspondingly unlimited. It certainly cannot be written down in its entirety. So there is no way in which one can identify the knowledge of X with the representation of that knowledge. Instead, what a logic lets us do is represent the knowledge of X as a finite set of expressions plus a process (the inference rules of logic) for generating the infinite set of other expressions that comprise X's total knowledge.

It is also important to see that logic is just one of many different ways of representing knowledge. It was a deliberate *choice* to use logic to represent X's knowledge. It might or might not be a good way of representing what X knows. It might be that X would show by its behavior that it knew $K(1)$ and $K(2)$ and $K(3)$ but would not exhibit any knowledge of $K(4)$. Then this logic representation would not describe X. It would be too powerful, implying that X knew things it didn't. We might try to fashion a new representation for X's knowledge by positing that X knew only what is expressed in exactly the set of expressions that are written down, a representation in which no additional inferences are permitted. For some purposes this might be useful, though with logics it isn't, because a logic carries with it a set of rules of inference and the notion of the free use of the rules.[5] If we accept our earlier story, X did not know $K(4)$, so in this case the revised scheme would be too weak, implying that X didn't know things it did. We might then cast about for other ways of representing knowledge that would provide an accurate knowledge-level description of X. There is no guarantee, of course, that we can ever find such a representation—X might not be representable as a knowledge-level system.

Although logic is only one of many ways of representing, it has many nice properties that reflect general properties of bodies of knowledge. Two bodies of knowledge can be combined to form a single body of knowledge, as when some knowledge is incorporated into an existing system. This corresponds to the conjunction of the two sets of expressions in the logic. If one adds to a body of knowledge exactly the same knowledge, then no new knowledge is obtained. This is reflected in conjunction being idempotent: $(A$ and $A)$ if and only if A. A particularly important feature is the indication of broad representational scope. In logics such as the first-order predicate calculus, essentially any knowledge can be represented. The indication is that other powerful representations—in particular, set theory—can be formulated in the logic. Such sufficiency is bought at the price of how that knowledge is represented. In fact, much work has been done in artificial intelligence and some in philosophy

5. Recently there has been some interest in using logics with restricted rules of inference, so that bounds can be given on the time to make inferences (Levesque, 1986).

External World

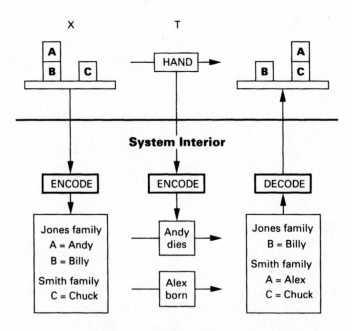

A block is clear if it corresponds to the youngest child

Figure 2-6. A representation of the blocks world.

on how to represent things in logical calculi. Much of the difficulty turns out to be that we don't understand what we want to represent, not that we can't find first-order ways of doing it. Another part of the difficulty is that the representation is often very awkward and indirect. Thus much research goes into finding alternative forms of logics (model logics, higher-order logics, sorted logics) that are easier to use or more perspicuous.

We can become clearer about what is involved in representation by pursuing how else we might represent our simple blocks world. The general situation is shown in Figure 2-6. There is an external world in which the blocks world occurs. In this example an action is taken (the transformation *T*) that moves the block *A* from atop block *B* to atop block *C*.[6] Besides the external world, there is the

6. I could have remained faithful to the prior example of whether block *B* was clear, but it would have been somewhat confusing, because it involves a change only in the knowing agent, not in the world.

system, in whose interior is another situation, the representation of the blocks world. This interior situation is equally part of the total world, of course, and consists of some physical system that goes through transformations as well, to produce another interior situation. The question is, What is the nature of the interior system for it to be a representation of the particular blocks situation in the external world?

I've chosen a rather unfamiliar way of representing the blocks world in Figure 2-6. Each stack of blocks corresponds to a family— the Jones family and the Smith family—and the children in a family are the blocks in order of age, youngest on top. The transformation is that people die and get born. If Andy Jones dies and Alex Smith is born, then the Jones family only has Billy and the Smith family has Alex and Chuck. To ask a question, such as whether a given block, say *B*, is clear, is to ask who is the youngest child in a family. In the initial situation, Billy is not the youngest, although after Andy dies, he becomes the youngest.

There is a clear correspondence between the external blocks world and family situations. Some of the properties correspond (being clear, and being the youngest), but not all (are the blocks square, or are the children boys or girls?). Some of the transformations correspond (moving blocks, and birthing/dying), but not all (blocks falling over, and the children growing older).

The representation is somewhat odd—I chose it to avoid the obvious ways we would create such representations if we were doing it on paper or in a computer—but it's actually not as far-fetched as you might think. According to a long tradition in anthropology (Laboratory of Comparative Human Cognition, 1982), when one attempts to get members of primitive tribes to reason on isolated, abstract logical tasks, they tend not to work with the abstract situations but to deal only with concrete situations with which they are thoroughly familiar. In fact, that is true with people in our own society. People are better on syllogisms if they are cast in concrete terms rather than expressed abstractly. For instance, reporting an experiment on syllogistic reasoning Johnson-Laird and Bara (1984, p. 20) noted that the data for one person had to be discarded because she said she couldn't imagine any particular concrete situation that corresponded to a particular syllogism, so she was unable even to work on the task (in fact, the scenario involved a family).

Let's describe abstractly what is going on in Figure 2-6. The original external situation is *encoded* into an internal situation. The external transformation is also *encoded* into an internal transformation. Then the internal transformation is *applied* to the internal situation to obtain a new internal situation. Finally, the new internal situation is *decoded* to an external situation. Suppose that the resulting external situation is the same as the situation produced by the external transformation. Then the internal system—the encoding process, the internal situation, the internal transformation, and the decoding process—has successfully been used as a representation of the external situation.

This is the essence of representation—to be able to go from something to something else by a different path when the originals are not available. We can cast this as a general law:

> *The representation law:*
> decode[encode(T)(encode(X))] = $T(X)$
>
> where X is the original external situation and T is the external transformation

This is called *the* representation law because it is the general form. Actually, there are myriad representation laws, one each for the myriad particular encode-apply-decode paths that represent an external path. Each encode-apply-decode path is unique exactly as required to reflect the aspects of the external path that are represented. The processes of encoding and decoding are part of the path, so they become an essential part of the law. There can be multiple forms of encoding, for there are many different situations that can lead to the same encoded situation. The same external situation can (on occasion) be viewed, heard, read about, or felt. Likewise, there can be multiple forms of decoding, for there are many different ways to interact with an external situation. The same external situation can be identified as another (that is, tested), selected out, constructed, or described (leaving the actual contact to someone else). The central claim behind the representation law is that if anything is used as a representation, then a law of the above form will be the essential ingredient that explains why the internal situation represents the external situation.

A representational system carries with it one other requirement. Namely, the internal system has to be controlled in some way. The application of encoding, internal transformings, and decoding must be executable at will, or at least sufficiently at will to serve the purposes of the organism. It is not necessary that freedom be complete, but representations must be at the service of other activities of the organism, and hence must be evocable at appropriate times and places. If the family representation in Figure 2-6 were to depend on real families being recalled or being perceived concurrently (or, worse, if it required waiting until children were actually born and died), it would not pass this requirement. On the other hand, the representational system need not be in the interior of the organism, although Figure 2-6 makes it appear that way. A representation can just as well occur in some exterior field, so long as it can be controlled—a scratch pad, an abacus, a computer, or even a friend.

This view of representation leads naturally to the following approach to representational systems. Consider a task for the organism that requires a representation—that is, that requires that the organism produce a response function that depends on aspects of the environment that are not immediately available. Then, the problem for the organism (or for evolution, it makes no difference) is to find the right kind of material with the right properties for encoding and decoding and the right dynamics for the transformation. If these can be found and brought within the organism's control, then a specific representational system can be constructed that will play the required role in doing the task. This is the *analogical* view of representations—each representing system is an analog of what it represents. Each analogical view is special—a particular adaptation to a particular representational need. This approach arises directly from applying the idea of the representation law.

However, there is a difficulty with this approach. The more capable the organism (ultimately ourselves), the more representational schemes are required. In the blocks world, we want to respond not just to blocks, but to their color and their size, to their stability and their shape, to the patterns on their faces and the relations between these patterns. We want to respond not just to properties and relations, but to transformations, which move beyond putting one block on top of another and clearing a block off to whether they're falling off, to their supporting each other, and their rotations. We wish to break out into new representational territory by putting together sequences of transformations, then giving blocks to other people, then painting them, and then selling them, then keeping accounts of the sales, then collecting and paying sales taxes. We want to do all these things vicariously (in our heads), in interaction and sequence. The more things that are demanded, the tighter are the constraints on finding some kind of material with the right dynamics. Finding feasible representations gets increasingly difficult with a richer and richer variety of things to be represented and richer and richer kinds of operational transformations that they undergo. More and more interlocking representation laws need to be satisfied.

This could simply be the way the world is in fact—a narrower and narrower eye of the needle through which to thread successful organisms with higher representational capabilities. That could have led to a world in which different higher organisms had largely disjoint representational capabilities. There is more than a little suggestion of this in the variety of the biological world, with its plethora of ingenious evolutionary solutions to problems of species success. The classical story that ethologists have told of the adaptive character of lower organisms seems to fit this picture (Tinbergen, 1969). Unfortunately, not all adaptations require representations, and the examples, from the digger wasp to the stickleback, are not sorted out to make it easy to see exactly what is representational and what is not.

It might have been this way, but it is not. Instead there exists an alternative path to obtain highly complex adaptive systems, which can be called *the Great Move*. Instead of moving toward more and more specialized materials with specialized dynamics to support an increasingly great variety and intricacy of representational demands, an entirely different turn is possible. This is the move to using a neutral, stable medium that is capable of registering variety and then *composing* whatever transformations are needed to satisfy the requisite representation laws. Far from representational constriction, this path opens up the whole world of indefinitely rich representations.

Figure 2-7 illustrates this path. It should certainly seem familiar, although its familiarity should not prevent the appreciation of its significance. The representational medium is a list structure, with sublists for the stacks of blocks, in order, starting with the table T. Let us go around the representation path again. We start with the encoding of the external situation into a list structure with T, B, and A for one stack and T, C for the other. Movement of the hand is

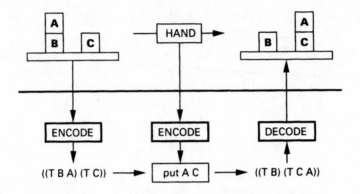

(put x y): If x last, move to end of sublist with y

Figure 2-7. List representation of the blocks world.

encoded into an internal process (put *A C*) that modifies the list structure: If *x* is the last item on its sublist, move it to the end of the sublist containing *y*. Although written in English, many readers will have instantly recoded this prescription into Lisp. This Lisp program is an expression composed according to a fixed scheme of interpretation (that of Lisp) so that it does exactly the transformation that satisfies the external transformation. This composed transformation depends, of course, on how the encoding of the situation was set up. If it had been set up so that the top blocks were first in the list and the table *T* (being superfluous) was dropped, then the program (put *x y*) would no longer satisfy the representation law (precisely not!). But a new Lisp function could easily be written that would. Nothing in the basic representational medium—list structures—bears any direct or necessary relation to the blocks world. What the representational medium does do is offer an unlimited variety of ways of encoding blocks-world situations such that, for each of them, Lisp functions can be written to satisfy appropriate representation laws.

We are now on familiar ground, for we understand well what it means to talk about *composable transformations*, however remote that might have seemed fifty years ago. Indeed, it is necessary to go back at least fifty years to become innocent of programmable systems. What is needed is a medium—in Figure 2-7 it is list structures, the same medium as the situations—and an interpreter that takes a structure in the medium and interprets it to carry out the processing specified. There is lots of freedom in how this is done. The medium in which the transformations are composed need not be the same as the medium in which the situations are encoded, nor the same as the medium that produces action at the time the transformation is required. It could equally be a medium of instructions for putting together a special-purpose machine—here, for (put x y)—that would simply carry out the transformation when started.

This great move has forged a link between representations and composable response functions. If a system can compose functions and if it can do it internally in an arena under its own control, then that system can represent. How well it can represent depends on how flexible is its ability to compose functions that obey the needed representation laws—there can be limits to composability. However, representation and composability are not inherently linked together. If the representations are realized in a special medium with appropriate (analogical) transformations, there need be no composability at all. Only for an organism that makes the great move does the connection exist. Then the linkage is complete.

Composable representation systems are sufficiently important that we should examine their requirements. First, the medium that is to be processed must have adequate variety. Even more, it must be capable of being in combinatorially many states. If not, then it doesn't provide enough scope, because the world is combinatorial in its variety. That is, the variety present in the world comprises many independent attributes, each with many possible values. Red flowers may be next to yellow ones or next to blue ones, and their height may be low or high, and they may be swaying in the breeze or quiet or being blown around vigorously, and the day may be hot or cold, and whatever holds now was different an hour ago, and different yet an hour before that, and on and on. Thus, the world of the organism can be in combinatorially many different states. Even if correlations exist between descriptors, and even if the organism attends only selectively to the environment,[7] the resulting set of possibilities that have to be encoded in any situation remains combinatorial. And if the world to be encoded is combinatorial, then the

7. Notice that selective attention, which serves to restrict variety, simultaneously contributes to combinatorial variability by allowing the system to be able to be focused at one place or another, independently of the state of the world, so that total variety becomes (possibilities for attention) × (possibilities for environment).

medium itself must equally be capable of combinatorial variety—which means there must be a set of independently variable parts.

Second, the medium must have high stability so that what is processed can be retained. But it must have low stability when it is being transformed, so that the transformation can be done at will. Furthermore, the energy costs must be modest relative to the actions ultimately involved, because doing a transformation at will in the service of other behaviors of the organism implies not often having to take the costs of doing it into account.

Third, there must be completeness of possible transformations. How much and what sort of variety is possible in the transformations translates directly into what representation laws can be satisfied. But even ignoring the issue of qualitative variety, there is again the issue of potential combinatorial variety in the transformations that arises (at the very least) from the combinatorial variety of their inputs and outputs.

Fourth, since these transformations must at some point be created, the ease of determining compositions is important. The demands of representation arise as the needs arise for novel action, which is to say, more or less continually, especially when considered in detail. A good representation system has the character that the organism can do with it what the organism wants, so to speak, not what the representation requires. This is just the opposite of what characterizes an analogical representation, where the organism does nothing, so to speak, and what the representation requires is what the organism needs. Thus, malleability of the medium and freedom of transformability are prime qualities of a representational system.

The transformations are expressed in some medium, which need not be the same as the medium used for the representation, though it might be and was in Figure 2-7. Its key property is *executability*. The medium itself can be passive, and then it must be interpretable by some other process, which is the familiar situation with programming languages. Alternatively, the medium can be active, and then it must be evocable. In either case, there is a dual aspect in which the medium is passive while being composed and then shifts at some controllable moment to being active. In addition, since transformations must be composed, the medium needs all the good properties of any representing medium. It might seem that there is an infinite regress here, because there is need for a composable scheme to compose the transformations, which requires its own medium, hence yet another level of transformations, and so on. But this regress stops immediately when the same medium is used for the transformations as for the representations. Then, it is all one medium and so there is self-application. This is a situation we are all familiar with in standard programming languages, and we know there are no fundamental difficulties. Again, problems of conception that would have been substantial fifty years ago are now of no moment because of the computerized world we live in, which makes familiar all these ideas and their basic consequences.

2.4. Machines and Computation

We have found our way to *computational systems,* via the back door, by focusing on the properties needed for representation. Computational systems turn out to be exactly those systems that provide composability of transformations. Let us begin the discussion of the nature of computation with the notion of a *machine,* which I have taken for granted so far. As often is true of general terms, there isn't a standard definition, but the understanding is common enough so that a suitable definition can be concocted for our purposes. Start with a general notion of a system as a region of the physical world that can be described by a set of interacting variables, shown simply as a box in panel *A* of Figure 2-8. If that system is capable of input and output, then we tend to call it a machine. Thus, a machine is something that defines a *function* (in the mathematical sense of a correspondence) from its input to its output, and will produce its output when given its input. Given the input, the output is determined.[8] This is shown in panel *B* of the figure. There is some kind of a medium that is processed, something to be input and something to be output. This, of course, is a way of describing systems—of imposing on them a descriptive viewpoint. Thus when we talk about automobiles as machines, as we routinely do, the media is physical space, the input is the occupants in one location, and the output is the occupants in another location. We don't always look at systems as machines. The solar system certainly fits any reasonable definition of a system, but we don't nor-

8. Sometimes the output is only probabilistically determined, but that comes to the same thing for our purposes.

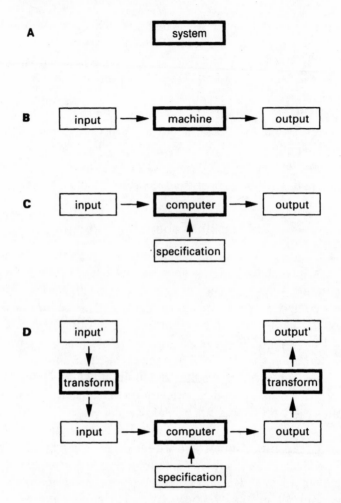

Figure 2-8. Systems, machines, and computers.

mally isolate some aspect of it as input and another as output, and so we don't see the solar system as a machine. We could, of course, and the use of the solar system as a sling to fling satellites out into far space is a viable point of view.

Given the notion of a machine, a computational system can be defined as a machine that can produce *many* functions. Again there is a shift of viewpoint. A machine determines a fixed function between its inputs and its outputs. A machine also *produces* its outputs, given its inputs, something not implied by being a function, which is just the correspondence. Thus, a priori, a computer produces one function, not many. To view it as producing many functions, some inputs must be viewed as providing the specification of the function to be produced. This is shown in panel C of the figure. The shift is straightforward. From the machine $z = F(x, y)$ one forms the computer $z = f[y](x)$, where y is now a parameter, rather than a second argument, of the function. For each y, the system produces a different function from x to z.

A simple but clear example is a hand calculator, especially one using postfix, such as an HP calculator. Two numbers are input, say 3 and then 5. The output is not yet determined. Then, with another button push, an operation is selected—plus, minus, multiply, or divide—and the output is now produced—8, -2, 15, or 0.6, respectively. The example even makes clear the arbitrary nature of the encoding, since many different schemes can be used to communicate to the machine the function to be computed—postfix (3 5 +), prefix (+ 3 5), or infix (3 + 5).

Although this view of a computer is quite general, it is not always employed. We don't always take the extra inputs to a machine as the means of converting it into a computer, even when those inputs operate to control the machine and shift the relations among the remaining inputs and outputs. For example, a television set has a brightness knob. This is certainly another input, and it changes the input-output function of the TV, where the input is the video signal and the output is the display. But we prefer to view this as *tuning* or *adjusting* the TV set, not as making it compute a different function. Similarly, we prefer to view the input to the TV set that determines the channel as *selecting* a channel, rather than determining what function the TV computes. It is easy to identify some aspects that tend toward a view other than that of the television being a computer. Continuity is certainly an important aspect of tuning. That the output exists as part of the input is certainly an important aspect of selection. The broader the variation of function that can be input, the more the machine seems like a computer. The matter is one of linguistic usage, of course, so we should not expect there to be too simple a characterization.

For our task of composing response functions, computational systems are exactly what is needed. When given different inputs, they produce different response functions. Consequently, computational systems are linked to representation—given that the representations are going to be formed by composing transformations to make the representation law hold. But computational systems do not inherently represent. They are devices that can be used to represent. It is inherent that a computational system provide the means to build representation systems. Only if the composed transformations obey representation laws does representation occur. And that depends on what determines what computations are done.

The prime question about a computational system is what functions it can produce. That's because the interest in viewing a system as a computer is precisely an interest in producing, on demand, different functions. The great move to composable transformations is necessary precisely because of the limitations of variability of special analog representations. Thus we are led down a familiar computer-science path that ends at *universal computational systems*—at universal Turing machines (Minsky, 1967). Though it is familiar, it is important to trace down this path, to describe it from the viewpoint of our enterprise of understanding representation, composable response functions, and knowledge systems.

The perfect computational system would be one that could produce *any* possible function. There is, however, a minor difficulty. Any physically realized computer is committed to fixed input and output ports, fixed places with fixed arrangements for embodying the medium. Panels *B* and *C* of Figure 2-8 are conveniently ambiguous about this, because they illustrate abstract systems. A computer cannot provide *any* function, but at best only any function between its particular inputs and its particular outputs. The tendency in discussing general matters of representation, computation, and the like is to work abstractly. So one tends to think only of the correspondence, but not of the particular input and output domains. This tendency must be firmly resisted, because physical realizability is an important constraint. In any event, as the panel *D* at the bottom of Figure 2-8 shows, the difficulty is only a small one in principle. Given some inputs' and outputs', arbitrary in form and location, the input' can be transformed and transferred to the input for the computer (at the input port of the computer), which then produces its output (at the output port of the computer), providing the required function. This output is then transformed and transferred into the output' that was originally specified. These transformations themselves, of course, provide functions, but they are fixed functions and hence can be realized by fixed machines. The job of the input transformation is to bring the real input' from wherever it might exist to the place where the input of the computer exists, and to produce an input to the computer that preserves all the necessary distinctions. The job of the output transformation is to take the output of the computer and ship it to the distant output', while converting its form to the form of this output'. Thus, these are fixed transformations that *select, transport,* and *transduce*[9] objects in the media. They do not perform the compositional transformations that the computer does.

There is also a genuine difficulty in this scheme. No system can produce *any* function if the input and output domains get too large. There are just too many functions. This can be seen easily by computing the number of functions that are possible. Let there be M different inputs and N different outputs. A function assigns to each input an output; that is, for each of the M inputs, a particular output is assigned from the N possibilities. The number of different ways this can be done is the number of different functions. This is N^M, or one of N output values independently for each of the M input values. This grows exceedingly rapidly, especially with M. If $N = 100$ and $M = 100$, both very modest, then the total is 10^{200}, an exceedingly large number. This growth is reflected in a theorem that says, if the inputs and the outputs are countably unbounded (such as letting the inputs and outputs have values over an indefinitely extended past history), then the number of functions becomes uncountably infinite (Minsky, 1967). But which function one wants the computer to provide must be specified by another input, which is also only countably infinite. Thus, there is no way for the computer to compute an uncountable number of functions—because which one to compute cannot even be specified.

This theorem deals with infinities, so it may not seem to be relevant to our finite world with its finite time. Indeed, the comment is often made that the theory of computability is irrelevant to our actual situation just because it applies only to infinite computations. But the theorem is just an elegant way of indicating a difficulty that is present in the finite case—and is apparent in the constrast between 100 and 10^{200}. The amount of input required to specify the function grows much faster than the inputs and outputs to the func-

---

9. Transduction, in this context, is changing representational form without changing content.

tion itself. Thus the specification of the function becomes a limiting factor on how many functions a computer can compute.

This result shows the futility of the hope for computers that provide *all* possible functions—which would have yielded the simplest answer to the question of what functions can be computed. Therefore, to pursue the question, we must characterize specific classes of functions and ask whether computers can be found that will provide all functions of such classes. There seems to be no difficulty at the low end. It is easy to specify, say, the six elementary trigonometric functions, sine, secant, cosine, cosecant, tangent, and cotangent, and to design a computer to do all of them. But our interest is at the high end—in computers that provide as large an array of functions as possible. Here, again, there is a difficulty. Any way of specifying a class of functions might amount to specifying a computer for that class. Hence there would be no way ever to specify a set that would not be computable, just by how it was defined.

The path that computer science has found for dealing with this specification difficulty is to shift from classes of functions to classes of machines. Each machine in a class realizes a different particular function. So we can talk about the class of functions realized by the class of machines. If the machines are very general in their character, they will define a correspondingly general class of functions. Then one can ask if there is a single machine in this class that can realize *any* function realized by *any* other machine in the class. Such a machine is called *universal* for that class—it can, upon specification, be any machine in the class. It is, of course, necessary to take some of the inputs to such a machine and use them to provide the specifications.

This scheme has two nice properties. First, the functions under discussion are, in an important sense, realistic. Each is realized by at least one particular machine in the class. Second, since the machines can be specified very generally according to principles for constructing them, the classes of functions can be very large. For instance, thinking physically, one might define all the machines that can be put together by chemical molecules. To work with this notion precisely, so as to be able to talk about all the functions defined by the chemical machines, we need to adopt some well-defined notion of a molecule, such as the classical chemical valence model. We also must adopt some conceptual way of identifying some molecules in some places as inputs and some as outputs. This produces a pretty big class of functions, though not quite as big perhaps as if we had adopted a richer chemical notion of molecules. But then we could consider that latter class of machines as well. Thus, we can work at the high end, where we consider *very* large classes of functions.

It turns out that universal machines exist for these large classes. Again, this comes as no surprise to us, familiar as we are with general digital computers, which are indeed universal machines. Conceptually, of course, this puts the cart before the horse. We are interested in what we should believe about the digital computer's ability to generate many different functions. We should not be using our intuitions about the computer to confirm for us that indeed computers can realize an immense variety of functions. In other words, the existence of universal machines gives us confidence that computers can exist that provide very large families of functions.

A limitation of these results would seem to be that the notion of a universal machine is relative to the class of machines. There would be universal machines for machines constructed with gears and pulleys, say, and universal machines for valence-style molecules. These two universal machines would clearly be different, but this turns out not to be a limitation after all. Investigations of universality have been carried out for many different ways of defining machines—where one tries to be as general as possible in the notion of machine. Computer scientists have analyzed Turing machines, Markov algorithms, Post production systems, recursive functions (which can be viewed as a form of machine), many variations on digital computers (such as models of random-access machines), and so on. Always, for these highly general classes of machines, universal machines exist. Furthermore, the classes of functions turn out always to be the same, once the ability is granted to transform inputs' to inputs and outputs to outputs', as in panel *D* of Figure 2-8. The upshot is that there is a single largest class of functions that can be realized by physical devices (machines). Not surprisingly, these have come to be called the *computable functions* and the machines that compute them are called *universal computers*. Thus, the answer to the question what functions can be computed, though not quite the simplest possible, turns out to be extremely elegant.

The way this issue has been formulated in theoretical computer science has resulted in a variegated set of definitions of this most general class of machines. That these all lead to the same class of functions, the computable functions, has seemed remarkable. It has become known as the *Church-Turing thesis*. It remains a *thesis*, rather than a *theorem*, on the grounds that it asserts something about the informal process of characterizing classes of machines. One can only prove theorems about what has been formalized. The only thing that keeps the Church-Turing thesis from becoming a theorem, however, seems to be a reluctance to settle the essential properties of what it means to be a physically realizable machine.

We have taken a rather long excursion to trace the story of universal computation. That is because computer science has a lot to tell us about this topic, and it is important because of the role that obtaining flexible response functions plays in mind-like behavior (recall Figure 1-7). We need to understand what sort of mechanisms are possible that can produce extreme flexibility. Universal computers provide the absolute maximum flexibility possible in physically realizable systems.

2.5. Symbols

Throughout the entire discussion of representation and computation, *symbols* have never once been mentioned. This could be taken as just a choice of terms. *Symbolic* could be defined to be essentially synonymous with *representational*. Anything that represents exhibits symbolic function. I choose not to do this, because this usage obscures an important issue that is closely bound up with what are normally called symbols, which are things that occur in expressions or other media. Symbols are certainly used to represent, as when "cat" in "The cat is on the mat" is used to represent a specific cat. But there is more going on than just that.

Let us focus initially on *symbol tokens*, rather than on *symbols*, the latter being abstract equivalence classes of tokens. Tokens occur as parts of the medium that gets processed—as regions within expressions or structures. A few familiar examples are shown in Figure 2-9. Particular words are parts of particular sentences. Number, letter, and operation-mark tokens are part of an equation. And so on. In the analysis of representation and computation of the previous two sections there was no need for anything such as sym-

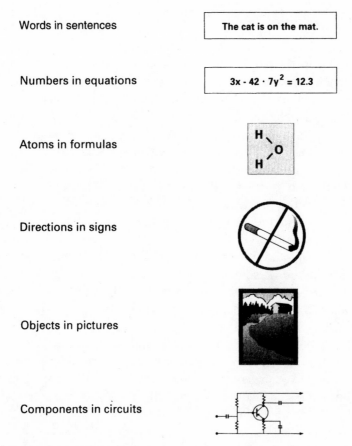

Words in sentences — The cat is on the mat.

Numbers in equations — $3x - 42 \cdot 7y^2 = 12.3$

Atoms in formulas

Directions in signs

Objects in pictures

Components in circuits

Figure 2-9. Symbol tokens are parts of structures to be processed.

bol tokens. Why is it the case that when we create representations we so often create arrangements that include tokens?

For a clue to what is going on, consider the standard view that symbols *stand for* something and that the token of a symbol occurring in some place in a structure carries the interpretation that the symbol stands for something within the context that is specified because of the symbol token's location. This implies at least that the knowledge required to process the structure is in part not available at that point. The token is a surrogate for that body of knowledge. The knowledge itself is at some other place. How that knowledge is to be used at this point is a function of both the local context and the knowledge itself, and the use can be determined only when that knowledge is acquired. What is certain is that the knowledge must be *accessed* and *retrieved*.

Figure 2-10 shows the general situation. It is a law of nature that processing in the physical world is always local, that is, always takes places in a limited region of physical space. This is equivalent to there being no action at a distance, or, somewhat more specifically, that causal effects propagate with an upper velocity of c, the speed of light in vacuo. Consequently, any computational system ultimately does its work by localized processing within localized regions in space. What guides or determines this processing task must then also be local. If the task is small enough or simple enough, then the processes could have been assembled within the local region and the task accomplished. Ultimately, there is no alternative to doing it this way. If the processing is complex enough, though, additional structure from outside the local region will be required at some point during the processing. If it is required, it must be obtained. If it must be obtained, then some process must do it, using structure within the local region to determine when and how to go outside.

The symbol token is the device in the medium that determines where to go outside the local region to obtain more structure. The process has two phases: first, the opening of *access* to the distal structure that is needed; and second, the *retrieval* (transport) of that structure from its distal location to the local site, so it can actually affect the processing. When to go outside is determined by when the processing encounters the symbol token in a fashion that requires the missing structure. Thus, when processing "The cat is on the mat" (which is itself a physical structure of some sort) the local computation at some point encounters "cat"; it must go from "cat" to a body of (encoded) knowledge associated with "cat" and bring back something that represents that a cat is being referred to, that the word "cat" is a noun (and perhaps other possibilities), and so on. Exactly what knowledge is retrieved and how it is organized depend on the processing scheme. In all events, the structure of the token "cat" does not contain all the needed knowledge.[10] It is elsewhere and must be accessed and retrieved.

10. It can of course contain some of it—symbol tokens can be codes. The virtue of coding knowledge into the token is apparent from Figure 2-10, for it avoids the need for access and retrieval.

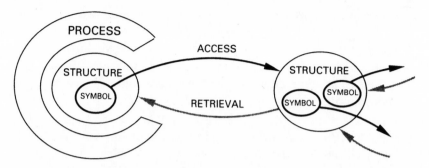

Figure 2-10. Symbols provide distal access.

Hidden in this account is the basic proposition behind information theory, namely, for a given technology there is a limit to the amount of encoding that can occupy a given region of physical space. In information theory this is expressed as the channel or memory capacity, and it is measured in bits. But its foundation is the amount of variety in physical structure, given that there is a limit to the amount of energy that is available to detect differences in structure (which is the aspect of the coding technology that is relevant). This limitation applies to all systems, discrete and continuous (Shannon, 1949). Thus, as the demands for variety increase—corresponding ultimately to the demands for variety in functions to be composed—the local capacity will be exceeded and distal access will be required to variety that exists elsewhere. There must be something within the local site that indicates that additional knowledge is needed and provides clues to how to obtain it. This requirement that complex systems require symbol structures, in the sense of embedded symbol tokens that provide distal access, is separate from the notion of representation. It is a requirement that arises from the constraints of processing, not from the constraints of establishing relations to the external world.

The scheme represented in Figure 2-10 shows symbol tokens as we normally think of them, as regions of a structure used to access distal data on demand, when processing occurs at that site. Some alternatives are possible. For instance, in the fashion of a drum machine, global sweeps of the total memory could occur periodically, rather than individual accesses on demand. A uniform access process of this sort might seem necessarily less efficient than individual accesses, but efficiency depends on the underlying technology (so, for instance, drum machines dictated such a scheme). In any event, such symbol systems could look somewhat different from the sort of symbol systems we are accustomed to.

We finally arrive at *symbol systems* (Newell & Simon, 1976; Newell, 1980a), a familiar notion in cognitive science.[11] Figure 2-11 lists the essential ingredients. Symbol systems are a form of universal computational system. This particular form brings out clearly the major assumptions in such systems while avoiding the highly particular arrangements that usually accompany the specification of a computational system, such as the sequential tape, reading head, and five-tuple of a Turing machine (Minsky, 1967).

There is a memory, which has structures that contain symbol tokens. The memory is independently modifiable at some grain size of the structure, because of the demand that the memory be capable of combinatorial variety. Within the grain size, structures may exhibit various dependencies, so that changing one part of the structure brings with it other changes. The constraints on the forms of language expressions and data structures are exactly such local dependencies. Symbol tokens are patterns in symbol structures that provide access to distal structures, namely, other structures in the memory. They are analogous to the symbols in Lisp, which are addresses that allow additional Lisp expressions to be obtained. There are symbol operations that compose structures from other structures. There are many variations on these operations, some building new structures and others modifying old structures.

Some memory structures (not necessarily all) have the property of determining that a sequence of symbol operations occur on specific symbol structures. These structures are called variously *programs*, *plans*, or *procedures*. The process of applying the operations is called *interpreting* the symbol structure. Interpretation can happen in a variety of ways. The program can be read to determine each successive operation, which is then evoked. Alternatively, the program can be compiled into a different program and the latter interpreted. Yet another alternative is to construct a specific special-purpose machine that embodies the operations and then execute it. These all come to the same thing—the ability to convert from symbol structures to behavior. Since this behavior can form

---

11. They are often called *physical symbol systems* to emphasize their origin in computer science and artificial intelligence, rather than in common usage, philosophy, or the humanities. In the current context, the shorter phrase will do.

Memory
Contains structures that contain symbol tokens
Independently modifiable at some grain size

Symbols
Patterns that provide access to distal structures
A symbol token is the occurrence of a pattern in a structure

Operations
Processes that take symbol structures as input and produce symbol structures as output

Interpretation
Processes that take symbol structures as input and execute operations

Capacities
Sufficient memory and symbols
Complete composability
Complete interpretability

Figure 2-11. Symbol system.

other symbol structures that guide behavior, this provides the capability to follow representation laws embodied as symbol structures and to create new symbol structures to embody required representation laws. Thus, interpretation of structures that represent symbol operations provides exactly the capability to compose functions and thus to represent.

Within this very general processing structure, the only additional requirements are some properties of sufficiency and completeness. On the sufficiency side, there must be enough memory and enough symbols. With insufficient resources, complicated transformations can be generated that the system is unable to perform, just because it runs out of the resources. On the completeness side, there are two requirements. First, there must be complete composability— the operators must make it possible to construct any symbol structure. Second, there must be complete interpretability—symbol structures must be possible that determine any arrangement of operation actions and the interpretation processes must be able to evoke the operations given the symbol structures. Without these forms of completeness there will be various things that a symbol system cannot do, and so it will fail to be a universal machine. Both forms of completeness need not be immediate in any sense, but may require lengthy and devious processing—just as long as the machine eventually gets there.

That is all there is to a symbol system, even though the specification seems extremely nonspecific.[12] A symbol system is sufficient for producing all computable functions (it is universal). It is as flexible as it is possible to be. But also, if the variety of knowledge and goals to be represented is large enough, a symbol system is necessary, both to obtain universality and to obtain distal access.

There may still seem to be a problem with symbol systems. How do the symbols in symbol systems represent something external to the symbol system? As it is often put, how do symbols acquire their *semantic function* of referring to things in the external world? Accessing in symbol systems is an internal operation—a symbol gives access to another symbol structure still in the internal memory of the system. How does it ever happen that a symbol actually *refers to* or *denotes* or *designates* or *stands for* or is *about* something outside the system itself? In philosophy this is called the problem of *intentionality*, after Brentano (1874). It still seems to be with us in the cognitive sciences. Even Pylyshyn (1984), who subscribes to a view of computation and symbol systems rather close to the one in this chapter, still maintains that it is not clear how symbols are *about* external objects.[13]

Within the framework set out here, the matter seems straightforward. Start out with knowledge systems. Knowledge is about its domain, which is external to the system being characterized. To have the knowledge that the block is on the table is to have knowledge about the block and about the table. Knowledge is a way of describing a system whose behavior can be computed (by an observer) with respect to an external environment. Symbol systems realize knowledge systems. At least some of them do, and these are the ones of interest here. They do so only approximately, of course, a matter to which we will return. Hence, symbol systems are about the same external things that the knowledge systems they realize are about. After all, it is the same system that is being described, just in two different ways. Symbol systems realize knowledge sys-

---

12. I have focused on the functional character of symbol systems. There are also implementation requirements not treated here. An important one is reliability. Structures must remain stable and operations must do the same thing every time. Some failure of reliability is not fatal but can imply styles of operation that involve redundancy and verification.

13. However, a recent treatment of the foundations by Fodor and Pylyshyn (1988) seems to indicate that he no longer takes this to be an issue.

tems by implementing representation laws so that the symbol structures encode the knowledge about the external world.

That's all there is to be said about intentionality, except for the details of how to build symbol systems that approximate knowledge systems closely enough. The details are clearly important, but they are details. Only if it were not possible to come close to realizing a knowledge system would there be an issue.

However, let us ask how a knowledge system acquires the specific knowledge it has about the outside world—for this specific knowledge is what leads to the symbols in the corresponding symbol system. Within the knowledge level the answer is uninformative. The knowledge was acquired from other knowledge sources that knew about the requisite outside world—what else? If the question is pursued at the symbol level, however, the answer is more useful. In Figure 2-2, the blocks-world situation, Y comes to know that block B is not clear. Inside Y there is a representation that supports that knowledge. That representation contains a symbol for B and an expression for B not being clear. And the symbol for B is about B, at least enough about B so that Y's knowledge that B is not clear is about B. No more, no less. How did Y find out that B is not clear? Y found it out because X told Y. How did X know that B was not clear? X knew it because X observed B. How did that observation yield knowledge to X? Because light reflected from block B was received by X's eyes, . . . Ultimately, there is some physical contact with the object. It may feed through any collection of agencies, supported by various other knowledge of physical laws and facts. But the laws of our physical world imply that there must be physical influence.[14] If an agent is in complete physical isolation, then ultimately nothing can be known. There are also issues of trust and presupposition. Why did Y believe what X told Y? Was Y warranted in its belief? Such issues are real and they affect whether the knowledge is valid or reliable, but they do not affect whether on occasion knowledge is transferred and with it the semantic function of the symbols involved.

Let us return to the issue of approximation and the realizability of the knowledge level. At every level of the computer-systems hierarchy (Figure 2-3) the description from below is not exact with

14. It can of course be the influence of an antecedent, with extrapolation being by physical laws and other inductions.

respect to its realization of the upper-level system. That is so for the symbol level realizing the knowledge level, the register-transfer level realizing the programming level, or whichever. Thus, symbol-level systems only approximate the knowledge level. Consequently, they do an imperfect job of being about the outside world. This point can be important. For instance, the arithmetic of computers is finite-accuracy floating-point arithmetic with a particular scheme for rounding. We generally use machine arithmetic as if it represents true arithmetic. Of course, it only approximates it, and the analysis of rounding errors and their propagation is required for serious numerical work.

It might seem that the approximation involved with knowledge-level systems is somehow special. One reason for this feeling might be that knowledge is almost always infinite, as is implied in its representation by the implicational closure of a set of logical expressions. It can be said that knowledge systems *inherently* can't be realized by symbol-level systems, because no finite device can realize an infinite set. This is true, but so are the inherent reasons why the other levels cannot be faithfully realized—why there cannot be computers with zero failure rates, or why settling time of digital circuits cannot be guaranteed to be finite. The pressing questions of approximation are how to attain good approximations in particular cases and in practice. To this there can be no simple or single answer. The entire field of artificial intelligence is, in a sense, devoted to discovering the symbol-level mechanisms that permit a close approximation to the knowledge level.

2.6. Architectures

Architectures are a key concept in this book. Unified theories of cognition will be formulated as architectures. Why this is so may not be obvious without reflection, but it will certainly become clear as we progress. The architecture of the mind is a major source of the communality in behavior, both within a person and across persons. Thus, we need to be especially clear on what an architecture is.

An architecture is the fixed structure that realizes a symbol system. At the top of the computer-systems hierarchy (Figure 2-3) is the knowledge level, below that the symbol level, and then the register-transfer level. Thus, the description of the system at the

Lifetime	10^9	sec	
Development	10^6	sec	ARCHITECTURE
Skill acquisition	10^3	sec	CHANGE?
Knowledge acquisition	10	sec	
Performance	1	sec	FIXED
Temporary storage	10^{-1}	sec	STRUCTURE
Primitive actions	10^{-2}	sec	

Figure 2-12. Fixed structure means changing relatively slowly.

register-transfer level is the architecture. More precisely, what is fixed mechanism (hardware) and what is content (software) at the symbol level is described by the description of the system at the register-transfer level. Of course, system hierarchies may exist that are different from the familiar one developed for computers, and then the architecture would be defined accordingly. To state the matter in general: given a symbol system, the architecture is the description of the system in whatever system-description scheme exists next below the symbol level.

It is customary to say, as above, that the architecture is the *fixed* structure and to talk about the architecture as genuinely immutable. For standard digital computers this is mostly true, and where it is not, as in systems that have levels of microcode, the changes are viewed as deliberate. Computer science has built up the notions of virtual machine, firmware, and dynamic configurability as appropriate ways to describe such structures. With natural systems (human cognition), a more general view is required, namely, that what counts is the relative rate of change. Figure 2-12 illustrates the situation. To tap into the reader's intuitions, it uses a human time scale, where task performance is taken to occur in the order of a second (1 sec). What is important is the relative time scale, not the absolute numbers.

The primitive atomic actions of the system take about a hundredth of a second (0.01 sec). To accomplish even a modestly complex task requires some data to be stored as intermediate temporary values. This occurs at a rate of about a tenth of a second (0.1 sec). Some number of these is required to produce task performance at about a second (1 sec). The architecture is the structure that is fixed while the system produces that performance. Clearly, not all structure is fixed over the course of a performance. Some structure holds the inputs and outputs for each primitive action, which operate every 0.01 sec. Some other structure holds the temporary data saved over several tenths of seconds to accomplish the task. In both cases, some structure must vary. Such momentarily varying structures are labeled the *memory content*.

Other processes can change the system more slowly. If there is feedback from the performance, the contents of the memory will change, but at a slower rate (10 sec). Skill acquisition might go on at an even slower rate (100 to 1,000 sec), and developmental changes might occur even more slowly (10^5 sec). Changes at all these different times scales are important. Some long-term changes might simply be content changes, namely just changes to the storage structures (0.1 sec). But others might change structures that were fixed during the performance (1 sec). Some or all of these might be taken to be architectural changes. Certainly what was fixed throughout the performance has now become variable. But some long-term changes, such as knowledge acquisition, may still seem better classified as *memory changes,* with only skill acquisition and other longer-duration changes taken to be architecture changes. This is all mostly a question of terminology. What is important to understand is that natural systems are changing at all time scales simultaneously. Such continuous plasticity does not invalidate the notion of an architecture as a *fixed* structure; it just makes the term *fixed* relative to the time scale.[15]

The important questions about architecture concern what functions are to be provided by the fixed structure. An architecture provides a boundary that separates structure from content. Behavior is determined by variable content being processed according to the fixed processing structure, which is the architecture. The fixed structure represents a communality for a wide array of processing. Thus, the natural question is, What is embodied in the architecture and what is moved out into the content?

It is given that an architecture must support a symbol system, as specified in Figure 2-11. But that takes the specification of the architecture only a little way. There are implementation issues as well as additional functions for the architecture to provide. Most of our experience with architectures comes out of computer science,

15. The picture is somewhat oversimplified. There are three different durations involved: *read time, write time,* and *residence time.* Read time is always relatively short, if the knowledge is to be useful. Residence time is independent of write time, although almost always longer. The fixity of the architecture is with respect to residence times.

Classical architectural functions
The fetch-execute cycle
  • Assemble the operator and operands
  • Apply the operator to operands
    The specific primitive operations
  • Store results for later use
Support access structures
Input and output

Historical additions
Exploit technology for power, memory, and reliability
  • Parallelism, caches, . . .
Obtain autonomy of operation
  • Interrupt, dynamic resource allocation, protection

Figure 2-13. Known functions of the architecture.

where there has been a fair amount of architectural exploration over the years. Figure 2-13 lists the main outcomes of these efforts. There are the classical functions that all computer architectures perform. All computers employ a division into operators and operands. To determine the next step of behavior the computer must assemble an operator and its operands, then it must apply the operator to the operands, and then it must store away the results for future use. This is the classic *fetch-execute cycle*. The specific operations available always include certain functions: moving data around from memory to memory, performing logical and arithmetical data operations, performing tests, and activating external devices for input and output. The actual operations are often much elaborated to enhance efficiency and ease of use. Implicit in the data-transmission operation is the support of the memory structure so the computer can access and retrieve information from it. These provide the basic functions for realizing a symbol system. Much that is important about them has been covered in the earlier analysis. Historically, these functions have been included in computers from the beginning—since it is not possible to build a working general-purpose computer without all of them.

More interesting are the additions to the architecture over the years. They have been of two kinds. One arises from the need and opportunity to exploit the available technology in order to gain power (operations per sec), memory (total bits available within a given time), and reliability (mean time between errors); and to reduce cost, space, and energy demands. For instance, parallelism, even massive parallelism, is a device not to introduce new functions but to exploit new underlying technology. The changes in the architecture may be radical, of course, and the technology may dictate the entire style of computation. Furthermore, although power, speed, and memory are continuous parameters, they can result in qualitatively different computations with every order-of-magnitude change. Real-time constraints especially reveal the effect of amount of computation available within specified time limits.

Interestingly, all the qualitative additions of functionality have served to increase the *autonomy* of computers—their ability to exist on their own. An important example is the *interrupt,* the ability for some agency external to the main cycle of operation of the computer to gain control of the behavior of the computer immediately, independently of what the computer is doing. Interruption is clearly an important function in interacting with a dynamic external world; it is also useful for many internal functions as well. Interrupt mechanisms have been with us for so long that many may not realize that early computers had no such mechanisms; instead, they polled the external world. They always had control and only when the program asked about the outside world could they find out anything about it. Not surprisingly, it did not take long before all computers had interrupt mechanisms.

Mechanisms for *protection* came along somewhat later. They provided reliable internal barriers (fixed in hardware) to keep activity in one part of the system from affecting other parts of the system. The need for protection arose as soon as multiple tasks were performed in a computer, either because of multiple users or because complex tasks were decomposed into subtasks that had permanent residence.

Dynamic resource allocation is another function that increases the autonomy of a system. In early systems, all memory was allocated in fixed arrays, as specified by the programmer. This implied a certain specificity of prevision on the programmer's part. Having the system keep a list of available resources from which the system itself can dispense new resources on demand, along with a collection operation to return unused resources to the list, not only permits the programmer to avoid planning these steps but permits the computer to accomplish tasks where the space required is unpredictable, even approximately, at the time the program is designed. Interestingly, dynamic resource allocation does not seem to require much if anything in the way of hardware support. The mechanisms (essentially list processing) are quite adequately realized in software. They must, however, remain in place and operate continually and permanently. Thus, they become an addition to the fixed structure, which is to say, to the architecture.

Dynamic memory allocation is a good example to emphasize that the distinction between architecture, as fixed structure, and content, as variable data, is not quite the same as the distinction between hardware and software. That is, many fixed mechanisms may be cast as software—the programs for doing allocation in our example, along with various data structures that are used to keep the list of available resources. That a software mechanism can be changed does not mean that it must be changed. It is thus that all sorts of software systems and software architectures are built up that transform one architecture into another.[16] What remains constant is that, at the bottom, there is a pure hardware architecture (what is often referred to as the *machine architecture* or the *machine language*). A number of factors impinge on whether a given fixed mechanism will end up in hardware or software—how fast it must operate, how expensive is its hardware realization, and how complex it is. There is a technological limit to how much complexity can be realized in hardware directly, without organizing that hardware as a computer so the complexity can be shifted into software.

The evolution of computers toward greater autonomy makes eminent sense, given their history. Computers are, in effect, *kept* systems. They have human keepers—trainers and operators—who do everything for the computers that computers can't do for themselves. When computers crash, their keepers pick them up and start them going again. When computers can't perform some task, such as getting information from another place, their trainers get the information and put it in a form that the computer can use. This is reminiscent of the old joke among psychologists of one rat remarking to another rat on how they have trained the experimenter to bring them cheese. The reason for computers' lack of autonomy is not hard to discern. The important criteria have always been eco-

---

16. For instance, Soar, the architecture to be used throughout the book, is realized as a software architecture programmed in Common Lisp, another software architecture, which itself runs on a hardware architecture.

nomic. As long as some task is rare enough and cheap enough for humans to perform, there is little pressure to make the computer perform that task autonomously. Gradually, of course, especially as computers have become more reliable and cheaper, and as we have discovered how to do increasingly diverse tasks, computers have evolved to become increasingly autonomous.

In any analysis of the architectures of natural systems, the concepts available from computer architectures are useful, although they hardly do the whole job. The autonomy of natural systems, especially humans, far exceeds that of computers—indeed, that is why humans can be the keepers of computers and not vice versa.[17] The issues of interruption, protection, and dynamic resource allocation arise in human functioning, and the mechanisms and solutions used in computers for these functions provide a framework for exploring how human architectures are structured. But the evolution of computers toward autonomy is hardly complete. It is part of our scientific task to understand what additional functions are required for architectures that support intelligence. For example, just to be concrete, a certain modularity of memory might be necessary for learning to take place autonomously.

As the specifications for architectures accumulate, along with the multitude of functions they should perform, it might seem that we are converging on a specific architecture in all its details. Whatever might be true when *all* of the constraints of Figure 1-7 are simultaneously applied is assuredly *not* true at the present stage. The systems are capable of great flexibility and immense variety. As Figure 2-14 illustrates schematically, many different symbol systems are possible, also many different architectures, and many different technologies. It is not just that there is variety, it is *radical* variety. Almost every sort of material can be fashioned into some sort of technology for general computation—magnetic, electrostatic, fluidic, biologic, mechanical (even the blocks world with rubber-band connections). Furthermore, the relationships between these levels are not one-to-one. Many different architectures can realize a given symbol system. Many different technologies can realize a given architecture. The same technology can be used to realize

17. We should not forget the ambiguity of the autonomy dimension of Figure 1-7. Humans are also strongly dependent on their embedding social system.

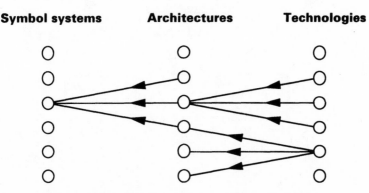

Figure 2-14. The potential for architectural variety.

many different architectures. (The only constraint seems to be that, by definition, a given architecture must realize a specific symbol system.) The variety is so great that we do not have any structural characterizations of its limits. All our characterizations are basically functional, such as the analysis of symbol systems that led to Figure 2-11. Essentially nothing is known about characterizing the properties of the machinery—except that it must provide these functions.

The only structural invariance I know is an empirical one—the computer-systems hierarchy of Figure 2-3. No matter what we do in computer science and engineering, this hierarchy appears to remain unshakable. The hierarchy did not emerge right away. Originally, there was essentially a fixed structure, the famous four boxes as shown in Figure 2-15, which could be found in any early textbook, such as Ware (1962). Architectures, as they are described here, emerged in the 1960s, when the complexity of the systems finally increased because of the decreasing cost of hardware and its increasing reliability (Bell & Newell, 1971). The enabling key appears to be the development of the register-transfer level, which is a system level with which one can describe complex architectures. Originally, there was only the logic level of combinational and sequential circuits built around the single binary variable (0 or 1). Since the register-transfer level was formulated in the 1960s, it has retained its basic form. The computer field has gone through radical transformations in technology, from individual logic components to ICs (integrated circuits) and on up the various scales of integration,

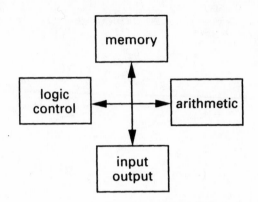

Figure 2-15. Early four-box standard architecture.

MSI to LSI to VLSI.[18] This last, VLSI, has introduced many new notions, such as area constraints and geometrical layout. Nevertheless, the register-transfer level has not changed an iota. There has been no evolution at all in terms of the level structure in computing systems.

We do not understand the force of this invariance. It may in fact be related to the engineering technologies we build or to the conservatism that now inhabits the computer field, with its concern for upward compatibility enforced by economics. Clearly, radically different technologies, such as biological ones, should change the hierarchy somewhat. One of the major challenges in the development of massively parallel connectionist systems is whether they will find a different hierarchical organization. In any event, the computer-systems hierarchy is an important invariant structural characteristic, although its seems to be the only one.

2.7. Intelligence

Intelligence is another central concept of cognitive science. Like the other concepts we have discussed, it has a long history unrelated to the attempts to shape it to the particular needs of cognitive science. Unfortunately, the history of the concept of intelligence is filled with contention, and in a way that the other concepts are not. The contention has spilled in from the larger political and social

18. Medium-scale integration, large-scale integration and very large-scale integration, respectively.

world via the development of intelligence testing and the importance it has assumed in the struggle of minorities and those without privilege. Contention surrounding the other foundational concepts we've covered, such as knowledge and representation, has managed to remain contained, for the most part, to the intellectual [*sic*] disciplines, such as philosophy.

The notion of intelligence is not only contentious, it expresses itself in the existence of a multiplicity of notions (Sternberg, 1985a; Sternberg & Detterman, 1986). These notions all bear a family resemblance, but the differences embody the needs to make intelligence serve different causes, so that synthesis and melding is precisely what is not permitted—which does not prevent recurrent attempts (Sternberg, 1985b). The notion of a single, universal kind of intelligence is set in opposition to multiple intelligences, such as academic intelligence and real-world (or practical) intelligence (Neisser, 1979), which distinction is in the service of arguments over education in the schools and its adequacy for life beyond the school. The notion of a single, universal concept of intelligence is also set in opposition to the relativity of the concept to the culture that defines it, which distinction is in the service of arguments over the dominance of Western ways of thought (Cole & Scribner, 1974). The notion of intelligence as a scientific construct defined entirely by a technology for creating tests is set in opposition to a notion of defining it by cognitive theories and experiment. In this last case, at least, there has been a vigorous and sustained movement to bring the two notions together (Sternberg, 1985a), although not one that has yet fully succeeded.

We cannot thereby simply walk away from the concept. Indeed, there is no reason to do so. Science engages in a continuous process of appropriation and refinement of concepts used elsewhere in society. Some notion is required of a graded ability or power of a mind-like system, which applies in some way to ranges or classes of tasks and ranges or classes of minds to indicate what minds can perform what tasks. There is little doubt about the usefulness of such a concept. It would seem that a theory of mind must contain such a concept. If it doesn't, the theory should tell us why such a notion is not definable or is definable only within certain limits.

In fact, the theory described in this chapter, whose key notions are knowledge, representation, computation, symbols, and architecture, contains within it a natural definition of intelligence:

> A system is *intelligent* to the degree that it approximates a
> knowledge-level system.

If these other concepts are accepted as we have laid them out, then
this definition is what answers to the requirements of a concept of
intelligence. It is a theory-bound definition, not an independently
motivated concept. Indeed, that is exactly what one wants from a
theory of the mind—that it should determine what intelligence is,
not that intelligence should be independently motivated.[19]

The formulation of intelligence just given is highly condensed. To
understand it, consider three arguments:

1. If a system uses *all* of the knowledge that it has, it must be
   perfectly intelligent. There is nothing that anything called intelligence can do to produce more effective performance. If all
   the knowledge that a system has is brought to bear in the
   service of its goals, the behavior must correspond to what
   perfect intelligence produces.
2. If a system does not have some knowledge, failure to use it
   cannot be a failure of intelligence. Intelligence can work only
   with the knowledge the system has.
3. If a system has some knowledge and fails to use it, then there
   is certainly a failure of some internal ability. Something within
   the system did not permit it to make use of the knowledge in
   the service of one of its own goals, that is, in its own interests.
   This failure can be identified with a lack of intelligence.

Thus, intelligence is the ability to bring to bear all the knowledge
that one has in the service of one's goals. To describe a system at
the knowledge level is to presume that it will use the knowledge it
has to reach its goal. Pure knowledge-level creatures cannot be
graded by intelligence—they do what they know and they can do no
more, that is, no better. But real creatures have difficulties bringing
all their knowledge to bear, and intelligence describes how well
they can do that.

19. I would argue that much of the contention over intelligence has arisen because of
its development in psychometrics without connection to the general theory of cognition.
This might have been the only way it could have developed during the first part of the
twentieth century, given the concurrent hegemony of behaviorism, which served to
repress cognitive theories. But the consequence remains.

Consider a concrete example. Suppose a man is shopping in a grocery store on a very limited budget. He compares the prices of the alternative products for each item he wants. He converts each quoted price to an equivalent price per unit to make them comparable. And he chooses the least expensive. This is an intelligent performance. It is the use of knowledge that the man has (how to do arithmetic, the fact that the cost for the same unit shows the contribution of the item to the total cost for a given amount of food) in service of his goal. If he knew all these things but just compared the stated cost, regardless of unit cost, that would be a less intelligent performance. Whether this is an act of perfect intelligence requires an analysis of the actual goals of the person and what else he knows that he might have brought to bear. Perhaps he knows about calories and thus could be computing cost per calorie. Then he could have been more intelligent. He brought some of his knowledge to bear, but not all of it. Suppose calories are not listed on the items. Then the failure to compute unit calories rather than unit weights or volumes is not a failure of intelligence but a failure of knowledge. Likewise, if the manufacturer has lied about caloric content, the man gets the wrong answer, but it is a failure of knowledge, not of intelligence. If, of course, he knows about the duplicity of the firm—it was just fined for false advertising and he read about it in the papers and discussed it—then he acts less intelligently if he decides on the basis of the firm's claims.

I could elaborate on the example indefinitely (it is my own example so no facts of the matter exist). Say we refine the man's goals—he is in a hurry, or he really does like a particular brand of peaches, so the extra cost is worth it—or change what the man knows—he knows about other aspects of a healthy diet (proteins, vitamins) and also about linear programming for proper optimizing. Assessing the intelligence involved in the performance of the task requires taking into account the actual goals and knowledge that are operative. This is just the way it is. Indeed, if we know that the man doesn't know something and we fail to take that into account and so judge him less intelligent—then we are not being intelligent ourselves.

This concept of intelligence has many properties that are exactly the properties that one would expect intelligence to have. A few are novel.

Intelligence is relative to goals and relative to knowledge. A system can be perfectly intelligent with respect to realizing some goals and making use of some knowledge, and not intelligent at all with respect to other goals and other knowledge. Intelligence as defined is not a measure, but a description of adequacy over the joint range of two complex domains, the system's goals and the system's knowledge.

An important consequence of the relative nature of intelligence is the need to keep distinct the task of acquiring knowledge to perform some other task. Let T be some task, say, purchasing items in a grocery. A person has a certain body of knowledge at the moment of performing T, and an assessment of intelligence is made with respect to that knowledge. If the person had additional knowledge, then the assessment would have been different. For instance, a person who does not know how to do arithmetic would not perform well. But this does not imply low intelligence. It might be thought that the person *should* know arithmetic, hence that there is a failure of intelligence. In that case, the task being assessed is not T but the task of acquiring arithmetic, call it AA. In other words, performance on AA might have been unintelligent, or perhaps the task of deciding whether to learn arithmetic (to do AA) was performed unintelligently. Assessment of the intelligence exercised in any of those tasks requires knowing the knowledge available at the time. A person's life is full of tasks, and each raises its own issue of how intelligently it is performed.

This definition sharply separates knowledge from intelligence. They are not the same thing at all. Many common intuitions of intelligence mix the two together. We expect an intelligent person to know certain things. Every intelligent person, we believe, should know how to add, should know how to get around in a city, should know, well, all kinds of commonsense things, as well as having learned what was taught at school. On the other hand, many common intuitions separate knowledge and intelligence. No amount of intelligence can arrive at brute facts that don't happen to be known, such as the lifetime batting average of Roberto Clemente. Of course, most intelligent members of a social community do know a common body of knowledge, because the society faces its members with many tasks of knowledge acquisition, and intelligent people succeed at these tasks, thus acquiring the associated bodies of knowledge. That knowledge and intelligence have some strong linkages does not imply that knowledge and intelligence are the same thing.

In general, the greater the intelligence, the better the performance. That is, the more the knowledge of the system is taken into account, the more will it attain its goals. Additional knowledge may not help—it may be irrelevant—but it cannot hurt. This ignores any processing costs of finding or applying the additional knowledge—because that is exactly what the knowledge level abstracts away from. It is of course easy to construct counter-examples, where a little additional knowledge leads a system astray. This can occur because the knowledge is in fact not true of the actual situation. Sometimes what seems to be going on is that the knowledge is not wrong, just incomplete. But then the knowledge that is wrong is the default assumptions that the system must use in order to produce action in the face of uncertainty.

Intelligence is a notion that applies only to knowledge-level systems. It does not apply to all machines. The question of whether an arbitrary machine is intelligent cannot be formulated within this theory. Intelligence does not even apply to all symbol systems, because not all symbol systems approximate knowledge-level systems (any more than all register-transfer systems approximate symbol systems).

Intelligence does apply to all knowledge-level systems—no matter how simple they are. This statement leads to a counterintuitive result: simple systems can have perfect intelligence. If the goal is narrow enough and the knowledge is delineated enough, then the system may not have to do much in order to use all its knowledge in the service of its goal. The thermocouple provides an example. Let the thermocouple be defined as having only one goal (to maintain a room temperature to a norm), one action (change the state of the furnace from *on* to *off* or vice versa), and only two items of knowledge (a general one: *on* increases the temperature and *off* decreases it; and a momentary one: the temperature is above or below the norm). Then, in its usual mode of operation, a thermocouple can be described as a knowledge-level system. As such, it has perfect intelligence. This arises from the simplicity of the thermocouple and not from any exalted status. It is the same old simple thermocouple it has always been. The change is only in the description. The same is true of the old (but still used) verbal tactic of describing a rock as intelligent because it seeks its level (Baars, 1986, p. 99, although the reference is actually to consciousness).

There is a strong temporal aspect to intelligence. This feature is seen clearly in the standard formulations of quantified logics. A common representation for knowledge is the implicational closure of a conjunction of sentences in a first-order logic, with goals being to establish the validity of sentences in the logic. The total knowledge of such a body is generally unbounded. It is not possible to access all knowledge from such a body of knowledge in finite time. In essence, this is what the theorems about undecidability of first-order logic proclaim—there is no way to guarantee that an arbitrary item of knowledge (a theorem) is or is not part of the knowledge. On the other hand, if one permits unbounded time, then it can be determined. Thus, given unbounded time, it is possible to have perfectly intelligent systems that have large bodies of knowledge and large sets of goals. But given only finite time, it is not possible to have such perfectly intelligent systems. To obtain systems with perfect knowledge, one must shrink down to very limited systems in terms of their knowledge and goals (as in the thermocouple example above).

It follows from the dependence of intelligence on the specific character of goals and knowledge that there can be no simple measure of intelligence. The variability and diversity are too great. It should be possible to have indexes that reflect the amount of intelligence, analogous to the gross national product and the economic productivity indexes. The gross national product reflects what is happening in the economy, but it can be accurate only up to a point, and not a very fine point at that. Goods and services are wildly diverse and the method of valuation (market prices) is the reflection of many factors. There simply isn't any such thing out there that *is* the gross national product that can become known accurately. Likewise, actual IQ measures are imperfect for many different reasons. An important one is that they confound knowledge and intelligence. But even beyond that, they try to summarize in a single number what is far too diverse.

The issue of the relation between knowledge and intelligence, though central to what is special about this definition of intelligence, is hardly new. The field of intelligence testing has continually attempted to develop concepts of intelligence that are, roughly speaking, independent of knowledge. The most famous of these is g, the general factor that is always present (if looked for) in factor analyses of intelligence tests (Spearman, 1927). The distinction is also captured in *fluid* intelligence (which can be used in diverse situations) as opposed to *crystallized* intelligence (which is cast permanently into a given form) (Cattell, 1971). A further reflection of this notion occurs in the concept of culture-fair tests, which are tests that do not depend on any knowledge that could vary with the culture of the individual. Actually, the same distinction lies behind the intuitive split between *domain knowledge* and *domain-independent knowledge,* in the expert-systems field.

One basis for communalities such as *g* and fluid intelligence comes from using the same underlying mechanisms over and over again. If different mechanisms could be used for different tasks indefinitely, there need not be anything in common in the abilities of people to solve different tasks. The existence of common mechanism starts, of course, with the architecture. Hence, one could expect more communality within a species, which presumptively has a common architecture, than across species or across more widely varying intelligent agents. And one should expect even more communality among people with common bodies of knowledge.

This theory of intelligence does not immediately provide what society has come to desire from a theory of intelligence, namely, a way to develop intelligence and ability tests that assign to any person one magnitude (or a few) on some scale indicating intelligence or ability. The theory here describes what intelligence is, not how to measure it numerically. No new measurement scheme flows instantly from the theory—which does not say that none can.

In sum, this definition of intelligence does not stand sui generis as an independently posited theory or basis for analysis. It has not been fashioned in order to be useful for this or that purpose. Rather, it flows from the fundamental framework of cognitive science and, within that framework, it provides a useful construct. Its relationship to the traditional psychometric notions of intelligence is problematical, but mostly because the relationship of cognitive psychology to psychometrics remains problematical, despite much recent scholarship.

2.8. Search and Problem Spaces

What processing is required for intelligent behavior? That is, how does a system behave in order to utilize its knowledge to attain its goals? The most general answer is quite uninformative—it will process the representations containing its knowledge and behave accordingly. But what can be said about the form such processing will take? For tasks that are relatively difficult, there is an answer—the agent will engage in *search*.

Search is fundamental for intelligent behavior. It is not just another method or cognitive mechanism, but a fundamental process. If there is anything that AI has contributed to our understanding of intelligence, it is discovering that search is not just one method among many that might be used to attain ends but is the most fundamental method of all.[20] The discussions of psychological processes involved in thinking, reasoning, and intelligence before the advent of AI in the mid-1950s show no particular emphasis on search (Johnson, 1955; Vinacke, 1952).

Two considerations lie behind the special role of search. One can be called the *existential predicament* of intelligent systems. When attempting to act, an intelligent system is uncertain. Indeed, that is of the essence of having a problem—it is not known what to do next. A system facing a problem exists in historical time. Its existential situation is that it must behave *now* but it is uncertain what to *do*. Thinking, here, is behaving—to think of one thing is not to think of other things. Suppose the system does not behave—does not think—then a little bit of the immediate future passes by and the same situation remains. It knows nothing further (it has not given any thought to the matter, so to speak), and it has just lost that bit of time. Thus, it is forced to act, even though, a fortiori, it is uncertain.

By itself this existential predicament generates search, indeed combinatorial search. In an uncertain situation, to act—to think the next thought—means to be wrong occasionally. (What else could uncertainty mean?) If the act is wrong, then recovery is necessary—recovery and trying again. But this situation cascades. A wrong act is taken while the system is still on a wrong path, and from that point of error still another wrong path is taken. This is exactly the pattern of behavior of combinatorial search.

Search need not exhibit the pattern of classical (chronological) backtracking. The system could return to some prior anchor point, or engage in some sort of dependency-directed backtracking, or attempt to repair the results of erroneous actions. All of these varia-

---

20. Actually, a case can be made that pattern-match processes are equally fundamental. They are what allows contact between stored memory structure and temporarily available task structure, as in production systems.

tions do not alter the fundamental fact that the system must search for a solution and that search tends to become combinatorial because new errors are committed before old ones are detected and resolved. Search will occur, whatever method is used to solve the problem, and the more problematical the situation the more search is required. Thus, intelligent behavior will be deeply involved with the processes that determine what spaces are searched and control search in those spaces. The character of any particular search will depend on many things, such as the memory available or the types of search steps that are possible.

The second consideration that implicates search in intelligent behavior can be called the *court of last resort*. If an intelligent agent wishes to attain some end—to find some object X, say—it must formulate that task in some way. It must arrange its activities in some way rationally related to finding X. It must do so—indeed, it can only do so—on the basis of its available knowledge. Even to seek more knowledge before acting is already to choose a particular way to formulate the task. The more problematical a situation, the less knowledge is available that says how to find X—that's what it means to be problematical. The formulation of the task that makes the least demands on specific knowledge is:

> *Formulation of last resort:* If it is not known how to obtain X, then create a space that is known to contain X and search that space for X.

This formulation has the feature that it can always be made to apply. A space can always be found that contains the desired object. The less knowledge is available, the larger the encompassing space has to be, and the more difficult and expensive must be the search. But the first step has been attained in any event—a task formulation has been adopted that is rationally related to attaining that task.

This formulation is indeed the court of last resort. It, and the corresponding method for working with it, is usually called *generate and test*. This method is often deemed too simple to be worthy of attention. But to ignore it is like the physicist ignoring continuity equations in fluid flow. It is the very groundwork within which all other activities are to be understood. For instance, all of the methods used in artificial intelligence are at bottom search methods, built up as further specifications on generate and test. Means-ends analysis, hill climbing, progressive deepening, constraint propagation—all are search methods of one kind or another. And all build on generate and test.

Search leads to the view that an intelligent agent is always operating within a *problem space* (Figure 2-16). This is the space the agent has created within which to search for the solution to whatever problem it is currently attending. It is the agent's attempt to bound the problem so it can be worked on. Thus, the agent adopts some problem space in which to solve a problem. The agent is then located at some current state in the space. There is available a set of operators for finding new situations. For instance, in the blocks world, the blocks are in some initial configuration on the table and the agent can move any block that is clear on top. Task attainment is formulated as reaching a recognizable desirable state (there may be many such desirable states). The search through the space can be made in any fashion, as long as only operators of the space are applied (and each operator may have its own conditions of admissibility).

Solving problems is not just a random search in the space. The space is a frame within which the agent brings knowledge to bear to search for the desired object. If the agent has enough knowledge, it need not search at all. It simply moves through the space directly to the solution. In any event, large or small, there is some body of knowledge available to control the search and implement the operators in the problem space.

There are two separate searches going on in intelligence. One is *problem search,* which is the search of the problem space just described. The other is *knowledge search,* which is the search in the memory of the system for the knowledge to guide the problem search. This search for knowledge is not always required. Given a special-purpose intelligent system that works on only one task with a general search algorithm (say branch and bound), then only a little knowledge has to be brought to bear (the evaluation function and the logic of branch and bound), and it is used at every state in the space. The procedure can be built right into the structure of the system, so that only problem search occurs. On the other hand, agents that work on a wide range of tasks—say, humans—have large bodies of knowledge. When a new task arises, that body of knowledge must be searched for knowledge that is relevant to the

LONG-TERM KNOWLEDGE

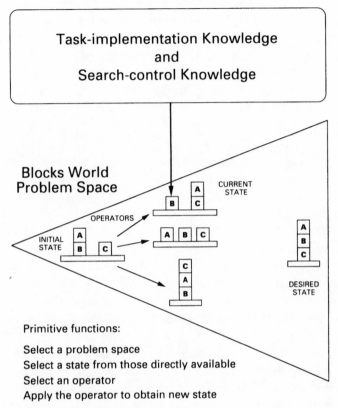

Task-implementation Knowledge
and
Search-control Knowledge

Blocks World
Problem Space

CURRENT
STATE

OPERATORS

INITIAL
STATE

DESIRED
STATE

Primitive functions:

Select a problem space
Select a state from those directly available
Select an operator
Apply the operator to obtain new state

Figure 2-16. The problem spaces and the two searches:
problem search and knowledge search.

task. Furthermore, in general this search is not a one-time retrieval
that initializes a small body of knowledge relevant to the task. Some
tasks have such a character, but generally at every state in the
problem space there is the possibility that some new knowledge,
available in the mind but not hitherto retrieved, has become relevant. Thus, the knowledge search goes on continually—and the
more problematical the situation, the more continuous is the need
for it. Knowledge search occurs in the inner loop of problem
search. Knowledge is used to select the operators for the problem
search and to evaluate their consequences; hence knowledge is
called upon within each state.

Knowledge search and problem search differ radically in their character. Problem search constructs its space. The only states that exist as declarative data structures are the current one plus, possibly, some that were generated in the search up to the current moment and have been saved to be accessed by memory operations. Each new operator application generates a new state, which has never been seen before by the agent. The problem space is necessarily combinatorial (with greater or less branching factor). Its topology could be reduced in dimension only if new states converged back on one another, as indicated in Figure 2-17. Convergence can happen only by comparison and identification of the states, since a priori it cannot be known what other states a newly constructed state might equal. Thus, the states have to be generated and then processed for duplication.

On the other hand, knowledge search occurs in a fixed, preexisting structure. The items being sought (the analog of the states in the problem space) preexist as data structures. The structure of the space (its connectivity and how paths through it are described) is preconstructed. Indeed, it is preconstructed to facilitate the search. The same place can be accessed through different paths and duplication can be immediately detected—just by marking the place when it is first encountered, something impossible in the problem space. Of course, it is possible to treat the knowledge search as if it were occurring in a problem space and to search it by the same combinatorial search methods. This is not the usual option, however, which is to exploit a specialized structure (indexes, hash tables, binary trees, balanced trees). In sum, the two spaces and the two searches are different.

There is much more to be said about problem spaces, which can only be touched on here. A problem space is a form of generate and test, with the operators comprising the generator and the recognition of a desired state being the test. Thus, the generator is realized by a sequence of operators; it is not a black-box process. Knowledge can terminate generation at many different points in the generation process (namely, after the application of any operator), thus opening the way for the generation to be intelligent. A major lesson from AI about generate-test situations is that it always pays to transfer knowledge from the test to the generator, so that candidate solutions need never be created at all. This is why multiple problem spaces should exist, rather than just a single large space with all conceivable operators. Packaging sequences of the operators of the

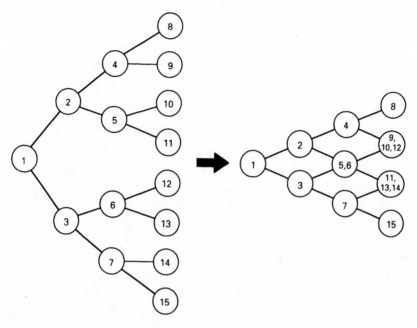

Figure 2-17. Combinatorial space becomes finite dimensional
through identification of nodes.

large space into larger operators (macro-operators) is a way of shifting knowledge from the test into the generator. Removing operators
known to be irrelevant is another way. Thus organizing the operators within many small problem spaces is a way of packaging
knowledge for efficient problem solving.

Another important aspect of problem spaces is the condition that
operators be freely applicable, that is, that a desired state be acceptable as the solution to the problem, no matter what operators
were used and in what order, as long as they are operators of the
space. Thus, the states preserve a certain set of properties over the
applications of the operators; it is these properties that are guaranteed to hold and do not have to be tested by the test for a desired
state. This free-application condition ties directly to the ability of a
system to search for solutions simply and efficiently. If the exact
sequence of operators were important, then the sequences would
have to be monitored, memory devoted to storing the sequence,
and processing devoted to managing that memory—search would
become a complex affair. In these terms, it is easy to see why
operators can have conditions of applicability associated with

them. These apply locally to the state at which application is being considered, hence do not complicate matters with memory and monitoring demands. In sum, the organization of processing in terms of problem spaces has deep roots in the basic efficiencies of problem solving.

2.9. Preparation and Deliberation

In general, intelligent systems engage in both knowledge search and problem search. This leads to the *preparation vs. deliberation trade-off*. It is also known as the store vs. compute trade-off, or sometimes the knowledge vs. search trade-off (although this terminology is misleading, because both preparation and deliberation provide knowledge—it is just from different sources). Whatever it is called, it is a fundamental trade-off for all intelligent systems.

The situation is shown in Figure 2-18. At some point there is an indication that a response is required. Then two types of processing enter into determining that response. The system can *deliberate*— engage in activities to analyze the situation, the possible responses, their consequences, and so on. In problematical situations, as we have seen, this will lead to a search for an appropriate response in some space. The system can also have various responses or aspects of responses already *prepared*. These must of course have been stored away. To use such preparations the system must access the memory, retrieve the prepared material, and then adapt it as appropriate to the case at hand.

Each specific situation leading to a response calls forth some mix of deliberation and preparation. That mix varies over the ensemble of total situations that the organism encounters. Overall, the organism itself can be characterized by its mix of activities—by the extent to which its response stems from deliberation or from its preparations. Thus, as in Figure 2-19, we can consider a space with deliberation and preparedness as dimensions.[21] Particular systems are located as points in the space. Actually, a system produces a cloud of points in the space, corresponding to the preparedness and

21. The preparation-deliberation space should not be confused with the generality-power space, which plots the scope of a problem-solving system against the difficulty of the tasks it can solve. This space also exhibits a trade-off, arising from the need to distribute limited developmental resources along one dimension or the other.

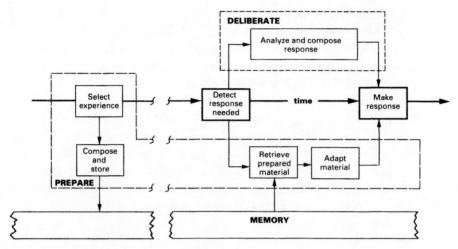

Figure 2-18. Preparation and deliberation processes.

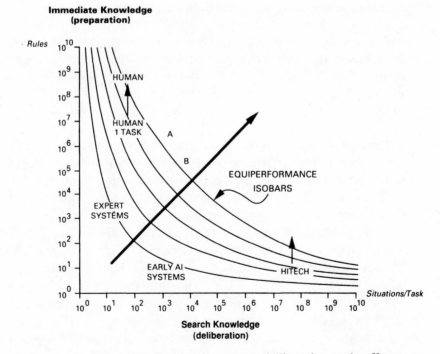

Figure 2-19. Preparation versus deliberation trade-off.

deliberation used in each task on which it works. The system itself can be taken as the center of this cloud. The vertical axis represents the knowledge that is encoded in the memory—the amount of the system's resources that is devoted to preparedness. In many current AI systems preparedness can be measured by the number of rules, or productions, it contains, 10, 100, 1,000, or more. The units are appropriately logarithmic. As more rules are added, they tend to cover special cases, so that more and more rules are required to get the same increment in coverage. The horizontal axis represents the knowledge that is obtained by considering multiple situations—by searching. In current AI systems deliberation can be measured by the number of situations considered, and again the units are appropriately logarithmic. With an exponential fan out of search, getting an additional increment of coverage requires considering a multiplicative increase in total situations.

The curves in the figure are *equal-performance isobars*. Systems at different points on the same isobar (*A* and *B*) will be equally effective, but they will attain that effectiveness by a different mix of immediately available knowledge, prepared ahead of time, and of deliberation about the current situation. In general, if a system is located at some point on an isobar (say point *A*), then there is another system that spends a little less of its time accessing rules and more of its time searching and that ends up at the same performance. The isobars form a family of roughly parallel curves, with performance improving as one moves up and to the right (along the big arrow), where both immediate knowledge and search increase.

The isobars represent curves of equal performance, not curves of equal computational cost. A family of *equal-cost isobars* also exists, as shown in Figure 2-20, for it takes computing resources to do either knowledge search or problem search. The cost isobars cross the performance isobars, just as in analogous forms of economic reasoning (which this situation strongly resembles). Cost isobars might even be almost straight. Thus, there is clearly an optimal mix for a system, where the cost isobars touch the highest performance isobar. The heavy arrow in the figure runs through these optimal-mix points. These constitute best trade-offs between amount of problem search and amount of knowledge search.

Particular systems are located at particular places in Figure 2-19. In fact, the figure can be used to sketch a history of artificial intelli-

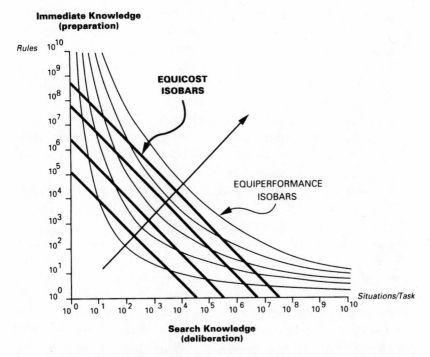

Figure 2-20. Equal-cost isobars and equal-performance isobars.

gence. The early AI programs had very little knowledge—not more than a dozen rules of domain knowledge. They did a modest amount of search, with trees of 100 to 1,000 nodes. That is the period that is often dubbed the *search period* of AI. Then came the awareness that lots of knowledge could be used—in what is called an *expert system* or a *rule-based system*. Expert systems can be seen as an exploration of what can be attained with very little reasoning or deliberation but with all the effort being put into accessing immediately available knowledge. Typical current expert systems are in the region of hundreds of rules of knowledge and only tens of situations explored deliberately. The biggest expert systems range up to about 5,000 rules and don't do much additional search.

Humans can be located on this same figure. If we consider expert behavior on a relatively narrow task, we find that tens of thousands of chunks of information are involved (Simon & Gilmartin, 1973). Humans do more search than current expert systems do, but only in the hundreds of situations, not in the many thousands. Of course, a human has expertise over many domains. Integrating over these domains might move the human up on the knowledge axis to about 10^6 or even 10^8 chunks but will not increase the size of the search, since this is relatively fixed by the externally fixed time to respond (here taken as a few minutes at best) and the rate at which the architecture does its basic operations, both of which remain constant. Hence, the diagram reveals a characteristic feature, that for a given system, with its fixed architecture, improvement comes from adding knowledge, not adding search volume. Thus, systems typically move up a vertical line as they gain knowledge.

The usefulness of Figure 2-19 for understanding the nature of intelligent systems can be seen in the story of Hitech.[22] This is the chess-playing program developed by Hans Berliner and Carl Ebeling (1988), which now has an official rating in human tournament play in the high master range (2,360). Hitech is a special hardware architecture with 64 parallel processors, which generates about 175,000 chess positions per second. This yields about 10^8 situations per move. Hitech is thus a system that operates by massive search. Like other such programs, Hitech does not use a lot of knowledge. Initially (1985), it had perhaps tens of rules—a few general rules such as alpha-beta and some more specific rules for evaluating positions. This characterization would locate Hitech over to the far right of the diagram. At this level of performance it was rated at about 1,900 points, essentially a high expert rating. Since then its rating has climbed about 400 points. All of that change occurred, of course, with fixed search capabilities—as noted, the architecture essentially fixes the size of the search. It was just as big when Hitech played at 1,900 as it is now when it plays at 2,350. Thus, Hitech has been moving up a vertical line in the figure, implying that more knowledge has been pumped into Hitech. And indeed that is true. Its knowledge is now up to perhaps a hundred rules.[23] (It is not easy to add knowledge to Hitech, since it must be applied at the speed of the move generator, which is only about 5 microseconds per position.)

---

22. Indeed, the particular analysis of the trade-off here is due to Hans Berliner, although of course the general idea has been common knowledge in computer science for a long time.

23. Hitech is not organized in simple rule-based form and no precise accounting of its stored knowledge has been attempted.

A final lesson can be taken from Figure 2-19. It is common in AI and cognitive science to talk about human intelligence and the intelligence of systems like Hitech in contrasting terms. Hitech is a brute-force searcher and it operates in an "entirely different way from human intelligence." Figure 2-19 urges otherwise. Certainly, different types of intelligent systems occupy different regions in the preparation-deliberation space, but systems like Hitech are to be analyzed in the same way as expert systems and humans are. They occupy different regions, but the analysis is the same. Hitech gets better only by the addition of knowledge, just as do other systems. Thus, the scientific objective in AI is to understand the entire space and the way systems in it relate to each other. Entire regions of this space are still unexplored.

The situation portrayed in Figure 2-19 is reminiscent of the situation in genetics. The analogy between them may be instructive, even though it is undoubtedly imperfect. In population biology, different evolutionary strategies for a species can be distinguished (Wilson, 1975). Two extreme strategies are the r-strategy and the K-strategy.[24] The r-strategy is to have lots of progeny and to spend as little energy on them as possible. Many progeny will die, but the species overpowers with numbers. The K-strategy is to have few progeny but to spend as much energy on each one as possible. This is the strategy of the big carnivores and of humans. Those two strategies define a space in which to understand the evolutionary possibilities. Some issues in population genetics become clearer when these different strategic possibilities are kept in mind. Similarly, the choice between high-knowledge and high-search strategies, which define the preparation-deliberation space, is an important choice for a species of intelligent systems.

2.10. Summary

This chapter has been a tour of the key terms that lie at the foundation of cognitive science. Iterating through these concepts seems a reasonable way to lay the foundations for the rest of the book. Figures 2-21 and 2-22 provide a summary that can serve as a ready reference when the concepts reappear in later chapters. Figure 2-21

---

24. The names come from the constants in the logistic equation used in quantitative population models.

Behaving system
A system characterized by multiple response functions on its environment

Knowledge
The medium of a knowledge-level system
What can be used to select actions to attain goals
 • Abstracted from representation and processing
The knowledge level is just another system level

Representation
A system that obeys representation laws

Composing transformations
A general approach to representing
Uses a nonspecific medium capable of combinatorial variety
Composes transformations to satisfy representation laws
Required if enough variety is required of the representation

Computational system
A machine that obtains multiple functions on some inputs and outputs by using other inputs to specify functions

Symbol
A mechanism for obtaining distal access
Required if enough variety is required of the system

Architecture
The fixed structure that realizes a symbol-level system

Intelligence
The degree of approximation to a knowledge-level system

Search
 Problem search: Search in the problem space to solve a task
 Knowledge search: Search in memory to guide problem search

Problem space
A set of states and a set of operators from state to state
 • Operators may have conditions of applicability
A task is to find a desired state, applying operators freely
The states are generated by the agent, they do not pre-exist

Deliberation vs. preparation trade-off
 Deliberation: Activity after task is set
 Preparation: Activity prior to setting of task
 Trade-off: The relative mix of two types of activity

Figure 2-21. Foundational terms for cognitive science.

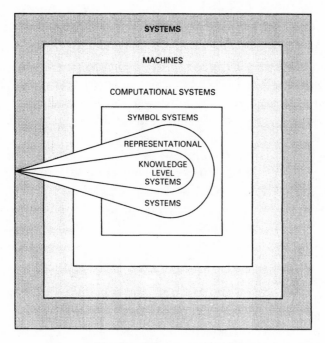

Figure 2-22. The different types of systems.

lists all the key terms and phrases teamed with short statements giving their essential character.

During the course of the chapter several systems were introduced. Figure 2-22 shows how they relate to one another. Focusing on the internal structure of the systems, it shows four nested classes of systems (the rectangles), each successively more specialized. The most general is just the class of all systems. Systems can be specialized to machines, which are systems that have a medium, so that inputs and outputs can be defined for them such that every machine effects a function from its inputs to its outputs (actually from the history of its inputs to its outputs). Computational systems are machines that are capable of producing multiple functions; they work by using some of their inputs to specify the functions that hold between other inputs and outputs. Symbol systems are computational systems with symbols, that is, with devices for distal access. The diagram doesn't reflect adequately that the diversity of computational systems is much greater than that of symbol systems, the diversity of machines much greater than that of computers, and so on, but the figure is sufficient to reflect our interest in systems that can support mind-like capabilities.

The two comet-shaped regions indicate the systems that support adaptation with respect to the external world. The larger class are the representational systems, which are systems whose internal structure obeys representation laws. Such laws support adaptation.[25] Within the class of representational systems are the knowledge-level systems, which are so structured that their behavior can be derived just from the content of the representations about the world and their goals. There are many representational systems that cannot be described at the knowledge-level.

Representational systems must be realized in some structure, so the two comet-shaped regions intersect the four types of system structures. Representational systems with substantial scopes for domains and goals require symbol systems for their realization, but as scope diminishes then structures of lesser capability can be used as well. The areas of intersection with these more general system structures become smaller and smaller, indicating their more specialized character. There are of course many structures of each type that do not satisfy representation laws, hence are not about the external world, and hence do not support active adaptation.

25. I did not discuss systems that support adaptation but are not representational. They would be another outer layer of the adaptational class of systems. The obvious candidates would be open-loop adaptations, such as those constructed by evolution and human designers. Examples would be a bird's wing or a wheel.

Human Cognitive Architecture

3

The basic concepts of intelligent systems—representation, knowledge, symbols, and search—apply as much to machines as to people, but human beings, of course, are unique in many ways. The constraints that shape the human mind, laid out in Figure 1-7, include some that are quite specific to the human situation: humans are constructed of neural technology, they are grown embryologically, they arose through evolution, they must be highly autonomous but social. Perhaps even development is specifically biological.

Our ultimate goal is a unified theory of human cognition. This will be expressed, I have maintained, as a theory of the architecture of human cognition—that is, of the fixed (or slowly varying) structure that forms the framework for the immediate processes of cognitive performance and learning. Thus, we need to set out that architecture. We will do so in stages. In this chapter I will attempt to derive some basic aspects of the human cognitive architecture, attending only to the way the human is situated in the world. This will lay the groundwork for proposing in the fourth chapter a specific architecture in detail. (Though, even there, some aspects will remain open.)

As an alternative presentation strategy, the architecture could be laid out as a total system. This would more closely approximate the axiomatic ideal. An advantage of a description presented in two stages, in addition to its possible didactic virtues, is that it separates what can be claimed about the human cognitive architecture on general grounds from what must be justified by detailed experimental data. This is a definite advantage for this book, given that the specific architecture is only an exemplar.

Thus, this chapter will be devoted to a quite general argument. As a first given, it will take neural technology to be the technology of the human cognitive architecture. As a second given, it will take an architecture to be a structure that supports mind-like behavior. From Chapter 2 we already have a characterization of what that means. To these two starting points this chapter will add what can be called the *real-time constraint on human cognition*. From these three constraints will be derived a number of key aspects of the cognitive architecture.

Whatever can be derived from these general considerations will no longer provide possible options in specifying the details of the human architecture. The wisdom of such a strategy—of attempting to divide and conquer—should be evident from the discussion in the last chapter. In Figure 2-14, for example, we saw that large degrees of freedom are available to construct architectures of symbolic systems. We also noted some assessments in the field that the architecture may be essentially a hidden variable—that there is no way to determine what representations or what control structures are used. Since any general (that is, universal) architecture can mimic any other, so goes this line, the situation is hopeless. (My response was to propose bringing knowledge to bear from many different sources.) Clearly, then, whatever aspects of the architecture that can be pinned down from the general situation within which the human architecture is constructed and operates can only help in making the internal details identifiable.

Here is another way to think about the enterprise of this chapter. Evolution is the designer of the human cognitive architecture. It will pick and choose systems that will aid in the survival of the species. Our problem as scientists is to guess what design evolution has settled for to date. We know a little about evolution as a designer. It never starts over, but always works with what is available. In Jacob's (1973) now famous phrase, evolution is a tinkerer. For instance, once a species is committed to a *K*-strategy (heavy investment in few progeny) evolution will not shift it to the opposite *r*-strategy (light investment in many progeny)—it is too hard to get from here to there. Evolution picks its architectures within the design constraints posed by the local situations in which the species finds itself. If we can discern some of these constraints, then we can delimit the field within which evolution must operate.

This chapter is speculative. Any attempt to get at general characteristics from general considerations must run this risk. I will comment on the risk at the end of the chapter, after the results are before us. Even if the speculations are wrong, they can be wrong in revealing ways.

Here is a preview of the results, as a guide for where we are going. Different cognitive worlds have different time scales. The different kinds of cognitive worlds that we see are governed by the time scales on which they occur—the neurological, cognitive, rational, and social. They have the character they do to enable mind-like behavior to emerge—to get to computational, symbolic systems. The temporal region within which cognition proper operates—about 10 ms to 10 sec—comprises four system levels. Within this cognitive band there must be a distinction between automatic and controlled processes, which again is a distinction in level. In addition, the architecture must be recognition based and there must be a continual shift toward increased recognition. This shift corresponds to continual movement along the isobar in Figure 2-19 toward increased preparation.

3.1. The Human Is a Symbol System

Chapter 2 was abstract in a very particular way. It discussed symbol-level systems and knowledge-level systems as the general structure that was necessary to obtain general intelligent behavior. It did not specifically make the case that humans were knowledge-level systems and symbol systems—though it was clearly understood that was what we were after. Rather, we settled for understanding the nature of these various systems, and what gives rise to them, namely, the need to deal with large amounts of variability in response functions.

At this point I wish to be explicit that humans are symbol systems that are at least modest approximations of knowledge systems. They might be other kinds of systems as well, but at least they are symbol systems. The grounds for this argument, as made clear by the entire previous chapter, is the variety of response functions that humans use. If the variety of response functions is immense enough, a system will be driven to compose its response functions by means of a computational system that constructs representations by means of composed transformations; and it will be driven to use symbols to obtain distal access in its long-term memory. That whole apparatus exists because of the demands of variety and volume. The groundwork has already been laid. I want here to be explicit about its application to humans.

One weak argument is that humans can undoubtedly emulate a universal machine. They might do it rather slowly, because they may have to spend a large amount of time memorizing new states. But, if we wait long enough, they can perform the operations of a universal machine. They are of course limited in their lifetimes (measured in terms of total number of operations they can perform) and ultimately in the reliability of their memory. But neither of these constraints is of the essence, just as they are not for computers, which also have limited lifetimes and reliabilities. In short, technically humans are the kind of beast that can be a universal machine. With that comes, again technically, all the other properties of universal machines. The argument is weak, however, because the imagined type of verification—instructing a human to be a specific universal machine (say a Turing machine) and then observing the person's execution of it deliberately and interpretively—is artificial. It is not an observation on the kind of life that humans lead. It could be the exploitation of a capability that is actually irrelevant to the regular style with which the human interacts with the environment.

The more substantial argument is to reflect on the variety of response functions that humans perform—not *can* do, but *actually* do. The fact is that they seem to create new response functions all the time. To adopt the well-worn device of the Martian biologist studying the human species, what would impress it most is the *efflorescence of adaptation*. Humans appear to go around simply creating opportunities of all kinds to build different response functions. Look at the variety of jobs in the world. Each one has humans using different kinds of response functions. Humans invent games. They have all different kinds of sports. They no sooner invent one game than they invent new ones. They not only invent card games, they collect them in a book and publish them, 150 strong (Morehead & Mott-Smith, 1959). That implies that people buy such books so they can develop yet new response functions by the score. Humans not only eat, as do all other animals, they prepare their food. But not only that, they invent recipes to do it in different ways. Hundreds of recipes, thousands of recipes—each a different way to prepare food, hence a different response function.

They also dance, write books, build houses, and have conversations. A conversation, whatever else it might be, is an opportunity to interact with the environment in a way that is different from prior interactions—that is, to build new response functions. Think of the Library of Congress as evidence of the variety of response functions that humans have exhibited by writing books, will exhibit by reading them, and want to exhibit by building buildings to make them available. To academics the mention of books suggests intellectual functions, as if all this was perhaps a phenomenon of the high end of the socioeconomic scale. What then of rapping? A creation of the black ghetto, rapping is a social invention to produce an opportunity for new responses to a highly dynamic environment. It serves other functions as well, but it builds on the human proclivity to invent new forms of responses. People create these opportunities. Indeed, our Martian biologist would not be wrong to conclude that the biggest biological puzzle about earthlings is why they have developed this efflorescence of adaptation.[1]

Ethology, looking at other organisms from digger wasps to herring gulls (Tinbergen, 1960, 1969), has properly become intrigued with the adaptations they exhibit. Each adaptation is seen as a unique biological phenomenon, to be curated one by one. Each is to be understood by exploring the behavioral and physiological mechanisms that support it. Not so with humans. There is no enumerating their adaptations—they will invent new adaptations faster than they can be recorded. The act of recording is itself one more adaptation—or rather a whole generator of adaptations, as the problems of such an ethnological scientific enterprise unfold and are responded to.

What I am saying here is not new, nor is it supposed to be. There are many ways of talking about the life of *Homo sapiens* so as to reveal the nature of the life of the mind. Always the same extraordinary characteristics of man as a biological organism are to be described. The issue is what it takes to convince ourselves that humans deal with so much variety that they must be symbol systems—that no system of less power and universality could suffice. I am attempting a description that takes as the givens obser-

---

1. Of course, if it could puzzle about it, then the Martian might a fortiori know the answer, because it would exhibit that same efflorescence. But no metaphor can be perfect.

vations on the *behavior* of humans, to wit, on the variety of that behavior. I wish to avoid judgments on the content of that behavior, for example, on its rationality or the success of its adaptation to the conditions that trigger it. I especially wish to avoid involvement with any internal or structural aspects of the human. My objective is to ground the assertion that the human is a symbol system on external behavioral aspects, so that it can serve as a design constraint for considering the nature of the internal structure.

To indicate this behavioral character of humans, I will use the phrase *unlimited qualitative adaptation*. Clearly, humans are not infinitely adaptive. That is easy to show. Just pit two humans against each other in a competition; one will win, the other will lose. The human that lost clearly was not sufficiently adaptive. Thus, the variety of adaptations is what is important—their range, qualitatively speaking. Here there seems to be no limit whatsoever. What might have seemed a limit, in terms of specific sensors and time-bound contact, humans manage to transcend by creating instruments and histories. They even bury time capsules so that some far-future human will have one additional opportunity to behave adaptively with respect to a past he or she might otherwise have missed.

This argument has a soft spot, which should be noted. It is an asymptotic argument. That is, as the variety of functions that can be exhibited by a system increases without limit, we know the set of functions becomes the set of computable functions. Furthermore, we know such a set can be generated only by a universal computational system (exactly so, since these two notions simply go together). If we consider systems that produce an ever greater variety of functions, at some point they must have the structure of a universal system, a symbol system. A human is capable of producing an immense variety of functions and does so in its everyday life. But is this actually enough variety so that the structure must be that of symbol system? Computational theory does not yet provide any useful answers to this question—in part because it hasn't sought them. In general, however, such questions are hard to answer in useful ways. It would be nice to have some theory that helps us here, but I don't know of any. It is instructive to observe that computers are in the same situation: to compute any computable function a computer has to have the structure of a symbol system. We construct computers so that they have this structure. But need we? Is the variety of actual functions that we want to compute such that we could get by with some structure perhaps far removed from a symbol system? It seems hardly likely, but there is no mathematical theory to provide definitive answers.

In sum, we will now take it as established that the architecture of human cognition is a symbol system.

3.2. System Levels

Let us turn to the technology out of which the human architecture is constructed. The first point is that, of necessity, intelligent systems are built up of multiple levels of systems (such as the computer-system levels in Figure 2-3). To analyze the levels in human cognition, however, we need to consider the topic more carefully. I wish to maintain that the human architecture is built up of a hierarchy of multiple system levels and that it cannot be otherwise structured. Thus, the discovery of the cognitive architecture can proceed with this assumption.

A system level is a collection of components that are linked together in some arrangement and that interact, thus producing behavior at that system level. In a system with multiple levels, the components at one level are realized by systems at the next level below, and so on for each successive level.

That engineered computer systems have a hierarchical structure, as analyzed in Figure 2-3, can certainly be taken as one pillar of support. Empirically, everything we understand about engineering systems to get intelligence tells us that building up multiple levels is required. This is one of the great empirical invariances. Although many different ways have been found to construct information-processing systems, they all still consist of a hierarchy of levels. Indeed, so far, it is always the same hierarchy.

A second pillar comes from Herb Simon's analysis of hierarchy (Simon, 1962). His argument was that stability dictates that systems have to be hierarchical. Attempts to build complicated systems without first building stable subassemblies will ultimately fail—the entire structure will disintegrate before it all gets put together. If stable subassemblies are created, layer upon layer, then each one has a reasonable probability of being constructed out of a few parts. Thus, there exists a general argument that stability dictates the existence of levels. The stability argument, of course, can be taken to underlie the entire hierarchical structure of matter, from nucleons, to atoms, to molecules, and on up. So the hypothesis about levels may have nothing to do with intelligent systems per se, but with the way all systems are put together in our universe. All we need for the argument is that intelligent systems will be hierarchical. We are perfectly satisfied if the universe in general is hierarchical because of evolution—because that is what survives.

Levels are clearly abstractions, being alternative ways of describing the same system, each level ignoring some of what is specified at the level beneath it. It all seems to be in the head of the observer, but there is more to it than that. Levels can be *stronger* or *weaker*, depending on how well the behavior of the system, as described at a level, can be predicted or explained by the structure of the system described at the same level. In standard treatments of systems analysis, systems are called *state determined* when their future behavior is determined by their current state. That is what holds for a strong level. A level is weak if considerations from lower levels enter into determining the future course of behavior.

In engineered systems (Figure 2-3 again), great care is taken to construct strong levels—to seal off each level from the one below. When dealing with logic circuits one need not understand the continuous circuitry underlying them—except when things go wrong. When dealing with programs one need not understand the register-transfer circuits that realize the operations and the interpreter—again, except when things go wrong. And so on. These are all very strong system levels, as evidenced by how small the failure rates are in commercially successful systems.[2] The strength of a system level is a property of nature, and not just something in the head of the observer. It is why, as noted in Chapter 2, being able to describe a system at a given level carries an empirical claim.

Many natural system levels are also very strong, such as the atomic and molecular levels. The stronger a level is, the more it forms a distinct world, in which nothing must be known about lower levels for it to operate. System levels need not be strong, however, and certainly it is an empirical matter how strong natural system levels are. In particular, though it may be assumed that intelligent systems are organized in levels, it cannot be assumed that these are all strong levels. There could be lots of ways in which

---

2. Indeed, the concept of *error* becomes useful just when a system level becomes strong enough so that it can be trusted most of the time.

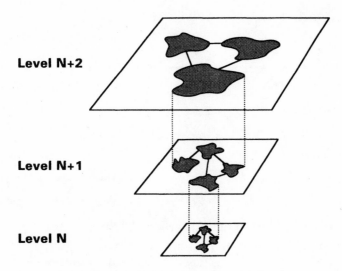

Level N+2

Level N+1

Level N

Figure 3-1. Expansion of space with levels.

phenomena from lower levels percolate upward, ways that are not to be described as errors.

As one moves up the hierarchy of system levels, size increases and speed decreases. This is an obvious, but important, property that follows directly from the nature of levels. Figure 3-1 shows the situation. At level N, a collection of K components, say of characteristic size S, are put together to form a component at level $N + 1$. The size of this higher component is at least KS, but it would be somewhat bigger because the level-N components are spread out in space, with a certain amount of interstitial tissue of some sort. A collection of K components of level $N + 1$ are put together to form a component of level $N + 2$. This higher component is at least $K(KS)$ in size, hence K^2S in terms of the bottom level. In general, components of level $N + m$ are K^m times the size of components of level N. Of course the number of components need not be the same at each level, so that the K is some (geometric) mean value. In summary, not only does the size increase with level, it does so geometrically, so that the appropriate scale unit is the logarithm of the linear size.[3]

---

3. In space of two or three dimensions, the components can be packed together so that the increase is by the logarithm of the area or volume; but it still comes to the same thing in terms of the logarithmic nature of the scale.

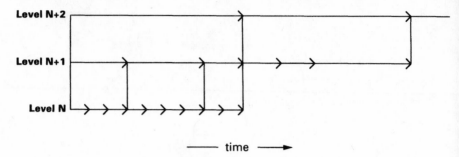

Figure 3-2. Expansion of time with levels.

Expansion occurs in time as well, as Figure 3-2 shows. Assume a system at level N takes time t to generate a response given a change in its inputs. If K such systems are connected together as components to form a system at level $N + 1$, then it will take this system longer to produce its outputs than is taken by the level-N components. How much longer is somewhat more complicated than in the spatial case. If the K components were arranged in series it would take Kt times as long. If they were arranged in a big loop, in which circulation continued until some state was achieved, then it could take $L(Kt)$, for as many iterations (L) as necessary; this could be indeterminately longer than t. If they were arranged in a binary discrimination net they might take only $(\log_2 K)t$. The time could be reduced to just t, but only if the K components didn't interact at all and each one simply delivered its output. This would be the limiting case, where the higher-level system does not exist at all as a system. Thus, what exact multiplier will exist depends on the processing organization at the level. But there will be some T such that the characteristic time at level $N + 1$ is Tt. Then, just as in the spatial case, the time for level $N + m$ is T^m times the time for level N, where T is some (geometric) mean of the time multiplier at each level. There is no invariant relationship between T (the temporal multiplier) and K (the spatial multiplier), except that in general T increases with K (perhaps sublinearly), because in general additional components play some role, though perhaps only conditionally. In summary, as one goes up the scale, everything slows down. Molecules behave more slowly than atoms; macromolecules in turn behave more slowly than molecules; cells behave more slowly than macromolecules—and so on up to planetary systems, and galaxies.

The scale is geometric, so that the appropriate scale unit is the logarithm of time.

We are interested in the smallest factor required to produce a new level. A level must be about a factor of ten bigger than the next lower level. Some number of components have to be put together and allowed to interact for a few cycles in order to get a new system level with new properties. It can't be done with two or three components and it can't be done with just a couple of component operation times. Novel behavior can't build up that rapidly. On the other hand, there are lots of cases where less than 100 or 1,000 components or component-times suffice.[4] Thus, we can take a factor of 10 to be the minimum characteristic factor to get from one level to the next. This factor is highly approximate, of course. It might be only 3 in some cases, it might be as many as 30 in others. Let us use ~~10 as a special notation to indicate such very approximate numbers. Perhaps "times or divided by 3" is a useful way to think of the approximation in analogy with the usual "plus or minus 3." A factor of ~~10 is both a symbol for the minimal growth factor for system levels and an estimate of its size as very roughly 10.

3.3. The Time Scale of Human Action

Let us now consider the time scale at which human action occurs, shown in Figure 3-3. At the left, time is measured in seconds, and ordered by a log scale. The next column to the right names the time units—microseconds (μs, or 10^{-6} sec), milliseconds (ms), seconds, minutes, and hours. Correspondence with real life is a little rough, because we don't live according to the metric scale of time; but it helps to keep the time scale calibrated to everyday life. The units themselves are, of course, geometrically related to one another. The next column names the system with the characteristic operation time. For us, time is the useful measure of the system level, not space. But of course the characteristic physical size increases correspondingly. Several adjacent levels group together in what are called *bands*. Different bands are quite different phenomenal

---

4. Systems can be much larger than the minimum. This usually implies a homogeneous iterative structure of some kind. Thus, a wire is a system that is almost indefinitely larger (longer) than the substructure out of which it is built. Simon's analysis of complexity indicates limits to how large, in terms of the number of immediate constituent components, a truly complicated system can be.

TIME SCALE OF HUMAN ACTION

Scale (sec)	Time Units	System	World (theory)
10^7	months		
10^6	weeks		**SOCIAL BAND**
10^5	days		
10^4	hours	Task	
10^3	10 min	Task	**RATIONAL BAND**
10^2	minutes	Task	
10^1	10 sec	Unit task	
10^0	1 sec	Operations	**COGNITIVE BAND**
10^{-1}	100 ms	Deliberate act	
10^{-2}	10 ms	Neural circuit	
10^{-3}	1 ms	Neuron	**BIOLOGICAL BAND**
10^{-4}	100 μs	Organelle	

Figure 3-3. Time scale of human action.

worlds, as shown in the right-hand column, and are described by different theories.

This figure provides an overview of where we are going. Starting at the bottom, there is the *biological band* of three levels—*neurons; organelles*, which are a factor of ten down from neurons; and *neural circuits*, a factor of ten up. As we'll see, neurons have a characteristic operation time of about a ms ($\sim\sim 1$ ms), and neural circuits of about 10 ms ($\sim\sim 10$ ms). Above the biological band, there is the *cognitive band*. Here the levels are unfamiliar—I've called them the *deliberate act, cognitive operation,* and *unit task*, each of which takes about ten times ($\sim\sim 10$) as long as the act at the level beneath. It will be the main task of this chapter to establish these cognitive levels and something of their character. Above the cognitive band lies the *rational band*, which is of the order of minutes to hours. All of these levels of the rational band are labeled the same, namely, as *task*. Finally, even higher up, there lies something that might be called the *social band*, which I will have only a little to say about.

A striking feature of Figure 3-3 is that each level is only the minimal factor of ten ($\sim\sim 10$) above its components. Each new level occurs, so to speak, as soon as it can in terms of numbers of components. For the levels of the biological band, this factor is a reading from what we know empirically, so it stands as a confirmation of the levels analysis. For the cognitive band, it is more a prediction of what we will find.

3.4. The Biological Band

We start at the neural level. We have to start someplace. We could, in fact, back down to the organelle, or even to the macromolecular band ($\sim\sim 10^{-5}$ to 10^{-7} sec). But the neural level is the obvious one, because it is so clearly the technology that is given for the human mind. Furthermore, we need only a few important facts from the neural level to lay the groundwork for developing the levels of the cognitive band. Figure 3-4, upper left, shows a neuron. Since neurons are biological cells, the neuron level is a cellular level, and it shares most of its properties, both of space and time, with all other biological cells. The characteristic linear size for a cell body is $\sim\sim 10$ microns (10^{-5} meters). Thus, in a brain of $\sim 1,000$ cubic centimeters, there are $\sim\sim 10^{12}$ cells, of which ~ 10 percent, or $\sim\sim 10^{11}$, are neurons, which has impressed many people as a lot to work with to construct a mind.

In terms of short-term operation, the neuron is a strong system level. Its inputs and outputs are clearly identifiable by synapses and its medium can be taken to be voltages, as measured across the cell membrane. Its characteristic action is to deliver a signal from the dendrites at one end of the nerve to the axon ramifications at the other end. This signal is a neural pulse or spike, shown in the upper right of the figure, if the distance is more than just a few characteristic distances (cell-body lengths), but it can be simply a dynamically changing output potential (graded potential), if the distance is short. Reflecting the immense strides in neuroscience made in the last

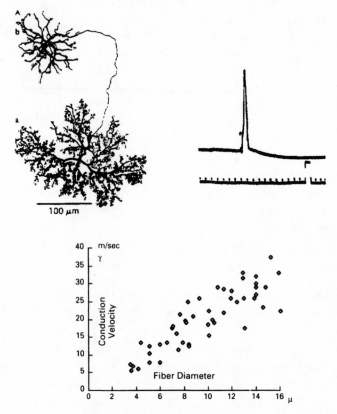

Figure 3-4. The neural level (adapted from Frank, 1959;
Shepherd, 1979; Tasaki, 1959).

decades, the operational behavior of the neuron is rather well understood in terms of cable equations in branching networks (Rall,
1977).[5] Current theory covers not only pulses and graded potentials
but also summation, inhibition, and the other integrative effects.
Thus, at the neural level there are strong behavior laws.

We need only two facts out of this wealth of detail. First, the
characteristic operating time is ~~1 ms. In the figure, the width of
the neural spike is about 1–2 ms, even for a sharp pulse. This is the

5. There are other forms of behavior of the neuron that are much slower (also, less
well understood), for instance, the transport functions that move transmitter supplies
down the axon to the vesicles, whose rates are in the range of millimeters per day.

time it takes to rise to its peak and come back down. Other processes in the neural signal are also $\sim\sim 1$ ms. For example, the time for graded potentials to move through a dendritic net is $\sim\sim 1$ ms and the time to make a synaptic transmission is $\sim\sim 500$ μs (which is actually a little less, as appropriate for a component action). Pulse rates vary accordingly, from high values of $\sim\sim 200$ pulses/sec (corresponding to one pulse every $\sim\sim 5$ ms) down to $\sim\sim 1$ pulse/sec (corresponding to one pulse every $\sim\sim 1$ sec). As a result, a single neuron can transmit only a few bits/sec.

The second fact is the speed of neural transmission. The nerve is specialized for rapid propagation of a neural pulse, and the speed increases with the diameter of the axonal fiber. The lower panel of Figure 3-4 shows the speed to be essentially linear in fiber diameter, and that it can attain speeds of $\sim\sim 100$ m/sec in large fibers. Large fibers occur only in the peripheral nervous system, where large distances must be covered ($\sim\sim$ meters); in the central nervous system the fibers are very small and the speeds are $\sim\sim 1$ m/sec. Specialization for speed is reflected in another technological innovation at the neural level, the myelination of nerve cells, which improves their speed by an order of magnitude.

From the entire discussion, it should be clear that we are in the standard realm of physical and chemical law. This is the familiar physical world, extended to the biological realm. Whatever might have been the lingering concerns of vitalism in the earlier part of this century, those concerns are long gone. We understand what is going on in the biological band by reducing phenomena to biochemistry and biomolecular mechanisms.

3.5. The Neural Circuit Level

We move up to the neural circuit level, that is, to where a collection of connected neurons together perform some function. Figure 3-5 will have to suffice as a picture. The world is a lot more complicated up here. Not only are there large numbers of neurons, but our measuring devices are still not up to multicellular records of the kind needed—hundreds or thousands of neurons. It is difficult to get a simple picture, to extract the few important facts needed for our argument. Nevertheless, here is a simple approximation to what the current art knows about neural circuits in the central

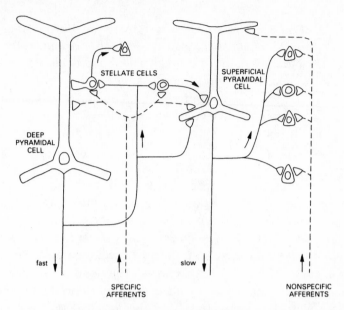

STELLATE CELLS

SUPERFICIAL
PYRAMIDAL
CELL

DEEP
PYRAMIDAL
CELL

fast

slow

SPECIFIC
AFFERENTS

NONSPECIFIC
AFFERENTS

Figure 3-5. The neural-circuit level (adapted from Shepherd, 1979).

nervous system (Shepherd, 1979). The brain can be viewed as a large collection of *local circuits*. These local circuits are of the order of a millimeter cubed ($\sim\sim 1$ mm^3). The local circuits are connected by *distal cables*. Those cables are of the order of centimeters in length (the brain volume is $\sim\sim 1,000$ cm^3, hence its linear extent is $\sim\sim 10$ cm).

Each local circuit contains on the order of $\sim\sim 5 \times 10^4$ neurons.[6] This might seem like a lot of neurons, but it probably isn't. There are several factors that force a body of neurons to be multiplexed. For instance, given how little information a neuron transmits ($\sim\sim 1$ bits/sec), neurons must be bundled into cables to get reasonable data rates (say a factor of ten). Also, coding seems often to be done by large populations of neurons with broad tuning—a form of distributed representation—so the distinct functional computing elements could easily drop by a total factor of 100, leaving about 500 elements for a local circuit.

6. With a cell body of $\sim\sim 10^{-2}$mm, there are $\sim\sim 10^6$ cell bodies per 1 mm^3. Nerve cells account for ~ 10 percent, with glial cells making up the rest. This would make for $\sim\sim 10^5$ neurons, except that distal cables occupy appreciable space, reducing the number to $\sim\sim 5 \times 10^4$ neurons/mm^3.

In any event, at the moment there is no way to go down and do more than peek here and there. So, we can think of a local circuit as computing an essentially arbitrary function of many inputs and outputs, with substantial provisions for bias and parameterization. But there is much evidence that local circuits are functionally coherent, and not a collection of independent, diverse computational processes (not like a miniature arbitrarily programmable microcomputer).[7]

Neural circuits are a distinct level. The medium is a continuous quantity, often called *activation*, which travels between parts of the circuit and between circuits. Activation is excitatory or inhibitory; it is summed and thresholded and otherwise transformed in the local circuits. Activation is some short-time statistical average of the neural pulses. The neural networks are often drawn as if the components are individual neurons, but in fact they actually are dealt with as if there were neural populations and the medium is almost always dealt with as if it consisted of continuous signals and not neural pulses.

The important fact for us is that the characteristic operation time of neural circuits is ~~10 ms. More precisely, ~~10 ms is the minimum time. Certainly, neural circuits can take longer to operate, ~~100 ms or even longer. However, we are concerned mostly with the minimum time. There are several different features of neural circuits, all of which support this general conclusion.

The most basic consideration is simply that of system levels. Neural circuits are built up out of neurons. Thus they will be essentially an order of magnitude slower than neurons, at best. If neurons are ~~1 ms devices, then neural circuits will be ~~10 ms devices. There is no way to put a collection of neurons together and get them to operate in the ~~1 ms range.

7. I am putting emphasis on temporal relations and ignoring what might be concluded from spatial considerations. Spatially, there are also multiple levels. The distributed networks with local circuits as components are up a level from the local circuits referred to here. The local circuits might conceivably be a single level. To be so, they would need to be some sort of substantial iterative construction, since 5×10^4 elements seems much too big for a single circuit (Simon's hierarchical argument again). One possibility is a factor of 10 for informational capacity, a factor of 10 for statistics, and a factor of 10–100 for an array that covers a field of some sort (such as a sensory field). This breakdown provides a total reduction factor of 10^3 to 10^4 and brings down 5×10^4 to 5–50. But there is certainly the possibility for another system level within the 1-mm cube, with connectivity via graded potentials. Such an additional level would not accord well with the temporal analysis, which would produce an interesting (and informative) situation.

A second indicator comes from communication times in the brain. The speeds of pulse transmission in the central nervous system are of the order of a meter per second, at the low end of the distributions shown in Figure 3-4, and the nerves are small in diameter and unmyelinated. Speeds go below a meter a second. Expressing this speed equivalently as ~~1 mm/ms, it is easy to see what it implies for neural circuitry. Within the mm^3 local circuits, the flow of pulses and the flow of graded potentials are all in the same temporal world (~~1 ms), which is consonant with the complex computational characteristics attributed to local circuits. The distance between local circuits is ~~1 cm (~~10 mm) and the time to communicate will therefore be ~~10 ms. Thus, time constants for anything involving more than a single local circuit will be ~~10 ms.

The third consideration begins with the fundamental generalization that neurons are statistical devices. The neuron is a statistical engine in which nothing occurs with precise timing. For instance, there has been much investigation into how information is encoded in the nervous system. All the encodings are forms of pulse-rate encodings. Stimulus intensity of sound, light, or pressure is encoded as the expected number of pulses per second. There is evidence for other sorts of codes, such as the interpulse interval or the variance of the pulse rates, but they are all statistics on the pulse sequences as a stochastic process. A major consequence is that precision, reliability, or stability in such codes requires at least one level of integration. Measurement has to take a sample of pulses. It may not be necessary to take large samples—sophisticated statistical operations might get by with small samples. But the latter still require ~~10 pulses. With ~~1 ms separation between pulses, at a minimum, any statistical integration will move up to the ~~10 ms region. Again we arrive at the proposition that neural circuits are ~~10 ms devices at a minimum.[8]

All of these considerations point in the same direction. An engineer would see the situation as indicating that the entire system is in balance (as opposed to it being a set of separate arguments from which you can reject one argument and buy another). He'd see a system that appeared to be cleverly engineered in transmission

8. Spatial averaging exists as well as temporal averaging, and it can diminish the need for temporal integration.

times and small-sample statistical techniques, all folded together to get rapid and reliable performance of the total system. The simpleminded way of putting these requirements together would end up with minimum times in the ~~10 ms level.

Let us end with the obvious, but important, observation that the neural-circuit level remains a realm governed by natural science. The types of laws are those of physics and chemistry. The style of analysis is similar to circuit engineering with stochastic signals, but that hardly changes the natural-science character of the systems.

3.6. The Real-Time Constraint on Cognition

Establishing the time order of neurons and neural circuits brings us to the *real-time constraint on cognition*. There is almost no time available for the neural system to produce fully cognitive behavior. To assess this behavior we need to establish the time order at which it begins to be observed. This is easy to do, because it only requires casual observation of our own behavior. A simple sentence is uttered, "Please pass the salt." It takes about a second. Reaction to it takes about the same time—the person addressed reaches for the salt in order to pass it. What transpired was cognitive activity of comprehension and decision, followed by implementation and movement. If the sentence had been, "You, gimme the salt!" the response might well have been quite different—no movement to pick up the shaker, but instead, "Are you addressing me?" A reflection afterward would reveal something of what went on— "He's always so rude, I just wasn't going to be pushed around." The time to do this might have been a little longer, perhaps a couple of seconds. But this is surely cognitive behavior.

Thus, characteristic interactions with the environment, which evoke cognitive considerations, take place in the order of seconds, ~~1 sec. If there has been preparation, it can be at the low end, say ~0.5 sec. Often, elementary reactions take ~2–3 sec. But if more time is available than that, say ~10 sec, then there is evidence that *lots* of cognitive activity can go on—implying of course that significant cognitive activity is occurring in ~~1 sec. A neat example is rapid-transit chess—whose rules establish that only ten seconds per move is available on average. There is ~~10 sec to take into account the opponent's move, understand the consequences, decide upon a move and make it. One can be pretty sure that within the ten seconds several cognitive acts are occurring. Moves are proposed internally, consequences are uncovered, realized to be bad, and alternatives are considered. Not many, perhaps, but some. A system could not play ten-second chess if it took one minute to engage in its first cognitive behavior. Humans cannot play one-second chess.

The point need not be belabored. A reasonable estimate for when the human engages in cognitive behavior is ~~1 sec, from which the constraint can be calculated. Neurons operate at ~~1 ms; neural circuits operate at ~~10 ms, and then cognitive behavior occurs by ~~1 sec. There is available only a factor of 100 between ~~10 ms and ~~1 sec. There are only about 100 ~~10-ms periods to accomplish all that is necessary to produce cognitive behavior. Just so we don't forget it, let us restate this principle, all by itself.

> *Real-time constraint on cognition:* There are available only ~100 operation times (two minimum system levels) to attain cognitive behavior out of neural-circuit technology.

This constraint has been observed by many people. In fact, it has become rather popular to do so recently. For instance, Jerry Feldman (Feldman & Ballard, 1982), one of the initiators of connectionism, coined the phrase "the 100 program-step limit" to indicate that if one wanted to accomplish with a serial digital computer what the brain does, one would have only 100 machine instructions.[9] As any system programmer will testify, hardly anything can be done in so few instructions. Jerry Fodor (1983, pp. 61–64), focusing on language, devotes an extensive section of *Modularity of Mind* to how fast people seem to understand and be able to respond to natural language. Much of the motivation for the observation has been to discredit the so-called symbolic-intelligence position. The negative point has been that the kinds of algorithms developed in computer science and AI for language and vision, which appear strongly serial in their operation, cannot explain how humans accomplish such tasks. The positive point has been that the computational system must be massively parallel.

9. Feldman was talking about the range from ~~1 ms, the neural-action time, to ~~100 ms, which he took as the time to produce a significant internal cognitive result, but the point is exactly the same.

In fact, the constraint has a much greater effect than just the elimination of programs with single threads of control in favor of massive parallelism. It binds all approaches. There are only a few cycles available for any kind of interaction. Parallel systems, even massively parallel ones, do not behave without interacting— without bringing the results of computations in one part of the network into contact with developing results in other parts of the network. In terms of the structure of the algorithms typically used with massively parallel systems, this interaction shows up as the number of successive propagations of constraints or as the number of steps to reach acceptably near the top in hill climbing, or to settle into equilibrium. These steps play the same role in massively parallel systems as program steps play in serial programs. And in all cases there are only about 100 such steps, end to end, to produce cognitive behavior.

In sum, all theories live under the same sword of Damocles. From a theorist's point of view, this is great. The harsher the constraint (providing it is true), the more chance of extracting some real knowledge about how the system is structured or operates. It may stump theoretical advance for a while, if no way can be seen for the system to operate within its limits. But that just provides the anvil against which to hammer out the right theory. Thus, the real-time constraint on cognition, although metaphorically a curse to the organism, is a genuine blessing to the theorist. I take no credit for being the first one to observe the constraint. However, I do want to put it to good use.

3.7. The Cognitive Band

We are now ready to start from neural circuits, at ~~10 ms, and climb up the levels of the cognitive band. We have established a clamp from above on how much time is needed for cognitive behavior to arise. It is possible to think of the gap to be covered in terms of a total of ~~100 steps, but it is better viewed as two minimal system levels. Each system level is ~~10 times longer in duration than the next lower level, so that two levels comprise ~10 × ~~10 = ~~100 steps. Thus, starting with neural circuits of minimal size, a system level can be built out of these and then, with the new systems as components, another system level can be built on top.

By that time some genuine, if perhaps elementary, cognitive behavior needs to be produced.

The base level for the cognitive band must be where the architecture starts. This must include the mechanisms necessary to accomplish the basic functions in Figure 2-13. Some mechanisms could obviously be slower, but only those that were not involved in the basic operational cycle and that are thus limiting factors on the speed of the entire system. In particular the base level has to provide the distal access associated with the symbol system (Figure 2-10). For a symbolic architecture, the symbols, with their ability to accomplish distal access, must sit at the bottom. Thus, distal access must be at the neural-circuit level. It can't be any lower—we've already seen that signals can't get across the brain in ~~1 ms. Thus the cognitive architecture itself has to be at the ~~10 ms level at least. This is looking at the architecture from above, as the beginnings of a symbol level. Seen from below, from the neural-circuit level, what are called symbol structures must be patterns of neural signals and symbol tokens must be things that open up access paths to distal parts of the brain.

It is important to understand the form of argument that is about to take place. We take a function (here, the basic distal access that identifies the lowest level of the cognitive band) and attempt to locate it at a given absolute time level. We wish to conclude that the basic architecture operates at ~~10 ms. We ask three questions. First, can the function happen faster? The answer here is no. There is no way the cognitive architecture can be faster than ~~10 ms, because the neural level (~~1 ms) cannot attain distal access. Second, can it happen more slowly? The answer here is maybe. It is not possible to argue directly whether distal access could take ~~100 ms or even longer—a minute or a month. Indeed, there could well be varieties of distal access mechanisms that take a long time. Instead, we defer the conclusion and proceed to stack up additional levels that are required to obtain cognitive behavior. Because these all have to happen before ~~1 sec, we will have the lower-level behavior hemmed in. Then we can conclude that the function must occur at the lower level (here ~~10 ms), because if it occurred at the next level up (here ~~100 ms) there would be no room for the other functions to be performed in order to get cognitive behavior (at ~ ~1 sec). Thus the answer to the second question becomes no only after the analysis is complete. Third, is it possible at the level proposed? Here the answer is yes, distal access in ~~10 ms seems possible. This question provides a sort of sanity check, no more. We know so little about the detailed mechanisms that we can only analyze it for plausibility. Still, checking plausibility is important, for it might show that having the function at the given level runs up against some strong counter facts. In sum, we will try to run this three-question test several times in an attempt to infer different aspects of the cognitive architecture.

From the architectural level, let us move up to the *deliberation* level of the cognitive band. This is the level at which the most elementary deliberations occur. If this were fifty years ago, use of the word *deliberation* would have been taken as moving the discussion over into some world of the exclusively mental. By now in cognitive science and AI, however, the operational meaning of *deliberation* is clear—to deliberate is to bring available knowledge to bear to choose one operation rather than others. Deliberation can be detected by observing the knowledge available in the system (encoded in some physical structure) flowing into a common site and being processed somehow. The right decision may not be produced, but at least the system is deliberating in order to make its choice. The actual choice is accomplished by physical processes such as those that perform a conditional branch instruction in digital computers.[10] The deliberation level is the lowest level at which this happens.

We now argue that the lowest level of deliberation must occur at the ~~100 ms level. This is up just a single system level from the basic architecture. The first question, then, is whether deliberation could occur faster, at, say, the ~~10 ms level? Figure 3-6 shows the essential minimal behavioral phases for deliberation. First, it requires symbolic access of remote knowledge. That's what deliberation is—bringing remote knowledge to bear. Within the local circuit there cannot have been pre-assembled all the knowledge that is relevant, for it was not yet known what knowledge to assemble. Furthermore, deliberation cannot be limited to a single distal access. At a local part of the system (the site of Figure 3-6), when

---

10. Actually, there are many physical processes that effectively take a choice between alternatives. An example is any process that takes a maximum of a function, $\max(f(x_1), f(x_2), \ldots, f(x_n))$ and allows the recovery of the value that led to the maximum, $x_1, x_2, \ldots, x_n$.

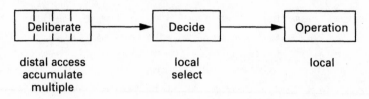

Figure 3-6. The necessary phases of deliberation.

some knowledge is acquired from some part distal to it, the content of that knowledge is not known. If it were, then the knowledge would have been already acquired. Thus, the acquisition of some knowledge may lead to the acquisition of more. It cannot be known in advance what the knowledge is that will be brought in. That is exactly the point of the local/distal distinction—that the knowledge that is encoded in neural structure at distal places cannot all be encoded locally. There may not be very many trips to the well, so to speak, but there can be no assurance that there will be only one. Take it to be some small number.

As the figure shows, more processing is required than just the multiple acts of deliberation, in which the knowledge is assembled and actually brought to bear. There must also be an act of decision and, after that, the selected operation must be performed. After all, the function of the elementary deliberation is to take some action or other. Each of these basic steps could take only of the order of ~~10 ms, which means that it is possible they could be accomplished by minimal neural circuits. But they are all functionally serial. The operation cannot be executed before the decision is made to do so—else there has been no decision. The decision to do so cannot be made until the knowledge is brought to bear—else there has been no deliberation. And later stages of deliberation cannot occur until the earlier ones are completed, because it is the earlier ones that contain the knowledge that leads to the further distal accesses. Thus, there is functional seriality in the elementary deliberation. There may of course also be lots of parallel operation. What the figure shows as a single access may pull knowledge from throughout the entire system simultaneously. When it arrives, all of the knowledge may be locally circulated and scrunched together concurrently. The figure doesn't indicate *all* that might happen. It indicates the *minimum* that must happen.

Figure 3-6 thus describes a system of components, each of which operates at the ~~10 ms level. The system itself, then, operates essentially one level up, namely at the ~~100 ms level. The figure specifies hardly anything about the number of components or their interconnection, or about what the upper bounds of the interactions are before a result is produced. But enough is specified to answer the question. No, deliberation cannot take place faster than at the ~~100 ms level.

The second question is whether deliberation could take longer than ~~100 ms. As with the symbol-access level, local considerations do not lead to a definitive answer on this. We must postpone the question until we fill in the cognitive band sufficiently to get cognitive behavior. Then we may get the constraint from the top that will permit us to assert that elementary deliberations could not be slower than ~~100 ms. The writing is on the wall, of course, since ~~100 ms is only one factor of 10 from ~~1 sec, the time at which cognitive behavior must be delivered.

The third question is about the plausibility of the elementary deliberation taking ~~100 ms. One consequence of minimality of the deliberation is that the action that is taken by the elementary deliberation cannot be a composed operation—that is, cannot be composed as part of the elementary deliberation. There is no way to have deliberated over what parts to put together, because the system is already down at the bottom level. It is the quickest level at which deliberation occurs. The action could have been composed prior to this decision to use it. Or this could be the decision to compose the operation, starting at this point but not yet knowing what operation it is that is to be composed (and thus be a different decision from the one made when the action is completely known). But the action itself cannot be composed of deliberative acts and still remain as part of a single elementary deliberation.

Such a level can be characterized as *automatic*. There is no way to get inside it to modulate it in any deliberate or controlled way. Of course, it can be interrupted—terminated and broken open, so to speak—but then other deliberate acts are involved in inspecting it and perhaps reconstituting it. But it can't be examined as it runs. There isn't any time for the examination to take place that could arrive at any judgment about it, so to speak—for that would take ~~100 ms itself. Of course, an organization might be possible that made the main-line elementary deliberation longer so that a quick

Automatic behavior	Controlled behavior
(Parallel)	(Serial)
Can't inhibit	Can inhibit
Fast	Slow
Load independent	Load dependent
Exhaustive search	Self-terminating search
Unaware of processing	Aware of processing
Target pops out	Target does not pop out

Figure 3-7. Properties of automatic and controlled behavior.

supervisory control could happen within it. But such a system moves the main-line deliberation toward ~~1 sec, which contradicts the hypothesis of ~~100 ms.[11]

One of the foremost developments in experimental cognitive psychology over the last decade has been the establishment of the automatic/controlled distinction. The label gained prominence after a famous pair of papers by Richard Shiffrin and Walter Schneider (1977), but the distinction began to be emphasized a little earlier (Posner & Snyder, 1975; Laberge & Samuels, 1974). The underlying intuition is that automatic behavior occurs by parallel processing and controlled behavior occurs by serial processing. But a whole battery of behavioral indicators separates the two types of processing, as shown in Figure 3-7. An automatic process can't be inhibited from being initiated. It is relatively fast. It takes the same time (or almost so) independent of the stimulus load. It cannot be terminated as a function of internal conditions (it is exhaustive). No detailed awareness exists of what processes are being carried out. If the task is perceptual, the answer appears to *pop out*. A controlled process has contrasting values for each of these attributes.

Figure 3-8 provides an example of this distinction, taken from Schneider and Shiffrin (1977). It shows the results of a single experimental task with two different conditions, one that results in automatic behavior and the other in controlled behavior. The essential experimental arrangement is shown across the top. The person

11. Recording all that happened might automatically occur, which could be deliberately analyzed after the fact, but that wouldn't affect the automatic character of each elementary deliberation. In a system that operates continuously in real time, such a scheme would raise some interesting issues about how to decide whether to use such records and on what time scale.

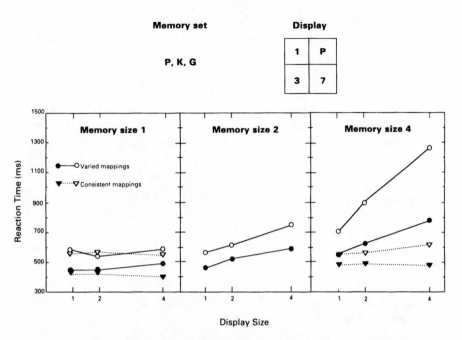

Figure 3-8. Example of automatic and controlled behavior (adapted from experiment 2 of Schneider & Shiffrin, 1977).

has memorized a set of characters, say *P, K, G* (the *memory set*), and is viewing a display, say the four characters *1, P, 3, 7*, arranged at the corners of a square (the *display*). The task is to determine whether any character of the memory set occurs in the display; in this case the answer is yes, *P* does. The display is shown only briefly, before being masked out. The person is supposed to respond by hitting a yes-button or a no-button as quickly as possible.

The total load on the person varies with the sizes of the memory set (1, 2, or 4 characters) and the display (1, 2, or 4 characters), thus producing nine different loads from (1,1) to (4,4). The reaction times range between 400 and 1,300 ms. These times include the time for perception and motor response. The ~~100 ms times we are concerned with are only the differences between the conditions, which exclude the time for these other activities. (Some of the larger differences are still much greater than 100 ms, because they reflect multiple deliberations.) The graphs give the reaction times for both positive trials (the solid points), when a memory character did occur in the display, and negative trials (open points), when no memory character occurred. The figure shows that negative trials always take longer than the corresponding positive trials, with the separation increasing as load increases.

The two different conditions are called *varied mappings* (solid lines) and *consistent mappings* (dotted lines).[12] The distinction concerns *targets* and *distractors*. In our example, the elements of the memory set (the targets) are letters. On positive trials one of these will also appear in the display. All the other characters in the display are distractors—in this case, digits. This is an example of a consistent mapping. The distractors are drawn from a different set of characters than the targets. An example of varied mapping would be having the distractors be other letters, say *X, C,* and *I* instead of *1, 3,* and *7* in the figure. On other trials the targets might use the characters that were used as distractors on this trial. Thus, in consistent mappings the targets and distractors are forever separate for the whole experiment, whereas for varied mappings the same characters were sometimes targets and sometimes distractors, depending on the trial.[13]

The point of all this is the way the two different conditions behave with changes in load. With consistent mapping reaction time hardly increases at all, either as the memory set increases or as the display size increases. With varied mapping, on the other hand, reaction time increases directly with the total load, as required by having to check memory characters against display characters. Thus, in the consistent mapping case, identification is automatic; in the varied mapping case it is controlled, in other words, deliberate. This experiment is just an exemplar of a whole stream of research since the mid-1970s that has established automatic and controlled behavior as a significant and stable feature of human performance.

In the light of this characterization of automatic behavior, the elementary deliberation of Figure 3-6 shows several points of correspondence. It is fast, there is no control, it is exhaustive, and there is no detailed awareness. Some aspects, such as load dependence,

12. Consistent mapping was run only with memory sets of size 1 and 4, which is why the middle panel of the figure is missing the dashed lines.

13. Letters for targets and digits for distractors are certainly separate. The perceptive reader will eventually ask about using the first half of the alphabet for targets and the second half for distractors. Are these separate or not? Shiffrin and Schneider (1977) showed they are not separate to start out with (they are all just letters), but with enough practice they can become separate.

cannot be verified as holding for the general scheme. Furthermore, no contrasting scheme of controlled processing has been delineated. But our task is not to provide a detailed theory of automatic and controlled processing, or any other specific body of experimental data. Rather, it is just to ask whether it is plausible that one should have a system level of elementary deliberations at the ~~100 ms level. This certainly seems to be the case.

3.8. The Level of Simple Operations

Let us now ascend another level. Figure 3-9 actually shows all four levels of the cognitive band. At the lower left-hand corner is an icon that stands for the symbol-access level, fashioned after Figure 2-10. This is the basic architectural level at ~~10 ms. Above it, slightly to the right, is another icon that stands for the level of elementary deliberate operations, fashioned after Figure 3-6. This is the ~~100 ms level and the one we have just discussed. The next two levels move up and to the right. The first is the ~~1 sec level and the second (in the upper right corner) is the ~~10 sec level.

We must now ask where the cognitive band needs to arrive—namely at a symbol system, which is to say, at the machinery for composing operations—so it can construct the response functions needed to interact with the environment. The elementary-deliberation level has produced a system that engages in knowledge search, but it does not engage in problem search. We need ultimately to build up to systems that engage in problem search with operators that are composed for the task at hand.

The elementary-deliberation level provides ways of executing preexisting actions. These operations can be put together into systems that will clearly work in the order of ~~1 sec, and these systems can compose some response functions. They are doing deliberations to select what they want to do. Figure 3-9 makes the activity appear to be a search. As we saw in Chapter 2, there must be the potential for doing search, because there is the potential for error. But, except for that, there need be nothing searchlike about the processing. If the knowledge of the system is good enough, what can occur is simply an extended computation, such as adding up a column of numbers or checking off a list of items. The important point is that of putting together a collection of deliberate acts in order to compose some way of responding.

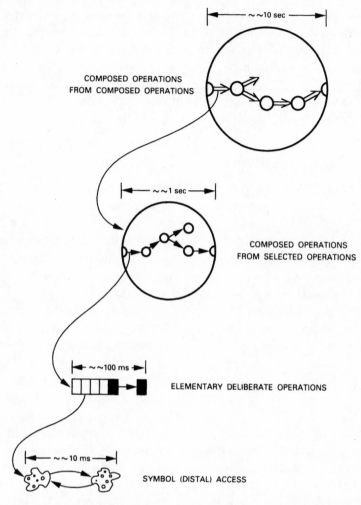

COMPOSED OPERATIONS
FROM COMPOSED OPERATIONS

COMPOSED OPERATIONS
FROM SELECTED OPERATIONS

ELEMENTARY DELIBERATE OPERATIONS

SYMBOL (DISTAL) ACCESS

Figure 3-9. The four levels of the cognitive band.

We have thus arrived at the time (~~1 sec) where we have to provide cognitive behavior, that is, reach a system that is able to compose responses. We would have succeeded completely in attaining cognitive behavior within the real-time cognitive constraint if the composition were in general problem spaces. However, this system level does have one limiting qualitative feature, namely, the operations cannot themselves be composed operations. That is, the actions must be elementary operations that have been selected, consequently they must have been around previously, and hence were not constructed for the to-be-produced response. This is a limitation on the adaptability of the system within 1 sec.

We need to ask our three questions explicitly, although the answers are already mostly apparent. Could one compose simple operations faster than ~~1 sec? The answer is no, because we have built up minimal level upon minimal level. There is no need to reiterate why there is no time to pack all the action at this level into less time. Could the composition of simple operations take longer than ~~1 sec? The answer is now a definite no, because we have reached the level at which we know cognitive operations must be available. Having reached this point, of course, we can finally settle the questions of whether the lower levels could themselves have been located at a higher level. They could not, because it would have pushed the level of simple operations higher than ~~1 sec, namely to ~~10 sec or above. And that would contravene the need to get the level of simple composed operations within ~~1 sec.

Finally, what of the plausibility of simple operations at this level? This involves an assessment of whether the cognitive actions that take place within ~~1 sec can be composed of simple operations. The most obvious observation concerns preparation and practice. It is a commonplace, especially of the psychological laboratory, that if a person is to give immediate speeded reactions in a task, then there must be adequate preparation and practice. The responses must be known and simple (press a button, vocalize a word) and if they are not, they must become so. Likewise the connection of the response with the eliciting situation (the stimulus) must be clear to the subject. If these conditions are not met, the response will take substantial time.

3.9. The First Level of Composed Operations

To move to general cognition is to move to general problem spaces where the operations themselves are composed to deal with the task. Each operator is produced by a system at the ~~1 sec level, and, as Figure 3-9 shows, this takes us to the ~~10 sec level. There is no available term for this level. Card, Moran, and Newell (1983) used *unit task* to refer to the tasks skilled users defined for themselves in human-computer interaction, which take from ~5 to ~30 sec.

Thus, the cognitive band, which can be defined as the apparatus necessary to go from neural circuits (the top of the neural band) to general cognition, requires four levels. It takes us from ∼∼10 ms up past the level of immediate external cognitive behavior at ∼∼1 sec.

Let us again ask our three questions. First, could general cognition have been obtained at a lower (faster) level? Again the answer is a clear no, because of how the levels have been constructed, each being a minimal system level. This seems true enough in terms of levels, but it might not be quite true in terms of time. We have now piled up several system levels and our simple assumption about how much time it takes in total might not hold true. If all the levels were somewhat shorter maybe full cognitive operations could be obtained in shorter time.

Let us examine this possibility a little closer. We have been using a factor of ∼∼10 for each step up in level and have cascaded three levels. Suppose we had taken ∼∼7 as the minimal scale factor for a level, rather than ∼∼10. Then the elementary-deliberation level would be ∼∼70 ms, the simple-operations level would be ∼∼500 ms, and the full-cognition level would be ∼∼3.5 sec—compared with ∼∼10 sec in the analysis above. This doesn't really make much difference qualitatively, given the degree of approximations we are working with. It might just about be wiped out, for instance, if the neural level were really ∼∼2 ms rather than ∼∼1 ms, which would place the fourth level at ∼∼7 sec.

Figure 3-10 gives a nomograph for assessing the sensitivity of our analysis to the particular numbers we have used, considering the scale factor between levels, the time of the base-level system (the neuron), and the critical time limit within which cognitive behavior needs to occur. The vertical is the system operation time (laid out on a log scale). At the right, along the horizontal, is the average scale factor per system level (from 1 to 12). The fanned-out lines give the operation times for each level, for the range of scale factors from 1 to 12, and these lines are labeled Level 0 to Level 5 at the far right. A vertical line has been drawn through the scale factor of 10, which is the assumption we have been using. At the left, along the horizontal, is the time of the neuron base system (from 0.5 ms to 5 ms, also a log scale). Changes in the base time simply shift the vertical scale. The locations of 1 ms, 10 ms, . . . 100 sec are shown by the isolines on the left. A vertical line has been drawn through the base time of 1 ms, which is the assumption we have been using.

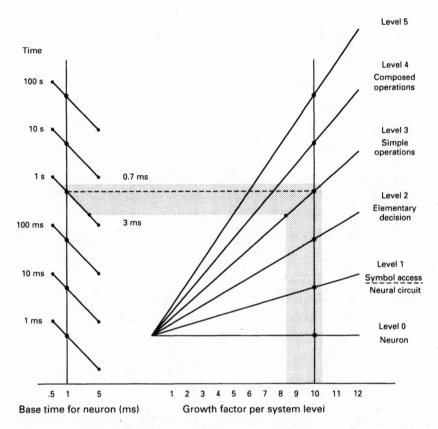

Figure 3-10. Nomograph for sensitivity analysis of scaling assumptions.

Its intersections with the isolines gives the ordinate to be used, if assuming a 1 ms base time. Thus, as the horizontal dashed line indicates, a 1 sec base time intersects the level 3 systems at a scale factor of 10, which is what our analysis has shown.[14]

Any combination of base times, scale factors, system levels, and critical time limits for behavior can be read off the figure, as well as ranges of base times and scale factors. For example, the stippled

14. The nomograph is simply a way to display time = (base time) × (scale factor)$^{\text{system level}}$ to make all four quantities apparent. The display is based on log(time) = log(base time) + [log(scale factor) × (system level)]. The base time is laid out logarithmically so that the isolines for 1 ms, 10 ms, . . . , 100 sec are straight lines. If each level is taken to have its own scale factor, the scale factor in the figure should be the geometrical average of the scale factors.

Subject and task	Seconds
S2 on CROSS + ROADS	1.9
S5 on DONALD + GERALD	5.6
S2 on chess position A	6.2
S8 on logic problem D1	7.7

Figure 3-11. Residence times for various tasks
(adapted from Newell & Simon, 1972).

band shows the range of scale factors that lead to satisfying the real-time constraint of simple operations (level 3) before getting to 1 sec, given that the base time for the neuron time-constant can vary between 0.7 ms and 3 ms (slightly smaller than the full range shown on the nomograph). We see that the scale factors can range from 9 to 11. The nomograph can also be used to see what it would take to get four levels within the 1 sec real-time constraint. If the neuron base time was 1 ms, then a scale factor of less than 7 would work. The consequence of such compression is that somewhat more complexly structured behavior would be available somewhat faster. The qualitative picture does not seem to change.

The second question is whether composed operators could take longer than ∼∼10 sec to obtain. The basis we have had for answering such questions has now been lost. We have already exceeded the ∼∼1 sec bound set by the time required for cognitive behavior. From now on the time limits on performance become a matter of the individual task and can vary tremendously. We will take up this issue again when we consider what lies above the cognitive band.

Third, we turn to the question of the plausibility of composed operators at the ∼∼10 sec level. A positive indication is provided by an interesting observation made some time ago. In *Human Problem Solving* (Newell & Simon, 1972), Simon and I noted that, in all of the problem spaces we had studied, people seemed to take several seconds for each step. Figure 3-11 reproduces the little table that lists the times. They range between 2 and 8 sec. The studies were not focused on temporal factors, but we thought the relative constancy was interesting. The constancy was especially striking since at least part of the complexity was due to the complexity of the operator just in data-processing terms. The ∼8 sec time was for the logic task, which had complex uninterpreted formal symbol manipulations for operations.

Figure 1-4 gave a fragment of the problem-behavior graph of a subject working in chess, taken from *Human Problem Solving*. According to Figure 3-11, it took a few seconds to make these moves. These are not moves in the actual game, but moves in the head, which the person is mentioning by talking aloud as he decides on a move. They form an internal search of the space of moves and countermoves. The accuracy of the representation is verified for the most part by internal cross constraints—if the person had been aware of features not stated, then he would never have searched in the ways observed, nor commented about the position as he in fact did. All that we want to observe about this search is how the times stack up. The moves are at the ~~10 sec level. These moves are indeed composed for this particular task. Almost always, the person diagnoses the situation to conclude the function that a move should perform—it should defend, attack, pin, move away, or whatever. This is followed by the generation of the actual move, which involves finding what moves in the particular position satisfy the function and then making the move on the board (though of course all in the person's mind).

These subtasks—diagnose the position, generate a move, and make the move—are all practiced tasks for a good chess player. The subtasks each take ~~1 sec, for they are not unitary acts but are themselves composite. Making a move requires removing the piece from its current square and placing it on a destination square, meanwhile adjusting whatever representation is held in the head (which is where this is going on) to take account of new relationships. Identifying the moves that provide a function (defend, for example) requires considering a nonhomogeneous set of possibilities—moving away, adding a defender, interposing against an attacker. And diagnosing the situation initially requires the consideration of a multitude of relations on the chess board. Many of these relations and their interrelations have been attended to and analyzed on prior positions, but the immediately prior move will have opened up some new considerations. Thus each act can be seen to take ~~1 sec and be itself composed of a set of acts. The microacts now appear as acts of observing a relationship and deciding to attend to it, or identifying the square to which to move the piece. They could be ~~100 ms in duration. None of this is pinned down carefully—we are not proposing the details of how people play chess. Rather, we are asking whether the amount of processing involved in solving problems seems plausibly commensurate with the time scales we have inferred. And we find that when a human works in a real problem space with composed operators the times are ~~10 sec.

That full cognition exceeds by one system level the ~~1 sec limit set for the emergence of cognition presents something of an anomaly. It does not show that cognition *cannot* be attained within the ~~1 sec limit. Rather, it shows that cognitive behavior does not arrive all at once, full blown. It is first limited in being primarily a selection from prepared possibilities. But if full problem solving is required then it takes longer.

One might take an evolutionary view on this and reason that since response time is a factor in adaptation—especially in a world of carnivores—then the race will go to the swiftest. Given a population of organisms who behave at the ~~10 sec level, if there is any evolutionary path for some of them to become faster, then that path will be found, and the response times will be driven down to ~~1 sec (or even lower, if it were possible). Of course, this is a typical weak evolutionary argument—explaining what is, without explaining the mechanisms or the evolutionary path by which it occurred. Even with the highly schematic situation we are using, however, the possibility of a mechanism can be seen.

The response time is driven down by an increase in preparation. Recall Figure 2-19, which showed the trade-off between deliberation and preparation with equal-performance isobars. Suppose response times reflected mostly deliberation. Then shifting along an isobar toward increased preparation leads to decreases in deliberation, and might even bring response times down from ~~10 sec to ~~1 sec. This requires that the system be able to package relevant knowledge in retrievable form. The mechanisms that would implement such a strategy cannot be clear. Our argument is too general for that. But it seems to be a plausible scheme.

Such a scheme requires that relevant knowledge be acquired and this must happen on specific occasions. The obvious source of such knowledge is the experience of the organism. In fact, on an evolutionary time scale, experience is the only source available. All other alternatives, such as reading, being instructed, watching video, and even conversing, require a developed society of intelligent beings. Experience also has the property of being relevant to future experience, at least on a statistical basis, so that it provides suitable occasions for knowledge acquisition. It would seem that learning on all or most available occasions would be warranted.

psychology has arrived at the possibility of uniting theories of cognition—
Theories that gain their power by having a single system of mechanisms
that operate together to produce the full range of human cognition.
I do not say they are here. But they are within reach and we should strive
to attain them.

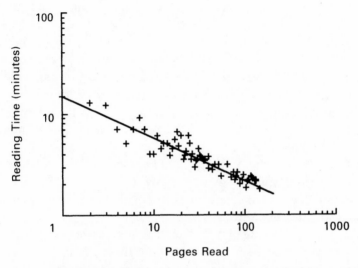

Figure 3-12. Reading inverted text with practice (data of Kolers, 1975; adapted from Newell & Rosenbloom, 1981).

The ultimate effect of such a strategy is to convert composed operators into simple ones. Whenever simple operators are applicable—that is, whenever they are retrieved as relevant to a situation—then the system is operating essentially in the ~~1 sec range rather than the ~~10 sec range. Actual behavior entails a mixture of fast and slow operators, and so the net effect is that, as the system learns, it gradually but continuously moves up the equiperformance isobar. I have described matters in terms of the shift from ~~10 to ~~1 sec, but longer operations come down accordingly.

The plausibility of this argument comes from the observation that humans learn continuously from almost everything they do. Figure 1-2 gave one example of human improvement with practice. Figure 3-12 shows another. The task is reading inverted text (Kolers, 1975). The paragraph in the figure is the introductory paragraph of the first chapter. It would take about 100 sec to read. If this whole book was written in inverted text, and if you could be motivated to read it all, then by the end of the final chapter you would be reading at about 20 sec for a short paragraph like this. This would still be slow compared to the 10 sec to read it in regular text, but most of the deficit would have been made up.

Practice in reading inverted text follows the same law that the choice-reaction task of Figure 1-2 does—the ubiquitous power law of practice. The qualitative characteristics sketched out above— the continual acquisition of experience that allows one to move along an isobar—are not specific enough to imply this quantitative law. Many mechanisms might be used to process experience and make it accessible, and many others for retrieving it and welding it into current behavior. But it takes only a few additional and very simple assumptions to obtain the power law, which were presented in Chapter 1. The ubiquity of the power law in human behavior might be taken as an additional indication of plausibility for this story of how it is that full cognitive behavior takes ~~10 sec (and up) and yet cognitive behavior is evident at ~~1 sec. Such a mechanism would dissolve whatever seemed anomalous in full cognitive behavior exceeding the ~~1 sec limit.

The argument made in this chapter is qualitative and does not say how far down such a mechanism could drive the time to respond. Figure 3-9 indicates why it is unlikely to extend down to the ~~100 ms level. The neural technology is fixed, or subject to only modest compression, and there is simply too much to do to obtain such a major compression. Empirically, we know that simple reaction times may be as low as 150 ms. But it is not just learning from experience that accomplishes that, but simplification, preparation, and carefully shaped anticipation all along the line.

A second plausible feature of this general arrangement is its consonance with the fast-read, slow-write characteristic often noted of human memory. Humans read out information from their long-term memory very rapidly, well under 100 ms. Figure 3-9 puts it at ~~10 ms. On the other hand all attempts to measure how fast humans write new information into long-term memory show it to be much slower—of the order of a few seconds for a chunk (Simon, 1975; Gilmartin, Newell, & Simon, 1976). These are measurements taken after minutes or hours, not after seconds—people remember a good deal about a situation immediately afterwards. Likewise, these are measurements of what *new* information is acquired, and it is necessary to separate out what was really novel in the situation versus what could be plausibly reconstructed. The measurements are of acquisition rates, not of the time between presentation and storage. The latter cannot be measured in the current art, since immediate responses are always mediated by temporary short-term memory. This fast-read, slow-write character of long-term memory is exactly what we would expect if the responses continually move from the $\sim\sim 10$ sec level to the $\sim\sim 1$ sec level. The occasions for learning new information show up in the $\sim\sim 10$ sec range. This is where knowledge is available from the environment about what to learn, namely experience attained in working at $\sim\sim 10$ sec. Thus, what would govern the slow-write phenomenon is the opportunity for acquisition. This locates its cause not in the time constants of a slow consolidation mechanism or the like, but in the occasions for learning. Of course, this is only another plausibility, for nothing in the picture of Figure 3-9 could exclude alternative mechanisms.

We have completed the climb up the four cognitive levels. All these levels are neurophysiological levels as well—it is the same system, simply under different descriptions—but the higher levels of organization have their own characteristics. They no longer appear simply as ever more complex neural circuits. In particular, with cognition we have left the realm of a world that works according to physical law. Instead, it is a world that works according to representational law. The processes have been so composed that they represent things—objects, relations, and activities—in the external world. The representational world remains mechanistic and, in Aristotelian language, it is still to be understood as a world of efficient causality. But the mechanisms are computational mechanisms and the laws are representational laws, which may be of arbitrary character. There is no mystery how these computational mechanisms and representational laws arise out of physical mechanisms and laws. In any reasonable sense, the cognitive realm is reducible to the natural science realm. But there is also no mystery about why reduction does not bring with it any change in theorizing about the cognitive realm or in our understanding of it. To predict and explain behavior requires attention to the computational mechanisms and the representational laws. Putatively, *all* that the lower-level systems of the biological band do is support the computational mechanisms, which in turn operate to enforce the representational laws. Of course, the systems levels are not perfectly strong, and there is substantial leakage between them. But that does not change the basic picture.

3.10. The Intendedly Rational Band

What happens as duration increases beyond the ~~10 sec level? What prevents there simply being more and more levels of the cognitive band? The elementary-deliberate level at the top of the cognitive band admits operators composed of simple operators. But operators can become increasingly complex, so that levels simply grow on top of levels. There must be a level whose operators are composed of composed operators. Why is there not simply an infinite tower of cognitive levels into the sky? In some sense this must be the way the system grows.

But what also happens is that cognition begins to succeed. We take the system to have goals with respect to its environment and its cognitive processes to be oriented toward the attainment of these goals (Figure 3-13 shows this simple structure).[15] The system will have some knowledge of this environment, but necessarily it will be limited. As discussed in the previous chapter, as the system has more time, the solutions it finds will reflect whatever knowledge it has. As that happens, we will have less and less of a chance of ascertaining what processing was involved in determining the solution. Processing will certainly go on, as indicated by the tree of arrows inside the box, for the solution will be determined by the knowledge available to the system. Thus, as time increases—which is to say, as the levels of problem spaces build up—there will be a shift toward characterizing a system as a knowledge-level system, that is, just by the goals and knowledge it contains, without regard to the way in which the internal processing accomplishes the linking of action to goals (of means to ends). To go back to the initial language of response functions, what determines the response functions will be only the external environment plus the goals of the organism.

In Figure 3-3 the system that operates at the knowledge level is shown to be in the *rational band*, but it is clear from the account above that it attains this status gradually as the levels ascend (implying more and more time to solve the problems). Thus, the justifiable name is the *intendedly rational band*.

---

15. Whence comes the presumption of mind being goal-oriented? Cognitive science in general assumes it. Ashby (1952) is one of the only people I know who has tried to derive goal behavior from general system postulates.

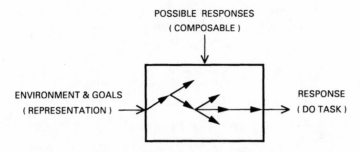

POSSIBLE RESPONSES
(COMPOSABLE)

ENVIRONMENT & GOALS
(REPRESENTATION)

RESPONSE
(DO TASK)

Figure 3-13. The intendedly rational band: knowledge-level systems.

The intendedly rational band consists of multiple levels, just as does any band. All the levels are labeled alike, however, as tasks (recall Figure 3-3). Each level of a lower band could be described and labeled in terms of its characteristic processes, structure, or medium—organelles, neural circuits, deliberate acts, unit tasks— but within the intendedly rational level, the internal structures are composed to fit the task structure, and so the organization at each level is that of the task. Thus, there is a task hierarchy, rather than a hierarchy reflective of inner structure. This hierarchy can continue upward indefinitely if tasks of indefinite complexity are undertaken.

We have now entered the realm of reason, as it is classically called. Behavior is not law-abiding in the usual sense. A law, in almost every sense we use the word, implies some form of context independence. A law is a guarantee that some rule can be applied taking into account only the finite amount of context that is stated explicitly with the law, against a background usually expressed as "performable by one skilled in the art." It is the glory of natural science that it finds such context-limited laws to be operational in nature. There seems to be no a priori reason that nature should have its behavior governed by sufficiently context-free rules to be discoverable by humans and communicable between them. At the rational level, on the other hand, the agent does whatever it can— whatever its knowledge permits—to attain its goal. The agent may go outside any prespecified context, as perceived by an external observer.[16] The longer the agent has, the more chance it has of

16. Especially since any physically realizable observer is itself only a device capable of taking into account a limited amount of context.

Scale	Time units	Band
10^{11}–10^{13}	10^4–10^6 years	Evolutionary
10^8–10^{10}	years–millennia	Historical
10^5–10^7	days–months	Social
10^2–10^4	minutes–hours	Rational
10^{-1}–10^1	100 ms–10 sec	Cognitive
10^{-4}–10^{-2}	100 μs–10 ms	Biological

Figure 3-14. Higher bands.

doing that. In short, behavior is no longer context free. The magic in all of this, of course, is the knowledge that the agent brings to the situation. If the agent knows nothing about the outside world—its structure, history, mechanics—then it has nothing to work with in escaping from the local context. It is of the essence of adult human minds that they bring a vast amount of knowledge into every situation they are in. The door to the room closes, the shades are pulled, but all the world is still there inside the human head. Not, of course, really there, only represented. But no outside observer, trying to predict the behavior of that human, can ever know all that is in its mind.

Note that in the cognitive band the system may be goal oriented, but that is not how it operates. It operates because it follows computational laws. We see the mechanisms of its attempts to be rational. Thus, the realm of the intendedly rational level is different from the cognitive realm.

3.11. Higher Bands: Social, Historical, and Evolutionary

What happens above the rational band? Or does this one just go on up forever? In Figure 3-3, the time scale trails off at the upper reaches, and for good reason: this book focuses on the structure and mechanisms of the cognitive band. However, a brief discussion will provide an outer context, so to speak. Figure 3-14 enumerates a sequence of speculative higher bands. Above the rational band comes the social band, above that the historical band, and above that the evolutionary band. Each spans a factor of about a thousand in time scale.

It is not clear that there actually are any higher bands. There are certainly realms that can be labeled social, historical, and evolutionary, and quite different things happen at different time scales. However, in order for systems levels to exist, in the sense we've been using them, they must be relatively strong. If the level has to be decomposed to lower levels to have any ability to explain and predict its behavior, then there may be little sense in treating it as a system level at all. Certainly, the evidence is not convincing that these higher levels are strong enough levels. Despite a long tradition of seeking laws of social or cultural dynamics (White, 1949), the current state of sociology does not give much hope of real social dynamics (Fiske & Shweder, 1986)—regularities, yes; an occasional inevitability, again possible; but societal-level information as a sufficient predictor of social change, hardly ever. At the historical level the case seems even more persuasive that strong levels do not exist. Although there has been much talk and writing about historical determinism, there is little to show for it and current developments in historical scholarship have moved off in contrasting directions, such as negotiated meaning (Toews, 1987).

One reason often given for this situation of apparent weak systemicity is that we humans are sitting within a level, looking upward, so to speak, at the social or historical system. We are the components of the higher level and so we naturally see our own dynamics and do not see the inevitable regularity of the higher level. I suspect that the real issue is not just that we are components but that we are intelligent components. Thus, we are not bound by local context, either in space or time. There are no regularities that hold at higher levels because they can always be defeated by actions at a level that has intelligence. None of the levels below us are intelligent—are at the intendedly rational level—so this problem of weak levels does not occur for us as systems. We are just below the first level that loses cohesion.

This hypothesis can be tested, at least a little. Evolution has always had a special problem with prediction. What path evolution will take is not predictable. The difficulty is rather well understood and it reflects the same issues as our arguments about the intelligence of the components. The act of adaptation depends upon the intimate details of the situation in which organisms find themselves. There isn't any way to express those details at a higher level, namely at the evolutionary level itself. To know what happens in evolution requires predicting the behavior of systems at the time scale of their lives.[17]

Another instructive example is found by going up even above the evolutionary band, say to $\sim\sim 10^{14}$ to $\sim\sim 10^{17}$ sec, which we might call the *astronomical level*. Here one seems to get again a strong level—there is a reasonable astrophysics of the heavens. It is clear why such a reimposition of strong levels can occur. The intelligence at our level simply does not command enough energy to make any difference at this higher level. The disruptive effects that we intelligent humans can inject into the levels just above us are no longer of any moment with another factor of a thousand in scale. Blow up the earth and the heavens will not blink.

The other side of the coin is why there should be a social band. Why shouldn't the intendedly rational level just extend upward? Why shouldn't rationality just get better and better, with increasingly available time? It would seem that rationality would dictate that—or at least intend it. The more time available the closer it could come to realizing a higher degree of rationality.

Before we may conjecture an answer, the situation must be delineated. As the time scale increases from days to weeks to months, the systems involved become social. They comprise multiple individuals in interaction. Humans do not lead solitary lives at the level of days and above. Thus, the system just above the rational level is the social face-to-face group and it moves up to encompass more distal organizations as the time scale increases further. The issue of continued upward extension and perfection of rationality is whether groups can be described as knowledge-level systems—as a single body of knowledge with a set of goals—such that the group's behavior is explainable and predictable by its use of knowledge in the service of its goals. In addition, the approximation should become better as more time becomes available.

That rationality fails for groups we all know directly from our own experience. The kernel of the reason appears to be the small bandwidth of communication between human beings. The compo-

---

17. One must admit other factors as well, such as the statistical character of mutation and the fact that genetic structure (on which mutation operates) determines performing structure (on which selection operates) by very indirect means.

nents of a social system—the humans—have too much knowledge relative to how rapidly they can communicate it to each other.[18] There is no way for a social group to assemble all the information relevant to a given goal, much less integrate it. There is no way for a social group to act as a single body of knowledge. This restriction applies to goals as well. Whatever advantages may be found in reconciling opposed or discordant goals, the limited means of communicating about goals and why they exist is sufficient to keep the organization from ever arriving at a single common basic goal structure.

Assessment of this constraint would seem to depend on the rates of communication between agents relative to the size of the knowledge bodies in each agent. In fact, it actually depends on the existence of an indefinitely large long-term memory in the human and the fact that learning from experience and communicating with the environment are fundamentally the same process. Let the rate of knowledge intake (or outflow) between the human and the environment be $\sim\sim K$ chunks/sec. Then this same rate governs the acquisition of knowledge prior to the meeting of the group that attempts to share knowledge by communication. The total body of knowledge in a group member is $\sim\sim KT$, where T is the total lifetime of the member. The amount that can be shared in the group meeting is $\sim\sim K\Delta T$, where ΔT is the duration of the group meeting. But the group meeting time, ΔT, is small compared to T, independent of K, the communication rate. This same limit does not affect the single human, who is organized differently—the rate of long-term memory acquisition is slow compared with the communication of knowledge for solving a problem.

The net effect is that the social band becomes characterized as a distributed set of intendedly rational agents, in which each agent has a large body of knowledge relative to how fast it can communicate it—that is, there is limited information flow. This characterization hardly accounts for everything at the social band, but it does account for a number of its salient features.

18. The constraint on communication indicates one difficulty with the use of society as a model for mind and intelligence (Minsky, 1986). The society-of-minds metaphor is built around relatively small communication channels, but inside each mind it is not that way at all.

3.12. Summary

The objective of the book is to be convincing that cognitive science is ready for unified theories of human cognition. So far, I have been laying the groundwork. I have introduced the major concepts needed to describe cognitive systems generally, and assayed the main outlines of the human cognitive architecture. My strategy is to present at the outset anything that can be discerned generally about the human cognitive architecture so there would be just that much less that would have to be posited in a proposed theoretical architecture.

I have proposed three ingredients as given, from which to extract these general features of the architecture: (1) the human architecture is constructed out of neural technology; (2) cognitive behavior is clearly evident at about one second; and (3) cognitive behavior requires a symbol system. Because cognitive behavior shows up rapidly in terms of how fast neural technology operates—the real-time constraint on cognition—they provide enough constraint to obtain some useful results.

First of all, different cognitive worlds attend different time scales of actions—the biological band, which is still in the realm of physical-chemical law; the cognitive band, which is the realm of representational law and computational mechanisms; the intendedly rational band, which is the realm of knowledge and goal-driven reason; and above that, with increasing fuzziness, the social, historical, and evolutionary bands. Our focus, however, was not on such a grand scale but on what could be said about the mechanisms and structure of the cognitive band, in which there are four levels. The lowest level is that of memory access, which occurs at ~~10 ms, the lowest level of neural circuits. The next level is that of elementary deliberations, which occurs at ~~100 ms. It is the level of automatic behavior. The next level is that of simple operations, which occurs at ~~1 sec and already provides minimal cognitive behavior. The fourth level is that of composed operations, which occurs at ~~10 sec. This is longer than the minimal time for cognitive behavior and shows a continual shift to a recognition-based system.

This chapter is highly speculative. It attempts to establish strong structural statements from highly generalized considerations. We don't understand the full variety of mechanisms that contribute to all these system levels. In fact, almost every aspect of the analysis has substantial uncertainty associated with it. That is no reason for not engaging in such speculation. The potential gains are very great, namely to get some general guidelines for the cognitive architecture regardless of any specific proposal. Moreover, taken with the right attitude, such speculation is almost totally benign. An argument has been laid out. It links together several general aspects of the human cognitive system. If some facts contravening the conclusion can be found, that is interesting. They can be taken back through the argument to find where the argument was wrong. That will be instructive, because the argument can be taken as the obvious line of reasoning. Thus, the form of the argument is important and needs to be shaped up. For instance, one can attempt sensitivity analyses, such as Figure 3-10, to make it easy to find the soft spots.

In the following chapters such concerns are put aside. Any candidate architecture for human cognition must exhibit these characteristics. The architecture must be a further specification of the outline sketched here.

Symbolic Processing
for Intelligence

4

This chapter deals primarily with the symbolic processing required for intelligence—with the details of a symbolic system that is capable of being intelligent in a real world. The prior chapters have laid out a set of general characteristics that a fully cognitive system must exhibit. But the details count. If there is any property that a theory of cognition must explain it is how intelligence is actually possible. *Necessary* characteristics are well and good, but they are substantially less than half the story. *Sufficiency* is all-important. Intelligence itself is a sufficiency of capability. To be intelligent is to be able to do certain things, to wit, to exploit (encoded) knowledge to attain whatever (encoded) goals the organism has at the moment. Unless the theory can actually demonstrate these capabilities, it cannot claim that it has explained intelligence. And to demonstrate sufficiency requires all the details. Therefore, this chapter shifts the focus from general considerations to a single system, realized on a computer, that can exhibit a range of intelligent behavior.

Soar, the system to be described, is also the architecture that provides the basis for the candidate unified theory of cognition. As the first chapter made clear, the only way to argue for unified theories of cognition is to present a specific candidate theory and put it through its paces. Doing so does not imply that the particular candidate theory can yet stand the full heat of scientific scrutiny as a fully developed theory. But an exemplar is needed and Soar is to be that exemplar.

A connection is still missing. I've made the claim that an exemplar unified theory of cognition is what is needed, yet I propose in this chapter to describe an architecture, Soar. Implicit therein is a claim that to specify a unified theory of cognition is to specify an architecture. That may not be the entire theory, but it is its center.

Given that the human is the kind of system described in the last two chapters, it is the architecture—the fixed (or slowly varying) structure—that underlies the communalities the system will show in behavior. An architecture is the system of mechanisms that accesses encoded knowledge about the external world held in memory and brings it to bear to select actions in the service of goals. If it works perfectly the actions reflect only this external knowledge— the system behaves as a knowledge-level system. Such a system has no psychology. Psychology enters in precisely as the processing of the encoded memory structures shows through. It is the architecture that determines the shape of this processing.

The focus through most of this chapter will be on how a total system can actually realize intelligent behavior. We will first discuss the architecture for central cognition, that is, for the symbolic part of the architecture, and next the phenomenon of learning from experience, which interpenetrates all of central cognition. Then we'll back off a bit and describe the total cognitive system within which the central system is embedded, namely perceptual and motor processing. With the total context in place, we will illustrate how the central system functions and attempt to characterize its abilities. As we move through all this, we will not attend to how these details correspond to human behavior. The architecture, of course, instantiates all the constraints described earlier, so it will be the right sort, generally speaking. Indeed, much about Soar will seem highly familiar given the groundwork that has been laid. At the end of the chapter, once the full specifications are before us, we will consider the mapping of Soar onto human cognition. The examination of the details and consequences of that mapping will be the task of the rest of the book. But by the close of this chapter we will be able to ask whether Soar describes a cognitive beast that is recognizably human.

4.1. The Central Architecture for Performance

The central architecture refers to the mechanisms of cognition, but not of perception or motor behavior. As already noted in Chapter 1, one thing wrong with much theorizing about cognition is that it does not pay much attention to perception on the one side or motor behavior on the other. It separates these two systems out. The

1. Problem spaces represent all tasks
   • Problem-solving architecture (no process substrate)
2. Productions provide all long-term memory (symbols)
   • Search control, operators, declarative knowledge
3. Attribute/value representation is the medium for all things
4. Preference-based procedure used for all decisions
   • Preference language: accept/reject, better/indifferent/worse
5. Goals (and goal stack) direct all behavior
   • Subgoals created automatically from performance-time impasses
   • Operators perform the function of deliberate goals
6. Chunking of all goal-results (impasse resolutions) occurs continuously

Figure 4-1. The main characteristics of central cognition.

result is that the theory gives up the constraint on central symbolic cognition that these systems could provide. The loss is serious—it assures that theories will never cover the complete arc from stimulus to response, which is to say, never be able to tell the full story about any particular behavior.

The reason cognitive psychology does not pay attention to these mechanisms is neither lack of awareness nor lack of desire. We all understand, especially when we take an evolutionary perspective, how intimate is the relation of perception, cognition, and motor behavior. Cognition no doubt grew out of systems largely devoted to perceptual-motor activity. Indeed, the view of mind-as-controller in the second chapter is responsive to such a general view. The difficulty is that the total system is too complex to handle all at once, and the sorts of considerations that go into perception and motor action seem too disparate to integrate. So the strategy is divide and conquer.

By describing central cognition first, I am committing this same sin in this section. I will rectify the situation, as least somewhat, before completing the chapter. But, in fact, the perceptual and motor systems of Soar are still nascent. This chapter stays as close as possible to what is firm and actual about Soar.

Figure 4-1 lists the main characteristics of central cognition in Soar. The rest of Section 4.1 presents the first five of these, which constitute the architectural structure that permits Soar to perform

LONG-TERM KNOWLEDGE

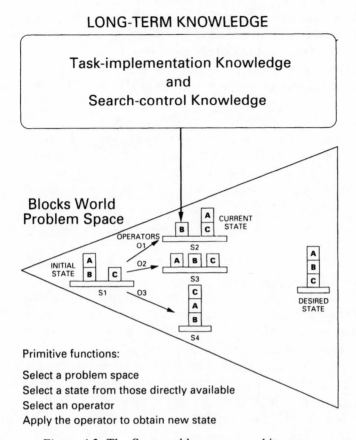

Figure 4-2. The Soar problem-space architecture.

tasks. I will put off to Section 4.2 the description of item 6, Soar's learning mechanism.

4.1.1. Problem Spaces for Formulating Tasks

Soar formulates all its tasks as problem spaces. Every system must somehow represent to itself the tasks it is to work on. The representation provides the framework within which knowledge is brought to bear and in which task accomplishment is assessed. Thus, for Soar, all cognitive action occurs within a search space.

Figure 4-2 gives a picture of a problem space, which should seem familiar from Figure 2-16 (even to the same blocks-world domain). The problem space is searched to accomplish the task—to construct the symbolic object that is desired. Here, the task is, starting at the *initial state* (s1), with blocks B and C on the table and A on top of B, to construct a *desired state* (s4), with A on top of B on top of C. When operating in a problem space, the system is always located at some *current state*. It can apply any of the operators of the problem space to the current state. The figure shows three operators, o1, o2, and o3, as possible operators to be applied to the initial state. These operators correspond to the moves of the various blocks: operator o1 moves block A to atop C, o2 moves A to the table, o3 moves C to atop A. This problem space is useful for solving problems in the blocks world precisely because there is a representation law that relates what the operators do to the data structure that is the current state and what real moves do to real blocks in the external world.

Operating in the problem space requires knowledge, both to implement the operators and to guide the search. This knowledge is held in the long-term memory of the system and it is brought to bear on the current state. (Thus, the figure actually shows the current state to be s2, which occurs after operator o1 has been applied to the initial state s1.) The long-term memory holds the knowledge to implement and guide searching through all the problem spaces of which the system is capable; a search of this long-term memory is required to find the knowledge that is relevant to this space and this current state. This is knowledge search and it is distinct from the problem-space search of applying operators to a state to construct new states. In particular, the knowledge search is through a physically existing memory, whereas the problem-space search generates the states one by one, so that only a single state exists physically at any one time.[1]

Every cognitive task that Soar does is represented by a problem space. Therefore, the primitive functions that Soar must perform are those that determine how it will operate with problem spaces. These are listed in the figure. They are to select a problem space to work in, to select a state within that problem space (if more than one is available), to select an operator of the space to apply to the selected state, and then to apply that operator to the state to take a

---

1. Old states, which have been generated, can of course be saved in some memory, for retrieval later; but this does not change the character of the problem space as being generated, state by state, rather than having all its states preexisting in physical space.

step in the space. These primitive functions are the acts of deliberation that this system must take. The Soar architecture is built to accomplish these functions directly. That is all it has to do to produce behavior. Hence, it may fairly be characterized as a *problem-space architecture*.

This organization can be contrasted with that of standard computer architectures, as they have developed in computer science. Such architectures take as the basic task to follow a sequence of operations, as determined by a data structure in memory (the program). The primitive functions are to assemble the operation to be performed (such as multiply), to assemble the operands to be the inputs of the operation (a multiplier and a multiplicand), to apply the operation to the operands, to save the result (the product), and to select the program structure to determine the next operation (recall Figure 2-13). It is commonplace in computer science to realize other processing organizations by programming an architecture in some available operation-operand organization of the classical kind. This can certainly be done for the problem-space organization, and it is exactly how we create a software Soar system to run on current computers. But if the problem space is the basic organization, in that nothing but operation in problem spaces occurs, then the primitive functions can be those of Figure 4-2 without ever dropping into another computational engine organized in some other way. The four functions in Figure 4-2 must be genuinely primitive; and much of the rest of architecture is devoted to accomplishing these functions.

It is standard in AI to use search spaces when problems are difficult (Rich, 1983). When tasks are routine, however, the standard practice is to formulate them as the behavior specified by a program in a language that permits sequential and procedural control, or, in other words, one that uses an operation-operand organization. With Soar, all behavior, however routine, is represented as movement through a problem space. Whether search is exhibited depends on what knowledge is available and brought to bear. If lots of knowledge is brought to bear Soar goes right to the goal, exhibiting routine behavior. If little knowledge is available, then Soar may do lots of undirected and combinatorial search.

This uniform use of problem spaces as the task representation is called the *problem space hypothesis* (Newell, 1980c). It is only one of several aspects of Soar where a uniform structure or process is adopted. The effects of such uniformities can be adequately assessed only in terms of the solutions they enable to system-wide issues. The uniform use of problem spaces strongly affects two such issues. First, the binding of control information occurs at run time, immediately before an operator is applied, whereas in standard (sequential and procedural) languages the binding occurs at the time the program is created. Thus, the problem space provides the opportunity to respond to each situation in terms of the knowledge available at that moment. It is a form of what AI calls a minimum-commitment strategy—never make a commitment until the choice is forced. Second, in a system that learns continuously, as Soar does, the movement from problematical (much search) to routine (little search) is continuous. It does not face at any point the requirement for a discrete change of representation. Offsetting these gains is the extra processing needed to make the binding decisions repeatedly at run time.

4.1.2. Production Systems for Long-Term Memory

The second feature of the central cognitive architecture is that all of its long-term memory is constructed as a single production system. Memory for everything is handled by the same structure, the same writing processes, and the same reading (or access) processes—for search control, for how to implement an operation, for declarative knowledge, for historical (episodic) knowledge, for everything. This is another uniform assumption. It is arguably the most contentious feature of the Soar architecture. Most people in computer science, AI, and cognitive science hold the view that declarative memory and procedural memory are fundamentally separate kinds of memories kept in separate kinds of structures. For instance, this is a key and much emphasized feature of Act* (Anderson, 1983). Many people also seek to create separate memory structures for episodic and semantic memory (Tulving, 1983). Soar is an exploration in trying to live with a single uniform memory.

Most cognitive scientists are familiar with production systems, also called parallel rule-based systems or sometimes pattern-directed inference systems (Waterman & Hayes-Roth, 1978). Figure 4-3 shows the structure. There is permanent memory of productions. There are three productions in the figure (P1, P2, P3), but there might be 3,000 or 300,000. There is a working memory, which is a collection of data elements (the Es). Each production has a set

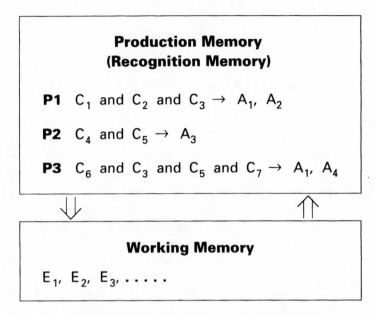

Figure 4-3. The Soar production system.

of conditions (the Cs). Each condition is to be matched with a working-memory element, someplace in working memory. If all the conditions are jointly satisfied, then the production is satisfied. It then fires its actions (the As), which enter new working-memory elements into the working memory.

The standard view of productions is that they are operator-like entities with conditions, which determine applicability, and actions, which occur when the conditions are satisfied. In this view additional search control may even be used to determine whether it is desirable to execute the production (Nilsson, 1980). However, a production system can also be viewed simply as a content-addressed memory. The right-hand sides (the As in the figure) are the content, the encoded knowledge in the memory; and the left-hand sides (the Cs in the figure) are the retrieval clues, the accessing structure. Thus, a production system is simply a form of *recognition system*—it recognizes patterns in the memory and responds by providing its content.[2] It is as much a scheme for accessing and

2. The terminology differs here somewhat from the usage in much of psychology and computer science, which assumes that the result of recognition should just be a yes or no.

retrieving declarative information as it is a scheme for procedural memory. In Soar, the production system plays both roles.

The Soar production system is realized within Ops5 (Forgy, 1981), a language that was developed in the late 1970s and has become a standard production system in the expert-system field (Brownston, Farrell, Kant, & Martin, 1985). Thus, the details of productions are taken from Ops5. Conditions are not arbitrary tests but patterns to be matched. The patterns can contain variables and the same variable can occur in more than one condition, in which case it must take the same value at all occurrences, providing in effect a test for equality. Conditions can test for the absence of an element in working memory as well as for the presence of an element. All possible instantiations are found on each cycle (that is, all possible sets of working-memory elements that satisfy each production, along with the bindings of the variables).

Figure 4-4 shows an example of a Soar production that proposes an operator to be used to take in information about a blocks-world task. An English paraphrase is shown at the top, then below it the actual production, then some working-memory elements that the production matches, and, at the bottom, the new elements that are added to working memory when the production fires.

Each working-memory element is a single attribute and value of an object. For instance, in the top line describing the working memory before the production fires, goal object $g3$ has the problem space $p14$ is one element; goal $g3$ has the state $s51$ is another element. Objects have an arbitrary *identifier* ($g3$), assigned by Soar when the object is created (the prefix, g, is simply a mnemonic to help the user); all attributes are marked by ^ and their values directly follow them. Also, as an aid to the user, all elements about the same object (here $g3$) are grouped together; elements can be distributed anywhere in working memory and in any order.

The production's name is *propose-operator*comprehend*; it has five conditions and three actions. The first condition matches the goal object (*goal . . .*), whose identifier $g3$ will be bound to the variable $<g>$ (all variables in productions are indicated by angle brackets). The goal element must have an attribute ^*problem-space*, whose value will be bound to the variable $<p>$; and an attribute ^*state*, whose value will be bound to the variable $<s>$. This first condition doesn't constrain the match beyond specifying that it be linked to an active goal element, since all the values are simply

English version of production
Propose-operator*comprehend:
   If the problem space is the base-level-space,
   and the state has a box with nothing on top,
   and the state has input that has not been examined,
   then make the comprehend operator acceptable,
   and note that the input has been examined.

Soar version of production
(sp propose-operator*comprehend:
   (goal <g> ^problem-space <p> ^state <s>)
   (problem-space <p> ^name base-level-space)
   (state <s> ^object <b> ^input <i>)
   (box <b> ^on table ^on-top nothing)
   –(signal <i> ^examined yes)
   →
   (operator <o> ^name comprehend)
   (preference <o> ^role operator ^value acceptable
     ^goal <g> ^problem-space <p> ^state <s>)
   (input <i> examined yes))

Working-memory elements before production fires
(goal g3 ^problem-space p14 ^state s51)
(problem-space p14 ^name base-level-space)
(state s51 ^object b80 b70 b64 ^input i16 ^tried o76)
(block b80 ^on table ^on-top-nothing)
(block b70 ^on table ^on-top b61)
(block b64 ^on b61 ^on-top nothing)
(input i16 ^advice a31)

Working-memory elements added by production firing
(operator o82 ^name comprehend)
(preference o82 ^role operator ^value acceptable
   ^goal g3 ^problem-space p14 ^state s51)
(input i16 ^advice a31 ^examined yes)

Figure 4-4. Example Soar production and working memory
before and after firing.

bound to variables. However, the next condition specifies that the problem-space element $<p>$ must have the name *base-level-space*. The third condition constrains the state $<s>$ in two ways. First (the fourth condition) $<s>$ must be a block that is on the table and has a clear top. Second (the fifth condition), it must have an unexamined input. This latter is given as a negated condition (marked by $-$), which is satisfied only if the condition itself is *not* satisfied by any elements in the working memory. State $s51$ actually has several blocks (b80, b70, b64), but only one satisfies the condition of being on the table and having a clear top. Thus, the conditions are being matched against specific elements—namely, attributes and values of an object—and not against an entire object. Note that the state also has another element (^tried o76), which does not enter into the match of this production at all.

If all the conditions are satisfied (as is true here), then the production fires the three actions, which put three elements into working memory. The first element creates a new operator o82, called *comprehend*. This is a new operator, because the <o> in the action element did not occur on the condition side and hence was not already bound to some already existing object described in working memory. The second element put into working memory is a preference element that asserts that o82 is an acceptable operator in the goal context (g3, p14, s51), where the goal, problem space, and state are those determined by the goal condition matching the element (goal g3 ^problem-space p14 ^state s51) already in working memory. The role of preference elements will be described in a moment. The third element is an additional attribute and value (^attention yes) to the existing input.

This is a typical Soar production, although some have more conditions and actions. A production can accomplish several sorts of computations (Newell, Rosenbloom, & Laird, 1989). It is a conditional computation, occurring only when its conditions are matched. It can modify existing objects by adding new attributes and values, and doing so in ways that depend on the existing working memory. It can create new objects and describe them with working-memory elements, again in ways that depend on existing working memory. This collection of computational abilities suffices to carry out the functions of a symbol system (Figure 2-11). The exception is that there is no way to change the long-term memory. Chunking (described in Section 4.2) is the mechanism that provides this capability.

Soar productions have two special properties, compared with Ops5 and many other production systems. First, the only action that a Soar production can take is to add elements to working memory. It cannot delete elements, modify elements, or take other actions. Thus, the Soar production system behaves like a memory, in that information is accessed (via the conditions) and retrieved (via the actions) and the new information in working memory does not destroy or replace the old, but monotonically adds to it. Elements must ultimately disappear from working memory, of course. This happens automatically when they become inaccessible because of the dynamics of problem solving (described below after the decision apparatus is introduced).

The second special property of Soar productions is that there is no conflict resolution. In general, given a set of elements in working ·memory, there can be no guarantee that only a single production will match with only a single instantiation. It is possible (and usually happens) that multiple productions with multiple instantiations occur. Ops5 calls this the conflict set. Ops5, and most other production systems, apply a fixed set of rules to resolve the conflict and to specify a single production instantiation to execute. Soar does no conflict resolution and executes all satisfied instantiations. Thus, the production system is an entirely parallel, uncontrolled system. In this respect, as well as that it only adds working-memory elements, the Soar production system operates like a content-addressed memory.

4.1.3. Objects with Attributes and Values for the Representational Medium

As Figure 4-4 shows, Soar has a very elementary representation of objects with collections of attributes and values. Both the attributes and values may be other objects, so that arbitrary attribute-value structures can occur. The grain size of the representation is the value of an attribute of an object. This is the unit that is independently readable and writable by a production. Conditions, actions, and working-memory elements are object-attribute-value triples. Consequently, an object is a collection of such elements. This is a medium that admits combinatorial variety and is easy to manipulate, as called for in Chapter 2. It is used for all representations.

Objects are defined by their set of attributes and values, so that two objects with the same attributes and values are taken to be the same. The identifiers ($g3$, $p14$, and the like) are simply temporary labels that serve to identify when a production is referring to the same object. Thus, the identifiers are created as arbitrary symbols by the actions of the productions, as occurred in Figure 4-4 when $o82$ was created to identify the new operator named *comprehend*.

The representation bears some affinity to object-oriented representations and frame (or schema) representations (Minsky, 1975),

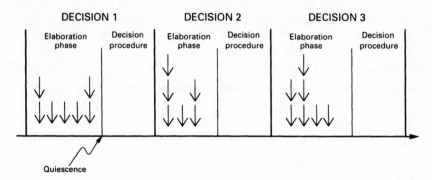

Figure 4-5. The Soar decision cycle.

but it is of the simplest sort. There are no default values, no attached procedures, and no automatic inheritance structures. It has none of the apparatus that would exist if the representation were extended in a framelike direction.

4.1.4. Accumulation of Preferences for Decisions

As Figure 4-2 indicated, the architecture of Soar is built around the problem space. Thus, the decisions that must be made are what problem space should be used (to attain a goal), what state should be used (within the problem space), and, finally, what operator should be used (to progress to the next state). These are basic operations of the architecture. They are all made by a uniform decision process, called the *decision cycle*. This is shown in Figure 4-5 (which shows three consecutive cycles). Each decision cycle has an *elaboration phase* followed by a *decision procedure*. The elaboration phase acquires the knowledge that is available about the current situation. All productions whose conditions are satisfied freely add new working-memory elements (the vertical arrows). There is no conflict resolution, so anything is free to flow in. This is a gathering operation, to pull everything in. Elements that arrive early may be used to access additional elements. The elements can be of any sort—about the blocks or tables or the relations between them, about what operators can move what blocks, about what block was moved in the past, and about what future arrangements of blocks are expected or desired. More abstractly stated, an intelligent system must be able to express its knowledge of situations and actions over the past, present, and future.

An intelligent system must also be able to express its knowledge

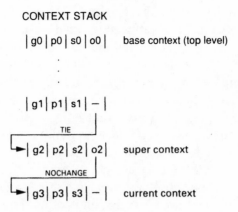

CONTEXT STACK

| g0 | p0 | s0 | o0 | base context (top level)

| g1 | p1 | s1 | − |

TIE

| g2 | p2 | s2 | o2 | super context

NOCHANGE

| g3 | p3 | s3 | − | current context

PREFERENCES PRODUCED BY ELABORATION PHASE

(s13 acceptable for supergoal state s2)
(s13 rejected for supergoal state s2)
(o2 acceptable for current operator)
(o7 acceptable for current operator)
(o7 better than o2 for current operator)
(o9 indifferent to o6 for current operator)

Figure 4-6. Soar performance elements and context stack.

about what actions *should* be taken. It must be able both to represent an action, without taking it, and to represent that an action should be taken, again without taking it. This latter may be a little less obvious, but if it were not possible, how could deliberation of what should happen occur? Furthermore, since it is the architecture that finally actually takes an action (even an operator, which is an internal action), there must be an architecturally defined and understood communication about what action to take. *Preferences* are Soar's means of such communication. Preferences will also accumulate during the elaboration phase.

The production in Figure 4-4 had a preference on its right-hand side that was put into working memory when the production fired. Figure 4-6 shows a possible collection of preferences that could be in working memory at the end of a given elaboration phase. A decision cycle takes place in the context of a stack of earlier decisions about goals, problem spaces, states, and operators (and called the *context stack*), as shown at the top of the figure (the arrows between the contexts in the stack will become clear in a minute).

The current context is goal *g*3, space *p*3, state *s*3, and no operator (that is, no operator has yet been decided upon). The supercontext consists of *g*2, *p*2, *s*2, and *o*2, and so on up to the top (which is called the *base-level* context). The first preference asserts that state *s*13 is *acceptable* for the supergoal context, in other words, that it should replace state *s*2. The second preference *rejects* this same state for the supergoal. Thus, what one preference proposes, another preference denies. The third preference asserts that operator *o*2 is *acceptable* to be the current operator. The next preference says *o*7 is *acceptable* for the current operator, so both operators are candidates. The next preference says that *o*7 is *better* than *o*2 for this particular decision. Finally, another preference asserts that operator *o*9 is *indifferent* to operator *o*6. There has been no other reference to *o*6 and *o*9, but if some production is caused to assert that preference there is no constraint against it. Any collection of preferences about any objects for any of the slots in the context stack is possible.

Let this collection of preferences be the ones in working memory when this particular elaboration phase runs to *quiescence*. The elaboration phase has kept going as long as additional elements have kept arriving in working memory. All the information available is gathered. When the elaboration phase runs to quiescence, the decision procedure occurs. Its function is to make the decision from the information available to it in the set of accumulated preferences. Many nonpreference elements will be in working memory at the same time, having entered it just now or on earlier cycles. Indeed, it is these other working-memory elements (representing the current state, possible operators, etc.) that have satisfied the productions that put preferences into working memory. But only the preferences are used by the decision procedure, and it uses all of them, whether input during this elaboration phase or earlier.

The decision procedure simply implements the semantics of the preference assertions. A preference always refers to a decision to adopt some object in a given slot in the existing decision context. It uses only a small set of decision concepts: *acceptable, reject, better* (*worse*), *best* (*worst*), and *indifferent*.[3] These have straightforward

---

3. As yet, we have no theory that determines the set of primitive decision concepts to be understood by the architecture, so there is continuing experimentation. For example, Soar4.5 contains *require* and *prohibit* preferences, which refer to immediate necessity with respect to goal attainment.

semantics. To be chosen, a decision must be acceptable. A rejected decision cannot be chosen, no matter what. If one decision is better than another (for the same slot) then, ceteris paribus, it will be chosen over the other; and analogously for worse decisions. *Best* and *worst* are simply the extreme points of the preference ordering (better than best isn't any better). A choice between indifferent decisions is to be made arbitrarily.

By default, the preferences that have been generated are assumed to constitute the entire corpus that has to be considered. Other preferences might apply and might have been produced. But the elaboration phase ran to quiescence and thus obtained all the preferences that were available without making some decision about how to proceed. Therefore this decision procedure must work with what it has. This is a *closed world assumption,* but not one that can easily be relieved.

If the decision procedure produces an unequivocal choice (in Figure 4-6 it would be that operator $o7$ should be selected to be the current operator), then that choice is implemented ($o7$ is installed in the operator slot of the current context) and Soar begins a new decision cycle. The context has now changed ($o7$ is now in the operator slot of the current context), so that the next elaboration phase can access new knowledge and propose preferences for yet another decision. In this case, the productions that implement $o7$, which have a condition that tests for $o7$ being the current operator, would be enabled and fire. Thus Soar moves step by step, accumulating the relevant knowledge and making the next decision. For example, starting with a new subgoal—that is, a context consisting of $(g, -, -, -)$— it might first choose a problem space $(g, p, -, -)$, then an initial state $(g, p, s, -)$, then an operator (g, p, s, o). Installing the operator releases the knowledge that implements the operator and produces a new state (s') in working memory, which might then be chosen on the next decision cycle to be the next state $(g, p, s', -)$. Then the next operator (g, p, s', o') is chosen, then the next state, and so on, to move through the problem space to attain the desired state.

The decision cycle is always the same. Any decision may be proposed—to choose any problem space, space, or operator for any of the slots in the total goal context, which includes the current context, the supercontext, the supersupercontext, and so on. Nothing, except the actual preferences that come forth, constrains behavior to any particular sequence of choices, say, to move along the state-operator-state path just described. For instance, in Figure 4-6 if the preference rejecting state $s13$ had not appeared, then the decision procedure would have chosen to change the state $s2$ in the supergoal rather than to install operator $o7$. Thus, at any point, any choice can be made.

All the knowledge that guides the problem solving resides in the productions. The decision procedure adds no knowledge of itself; it just implements the fixed semantics of the concepts, accept, reject, better, best, worse, worst, and indifferent. Behavior, of course, needs to be directed. The goals and the goal stack provide the context that lets that happen. Each level of the stack specifies a subgoal of the level above, so the goal stack produces a goal-subgoal hierarchy. In this respect, Soar is like most complex AI problem-solving systems. In fact, one of the main things that has been learned in AI is the effectiveness, and apparent necessity, of a goal hierarchy, with goals, subgoals, and alternative subgoals, for controlling behavior to achieve intelligent performance.

4.1.5. Impasses and Subgoals for Resolving Difficulties

So far, we have taken the context stack (the goal-subgoal hierarchy) as given. The Soar architecture creates the goals dynamically as it goes along. This is an important feature of Soar that contrasts substantially with the current state of the art. In essentially all AI systems, subgoals are created dynamically, but only as predetermined and stored in memory. Cast in terms of productions, the situation is like that shown in Figure 4-7. The production reads: if you are attempting to attain goal $g0$ and if other conditions, C_1, C_2, and so on, are satisfied, then set up $g1$, $g2$, and $g3$ as subgoals to be attained. The subgoals are created deliberately in terms of the methods the system has available to it.

Soar creates subgoals dynamically when it runs into *impasses*. It might have occurred to the reader that there was something odd about the decision cycle, as described above. Given an arbitrary collection of preferences, what guarantees that the decision procedure will yield a clear choice to be taken next? All kinds of things could happen to prevent that. Suppose, just to be extreme, no production proposed *any* new preference! What then? The extreme simplicity of the decision cycle would seem illusory, because substantial complexities still need to be taken into account.

Create-subgoals:
  If goal g0 is desired,
    and condition C_1 is satisfied,
    and condition C_2 is satisfied,
  then attain goal g1 and goal g2 and goal g3

Figure 4-7. Example of a typical AI goal-setting production
(not used in Soar).

Indeed, there need not always be a clear choice. All the untoward things can happen. They prevent the decision procedure from choosing a unique decision and hence they prevent Soar from moving forward. They are impasses. When Soar finds itself in an impasse it creates a subgoal to resolve the impasse. Thus, subgoals arise dynamically because Soar is unable to proceed. Furthermore, this is the only way subgoals can arise. If Soar knows what to do next, there is no need of a subgoal.

The possibilities for impasses arise from the different ways in which the decision procedure can fail. The decision procedure can be thought of as getting rid of all the decisions that can't possibly be chosen. First, it attends only to decisions that are acceptable. Then, it gets rid of all the decisions that are rejected. Of those remaining, it throws away all that are worse than some other acceptable and not-rejected decision. Finally, it considers only the decisions concerned with the highest subgoal. Any change in a goal at some level—a change in problem space, state, or operator—completely preempts all changes about subgoals, because these latter were all created in response to the impasse at this higher level.

Given the finally remaining set of decisions, just four ways exist for impasses to arise. First, there can be a *tie impasse*. When all things that are not to be chosen are cleared away, there can be left a collection of alternatives that can't be discriminated. They are all acceptable, none have been rejected, none are preferred to any of the others, and they are not indifferent.[4]

Second, there can be a *no-change impasse*. After all is said and done, there are no choices available. Either they have all been rejected or nothing was ever declared to be acceptable. This might seem a rare situation, but it happens all the time. For example, an

---

4. Indifference is the definite preference that any of the indifferent elements be selected.

operator has been selected, but not enough is immediately known to produce a new state as a result (*immediately known* means that the required productions do not fire within the elaboration phase). Hence, even though many things may have happened (new objects created and old objects augmented with new attribute-values), no production puts forth a preference for selecting a next state to be the result of the operator. Furthermore, no productions propose that the situation should be abandoned, by proposing a different operator, for example, or a new choice in a higher context. The upshot is a no-change impasse.

Third, there can be a *reject impasse*. The only preference may be one for rejecting one of the decisions already made. For example, in Figure 4-6 there might also have been a preference to reject $s2$ in the supergoal state. Rejection, of itself, doesn't say what to do to gain any additional knowledge, so an impasse occurs.

Fourth, and last, there can be a *conflict impasse*. One production can provide a preference that operator $o1$ is better than operator $o2$, and another production can provide a preference that operator $o2$ is better than operator $o1$. And when the smoke clears that is all that is left. Since no constraint exists on what preferences are generated, such an eventuality can certainly happen (although in our experience it does so only rarely). Given the semantics of preferences, there is no way to proceed, hence an impasse occurs.

These, and only these, four different generic situations create impasses. Analysis of all possible situations, starting from an arbitrary collection of preferences, shows that these are the only situations that can occur that lead to an impasse. In the rest, a single choice emerges as the one to be made. Of course, the impasse itself is hardly completely characterized by being one of these four types. The impasse is caused by the entire state of working memory in conjunction with the entire recognition memory. No description of this situation exists other than the total state of the system. Thus, the impasses signify the full variety of deficiencies of knowledge of which the system is capable.

An impasse does not mean that Soar is stymied and therefore halts. Soar responds to an impasse by creating a subgoal to resolve it. What resolves an impasse is knowledge that would lead Soar not to make that impasse at that decision point. There are many ways in which this might happen. What these are or could be depends not only on the current working memory, but also on all of the knowl-

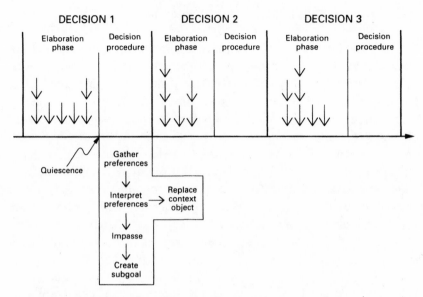

Figure 4-8. Complete Soar decision cycle.

edge in the long-term memory. But it must include some preferences that make the decision occasion that produced the impasse
now yield a clear choice. This does not require any formulation of
the set of possibilities for what could resolve the impasse. The
decision procedure itself determines that. Nor does it require any
specific reconsideration of the decision situation. At every decision
cycle all choices are open to be made and are considered in the
context of whatever alternative choices have been proposed. Preferences can be produced at any time that make a choice at the site
of the earlier impasse. Then that choice will simply be taken and the
processing will move on from there. Alternatively, preferences
could be produced that make a choice somewhere higher up in the
context stack, in effect abandoning all the lower processing. All the
processing in the subgoal and subgoals generated by the higher
impasse will become moot and can just be aborted.

We can now complete the picture of the decision cycle. Figure
4-8, which is the same as Figure 4-5 except for the addition of the
impasse mechanism, shows where the goal stack comes from. With
each impasse a new subgoal context is created, which has a goal but
no problem space, state, or operator. Contexts are removed from
the context stack when a decision changes something higher in the

subgoal stack, thus rendering the ongoing subgoal processing below it irrelevant.

The removal of goal contexts causes the disappearance of working-memory elements associated exclusively with the discarded contexts. Only working-memory elements connected to elements of the goal context stack can be accessed. To be accessible an element must be part of the context (an established goal, problem space, state, or operator) or occur as the value of some attribute of an object that is accessible. (An element may be connected to the goal context stack in several different ways.) Productions conform to this connectivity constraint by matching only along chains of working-memory elements that start with objects in the context stack. The production in Figure 4-4 satisfies this constraint. Its first condition matches a goal element; the next two elements for a problem space and a state are linked to the first condition (the identifiers $<p>$ and $<s>$ occur in both conditions); the last two elements for a block and an input are linked to the state (the identifiers $<b>$ and $<i>$ occur in both conditions). Thus, the removal of objects from the goal context stack cuts other objects out of ever being accessed, and so they disappear from working-memory. This is the other side of the coin of the fact that all the production system ever does is add knowledge to working memory; removal takes place automatically.[5]

It is a key feature of Soar that the goal context stack is generated entirely internally and that impasses are the sole source of subgoals. Such a scheme can generate all the sorts of subgoals that we have become familiar with in AI systems. Tie impasses produce subgoals to choose between operators or between states. They also produce subgoals to choose between problem spaces, to choose, in other words, how to formulate or represent a task. These latter rarely show up in AI systems, and indeed so far they arise only in quite limited ways in Soar. No-change impasses on operators can produce subgoals that implement the operator. They can also produce what are called precondition subgoals or operator subgoaling, namely, the goal to find a state where the operator does apply. They can also produce subgoals to specialize or instantiate an operator. A moment's reflection will show that all three of these common situations—not immediately knowing the result of applying an operator,

---

5. In the Soar software system, these inaccessible elements are garbage collected.

not having a state in which an operator applies, and not having a generalized operator instantiated to the present situation—all should lead to no-change impasses on the operator. On the other hand, a no-change impasse on the state produces subgoals to find or construct an operator, because no operator at all was proposed. And so it goes. Any lack of knowledge that prohibits the situation from moving forward leads to some kind of an impasse and hence a subgoal to resolve that impasse.

The internal subgoals determine what Soar will do once it starts to pursue something. It then has an end, and any lack of knowledge in attaining that end leads (via impasses) to attempts to obtain that knowledge. But this decision cycle doesn't account for why Soar wants to stack blocks in the first place, or play chess, or whatever. Further, it does not account for how Soar represents to itself such wants. In Soar, deliberate goals take the form of operators, which are defined by whatever combination of partial procedural and end-state specification is available at the time the operator is created. Thus, the goal to stack the blocks in a particular configuration is, in the first instance, an operator to stack them. Such an incompletely determined operator produces a no-change impasse, which generates the subgoal that leads to selecting a problem space in which to solve the problem. Indeed, whether stacking the blocks is in fact a problem or is something that Soar can just do (an immediately performable operator) is not intrinsic to the task to be accomplished, but is determined in terms of what is known right at the moment of the attempt to stack the blocks.[6]

Some additional insight into the Soar architecture can be gained by contrasting Soar with standard computers. Impasses also occur in standard computers. For instance, dividing by zero produces an impasse. However, if division by zero occurs, who knows what's wrong? There is no way that the architecture can respond to this impasse, other than to produce an error message and then abandon ship. That is because a computer architecture has no relationship to what is being computed. Its operation-operand structure relates it

6. AI systems have typically made a basic structural distinction between operators and goals, which has long needed clarification. Pragmatically, it has simply been the designer's decision to cast some aspects as given and some as to-be-sought. But this is clearly unsatisfactory. The solution offered by Soar seems fundamentally satisfying. Operators and deliberate goals are the same thing; operationally, goals arise from a lack of knowledge at the moment when that knowledge is needed.

to only one task, following a program in memory. The Soar architecture, on the other hand, is structured in terms of problem-solving requirements. Its primitive actions—what corresponds to *divide* and *branch-on-zero*—are functionally important actions in terms of Soar's overall behavior—selecting problem spaces, selecting states, selecting operators, and applying the operators. When an impasse occurs there is a functionally appropriate action the architecture can take. Setting up a subgoal, which records the type of impasse and points to the implicated objects, is analogous to the error message. But the form it takes shows that the architecture knows what needs to be done with it—attempt to resolve it—and knows how to go about that—set up a subgoal that can evoke the knowledge in the system that can guide such an attempt. The standard computer architecture not only does not have a goal structure it can use to pose the task of resolving the impasse; even if it did, there would be no way for it to formulate the task to be done, because the formulation would be buried within the semantics of the program being interpreted. Soar's ability to define its subgoals is one gain from casting the architecture in terms of problem spaces and not in terms of operations and operands.

4.1.6. *Operators and Context*

Typical problem-solving systems in AI use search in problem spaces in order to solve problems (often under somewhat different guises and terminology, in accord with their total systems organization). The typical arrangement is that the operators in a problem space are specified in a standard procedural or functional language, such as Lisp. Likewise, the search control to select the operators is realized in a standard program, perhaps with essential parametric input, such as the weights of an evaluation function. Such systems have two layers—a problem-solving layer and a program layer. It is important to see how Soar differs from this organization. Figure 4-9 is meant to emphasize that Soar operates in problem spaces all the way down. Suppose Soar starts out working on a task in the top problem space (*p*1). There might be several operators proposed that cannot be differentiated—a tie impasse. This leads Soar to set up a problem space (*p*2) to make that selection. The operators of this space evaluate the alternative operators. One is selected, but it may not be possible to carry it out in terms of immediate knowl-

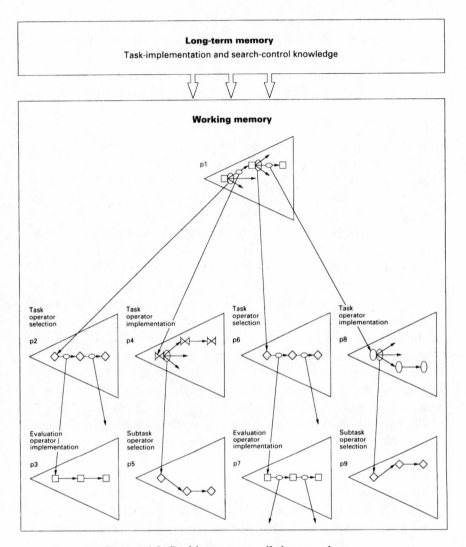

Figure 4-9. Problem spaces all the way down.

edge—a no-change impasse. This leads to a problem space (*p3*) that is concerned with implementing evaluation operators. Thus, Soar keeps running into impasses and dropping into subproblem spaces to resolve them. Ultimately it bottoms out when the knowledge immediately available in a space is sufficient to enable it to act—a result is actually produced. Of course it may run out of knowledge entirely. That could lead it just to try out the operators at the top (which means it has the search-control knowledge of what to do if no task-specific knowledge is available).

Operators with no-change impasses are analogous to procedure calls, with selecting the operator being analogous to calling the procedure, searching in the problem space being analogous to executing the code body, and the context stack being analogous to the procedure stack. This analogy immediately highlights two operations that are missing in Soar: communicating down to the operating context of the procedure body the input parameters; and communicating back to the initial (calling) context the results of the computation. For standard programming languages these communications are highly formalized operations with corresponding disciplines (such as call by value or call by name). By contrast, in Soar there are no communication operations of this sort. All processing occurs in one large open context, as demonstrated by the fact that decisions can be made at any level in the context. Often additional knowledge must be added to a state to instantiate an operator, and this is functionally equivalent to specifying parameters. Equally, knowledge is simply retrieved from the higher levels when it is needed. Likewise, there is no packaging of results in some standard form. Anything that is linked to a higher level in the goal context stack is a result at that level, because it can be accessed at that level and will not disappear along with the lower level when the impasse is resolved.

4.1.7. Example Trace of Performance

To make all this concrete, Figure 4-10 gives a trace of Soar as it works on the simple block-stacking task of Figure 4-2. The initial situation is that block *B* and block *C* are on the table and block *A* is on top of block *B*. The task is to get to the desired state where *A* is on top of *B* is on top of *C*—it is desired to stack up all the blocks in a specific order. Soar is provided initially with some knowledge. It must know about the blocks-world problem space, what its operators are and how to perform them. It must also know how to react to various impasses, that, for example, upon a tie impasse the selection problem space should be used to attempt its resolution. It also has the knowledge about the selection space itself. It knows some simple heuristics: not to propose an operator that immediately undoes what has just been done; and not to propose moving some part

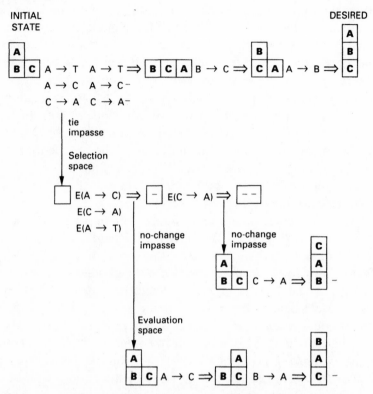

Figure 4-10. Behavior of Soar on a simple blocks-world task.

of the state that is already in its desired position. This latter is a simple form of means-ends behavior. This body of knowledge is all encoded in productions—it is the initial contents of Soar's long-term memory.[7]

Soar proposes all three acceptable operators in the problem space: move A to the table ($A \to T$), move A on top of C ($A \to C$), and move C on top of A ($C \to A$). This leads to a tie impasse, because Soar has no knowledge of which of these moves is worthwhile for the goal. The architecture sets up the tie impasse's subgoal, and the next decision cycle chooses the selection problem space.

7. Except for the task-specific knowledge of the blocks world, this knowledge is usually taken as given in any task; it is part of Soar's *default* knowledge.

The task in the selection space is to resolve the tie between the three operators. This particular space has an operator E to evaluate an item (a move operator). Since all three move operators are to be evaluated, there are three corresponding applications of the evaluation operator. However, Soar is indifferent to which evaluation operator is applied first, because it intends to do them all. Thus, it does not get another tie impasse between the three evaluation operators, but simply picks one arbitrarily. It happens to evaluate moving A on top of C first. It gets a no-change impasse, because it does not know how to evaluate the move using the productions that are available in the selection space. The selection space is not task-specific and only knows about applying an evaluation operator to all tied items and considering the results.

The no-change impasse leads Soar to set up the evaluation space, which implements E applied to $A \rightarrow C$. There could be alternative evaluation spaces. This particular one is a look-ahead space, which works only for evaluating operators. It embodies the notion of trying the operator in the original space to see what happens, in order to evaluate the results. Therefore, the move operator is applied to the original blocks situation. This might seem to be doing just what it avoided doing by getting the tie impasse in the first place—namely, making a specific blocks move. But there is a critical difference. In the top space the move is in the service of reaching a particular desired configuration; in the lower space the move is in the service of evaluating the desirability of making the move. The structure of these spaces neatly separates out these two separate functions and generates the search in the blocks-world space implicitly. After making the $A \rightarrow C$ move, there is only one move that can follow it. The others are eliminated by the heuristics not to back up immediately, to preserve parts of the result that are already in place, and not to move a block twice in a row. Hence, no tie impasse arises, and Soar ends at a state that is not the desired state. The recognition that it has not reached the desired state is directly available, so it records that information in the selection space as the result of the evaluation operator (the − mark).

Soar then selects the next operator to be evaluated. This happens to be moving C on top of A, which leads immediately to a recognizably bad position. At this point, two of the three original alternative moves have been declared no good, by exploring their consequences. The negative evaluations $(-)$ are converted into preferences to reject the operators in the original context, where they had been proposed (part of the knowledge of the selection space). This immediately resolves the tie impasse, since the only choice left is forced. So this move ($A \rightarrow T$) is actually made in the top space, not in the evaluation space. (It occurs by the operation of the decision procedure to select from all the options—in this case, between the option of evaluating the move in the selection space and the option of selecting the move in the top space.) Having moved A to the table, the available elementary heuristic search-control knowledge sees that one of the things wanted can be attained in a single move, namely, to move B onto C, as specified in the desired state. At this point, there is only one move that can be applied without taking back an immediately made move, so Soar gets to the final state, which is indeed the desired state.

This example provides a bit of typical Soar behavior as it performs a simple task. Soar simply proceeds to apply operators to do the task, and its lack of knowledge about how to proceed drives it to solve a variety of subgoals, which result in a pattern of behavior that is a look-ahead search. This behavior, of course, is not just determined by the architecture. Plenty of knowledge is brought to bear.

4.2. Chunking

We now have seen how Soar performs—by using problem spaces and moving through them to attain its tasks, detouring as necessary to resolve whatever impasses arise. We come now to the final component of the architecture in the list of Figure 4-1, namely chunking. Chunking is learning from experience. It is a way of converting goal-based problem solving into accessible long-term memory (productions). Whenever problem solving has provided some result, a new production will be created, whose actions are these just-obtained results and whose conditions are the working-memory elements that existed *before* the problem solving started that were used to produce the results. This newly minted production will be added to the long-term memory, and will henceforth be available to add its knowledge to the working memory in any future elaboration phase where its conditions are satisfied. For reference, Figure 4-11 lists the key properties of chunking, which will emerge as we proceed through the discussion.

1. Chunking converts goal-based problem solving into productions
   - Actions are based on the results of the subgoal
   - Conditions are based on the pre-impasse aspects necessary to produce the action

2. Chunks are active processes (productions), not declarative data
   - Chunking is a form of permanent goal-based caching

3. Chunks are generalized implicitly
   - Ignores whatever the problem solving ignored

4. Learning occurs during problem solving
   - Chunks become effective as soon as they are created

5. Chunking applies to all impasses, hence all subgoals
   - Search control, operator implementation, . . .
   - Whenever knowledge is incomplete or inconsistent

6. Chunking learns only what the system experiences
   - Total problem-solving system is part of the learning system
   - Chunker is not intelligent per se, but a fixed mechanism

7. Chunking is a general mechanism to move up the preparation-deliberation isobar

Figure 4-11. Properties of chunking.

Figure 4-12 shows what is going on in chunking. It is a display of working memory, as time flows from left to right. I have spread out the working-memory elements (the little circles) vertically just to make it easier to see what is happening. This is a picture at the production-system level, in which elements come into the working memory one at a time, without regard to what problem spaces are controlling the productions that fire. Any working-memory element is produced by some production instantiated to some prior working-memory elements. These causal linkages are indicated by the lines in the figure. For instance, the element *B* is the result of some production being instantiated on the elements *4* and *6* to its left in the figure. In reality, productions have many conditions and hence there should be many lines back from each working-memory element; but the figure is just schematic. Decision cycles are shown by the dashed vertical lines. At some point an impasse occurs. This is shown by the left-hand solid vertical line. The nature of the impasse is not shown, because it does not enter into the story. Soar creates the new subgoal context (as additional working-memory elements) and proceeds to generate more working-memory elements. These, of course, are dependent on available elements, some of which

Working Memory

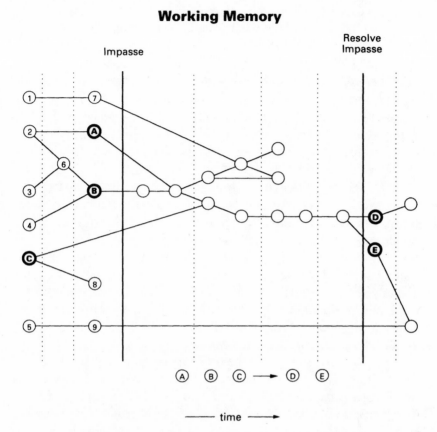

Figure 4-12. Diagram of behavior of Soar during chunking.

existed prior to the impasse and some of which arise after the impasse. The problem solving may go down some path (toward the top) and then abandon it and pursue another (toward the bottom). Finally (let us suppose), two elements, *D* and *E*, are produced that resolve the impasse. They would include at least one preference element that applied to the decision in the higher context (where the impasse occurred) and that is effective in getting a decision made there. The next decision cycle would then move ahead in the higher context, as marked by the right-hand solid vertical line.

At this point, having resolved the impasse, a new production (the chunk) is created, which is indicated at the bottom. Its actions are formed from the results, *D* and *E*. Its conditions are formed from the three elements, *A*, *B*, and *C*, that gave rise to the results and that also existed prior to the impasse. These are obtained by working backwards—by doing what is called in machine learning *back-tracing*. Starting with the results, the elements that gave rise to them are located, and then the ones that gave rise to these, and so on. The backward search terminates when elements of the prior context are encountered, in this case A, B, and C. Notice that this avoids picking up elements that were used in exploring paths that did not succeed (element 7 that fed the upper exploration). The new chunk is added to the total set of productions and henceforth functions just as any other production.[8]

Suppose Soar comes exactly this way again. At the particular point when the impasse that occurred originally is about to occur again (the left-hand solid vertical), the chunk will fire because its conditions will all be satisfied on available elements A, B, and C. It will put its two actions, D and E, into working memory. They will enter into the decision procedure and the impasse will not occur. Exactly the preference elements that finally resolved the impasse originally (at the right-hand vertical) are now all assembled ahead of time, so problem solving will simply proceed. Consequently, the action of a single production will have replaced all of the problem solving that was required on the original occasion. The figure shows only a little bit of processing, but additional impasses could occur and further subspaces be explored, and so on, just as in Figure 4-10. The gains in time (that is, efficiency) can be considerable—indeed, indefinitely large. Thus chunking is a form of learning by experience, in which the results of solving problems are remembered in a way that lets them be accessed to solve recurrences of the same problem.

Figure 4-13 shows an actual chunk, learned during the blocks-world task of Figure 4-10, rewritten in English. A chunk looks like any other production (compare Figure 4-4). It knows exactly what operator to apply if Soar is in a certain specified state and only one

8. The above description of chunking is simplified in several respects (Laird, 1986). First, each independent result leads to an independent chunk, so that several chunks can be created from a single impasse. Second, chunks are created whenever the results they capture are created. These results can never be modified or undone, in any event, so the chunks can be built right away. Third, various processes are performed on the chunks to make them more effective and efficient: conditions that can always be satisfied, hence provide no constraint, are eliminated; additional tests are inserted to keep instantiated variables distinct; sometimes a chunk can be divided into two independent chunks; and the conditions of a chunk are ordered to improve efficiency of matching.

Chunk1:
  If the problem-space is simple-blocks-world,
      and the state is one proposition different from the goal,
      and the state has block 1 and block 2 clear,
      and block 1 is on the table,
      and the desired state has block 1 on block 2,
  then make a best preference for the operator that moves
      block 1 onto block 2

Figure 4-13. An example chunk from the
blocks-world trace of Figure 4-10.

step from the desired state. The conditions express this in a way derived from the original formulation. The first condition is that the problem space is the simple blocks world. That may seem like a boilerplate instruction, yet it is critical for not overgeneralizing this knowledge, which is specific to the blocks-world problem space. The second condition specifies that the system is one step away from the goal state. It does this in terms of how many propositions are not satisfied. This implies a particular representation for the blocks world, in terms of little propositions such as (onto *B C*), and operators that change these propositions. This condition is also dependent on the problem space. The third and fourth conditions specify the actual contents of the state and desired states.

The analysis just given posited the recurrence of *exactly* the same situation. So chunking appears to be a scheme that simply speeds up processing. But the *exact same situation* means that *all* the elements in working memory at the time of the left-hand solid vertical are the same. Yet, only elements that were relevant to producing the result were picked out in building the chunk. All the rest are irrelevant. The chunk production will not test for any of these. Hence, the chunk will be evoked in any situation that has elements that match its conditions (*A, B, C*), no matter how different the situation is otherwise. Thus, chunking produces *implicit generalization*. This production will work not only in the exact same situation, but many other ones as well, producing transfer of learning. This production could introduce inappropriate elements into working memory and lead problem solving astray. If it does, it would produce negative transfer or, to use an alternative term, *overgeneralization*. How efficacious and safe implicit generalization is cannot be determined at a glance. It turns out to be extraordinarily powerful, as will be apparent throughout the rest of the book. But both overgeneralization and overspecialization remain ever present, important issues.

Now that chunking has been described, let us pick up some of the additional points in Figure 4-11. A convenient way to think about chunking, especially for computer scientists, is that it is permanent caching of goal results. Building a cache avoids the processing that was used to generate the cache. This description would be quite accurate, except that generalization to new situations occurs—which is not part of the notion of caching. It is important to realize that what gets ignored is a function of the problem solving and also a function of the representation. Whatever prior knowledge is considered in arriving at results will be included in the conditions. If the problem solving doesn't consider it, then it will be ignored. On the other hand, if some knowledge is actually unnecessary, but the representation is such that it must be considered, however superficially, then the result will be taken to be dependent on it. Therefore, there is a very strong dependence of the learning upon the problem solving and the task representation.

Not only does learning depend intimately on problem solving, problem solving depends equally strongly on learning. The chunks get built and become operational as soon as the result is obtained. Thus, learning is going on all the time and it can become effective in the next decision cycle. Behavior is not divided cleanly into two distinct phases—first a performance phase, then a learning phase. The two activities are completely intertwined.

Chunking applies to all subgoals. The mechanism is completely general. Indeed, the chunking mechanism works at the level of productions, not in terms of problem spaces and their function. For instance, it deals in impasse resolution, not success and failure, semantically defined. Hence, it learns both from experiences that succeed and those that fail. Since everything that Soar does occurs by means of subgoals, from the most complicated concerns to the most trivial selections, Soar can learn about all aspects of its performance. Every new activity that Soar engages in will first be encountered via an impasse, because it does not know how to proceed. It will then require problem solving in subgoals—perhaps extensive, perhaps slight. In all cases, it will chunk the results and thus will learn about them. Thus, Soar will learn how to implement operators, learn search control, learn about how to get new problem spaces, learn anything and everything that Soar sets up sub-goals for. Such a general description cannot be taken completely at face value—it is not obvious how well chunking will work. How-ever, we will see many demonstrations throughout the book that lend credence to this description.

That Soar can learn anything does not mean that Soar will learn everything. Soar learns only from what the system experiences. It is experience-based learning. Thus, the key question is, what will Soar experience? But this is essentially impossible to ascertain. What tasks will Soar attempt? This question has both an external and an internal aspect, or, better said, a macro aspect and a micro aspect. At the macrolevel, what tasks come Soar's way from the environment is both important and strongly influenced by aspects outside Soar, such as what task users feed to it. But how Soar takes these tasks and decomposes them into problem spaces (the mi-crolevel) is also important. The learning that finally occurs (the chunking) depends intimately on the microstructure of these spaces, which in turn depends on the knowledge that has been built up by all of the prior experience. Furthermore, these aspects feed back on each other, since the learning that occurs determines the spaces that occur subsequently. In sum, any theory of what Soar will learn must occur within a larger theory of the environments Soar inhabits, how tasks arise, and how they get defined—in short, a total theory of Soar as an agent in the world.

Figure 4-14 provides some feeling for what chunking achieves. The figure shows the problem space of the three-blocks world. Each point in the space represents a given configuration of three blocks. Blocks-world problems are to go from some initial configu-ration to some desired configuration. The blocks are labeled A, B, and C so it can be seen what blocks must move into what positions. There are effectively only three desired arrangements (heavy out-lined in the figure): three one-block stacks, one two-block stack and one one-block stack, and one three-block stack. All other arrange-ments differ only in their labeling; but the labels themselves are arbitrary, so we may use the desired arrangement to set the labels in a fixed way. Hence, all possible blocks-world problems can be given by picking any one of the 13 points in the space as the initial point and any of the 3 desired points as the goal state (hence there are only 3 × 13 = 39 distinct problems, including the 3 identity problems, out of the 13 × 13 = 169 problems defined as going from

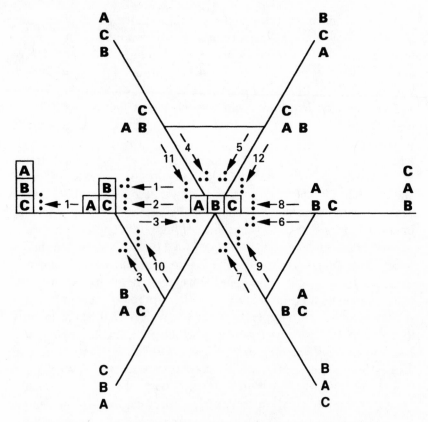

Figure 4-14. The twelve chunks that comprise learning
in the three-blocks world.

any point to any other point). There are correspondingly bushier
problem spaces for larger numbers of blocks, in which there would
be many 3-block subspaces.

As Soar does tasks in this space, it builds chunks. A chunk is
indicated by an arrow on the diagram with a little three-dot figure at
its head, which indicates the desired configuration. The chunk of
Figure 4-13 is chunk number 1. It occurs in two places, but consider
the one at the far left, pointing at the state $A/B/C$ (A on top of B on
top of C). It will be evoked at the state at its tail, the state $A,B/C$.
At that state there is a choice for which way to go. The chunk is a
search-control chunk that says that if the desired state is a stack of
three blocks ($A/B/C$) then go to the left, toward the desired configuration, although this configuration of course cannot be "seen"
from this state.

There are a total of twelve chunks in the figure; ten of them get evoked in only one situation, but two of them (chunks 1 and 3) get evoked in two. These twelve chunks completely learn the space, in that they let Soar move on a direct path from any state to any other state. The chunks do not depend on the actual labels used on the blocks, only on the relevant source-destination relations. Thus, if we consider tasks as they are actually encountered by the problem solver, these same chunks will actually be evoked in many different situations, and they will guide Soar on a direct route for any task.

These chunks will get built any time Soar passes through a choice point where the chunk will apply. For instance, in any task heading for $A/B/C$, Soar will finally arrive at $A,B/C$ and in taking the last step it will build chunk 1. Once built, the chunk will apply in all the other places and in any other task that passes this way. Thus we get a bird's-eye view of what transfer of learning means in this blocks world. Soar needs to accumulate the 12 chunks to learn the whole space, and it doesn't make any difference what set of tasks is used to learn these 12 chunks, as long as there is coverage. From the point of view of individual tasks, of course, the accumulation of chunks implies transfer of learning from one task to another.

Finally, it is useful to return to the preparation vs. deliberation trade-off space in Figure 2-19. Chunking, considered as a caching mechanism, is a general way for the system to walk up an isobar, continually shedding search and replacing it with more directly available knowledge, that is, with prepared patterns that can be recognized. As such, it provides a mechanism that satisfies the requirement analyzed in Chapter 3 for continually compressing the $\sim\sim 10$ sec level down toward the $\sim\sim 1$ sec level. Interestingly, there seems to be no corresponding uniform mechanism for moving down the isobar, giving up recognition knowledge and doing more search. As with caching, this picture would be satisfactory except for the possibility of transfer. The transfer of learning complicates the situation substantially. But it is still useful to think of chunking as a shift upward along the isobar.

4.3. The Total Cognitive System

We have now described the central cognitive structure of Soar (Figure 4-1): problem spaces, the recognition memory (production system), attribute-value representation, the decision cycle, preferences, impasses, subgoals, and chunking. This structure sits within a larger system that includes perception and motor behavior. We will call it the *total cognitive system,* not wishing to oppose cognition to perception and motor behavior. We need to describe this structure as well, for it is critical to a unified theory of cognition. Not even a simple stimulus-response arc can be treated without including perception, cognition, and motor behavior.

The treatment, at this point, of the total cognitive system will be brief and superficial. We need to keep our attention focused on central cognition, to understand it thoroughly. Thus, after embedding central cognition in the total system, we will immediately turn back for the rest of this chapter to illustrating and exploring the central mechanisms. The total cognitive system will get more attention again in Chapter 5, when we consider the complete arc from stimulus to response. Even then, however, the treatment will be limited. Operationally, Soar is still largely focused on central cognition. This is one respect in which Soar provides an imperfect exemplar for a unified theory of cognition, which demands a complete treatment of all parts of the mind.

The treatment of the total cognitive system will thus be largely theoretical and not backed up in detail by an operational Soar system. It is important to recognize both sides of this coin. On the one hand, a unified theory of cognition is a theory—a body of knowledge about the nature of the human mind. As with theories generally, it need only exist in written form as assertions about the mind. Thus, the sketch of the complete cognitive system below and in Chapter 5 is perfectly legitimate, and a certain amount of any unified theory of cognition will exist only in declarative form. On the other hand, for a system as complex as the mind, it is difficult to have much faith in a theory without having it instantiated in some operational form. This will be especially difficult as unification increases, making the relation of disparate aspects important. Consequently, though throughout the book I will continually put forth theoretical tendrils that extend beyond the operational core of Soar or modify it in various ways, I will always do so with a certain amount of diffidence and uncertainty about the nature of the theoretical ideas themselves (even apart from the relation of these ideas to the empirical phenomena they purport to explain).

Figure 4-15 shows the total cognitive system. We return to the view of Chapter 2 (Figure 2-1), that the mind is a controller of a dynamic system interacting with a dynamic external environment

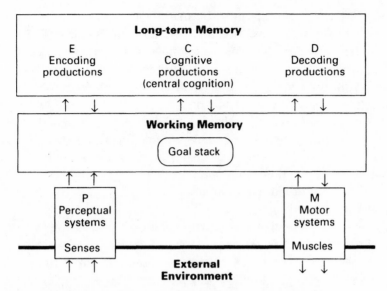

Figure 4-15. The total cognitive system: perception, cognition, and the motor system.

(located across the bottom of Figure 4-15). Much of the design of the total system is driven by requirements of this controller task. There must be some processes that transduce the energies in the environment into signals for the system. These are collectively called *perceptual systems (P)*, although they are tied down only on the sensory side (transduction from the environment). Similarly, there must be some processes that affect the environment, injecting, so to speak, the organism's energies into it. These are the *motor systems (M)*, although they are tied down only on the physical-action side. Because the environment is a dynamic system, producing a stream of unpredictable events, there must be a buffer memory, so that the cognitive system can get some temporal room for its own processing. This is the working memory—the same memory into which central cognition *(C)* works. Thus, the working memory becomes the communication device for all the components of the total system. It is a bus as well as a buffer.

This arrangement of working memory as bus and buffer is the simplest structural assumption, given the apparatus already in place for central cognition. However, this assumption is worth examining. The functional imperatives are that buffering must occur and that ultimately contact must be made with cognition. On the perceptual side, there could be other buffers embedded in *P*. *P* could put elements into some special memory and another special device could move them into the working memory. The figure is simply silent on this. One might think that cognition could perhaps examine directly such a structurally distinct buffer. But it is doubtful that this proposal differs from having productions with conditions that match working-memory elements with distinguishing tags, because productions are the only way cognition has of examining anything, and what productions examine is called working memory.

On the motor side, additional buffering could exist within *M*, to make information available to internal components of *M* at appropriate times. The figure is equally silent on this. However, motor actions could be *direct actions* of productions that went to such special motor memories, without ever showing up in the working memory. This direct-action scheme might seem simpler than the indirect one of Figure 4-15, where cognition puts elements in working memory to be communicated to the motor system. Indeed, almost all existing production systems (including Ops5) employ general right-hand side actions and not the indirect scheme. Direct action has a fatal flaw, however. It implies the possibility of *sudden death*. If a production containing a dangerous motor command (say, *kill thyself!*) were ever triggered, there would be no way to sense or revoke it. Motor commands, of course, affect the external world and, as such, are ultimately irreversible. So the question is what types of security are to be provided for such operations, not whether commitment can be avoided completely. Direct action implies that responsibility resides in the assurance that a sudden-death production will never be fired or will never be created. But this is untenable given the design of central cognition in Soar. For Soar, security resides in the decision cycle, which has been judiciously set up to provide protection against irreversible actions, including internal ones. The elaboration cycle is totally permissive, but it runs to quiescence precisely to permit whatever is known immediately to be brought to bear. The decision procedure is the watchguard to ensure that some rogue production producing a rogue action will at least have a chance of being sidelined. Thus, although on formal grounds direct motor action from production actions might be simpler, such a design is not admissible for Soar.

The total system consists of more than *P* to *C* to *M*. There is a set of productions called *encoding productions (E-productions)* and another set called *decoding productions (D-productions)*. These productions are identical in form and structure to the productions of central cognition (which can be called *C-productions* where needed). They differ in being entirely free of the goal context stack. For them there is no such thing as the decision cycle, running to quiescence, or impasses—they fire at will. In contradistinction, cognitive productions are tied to the goal context stack by the connectivity constraint. Each condition must either match a goal-context element or must match an element that links (perhaps through an explicit chain) to a goal-context element. Encoding and decoding productions are distinguished from each other only by the functions they perform.

On the input side, as elements arrive autonomously from the perceptual system, the encoding productions provide what can be termed perceptual parsing, putting the elements into a form to be considered by central cognition. Likewise on the output side, the decoding productions provide the expansion and translation of the motor commands produced by the cognitive system into the form used by the motor system. The motor system itself may provide elements back into the working memory, indicating the processes the motor system is undergoing as commands emerge into action. Such proprioceptive elements can themselves undergo perceptual parsing prior to consideration by cognition.

All this activity is not under control—these productions recognize and execute at will, concurrently with each other and concurrently with central cognition. Control is exercised by central cognition, which can now be seen to consist of just the decision apparatus, from which flows the decision cycle, impasses, the goal context stack, and the problem-space organization. Since there is not only the autonomous entry of elements into the working memory, but also a flurry of activity with the encoding and decoding productions, it can be seen that central cognition operates essentially as a form of supervisory control.

Central cognition is indeed serial—that is what the decision mechanism enforces—and so it can consider only some of what goes on in the working memory. Indeed, the functional requirement of the encoding productions is to shape up new arrivals so that the limited efforts of central cognition are well spent. In terms of the issue of sudden death mentioned above, motor actions take time to develop, from the decoding of the commands to the firing up of muscles. Central cognition can operate in supervisory control over these as well, using the products of decoding as well as whatever the motor system leaves in working memory (as elaborated by other encoding productions). Central cognition has a chance to issue new commands, providing mid-course corrections or aborting an action.

You might wonder why, in terms of this picture, the encoding productions cannot further elaborate the objects that central cognition is working on. But the answer is clear, for the productions that rain down during the elaboration phase are indistinguishable from encoding and decoding productions. That is, within an elaboration phase it is open season, and whatever productions of any kind that can fire will fire. The essential point is that the decision mechanism detects the quiescence of the products of cognitive productions as the signal to move into the decision phase and ignores the continuing pitter-patter (or torrent) of encoding and decoding.

The total cognitive system can be viewed either functionally or structurally. The top half of Figure 4-16 shows the functional view. In it, perception is really $P + E$. P is the sensory component and E is the perceptual encoding of it.[9] The motor system is really $D + M$. D is the decoding and local-control component and M is the actuator. Then C is a supervisory system. The bottom half of the figure shows the structural view. Here, P and M are composed of unspecified collections of mechanisms, quite different in some ways at least from the apparatus of cognition—it must transduce energy to representations, on the one side, and it must take real effortful actions, on the other. $E + C + D$ all are similar stuff, productions, distinguished by their content. The two diagrams group the components for the total system quite differently.

The importance of these two alternative views is revealed by an interesting hypothesis. It is a genuine hypothesis but it cannot yet be put to the test in Soar, because the total cognitive system is not yet fully developed operationally. The hypothesis concerns the

9. The temptation is strong to call the P module the *senses*, but the distinction between the senses and perception is so complexly grounded that the issues are impossible to disentangle and labeling as senses versus perception is best avoided. The interface between P and E (that is, what P delivers for E-productions to elaborate) is an essentially open issue at this point in terms of the Soar architecture.

In terms of function

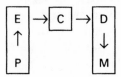

In terms of structure and learning

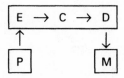

Figure 4-16. Two views of the total cognitive system.

genesis of encoding and decoding productions. The hypothesis claims they arise from chunking, just as do the productions of central cognition. After all, E-productions and D-productions are just productions. Why should they arise any differently from the way other productions arise, namely chunking? The only feature that distinguishes C-productions is that they are tied to the goal stack indirectly by the connectivity constraint.

Consider then a new chunk about to be built. It will be a C-production, if its conditions specify goal-context elements or specify links to linked elements. But if the implicit generalization involved in its creation abstracts away from the goal-context stack, then it could become some other kind of production, say an E-production or a D-production. What happens depends upon the abstraction that occurs when the chunk is created (by implicit generalization). This, in turn, depends on the details of the representation and the problem solving, as was emphasized in the discussion of chunking in Section 4.2. It is at least plausible that under the appropriate conditions, chunks will get free of the goal context and become free-floating E-productions and D-productions.[10] Many de-

10. Lest it be supposed this is unlikely, such extreme context-free productions already arise, although they usually indicate overgeneralization errors.

tails affect the issue, including aspects of the total system that will not be taken up until the next chapter, and some of the details apply only to perception or only to motor behavior. It is also possible that small refinements of the architecture will be discovered to make a large difference, so the hypothesis is not one that is pointed exactly at the current Soar architecture as cast-in-concrete. The importance of the hypothesis, if it were to prove out, is considerable. It provides at one stroke a theory of both perceptual and motor learning, and it defines how they relate to deliberate cognitive learning. The hypothesis is worth stating here because it highlights the integrated structure of the total Soar architecture.

We now put aside the total cognitive system and return to central cognition, in order to make sure its operation and scope are understood. From now on, however, the central cognitive mechanism should not be assumed to be floating in a vacuum—or forever lost in thought, as Guthrie would have it of Tolman's rats with their cognitive-maps (Guthrie, 1953). Rather, central cognition is the control structure of a behaving organism.

4.4. R1-Soar: Knowledge-Intensive and Knowledge-Lean Operation

Let us look at examples of how Soar behaves. The blocks world is a toy example that is useful for understanding the mechanics of how Soar operates, but it does not reveal much about whether these mechanisms constitute an intelligent system. The best examples to use are the tasks that have made the largest demands for intelligence. These come from the efforts to develop Soar as an AI system.

R1 (also called XCON) is an expert system developed by John McDermott at CMU jointly with Digital Equipment Corporation (McDermott, 1982). R1 has become one of the most commercially successful expert systems (Bachant & McDermott, 1984). Every Digital Vax computer has its order processed through R1, and this system sits at the center of a collection of expert systems at Digital that control and structure the sales and manufacture of Vax computers.

R1 takes as input the order that comes from the salesperson in conjunction with the customer ordering the Vax. R1 verifies that the order is correct, that is, consistent, and then it fills out the order. There are many things to be specified beyond the main items that the customer specifies, for example, cable lengths and power supplies. R1 lays out the components in cabinets and modules. Its output is a schematic that describes all of the details of the system and how it is to be assembled. In specifying this configuration, it takes into account large numbers of facts and considerations—the cost of components, the power demands, cable lengths, comparability constraints between components, and so on.

Configuring Vaxes is a good example of a knowledge-intensive task done relatively well by human experts. Anyone of reasonable intelligence, general technical education, and diligence can configure Vaxes. However, the person does have to know all about Vaxes and know about them in gritty detail. Given a lot of practice and access to the information on Vaxes in manuals, tables, production specs, and the Digital production organization, a person becomes skilled at the task. Even with reasonable familiarity, humans engage in some amount of search—of fiddling to find an appropriate configuration. Only with time does the skill build up and require hardly any search.

R1 is a good example of an AI expert (or knowledge-based) system that is capable of expert-level performance. R1, however, is not quite a typical expert system. Configuration is a simple type of design task, and most expert systems perform diagnostic tasks. Moreover, R1 is one of the largest expert systems. It comprised about 3,300 rules at the time of the Soar study (1984), with a data base of about 10,000 components, and has grown substantially since then.

R1-Soar was created early in Soar's career, as the first attempt to work with a realistic task (Rosenbloom, Laird, McDermott, Newell, & Orciuch, 1985; van de Brug, Rosenbloom, & Newell, 1986). R1-Soar does a substantial component of the Vax configuration task. It does not do it the same way that R1 does. The project was not to simulate R1 in Soar, but rather to use exactly the same knowledge, so that exactly the same configurations will be obtained, which maximizes the opportunity for learning from the comparison of R1-Soar with R1. R1-Soar provided about 25 percent of the total functionality of R1, mainly configuring the unibus, which was deemed to be the demanding part of R1. This is enough cover-

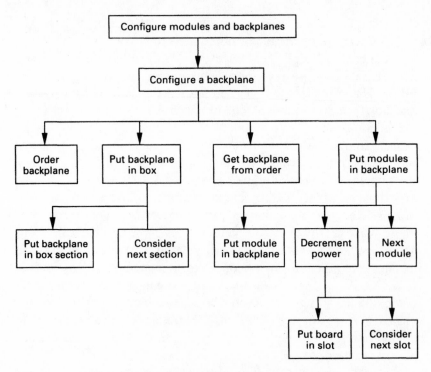

Figure 4-17. Operator implementation problem spaces
of R1-Soar (version 2).

age to provide assurance that all of R1's functionality could be
provided just for the expenditure of the requisite effort.[11]

Figure 4-17 gives the hierarchy of problem spaces of R1-Soar.
This structure comes from the second, more-complete version (van
de Brug, Rosenbloom, & Newell, 1986). These are the operator-
implementation spaces. Each one gets invoked when an operator in
another (higher) space is selected and cannot complete its task just
by the knowledge directly available (that is, in productions in the
higher space). Then a no-change impasse occurs and the appropriate space to do the processing for the operator is selected. This

11. A methodology called RIME (Bachant, 1988) has been developed at Digital in
which to produce a revision of R1. RIME adopts some task-structuring features of R1-
Soar, namely, problem spaces and some method schemes, although not impasses or
chunking. On the one hand, RIME provides some verification that the total R1 system
could be constructed along the lines of R1-Soar. On the other, the current R1/XCON
system at Digital has grown in size, functionality, maintainability, and modifiability, so
that the original R1-Soar now appears as a very modest part of the total system.

hierarchy corresponds to a standard subroutine hierarchy, in the sense that the knowledge of the system is captured in this collection of problem spaces. For instance, the top space in the figure is the space to do the total configuration task by configuring modules and backplanes. The operator to configure a backplane leads to the space by the same name. In that space the operator to put a backplane in the box might be evoked, or the operator to get a backplane from the order, or one of the other operators. Each space contains some knowledge about how to do part of the task.

R1 itself is realized in a relatively flat organization, typical of many expert systems. There is one substructure, called a context (not to be confused with the goal contexts of Soar), which essentially organizes a single subtask. Increasing the functionality of R1 occurs by adding more and more separate contexts and their associated rules from the global knowledge of a human expert (knowledge both of R1 and Vax configuration). The 3,300 rules involve a couple hundred such context situations. In the jargon of expert systems, R1 is a relatively *shallow* system, in which the rules are created as much as possible to reflect the expert's judgment of what ultimate useful actions should be, but the system is given no ability to reason about the task in terms of its structure.

In mapping R1 into R1-Soar, we moved to the opposite end of the scale, to a *deep* structure. We provided a set of basic spaces in which Soar could carry out the basic manipulations of the task of configuring computers. It was important to provide a formulation that would let Soar solve the same task as R1 by just searching around without any heuristic knowledge. It needed knowledge of the domain—these deep spaces. It also needed knowledge of the task—constraints on well-formed configurations and evaluation functions on different aspects of the configuration, such as costs, power limits, and the like. This deep formulation is not conceptually profound. It is essentially a blocks-like world of gross manipulation and connection—selecting containers, such as cabinets or backplanes, putting various objects into them, such as components and cables, and evaluating the result in terms of constraints and costs. It is an engineered, hence discrete and reliable, environment. Nevertheless, it is a formulation that has exactly the characteristics of the deep end of the shallow-deep task continuum in expert systems. Configurations can be constructed provisionally and evaluated.

	No learning	During learning	After learning
Base: no search-control knowledge	1731* [232]**	485 [+59]	7 [291]
Partial: two key search-control rules	243 [234]	111 [+14]	7 [248]
Full: search control equivalent to R1's	150 [242]	90 [+12]	7 [254]

* decision cycles
**[number of rules]

Figure 4-18. Performance and learning by R1-Soar (adapted from Laird, Newell, & Rosenbloom, 1987).

Figure 4-18 shows the behavior of R1-Soar on a small configuration task. Consider the No-learning column. The *base* system is the one without any heuristic search control at all, just the basic definition of the task in terms of spaces with their operators, plus the evaluation functions. Soar obtains the configuration in 1,731 decision cycles, essentially by hill-climbing search with some backup. Analysis of this performance (by humans) leads to proposing two productions of search-control knowledge, which can then be added to create the *partial* system. With these two additional productions, R1-Soar can attain the configuration in only 243 decision cycles (attaining the identical final configuration). Adding 8 more search-control productions gives R1-Soar exactly the same knowledge as R1, to create the *full* system. We were working from the actual set of R1 productions, so the characterization of having "exactly the same knowledge as R1" is reasonably grounded. At this point, R1-Soar can attain the same configuration in 150 decision cycles (bottom left number). It moves directly from the order to the confirmation without search, much as R1 does. The factor of ~10 from 1,731 decision cycles to 150 gives an indication of the value of the search-control knowledge embodied in R1.

The No-learning column demonstrates three things. First, it shows that Soar can work on modest-size tasks. Vax configuration is not a huge task, but it is a real task.[12] Second, it shows that Soar

12. This run is on a small task and with the initial version of R1-Soar, which covered only ~15 percent of R1. The second version covered ~25 percent and was run on a batch of 15 normal-size tasks; see Laird, Newell, and Rosenbloom (1987) for a table of the data.

can behave like a knowledge-intensive system. There is an oft-expressed dichotomy in the expert-systems field, with knowledge-extensive systems on one side and knowledge-learn (or general problem-solving) systems on the other (Chandrasekaran & Mittal, 1983; Hart, 1982). Soar, as it comes from the factory, so to speak, is in the general problem-solver mold. Thus, it is of interest that it can also behave like a knowledge-intensive system. Third, the left-hand column shows that Soar can move smoothly from one type of problem solver (at the top) to the other (at the bottom), just by adding productions. Soar is capable of intermixing general problem-solving and knowledge-intensive behavior, depending on the occasion. These three points might all have been apparent just from an examination of Soar's structure; but their empirical demonstration is nevertheless welcome. Besides these demonstrations, it is interesting that the number of rules is relatively small, both in total size (242 for the R1-Soar equivalent) and in the small increments to take Soar from the base system to the full system (adding just 10 productions). The R1 system, to which this version of R1-Soar is equivalent, is about 500 rules.

In moving down the left-hand column, Soar is actually walking back up along an isobar in the preparation vs. deliberation space in Figure 2-19. It starts by taking 1,731 decision cycles with 232 rules' worth of immediately available knowledge. Then it moves to taking 243 decision cycles with 234 rules' worth of knowledge. Finally, it takes only 150 decision cycles with 242 rules. In all cases the system performs exactly the same task, so it is indeed traversing an isobar. Thus, a diagram like that in Figure 2-19 is more than just a conceptual device; it is possible, at least sometimes, actually to locate and plot systems on it.

Next is the question of learning. When the R1-Soar effort started, Soar was not capable of chunking, which had not been part of the initial design. However, by the time R1-Soar was operational, it had been discovered that chunking could be realized in Soar (Laird, Rosenbloom, & Newell, 1984). What, then, will Soar do with this task if chunking is turned on, starting from the base system (which took 1,731 decision cycles)? The top row gives the data. What happens is something of a surprise, especially to psychologists who are used to pretest/posttest learning designs. The middle column is called During learning, because it measures the performance with learning turned on. As Soar starts this task, it is exactly the base system. Then it begins to build chunks and these chunks are actually utilized before Soar finishes this first configuration. Instead of taking 1,731 decision cycles, R1-Soar takes only 485 decision cycles, a substantial decrease. That is, there is *within-trial transfer*. Soar learned 59 productions during this run.

Figure 4-18 shows the data for a single task. Consequently, if a standard posttest is performed after finishing up the learning trial, we find that Soar has learned everything it can and now takes only 7 decision cycles (the After-learning column). These are just the moves at the very top level, which cannot be chunked because they did not occur in response to impasses higher up. The other two rows in the figure correspond to the top row, except with different starting points. They show that, if the system is primed with some other productions (here produced by hand), then chunking still provides additional within-trial transfer. In all cases, the learning is complete in a single trial, ending up with the same 7 decision cycles. Even if, in the bottom row, the system is primed with all the knowledge that was in R1, it still becomes faster with learning. The gains gradually diminish with the amount of priming, from 72 percent to 54 percent to 40 percent, but that is to be expected.

That R1-Soar learns completely in a single trial seems a bit odd for a task as complex as configuring Vaxes. There is a reason for such speed, and it comports well with theories about human learning. The theory of chunking in human cognition (as described briefly in Chapter 1) has the human continually constructing chunks that are symbolized groups of the symbols that are available in immediate experience. The chunks then become available in immediate experience at a later time, to build up yet additional chunks. Thus, the chunk hierarchy builds up one level at a time by multiple experiences through the same part of the world. Soar, however, learns chunks at all levels simultaneously. It can do so because it can keep the memory of the antecedent conditions for each impasse until that impasse is resolved. This could require an indefinitely long delay, with a consequent requirement for large amounts of intermediate memory. Soar can also run with what is called *bottom-up* chunking, which creates chunks only for impasses that have no subimpasses—no chunking occurs if anything interrupts the learning experience. This scheme requires little short-term memory but requires multiple trials to learn the full behavior.

The two learning columns of Figure 4-18 show two things. First, they show that Soar can become knowledge-intensive by chunking, that is, by learning. This learning occurs in a reasonably complex nontoy task. We cannot see from the figure exactly what is learned by the chunks, although it is evident that it takes many chunks to equal the couple of manually contrived productions. Second, problem solving and learning intertwine. Given a system that always ran with chunking, analogously to the way humans learn continuously from experience, there would be continual instantaneous feedforward from chunking to the immediately following performance. Thus we are led to describe within-trial transfer in contradistinction to the usual between-trials transfer. Within-trial transfer seldom shows up in psychological studies, because there is no convenient way to obtain the baseline of behavior without learning required for the comparison. Human learning cannot be turned off.

R1-Soar provides a nice demonstration of many characteristics of Soar, with respect to both performance and learning. However, this is a typical AI-oriented analysis, which uses expert systems to provide the basis of the significance of various aspects of the system. We need to reflect on what this example means for a unified theory of cognition. Soar is a model of the human cognitive architecture— that is, it embodies the theory. A central prediction of any such theory is that humans can behave intelligently. The only way we know to get this prediction from a theory is to show concretely that a system designed according to the theory (Soar) behaves intelligently. If one had an independently established theory of what mechanisms are sufficient for intelligence, then various alternative demonstrations might be available to show that a proposed unified theory predicted intelligent behavior. But no such theory is in sight and it is not clear what one would be like. Thus, we must demonstrate directly the sufficiency of these mechanisms to produce general intelligent behavior. It is important that this demonstration show as much intelligent capability as possible. Doing some small toy task, such as moving blocks around on a table, no longer suffices. We know many ways of doing such tasks that are not convincing as demonstrations of intelligence in more general and difficult situations (although we understand fairly well the kernel of truth they contain). Soar needs to be able to work on real tasks, and indeed on a variety of real tasks. R1-Soar makes a positive contribution in this direction.

4.5. Designer-Soar: Difficult Intellectual Tasks

Let's consider another example of Soar behavior, also in the direction of substantial intelligence but somewhat different from R1-Soar. The system is called *Designer-Soar* (Steier, 1989). Its task is to design algorithms. This is an intellectual task, taught in advanced undergraduate courses in computer science (Sedgewick, 1983). A simple example task would be to design an algorithm to find if an element is a member of a given set. A somewhat more difficult task would be to design an algorithm to sort a set of numbers in ascending order. That is, if the input were the numbers (5, 8, 6, 3, 7, 3, 2) then the sorting algorithm should produce (2, 3, 3, 5, 6, 7, 8). The task for the problem solver is not to sort these particular numbers, or even to be able to sort any given sequence of numbers. The task is to find an algorithm—the essential steps of a program or procedure—that will sort any sequence of numbers.

Designer-Soar is the work of David Steier. It has its roots in two earlier non-Soar AI systems to design algorithms. One was Designer, developed by Elaine Kant, David Steier, and myself a few years ago (Kant & Newell, 1983; Steier & Kant, 1985). The other was Cypress, developed by Doug Smith (Smith, 1985). Versions of Soar were created for each of the systems (see Steier, 1987, for Cypress-Soar). The current Designer-Soar (Steier & Newell, 1988; Steier, 1989) is a successor that amalgamates a number of important features of both these systems.[13]

There are interesting issues about how to formulate the task of algorithm design. The first issue is, What is desired? An algorithm, in contrast to an actual computer program, provides only the essential steps that have to be done. Given an algorithm, a program must still be written in a specific programming language (Lisp or Pascal); but the general plan is now available. Thus, whereas the task of programming has a well-specified desired object (the code), algorithm design does not. Still, an algorithm must be cast in some representation. There is no consensus in computer science about what this must be, largely because the desired result really is the knowledge on the part of the designer about how to proceed, which could be represented in many different ways. The issue is analogous to what is desired when a person reads a paragraph to com-

---

13. In the spring of 1987, when I gave the William James Lectures, I discussed these earlier systems; the current Designer-Soar was created in summer 1987.

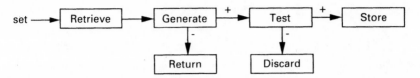

Figure 4-19. Subset-test algorithm.

prehend it. In any event, Designer-Soar uses a very general set of functional operations: *generate, select, test, retrieve, store* (put in memory), *discard* (ignore the item), *apply* (an operation), and *return* the result at the end of the algorithm. To have an algorithm is to have a procedure described in terms of these operators. Figure 4-19 gives the algorithm for finding the subset of positive elements of a set of numbers (the *subset-test*). This is about the simplest example of algorithm design that can be imagined.

The second issue is, What is given? Here matters are even more problematic. In fact, the issue is also problematic for the tasks of programming or coding, where the desired result can be clearly stated. What is given when a person goes to construct a program? The studies in AI and theoretical computer science have been extremely varied on this score, from input/output specifications in some formal language, to sets of input/output examples, to sets of specific program traces, to generic programs that are to be transformed to more efficient ones. Each type of givens sets a different task.

An important distinction is whether a designer already basically understands the process for which the algorithm is being sought. No human ever designs an algorithm for testing a subset without already knowing what the test is and indeed knowing how to test for the subset if given a specific input. The task of the algorithm designer is how to express this knowledge in terms of an explicit algorithm, rather than simply to have it as a cognitive skill. This distinction is not observed in AI efforts on automatic programming or on algorithm discovery, since the systems are never taken to be repositories of substantial preexisting knowledge. Consequently the AI systems really work on a dual task—to discover how to test for a subset and to discover an algorithm to test for a subset. Soar takes as given a knowledge of how to test a subset. This is expressed as a *task-domain* problem space with a set of basic operators for manipulating sequences plus search control for selecting them to do the subset test.

To design such an algorithm, Soar must cast it as search in a problem space. Soar is trying to find a conditional sequence of operations (Figure 4-19). To find such a thing requires a problem space of partial algorithms—fragments and parts of Figure 4-19. The initial state is the null algorithm (no algorithm at all) and a desired state would be the algorithm of the figure (verified to find the subset of positive items in a set). The operators would construct, modify, and combine fragments of algorithms. Both Designer and Cypress formulated the task this way, and so did the Soar systems based on them.

However, there is another option. This takes the abstract operations of the algorithm—generate, test, and the rest—as the operators of a space. The states of this space are partially tested sets of items. The initial state is the initial set and the desired state is the set fully tested. If a sequence of operators can be applied to the initial state to produce the desired state, then that sequence certainly provides a way of testing the set. If Soar chose the operators because of the particular items in the initial state, then Soar would just have done a particular test. But if the states represent a general set of items, and Soar is still able to test it, then the sequence of operators that it goes through must be a general algorithm. Of course, no simple preset sequence of operators will suffice. There must be conditionals, which is what algorithms are all about, namely, specifying conditional steps on the basis of the actual data already input. In fact, general operators, such as test and compare, actually don't do anything to a set of items, they just acquire information about it on which to base decisions of what operations to apply later. Thus, the actual states of this space are not just partially tested subsets of items; they also have a representation of what is known about the subset. That is, the items are augmented with assertions about their status or what prior operations have been performed on them—knowledge on which to base the decision of what operation to apply next.

Designer-Soar uses this second option. It might seem a little arcane, as described, but it is a very common strategy both for humans and for AI systems. For instance, consider theorem proving in logic, for which many computer programs have been built (Loveland, 1978). If the task is to find a proof, then the natural problem space to work in is that of proofs. The initial state is the null proof and a desired state is a fully written-out proof—precisely analogous to the problem space used by Designer and Cypress. But hardly any theorem provers do that. Instead, they use the second option. They start with the premises or axioms and apply valid inference rules as they try to reach the to-be-proved theorem.[14] What they really desire is the successful sequence of steps taken, not the final state reached. Just as in our second option, the final structure is not a simple sequence but a tree or network. I have called this the *element strategy* (Newell, 1983), since it takes the states of the space to be elements rather than sequences or networks of elements.

Figure 4-20 shows a high-level trace of Designer-Soar on the subset test. Designer-Soar prints out a preformed message whenever it does various critical things. Much information is suppressed, but it lets us focus on the way Designer-Soar goes about its problem solving. Designer-Soar starts by requesting the problem and then simply printing it back out (decision cycle 2, or dc 2). It first attempts to go through the problem completely symbolically, that is, assuming a symbolic input and operating on it by its general operators. It manages to retrieve the input set and then gets stuck because there is nothing specific enough to select the next thing to do (dc 106). *Retrieve* is one of the generalized functional operators, which will become components of the algorithm, so it is printed in boldface. In the course of evaluating which alternative to choose, it considers *generate* and then *test* (dc 112, dc 118), which appears (to it) to satisfy the specs. All of this has been done entirely symbolically on an input about which it knows only what the specs tell it, namely that it is a set of integers. It avoids doing any actual computation by abstracting away from the values of generate and test and considering only the types of their inputs and outputs (Unruh, Rosenbloom, & Laird, 1987). What this abstract evaluation process yields is a plan, since Soar knows it has abstracted the situation and now must do it in full detail (dc 158).

Returning from the evaluation, Soar proceeds to generate one integer from the set and then to test it (dc 162), still symbolically.

---

14. So-called refutation-formulations, such as Resolution, seek to find a contradiction, rather than the desired theorem; but it all comes to the same thing as far as these two different types of formulations are concerned (Loveland, 1978).

dc 2. What's your problem?   Subset
      3. The specification is:
         The input to the algorithm is a set of integers, and the output is
         the largest subset of the input set whose elements are all positive.
     17. A general solution is: [symbolic execution]
     21. **Retrieve** the input   [consult spec]
    103. A set of integers
    106. What's next?   [tie impasse]
    111. Let's try to do this: [evaluate]
    112. **Generate** one integer in the set
    118. **Test** if it is member-of-output-set   [consult spec]
    158. The plan looks good
    160. **Generate** one integer in the set   [symbolic execution]
    162. **Test** if it is member-of-output-set
    172. But how do I implement this test?
    173. Run it on some sample input   [test-case execution]
    177. **Retrieve** the input
    250. A set of size 2 with elements 1,0
    252. **Generate** one integer in the set
    261. The order to generate items is arbitrary
    261. The value of the item generated is 1
    266. **Test** if it is member-of-output-set
    277. Implemented as a test for it being positive   [test in domain]
    278. The test returns true
    280. **Store** the item in output
    301. Go again   [test-case execution]

Figure 4-20. High-level trace of Designer-Soar on subset test.

Now, it must actually do the test. Not only is nothing specific
known about the value of the symbolic element, but nothing specific is known about the test. Soar recognizes this problem (dc 172)
and knows to try a specific case (dc 173). It starts over again by
retrieving the input (dc 177), but now it determines a case using the
heuristic of the simplest case that is not degenerate—a set of size 2
(not size 1) with elements 0 and 1, selected from the beginning of
the integers (dc 250). Now, when it generates an element, it can
actually pick one, which turns out to be 1 (dc 261). When it applies
the test to it, it can see from the specs that the test should be that
the element is positive. Soar knows this test from its domain knowledge, so it can implement the functional test in the algorithm with
the domain test (dc 277). But even more, it knows the result of the
test to be true (dc 278). At that point it can see from the spec that it

302. **Retrieve** the input
303. A set of size 2 with elements 1,0
305. **Generate** one integer in the set
305. The order to generate items is arbitrary
313. The value of the item generated is 0
317. **Test** if it is member-of-output-set
317. Implemented as a test for it being positive   [test in domain]
328. The test returns false
330. **Discard** the item
331. Go again   [test-case execution]
332. **Retrieve** the input
333. A set of size 2 with elements 1,0
335. **Generate** one integer in the set
335. The order to generate items is arbitrary
335. There are no items left to generate
336. **Return** the result
336. A set, with elements 1
337. And we've got the answer
343. But did I get all the cases?   [test-case execution]
349. We've looked at cases where the generator in step 2 can generate elements and where it is finished.
351. We've looked at cases where the test for member-of-output-set in step 3 returns true and where it returns false.
354. Looks as if all the cases have been considered
357. So we're done with this problem
358. Goal design-algorithm achieved

Figure 4-20 (continued).

---

needs to store that element in the output set (dc 280). This store operation was not in the plan, which was just to generate and test, because the evaluation did not require looking further in advance to decide the actual next step.

The store operator completes the computation. But the knowledge about using test cases includes the fact that no single test case can establish a complete algorithm. Therefore Soar begins all over again (dc 301). It retrieves an input, gets the same test case, and generates an element. An additional part of the knowledge about using test cases is to make a different choice if one is possible, so it generates the item 0 (as opposed to 1, which it looked at first). Soar applies the test of membership and gets false (0 is not a positive integer). It can see from the specs that this item is not part of the result, hence is to be discarded. This ends the third pass through the task, one symbolic execution and two test-case executions. Soar follows the same path repeatedly—retrieve, generate, test—because it has learned search control for doing this, not because it has a data structure that it follows. This was true even of the plan it developed originally, which is remembered as what steps to prefer under what conditions, not as a declarative plan.

Soar (dc 331 to dc 335) repeats the behavior of (dc 301 to dc 305), retrieving the input and generating an element. By now it has looked at all members of the input set (both of them), hence can return the result (dc 336 to dc 337). This completes the computation, but Soar was doing this computation to obtain an algorithm. The criterion for the latter is that all the potential places in the existing algorithm where branches could occur have been investigated. It knows to do this (dc 343), proceeds to do so (dc 349 and dc 351), and concludes that there is nothing more to be covered (dc 354). Thus, it concludes that the algorithm has been designed (dc 358). In fact, this is not a proof of the correctness of the algorithm, for in general one cannot verify an algorithm by examining a finite set of specific cases.

As we have said, Soar learns on whatever it does. So we should expect some learning as it attempts to design algorithms. Figure 4-21 gives a summary picture of two pairs of algorithms: a pair of simple ones, *find the subset of positive elements of a set* (the latter being the one used for illustration) and *find the intersection of two sets,* and a pair that is slightly more complex, *merge sort* and *insertion sort.* In each case, one member of the pair was done and then the other. For each pair, the upper line is the behavior (total decision cycles) without learning, and the two lower lines show the behavior with learning.

Consider first the lower learning line (*all goals*). Both pairs tell the same story. There is within-trial learning from the beginning of each task to the end of it. There is also between-trial learning from the first member of the pair to the second. This can be seen most easily in the bottom graph showing the sort routines. If there was no transfer from doing the insertion sort to the merge sort, there would be only the within-trial transfer for the merge sort. This should produce a curve that was just barely steeper than the learning curve for insertion sort, corresponding to the fact that the no-learning curve is barely steeper. Instead, the learning curve for merge-sort is actually flatter, showing the effect of the between-trial

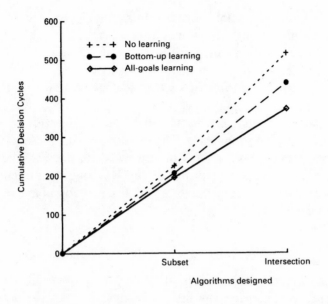

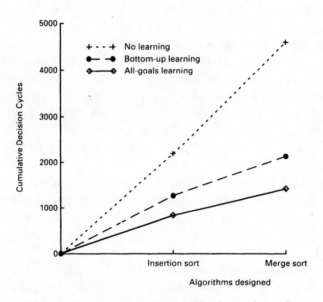

Figure 4-21. Learning and transfer in Designer-Soar.

transfer. One might conjecture that this effect is really just a slightly larger within-trial effect for merge sort—after all, the amount of within-trial transfer varies for different tasks. But a direct check of the amount of within-trial transfer on a run of merge sort in isolation (the appropriate control) shows the effect to be real.

The second learning curve (*bottom up*), shows what happens when Soar chunks only if the goal has no impasses—in other words, is at the bottom level. The learning is less, as shown by the fact that the curve is higher. But otherwise the story is the same. If the task was repeated with bottom-up learning, then eventually it would arrive at the same place as with learning for all impasses on a single trial.

4.6. Soar as an Intelligent System

We have seen examples of Soar's behavior on two different tasks requiring intelligence. The first, configuring Vaxes, is knowledge-intensive but moderately routine. The second, designing algorithms, is more difficult intellectually, although it too required substantial knowledge. The two corresponding systems, R1-Soar and Designer-Soar, consist of the Soar architecture plus the various problem spaces and search control. One should think of these two versions being added together to make a single Soar system with the knowledge of the two tasks. They are kept separate simply because they are worked on by separate investigators at different times. Indeed, the knowledge of the two domains of sorting and sets by Designer-Soar is an example of such a combined system. There is, of course, communality between the two algorithm design tasks. They used some of the same spaces, such as the algorithm space. But a truer measure of their communality might be the transfer of the learning from one to the other, which hardly existed in this case (only 1 percent).

We have used these two tasks to provide evidence that Soar, as our exemplar unified theory of cognition, predicts that humans will be intelligent. Of course, the architecture by itself does not exhibit intelligence. It must be augmented with knowledge, represented in the form of problem spaces and associated search control. This is exactly what we've done by providing Soar with the appropriate problem spaces.

One swallow, even two, does not make a summer. Thus, it is

Many small and modest tasks (21), many methods (19)
Eight Puzzle, Tower of Hanoi, Waltz Labeling
Dypar (NL parsing), Version spaces, Resolution theorem proving
Generate & test, Hill climbing, Means-ends analysis
Constraint propagation

Larger tasks
R1-Soar: 3300 rule industrial expert system (25%)
Designer-Soar: algorithm discovery (also Cypress-Soar)
Neomycin-Soar: revision of Mycin
Merl-Soar: production scheduling of replacement windshields

Learning (chunking)
Learns on all tasks it performs
• Learns search control, operators, problem spaces
• Improves with practice, transfers to other tasks
Explanation-based generalization
Abstraction planning (by chunking)
Constraint compilation (by chunking)

Interaction with external world
Acquires new tasks from external specs (by chunking)
Takes guidance (by chunking)
Robo-Soar: simple robot controller of a Puma arm with vision system

Figure 4-22. Summary of tasks accomplished by Soar.

useful to provide a summary of the things that have been done with Soar (Figure 4-22). Each one helps to flesh out the evidence that Soar is capable of general intelligent action.

First, Soar has done just about all the toy problems that have become the stock in trade of AI: Tower of Hanoi, Missionaries and Cannibals, the Eight Puzzle, and many more. In doing these tasks it has exhibited just about all the different methods that have been important enough in AI to have acquired names, like hill climbing and means-ends analysis. It has often used multiple methods on the same task and the same method on multiple tasks—just what might be expected. Soar has done a few modest-sized tasks, such as forms of parsing like Dypar-Soar (Boggs & Carbonell, 1983) and version spaces (Mitchell, 1978), a scheme for learning concepts. Soar has done a few large tasks. Besides R1-Soar and Designer-Soar, which have been discussed, there is also Neomycin-Soar (Washington & Rosenbloom, 1988). Mycin is a system that does medical diagnosis; it is one of the granddaddy expert systems (Shortliffe, 1976). Bill Clancey built a revised and much rationalized version called Neomycin (Clancey & Letsinger, 1981), in order to use the knowledge in Mycin in an intelligent tutoring context. Neomycin-Soar attempts to do exactly the task of Neomycin with exactly the same knowledge, so that, as with R1-Soar, we can learn as much as possible from the comparison of the two systems.

With respect to learning, summarizing by specific task does not make sense, since Soar learns in all the tasks it performs. But it does learn the different components of its own internal structure—operator selection, search control, operator implementations, new operators, problem spaces. Soar provides a form of *explanation-based generalization* (Mitchell, Keller, & Kedar-Cabelli, 1986), which means it learns from examining single cases, analyzing the behavior in detail, and using an underlying theory of the domain to derive some heuristics from the case that can be helpful in later problem solving (Rosenbloom & Laird, 1986). Soar does other forms of learning, but these will be discussed more in Chapter 6 on learning, memory, and skill. Soar does a simple form of abstraction planning, also using chunking (Unruh, Rosenbloom, & Laird, 1987; Unruh & Rosenbloom, 1989). In evaluating an operator, pursuant to resolving a tie impasse, it abstracts away from various aspects of the situation that keep the operator from being applicable, thus letting its look-ahead evaluation proceed. As it does so, it builds chunks (automatically, of course, because it is always chunking). These chunks can transfer to the fully detailed situation to help make selections. Compared with the usual form of abstraction planning (Sacerdoti, 1974), Soar is not making deliberate decisions to plan—it plans automatically just by the decision to abstract. Furthermore, it is not making any deliberate decisions to implement a plan—the chunks simply get evoked in the appropriate context.

The effort to use Soar for constraint compilation provides an interesting point. Recently, programming languages have been developed that make use of constraint propagation. Much of this work was pioneered by Gerald Sussman at the MIT AI Laboratory, and a particularly useful point of reference is Guy Steele's thesis from that group (Steele, 1980). From the standpoint of a programming language, the user simply writes down a set of constraints and the system compiles code to produce the values of the variables that satisfy the constraints. Soar can be given the knowledge about constraint propagation so that it can solve a constraint-propagation problem.[15] If the problem is approached with the right formulation, then the chunks that Soar creates are the equivalent of a deliberately coded constraint compiler. That is, if one takes productions to be the target language into which the compiler works, then the productions produced by chunking, given the experience of solving the constraint problem, are exactly the productions that should be produced by such a compiler. The point is that chunking is emerging as a powerful and natural way to convert experience into future capability.

The last item in Figure 4-22 is interacting with the external world, which we have glossed over—how Soar acquires tasks, how it affects the world, how it gets feedback, and so on. In describing the total cognitive system (Figure 4-15), we discussed the underlying architecture for interaction with the external world. But there must also be substantial knowledge about how to accomplish the interaction collected in problem spaces. Soar can take outside guidance by using chunking (Golding, Rosenbloom, & Laird, 1987), requesting some information from an external user that will help it make a choice, and then incorporating that information into itself by chunking. There is also a version of Soar, TAQ-Soar, that takes external specifications of a task and builds the internal problem spaces required to perform that task (Yost, 1988). It interprets the input language, creates internal representations of what the expressions mean, and then by executing the task interpretively creates the chunks that implement these spaces, just as if some person had written down the productions directly (which is how most Soar systems have been constructed up to now). We will see more of TAQ later. Finally, a recent version of Soar, Robo-Soar, does a simple robotic task, viewing an external set of blocks with a TV camera and giving commands to a Puma arm to move the blocks (Laird, Yager, Tuck, & Hucka, 1989). The vision and robot-arm software are the *P* and *M* modules (Figure 4-15) that communicate with central cognition via working memory. The main point for us here in these systems is that interfacing with the external world is something that Soar performs, just as it performs other tasks.

Thus, there is considerable evidence that Soar can exhibit intelligent behavior. The evidence is as good as is available in AI at the

---

15. This is work by Olin Shivers.

moment, for Soar is a state-of-the-art AI system, and indeed it is breaking new ground in its integration of learning and problem solving. However, there is much that AI still has to discover about mechanisms of intelligence and much that it has to demonstrate about how they combine to produce intelligent action on complex and difficult tasks. Thus, the demonstration that Soar can exhibit intelligence is only as good as the current state of the art. Indeed, this question must be re-asked continually as AI advances—Soar must keep up with the art, if we are to be able to assert that it predicts that humans are intelligent, according to an increasingly improving view of the nature of intelligence.

Our technique so far to understand Soar as an architecture for intelligence has been to look at its behavior on a sample of tasks. In Chapter 2, we arrived at a definition of intelligence as the degree of approximation of a symbol-level system to a knowledge-level system. Thus, we should also examine how well Soar approximates a knowledge-level system.

The definition of a knowledge system, with its multiform relations between specific goals, specific actions, and specific knowledge linking actions to goals, shows that no general metric can exist for the degree of approximation, whether a single number or a fixed vector of numbers. However, the mechanisms in Soar can be examined to see how they bring Soar closer to a knowledge-level system or, conversely, put barriers in its way.

To start, Soar is computationally universal. This is certainly a necessary characteristic, but it is hardly of singular notice, being shared by many systems that do not otherwise seem useful models of general intelligence. As Figure 1-7 made clear, universality does not address constraints other than flexibility and symbolic capability. In particular, it does not address real-time constraints. However, production systems are a direct attempt to deal with the real-time constraint. They make Soar a recognition problem solver that attempts to bring all its information out as quickly as possible. Chunking is part of this attempt to deal with the real-time constraint by continually shifting more knowledge to recognition. It is applicable in all situations; this flexibility flows from the uniform use of problem spaces and impasses, which is a necessary condition to being able to approximate the knowledge level.

The lack of a fixed mechanism for conflict resolution is strongly related to approximating the knowledge level. Its advantage can be seen by reflecting on the conflict resolution scheme of Ops5, which Soar abandoned. The Ops5 conflict resolution is a fixed mechanism, which always controls what productions to fire, which has only fixed knowledge (prefer a production that instantiates more recent elements, prefer a production that is a special case of another), and from which there is no recourse if its knowledge is inadequate. But its knowledge is only heuristic and thus when it fails (as it must in some situations) Soar cannot possibly operate like a knowledge-level system, even if the knowledge is encoded elsewhere in the system. Soar abandons the fixed conflict-resolution mechanism and thus keeps itself free to move toward a closer approximation to the knowledge level. It does not, of course, abandon conflict resolution. The decision structure of Soar is the conflict-resolution mechanism. The impasses are the conflicts and setting up the subgoal initiates the process of conflict resolution. Setting subgoals is not like evoking a fixed mechanism, because all of Soar's knowledge and problem solving can be brought to bear to resolve a conflict.

This discussion reveals a major criterion for attaining a knowledge-level system: no *trap-state mechanisms* are allowed. Anytime a system has a mechanism that is both local (contained within a small region of the system) and whose result must be accepted, then a fixed gap has been created between the system and the knowledge level. For the mechanism itself can (by assumption) only be a source of a finite amount of knowledge; and when that knowledge fails (as it must, if the tasks are diverse enough) there is no recourse (also by assumption). Thus the system is trapped in its state of knowledge, even if the knowledge exists elsewhere in the system. Our example was the fixed conflict resolution, but there are many others, such as fixed Lisp functions to perform operator selection or to determine the order in which operators are to be applied.

Within the decision process, productions are allowed to run to quiescence, as opposed to taking only a single cycle or terminating after a fixed number of cycles. This design feature is clearly a response to obtaining all the information that is immediately available. Impasses are a device for preventing the system from operating short of its full knowledge. They are the device that detects that the immediately available knowledge is not sufficient and thus keeps the system open to attempts to extract other knowledge available through symbolic manipulations (that is through deliberation). They keep the production system itself from being a trap-state mechanism. These two mechanisms cannot assure that all the knowledge available in Soar is brought forth, only that there is not some local mechanism that precludes it.

In sum, the mechanisms of Soar can be viewed in terms of their specific functional contribution to bringing the system close to a knowledge-level system, especially if one expands the view to include constraints of real time as well as completeness.

The picture this discussion paints is of a system that tends continuously to move in the right direction. We know that no form of system could actually be a knowledge-level system over any reasonably rich set of knowledge and goals. So the fact that Soar only approaches such a state is acceptable. However, we do not have any proof that no trap-state mechanisms exist in Soar. Indeed, since chunking adds productions permanently, the behavior of Soar under the impress of bad chunks could constitute some form of trap state. Moreover, this analysis provides no information on the rate of convergence or whether there are alternative mechanisms and arrangements that would converge faster or more uniformly.

There are aspects of Soar whose relation to knowledge-level approximation is unclear. For instance, Soar's knowledge resides in a large collection of problem spaces. How is this knowledge shared among spaces? Also, what of memory-resource sharing? Do many spaces have essentially the same knowledge, so there is really redundant coding? Transfer of knowledge between problem spaces is a related, open issue. Chunking in Soar is a transfer mechanism, as we have seen in the implicit generalization of chunks. Perhaps the full answer is already contained within the chunking mechanism, if we could ferret it out. What of the universality of chunking? How far does it reach? If other learning mechanisms are needed, then the Soar system as it stands must have places where it cannot adapt. This issue of the universality of chunking—the sufficiency of chunking for all learning in Soar—is an issue of contention within the machine-learning field. We who have built Soar believe the hypothesis is a good bet, though many scientists in machine learning believe it is not credible.

4.7. Mapping Soar onto Human Cognition

We now need to map Soar onto the human cognitive architecture. According to the familiar axiomatic view, a theory exists as an abstract symbol structure independent of the domain it purports to describe. It needs to be completed by a set of identifications, and there may be many ways in which such identifications might occur. Indeed, the long-standing practice in cognition has been generally to treat theories of cognition as relatively autonomous with respect to their neural realization. In any event, describing Soar as a distinct system with AI roots creates the need for an identification of the features of the Soar architecture with those of the human cognitive architecture.

Given the development so far, it should simply be an exercise for the reader to say exactly how the mapping goes. For indeed, it can go only one way. The four levels of cognition, as laid out in Figure 3-9, provide the target. Given the structure of Soar as described in this chapter, we are then forced into the mapping shown in Figure 4-23. We need to keep distinct the terms from the analysis of the human cognitive architecture and those from Soar, even where the same words are used; hence, I will prefix some terms and phrases with *Soar* when necessary—for example, Soar long-term memory vs. (human) long-term memory.

Productions correspond to symbol structures. Matching the productions to the elements in Soar's working memory corresponds to the process of accessing distal structure. Thus, the production system forms the recognition system, at the bottom of the cognitive level, and hence all of long-term memory. The operation is totally parallel at this level, as reflected in there being no conflict resolution for the production system. Action is involuntary and there is no awareness of individual firings.

It follows that the duration of a production cycle (matching and executing one or more productions in parallel) takes place at the $\sim\sim$10 ms level. We need to be mindful that $\sim\sim$10 ms is a highly approximate quantity, which might be as fast as 3 to 4 ms and as slow as 30 to 40 ms (see Figure 3-10). Part of this large variability stems simply from the time constants not having been pinned down against detailed data of human behavior, but much variability will remain, both between humans and within an individual human over time and occasion. Within the individual, the variability can arise from multiple sources: tasks, component subsystems, long-lived internal states, or momentary state.

It is unclear what factors should determine the duration of a production cycle. We could simply assume this to be the bottom

Soar	Human cognitive architecture	Properties
Productions	Symbol system • Access LTM • Retrieve from LTM	~~10 ms level Recognition system (content addressed) Parallel operation Involuntary Unaware of individual firings Duration: depends on complexity (simpler match than Ops5)
Decision cycle	Smallest deliberate act • Accumulates knowledge for act, then decides	~~100 ms level Smallest unit of serial operation Involuntary (exhaustive) Aware of products not process Duration: longest production chain (to quiescence)
Primitive operators	Simple selective operations	~~1 sec level Serial operations Primitive observable thinking acts Duration: decision-cycle sequence (minimum of 2 decision cycles) Goal-oriented
Goal attainments	Full problem spaces	~~10 sec level Smallest unit of goal attainment Smallest nonprimitive operators Smallest unit of learning (chunk)

Figure 4-23. Basic mapping of Soar onto the human cognitive architecture.

layer of the Soar model of the architecture and assign whatever timing functions fit the human data. However, the computational requirements of matching are as much a requirement on the biological system as on any other computational system. The possible algorithms that accomplish pattern matching need to be explored to understand how long they take and what dependencies they exhibit. One constraint is definite. The pattern match should be an associative memory structure with the same computational powers as the cognitive architecture. We will see in the next chapter some indications that the current Soar production match is too powerful and that some weaker match might give us a better picture. All we need at this point is that production cycles take ~~10 ms.

The Soar decision cycle corresponds to the elementary deliberate operation. The elaboration cycle corresponds to the repeated accessings of knowledge that constitute deliberation. It accumulates knowledge and uses it to make a decision about what to do. The Soar run-to-quiescence cycle corresponds to the exhaustive character of the elementary deliberate operation. Hence, the Soar decision cycle is involuntary and automatic. Once initiated, it simply completes of its own accord. There is awareness of its products, since they emerge in working memory at the end, but not of what goes on to produce them.

It follows that the decision cycle occurs at the ~~100 ms level. Its duration will be determined by the longest production chain to quiescence. This adds another source of variability to the duration of this system level—it is not just the sum of random durations of lower-level components, but the number being summed is also variable. Indeed, the decision phase has the peculiar feature that its duration can be governed by irrelevant productions that have nothing to do with the task and bear no functional relation to it.

The Soar simple operator corresponds to the sequence of deliberately selected operations. This selection is a serial process and is the primitive level of observed thinking. It constitutes the acts of immediate-response behavior. The duration is determined by the sequence of decision cycles needed to carry out the operator. There's a minimum of two: one to select the operator and one to apply it. Simple operators must take ~~1 sec, although minimal operators might be much faster if they required only two decision cycles.

General Soar problem spaces correspond to problem spaces where the operators themselves can be composed. This is the top of the cognitive band, just before we enter the upward-reaching hierarchy of problem spaces piled on problem spaces that is the intendedly rational band. The time for this level is ~~10 sec. The problem space is the smallest unit of goal attainment; the system works in the space and finds a resolution. Chunking corresponds to the continuous shift from deliberation to preparation that comes with experience.

The general mapping of Figure 4-23 seems to be the only one possible for Soar. That is, it is not possible to make Soar productions correspond to something that happens at the ~~100 ms or the ~~1 sec level. Nothing else fits. Soar might not be right—as with all theories about the real world, it could be a little bit wrong or it could be just plain wrong. Either option, or anything in between, always exists as a possibility for a scientific theory. But given that Soar is a reasonable model of human cognition, then there is a clear indication of exactly how to go forward in detail. The bridging rules for Soar as a unified theory of cognition are set. They make clear how to use Soar as a theory and how to bring specific experimental data to bear on Soar to assess how good a theory it is.

4.8. Soar and the Shape of Human Cognition

Pursuing in detail the consequences of this mapping starts in earnest with the next chapter, on immediate responses. Before starting that enterprise, let's step back and take a more global view. Does Soar have the general shape of human cognition? Are its global features, as revealed in this chapter, of the right kind? Contrariwise, does it present some caricature of a human? Or is it simply wide of the mark in some respect? A unified theory of cognition must be a good theory in the large as well as in the small.

Figure 4-24 gives a sample of the qualitative global characteristics of Soar and human cognition. Unfortunately, no hard data are available upon which to base such a listing. I know of no good existing lists of characteristics that can be taken as a useful standard, though certainly a massive amount of writing, observation, and folk psychology bears on the general character of human nature. Indeed, these are the kind of phenomena where Everyman is king and the servants count equal to the nobility. It would be extremely useful if there were lists of this sort to provide some objectivity and discipline to global comparisons. Then, at least, the same questions about qualitative features could be asked of all candidates for unified theories of cognition. And those attempting to address the list would not have to be its creators.

In any event, Figure 4-24 is one list. The convenient idiom is to talk about Soar having such and such properties, as if it were a modal human. This is shorthand for circumlocutions that say that the unified theory of cognition, of which Soar is an operational

1. Has the general features derived from the real-time constraint
   - Symbol system, automatic/controlled behavior, recognition-based, fast-read/slow-write, continual shift to recognition (learns from experience)
2. Behaves intelligently
   - Not completely rational (only approximates knowledge level)
3. Goal oriented
   - Not just because it has learned goals
   - Goals arise out of its interaction with environment
4. Interrupt driven
   - Depth-first local behavior, progressive deepening
5. Default behavior is fundamentally adaptive
   - Does not have to be programmed to behave
6. Serial in the midst of parallelism
   - Autonomous behavior (hence an unconscious)
7. Recognition is strongly associative
   - Does not have deliberate access to all that it knows
   - Remembering can be a problem, but can be taken as a task
8. Doesn't know how it does things
   - Learned procedures are nonarticulable; chunking accesses working-memory trace, not productions
   - Can work interpretively from declarative procedures
9. There is meta-awareness or reflection
   - Can step back and examine what it is doing
10. Uses indefinitely large body of knowledge
11. Aware of large amounts of immediate detail
    - But focused, with a penumbra
12. Distractible

Figure 4-24. Characteristics of Soar that agree with the basic shape of human cognition.

embodiment, describes (or predicts) humans as having the properties in question.

To see the importance of such a list, we start with distractibility. It is the last item (12), but it provides a specific lesson. In the early 1960s, Walt Reitman (1965) developed an entire research path in reaction to the single-mindedness of GPS, an early simulation of human problem solving (Newell & Simon, 1963). GPS seemed to have none of the distractibility so characteristic of human behavior (as we can all testify, with little need of hard data). Reitman thought

GPS's basic structure precluded it from being appropriately distractible.[16] This seemed to Reitman a fatal flaw, and he went on to develop the Argus system, whose central point was to exhibit appropriate distractibility. Soar's decision cycle is indeed structured so that distraction can occur, although it is not so structured *in order to be* distractible. There is no constraint on what productions fire, except the content of the existing working memory. Any decision can be made at any time—there is no top-down mode setting or conditioning of what decision is to be made at a given point (such as *now* select a state, *now* select an operator, or *now* return the result). Indeed, Soar is a distractible system in exactly the sense that Reitman was after, although it attains this characteristic without the massive architectural alterations that Reitman put into Argus (to produce a system that would be seen today as somewhat connectionist in spirit). I bring up this example only to point out that one sufficiently glaring failure of a global qualitative characteristic can doom a theory of human behavior. Thus, it is worth examining a list of global characteristics before we start applying the theory to details.

Proceeding now from the top item (1), Soar has all of those characteristics that were developed in Chapters 2 and 3 and that have just been linked to Soar by the mapping in Figure 4-23. Soar has symbols, both automatic and controlled behavior, a basic recognitional mode of operation, a fast-read slow-write long-term memory, and a continual shift to recognition with experience. We argued for all of these as features of human cognition, and Soar exhibits them as well. More globally, with the given mapping, Soar has the same temporal bands and levels that stratify the different cognitive worlds in humans. We know nothing about Soar above the intendedly rational band, but that is about as high as our analysis of human behavior goes in any event.

(2) Soar behaves intelligently. In simple cases its behavior can be predicted just by what it knows and wants. However, it is not completely rational and only approximates a knowledge-level system.

(3) Soar is goal oriented, but not just because it has learned goals

16. The lack of distractibility was characteristic of essentially all AI programs of that era, but GPS was also a system that embodied a psychological theory, so it was a natural focus for this criticism.

in its memory. It is goal oriented because its goals arise out of its interaction with the environment. It builds its own goals whenever it can't simply proceed.

(4) Soar is interrupt driven—another general characteristic of human behavior. If, in reaching for a pencil at my desk, I knock over a little picture stand, I reach for it instantly (*reflexively* we often say) and may even catch and right it before it topples over— and then I just return to reaching for the pencil. I have processed the interrupt without missing a beat. Human behavior is strongly interrupt driven and Soar behaves the same way. That is what the open character of the deliberation cycle is all about. Depth-first behavior and progressive-deepening behavior are natural modes of operation, for both Soar and humans.

(5) Soar's default behavior is fundamentally adaptive. Given that it doesn't know anything except that it is faced with some task, it commences to work on that task, even if uninstructed. Like humans, Soar doesn't have to be programmed to do something. Its natural default behavior is not to do nothing. Of course, for Soar to have a task is for Soar to already have a formulation in a problem space. So this characterization does not address the initial formulation of tasks.

(6) Soar is serial in the midst of being parallel. There is the serial central cognitive structure that leads to one operator at a time. But this is embedded in a sea of autonomous stuff out in the perceptual and motor fields. Soar clearly has unconscious processing that goes on, outside deliberately controlled central cognitive processing. This is just the way it is with us.

(7) Soar's recognition system is strongly associative, behaving like a content-addressed memory. From this characteristic comes some important human-like properties. Soar does not have deliberate access to all it knows. The only way to make an associative memory work is to put retrieval cues in the working memory and see what they draw down. There is no way to know for sure what is out there in an associative memory. Remembering—finding out what was put there at some earlier time—can be a genuine problem (for humans as for Soar). But the task can be formulated to try to search its own long-term memory by manipulating the cues put into working memory.

(8) Soar does not know how it does things. The learned procedures—all the things it chunks—are not articulable. This property

is often commented upon with respect to human behavior—as if it were an especially telling feature with respect to logical or rational behavior that humans can not articulate their skills (Polyani, 1958; Mandler, 1985). In this respect, it is worth noting that chunking does not gain access to the productions. Chunking is done entirely in terms of the trace that is laid down in the working memory, with no access to the productions and how they are represented. Soar can also work interpretively from specified instructions, held as data structures in working memory, and it can then be articulate about them. And humans likewise.

(9) Soar has a certain reflectiveness, which arises from the impasses. Taking an impasse amounts to stepping back from what was being done to examine the larger context. Reflection is always possible for Soar, since the taking of impasses is built into the architecture. Hence Soar is indefinitely reflective. This certainly is one sort of human reflection. Whether it corresponds to all the kinds of reflectiveness is unclear. There does not seem to be any useful taxonomy of the flavors and varieties of reflection in humans.[17] However, it is a strong feature of Soar's reflection that it is driven by inadequacy (by impasses) and does not occur as a deliberate act.

(10) Soar is structured to have a very large knowledge base. That is what the production system provides and the design is for Soar to have a large number of productions ($\sim\sim 10^6$ or more). However, none of the tasks explored with Soar has dealt with such large memory, so we can only project that Soar would behave plausibly under such conditions.

(11) Soar's immediate temporary environment (its working memory) can contain a large amount of detail, but Soar is always focused on some part of that detail, and most of it remains unprocessed.

4.9. Summary

Iterating through the list of Figure 4-24 instills confidence that Soar is a good candidate for a unified theory of cognition. That is, of course, deliberate on my part. One wants as complete a picture as

17. But see Maes and Nardi (1988) for a variety of reflections in computational systems.

possible, however, so I list here some of the problems and issues that Soar faces.

Soar, like any computer system, is a system always in a state of becoming something else. Many aspects are not yet operational, or only operational in some limited way. I describe here a current version, Soar 4.5, but then immediately claim that certain improvements are coming in Soar5, the next major release. These include some important aspects, otherwise we would not be modifying or enhancing Soar to include them. Of course, some of these changes will not make it even then, so it will have been premature to speak of them. It is a genuine Tristram Shandy situation. In the two years since I delivered the William James Lectures, Soar has changed significantly. In particular, Soar5 has gone from the design stage to implementation and is now being introduced. To update the book to take into account Soar5 would require extensive rewriting, during which Soar would change some more. Thus, what is represented to be Soar is really a moving average through a two-year window.

It is easy enough to enumerate specific examples of important aspects of Soar in this in-between state. The main new aspects of Soar5 are components of the perceptual and motor systems and the adoption of the principle that Soar5 is able to remember only a single state within any problem space, as opposed to Soar4's current capability for remembering all of the states that have been visited. Beyond Soar5 are modifications to reduce the power of the matching capability of productions. The current one, inherited from Ops5, seems in some ways clearly too powerful for what can be done in a single recognition. A more minor issue concerns the requirement for some productions to keep Soar from descending into infinite impasse pits. Somehow, one feels that the default behavior ought to be defined entirely in the architecture, but this has not occurred yet.

Certain things have not been demonstrated with Soar, although nothing in our current understanding indicates where the difficulties will arise. One long-term goal of artificial intelligence has been to construct *nonbrittle* systems—systems that do not abruptly fail when they move out beyond some predefined task scope. Certainly humans show some degree of nonbrittleness, although we may overestimate it (transport a steelworker to the floor of the stock exchange or a psychoanalyst to the old manual Vax-configuration task, and see what happens). Soar has enough attributes of general intelligence that it might permit a significant step in that direction, but no direct demonstrations of that have been attempted yet. Whether chunking covers the full range of learning remains another issue on which the current demonstrations, being simply enumerative, are not definitive.

Finally, it is easy to name aspects that are simply missing in the version of Soar developed to date—emotion, dreams, imagery. These phenomena might require entirely new structures, different in kind from the current mechanisms of Soar. Insofar as that is not the case, the burden of proof rests on Soar to show how such phenomena are to be explained within the current architecture. This has not been done yet.

One other summary of Soar might be useful. In Chapter 1 we considered a list of the many different constraints that impinge on the nature of mind. One reason we need a unified theory is to bring to bear all those different constraints within one theory. We must first ask if Soar is adequate in terms of the constraints it was designed to take into account. It is a separate question whether it might also be responsive to other constraints. Let us start with design intentions. Figure 4-25 lists the same constraints given in Figure 1-7, but added to it are indications whether Soar was designed to deal with each given constraint.

Much effort went into making Soar flexible, for flexibility is required for universal computation and is shared by all reasonable computational systems. We also focused on the constraint of operating in real time. This is probably the biggest new constraint we tried to respond to. The inability to put universality and real-time response together in the same system removes whole realms of computational systems, such as standard theorem provers, from the list of candidates for unified theories of cognition.

With respect to the richness of the environment, we deliberately designed for having vast amounts of knowledge. This is embodied in the notion of an indefinitely large recognition system (production system). But the other two aspects of interaction with the environment—the rich perceptual input and output having large degrees of freedom—received very little attention. The design of the total system (Figure 4-15) only begins to address some of the issues and is silent on the issues of scale and complexity, which is the real import of the constraint.

Soar is fully responsive to having symbols and abstractions. This

1. Behave flexibly	yes
2. Exhibit adaptive (rational, goal-oriented) behavior	yes
3. Operate in real time	yes
4. Operate in a rich, complex, detailed environment	
• Perceive an immense amount of changing detail	interface only
• Use vast amounts of knowledge	yes
• Control a motor system of many degrees of freedom	interface only
5. Use symbols and abstractions	yes
6. Use language, both natural and artificial	no
7. Learn from the environment and from experience	yes
8. Acquire capabilities through development	no
9. Operate autonomously, but within a social community	no
10. Be self-aware and have a sense of self	no
11. Be realizable as a neural system	no
12. Be constructable by an embryological growth process	no
13. Arise through evolution	no

Figure 4-25. The design of Soar and the multiple constraints on mind.

does not have to do with Soar per se but with the conjunction of these two requirements with computational universality. Thus the three of them come along together. On the other hand, we paid no attention to the requirements of natural language. The major issue about natural language, from the point of view of a list of constraints on cognition, is whether it provides constraints in addition to those elsewhere in the list—universality, real-time operation, symbols, abstraction, and on down to learning and socialization. This is one way of phrasing the current modularity hypothesis (Fodor, 1983). By embodying many of the other constraints, Soar may have something to say about this one. But in any event, there are no aspects of Soar's design that are deliberately responsive to specifically linguistic requirements.

The Soar architecture is fully responsive to learning, through its built-in chunking mechanisms. As noted earlier, however, learning was one major constraint that was not at all involved in the original design (Laird, 1984); it was achieved only after the system had become fully operational.

No attempt has been made to design Soar to satisfy the rest of the constraints—development, living in a social community, self-awareness, realization as a neural system, or its construction by the processes of embryology, and ultimately of evolution. Chapter 3 showed that the real-time constraint, in concert with using neural technology, determines a lot of features of the architecture—and that these features are largely present in Soar—but such considerations did not enter into the Soar design and had not been articulated then.

Finally, the description of our candidate architecture for a unified theory of cognition is complete. The candidate has become very specific, not only in its mechanisms, which exist in integrated operational form in Soar, but also in the mapping between the architecture and human cognition. The task for the rest of the book is to illustrate, by bringing this candidate into contact with many different facets of human cognition, in varying degrees of detail, what a unified theory of cognition should provide.

Immediate Behavior

5

The preparations are complete. Our candidate unified theory of cognition, Soar, has been described in detail, along with how it is to be mapped onto human cognition. In this chapter we begin the consideration of Soar in specific domains of human behavior.

As we start to take Soar seriously, I want to reiterate a point made in Chapter 1. This book argues for unified theories of cognition—the plural, not the singular. I am not trying to make the case that Soar is the only or even the prime candidate in all the land. I believe it is an interesting candidate and hope that you will find it interesting too. It is certainly the candidate that I personally wish to work on. However, the central claim in the book is that it is possible now to have theories that apply from the level of immediate behavior to the level of problem solving and learning. I am much more concerned with figuring out how a theory could put it all together, and what could be the plausible yield from doing so, than I am for arguing that a particular candidate (to wit, Soar) is the best or even the favored choice. This focus also lets me avoid the task of making continual cross-assessments with other possible candidates and defending the preferred status of one theory. The task of laying out a unified theory of cognition is sufficiently demanding that such an additional burden would be a genuine distraction. I am not attempting to avoid comparison of Soar with competitive theories. As Soar begins to be a genuine candidate, as opposed to being an exemplar, then it will be both necessary and appropriate to make comparisons.

This chapter focuses on *immediate behavior*, responses that must be made to some stimulus within very approximately one second (that is, roughly from ~300 ms to ~3 sec). There are good reasons for taking up this arena first, other than just that a unified theory of cognition should apply to all areas of cognition, hence why not to this one? For one, Soar comes with the appearance of an AI problem-solving and learning system. In AI generally, it is simply not done to construe the details of behavior of such a system as a model of human behavior, whatever might be asserted about its global intelligent behavior. The details seem all too evidently dependent on the programming languages and environments in which the system is built and on the need to write procedures to do the low-level tasks. Thus, showing that Soar provides a theory of immediate-response behavior makes a critical statement about Soar being a genuine candidate for a unified theory of cognition. However, the really important reason for beginning here is that immediate behavior is where the architecture shows through—where you can see the cognitive wheels turn and hear the cognitive gears grind. Immediate behavior is the appropriate arena in which to discover the nature of the cognitive architecture.

We will first discuss in some detail the scientific role of immediate-response behavior in discovering the architecture. Then we will make two preparatory steps: discussing some methodological preliminaries and analyzing how the architecture will handle immediate behavior. This latter includes paying additional attention to perception and motor behavior, since these are so intimately part of immediate behavior. Only after that will we apply Soar in varying amounts of detail to a succession of experimental paradigms— simple and choice reaction tasks, stimulus-response compatibility, item recognition, and transcription typing.

5.1. The Scientific Role of Immediate-Response Data

When you're down close to the architecture, you can see it, and when you're far away you can't. As we have already discussed, the appropriate scale is temporal, not spatial. The architecture works in the region of $\sim\sim10$ ms to $\sim\sim1$ sec, so only tasks that are carried out in this time frame will reveal the architecture. As the tasks move away in time, by a factor of ten to durations of about ten seconds or even further away to minutes and hours, less and less specific features of the architecture can be seen in the performance of the task. The fading with increasing temporal distance is not caused by some fixed mechanism, analogous to the inverse square law or (a better analog) statistical smearing. Rather, the fading occurs because of adaptive behavior, which to the extent it is successful necessarily operates to obscure the internal mechanisms by making behavior exclusively a function of what the system's goals depend upon, namely, the external environment.

Not only are the particulars of immediate behavior important, psychology has learned to find regularities at this level. Literally thousands of regularities have been discovered, verified, and now reside in the archival literature. My best estimate is ~~3,000, that is, anywhere from a thousand to ten thousand. This way of talking about it may strike experimental psychologists as somewhat odd. We normally think of scientific regularities as unique discoveries, to be discussed one by one. We do not think of them as being garnered by the bushel basket and served up a dozen at a time, for sixpence.

Yet it is true that there are thousands of healthy, robust regularities of immediate behavior. Almost all are quantitative, many are parametric with external task variables. Many are so clean they take your breath away, like Fitts' law (Figure 1-1) and the power law of practice (Figure 1-3). Every good experimentalist should ponder that finding one more regularity is simply adding one to this dazzling field of ~~3,000. It is unlikely that the next regularity will sparkle and shine in a different way from the regularities already in the archives—a diamond to the zircons of the past. The next regularity will not be different in kind. Recency does not add scientific luminance, or at least should not. Each new regularity will become one with its fellows, and they all will sparkle, each according to its individual light in revealing facets of our cognitive nature.

The great array of regularities has not yet been integrated into any general theoretical structure. Of course we need more data, and especially more regularities. But if we ask whether new energy should go to building integrated theories to bind these regularities together, or go to finding one more regularity to add to the field, then the issue is worth pondering. Indeed, this book constitutes an extended argument for shifting the energy of psychology to theory building. It goes without saying that Soar must be a theory that applies to these regularities.

Of course, I shouldn't simply assert that ~~3,000 regularities exist without citing evidence. On the other hand, it wouldn't be possible to assert each of the ~~3,000 regularities separately, one by one. It *is* possible to illustrate. Consider *transcription typing* (hereafter just *typing*)—looking at a text manuscript and producing a copy by means of a typewriter. It is a common enough activity, though a relatively minute and arcane corner of the psychology world, out of the mainstream of experimental activity. Actually, there is a long history of investigation of typing, and more recently a modest flurry of activity (Cooper, 1983), but it doesn't compete for attention or resources with many other areas of experimental work, such as lexical access, automaticity, or short-term memory. In late 1986, however, Tim Salthouse published a paper in the *Psychological Bulletin* in which he listed 29 robust regularities for typing. Figure 5-1 lists them in abbreviated form (Salthouse, 1986). These regularities had been confirmed by more than one investigator, often in many studies, so there is reasonable confidence they exist. All of these 29 regularities constrain the architecture. Any proposed cognitive architecture must produce them. Of course, the architecture alone cannot do so. An architecture by itself can't do anything. It must be augmented with procedures, plans, programs, or whatever is the form that procedural content takes in the architecture. Therefore, all glimpses of the architecture require disentangling the effects of the content from the architecture. But typing involves rapid response to the environment. The typist takes in text from manuscripts and strikes keys to reproduce them, continuously, at ~~1 word a second (~~60 wpm). This behavior is fairly close to the architecture, then, but whereas every candidate architecture can type, we can confidently expect that not every one will also exhibit all 29 of these regularities.

Let us go through the list briefly, in order to get some feeling for what such a collection of regularities amounts to. It is important to see that discovering the cognitive architecture is not like the task of finding a physical principle to explain a single parabolic curve that describes a ball rolling down an incline. The desired architecture must satisfy the conjunction of a huge set of regularities.

To begin with phenomenon (1), typing is faster than a reaction time. The time between hitting one key and the next, called the *interkey interval* (177 ms in one experiment, or 68 wpm), is over twice as fast as the time it would take to see the letter and select it (516 ms in the same experiment).[1] However (2), typing is slower

---

1. The actual two-choice reaction task was *L* or *l* to one key, and *R* or *r* to another key. This is more complex, hence slower, than the simplest two-choice reaction task (*L* to one key, *R* to another), which takes about 350 ms, but even this latter is slower than going from any letter to its key.

Salthouse's regularities

1. Faster than reaction time: 177/560 ms interkey/2CRT
2. Slower than reading: 60 wpm vs. 250 wpm
3. Skill/comprehension independence: ρ insignificant
4. Word-order independence: ρ = .99 meaningful/random
5. Slower with random letter order: to 60%
6. Slower with restricted preview: all, 200 ms; 1 character, 690 ms
7. Faster alternate-hand keystrokes: 30–50 ms faster
8. Faster frequent letter pairs: 52 ms/log-unit of frequency
9. Word-length independence: on interkey interval
10. Word initiation effect: first keystroke 20% slower
11. Specific preceding letter-context counts: 1.8 characters
12. Dual task independence: for highly skilled typists
13. Copy span size: 13.2 characters
14. Stopping span size: 1–2 keystrokes
15. Eye-hand span size: moderate typists, 3–8 characters
16. Eye-hand span less as meaning decreases: 3.5–1.7 characters
17. Replacement span size: ~3 characters
18. Process-detectable errors: 40–70% detected
19. Substitution errors mostly adjacent-key errors: 70%
20. Intrusion errors mostly short interkey intervals: 40%
21. Omission errors followed by long intervals: ~2 (median)
22. Transposition errors mostly cross-hand errors: 80%
23. 2-finger digraphs improve faster than 1-finger digraphs
24. Tapping faster with typing skill: ρ = −.4
25. Decrease of variability with skill: ρ = −.7
26. Increase of eye-hand span with skill: ρ = .5
27. Increase of replacement span with skill: ρ = .6
28. Moderate increase to copy span with skill: ρ = .5
29. Increase of stopping span with typing speed: ρ = .6

Additional regularities

30. Speed-accuracy trade-off?
31. Skill-acquisition rate?
32. Transfer to other keyboards (positive and negative)?
33. Relation to Fitts' law?
34. Detailed distributions on many of above?

Figure 5-1. The Salthouse 29: robust regularities about typing (wpm = net words per minute, ρ = correlation coefficient).

than reading. People read at 250 wpm and they type at 60 wpm (to use conventional numbers), a difference of almost a factor of four. Both these phenomena are fairly obvious to careful observation, and they might therefore seem uninteresting. On the contrary, they eliminate whole classes of architectures. The first says that typing can't occur just by iterating isolated responses to each letter. The second says that typing is limited by some other process than that involved in perceiving and reading text. It does not identify the other process, but it eliminates the class of architectures with relatively slow perceptual mechanisms.

(3) People vary in their typing skill (wpm) and they also vary in how much they comprehend what they type. But there is no relation between the two—the high comprehenders are not the fast typists (as if typing depended on understanding); but the high comprehenders are not the slow typists either (as if comprehending interfered with typing). (4) Typing speed is independent of word order. So the sentence, "For come now is party time the men all good to to aid the their of," is typed just as fast as, "Now is the time for all good men to come to the aid of their party." Thus, not only sense but syntax seems not to make a difference. On the other hand (5), if the letters are scrambled, typing slows down appreciably to about 60 percent. "Won is hte mtei fro lal dogo mne ot coem to hte dai fo ehitr ptyar" takes a while.

(6) Normal typing has an unrestricted preview of the coming text (at least to the edge of the page). If the preview is restricted to a fixed set of characters, then the interkey interval increases. For example, it goes from 200 ms to 690 ms if only 1 character can be seen (from 60 wpm to 17 wpm). (7) Typing successive keystrokes from alternate hands is faster than typing them with the same hand. This seems fairly obvious—the finger of one hand may start while a finger of the other is still hitting the key. This illustrates again that obvious regularities can be just as useful as novel ones in constraining the nature of the architecture. A rigidly programmed motor system would not show such a variation. (8) Frequent letter pairs are faster—there is a word-frequency effect, although it turns out not to be very big.

(9) Typing speed (interkey interval) is independent of word length. People type short words and long words at exactly the same rate. On the other hand (10), there is a word initiation effect. The first keystroke of a word is slower than the others by about 20

percent. (11) There are also a lot of specific differences in the inter-keystroke intervals depending on the exact context, namely, the exact preceding characters. (12) Skilled typists can do many other tasks at the same time as they type. They can type and read something else concurrently, or type and listen to something else concurrently. This automaticity is greater the more skilled the typist.

We now arrive at various *spans*, which are measured to find out how much information is kept in the system under various conditions. (13) There is the *copy span*. If the text is suddenly removed, how long can typing continue? The copy span is about 13.2 characters. (14) There is the *stopping span*. If a stop signal is suddenly given, how quickly can typing cease? That's 1–2 characters. (15) There is the *eye-hand span*. How far ahead in the text are your eyes looking from where you are typing? Quantifying this span depends on accurate measurement of gaze direction. The eye-hand span is between 3 and 8 characters, somewhat less than the copy span. (16) The eye-hand span decreases as the meaning of the text decreases. It drops from about 3.5 characters for fully meaningful text to 1.7 characters for meaningless text. (17) There is the *replacement span*. How many characters can be surreptitiously replaced without any effect on the typing (or the typist noticing it)? A special experimental arrangement is required to make these changes in a controlled way dynamically. This span is ~3 characters. All these different spans tell something about what is going on inside the typist's head. They result from a combination of the method used in typing and the architecture. Different architectures would lead to different profiles of these spans. With a simple enough architecture, several of them would be the same.

The next set of regularities is about errors. (18) Typists can often detect that an error has been made even though they have no perceptual feedback about what they typed (40–70 percent of the time). That they know an error has occurred implies something about a self-monitoring capability of the architecture. (19) *Substitution errors* occur when one letter is typed in place of another, *bpat* instead of *boat*. Such errors usually involve adjacent keys. (20) *Intrusion errors* occur when an additional letter is inserted, *bioat* for *boat*, and most happen very quickly (short interkey intervals). (21) *Omission errors* occur when a letter is left out, *bat* for *boat*. Such errors tend to be followed by long interkey intervals, about twice the median size. (22) *Transposition errors* are the interchange of adjacent letters, *baot* instead of *boat*. Such errors occur mostly when the two characters are typed by fingers of opposite hands. Once more, it seems apparent why transposition errors have this propensity, namely, controlling the timing between the two hands is more difficult than controlling the timing between two fingers of the same hand. But the architecture still has to permit such an effect to show through. For instance, if an architecture were to treat each keystroke as an independently initiated event, the effect would not occur.

Finally we come to some skill-related regularities. (23) Not only does the interkeystroke interval decrease with practice (which must happen for typing speed to increase with practice), but sequential pairs of keystrokes (digrams) also decrease, and some decrease faster than others. Interestingly, the digrams that involve two separate fingers (whether on the same hand or not) decrease faster than the digrams that involve only a single finger (whether the same letter or not). That is, *st* (the ring and index finger of the left hand) improves faster than *ft* (left index finger). Who would ever care about such a regularity? It shows up in Salthouse's list, I would hazard, because several investigators looked generally at improvement of sequences of characters (chunks) and the slow rate for one-finger digrams showed up reliably. But whether it is interesting from any larger view (could it possibly be relevant to training?), it can still be interesting as a constraint on the cognitive architecture.

(24) People who are fast typists *tap* faster. This is an important correlation that ties typing to other tasks. It is an opposite kind of regularity to (3), which showed that comprehension and typing skill were independent. (25) Skill in any complex domain exhibits variability. In typing, the speed fluctuates over short stretches of text. As skill increases this variability goes down. That is, the skilled typist is a steady typist. (26) There is an increase in the eye-hand span with skill. This is the third regularity on eye-hand span, which probably reflects the long-standing popularity of studying eye-hand span in typing. (27) There is an increase of the replacement span with skill. (28) There is also a moderate increase of the copy span with skill. Finally (29), the stopping span increases with skill.

There we have the Salthouse 29. It seems like a lot of regularities, and it was somewhat obsessive to go through the entire list. Even so, there are some important regularities that did not make the Salthouse list. I have added a few to the bottom of the figure, as questions. (30) What is the speed-accuracy trade-off? If a person attempts to type faster, how much will errors increase? Unlike regularity (23) on the improvement of digrams, whose significance is not generally clear, we all believe that speed-accuracy trade-offs are highly relevant. (31) How fast do people learn typing? Does learning follow the power law? We would predict assuredly yes; and it is nice to have the regularity confirmed (Gentner, 1983). (32) Essentially all of the results have been taken on the standard QWERTY keyboard. What are the positive and negative transfers to keyboards of other layouts (such as the Dvorek or the alphabetical keyboard)? (33) What is typing's relation to Fitts' law (Figure 1-1)? After all, the situation involves moving a finger a certain distance to hit a target of a certain size (the key), so Fitts' law should apply. (34) One last omnibus issue: Almost all of Salthouse's regularities are quoted as comparisons, shifts, frequencies, and correlations. Behind them lie detailed distributions, which are also a function of skill level and must show individual differences. Knowing these details would perhaps not lead to new distinct regularities, but they would certainly add constraint to the architecture.

Thus, we arrive at about a third of a hundred regularities about this one small area alone. Any candidate architecture must deal with most of these if it's going to explain typing. That was Salthouse's aim—to put forth a profile of results that characterized the behavior of the area. Of course, there is no reason to focus on typing. It is just one of a hundred specialized areas of cognitive behavior. It takes only a hundred areas at thirty regularities per area to reach the ~~3,000 total regularities cited at the beginning of this chapter. I haven't tried to enumerate either the areas or the regularities within areas, but a scattering of regularities has already been mentioned—Fitts' law, the power law of practice, a few automatic/controlled search results in item recognition (Figure 3-8). There will be others. Any architecture, especially a candidate for a unified theory of cognition, must deal with them all—hence with thousands of regularities.

This is for me *the Great Psychology Data Puzzle*. My bet is that enough constraining regularities already exist in the literature to identify the architecture to all intents and purposes. We could stop doing experiments entirely and, just from what now exists, discover what the architecture is. This is not to say we must identify some specific genius who will solve this puzzle for us. Rather, this is an argument that lots of us should try to do so. There exists a sufficient collection of reliable results about the microstructure of behavior that an architecture has to satisfy, so we could, with immense profit, spend our time theorizing about the architecture.

This attitude clashes sharply with a repeatedly voiced concern over nonidentifiability in psychology. It is not possible to determine whether item-recognition tasks are being done by serial or parallel processes (Townsend, 1974). It is not possible to identify what representation is being used (Anderson, 1978). This issue was mentioned in Chapter 1, but it obviously bears directly on the present contention, so I repeat myself. This concern over nonidentifiability seems to me a methodological artifact. It shows up only when attention is focused on one specific task, one specific type of data, and one specific inference situation. If one considers only a specific item-recognition task, only reaction-time measurements, and a theory that is completely sui generis so no general architectural principles hold—then, and only then, do essential difficulties of identification arise. Demonstrations of nonidentifiability require formalization; and formalization leads, of itself, to lean, abstract situations (the rest are too complex to formalize), so the search for demonstrations of nonidentifiability tends to be successful. But the actual situation of psychology is just the opposite. There is an immense diversity of specific experimental constraints, along with general bounding principles (such as those derived from the real-time constraint of Chapter 3). These are sufficient, I believe, to pin down the architecture in most of its major aspects. We are faced with an embarrassment of riches and our problems are how to cope with the complexity of it and how to have the courage to deal with it. Of course, there can be no prior demonstration of the sufficiency of any fixed collection of regularities. We will know that the architecture is identifiable only when it is identified. So what I have expressed here is an opinion, although I trust an informed one.

The point is not that further experimentation should not occur. That is a foolish extrapolation. There are vast fields of human behavior that are essentially unexplored and often a direct experimental attack on a question is by far the most efficient way to get information. The point is to increase the relative energies devoted to theoretical integration of the vast collection of regularities that we already have in hand. The point is also to increase awareness of how unlikely it is that any new regularity will make a bravura appearance rather than simply take its place as another member of the chorus. It is the web of regularities that count, not any one of them.

As we have noted repeatedly, behavior gradually moves away from the architecture as the time scale increases and adaptation blurs its sharp edges. That might lead to the conclusion that architecture is unimportant except for dealing with immediate-response tasks (which, notably, would include perception and motor behavior). Behind this conclusion is an important kernel of truth. This kernel has helped cognitive science be successful in many studies of problem solving, memory organization, and language, which needed only general notions of the information-processing characteristics of humans, or in creating simulations that were embedded in patently wrong details but still gave good results at the more aggregate level.

In fact, the kernel of truth stretches out along a continuum, for as one moves away from immediate-response behavior, the features of the architecture do not all fade into irrelevance at the same rate. There is a continuum of more abstracted models of the architecture, and this continuum captures the architectural constraints that continue to operate as tasks increase in duration. A good formulation of this abstracted architecture can be found in Simon (1989, p. xii): a small short-term memory; an unlimited long-term memory of schemas, organized associatively in terms of both indexes and productions; tasks organized in problem spaces, in a representation defined by mapping processes on the perceived environment; with learning accomplished by growing the indexes or adding productions or schemas. Augmenting this qualitative picture with a few constants, such as chunk size and acquisition rate (Simon, 1974), permits many analyses of long-duration cognitive behavior. In a similar vein, the MHP of Card, Moran, and Newell (1983), discussed in Chapter 1, can be taken not as a poor approximation, reflecting our incomplete knowledge, but as an abstract architecture, useful as one moves away from immediate behavior. In terms of the details of its definition, it lies somewhere between Simon's formulation and that of Soar.

Still, it is important to get the architecture right—for all of cognitive science and not just the parts directly involved in immediate behavior. Wanting to get it right has somewhat the character of an act of faith, at this point. The argument is that if the architecture is right, then everything else will go smoothly. Hypothesizing what is natural and simple, given the architecture, can be relied upon as a guide—it will very often be the way things are. The abstracted architectures discussed above clearly capture some of what is simple and some of what remains apparent the longest as the duration of behavior increases, but other details and how the parts fit together are also important. Thus, the architecture has a heuristic impact further up the temporal scale than might be imagined from the actual detailed processes.

In sum, the major scientific function of immediate-response data is to identify the architecture, which will set the terms for a unified theory of cognition—and the syntax as well.

5.2. Methodological Preliminaries

Before we can take up specific cases, we need to consider some preliminaries to set the stage, especially since we are using Soar to illuminate the situation for unified theories of cognition. How should we expect to use Soar as a theory at the immediate-response level? What are the varieties of explanations and predictions it should offer? How complete and well specified should such a theory be?

5.2.1. How to View Using Soar as a Theory
Some things are obvious. Taking Soar seriously as a theory of cognition means it should explain and predict cognitive regularities, such as the ones just enumerated for typing, and it should reveal how they are related to other regularities and on what aspects of human cognition they rest. Taking Soar seriously as a unified theory means that it should explain and predict the empirical regularities from all the other domains of immediate behavior. But other things are not quite so obvious. What else is implied by Soar being a unified theory? By being cast as an architecture? Be being embedded in a running computer system? A clear view of these implications helps us to see how to apply Soar in specific cases.

Soar should explain and predict, but it should not necessarily offer novel explanations—explanations that no psychologist has ever thought of. Just the opposite. The objective in a unified theory is synthesis. Soar should incorporate what we now understand most solidly and fully about human cognition. In addition to the empirical regularities, there are many microtheories of limited task domains that reveal rather clearly the mechanisms involved. Soar should incorporate these successful microtheories. It should assimilate and absorb them into the total architecture rather than pose radical alternatives. It remains to be seen how extensively this can be done. There are clear indications that theoretical action comes from having mechanisms of a given general sort and that specific models instantiate such mechanisms so that concrete analysis and predictions can be made. Remember the example in Chapter 1 of many similar random-walk models of the decision processes for perception and memory retrieval (Figure 1-11). That should remind us that, at a given stage of scientific development, it is often not possible to extract the essential mechanisms in pure terms. All we can do is find a collection of equipotent models with a family resemblance. Thus, we can expect a number of places where the mechanisms in Soar that account for various regularities are the Soar-images of the mechanisms in microtheories that account for these same regularities.

Explanations and predictions should follow naturally from Soar. A scientist should be able to think in terms of the architecture—it is after all a way of coping with nature and one should be able to take its stance. More often than not, seeking the natural way for Soar to do a thing should lead to an explanation. I think of this as taking a *Diracian* attitude toward the theory and its relation with nature. P. A. M. Dirac (1902–1984) was an eminent theoretical physicist. One of his cardinal attitudes when confronted with a problem was to find the simple and elegant solution; he was sure that nature would be found to have solved it that way. That is the way we should treat Soar. We should take it seriously and go with the architectural flow.

Soar should not be treated as a programming language. It may be tempting to think of Soar this way (recall item 9 of Figure 1-6). After all, Soar can be programmed and there is a manual for it (Laird, 1986), but being a programmable system is part of its theory of cognition. All the features of Soar implicitly carry the claim that they correspond to features of the human cognitive architecture. These claims may be wrong, either a little wrong or radically wrong; but they're relevant. Thus, to get Soar to explain or predict some human behavior, one does not program in an explanation in terms of some other theoretical elements, as if Soar were just a way of simulating this other structure. Much has been made about the value of the cognitive revolution in providing psychologists procedural languages that helped them to be operational about the processes going on in cognition. Soar provides much more than that (Newell, 1970), namely a theory of the human cognitive architecture.

Soar does not automatically provide an explanation for anything just because it is a universal computational engine. There are two aspects to this assertion. First, from the perspective of cognitive theory, Soar has to be universal, because humans themselves are universal. To put this the right way around—Soar is a universal computational architecture; therefore it predicts that the human cognitive architecture is likewise universal. Second, universality refers only to the class of functions that can ultimately be composed. It doesn't deal with the sorts of errors that will be made, with how fast Soar will run, and with what profile of durations of its various subcomponents. Most ways of attaining a given result can be seen not to be a way that humans do it, or indeed could do it. The commonly heard argument to the effect that if something is a universal system it can explain anything is simply fallacious.

Soar's programs are part of the theory that predicts behavior and regularities. Having programs is inherent to architectures—they are exactly the kinds of systems that have content that shapes and determines their own behavior. Again, said the right way around, Soar claims that humans have programs, indeed, that they have analogous programs. However, the human programs are not arbitrary. They must be acquired somehow—by experience, by instruction, by some process that itself is a function of the human architecture. Correspondingly, Soar must acquire its programs, and by processes analogous to those occurring in humans. Treating Soar as a unified theory implies that the acquisition process cannot lie outside the theory. Such a demand cannot actually be met most of the time, not just because of the frailty of theory but because humans acquire their programs over vast reaches of past experience and arrive at a current task or experimental arrangement with a mind packed full of programs and other knowledge. Mostly, then, the theorist will load into Soar a program (a collection of productions organized into problem spaces) of his or her own devising, proposing the resulting programmed system to be an explanation of some phenomenon. The positing of theorist-programmed versions

Types of agreement between theory and data
Parametric: explains variation with experimental parameters
Quantitative: explains mean or typical values
Qualitative: explains order, presence or absence of effects
Consonant: assigns explanation elsewhere
No explanation
Contradiction

Constraints on the specification of the model
Posit existence of problem spaces by function
Posit existence of operators by function
Posit specific productions
Posit tasks that create the productions by chunking
Generate tasks that create productions by chunking

Figure 5-2. Types of explanation and prediction.

of Soar will occur at every turn, but this necessary scientific tactic should not be confused with inherent lack of constraint. The additional claims are always there—Soar can acquire such a program, Soar will acquire such a program in the circumstances of the task being explained, and Soar will not evoke other behavior, available from other learning, in place of the given behavior. The obligation is on the theorist to cope with the flexibility of human behavior in responsible ways.

5.2.2. Types of Explanation and Predictions

Not all explanations of human behavior are of the same character. First, of course, an architecture is to be used to explain behavior at different time scales. In this chapter, we are focused on immediate responses, but in later chapters we will focus on other time scales.

Different kinds of agreements can occur between theory and data. The top part of Figure 5-2 exhibits a range of possibilities. At the strong end, a theory is able to deal with the full *parametric* detail. For example, it explains how choice reaction time depends on the number of alternatives being chosen among. Less strong, but still noteworthy, are theories where the data are *quantitative* but where only characteristic values are found, such as means or perhaps variances. Weaker, but still useful, are theories that provide only *qualitative* explanations, even though sometimes quantitative evidence is available. Qualitative theories predict the existence of an effect, for example, or that one variable will be larger than another. Sometimes a theory is merely *consonant* with the data, in that the theory assigns a phenomenon or regularity to some other mechanism outside the immediate context. It is critical that a theory not be forced to provide an explanation for something it shouldn't explain. If some phenomenon is really caused by the motor system and a theory that does not include the motor system is stretched to provide an explanation for it, then that theory is headed for deep trouble at some point. Consonance is to be distinguished from *no explanation*, and the latter, of course, from *contradiction*, where the theory gives an explanation that is demonstrably incorrect.

Theories are to be used in many ways. We want a unified theory of cognition to provide power and ease over the full range of theoretical uses. In the main this variation corresponds to what the theorist posits as the givens from which to attempt to derive predictions and explanations. The bottom part of Figure 5-2 shows this range for Soar. At the abstract end, only the existence of problem spaces is posited, in essence, the existence of microdomains of expertise. Soar will be assumed to have some spaces and not others. Sometimes Soar can be posited to have certain operators that accomplish certain functions in appropriate problem spaces, but without specifying exactly the details of the productions or even of the conditions of evocation. Alternatively, the full task specification could be given, that is, all the productions in their full glory, hence enough to run simulations on fully specified inputs. This is the standard case, but it is not the strongest case for a theory, such as Soar, that includes learning. The tasks could be posited that give rise to the specified productions by chunking. Finally, it is possible to go even further and posit some general arena of interaction of Soar with an environment that would generate the tasks that are to create the productions by chunking. Each of these steps of concretization provides something closer to a full explanation of the phenomena under consideration, but all levels are useful. Indeed, the more abstract bases for explanation have a force and charm of their own. They permit us to extract conclusions from a theory without knowing everything about the situation. Scientifically, this is of the essence, because both the scientist and the applier of science always fail to know all aspects of the situation to be explained.

1. **Single-state principle: one state in a space**
   Operators modify states (delete/replace)
   Elaborations are maintained as the state changes

2. **Limited instantiation mechanism: one cycle/instantiation**
   Independent productions execute in parallel
   A resource limitation, but also a functional capability

3. **Limited match power: weaker than Ops5**
   Not satisfy equality constraints on the fly
   Not permit (state ^A <x>) (state ^B <x>) → . . .
   But only (state ^A <x> ^B <x>) → . . .

4. **Duration of match: depends on object complexity**
   Complicated because of space/time trade-offs in match

Figure 5-3. Variant microcharacteristics of Soar.

5.2.3. Underspecification of Soar

Architectures, like other large systems, are never completely specified, fixed, or finished.[2] Soar is no exception. There is, of course, a Soar that is the code that exists as of a given date, say 18 February 1987, when the first William James Lecture was delivered. But Soar is always in a state of becoming. These micromodifications almost never change Soar's essential nature, but they can have important effects on how well Soar explains various psychological phenomena. Figure 5-3 provides four examples of scheduled modifications and completions to Soar4, which are also relevant to Soar as a cognitive theory. These underline Soar's actual nature as a family of closely related systems. By extension, they help us to see that unified theories of cognition will be more like Lakatosian research programmes than like Popperian theories. There will always be a certain chameleon quality about them; they cannot be completely pinned down, for they could just as easily be slightly different, or exist in multiple variations, or be on the verge of a change.

The *single-state principle* states that only a single state of a problem space is kept in working memory while Soar searches the space. Currently, Soar4 keeps the entire path, adding each state as it is generated. Soar4 has the potential to back up to any of these

---

2. Actually, the human architecture itself may never attain a fixed state; certainly biological entities are not static structures (recall Figure 2-12).

prior states. The single-state principle has Soar keep only the current state, and so the system can go back only to the current state in a higher space or to the initial state (which can be reconstructed). Many indications converge on the adoption of this principle. Soar almost never actually backs up in the same space. It usually does its search by dropping down into selection subspaces, as illustrated for the blocks world in Figure 4-14. Even in more sophisticated searches, such as progressive deepening, as illustrated for algorithm design (Figure 4-20), it comes back to the initial state and begins over again. The current scheme is computationally inefficient, requiring each new state to be copied, because the older state is still viable. Most important psychologically, the current scheme is unrealistic in terms of short-term memory. Whether difficulties arise from the amount of material to be remembered or from interference from highly similar states, maintaining multiple states is unlikely. Thus, an initial version of the single-state principle will be installed in Soar5,[3] and we will treat Soar as obeying the principle. This change would seem to have little impact on immediate behavior, since searches of multiple states in problem spaces do not occur. On the contrary, it is actually essential to deal with perceiving sequential input without inappropriate state copying.

The *principle of limited instantiation* is that each production produces only one instantiation per elaboration cycle. Currently Soar4 adopts a simple parallelization of the Ops5 match. Soar finds and executes all the possible instantiations of all productions, whether 1, 10, or 10,000, all in one cycle of the production system. By our mapping of Soar to human cognition, this must happen in $\sim\sim 10$ ms. Two distinct assumptions are required for this. First, productions are processes that operate fully in parallel. It seems reasonable to assume this; they can be independent mechanisms in separate locales. Second, all the instantiations of the same production can be produced in parallel.[4] Since a single production implies a common structure, it is much less plausible to accept this assumption. It seems more appropriate to take the common structure as imposing

---

3. This feature is called *destructive state modification,* because the current state is modified to create the new one.

4. Recently the Ops5 match has been shown to give rise to *expensive chunks* that produce combinatorially many instantiations, providing additional grounds for modifying the match (Tambe & Newell, 1988; Tambe & Rosenbloom, 1989).

some sort of resource limitation. Such an assumption has shown up in earlier designs (Newell, 1980b; Rosenbloom & Newell, 1987). One simple formulation of this constraint is that each additional instantiation takes one additional production cycle. By affecting how much parallelism is available within a decision cycle, this principle can affect the time taken in immediate-response tasks while leaving the general functionality essentially unchanged.

The *principle of limited match power* is that equality tests cannot be performed between separate condition elements. Soar has been constructed by assuming the conventions of Ops5 and modifying them as needed. The most important unanalyzed conventions are those that govern the matching. They determine how much computation can be accomplished in a single production cycle. Some aspects of this match are quite limited. Soar does a pattern match, rather than permit arbitrary computations to test if a production is satisfied. In other ways, however, the match is quite powerful. Soar permits the same variable to occur in many different condition elements, where it must have the same value. Thus, if there are M elements in the working memory, a production with K conditions can be forced to consider of the order of M^K possibilities for instantiation, satisfying a fixed but arbitrarily large set of equality tests among the possibilities. Indeed, this matching scheme is sufficiently powerful to be NP-complete (Garey & Johnson, 1979), meaning (for instance) that one can encode into the matching of a single (horrendous) production the requirement to solve a traveling-salesman problem. Humans do not have this much power in the recognition match, so the Soar match needs to be replaced by a weaker capability. One simple but plausible version (noted in the figure) is not to permit equality testing of variable bindings between condition elements, as now, but to permit testing within a single condition element. This makes equality testing a localizable process, rather than one that can be done between arbitrary subsets of elements in working memory. This principle also can directly affect the time taken for immediate responses.

The *duration of the match* is an unspecified aspect of the architecture that exists even after we have prohibited unlimited instantiation and curbed the logical power of the match. How long the match takes and on what parameters it depends have not been fully specified in the Soar theory of human cognition, although of course they are determined for any current computer implementation.[5] The basic assumption is that the match cycle always takes approximately the same time, but the constancy need only be approximate. Other aspects could have important temporal effects, such as the number of conditions, their size or complexity, and so on. Assumptions should arise naturally from an understanding of the algorithms that could govern the match in the human. The issue is complicated, because an entire space of algorithms exists, varying along dimensions, such as how much state is saved from cycle to cycle and how much seriality is involved (Gupta, 1986).

All these proposed modifications and further specifications are slated to be made in Soar in some form or another. They all have some effect on aspects of immediate behavior, which is our concern in this chapter. However, they will still leave Soar essentially the same architecture described in Chapter 4.

5.3. Functional Analysis of Immediate Responses

The tasks that involve responding immediately to a presented stimulus comprise a family with many common characteristics, although of course each task has its own unique features. The first step in considering how Soar behaves for such a family is to see if these common characteristics permit Soar to be specialized. In this respect, theories of the architecture are like the general partial differential equations of physics, such as the wave equation or Maxwell's equations. They give rise to specialized theories for specialized classes of initial and boundary conditions.

This is likely to be the case with immediate behavior. The common properties are extremely constraining, especially when we focus on the chronometric experiments typical of the psychological laboratory, from which most of the regularities have come. The defining characteristic of immediate response is that not many steps occur between the external presentation of the situation (the stimulus) and the resulting external action (the response). Several additional conditions hold as well. First, the task is speeded. To enforce this, experimenters make the instructions command and the payoffs reward responding as fast as possible. Second, the per-

---

5. Actually, they differ significantly between the existing uniprocessor and multiprocessor implementations (Tambe, Kalp, Gupta, Forgy, Milnes, & Newell, 1988).

son is well prepared, so the task is simple, understandable, and explainable, and ample opportunity is given for the person to understand and practice all relevant aspects of the task. Third, the task environment is well behaved, so care is taken that untoward things do not happen and the situation is not open ended and uncertain. Often, of course, the experimental design deliberately includes elements of uncertainty and surprise, but these are limited to specific task dimensions and inserted in highly controlled ways. The net result of all these constraints and enforcements is a specific central paradigm for immediate-response tasks: the presentation of a stimulus in a familiar class, to which the person generates an immediate (speeded) response in a familiar class, according to a simple rule or correspondence that the person has become skilled in using. This central paradigm can be elaborated in many ways—a preparatory phase, a sequence of two presentations, an occasional surprise. But the boundaries of the paradigm are exceeded when the person begins to be error prone, puzzled, surprised, forgetful, or unmotivated. In all these cases, task duration also tends to exceed ~~1 sec.

To explore how these task conditions specialize Soar, we first lay out the problem space in which immediate behavior takes place. This is the space where perception and motor behavior interface with cognition. Hence, this discussion augments the brief treatment of the total cognitive system given in Chapter 4. Next we specify the functions that the operations in this space must perform to do the task, abstracting away from some of the details of their full operation. Finally, we specify the basic temporal parameters required to obtain numerical predictions of response time. The result of this section will be an abstract analysis scheme that can then be applied to several examples.

5.3.1. The Base-Level Problem Space (BLS)

Like all other behavior, immediate response occurs in a problem space. This is the space in which the working-memory elements created by perception (via encoding perhaps) become available for cognitive consideration; and in which the commands are issued that result (via decoding perhaps) in the motor system taking action. Both input and output occur in a single space, since otherwise taking an impasse would also be required for taking an action, and this would imply some permanent lack of knowledge. This space is

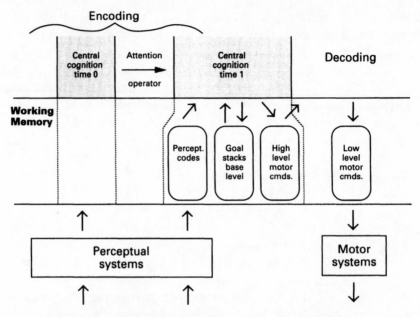

Figure 5-4. The base-level problem space (BLS).

called the *base-level problem space (BLS)*, because it is the one that governs interaction with the external world (Rosenbloom, Laird, & Newell, 1988a). Figure 5-4 provides a picture.

The base-level problem space is also the one space that doesn't arise from an impasse and is always in place as the top of the context stack (hence it is also called the *top* space). It is the space within which an initial impasse occurs and from which the stack of contexts grows as impasses occur within impasses. A moment's thought shows that one space must exist that does not arise from an impasse. Just ascend the stack of goal contexts—it is a finite structure and must terminate in some top context, which then necessarily did not come from any impasse. Suppose this top space of the context stack were not also the base space that contains perception codes, motor commands, and the operators that deal with them. Then somehow there would have to be some lack of knowledge in this space that would force an impasse into the base (I/O) space. It is a little hard to imagine what that lack would be, especially since it must be related to what is going on in the top space.

For immediate-response tasks, almost all the internal action takes place in BLS. Only when an impasse occurs will other problem spaces be selected and entered. In simple, speeded, practiced tasks, where expectations are almost always fulfilled, such impasses will be rare.

BLS interfaces with perception and motor behavior. In the last chapter we sketched the total cognitive system (Figure 4-15), but now it is necessary to fill out a few details of the perceptual and motor processes, and how they operate. When the system is alert and in contact with the external world, working memory is full of perceptual and motor elements. In the midst of this continually changing population of elements exist the elements of central cognition, all tied to the goal stack, which itself is a collection of elements in working memory. Perceptual subsystems, encoding productions, decoding productions, and motor subsystems read these elements and fire at will, in various ways depending on their individual nature.

The arriving perceptual elements and the encoding activity are outside central cognition, that is, inaccessible to it. How will cognition ever make contact with them? This is not an issue on the motor side. Central cognition can insert into working memory an element that is a command to the motor system, or one that can be decoded into a command. The decoding productions and the motor system can be assumed to be able to detect and acquire any elements addressed to them (put another way, working memory acts like a typical bus). The problem is on the perceptual side. How will an element not in central cognition become part of central cognition? The conditions of the central productions have no access to these elements—they do not even know they are out there. Some kind of active process is necessary to acquire these elements and make them accessible—to bring them inside cognition.

The *attention operator* is the required active process. It can be executed, as can any other operator, by central cognition. It is given a search specification, and it finds an element satisfying this specification from anywhere in working memory. The result of the attention operator (if successful) is that it switches cognition to be at the place of the attended element. The attention operator is like a *channel selector*. The parts of the working memory into which the perception systems put their elements (that is, the new perceptual elements) are organized as topographical *fields*—as metric spaces with relations of *at, near, far,* and *direction*. The perception subsystems (*P*) deliver information at *places* in these fields. The

E-productions build up structures (augmentations and links) around these places and between places. Attention is an operator that establishes the cognitive system as attending to some region in a given perceptual field. Once there, the additional input from perceptual systems and E-productions that are linked to that place continue to occur within central cognition, so that additional acts of attention are not required for processing of the incoming perceptual knowledge to continue.

Channel selection requires some explication, for the obvious assumption might seem to be for the attention operator to bring the new element *into* central cognition, for example, to link the element to the current state in which problem solving is proceeding. However, an element-transfer operation of this sort suffers a major difficulty. It must be deployed repeatedly in the inner loop of any activity involving dynamic perception, in order to continually bring into the current state the encoded image of the perceived world. More generally, this would make the connection of central cognition with the perceived world indirect, through a deliberately deployed low-bandwidth communication channel. Central cognition would be a sort of inner homunculus. Channel selection puts central cognition in direct contact with the part of the perceptual world to which it is attending, with an indirect relation to those aspects to which it is not attending.

The attention operator has primitive capabilities, hence it is an architectural mechanism. Its search specification is correspondingly fixed in character and basically simple, corresponding to the primitive attributes made available by perception. There is abundant evidence in the psychological literature for the simplicity of automatic search processes for the visual field (Treisman, 1986). The exact role that the Soar attention operator plays in accomplishing such tasks requires detailed consideration. But even without a full understanding of Soar's operation we know the attention operator, as an automatic process, could not have the ability to accept and use elaborated high-level descriptions as search specifications. Such power runs counter to the entire design of the architecture, as well as it no doubt would to these empirical results.

The attention operator is voluntary. It can be chosen by deliberation, just as can any operator. But attention can also *interrupt* cognition. Interruption occurs by the architecture having the capability of proposing the attention operator. The architecture simply makes a best preference for the attention operator, which will then be selected at the next decision cycle. This is an interesting example of a tiny change to the architecture (the ability to create a specific preference) that provides an important function, namely, interruption. It has two minor but interesting properties. First, the interruption does not occur instantly, it must wait until it is selected by the decision procedure when that executes next. Thus, there are variable delays in responding to the interruption. Second, the interruption need not be taken. Given a best preference, nothing can be taken over it, but if another best preference occurs then a tie impasse emerges and Soar is given the option of deciding.

When we turn to the nature of human motor action we find ourselves in an unsatisfactory state. The starting point for the extension of a unified theory of cognition into motor behavior is the interface between central cognition and the motor system. Cognitive intention produces a command to release motor action. But what is the language of commands that cognition uses to send messages to the motor system? Knowing that would be enough to get started. The command language structures the way the motor systems appear to cognition, and thus it determines cognition's tasks.

Unfortunately, the nature of the command language to the motor system is exactly where obscurity is deepest. Much is known about the motor system, both in behavioral and neural terms (Brooks, 1986; Stelmach, 1976, 1978; Stelmach & Requin, 1980; Kelso, 1977; Schmidt, 1982). The field has moved from a simple point-response, so to speak, to motor programs, and to elaborations of these, such as hierarchical programs (Rosenbaum, 1988). But nowhere is there any real clue about the language of the programs—only that it exists, or can appear linear or hierarchical under suitable tasks. Some experiments have attempted to determine directly whether the language of commands includes time, force, final position, or firing rates. These experiments are aimed in the right direction, but as yet they yield no integration. Their results can perhaps be summarized by saying that all the above are used, though in various not-well-understood situations and occasions.

D-productions might seem to offer a way out. They decode from some *high-level motor-command language* down to primitive commands. Thus, so goes this hope, one can adopt whatever motor-command language one wishes and simply stipulate that this will be converted into some unknown, but certifiably primitive, commands that the motor system can process. But this will not do. An arbitrary language will lead to arbitrariness in the cognitive tasks performed. The issue is precisely *not* to adopt whatever command language one wishes, but to find the one used by nature, which will presumably provide for smooth and rapid transduction of cognitive command to motor action.

One problem in thinking about this is the limited forms of command languages used in computer systems, even when extended to robotics, which are procedure calls (operations with predefined numerical parameters) composed in sequential hierarchical programs. It is useful to expand the possibilities. *Coordinative structures* or *synergies* (Kelso, 1982) form the motor system of *composed dynamic systems* (Saltzman & Kelso, 1987). For example, the way to get a finger to move to touch a given place is for the system to set up a temporary dynamic system that has its equilibrium position where the finger is supposed to come to rest. Think of it as an assemblage of springs that comes to rest at the desired landing place. Having created that dynamic system, the system turns it loose and the finger automatically homes in at that place. If something disturbs its trajectory, then self-correcting behavior occurs simply by continuing to move toward the equilibrium point; it is not due to any feedback-control system that senses the deviation and reacts to it. This research tradition originates in the work of the Russian Nicolai Bernstein (Bernstein, 1967). Its focus has not been on characterizing the command language (or even acknowledging an interface between cognition and the motor system), but on the evidence that the motor system runs in terms of such coordinative structures.

In this scheme, the command language is the set of specifications for building composable dynamic systems. The systems themselves can behave for durations of between ~100 and ~1,000 ms and longer. The approach accommodates such tasks as handwriting, which can be seen as a very long term (~~10 sec) advancing, oscillating system, modulated to give the individual letter shapes (Hollerbach, 1980). This is in contradistinction to more classically organized command schemes that have the motor act micromanaged by the setting and changing of command-parameters every 10–20 ms.

Coordinative structures are a nice example we can use to enrich the view of composable systems developed in Chapter 2. There, the examples of composable transformations obeying representational laws were programs—passive data structures to be interpreted to yield action. We argued that the concept was broader than that. These composable, dynamic motor systems (synergies) satisfy all the requirements of composable transformations, but instead of being programs that are interpretable, they are designed systems that behave. Their purpose in the context of the motor system remains exactly that discussed in Chapter 2, namely to obtain an extremely wide diversity of response functions.

For many cognitive activities (though far from all), the motor system operates almost as an exterior appendage. This is true of the speeded response tasks we are considering in this chapter, which are actions such as a button push, a keystroke, or an uttered single word. These are overlearned skills that are tightly coordinated and under good control, whatever the internal dynamics of their realization. Some crude timing model is needed for the motor system to fire up and execute, in order to compute the total time from stimulus to response, but that is entirely phenomenological. Thus, a model of the motor system adequate for the purposes of immediate speeded tasks employing simple discrete responses can avoid most of the complexity inherent in the above picture. This situation is of some comfort, given the uncertainties attending on the nature of motor commands. But, equally, it is just a stopgap, from which little can be expected in the way of unifying cognition and motor behavior.

5.3.2. Functional Operations for Immediate Response

We can now develop the operational scheme for speeded, well-prepared, immediate-response tasks. We know the overall task is to produce a simple response dependent in some well-specified, direct way upon the presentation of a stimulus. We know what space must be used and (up to a point) how it connects with perception and motor behavior. We know that operators in this space will be used to connect the encoded stimulus with an encoding of the response. We know the person will have whatever search control is appropriate to the task (because of instruction, preparation, and practice), so that there will be no superfluous activity and (to first approximation) no failures of activity.

Given the above, we can simply write down what functions must be accomplished. These will either be accomplished by perception or motor behavior, or by operators and search control in BLS. We

Central Cognition

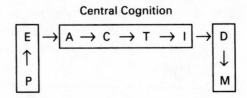

P Perceive: sense the environment
Duration: uncontrolled, decreases with intensity

E Encode: perceptual parse (production sequence)
Duration: Increases with complexity, not required for detection

A Attend: focus on input (operator)
Duration: Delay + search, decreases with preparation (to null)

C Comprehend: analyze for significance (operator)
Duration: Increases with complexity, decreases with preparation
(must exist)

T Task: set what task is to be done (operator)
Duration: decreases with preparation (to null)

I Intend: determine and release action (operator)
Duration: decreases with preparation (must exist)

D Decode: convert commands (production sequences)
Duration: increases with complexity, decreases with preparation (to
null)

M Move: make the commanded movement
Duration: uncontrolled, decreases with force, imprecision, preparation

Figure 5-5. Minimal scheme for immediate response
in the Soar architecture.

will take each function to be accomplished by a distinct operation. Figure 5-5 gives the minimal complete functional path from stimulus to response. It goes from perception (*P*) to encoding (*E*) to attending (*A*) to comprehending (*C*) to tasking (*T*) to intending (*I*) to decoding (*D*) to motor action (*M*). These are not stages in the sense made familiar by Sternberg (1969), but they can become stages as soon as data dependencies show up, where the output of some productions becomes the input of others.

A functional analysis always raises questions about uniqueness. Some freedom or indeterminism always exists, and understanding it is critical to using a functional scheme. We will discuss the general issues below. One type of variation, however, is an important part of the scheme itself. Depending on the specifics of the task, some operations can be performed prior to the occurrence of the stimulus (at *P*) by suitable *preparation*. Since adequate and appropriate preparation is assumed, these possibilities are important in determining the behavior.

Let us go through the sequence, defining the functions and why they are necessary. We will assume the paradigm immediate-response task: a stimulus is presented, the person must immediately produce a response that is some direct function of the stimulus. We will also note factors that affect the duration required to perform the function and the possibility of preparation, which could remove the function entirely from the analysis.

Perceiving the stimulus must occur first. The architecture provides no alternative to this being done by *P*, the perceptual module. *P* runs autonomously and is not modified by experience (it could also be said to be impenetrable). Thus, its duration is uncontrolled by central cognition. The duration is a function of specific stimulus properties. For instance, as stimulus intensity goes up, the perception time goes down.

Encoding occurs next, a process of perceptual parsing that produces a representation of the stimulus in task-independent terms. This is a comprehension function that is obligatory, given the structure of the architecture. It is composed of a sequence of production executions, whose duration is simply the sum of the serial chain of E-productions that fire. Duration will increase with the complexity of the stimulus. However, just detecting that a stimulus is there requires no encoding at all (with suitable preparation). The arrival of the stimulus elements from *P* can be enough for the system to trigger further responses.

Attend is the operator that brings cognition to focus on the stimulus element. The duration associated with attend has several functionally necessary components. For voluntary attention, there may be a delay prior to selection of attend, measured from when the stimulus element is available in working memory. Such a delay would be absent for an interruption. There must be a search for the stimulus elements, though this is likely to require an essentially fixed duration, since all of the usual problems associated with search (choice of directions, rejection of candidates, and the like) occur at the level of a decision cycle. It is important to note that preparation may be possible so that attend need not occur at all.

The system must already be located at the place where the stimulus element will arrive, and must expect it there. Note that attend is not an eye-movement operation.

Comprehend is the function of assuring that a new perceptual element is what was expected and in the form needed for continued processing. It involves both recognition and labeling or re-representing, as required. This interpretive function in general cannot be moved out into the E-productions. There is no way to produce new E-productions in the short term, in response to particular demands, and they cannot be controlled as a function of the task— once there, they will just fire. So E-productions cannot be organized to be a task-responsive system. The application of this principle requires some care. E-productions, of course, are conditional, so they can have some task conditionality built in, but their conditionality is built in once and for all at the time of creation (which occurred long prior to the task under consideration).

Comprehension is performed by an operator. If a sufficiently complex comprehension is required, then this operator has to break out into an implementation space, but there are limits to the amount of processing that can occur for immediate-response tasks. The duration of comprehend increases with the complexity of the stimulus object—what it takes to identify it and its task-relevant aspects—and decreases with preparation, which is again the extent to which the comprehension task has been narrowed down to what is essential. How much preparation is possible depends on the details of the task.

Tasking is the function of setting a task to be performed. This task cannot be set by an impasse occurring, since the system is already at the top level. Thus, tasking must occur by an operator being selected in BLS that augments the current state so that both comprehend and intend can know what to do. This operator and the search control that proposes it must be a part of the system's long-term memory. There is, therefore, a question of how such operators got created and established in the first place. Pursuing this would take us far from immediate behavior. The answer for most immediate-response tasks is in terms of prior instructions and preparation. But additional questions lie behind that answer, such as why the person accepted the instructions.

For immediate-response tasks, it is always possible to perform the tasking operator prior to the presentation of the stimulus. In fact, doing so is a necessary part of being prepared—that the person knows exactly what to do and only must execute the task. We might have put *T* as the initial function to be performed, rather than after *C*. In general, however, the task to be attempted is evoked by what is comprehended about the environmental situation, so it seemed better to indicate the general situation and not imply that the task is always set ahead of time. In any case, *T* will not show up in any critical-time paths and it effectively drops out of the analysis, even though it is an essential function for accomplishing a complete task.

Intend is the function of committing to a response. There must be such a function or there will not be a response from the person, though there might be behavior of the person's body. The intention is not the response itself, which is produced by the motor subsystem. Instead, it is the issuance of a command to the motor system that commits the system to a particular response. With the successful completion of an intention, expressed as an encoded command in working memory, control escapes from central cognition. Control can possibly be regained, if enough time elapses before the motor system passes beyond the point of no return and suitable abortion or modification commands are possible, hence can themselves be intended. But such control is a new task and problem, distinct from the original intention.

Intending is performed by an operator. It determines which external action to take and issues the motor command to working memory. With suitable preparation it may be very simple and hence short. It can also expand indefinitely if there are difficulties in determining what response should be made. However, it must always occur, for it is the point where behavior is controlled.

Decoding, like encoding, is an obligatory function, consisting of a sequence of productions. Decoding of the command occurs autonomously, outside the control of central cognition. Its duration increases with the complexity of the motor command and can be influenced by preparation.

Motor behavior is the function of actually affecting the external world—clearly necessary for accomplishing a task. Like perception, its duration is not controlled by central cognition. It is intrinsic to the motion required and not penetrable by cognition. If we think in terms of a composed dynamic system, however, its operation may be quite complex and may last a relatively long time, compared with the fast cycles of the system. The motor system might have some properties that could be changed by preparation, such as being in a state of tonus, but our model for the motor system is not good enough to specify this kind of modification.

This *P-E-A-C-T-I-D-M* scheme is defined by the functions that are *necessary* to perform the task. Remove any of them and the task fails. It is easy to show these functions are also *sufficient* (within the Soar architecture) simply by specifying operators and productions that implement the functions that actually perform the task. This will be straightforward for the immediate-response tasks under consideration. Each operation simply reads and writes some definite information on the state received from the prior operation. Furthermore, the assumption of adequate preparation implies that operators and selection productions will have whatever conditionality is appropriate.

So straightforward is the operation of these systems that an important simplification becomes possible. We can assume that, if the knowledge has been encoded in the state, then the appropriate operators will be selected and executed to provide the next stage in the path. Hence, there is no need to be explicit about either the encodings or the conditions of the operators and productions. We can simply assume the knowledge is encoded and write down the sequence of *P, E, A, C, T, I, D, M* operations that generate the right knowledge at the right time.

This abstraction moves the focus away from the production system entirely and to a sequential scheme for specifying behavior. This level of analysis, the level of *abstract functional operations*, is not a new general system level that somehow squeezes in above the level of immediate deliberation and below the level of problem spaces (Figure 4-23). Rather, it is a simplification of the level of simple operations. Moreover, its abstraction—ignoring conditional linkages, using the operators dictated by perfect task analysis, and assuming no problem solving—holds only under the special conditions of prepared, speeded, simple immediate-response behavior.

The abstract functional operations (*P, E, A, C, T, I, D, M*) are both necessary and sufficient for these immediate-response tasks. They are not necessarily unique, however. There could conceivably be different decompositions of the functions into a sequence of operators and productions. We already incorporated into the scheme one way in which this happens, namely, that preparation removes some function from having to be performed between the stimulus and response, and lets it occur in advance. Generally, such advancements do not provide alternative decompositions of behavior. The speeded nature of the task and adequate preparation implies that the minimal time arrangement will occur.

Other questions about uniqueness need to be asked. Can the functions be carried out in different orders (given the Soar architecture)? For example, is *D-C-A-M-I-P-T-E* possible? The answer is no. *T* will always occur in advance. The initial sequence of *P-E* is dictated by the architecture, as is the final sequence of *D-M*. *A* always occurs after *P-E*, if it has not occurred in advance of the task. The remaining possibility is *C-I* versus *I-C*. But *C* always has to precede *I*, since *I* terminates the act of cognition on the response. Thus, since the function of *C* (comprehension of the input) is necessary, it must be performed before *I*.

How about variation in how the functions are implemented in productions and operators? Different kinds of uncertainty must be distinguished. The first is our scientific uncertainty about the boundaries between parts of the system. In our present state, we are unable to determine sharply the boundary between *P* and *E, I* and *D*, and *D* and *M*. We do know, however, that even though we do not know the actual boundary, it is fixed and does not vary with task or person.

A second kind of uncertainty is variation depending on the task and on the properties of the study population. There can be uncertainty between *E* and *C*, since they both involve the analysis of the stimulus. What analysis goes in *E* and what in *C*? The key discrimination is task dependence. The stimulus analysis carried out by *E* is totally task independent—*E* involves automatic encoding and cannot be augmented or changed for a specific task. All task-dependent stimulus analysis occurs within cognition. However, what is task independent can depend on the population. Some populations recognize the letters of the Hebrew alphabet perceptually; many others do not.

A third kind of uncertainty is that multiple organizations are possible, given the types of knowledge of the people performing the task and the lack of detailed knowledge on the part of people analyzing the performance (the scientists). For instance, there can be uncertainty between *C* and *I*. Multiple functions must be accomplished—verifying the relevance of the stimulus, encoding the stimulus in task-dictated ways, selecting or constructing a response, and composing and issuing commands to the motor system. These could be packaged as two operators, C and I (as we have done it) or as suboperators of a single CI operator. Then, although the boundary functions of verification at the beginning and commanding at the end are fixed, task encoding and response selection or composition could intertwine in whatever way is most efficient. On the other hand, a CI operator might be composite and require an impasse and subspace, so the decomposition into C and I each as simple operators might be faster.

Even with a fixed functional decomposition, functions may require implementation by multiple productions and/or multiple operators. The power of a production or a simple operator (an operator realized within a single problem space) is dictated by the Soar architecture and bears no necessary relationship to a general function such as comprehension or intention. The architecture dictates the boundary conditions: P and M are fixed; E and D are realized by collections of free-firing productions, and A is a single primitive operator. C and I are operators that can be as complex as the task requires, but whose complexity remains limited by the demands of the immediate-response task.

That functions can be realized in specific operators in multiple ways is just the familiar point that there is more than one way to skin a cat. Especially as the task to be performed (stimulus analysis and response construction) becomes more complex, more alternative ways of carrying it out become possible. This is just the point that psychologists must always be prepared for multiple methods on the part of their subjects (Newell, 1973b; Siegler, 1987). Considerations of efficiency weed out some methods, but there will still be alternative plausible ways of accomplishing a task.

5.3.3. Making Quantitative Predictions
To make quantitative predictions of response time,[6] it is not enough to write down the functions to be performed or even to specify the way they map into operators. It is necessary to provide times for

6. Errors are another type of quantitative prediction. However, error rates are extremely low in the class of immediate-response tasks under consideration, and designedly so. Thus, the functional-operation abstraction does not retain the aspects of the situation needed for an analysis of errors. Response time is the relevant quantitative prediction.

each of the operations. Perception (*P*) and motor behavior (*M*) are primitives as far as our analysis is concerned, but encoding (*E*) and decoding (*D*) consist of sequences of production cycles, and the others, *A, C,* and *I,* involve operators, which are composed of decision cycles, which themselves are composed of production cycles and the decision procedure. Independent productions will fire in parallel during one cycle, of course, so that sequences of productions arise only with dependency.

For simple speeded tasks, most of the functions can be accomplished with a *minimum operator* that simply detects or reads some code in the current state and records or writes some other code. Even when the required processing is slightly more extended, the steps will still be quite independent, with the result that the total function will be a sequence of minimum operators. Thus, the time for the minimum operator provides a basic time unit for the analysis. The minimum operator requires one minimum decision cycle to select the operator and one minimum decision cycle to apply the operator. The minimum decision cycle is one production cycle and one minimum operation of the decision procedure. This is true both for selection (a single production enters an acceptable preference) and application (a single production augments the state with a code or sets a motor command). Thus, the minimal operator will take 2 × (production-cycle-time + decision-procedure-time).

Numerical values for the parameters are required if we are to produce quantitative predictions of behavior. The usual practice in psychological experimentation is to treat each experiment or experimental series as essentially an independent unit with respect to quantitative predictions. The rationale has two parts. On the negative side, each experimental situation has many unique features, so absolute parameters cannot be expected to apply across experiments and laboratories. On the positive side, the purpose of an experiment is to reveal some phenomenon or regularity, and the full quantitative details are almost always irrelevant to this. Each immediate-response experiment usually has a single estimated parameter that bundles together all the unique perceptual, motor, and cognitive processes. These often show up as the intercept on some plot, where the quantities of interest are the changes with condition or sometimes the slopes. The experiments on automatic and controlled behavior in Figure 3-8 provide a typical example.

Cognitive psychology does believe that cognitive mechanisms

take characteristic times that transcend the unique experimental situation, perhaps as functions of as yet undetermined aspects of situations plus a stochastic component. Thus, psychology is sensitive to estimates of parameters turning out to be approximately constant. For instance, the Posner naming task (Posner, 1978) presents a person with a pair of letters and asks whether they are the *same*. Comparing the judgment time for the *same percept* [a a] versus the *same letter* [a A] (against foils such as [a b] or [a B]) shows that it takes ~80 ms to retrieve the letter code given the percept. Furthermore, this value of ~80 ms is quite robust and has been obtained in many experimental variations. Its invariance has contributed much to the importance of this paradigm. On the other hand, confidence in factor analysis of intelligence tests seriously eroded because the factors never turned out to be independent enough of the specific tests—so it was difficult to believe in the reality of underlying factors that the factor analyses were just revealing from different angles.

A unified theory of cognition necessarily takes a strong position with respect to developing constants that can be used in all situations. A unified theory claims to present the mechanisms of cognition that operate in all tasks. For Soar, these are the mechanisms of the recognition memory, the decision procedure, the chunker, and the modules for perception and motor behavior. The timing and reliability constants associated with these mechanisms might be functions of various characteristics of the cognitive architecture and might be stochastic. Depending on the exact situation they would then be constant functions or constant parameters of distributions, but they would still be constants over all situations. To use Pylyshyn's term, these constants are not penetratable by the content of each task. Of course, the need for constants does not eliminate the variability in nature that led to the general acceptance of experiment-bound constants.

Nevertheless, a major enterprise for a unified theory of cognition will be to develop these constants. One approach is to design experiments that attempt to measure a particular constant in as pure a form as possible. This is analogous to doing experiments to measure the speed of light. A second approach is to assemble the analyses of a large diversity of tasks involving all the various constants in different combinations. On the whole, it is not possible to find pure experiments, and several constants enter into the prediction of

Decision procedure	~10 ms
Production cycle	~20 ms
Minimal operator	~60 ms $= 2 \times (20 + 10)$
Perception	~40 ms
Simple motor act	~60 ms

Figure 5-6. Stipulated time constants.

each experimental result. This approach accepts this limitation and treats the analyzed experiments as a very large set of simultaneous constraints on the constants. The yield is the adoption of values that produce relatively good results across the breadth of behavior, including estimates of variability and indications of functional variation in the constants. The attempt to determine the constants is not a one-time affair but a continuous activity. Indeed, this activity could become a major indicator of the scope and the accuracy of a given unified theory.

Coming back to the enterprise of this chapter, we wish to illustrate how Soar can be used to make predictions at the immediate-response level. The previous analysis has identified three or four constants that enter into the formulation. The perceptual module, the minimal operator, and the motor module form a set of three. If encoding and decoding productions also occur, then we need the production cycle as well. In the latter case, we could take the decision procedure as another constant and then derive the minimal operator as two production cycles and two decisions; this provides an alternative set of four.

We do not wish to engage in a mini-version of the parameter-setting exercise described above. Even initial attempts should be done against the background of the sort of analysis we are about to commence, so it would put the cart before the horse to set them by some form of data analysis before we start. Instead, we simply stipulate a set of values in round 10 ms terms (Figure 5-6). This set will turn out to be fairly close to the mark for the several experimental paradigms we will discuss. These constants may be viewed in one of two ways, and it probably doesn't make much difference which. First, they can be viewed as if they were established by an analysis of a set of independent experiments. Then they are indeed constants for the purposes of the analyses to come. Alternatively, they can be viewed as if they were determined jointly by the set of experiments to be described. Since quite a few experiments are involved, with independent data sets, the constants may be taken as having been amortized broadly over many data points.

These constants are at least plausible. Consider the central processing constants—the decision procedure at ~10 ms, productions at ~20 ms, and minimal operators at ~60 ms. The decision procedure and the production cycle are toward the lower end of the ~~10 ms range we have been using all along. The minimal operator is far below the general ranges we have specified, ~~100 ms for a decision cycle and ~~1 sec for a simple operator, but this is just the result of seeking the absolute minimum. Normally, many productions would fire within a decision cycle, since the situation is open to any production at all, whether or not relevant to the task. One feature of immediate-response tasks is the removal of extraneous firings. In addition, multiple preferences would be expected to increase the decision processing. On the empirical side, Card, Moran, and Newell (1983), after considering diverse experimental results and analyses, adopted a characteristic value of ~70 ms for the cognitive processor cycle (τ_c) of the Model Human Processor, with a range of ~25 to ~170 ms (see Figure 1-9 in this book). They deliberately avoided decomposing the central processing of these tasks in any uniform way, taking at face value the conceptual units of the original studies (which explains the large total range). Thus, these values mostly, but not uniformly, reflect activity a level above the production cycle and decide time. Thus, the decision-procedure and production-cycle durations should be a modest submultiple of ~70 ms, say between ~10 and ~40 ms. On the other hand, the minimal-operator duration of ~60 ms seems quite consonant with the ~70 ms central cycle.

The perceptual-module time of ~40 ms can be compared with the Model Human Processor value for the perceptual processor of ~100 ms with a range of 50 to 200 ms. The perceptual processor covers both P and E, so we would expect P to be down toward the lower end of the range, namely ~50 ms. For perception it is possible to find confirmation in physiological measurements, something not possible for central cognition. For instance, measuring evoked potentials as they come up the stations of the auditory nerve yields times of ~20 ms before the cortex is reached. Similarly, measuring the stations of the optic nerve yields similar times before the visual cortex is reached. The basic duration of P should be slightly longer than this.

The motor-module time of ~60 ms can be compared with the

"Press the button when the light goes on."
Adequate preparation, warning, intensity, within fovea

		ms
P	Minimum	~40
E	None: only detection required	0
A	None: subject is prepared, already fixated on light	0
C	Single operator to verify, no impasses	~60
T	None: subject is prepared, T is incorporated in C	0
I	Single minimal operator, no impasses	~60
D	None: simple practiced response	0
M	Minimum	~60
	SRT	~220

SRT = P + C + I + M

Figure 5-7. The simplest response task (SRT).

Model Human Processor value for the motor processor cycle of 70 ms, with a range of 30–100 ms. This is within the range, but it seems a little high if we consider the motor processor to be $M + D$, for this assumption implies that M should be down toward the low end.

5.4. The Simplest Response Task (SRT)

At last, we are now prepared to deal with simple immediate-response tasks. Figure 5-7 shows the simplest task: Press a button when the light goes on. This is the minimum arc from stimulus to response, assuming (as we do) that there is adequate preparation, including an immediately preceding warning, and that the stimulus has adequate intensity and occurs within the fovea so no eye movements are required. The figure provides an accounting of the processes and how long they take, from which we obtain a prediction of the time. Perception (P) is taken to be ~40 ms for a stimulus of adequate intensity. For this simple response task, only detection is required, not stimulus encoding, so 0 ms is required for E. Likewise, attend occurs prior to stimulus occurrence, when the fixation point is presented. So 0 ms is required for *A*. A single comprehension operator (*C*) is required, but it will be minimal (~60 ms) because everything is defined in terms of an expected sequence and that expected sequence occurs. The task is prepared in advance, hence 0 ms for *T*. There is an intend operator (*I*), which can execute as soon as *C* labels the stimulus object as the correct one. All it has to do is lay in the command, so it is also a minimal operator (60 ms). The motor movement itself is a simple highly practiced action. Thus, no decoding of the command by D-productions is required (0 ms for *D*). Finally, *M* is ~60 ms, which is the duration of a minimal motor action. Adding up the column gives ~220 ms for the total time of a simple reaction time task.

What has been done in getting to the result of Figure 5-7? We started with Soar and the mapping of it into the time scale of human cognition (Figure 4-23). We then produced an analysis of its behavior in extremely simple situations, which permitted us to come up with an a priori rough estimate of human simple reaction time. The actual times are ~200 ms, although there is lots of variability, both from trial to trial and depending on aspects of the stimulus situation, such as modality, intensity, and immediate prior task (Luce, 1986). Thus, we see that Soar is to be used not only as a theory for problem solving but as a detailed model of microcognition. Many questions are raised by the particular style of analysis and approximation used here, but let us delay these questions until we consider some more examples.

5.5. The Two-Choice Response Task (2CRT)

Figure 5-8 shows a *two-choice reaction-time task (2CRT)*: Press the button under whichever light goes on. Again, we assume adequate preparation, the location of both lights within foveal vision, and so on. This situation is just barely more complex than the SRT task. Let us go through the accounting.

Perception still takes the minimum time; both stimulus representations of the two lights occur concurrently. Now, a distinguishing feature has to be noted about these two stimuli. The standard 2CRT experiment is designed so that a highly available feature is made highly salient, one light being turned on (with the other left off). This feature is detected and noted by an E-production. At minimum

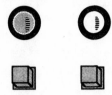

"Press the button under whichever light goes on."
Adequate preparation, warning, intensity, within fovea

		ms
P	Minimum	~40
E	1 production to encode property	~20 +
A	1 operator	~60 +
C	1 operator to verify	~60
	1 operator to discriminate	~60 +
T	None: subject is prepared, T is incorporated in C	0
I	1 minimal operator	~60
D	Command can't be given in advance	~20 +
M	Short	~60
	SRT	**~220**
	Additional times for 2CR	**~160**
	Total 2CRT	**~380**

Figure 5-8. The two-choice response task (2CRT).

it takes only a single production, which is to say, it is a feature that would normally be encoded for the type of perceptual objects being used. (The stimulus is not, for instance, the choice between a single geometric figure being a triangle or a square, which would require more perceptual encoding.) Thus E is ~20 ms, marked with a plus to indicate that the value is in addition to that for the SRT task.

In this experiment, with two spatially separated lights, an attend operator is required. The standard arrangement is to have the person attend to a neutrally placed fixation point, so that an attend operator is required in all cases. If the person were to attend to one place or the other, response could have improved to the attended choice but would have been slower to the unattended choice. We are not talking about eye movements in this situation; all vision is within the fovea; but there is no doubt that attention shifts occur within fixations (Posner, 1978). Thus, attend requires ~60 ms. The comprehension operator must still occur. Attend only acquires the stimulus, it does not verify nor label it. But verification is not the discrimination, to be used as the basis for the choice of action, so labeling requires another operator, for another ~60 ms. The intention operator takes the same duration as in SRT. However, if discrimination is located in the comprehension operator, which produces a discriminating label, then there are in fact two intend operators, one for each response, only one of which fires. The motor command cannot now be totally given in advance, so it needs at least minimal decoding (20 ms for D), but the motor behavior is the same ~60 ms as was used in the SRT task. Summing up the result gives a total of ~380 ms, which is the original ~220 ms of SRT plus another ~160 ms that represents the additional activity needed to deal with the complexity of a simple choice. Actual 2CRT times for humans are ~350 ms, with (as always) substantial variation.

We now have a second example of using Soar to make rough predictions of the time it takes for a human to do immediate-response tasks. Let us consider one more example, to have a suitable basis for discussion.

5.6. Stimulus-Response Compatibility (SRC)

Stimulus-response compatibility can be simply illustrated by an elevator control panel (Figure 5-9). If the UP button is located above the DOWN button, then calling for the elevator is straightforward. On the other hand, if the DOWN button is located above the UP button, then there is some difficulty. People will make more errors in hitting the button and they will take longer to hit the correct button. UP above DOWN is compatible with the desired direction of travel; DOWN above UP is incompatible. In general, arrangements that are more incompatible require longer response times and result in more errors. That seems sensible enough—downright intuitive, as a matter of fact.

Stimulus-response compatibility is easily shown experimentally. Figure 5-10 shows a typical experiment (Duncan, 1977). Four buttons are located below four lights (Duncan's setup was slightly different). There are four conditions, each dictating a response with a different compatibility between stimulus and response. Most compatible (*corresponding*) is to press the key directly beneath the light. Of intermediate incompatibility (*opposite*) is to press the cor-

ELEVATOR BUTTONS

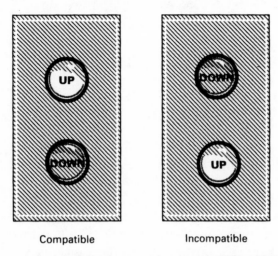

Compatible   Incompatible

Figure 5-9. Stimulus-response compatibility (SRC).

responding key on the opposite side of the light that displays. More incompatible are the two mixed conditions: *mixed-inner*, where an outside light corresponds to the button immediately below it but an inside light corresponds to the opposite inside button; and *mixed-outer*, where the center lights correspond to the center buttons and the outside lights correspond to the opposite outside buttons. It can be seen from the figures that response times vary with the different conditions. (Duncan reported only the average of the mixed conditions.)

The empirical demonstration of SRC actually goes back to Fitts and Seeger (1953). Again, we find Paul Fitts at the discovery of an important phenomenon. Paul Fitts is one of the heroes of experimental psychology, as far as I'm concerned, although he is known mostly to engineering psychologists. He introduced several important quantitative laws and initiated the investigation of stimulus-response capabilities. SRC is of major importance in human-computer interaction and human factors. A large part of what makes displays and buttons easy to operate is whether stimuli and responses are compatible. Questions of compatibility show up in mundane ways, too, such as the common error of increasing the hot water in the shower when cooler water is wanted because no natural arrangement exists on which to base a compatible response.

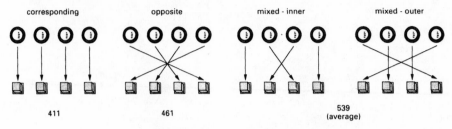

Figure 5-10. Experiment demonstrating SRC (Duncan, 1977).

Indeed, SRC phenomena are pervasive in all immediate-response situations.

Our concern here is not with SRC's practical importance but its use as an example of an immediate-response situation that is somewhat more complex than the SRT and CRT situations analyzed so far. If we accept the analysis used for the simpler tasks, it should be possible to analyze SRC phenomena within Soar. That there is indeed something to be analyzed can be seen in Figure 5-10. Although it might not require explanation why the *corresponding* case is least expensive (in time), the issue is not at all clear between the *mixed* case and the *opposite* case.

Until recently the state of the art in SRC research was a body of much empirical data plus two qualitative propositions: the more complex the mapping, the more incompatible; and simplicity is defined by population stereotypes. These permitted intuitive assessment of the comparative compatibility of sufficiently obvious situations. In 1983, Paul Rosenbloom proposed a quantitative theory of SRC, which was followed up by Bonnie John (John, Rosenbloom, & Newell, 1985; John & Newell, 1987). This theory was in the style of the Model Human Processor (MHP) developed for application to human-computer interaction (HCI) by Card, Moran, and Newell (1983) and described briefly in Chapter 1 (Figures 1-9 and 1-10). The MHP supports a technique for predicting the time to do a routine cognitive skill by writing an explicit algorithm for the mental operations that are performed, in a language composed of *Goals, Operators, Methods, and Selection rules* (hence called *GOMS* analysis). GOMS had been applied to text editing where the operations take ~10 sec. For the SRC task, the GOMS analysis was refined to use very rapid internal operators in an explicit algorithm for doing the mapping from the stimulus to the response. This quan-

task: intend to **delete**   type **dlt** (vowel deletion)

		ms
P	Minimum	~40
E	1 production/letter (6 letters)	~120
A	1 operator	~60
C	1 operator to verify	~60
	Perception$_{bj}$ = 314	~280
I	Get each syllable: 2 operators	~120
	Get spelling of syllable: 2 operators	~120
	Get each letter: 2 + 4 = 6 operators	~360
	Identify each letter: 2 + 4 = 6 operators	~360
	If constant link to save: 3 operators	~180
	Issue command to type letter: 3 operators	~180
	Mapping$_{bj}$ = 66 × 25 = 1650	~1320
D + M	Keystroke (can't split D, M): 3 × 180	~540
	Motor$_{bj}$ = 203 × 3 = 609	~540
	Totals: Total$_{bj}$ = 2573, Obs avg = 2400	~2140

Figure 5-11. SRC example: recall command abbreviation.

titative theory is quite successful at predicting the times humans take to do an SRC task. Its interest here is that it permits us to show an important way to proceed with Soar as a unified theory of cognition—to *incorporate* another successful theory, rather than replace it by proposing an entirely new theory.

Let us start with the qualitative structure of the theory. The mapping of stimulus to response must be done between representations. There will be a representation of the stimulus situation as it appears to the person, and this representation must be operated upon to produce a representation that is now in terms of the output situation. Thus we get *encode* → *map* → *respond*. The mapping is done by applying one operator after another. It must occur very rapidly but it still must be done in a controlled fashion, for the mapping is determined by instructions for the task and can be changed at any time. In Soar terms the mapping must be done by operators (minimal ones to be sure) and not by encoding or decoding productions, which admit no control. Hence the mapping is serial.

We wish to convert this general theory into Soar terms, which means that we must specify the mapping algorithm. Figure 5-11 shows an example. The task is taken from work by John (John, Rosenbloom, & Newell, 1985). She is exploring SRC in human-computer interaction, so this task is to recall command names for a computer system. The commands are abbreviations and they must be obtained in response to thinking of the complete name for the function, in response to the demands of the task. Thus, in the figure, the user intends to *delete* something but must think of the command name *dlt* to type it at the keyboard. In the experiment, *delete* appeared on the display and the user was to type *dlt*. This might not seem to be an example of SRC phenomena, since the usual examples of it are spatial (as in Figure 5-10), but it is. A highly compatible condition would be the rule of identity—type *delete* in response to the display of *delete*. Highly incompatible would be labels based on remote functional descriptions, such as *gro* from *get rid of* for *delete*. An intermediate case would be an arbitrary prefix character plus a one-letter code, for example, /d for *delete*.

The particular abbreviation rule in the figure is called *vowel deletion*. Going from *delete* to *dlt* is a mapping. In the figure, we write down the process of carrying out this mapping as Soar would perform it, namely in terms of our scheme of *P-E-A-C-I-D-M* (leaving out *T* as already having been performed). We have an algorithm from John's work against which to compare.

The initial requirement is to read in the displayed stimulus (*delete*). The first step for Soar is perception *P*. This just takes the basic perceptual time of ~40 ms, as used for SRT and CRT. The result has to be encoded for Soar to recognize the word. This task requires a minimum of one production a letter. Encoding is essentially name recognition, and empirically it turns out to take about 30 ms per letter, for both reading and isolated word naming (Just & Carpenter, 1987; Henderson, 1982). We will use ~20 ms per production, the time we adopted. Encoding *delete* will take six productions for a total of ~120 ms. Then there's the *A* operator to attend and a *C* operator to verify. If we add up this part we get ~280 ms. In John's theory, this entire phase is summarized in a single perceptual operator of 314 ms, which was a parameter estimated from her data. Our prediction is a little low, but in the ballpark.

Soar does the mapping by getting each syllable of the word (*de, lete*), then the spelling of each syllable (*d, e*), and then deciding whether to type each letter (*d*—type, *e*—don't type). The figure shows the number of operations, aggregated over each stage. There are two syllables in *delete*, so two operators are required to get the syllables, one for each. Likewise, two operators are required to get the spelling. An operator is required to obtain the letter from the syllable, which yields 6 operators for the letters. Obtaining each letter provides the decomposition to obtain the letter in the next place. Consequently, each letter must be identified as being a consonant or a vowel (6 more operators). Then the discrimination must be made. This is handled by an operator to pick out the consonants and ignore the vowels. Here, there are only three operators, one for each consonant and none for the vowels. In this particular algorithm, the whole abbreviation is obtained before it is typed out. Three commands need to be issued, one for each letter, so that requires 3 more operators. Adding up all the times corresponding to these operators gives ~1,320 ms. John's algorithm has almost the same operators (25 instead of 22) but uses 66 ms per operation instead of 60 ms, giving John's algorithm a total of 1,650 ms, slightly higher than Soar.

The motor operation $(D + M)$ has been lumped into a single value of ~180 ms per letter. Given our lack of clarity about a model of autonomous composed dynamic systems, it is hard to separate D and M, except in the simplest possible cases, as we did earlier. The choice of ~180 ms will be justified to some extent later. At the moment, it at least permits us to get final aggregate times. John's (experimentally estimated) motor time was 203 ms per keystroke, so she gets a slightly higher total again, namely, 609 ms versus ~540 ms. Finally, we end up with Soar making a prediction of how long it will take a person to react in this situation—to type *dlt* after seeing *delete*. Soar's prediction is ~2,140 ms. John's prediction is considerably higher, ~2,573 ms. In fact, the observed average time is 2,400 ms, which is in the middle. The errors of prediction are 12 percent over and 7 percent under, respectively.

Figure 5-11 is an analysis of a single task and made one prediction. In fact, theoretical predictions have been made with John's theory for 27 SRC situations, including many of the original basic studies on SRC and the one by Duncan described earlier. Figure 5-12 presents all the results, in a plot of predicted (on the horizontal) versus observed (on the vertical) response times. Each point represents one condition of one study, each of which presented a specific situation in which an SRC time could be modeled and computed. The average accuracy is 12 percent. As can be seen, the

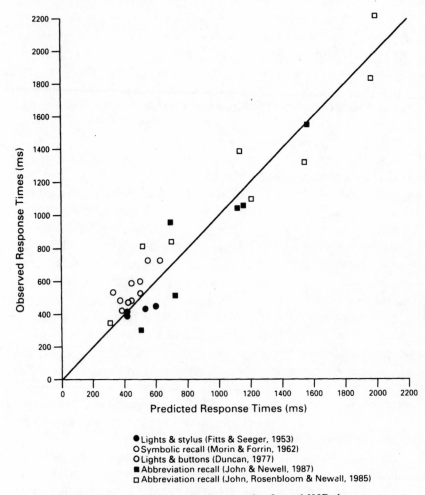

Lights & stylus (Fitts & Seeger, 1953)
Symbolic recall (Morin & Forrin, 1962)
Lights & buttons (Duncan, 1977)
Abbreviation recall (John & Newell, 1987)
Abbreviation recall (John, Rosenbloom & Newell, 1985)

Figure 5-12. SRC prediction results from MHP theory
(John & Newell, 1987).

MHP theory does a good job of predicting the time taken to respond in SRC situations. By the same token, Soar does a similar job, because it incorporates the MHP theory, though the details will not be the same.

5.7. Discussion of the Three Analyses

We now have three examples before us: SRT, 2CRT, and SRC. Let us step back and see what we have been doing. We are taking Soar seriously as a theory of cognition. The domain is quite specific—immediate speeded reaction-time tasks—but it is an especially important one for Soar, for the theory as developed originally and described in Chapter 4 was oriented toward problem solving and learning, not toward immediate-response data. Thus, one aspect of this exercise is to establish that a unified theory of cognition must stretch across the full spectrum of tasks.

We did not construct our models by writing production systems that performed the tasks. Instead, we established a more abstract level of analysis. By an analysis of the general task situation—speeded, low-error, immediate-response tasks—in conjunction with the Soar architecture as a constraint, we established a set of functional operations (P, E, and the others). These operations do not define an independent system level, but they approximate what could have been obtained by the more extensive analysis using operators defined completely by productions, plus the E and D productions.

The key element in the functional level of analysis is that the actual programs that perform the task are not written. The basic assumption is that, if the knowledge is encoded in the current state in working memory, then the recognitions and discriminations (to wit, the search control) can be taken for granted to execute in the right order the actions that are necessary. Furthermore, the costs of that control can be captured approximately, simply by the need to select operators. This assumption gets rid of the need actually to program the tasks.

It should not have escaped notice that Figure 5-11 is a single specific algorithm. There are many minor variations in the way processing could have gone. The typing could have been generated as each letter was attained, the breakdown might not have been via syllables but directly from the whole word, and on and on. It is unknown which variation a given person uses. Indeed, different people will use different algorithms, although they all satisfy the same broad functional requirements. John's original theory of SRC handled this problem by considering all reasonably efficient algorithms and averaging over them to get its final prediction (the 2,573 ms quoted above). There were actually about 50 different algorithms, most of which were within a few hundred ms of each other and constituted minor permutations of a few basic schemes.

The predictions made here by Soar (and the MHP) have a special characteristic, compared with what most psychological theories provide. They are *no-parameter* predictions. That is, the numbers that enter into these predictions are not derived from the data being predicted. They were, of course, obtained from other experiments at other times. There are only a small collection of such numbers: productions take ~20 ms, the minimum time through the perceptual system (P) is ~40 ms, the perceptual time decreases with intensity according to a power law with certain constants (Luce, 1986), and so on. After a while they gain the status of constants, which are simply part of the cognitive theory.

The values adopted here for these constants in Soar are quite approximate, even just illustrative. There is good reason to be relaxed about these values. The functional-operation level, with its tendency toward gross approximation, is not the best environment in which to establish good mean values with ranges of variation. Indeed, it would not have made much difference to the exercise we were doing whether the minimum P value was ~40 or ~50 ms (Figure 5-6). What is important here is that Soar offers a way of reasoning about the total system from first principles and finding absolute (though approximate) results. This is an extremely useful property for a theory. Also, as has been argued vigorously on other occasions (Card, Moran, & Newell, 1983; John & Newell, 1989; Newell & Card, 1985), it is important for areas of application, such as HCI, that need no-parameter theories to help in design. Realistic values for the basic constants should be set on the basis of wide coverage of phenomena.

Our use of an abstract processing model in this section makes a general point. A theory (here, a unified theory of cognition) is a body of knowledge about a domain. Ways must be found to bring that knowledge to bear to meet the variety of demands that a theory should serve. Theories of cognition can be expected to be very complicated and detailed. Approximate ways of using them are needed. The functional-operation level of theory is such an approximate level of analysis. We didn't invent this level for Soar, of course. It corresponds to the GOMS level of analysis (Card, Moran, & Newell, 1983) taken over into Soar, along guidelines laid out by research on SRC.

Approximation at this level has its risks, as can be illustrated by the present examples. The unit of accounting has ended up being ~60 ms. This is an ambiguous number. It could be a minimal operator, composed of two decision cycles of ~30 ms each. That is small for such an interpretation, though not implausible as a minimum. But 60 ms is also enough time for several productions within a decision cycle. This shift of interpretation could be radical. The issue can be resolved, though, because the functional-operation level is not autonomous but an approximation to the actual behavior of Soar. Thus, whatever ways are devised of organizing Soar to perform these tasks and learn how to perform them will determine which interpretation is correct (or whether both are possibilities under suitably different conditions).

Finally, I want to end this discussion of response tasks by re-emphasizing the importance of incorporating different theories into a unified theory of cognition. Theories do not always have to compete with each other. Rather, they can feed each other. Incorporation into Soar, even if complete (which has not been accomplished yet), does not show that the GOMS theory has been overturned or rejected. The GOMS theory posits a set of mechanisms and structures, and the particular formalisms used are secondary. Of course, incorporation into Soar is not just a change of formalism. It links GOMS up with many other phenomena in a way that was not possible in the earlier formalism.

5.8. Item Recognition

Let us consider another immediate-response task, *item recognition* (Sternberg, 1975). A sequence of *target* digits is presented to a person, such as 3, 6, 1, 7. Then a warning signal is given to indicate the end of the targets and the imminent arrival of the *probe*, say 6 in this case. The task is to indicate whether the probe item (6) is a member of the set of targets just presented. In this case the answer is *yes* (it is the second item).

The graph in Figure 5-13 shows the basic phenomena discovered by Saul Sternberg (1966), which have become the hallmark of item recognition. If the reaction time (*RT*) is plotted against the size of the target set *s* (which is 4 in our example), then under appropriate conditions—such as the mixing of positive (*yes*) and negative (*no*) responses, with significant proportions of each—three regularities emerge. First, *RT* increases linearly with set size. The increase is very linear indeed—increase the size of the set by one, and the time to perform the task increases by a constant increment. Second, this

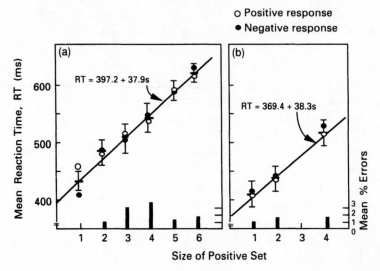

Figure 5-13. Basic Sternberg phenomena.

increment (the slope of the line) is ~40 ms. This is very fast. For instance, it is much faster than people can deliberately iterate through a list in their heads (say counting from 1 to 10), which is about 130 ms per item (Landauer, 1962).

The third result is what makes behavior on this task seem extraordinary. The strong linearity is prima facie evidence for some sort of search—given the probe, a check is made of each of the target items. An obvious consequence is that the slope of the line should be different for positive cases (the probe occurs in the list) and negative cases (the probe does not occur in the list). In the negative case the entire list needs to be searched; in the positive case, the search can stop when the probe is found—on average, half-way through the list (assuming suitable randomization, which experimenters provide). For positive cases the plotted slope against s should be half that for negative cases (or the same slope if negatives are plotted against s and positives against $s/2$). As Figure 5-13 shows, however, this does not occur. Instead, the two lines are exactly parallel. Thus, the sort of *terminating* search envisioned by the simple search model could not be taking place. Identical slopes would be exactly the result, however, if search were *exhaustive*, if the entire list had to be searched whether the probe item was found or not. But there was no particular reason to expect exhaustive

1. Linearity: RT = intercept + slope × (set size)
2. Fast processing: slope = 40 ms for digits
3. Parallel slopes: same positive and negative slopes
4. Flat serial position: no serial-position effects
5. Unawareness: mostly unaware of processing details
   [The first five phenomena constitute the hallmark set]
6. Presentation-mode invariance: holds for fixed sets and varied sets
7. Perceptual-mode invariance: holds for visual and speech presentation
8. Negative-set independence: RT not depend on negative set size
9. Limited positive-set size: less than 6 to 8
10. Multiple stages: intercept is about 350–400 ms
11. Encoding stage: associated with linearity
12. Slower rate with low legibility with little practice
13. Comparison stage: associated with linearity
14. Decision stage: associated with deciding on response
15. Response stage: associated with positive-negative frequency
16. Item-type independence: wide range of item types
17. Cavanagh's law: slope × memory-span-for-item types = 245 ms
18. Age invariance: holds over age (but slower)
19. Mental ability invariance: holds for retardates (but slower)
20. Practice invariance: extended practice does not affect slope
21. Fast-recency effect: if positive set and probe both rapid
22. Repeated-items effect: fast if probe in positive set
23. Probe-probability effect: fast if high expectation
24. Distinguished-item effect: nonlinear response
25. Increasing min-RT: increases with positive set size
26. Variance increase: target-set linear, positive = negative
27. Dual-task independence: for various tasks
28. Translation effect: increased slope if probe is a translation
29. Sublist effect: strong effect of positive set in categories
30. Positive-set-selection effect: large if done at probe time
31. Self-termination slow: slope greater than 100 ms
32. Self-terminating if item-dependent response

Figure 5-14. Basic Sternberg regularities.

search. Thus this result, so beautiful in its regularity, provides a neat puzzle—the very stuff of which great science is made.

The three regularities I've mentioned are only the tip of the iceberg. A huge number of phenomena may be found in item-recognition behavior. Figure 5-14 lists 32 of them, starting with the three just mentioned.[7] This isn't an exhaustively researched list—

7. Almost all of these are touched upon in Sternberg (1975); additional sources are Sternberg (1969) and Nickerson (1972).

the number of regularities could probably be pushed toward 50 or even higher, for the Sternberg phenomena have received extensive attention from the experimental community. Added to the list of regularities in typing, this list supports my claim about the Great Psychology Data Puzzle. Any theory of cognition must ultimately explain all these regularities and more. Any theory that gets through the eye of this needle, with its ~~3,000 obstructing filaments, is likely to enter the heaven of being fundamentally correct.

We should not be diverted to examine all the regularities of Figure 5-14, but a few are worth touching on. We have already discussed the first three, linearity, fast processing, and parallel response. (4) There are no serial position effects—it doesn't matter where in the list the digit occurs that matches the probe. (5) There is no awareness of the processing details—people do not know how they do the task. These five regularities comprise a basic set whose joint occurrence are the signature of the Sternberg effect.

(6) The basic set of phenomena is found for *fixed* or *varied* sets. With a fixed set, the targets are presented at the beginning of a block of trials and then held constant, while probe after probe is presented. With a varied set, a fresh set of targets is presented just before each probe. The results are the same in both cases. (7) The basic phenomena are found whether the modality of presentation is visual or auditory. We have looked at only the first seven regularities, but this is enough to see that each one adds strong constraints to the nature of the architecture. Some implications of these constraints are reasonably clear, even without detailed analysis to separate out the contribution of the architecture from that of the memory content. Such implications serve to eliminate outlandish architectures. The central issue, however, is what architecture is consistent with *all* of them—and that is a constraint of a different color.

Because of the puzzling fact that simple terminating search does not explain the basic, highly regular data, a great deal of theoretical activity has been invested in the Sternberg phenomena. The first alternative model, put forward by Sternberg himself early on, was exhaustive search. It was easy enough to stipulate a computational structure with this property, but it never had any particular reason for existing. Both models were serial. Soon various parallel models were invented that would yield the basic phenomena, then even some self-terminating serial searches that would. The models have

Analysis of varied-set paradigm
Items are attached to the current state as they arrive
They are represented in identical fashion
A single state moves through time during the arrival of items
A probe enables productions that instantiate each item
The processing is simple enough to occur within elaboration phase
There is no commitment to whether the process is search, assembly, activation . . .

Conclusions
1. Linear, because instantiations are not concurrent
2. Fast, because happens at production rate
3. Parallel slopes, because runs to quiescence, hence exhaustive
4. No serial position effects, because runs to quiescence
5. Unaware, because happens within a decision cycle

Figure 5-15. Qualitative analysis of the basic Sternberg task.

proliferated until almost any type of model can be generated (Townsend & Ashby, 1983). An abundance of models is characteristic of psychological data in the chronometric area. If attention is limited to a few quantitative regularities, even if they are fine-grained parametric curves, many technically distinct quantitative theories can be invented to explain them. (Remember the collection of random-walk models for dealing with same-different judgments in Chapter 1.) On the other hand, no one that I know of has a theory that explains all 32 regularities, much less the 50 or more that could probably be tracked down. The theories put forth so far explain 2 or 3 regularities, maybe occasionally 6 or 7 regularities, but the rest are never attended to. Soar will not provide a complete sweep either—it is only an exemplar—but the long list stands as a reminder of the sources of constraint that exist for unified theories.

Let us consider how Soar provides a *qualitative* explanation of the basic Sternberg phenomena (Figure 5-15). Ultimately, of course, Soar must do better than this. Just as with the functional-operation level of analysis, however, it is interesting to see Soar used in a qualitative way. At the top of the figure is the analysis of how the task is accomplished, at the bottom the derivation of some of the major regularities of the paradigm.

We consider the variable-set paradigm, in which the targets are received in sequence just before the probe. Soar's attention will be focused on the place of receipt of the target items. As each item arrives, it passes through a *P-E-C* sequence of operations and becomes attached to the current state. The items are all attached to the same state (this arrangement follows the *single-state principle* of Figure 5-3) and in the same way. This is because the items are presented rapidly (500 ms between items), so there is no time between items to engage in any discriminating processing. The simplest representation is that each item is linked by an attribute, *target*, to the current state, and the same attribute is used for all items.

The warning signal arrives, passes through its own *P-E-A-C* stages (there may or may not be an attend operator, depending on the experimental arrangement). Its arrival enables the resetting of the context (by a *T* operator) so that the probe will be handled differently than the target items. The preoccurrence of the warning signal is usually all that differentiates the targets from the probe. The time between warning and probe is usually quite short (~500 ms), which means that other tasks cannot be completed reliably before the probe arrives.

Then the probe arrives, passing through its own *P-E-C* stages (but not *A*, since attention will already be focused on the impending probe). The probe causes some kind of process that involves instantiating each of the targets by one or more productions. This occurs as part of the C-operator, as the system ascertains whether the probe has the property *is-a-target* or *is-not-a-target*. All the targets are identical, all being values of a single attribute (*target*). Thus, any production (within *C*) that matches against one target matches against all and hence will be instantiated against all. The execution of this production all occurs within a single elaboration phase. Furthermore, we know from the *limited-instantiation mechanism* (Figure 5-3) that one production cycle is required to produce the instantiation associated with each target. As a result of this, some contact is made between the probe and the target, resulting in an augmentation that says *is-a-target* or *is-not-a-target*. This is detected, an intention is generated (an I-operator), and a response is produced, in a fashion familiar from the SRC examples.

In this qualitative explanation, the details of the comprehension-operator productions are not specified. They could be conducting a search, attempting to assemble the targets in some form for subsequent testing, or performing some other function—it doesn't make any difference. What is imperative is that all the targets must be touched in some way, hence by a single production (because they are indistinguishable), hence producing an instantiation for each, hence executing by a temporal sequence of actions, one for each target.

Given this processing picture, let's return to the basic Sternberg results, taking them in the order of Figure 5-14. (1) *RT* is linear in set size. The linear effect comes from the sequential effect of the instantiation (per above), whatever the exact function that is carried out. There is also, of course, an intercept (all the operations that execute only once for the entire set of items, namely, *P* and *E* for the probe, and *I*, *D*, and *M* for the response). (2) The time per target item will be fast, because it happens at a rate of actions per instantiation. The function to be performed being very simple, it is probably simply ~20 ms per item, but it could be some small multiple of ~20 ms, if more than one production has to execute, instantiated over the whole set. (3) The linear effect is exhaustive, because the decision cycle runs to quiescence. Thus whatever happens within a decision cycle will run to completion. Quiescence is a functional feature of the decision cycle; it is not posited to explain the Sternberg results. (4) There are no serial position effects, because the decision cycle is exhaustive (what is measured is the aggregated effect over the entire set). (5) Soar is unaware of the processing details, because they happen within a decision cycle and Soar has no access to the interior of a decision cycle. This is the basic signature set.

(6) The analysis just given is for the varied-set task, and possibly it is dependent on the fact that target items arrive sequentially. It does not automatically follow that the phenomena also hold for the fixed-set task. Whether they do depends on an investigation of the representation used for sequences in long-term memory, and whether when they are brought into working memory they would be the same as for the varied set. This investigation is beyond us at this point in the book. (7) On the other hand, there is nothing in the procedure that is different for visual and auditory perception, at least as far as the qualitative results.

This qualitative level of analysis doesn't yield results as strong or as reliable as the functional-operation level of analysis used for exploring stimulus-response compatibility. For instance, it could not be expected to provide explanations for others of the 25 additional regularities associated with the item-recognition paradigm. It does give quite a bit of explanation, however, and its extra degree of abstraction helps us to see the essentials of the explanation. For instance, exhaustiveness is seen to depend not on whether a search-

and-test or an assembly/activation process was being performed, but only on the exhaustiveness of the decision cycle. The qualitative level provides yet another example, in addition to analysis by functional operations, of reasoning with Soar as a theory of unified cognition, without requiring us to carry out a detailed simulation. It helps debunk the stereotype that programmed information-processing models always require detailed simulations.

The Sternberg task provides a good opportunity for exploring analysis at the detailed level of a fully specified Soar system. What would happen if we tried to specify a fully detailed model—that is, specify the productions—for the item-recognition task? The example will show why it is not always profitable to work at this fine-grained level.

The top of Figure 5-16 shows the memory elements that would be built by the schematic procedure set up in the qualitative analysis. There is a state $s1$, with an attribute ^items, which has four values, $d1, \ldots, d4$. This is the standard Soar encoding, where an attribute can have multiple values. Each value represents a particular item. Item $d1$ has the value 3, $d2$ the value 6, and so on down the list. The probe is represented as attribute ^probe; it is item $d5$, which has value 6. The values of $d2$ and $d5$ are actually the same, but of course Soar doesn't know it.

Several productions are written in the figure below the working-memory data structure. The first production (*item-test-1*) does the essential task of declaring success if the probe matches a target. This occurs as part of the comprehend operator. It is just the positive response; it takes another production to handle the negative response. The first condition picks up an item $<x1>$ and the probe $<x2>$. Among other things, this first condition will keep this production from firing unless both target and probe have arrived. The second and third condition pick up the element of the target and probe, respectively, but only if they have the same value. This step is enforced by using the same variable $<v>$ for both values. Thus, these two condition elements, by having the same value, are applying an equality test constraint during the course of the match to select a satisfied production. If there is a matching target and probe, this production will find it and fire, declaring success.

How long it takes such a production to execute depends on the assumptions about the details of the match. Figure 5-3 outlined various options, indicated on the figure above. (A1) If we assume the standard Ops5 computational model that the time for a produc-

Working-memory elements built after acquiring the items
(state s1 ^items d1 d2 d3 d4 ^probe d5)
(item d1 ^value 3)
(item d2 ^value 6)
(item d3 ^value 1)
(item 34 ^value 7)
(item d5 ^value 6)

Single production to do essential task (Ops5 match)
(sp item-test-1
  (state <s> ^items <x1> ^probe <x2>)
  (item <x1> ^value <v>) (item <x2> ^value <v>)
  → (state <s> ^result success))
(A1) Constant time/cycle: 1 cycle, independent of set size
(A2) Constant time/instantiation: 1 cycle/item (~20 ms)

No equality tests in match
(sp item-test-setup-2
  (state <s> ^items <x1> ^probe <x2>)
  (item <x1> ^value <v>) (item <x2> ^value <p>)
  → (state <s> ^test-item <t>)
  (test-item <t> ^value <v> ^probe <p>))
(sp item-test-2
  (state <s> ^test-item <t>)
  (test-item <t> ^value <v> ^probe <v>)
  → (state <s> ^result success))
(A3) 1 cycle/item (~20 ms) or 2 cycle/item (~40 ms)

Figure 5-16. Detailed Soar models of the Sternberg phenomenon.

tion cycle is constant, then the production duration is independent of target-set size—and none of the Sternberg phenomena occurs. (A2) On the other hand, if we assume the limited instantiation mechanism, the production executes in one cycle per item. Then we get all the basic Sternberg phenomena, as in our qualitative analysis. However, the slope of the Sternberg plot is ~20 ms, rather than ~40 ms (the empirical value), if we retain the value of ~20 ms per production cycle.

(A3) Finally, if with A2 we also assume limited match power, then equality tests cannot be done on the fly. Two productions are required. The *item-test-set-up-2* production creates elements (*test-item . . .*) that hold the candidates for testing. This production looks like the original *item-test* production except that it has different variables in each condition (<v> and <p>). The *item-test-2* production then does the equality testing with a single condition element (*test-item . . .*) with two <v>s. In this case, depending on what assumption is made about the timing of a production cycle, the time could be ~20 ms per item or ~40 ms per item (one ~20 ms contribution from each production).

The point of this exercise is to observe that minor changes in assumptions move the total time accounting in substantial ways that have strong consequences for which model fits the data. In assessing the form that detailed productions should take, one must take all possible constraints into account. A major constraint is how the system would ever acquire a particular set of productions. Throughout this entire discussion of immediate-response tasks, we have simply been writing down whatever problem spaces, operators, and now productions we thought appropriate to the task. But Soar (and correspondingly the human) must acquire these ways of behaving. Soar specifies the basic mechanisms by which behavior is acquired—chunking while problem solving to do tasks—but it will require much investigation to see how chunking actually affects the explanations.

The appropriate research strategy is to delay commitment to the details of the explanation until all the constraints can be brought to bear, or at least enough of them so that no important degrees of freedom remain. The evidence should be assembled from a large and diverse variety of tasks, using the approximate analysis of the functional-operation level. Then the total evidence should indicate which detailed assumptions are correct. There could be as many as ~100 diverse experimental paradigms, each with several regularities. These would provide the opportunity to treat the problem of theory discovery and evaluation as a constraint-satisfaction task. Such a path is open to a unified theory of cognition, in a way that it is not open to microtheories of single paradigms. For the latter, the refinement of theories must come primarily from more accurate and fine-grained parametric data. That is of course crucial, and (as Figure 5-13 shows) the yield from elegant data can be very great, but we need to bring together data from radically different tasks, whose explanatory mechanisms may intersect, if we are to achieve any stability in our theories. This enterprise should be a major yield of unified theories.

5.9. Typing

Let us consider one final example. Typing served at the beginning of the chapter as an example of multiple regularities, the implied promise being that we should ask how Soar explains these regularities. Typing also provides us with a simple perceptual-motor skill. Until the total cognitive system is more fully developed, Soar is limited in its ability to deal with perception and motor behavior. Typing involves coordination of perception, cognition, and motor behavior, but it is still simple enough to be analyzed without undue dependence on perception and motor phenomena. Furthermore, lots of regularities are at hand—the Salthouse 29. Finally, as it turns out, typing offers another example of incorporating existing theory. The initial developments here were the work of John, using the version of the Model Human Processor (MHP) that she had applied to stimulus-response compatibility (John, 1988). She developed a detailed theory called the *Model of Expert Transcription Typing (METT)*. Having established the general way in which SRC theory maps into Soar, we can simply extend the same analysis to typing.

Figure 5-17 shows how Soar would type. Soar would get the next word, get the spelling of the word, get a letter within the spelling, and then issue the command for a keystroke to type the letter. This is a straightforward way of typing, given that the words being typed are known and that letters are available more quickly via word recognition than by reading each letter from the page. It forms a natural pipeline in the *P-E-A-C-I-D-M* sequence, in the functional decomposition of Figure 4-16. There are three processors. *P-E-A-C* is a serial component that obtains successive words. *I* is the central cognitive component that moves from spelling to letters to keystroke commands. It too is a serial component, because central cognition is serial, but it operates independently of *P-E*. Finally, the motor system *M*, with any required prior decoding *D*, operates independently of cognition and, even more so, of perception. This is a loosely coupled pipeline, with buffers in working memory (the outputs of *P-E-A-C* and *I*, respectively), that permits each processor to proceed at its own pace. If the buffers become empty for too long, the downstream processors run out of work and the throughput diminishes.

The figure shows how such an arrangement operates. The actual throughput is given by the critical path (the heavy line). Different processors become critical during different intervals—first the perceptual processor, then the cognitive processor, then the motor processor for just a small time, and then back to the cognitive processor. In the example of the figure, which corresponds to the

Basic procedure

> get word $\rightarrow$ get spelling $\rightarrow$ get letter $\rightarrow$ do keystroke

Three processor pipeline

> $[P - E - A - C] - - - (I_{spell} - - (I_{letter} - - I_{keystroke})) - - - < D - M >$

> $[in] - [the] - [red]] - - - - - - - - [box] - [t$
> $(i,n,\#) - (^) - (i) - (n) - (\#) - (t, h, e, \#) - (t) - (h) - (e) - (\#) -$
> $< ^ > - < i > - < n > - < \# > - - - - - - - < t > - < h > - < e > - <$

Processing assumptions

1. P - E - A - C   must complete before I_{spell} begins
2. I_{letter} of same hand waits for $M_{prior-letter}$
3. P - E - A - C must not get too far ahead (3 words)
4. Use SRC perception (314 ms) and operator (66 ms) times

Figure 5-17. Soar's model of typing (adapted from John, 1988).

work of an expert typist, the cognitive processor occupies the critical path most of the time. If the motor operator were slower, as with a less expert typist, then the motor processor would be on the critical path more frequently. To specify this model fully, we would have to make a number of additional assumptions, which are listed in the figure. (1) The perceptual process must be complete before I_{spell} can begin. That is, the word has to be identified. (2) I_{letter} has to wait for the prior motor operator ($M_{prior-letter}$) to finish, if it is on the same hand but not if it is on the opposite hand. This constraint reflects the buffering between I and M, in particular, the nonability of M to sort out commands or to have any local memory of them. (3) There is also a short-term memory assumption on the capacity of the buffer between perception (*P-E-A-C*) and cognition (*I*). This is simply set at 3 words, which we just accept as an approximate fixed number. Finally, in line with the SRC theory and with our initial development of this model in terms of the MHP, we use the same times as John did in her analysis: 314 ms for perception (*P-E-A-C*) and 66 ms for a cognitive operator (any of the *I*s). We

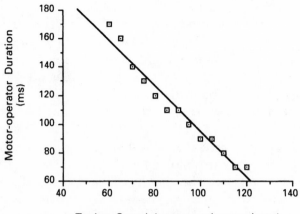

Figure 5-18. Motor operator versus typing speed (John, 1988).

saw earlier in the analysis of SRC (Figure 5-11) how those times correspond to some numbers for Soar (280 ms and 60 ms, respectively). Use of our own parameters would change the results marginally but would force us to redo the entire analysis for all the tasks.

We have not posited a time constant for motor operation ($D + M$), because, in fact, it isn't constant. People vary in their typing speed from ~10 to ~100 words per minute. At the slow end, many additional operations of perception and cognition are involved in hunting and pecking, making behavior more complex than the model of Figure 5-17. But as skill increases the simple pipeline model becomes an increasingly good approximation. Given this model, changes in typing speed (corresponding to changes in typing skill) imply changes in the constants of the model. Neither perception nor cognition are likely candidates for substantial change. This leaves changes in motor-operation time as the major parameter in changes in typing speed.

We can use the model to plot the typing speed that arises from each duration of the motor operation (Figure 5-18). The main use of this graph is to obtain the motor-operation time for a person whose typing speed is known, an individual-difference parameter that is often available. The figure also provides some interesting general knowledge. Knowing that maximum typing speed is ~120 words/ min, we know that the motor operator never gets faster than

~60 ms. This is an indirect indication that taking the minimum motor operator as ~60 ms in the analysis of SRT, CRT, and SRC may not be too far off the mark. The graph in Figure 5-18 is an independent way of estimating the motor operator (and there are many others) that would leave these earlier predictions of reaction times zero-parameter predictions.

This model can now be applied to all of the Salthouse 29 regularities in Figure 5-1. That takes a little doing. Each regularity is an exercise in theory application—like the problems in the back of a first-year engineering textbook on mechanics. Figure 5-19 displays the individual results. The theory explains one-and-a-half parametric results, where the actual parametric detail was predicted; eight quantitative results, where the quantitative number was predicted; a few qualitative results for those Salthouse regularities that were only qualitative; and twelve qualitative results. Thus the theory deals with about three-quarters of the phenomena in some way and is silent on the rest.

The theory produces its results in zero-parameter fashion, since no constants were estimated from the typing task. Actually, in many cases the results depend on the skill of the typist and variations in that skill, which is estimated by typing speed. This is, of course, a measure on the person but it is one that is obtained independently (from a typing test or the person's self-report). Then the parameter to be used in the theory, the motor-operator time, is obtained through Figure 5-18. It remains true that no constants are estimated from the typing experiments that are explained.

We will not go through all 29 predictions in detail, but we should look at some of them. Consider the first prediction (1). We have a model for 2CRT (Figure 5-8), which yields a response time of 380 ms. This is much slower than the 200 ms interkey interval for a 60 wpm typist, thus producing the correct prediction

(2) We do not yet have a Soar model of reading (though it is ultimately necessary to obtain one), so reading rates must be taken as empirical (~250 wpm). However, it is comforting that Soar predicts that even the maximum rate of typing (~145 wpm) is substantially less than the average reading rate.

(3) That skill and comprehension are independent can be seen by inspection of the algorithm used in the model. Nothing in the algorithm depends in any way on comprehension. Therefore, if any variance in comprehension exists at all, there will be independence.

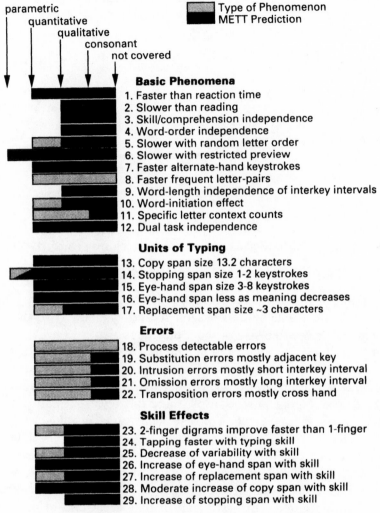

Figure 5-19. Typing results (John, 1988); METT is the
Model of Expert Transcription Typing.

(4) The algorithm picks up each word independently of context
and processes it (for spelling and letters). This shows directly that
word order doesn't make any difference.

(5) This same algorithmic structure demonstrates directly that
letter order does make a difference, and a large one. If the system
can't recognize a word, it can't get its spelling and hence its letters.
It must then process each letter one at a time, which implies much

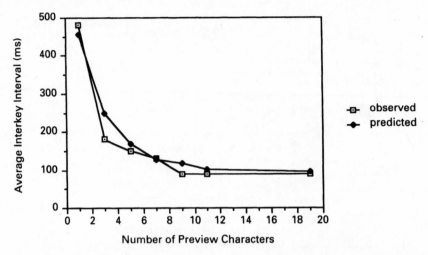

Figure 5-20. Restricted preview and stopping span (John, 1988).

more time in both the perceptual and the cognitive processor. What the total effect will be depends on the critical-path analysis and hence on the relative size of the motor operation.

(6) The same mechanism of having to deal with units—syllables and letters, as opposed to words—accounts for effects of restricted preview. Recall that this is where the experimenter makes available only *K* characters to the right of where the keystrokes are occurring. The restriction lets the typist see only fragments of words, and hence the ability to deal in whole words is lost. This mechanism seems to account for most of the effect, as Figure 5-20 shows. Actually, the syllable shows up as an intermediate unit. If the typist can see a syllable in the preview window, then he or she has direct access to its letters. At first blush, it may seem odd to obtain a continuous curve of speed versus preview size, when the mechanism involves only discrete units, the letter, syllable, and word. However, the statistics of language smoothes out the curve.

And so it goes through the Salthouse 29. Soar gets the other regularities (that it does obtain) through analyses analogous to those in John's original METT model. This model, although impressive, does not explain all the regularities, and for those it does explain it does not do so as completely as the data permit. We should expect Soar to provide an improvement on METT, because it provides the extra mechanisms.

Interestingly, the major barrier to a more complete explanation is the poorly defined motor system in Soar. The major failure in the original METT analysis concerns the five regularities about errors (items 18–22). All these error regularities appear to involve primarily the motor system. Four of them (19–22) arise directly from the motor system. As a physical dynamic system, the fingers, hands, and arms must be subject to analog errors in space and time, independent of the details of their control system. Thus, spatial-accuracy errors would be expected—substitution errors to adjacent keys (item 19). Likewise, temporal-accuracy errors would be greater the more independent the physical linkages—transposition errors occurring more frequently for opposite-hand than same-hand keystrokes (item 22). Similarly, though perhaps not quite so obvious, intrusion errors would arise from a finger striking two keys (hence short interkey intervals, item 20) and omission errors would arise from a finger failing to strike a key (hence long interkey intervals, item 21). In all these cases, the likely source of the errors is not in perception or cognition (the controller) but in the motor system. For Soar to predict these errors requires an elaboration of the motor system and the way it is controlled.

The motor system even influences item 18, detecting typing errors without visual feedback. Here Soar does have something to say. Error detection requires the ability to compare what should have happened with what actually happened. The process of Figure 5-17 cannot detect errors in perception or in cognition, at least of most kinds, because the requisite knowledge isn't available. On the other hand, the keystroke command issued by the *I*-operator can be compared with the keystroke that actually occurred, either through proprioception, which permits cognition to do the comparison, or through the motor system. Thus motor-system errors could be picked up internally. To move beyond this basic qualitative prediction brings us back to the motor system and our current limitations.

5.10. Summary

We have been exploring Soar as a theory of immediate behavior, at the level of about one second, for at this level the architecture is revealed. Besides being an interesting testing ground for Soar, immediate-response data are needed to identify the architecture. Fortunately, there is an immense amount of elegant data at this level—

data that together pose what I like to call the Great Psychology Data Puzzle. The information is already there—all we need to do is put the puzzle together.

We examined several immediate-response tasks, familiar from the experimental literature: simple reaction-time tasks (SRT); two-choice reaction-time tasks (2CRT), stimulus-response compatibility (SRC), item recognition (the Sternberg phenomena), and, finally, typing. This is not a very wide range of immediate-response tasks. There are also same-difference judgments, counting, inequality comparisons, the Posner letter task, psychophysical judgments— the tasks go on, if not endlessly, at least for quite a while. But the diversity we have shown is sufficient to indicate how Soar can model them and that it can do so within some margin of approximation. How successful Soar will be in the other tasks cannot be determined until the analyses are actually made. Likewise, how much Soar will be refined to more fine-grained explanations cannot be determined in advance. But for illustrating the reach of a unified theory of cognition, the point is made. A unified theory of cognition should generate explanations and predictions over the whole range of immediate-response tasks.

The examples analyzed in this chapter were chosen to make a number of points in addition to the basic one about providing explanations over a wide range. First, Soar moves toward making zero-parameter predictions. This is unusual for current theories in psychology, but it should be a feature of any unified theory of cognition. The problem is not that the constants are missing. Rather, constants measured in one situation must work as well in indefinitely many other situations. Second, we illustrated multiple ways to use Soar as a theory, from the qualitative analysis in the Sternberg task, to the functional-operator level in the reaction-time and typing tasks, to the production-level analysis, also for the Sternberg task. We will see additional ways before the book is over. A theory is a body of knowledge, and it does not dictate the ways it can be brought to bear. Third, we used stimulus-response compatibility and typing to illustrate the incorporation of existing theories into Soar. Especially for unified theories, the relationship of a new theory to existing theories is not always one of competition—of which one is right. Soar now provides the same explanations of SRC as the MHP does. Soar is instantly enriched and its scope increased; the MHP is in no way diminished. Indeed, the MHP's

1. How humans are able to exhibit intelligence (Chapter 4)
   • To the limits of our knowledge in AI
2. Many global properties of human cognitive behavior (Chapter 4)
   • Though without careful characterization
3. Human immediate behavior (~~1 sec) (Chapter 5)
   • Quantitative, using functionally defined operators
4. Discrete perceptual-motor behavior (Chapter 5)

Figure 5-21. The coverage so far of Soar
as a unified theory of cognition.

whole style of analysis has been incorporated as well. Furthermore, the MHP was itself not an attempt at new theory but a synthesis of existing knowledge in cognition.

It is important not to forget the rest of Soar while grubbing around down in the 100 ms trenches. This is the same Soar that designs algorithms and does computer configurations, the same Soar that learns about the blocks world. It is *really* the same Soar, not just the same in some generalized manner of speaking. The decision cycle and the operators, which are the heart of the explanations in this chapter, play central roles in these larger tasks. If we had moved to slightly more complex tasks in this chapter, we would have seen much of the rest of the mechanisms emerge. Thus, Soar is moving toward being a genuine candidate for a unified theory of cognition—or, to stay with our rhetoric, a genuine exemplar.

Finally, let us take stock of where we have arrived. We wanted to illustrate how Soar, as our candidate theory of cognition, handles various domains of cognitive phenomena. Starting with this chapter, we begin to summarize explicitly the domains that Soar has covered. Figure 5-21 is the initial list, and we will add to it as we proceed. Right now we are not concerned with exactly how good a theory Soar provides of each item in the figure. We are interested in *coverage*—in whether a single theory, as an integrated conceptual structure, can address many different cognitive phenomena, ranging in time scale and task. After all, Soar is only an exemplar, and we can excuse it for dealing with a given area only approximately, as long as it can make serious assertions about the phenomena.

From Chapter 4 we get two items in the list. First, Soar shows how humans are able to exhibit intelligence. This functional constraint is of fundamental importance for any cognitive theory to explain. Second, Soar exhibits many global qualitative properties of human cognitive behavior. Although we had only a catch-as-catch-can list of properties, presenting the right global picture of the nature of human nature is also of fundamental importance. From this chapter, we can say that Soar is a theory of immediate-response behavior. It provides a quantitative theory at the level of functionally defined operators. The tasks covered were simple and two-choice reaction times, stimulus-response compatibility, and item recognition. It is evident that many similar phenomena could equally well have been covered, although with what success will have to be seen. Finally, we have put forth typing as yet another extension of explanation, into discrete but ongoing perceptual-motor behavior. Nonetheless, Soar has not yet dealt with any of the central phenomena of perception or motor behavior.

Memory, Learning, and Skill

6

In Chapter 5 we focused on the simplest of behaviors, such as pressing a button in response to a clear stimulus. We treated these behaviors as pure performances—as if the human was not changed at all in doing these tasks. But that of course is not so. Humans learn continuously from all tasks they perform, at whatever scale the tasks occur. As our candidate unified theory of cognition, Soar must address the phenomena of memory, learning, and skill, as well as the immediate-response tasks of Chapter 5.

First let us be clear about our terminology (see Figure 6-1). *Learning* is not exactly a term of art, but is used quite broadly. As behaviorism amply demonstrated, it can be used in a way that avoids positing a *memory*. If the memories of a system are identifiable, however, it is useful to refer to learning with respect to each memory. Where there is a memory, there is also a set of functions for using it: the *acquisition* of knowledge by this memory and the *retrieval* of knowledge from the memory, to which *access* is required to determine what is retrieved. The term *learning* usually refers to the acquisition side, but people are not usually considered to have learned something unless, under some circumstances, they can access and retrieve the learned knowledge from the memory and use it in a response. It thus tends to be used to stand for the entire process (which is the way the figure shows it).

This chapter covers all of memory (with the associated learning)—short-term and long-term memory, procedural (skill) memory and declarative memory, episodic and semantic memory. We will start with Soar's theory of memory and learning, and see how it is to cover all of these. This will lead us to something called *data chunking*, which relates to episodic memory. Then we will talk about skill acquisition and, finally, short-term memory.

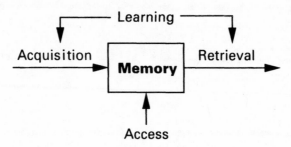

Figure 6-1. Basic terms in analysis of learning.

This chapter has a secondary theme. To paraphrase a famous line: there are more things in an architecture, Horatio, than are dreamt of in your theorizing. An architecture should be taken seriously and out of it will come interesting and important things about the nature of cognition. It is the same with any good theory. For instance, if one tries to think directly about the nature of semantic memory or episodic memory, one hardly understands the possibilities that exist for realizing such memories. When presented with a full-fledged architecture, the possibilities simply emerge. Different architectures, of course, offer different possibilities. A single architecture exhibits only one arrangement of the possibilities. An important aspect of each architecture-embodied unified theory of cognition is its capacity for generating new possibilities. This will be true of any such unified theory, not just Soar, but it is an important lesson to be taught through Soar.

6.1. The Memory and Learning Hypothesis of Soar

Three fundamental assertions capture much of what the Soar architecture implies about human memory and learning. They are a good place to start.

The first assertion is the *functional unity of long-term memory (LTM)*. All long-term memory consists of recognize-retrieve units with a fine grain of modularity. In Soar these are productions, but productions should be taken simply as a convenient computational realization. There may be other ways of building memory systems that are both recognition memories and fine grained. On the other hand, given these functional specifications, the major variation remaining is the specific recognition scheme—the power of the match, as we termed it when discussing the Sternberg phenomena in Chapter 5.

It follows that episodic, semantic, and procedural knowledge must all be encoded in this same memory. Uniformity at this basic memory level has many consequences. However, there are some consequences it does *not* have. It does *not* imply a single encoding for *all* knowledge. A uniform level of encoding at one level can be used to create multiple codes at higher levels. This process is transparent with computers, which at one level have a uniform representation of bit vectors and use that coding to produce at higher levels an indefinitely diverse set of representations—numbers, arrays, lists, attribute-value systems—and above these yet other diverse application systems with their own domain-dependent representations, ad infinitum.

And for the lower level of the neural-circuit implementation, uniformity at the memory level does *not* imply the same structure and mechanisms, for example, realization as a fixed uniform neural circuit. One reason we do not assume similar structures at the two levels is that a given function can be realized by many alternative mechanisms—this rule certainly holds for architectures (Figure 2-14)—but there are more specific reasons. The productions of a production system do not interact directly but only via the elements they deposit in working memory. A production *system* might better be called a production *collection*. This is especially true for Soar, where conflict resolution, which does make productions interact, is entirely removed.

This point is important, because there is a tendency simply to believe that the functional homogeneity of production systems conflicts with the evidence of heterogeneity of neural organs and their dedication to special computational functions (Geschwind, 1981). Figure 6-2 shows how an apparently homogeneous production system can actually be composed of several heterogeneous production systems. The figure is looking down on working memory, broken up into a set of regions, each region realized in separate parts of the nervous system. Each region has its own production system, with its own matching rules, each takes somewhat different times to execute, and so on. Several things must hold for this sort of separation to work. Some production systems must function as communication devices, transmitting working-memory elements from one region to elements in another, possibly with transduction (remap-

Working Memory

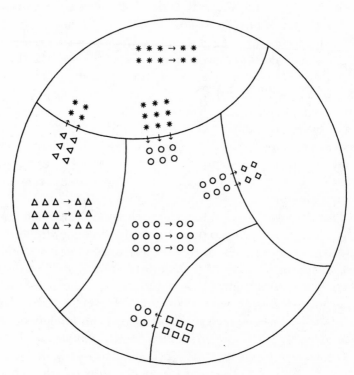

Figure 6-2. Structurally heterogeneous productions
form a common system.

ping and recoding). The construction of chunks must respect the homogeneity of production conditions and actions. The obvious scheme would be to construct extra chunks to do the mapping, but other schemes are possible. Finally, the decision apparatus must maintain common control, though there is nothing that prevents some of the local production systems from being like the E-productions of the total cognitive system. What remains constant in all this is an information-processing system that in all of its subcomponents works as a freely responding recognition memory. The point is to deny the inference from functional homogeneity to structural homogeneity.

The second assertion is the *chunking-learning hypothesis.* All long-term learning occurs by chunking. The units of learning are chunks, the recognize-retrieval units of the memory, which are formed by immediate goal experience—the features with which we have become familiar. This assertion is probably the most contentious aspect of Soar, in the view of the AI field, which is where Soar got its start. Soar is seen as an interesting system and chunking as an interesting learning mechanism, but it is hardly the only learning mechanism around. The field is currently investigating lots of different kinds of learning (see the journal, *Machine Learning*) and it is believed, generally speaking, that many different learning mechanisms will be developed for many different situations. Chunking is seen as one mechanism located in the corner of the space of learning mechanisms that are low level and unintelligent. (Intelligence here is measured by the amount of knowledge and analysis that goes into creating a specific addition to the performance system.) Thus, from an AI standpoint, the assertion that chunking is a sufficient mechanism should be considered a speculative and a priori unlikely hypothesis. I share some of this assessment, and I would not be unduly surprised to see the assertion overturned. Chunking could become only one of several mechanisms in a general intelligence. However, the indications from our experience on Soar so far are certainly all in the direction of supporting this hypothesis.

The third assertion is the *functionality of short-term memory (STM)*. Short-term memory arises because of functional requirements. All architectures bring together elements out of which behavior is composed. A memory is needed to hold these elements and keep them assembled together. This is functionally a working memory and this is what it is called in Soar. By its nature, a working memory is temporary, since it must change at a rate commensurate with the rate of operations. Thus, this memory will give rise to short-term memory effects. Other sources of short-term memory effects might be other functional aspects of the total architecture, especially those involved with perception and motor action, where timing constraints are important. The current Soar architecture is entirely functional—all of its mechanisms and structures exist to provide functionality. No mechanisms or structures in Soar have been posited just to produce some empirically known effects. It is entirely possible that short-term memory effects in humans arise from limitations of the underlying neural technology that has no relation to functionality at all. To exhibit these effects, Soar would need to be augmented with additional architectural assumptions about these mechanisms and their limitations. With the current Soar architecture, the only short-term memory effects we will be able to derive are those rooted in mechanisms that have some functional role to play in the architecture as a whole.

As we focus on learning, a reminder is in order that learning and memory cannot be separated from the rest of Soar—from impasses, problem spaces, preferences, and the decision cycle. Learning is a side effect of experiencing and indeed of micro-experiencing—that is, experiences that arise and dissipate in a few seconds. Hence, whatever determines local experience plays a major role in what is learned. This is also a somewhat radical and contentious proposal within AI, where the tendency is to separate the learning system from the performance system and treat them as separate subsystems of comparable complexity, each with its own sources of knowledge.

These strong assumptions of Soar are substantively interesting, but we ought not let the question of their truth or falsity get too much in the way of Soar as an exemplar unified theory of cognition. Other candidate unified theories have quite different assumptions. For example, Act* has a sharp structural separation of declarative and procedural memory.

6.1.1. A Review of Learning Mechanisms in Soar
Chunking and what we have learned from it underlie this whole chapter, so I want to be sure the concept is clear at the outset. The occasion for chunking is an impasse. A chunk is built for each result involved in resolving the impasse. The action of the chunk is built from the result. The conditions of the chunk are built from the working-memory elements that existed before the impasse occurred and that led to the production of the result (by a sequence of production firings, as shown in Figure 4-12).

Chunks are active processes, not passive data. The fact that we write them down on paper as $C_1, \ldots, C_m \rightarrow A_1$ does not make them declarative structures. Soar has no access to them as data. That is, they do not appear as elements in working memory to be examined by other productions. They could be realized in a radically different way than the notation indicates (and they are in our computer implementations, where they are realized by Rete networks; Forgy, 1981). Since chunks are not declarative structures, they are not rules, as that term is used in discussions of rule-following behavior and whether humans do or do not follow rules. As the mapping at the ~~10 ms level indicates, chunks are memory accesses. But they are active because the recognition memory is active, initiating the entry of its contents (the actions) whenever its conditions are satisfied.

Chunking can be viewed as a form of permanent goal-based caching. Chunks generalize to new operating contexts, but they do so implicitly, because many elements in working memory when the chunk is created do not become conditions in the chunk. Learning occurs during problem solving and takes effect as soon as the chunk is created. Chunks are created for all impasses, hence for all subgoals; and since subgoals arise for all aspects of Soar, chunks are formed for search control, operator implementation, and many other things. But Soar learns only where the system has its experiences, for it only impasses because of its current activities.

There is no way to address directly the sufficiency of chunking as a learning mechanism. No taxonomy of all types of learning exists, against which chunking can be tested, and no such taxonomy should be expected, given the broad usage of the term. What is clear is that humans learn in all kinds of ways—that their learning is not strongly channeled. This is just another way of expressing what we termed in Chapter 3 their extreme qualitative adaptiveness. Hence, the diversity of learnings that Soar has engaged in so far is relevant to the sufficiency of chunking. It cannot settle the question definitively, but it can provide a positive indication or, contrariwise, reveal that chunking is a narrow mechanism.

Figure 6-3 shows the current situation for Soar (Steier et al., 1987). This characterization is nonsystematic—it simply gathers up and organizes the types of learning that have shown up in our aggregate experience with Soar. There have been no deliberate attempts with Soar to produce any specific sort of coverage— although we have been intrigued, and occasionally delighted, as new forms of learning have emerged.

Let's start with types of transfer, where the learning that occurs in one situation is used in a different situation. Soar exhibits within-trial transfer (recall Figures 4-18 and 4-21). That was the initial surprise with chunking: chunks formed early in a task applied immediately before the end of the task. In retrospect, that should not have surprised us. I suppose we were caught off guard because

Types of transfer
Within trial, across trial (practice), across task

Sources of knowledge for learning
Internal: Generated by problem solving
External: Advice, examples, task definitions

What is learned
Operators: Implementations, instantiations, macro-ops
Search control: Operator selections, plans, strategies
Declarative data: Recognitions, recalls, descriptions
Tasks: Problem spaces, initial and desired states

Types of tasks
Puzzles, games, decisions, designs, instructions, . . .

Occasions for learning
All tasks, with both success and failure

Figure 6-3. Varieties of learning by Soar (circa 1987).

psychologists so seldom adopt paradigms that reveal within-trial transfer, preferring instead paradigms with a pretest, followed by a learning session, followed by a posttest, in which all opportunity for using the learned material in the learning session is carefully excluded. The main exception is the standard practice situation where improvement occurs over a sequence of trials. This setup involves across-trial transfer, since almost always each trial in the sequence differs in some way. Soar exhibits this practice effect. Soar has also exhibited across-task transfer, which is the classical paradigm of learning in one situation and testing in another. Learning in the blocks world (Figure 4-14) is an example, although the data was not presented in the standard way.

Learning is a process of knowledge transfer—knowledge from some source becomes part of some target system. For chunking, the source is the experience that occurs in a problem space, and the knowledge (of what is effective to resolve a specific impasse) is transferred to production memory. This experience is an *internal knowledge source*. Soar can also learn from *external knowledge sources*—from advice, from examples, from definitions of tasks. (These will be illustrated below.)

By now Soar has learned almost all the kinds of things that are of interest in AI systems, in at least some form—though often in elementary embodiments. It has learned operator implementation, operator instantiation, and macro-operators. It has learned to do operator selection, to build plans and then use them to control search. These aspects pertain to the procedural side of memory. On the declarative side, Soar has learned to recognize objects and to recall objects when given some cues. With respect to tasks, it has learned problem spaces and also initial and desired states. All of this learning is accomplished through chunking—by doing some task whose result is the building of chunks that resolve impasses. By its nature, chunking works on any type of task, and it has in fact been demonstrated in a miscellaneous but diverse collection of puzzles, games, design tasks (such as R1-Soar and algorithm design), and diagnosis tasks (such as Neomycin-Soar). Again, by its nature, chunking occurs on all conceivable occasions, but it is comforting to know that this actually happens. This includes, by the way, learning both on success and on failure. Chunking is not sensitive to success and failure, only to whatever resolves an impasse. An impasse can be resolved as much by failure—the decision to leave a space as unprofitable—as by success.

In sum, the demonstrations of learning in Soar are scattered widely throughout the range of our experiences with it. Soar is not limited to learning that is somehow narrowly focused on specific types, occasions, or experiments. The ubiquity of learning is clearly a phenomenon that characterizes human behavior, and one that a unified theory of cognition should explain. Although we have no systematic way to assess the diversity and pervasiveness of its learning, Soar as a theory of cognition can be taken as predicting this characteristic of human behavior.

No examples have been provided yet of learning from an external source of knowledge. Here are two from the work of Andy Golding (Golding, Rosenbloom, and Laird, 1987). Figure 6-4 shows a case of taking direct advice. The task domain is very simple—solving elementary algebraic equations. The initial state contains an equation, $a \cdot b = -c - x$, which is to be solved for x. The problem space contains operators that modify the form of the equation while preserving equality. We are not interested in this trivial bit of problem solving; it serves only to show how Soar obtains guidance from outside. Soar runs into a tie impasse immediately, because it does not know which operator to try. The tie impasse leads it into a selection space to resolve the tie. This selection space has operators to evaluate alternatives (the alternatives in this case being operators in the higher space). So far, this is just like blocks-world

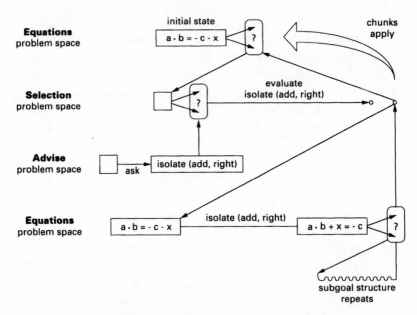

Figure 6-4. Learning from external advice
(Golding, Rosenbloom, & Laird, 1987).

problem solving (Figure 4-10). Again Soar reaches an impasse because it doesn't know which alternative it should evaluate first. The
response to this impasse is to go into an *advise space* in which it
seeks knowledge from outside (by executing the *ask* operator). The
external advisor then indicates a specific operator, namely, to isolate the variable by adding to the right-hand side. This tells Soar
which operator it should evaluate—not which operator to use, but
the one to evaluate. Thus, Soar can reject the advice, if its own
evaluation leads it to another conclusion. The figure shows the
evaluation proceeding positively. Soar's approach to evaluation
now continues as in the blocks-world task, namely, to look ahead to
see the consequences of using the operator. It proceeds to solve the
problem, which requires some more problem solving, indicated
without detail by the wavy line in the figure. This evaluation activity leads to building chunks. Thus, when Soar attempts to solve this
particular problem again, these chunks incorporate the knowledge
of how to make selections in the original space. In sum, it asks for
advice on what operator to try; then evaluates that advice; and the
evaluation leads to chunks being built that transfer the advice
knowledge to where it is finally used.

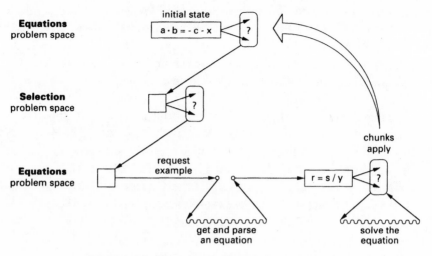

Figure 6-5. Learning from external example
(Golding, Rosenbloom, & Laird, 1987).

Figure 6-5 shows a case of learning from an illustrative example, using the same simple algebra task. Again, there is the initial tie impasse; again, the selection problem space to resolve it; again, the tie impasse on how to proceed with the evaluation; again, the advise problem space to ask for guidance. This time the request is for the advisor to give another example task to solve. There is additional activity (the wavy line) to input the new equation and the variable to solve for. Then Soar tries to solve the new equation, $r = s/y$, for y. The figure doesn't detail the activity to do this. It could solve it by brute force, or by getting further advice, or whatever. In any event, in so doing some chunks get built. Those chunks transfer to the original space. That is, the chunks that summarize the selection of operators that solve the illustrative example also apply to select the operators in the original task.

These two examples show that knowledge can enter the system from outside by chunking, in one case by advice about which operator to evaluate first, and in the other case by an example to try. Chunking is playing the role of a knowledge-transfer mechanism. This is a perfectly reasonable way of looking at learning, even if not the usual one. It makes learning look analogous to a data link in a communication system. The key is the transfer of learning (that is, generalization), rather than the compilation effect for more efficient repetition. Chunking is also playing the role of assimilator.

It is solving the problem of how to fit the external knowledge into a context in the rest of the system, where it can be successfully used. The external advisor is ignorant of the internal workings of Soar, which means that communication from the advisor requires assimilation. In the selection-advice case it is perhaps plausible that both Soar and the external advisor know what knowledge is to be communicated—to wit, that a certain operator be applied—and so the device of asking for this knowledge within the evaluation space, rather than the original space, may seem to be simply a device for getting some distance between Soar and the advice so it can be rejected. It keeps Soar from letting the advisor grab absolute control of it. In the illustrative-example case, however, the advisor does not know what knowledge might be useful. Indeed, what transfers is whatever results from solving the example. The advisor did not have to formulate this, and neither did Soar. In fact, the advisor will never know what was actually useful, without an analysis of the internal state of Soar.[1]

In these two examples we begin to get a sense of the multiple and unexpected ways in which chunking enters into the life of the intelligent agent, becoming an integral part of its performance and not just something that "improves its behavior on the next trial."

6.2. The Soar Qualitative Theory of Learning

Soar presents a definite global qualitative theory of memory, learning, and skill (Figure 6-6). In Chapter 4, when we first described how Soar was to be taken as a theory of human cognition, we listed many global properties of Soar that corresponded to human cognition (Figure 4-24). Naturally, several of these concerned memory, learning, and skill. This list may be taken as a refinement and expansion of the earlier one. A little redundancy will not hurt. In particular, it will reinforce the point that, whatever detailed predictions and explanations Soar might provide, its global character is

---

1. This case is actually an example of what I termed a *wild subgoal* (Newell, 1983), namely, one without any predefined relation of the subgoal to the supergoal, one where the problem solver simply attempts to exploit whatever results from solving the subgoal. Polya's heuristic examples depend on wild subgoals and (to 1983) no AI system had the ability to use them. That may be why no AI system has solved the examples in Polya's books (Polya, 1945).

1. All learning arises from goal-oriented activity
2. Learn at a constant short-term average rate ~.5 chunk/sec (the impasse rate)
3. Transfer is by identical elements and will usually be highly specific
4. Learn the gist of a sentence, not its surface structure, unless focus on it
5. Rehearsal helps to learn, but only if do something (depth of processing)
6. Functional fixity and Einstellung will occur
7. The encoding specificity principle applies
8. The classical results about chunking (such as for chess) will hold

Figure 6-6. The Soar qualitative theory of learning.

important—especially if it turns out to be counterintuitive or strikingly dissonant.

(1) All learning arises from goal-oriented activity. One learns by doing, as Dewey (1910) said. This is arguably the most important single feature of chunking. In order to learn, the organism has to be goal oriented. It does not have the goal of learning, of course—learning is not deliberate. Rather, it learns about only what it is goal-oriented about. Furthermore, it does not learn directly about what it deliberately wants. Rather, it acquires the knowledge it needs to obtain what it deliberately wants. Thus, to do learning of some specific type, the learner must get itself into a situation which is goal oriented in the right way. Many consequences follow from this requirement.

(2) Learning occurs at an approximately constant rate—the rate at which impasses occur in the system. In Chapter 3, in setting up the order-of-magnitude time scales, I estimated the rate at a chunk every couple of seconds. Let us now refine this. We assume that humans chunk bottom-level impasses, that is, impasses whose resolution is not interrupted by further impasses. In Soar we call this *bottom-up chunking* to distinguish it from *all-goals chunking*. Figure 4-21 showed both types of chunking on the same algorithm-design task. Suppose a bottom-level impasse resolution takes on average M simple operators to resolve. Each simple operator in Soar takes just two decision cycles, one to select it and one to implement it. It cannot take more than that without an impasse occurring, either a tie impasse in selecting the operator, a no-change impasse in implementing the operator (if it required a sub-

space to implement it), or some other impasse. Furthermore, suppose each decision cycle takes on average K production cycles. The average time to create a chunk is $C = 2MK\tau_p$, where τ_p is the time of a production cycle (20 ms). There are 2 extra decision cycles at the beginning to select the problem space and initial state, but we can think of this as equivalent to adding an extra initialization operator. In Chapter 5 we worked with minimal operators (selection plus execution) for speeded response tasks, which we took to correspond to the case of $K = 1$, only a single production cycle per decision cycle. Simple operators will in general require several production cycles, corresponding to $K = $ about 4 or 5. So each chunk might take on the order of $\sim 200M$ ms. Soar tasks typically build a new chunk every 5 or 6 operators (including the initialization "operator"), which yields just ~ 1 chunk per sec. This is a little faster than the empirical rates but close enough to be in the ballpark.

The chunking rate is a good example of an approximate constant. In the long term, the system cannot deviate much from a constant rate of impasses that is moderately close to the minimum and corresponds to relative constant rates for K and M. When impasses occur there is a lower limit to the number of operators it takes to diagnose and resolve an impasse; this puts an upper limit to the chunking rate. But when impasses do not occur, chunks get built that substitute for long sequences of simple operators, hence shortening the time to the next impasse and raising the chunking rate until it presses on the upper limit.

(3) Transfer is by *identical elements*, in the sense that Thorndike used the term in his theory of transfer (Thorndike, 1903).[2] The identical elements of Thorndike were concrete stimulus-response associations and were sufficiently hypothetical to not be really countable. Here they are productions with their abstract conditions and actions. Abstraction is important, of course, because it permits the same productions to be evoked in different situations. Indeed, productions can be seen as the appropriate form for a stimulus-response theory to take so as to attain universal computability. In

---

2. Mark Singley and John Anderson have taken this as a theme of their recent book on transfer (Singley & Anderson, 1989). They use Act* as their theory and, as noted, Act* productions correspond to Soar operators, not Soar productions; but otherwise the transfer theory they develop in quantitative detail could be incorporated into Soar in the same way we have done with the SRC theory in Chapter 5.

this sense, Soar retains the flavor of identical elements. Most important, elements can be actually counted, the amount of transfer measured, and the quantitative predictions of learning times verified (Polson & Kieras, 1985; Polson, Muncher, & Engelbeck, 1986; Singley & Anderson, 1989).

Transfer by identical elements implies that learning will tend to be highly specific. That can be seen in the way chunks are built up from the specific case. Thus, in general, there is little transfer to different situations. This agrees with the central conclusions of the stream of educational research that Thorndike initiated (Singley & Anderson, 1989, chap. 1). However, it need not always be the case—transfer occurs if the original productions (the identical elements) apply in the new situation. Transfer can be highly general if the productions are appropriately abstract. As Soar shows, this happens only if the representation is just right. For instance, when Soar solved a constraint-satisfaction problem, the chunks captured the general program for solving that constraint on later occasions. But the norm is for chunks to be specific, because they have incorporated specific features of the local task environment in their conditions.

Psychology often casts the issue of transfer in terms of generalization gradients and similarity metrics to explain how transfer and generalization occur (Osgood, 1949). These metrics are seen as part of the structure of the task environment. Soar says that such metrics can be found. The conditions of chunks, which determine whether transfer occurs, test the structure of the environment— two environments must be alike in some specific way if the chunk is to transfer. Metrics will always be approximate, however, because they are based on functional grounds. Variation can occur on every new use, because what features are attended to depends on the details of the task to be solved. Hence, similarity metrics are never going to be highly reliable, because they are grounded in the shifting sands of function.[3]

(4) The theory suggests that when people read sentences, they learn the gist of the sentence but not the verbatim sentence (Barclay, Bransford & Franks, 1972; Fillenbaum, 1966). In terms of

3. This conclusion applies to cognitive skills; the issue of perceptual or motor gradients need not be the same (Shepard, 1987). For Soar the nature of similarity metrics depends on what role chunking plays in perception and motor behavior (E and D of the total cognitive system).

Soar, the task in reading is comprehension, which will lead to chunks that relate the sentence to its meaning but not to chunks that relate to the verbatim text. On the other hand, if Soar is given cause to focus on the surface structure, then clearly the text can be learned. Learning depends upon what task is performed. Chunking, of course, applies to all the subgoals generated by whatever impasses occur, many of which are microscopic in comparison with the grand goal of reading the sentence. Hence, it is entirely plausible that various bits of the text will be learned in any event in the course of reading.

(5) Rehearsal is the attempt to retain information in the short term by repeating the material to oneself in some fashion. It has been much studied, in part because it has been linked to the retention of knowledge in the long term. In the classic Atkinson and Shiffrin (1968) model, rehearsal was considered the sole transfer mechanism from the short-term store to the long-term store. This model was challenged by the *depth-of-processing* theory (Craik & Lockhart, 1972), which demonstrated that so-called *elaborative* rehearsal, which involves substantial processing of the material, does lead to long-term retention; whereas so-called *maintenance* rehearsal, which involves simply repeating the words, does not. The Soar theory indicates that there will be positive effects of rehearsal if rehearsal entails tasks for which the information is needed, so that chunks get built. But if no tasks are performed, if the aim of rehearsal is simply getting some sort of behavioral loop going, then long-term acquisition cannot be expected. Furthermore, in accord with the depth-of-processing theory, the more elaborative the processing the better. That is, the more diverse the rehearsal tasks and the more they involve existing material in long-term memory, the greater the likelihood that some of these chunks will contain the to-be-remembered material and will fire within the recall context.

(6) Soar predicts the occurrence of *Einstellung* and *functional fixity*, two related phenomena in human problem solving. Einstellung (Luchins, 1942) is the preservation of a learned skill that is not useful in a new environment. If a method is used successfully on a sequence of problems, then even when it becomes inappropriate it may continue to be used.[4] Einstellung shows up not only in longer

---

4. The new problem must appear amenable to the same method—no one would try to make a bed by the same method just used successfully to wash dishes!

solution times, but in the inability to solve the new problems at all. Functional fixity (Duncker, 1945) is the inability to think of (recall from memory or notice in the environment) objects as parts of a problem's solution if the objects have been previously used for a function different from that demanded by the current problem. A typical experimental demonstration might involve the failure to use a brick as a measuring instrument (that is, as a standard length) if it has just been used to hold up a shelf. Both of these phenomena involve the chunks that are built, either for recall or for recognition, and their essential meaning is that the conditions of accessibility are related to the function or tasks in which the learning occurred. This is just a restatement that learning is related to the goals operating at the time of learning.

(7) Related to both these phenomena is the *principle of encoding specificity* (Tulving, 1983), which, in its simplest form, asserts that accessibility depends on the cues that are noticed at the time of learning. Soar chunking is a strong form of this principle. In general, learning systems composed from production systems obey the encoding-specificity principle, since the conditions (which determine accessibility) are constructed at learning time from the materials that are available then. Thus, as in many other cases throughout the book, Soar has various properties because of specific mechanisms, and these properties are shared by large families of architectures. The Soar explanation is strengthened by the observation that the specification of the encoding is related to the task being done (although this too is a general property shared by a subfamily of architectures).

(8) The psychological literature contains many results about chunking as the organization of memory. Some of these, such as the original short-term encoding results on which Miller based his original paper (Miller, 1956), are not pure long-term memory results and do not flow from the aspect of Soar we are considering here. But others, such as the chess-perception results (De Groot, 1965; Chase & Simon, 1973), can be seen as direct analogs to Soar's theory of chunking. A person views a chess position from the middle game of a tournament game for five seconds and then attempts to reproduce the position from memory. A chess master will do a good job (23 out of 25 men correctly placed); but a novice will do very poorly (3 or 4 out of 25). In fact, this perceptual-memory test is the best quick test there is for chess skill. The models that explain this phenomenon do

so in terms of chunking—that the chess master acquires, through extensive experience, spatially and functionally related groups of chess pieces that are treated as single units, both in terms of perception and memory. Chunking permits the master to characterize a complex arrangement of many pieces in just a few chunks, whereas the novice, who has essentially one chunk per piece, can grasp only a few pieces. There are a number of interlocking results in this area, including simulations of the chunking and retrieval behavior, and they provide one of the major pillars of empirical evidence for chunking in humans. Soar is entirely consonant with this theory, including the fact that the chunks have a strong functional character (and also a strong spatial-contiguity character).

The items in Figure 6-6 are recognizably similar to the characteristics of human learning and memory, both in terms of casual observation and in terms of the broad picture painted in the psychological literature. The list is no more than a broad-brush qualitative picture and it is not intended to be otherwise. One of its deficiencies, in common with the analogous list in Figure 4-24, is the lack of any systematic principle of generation for the items of the list, even a principle of generation independent of the theory (here Soar). This deficiency cannot be solved in this book. I present the evidence just as one dimension of evaluation of a unified theory of cognition. It is important, however, that a candidate theory be evaluated at this gross qualitative level.

6.3. The Distinction between Episodic and Semantic Memory

A unified theory of cognition must give an account of the major types of memory that have been found empirically. Psychology has developed a small taxonomy of memories. Ultimately, what must be explained are the (many) specific experiments that gave rise to the particular memory distinctions. But at a global level it is useful to ask how such a theory—here Soar—handles memory, as standardly conceived.

One important example is the distinction between *episodic memory* and *semantic memory*, introduced by Endel Tulving in 1969 and discussed extensively by him more recently (Tulving, 1983). The distinction arises as a late development in the central learning tradition of American experimental psychology, which has focused on verbal learning. This tradition is concerned with using verbal mate-

Study trial

BOOK	13
HOUSE	45
BRICK	84
. . .	
GLOVE	12

Test trial

HOUSE	?
BOOK	?
. . .	

Figure 6-7. Paired-associates verbal-learning paradigm.

rials—letters, numbers, words, phrases, and sentences—to conduct experiments in which people deliberately learn various lists of items and then demonstrate that learning at a later time by carrying out various tasks that depend upon it. This is the world of Ebbinghaus' nonsense syllable and the origin of many familiar experimental paradigms—item recognition, serial recall, paired associates, free recall, cued recall, and so on.

Figure 6-7 shows an example of a paired-associates task. The tasks starts with a *study trial*, in which a sequence of pairs is presented to the person: *book—13, house—45, . . .* This is followed by a *test trial*, in which the person is presented the words that occurred earlier and asked to state the associated number: *house—?* (the person says *40*), *book—?* (the person says *13*), *horse—?* (the person says *17*), and so on. The pairs are presented in random order.

As Tulving (1969) made abundantly clear, the memory involved in learning verbal material is special. It is learning what occurred in a particular *episode*. Thus, having learned in one session the paired associates as in Figure 6-7, in the next session the person might be asked to learn *book—45, house—13 . . .* just the opposite from the first session. What is being learned is not that *book* and some number, say *45*, belong together, but that they belong together on a particular occasion. This situation seems to contrast sharply with learning that *2 + 2 = 4* or that *canaries have wings*. These are permanent facts independent of the occasion for learning them, and they belong in a memory called *semantic* memory, in accord with the name being used at the time for studies of memory and knowledge organization in AI (Quillian, 1968; Collins & Quillian, 1969). In fact, it was the emergence of the work in semantic memory that finally brought the contrast between it and episodic memory to where it could not be ignored.

Making such a distinction immediately raises the question of whether two distinct memory structures exist, one for episodic memory and one for semantic memory, or whether only a single memory exists that somehow encompasses both types of information. And, indeed, a small, lively literature exists on the topic (Tulving, 1983). Clearly, a unified theory of cognition must provide an answer to this question. Indeed, we should be able simply to read out of Soar its explanation.

First, Soar must say that episodic and semantic information are held in the same memory—there is only one long-term memory in Soar. This is not quite the whole answer, however, for we must detail exactly how Soar deals with episodic memory and how it deals with semantic memory. Take the episodic side first. Chunks from selection spaces produce search-control productions that reproduce the operators that were selected on a prior occasion. Lived history, for Soar, is a sequence of operators. To the extent that it is caused to focus on some of these operators in order to select them, it will remember their selection (as chunks) and be able to reproduce their occurrence. Indeed, the right-hand column of Figure 4-18, which shows what happens when R1-Soar is presented the same situation over again, provided a scrap of such a history. This form of history has certain peculiarities. It is selective—what is remembered depends on what Soar is doing with the information at the time. It is also self-oriented—it is cast very much in terms of what Soar is doing, not as a record of the objective situation. To attain the latter, Soar must be attending to the ongoing stream of events so as to capture them in some kind of operators. Both of these properties also characterize human episodic memory.

Now take the semantic side. Chunks generalize to new situations. When they do, they become Soar's abstract, episode-free knowledge. For instance, Figure 4-14 showed the twelve chunks that constitute knowledge of the three-blocks world. These blocks chunks are no longer tied to any history; they simply describe the structure of the space so that Soar can get around in it (when solving problems). These same chunks could have been learned in the pursuit of many different specific tasks in many different orders, so there is no trace left of any historical information. The situation need not be as ahistorical as the blocks-world case. Chunks can exist in arbitrary mixtures, some tied to the historical moment of their birth and some abstracted from various aspects of that moment, including the temporal. Furthermore, various kinds of mixed dependence can show up above the level of the individual chunk—for example, prior episodic information may be remembered and then used by deliberate analogical means in solving a current task. Soar can behave in these ways too, but this is a property of the spaces and impasses that obtain and not just of the chunks.

Many points can be made from this brief discussion of the distinction between episodic and semantic memory. First, it is important to be able to use a unified theory of cognition to answer questions that have been raised about the nature of human memory. In this regard, we have sketched a qualitative answer but have not gone back to the original data to see how satisfactory the story is in detail. Second, a unified theory must contain the answer to the question of the basic nature of the episodic/semantic distinction. One does not add new information to the theory to obtain it. One simply goes to the theory and reads out the solution. In fact, there may be still other ways in which both episodic and semantic memory can be encoded in Soar, ways that we have simply not discovered.[5] Third, the solution that the Soar architecture proposes has elements of novelty. It does not just point to one of the alternative schemes that exist in the current literature. This is what I meant at the beginning of the chapter about there being more things in an architecture than are dreamt of in theory. Very few of the possibilities for how to handle episodic and semantic memory are available upon direct thought—from the top down, so to speak. They can only be discovered by examining essentially complete architectures. Fourth, the answer to this episodic-semantic question occurs within a total context of other processing mechanisms. On the supportive side, this solution already fits within a theory that agrees with many other aspects of human behavior. So it instantly gains plausibility in a number of ways.

Finally, the solution here is the solution of *this* unified theory of cognition. Any other unified theory will also provide mechanisms for remembering both episodic and semantic information. These could look the same, similar, or quite different.

5. A recent treatment of this topic can be found in Rosenbloom, Newell, and Laird (1989).

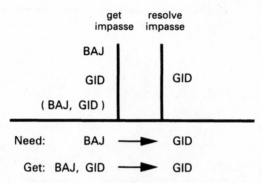

Figure 6-8. The data-chunking problem.

6.4. Data Chunking

We have been proceeding to read out from Soar the global characteristics of its theory of learning and memory. Unfortunately, there is a very large fly in this ointment. Figure 6-8 shows the problem. Assume a paired-associates task, with nonsense syllables (*BAJ-GID*). The pair is presented on a study trial. The person knows he is supposed to study the pair, so that at some later time, when given *BAJ*, he can respond with *GID*.

How will Soar do this task? Soar can learn only by solving problems. When presented with instructions for a task, it must pose itself a problem that will result in the kind of learning that it needs. In this case it must create a task that builds a chunk something like *BAJ → GID*. This is Soar's self-posed task. Let's look at this situation in the same way we explained chunking in Figure 4-12, that is, by focusing on working memory as the elements show up. The exact task that Soar poses for itself, to learn the paired associate, need not be spelled out. We know, however, that at some point the critical impasse must take place (indicated by the left-hand vertical) and that the chunk that resolves the impasse will be the desired chunk. The requirement for the problem solving for this impasse (between the two verticals) is to produce the response item (*GID*) plus some preferences that resolve the impasse). Where will *GID* come from? It will come from some production that picks up *GID* on the left-hand side (possibly in isolation or embedded in some larger structure). But if this happens, then *GID* will turn out to be part of a condition of the chunk. That would mean that the chunk cannot be evoked without *GID* being already available—just what cannot be the case if the paired-associates task is to be performed.

This is what we call the *data-chunking problem*—that chunks that arise from deliberate attempts to learn an arbitrarily given data item will have the item itself somewhere in the conditions, making the chunk useless to retrieve the item. Normally, chunking acquires procedures to produce an effect. When what is given is a data item, not a bit of behavior, the attempt to convert it to procedural learning seems stymied.

What is going on here is interesting from the point of view of a unified theory of cognition. At the highest level, the story about learning and memory has been proceeding satisfactorily. When we examine the phenomenon of learning in Soar one level deeper in terms of its mechanisms, however, we find something that calls the entire enterprise into question. In fact, those of us who were developing Soar were unaware of the problem for a long time, since chunking was quite successful and continually exhibiting new and interesting powers. We stumbled across the data-chunking problem only when we turned to look at verbal learning phenomena. It came as quite a surprise to us, and especially so when it turned out to be not just an issue of a bug or a little programming, but something that seemed of the essence.

Let's review how we got in this jam. Chunking originates in psychology as a notion about how people organize data in memory, and its introduction was one of the earliest events of the cognitive revolution. George Miller presented the idea in 1956 to explain why short-term memory wasn't constant when measured in bits (the coin of the realm in the mid-fifties), but was (roughly) constant when measured in terms of new units he called chunks. Suppose someone is given the following task:

Repeat back: R, C, A, C, B, S, A, P, A

Normally, the person would miss several items when reciting the list—the sequence exceeds the normal letter span we are able to remember. But suppose the person had heard, instead:

Repeat back: RCA, CBS, APA

If the person knew the three-letter abbreviations, then the sequence would be easy to remember, although the person would have to decode *RCA* (the chunk) to *R, C, A*, when providing the output. At some earlier time the *RCA* chunk was created from a set of existing chunks, *R, C,* and *A*, which themselves had been formed yet earlier. If, for instance, *RCA* and *CBS* had featured jointly in the news, say some prominent executive moving from *RCA* to *CBS*, the person might have formed yet a higher chunk, (*RCA, CBS*). Or the person might form such a chunk deliberately for himself. Thus, chunking is recursive—memory becomes organized hierarchically.

Much experimental evidence exists that chunking goes on all the time. For instance (McLean & Gregg, 1967), people can learn to recite a permutation of the alphabet:

Repeat back: G K M Z I F O B X L J N P R C U S Q T V W E A Y

The sequence was presented to some people in groups of two and to others in groups of three:

GK MZ IF OB XL JN PR CU SQ TV WE AY
GKM ZIF OBX LJN PRC USQ TVW EAY

The string is learned either way, though it takes quite a few repetitions, and it can be recited smoothly. But if (surprise!) people who learned the list in subgroups are asked to recite the sequence *backwards*, then the chunking is revealed. They can recite backwards, but they produce the sequence in little bursts of letters. They recollect each chunk as a unit, unpack the chunk into working memory (which arrives in forward order), and then invert the order for the small sequence. They recite the list as *YA, EW, VT, . . .* or *YAE, WVT, . . .* , depending on how they learned it. This experiment is particularly revealing because it demonstrates actual chunk formation. The units of twos and threes certainly did not exist beforehand.

Although the concept of chunking is well established and well known in cognitive science as a form of memory organization, it has generally played second fiddle to other concepts for the organization of long-term memory, such as semantic nets, frames, and schemas. The reasons are not entirely clear. My own conjecture is that operational systems were built using semantic nets, frames,

PARALLEL				SERIAL			PARALLEL		
HIERARCHY							HIERARCHY		

		encode			map			decode	
s	— s	— s	→ c	d —	g	→ d	d	→ r	= r
↑	↑	↑	↓	↑	↑	↓	↑	↓	↓

s	s	s	c	= c	g	d	= d	r	r

WORKING MEMORY

Figure 6-9. Xaps2 chunking scheme.

and schemas, but no AI systems were built using chunks. At least one simulation of chunking was developed (for the chess-perception experiments; Simon & Gilmartin, 1973), but it was narrowly focused. Chunking remained mostly a way of analyzing experimental results.

In 1982, Paul Rosenbloom built a system, called Xaps2, that used chunking to deal with the power law of practice of Figure 1-3 (Rosenbloom & Newell, 1987). As shown in Figure 6-9, chunks were realized by productions. A chunk actually requires three productions. One encodes the stimulus items into a chunk: if *R, C, A*, then put *RCA* in working memory. One decodes a chunk name into separate elements: if *RCA*, then put /r/, /c/, /a/ into working memory. (Note that the name is not decoded into the same stimulus elements as were originally given but into response codes). The third production arises from the need to control when the decoding is to happen—when the response is to be given. Rosenbloom called this a *mapping* production, for taking the internal stimulus code into the internal response code, but with additional conditions for goal elements, to provide control. In Xaps2, there was a hierarchy of stimulus (encoding) productions, which all ran freely in parallel. Correspondingly, there was a hierarchy of response (decoding) productions, which also ran freely in parallel. The mapping productions were controlled by the task, which allowed them to gate which response would occur. The Xaps2 system produced the power law of practice.

The original Xaps2 version built chunks according to experience—just as indicated by the original psychological work on chunking. Chunking gathered up whatever was delivered into short-term memory by ongoing experience and created new chunks continuously. Making such a system really work, however, drove us to link chunks with goals. Rosenbloom constructed a successor system, Xaps3 (Rosenbloom, 1983), to have the goal-caching character, from which we went to the scheme in Soar (Laird, Rosenbloom, & Newell, 1984). The major evolution was the step from the fairly complicated three-production scheme to the one production scheme described in Chapter 4. The second achievement, whose essential details are harder to articulate, was to integrate chunking into the existing Soar system (which had not been designed with learning in mind) so that chunking could work anywhere.

Through all the history of Xaps2 and Xaps3 to Soar, we never asked whether the chunking would apply to data, such as learning to recall verbal items. There never has been any question that chunking provides effective learning—we've seen lots of examples with Soar. It seemed obvious that the procedural chunking schemes would work in the situations that gave birth to the idea. Only when we finally got around to getting Soar to perform the classical tasks of paired associates and serial recall did the problem of data chunking emerge. Thus, we have another example of the architecture having its say—in this case, telling us of difficulties of which we had been quite unaware.

What is to be done about the data-chunking problem? Two radically different paths could have been taken—switch or stay. One path (switch) would be to change the architecture, by, for example, adding a separate declarative memory. This step would abandon the uniform-memory principle—all memory is stored by productions—and replace it with a dual-memory system. This arrangement appears in Anderson's Act* (though not in reaction to the data-chunking problem, of course, but as a fundamental principle). In a dual-memory system the two kinds of memory, declarative and procedural, are kept completely distinct and have different processes. Permanent storage into the declarative memory (which is what is at issue here) occurs autonomously. That is (to continue with Act*), there is a small constant probability that any entry of an item into working memory will also become a permanent part of declarative memory.

A second way of changing the architecture is to add a mechanism to manipulate the data in working memory without Soar becoming aware of the data. The data-chunking difficulty can be localized to the chunker creating conditions (for the to-be-built chunk) for everything Soar became aware of in resolving the impasse and in particular for the response datum (*GID*), input from the outside. If Soar could avoid attending, so to speak, while it moved the datum over to be the result, then it could build chunks that would perform perfectly well. This does lead to a rather bizarre view—that the memory is built up of items that Soar is guaranteed not to know about! Of course, Soar will find out about them eventually, when they arrive in working memory at some latter time, but still the whole setup seems to fly in the face of a system remembering what it focuses attention upon.

Despite the seeming oddity, we actually explored this path, in part because such schemes have actually been tried, though not to solve this difficulty. PSG, an early production system (Newell, 1973b), had a primitive action *Notice(<pattern>)* that searched working memory for an item satisfying *<pattern>* and brought it within the attentional scope of other productions. This mechanism, which seems quite reasonable, has exactly the property of being blind to the item (since it occurs on the right-hand side of a production); and an addition of *Notice* to the action repertoire of Soar productions would solve the data-chunking problem. It would have other effects as well, such as destroying the uniform principle that *all* actions simply put elements in the working memory and making it problematical how chunking would create productions containing *Notice*.[6]

The other main path is to stay with the architecture. If Soar is the right architecture, then there must be a solution for the data-chunking problem somewhere in the current behavioral repertoire of Soar. We should listen to the architecture to hear what it says. This is the path we followed. Not only is there a way to chunk data in the current version of Soar; data chunking has some interesting properties.

Figure 6-10 gives the essential elements of the solution. The key idea is to separate generating an object to be recalled from testing it. The desired object here is *GID*. We want the process that generates *GID* not to know that it is the response that is to be made—not to be the process that tests for the item. Thus, to achieve the required

6. Another possibility is partial matching to evoke the chunk for *GID*, even though the *GID*-condition in the chunk fails to match.

1. Separate generated object from test if it is correct
2. Test can contain result object in conditions
3. Generator must not consult result object
   Producing result is separate from efficiency
   Search control is never chunked, as it affects only efficiency
4. Multiple approaches exist for generator
   Construct object (object is search control)
   Search for object (cue object is search control)

Figure 6-10. Basic principles of Soar's solution
to the data-chunking problem.

learning, Soar should create for itself a task to be solved by generate and test. It is alright for the test to contain the result, namely *GID*. The test is to find an instance of *GID*, so the test not only can have *GID* in some condition, it *should* have it. As long as the generator doesn't produce *GID* by consulting the given object (*GID*), then *GID* will not occur in the conditions of the chunk that will be built.

How might such a generator of *GID* be achieved? One way would be just to start generating —*GAA, GAB, GAC, GAD*, and, eventually, *GID*, at which point the test, which is looking for *GID*, will say *that's it!* This method indeed solves the data-chunking problem, because nothing in the generator has consulted *GID* in producing its results, hence the chunk has *BAJ* in the condition and *GID* in the action.

You may be thinking, Yes, but at what cost! Indeed, a generation of this sort could take a fair amount of time. After all, it could not actually start with *GAA*, but would have to start with something like *AAA*, and maybe not even *AAA* but with *A*, and all single letters, before starting over with *AA*, and then all pairs, before even getting to *AAA*. Thus, although the solution is feasible, it could be extremely costly.

This leads to the next part of the solution. In problem spaces, producing a result is separate from the efficiency of producing the result. A problem space is given by a set of operators (with the set of states to which the operators apply). A problem is given by starting at an initial state and finding a desired state. A solution is attained by applying one operator after another until a desired state is produced, without concern for what operators are applied or in what order, as long as they are in the space. The search in the space can go on for a long time, with many backtrackings, or the path can zip directly to the solution. All that is required is that a desired state is attained. Efficiency is a question of search control, not of whether the solution is acceptable.

This separation has an important consequence for chunking. Working-memory elements that enter into search control (by evoking search-control productions) do not enter into the chunks. To use them would be to tie the solution to the exact path that was chosen, whereas what is known when a chunk is built is that a solution has been found legitimately, and the particular path is not important. This means that any search control whatever can be used to guide the operators to the solution.

There are several ways to exploit the possibility of search control to create an efficient generation of *GID*. For instance, the answer might be guessed. Starting from the stimulus *BAJ*, one might guess *RAJ*, then *RAG, GAG, GIG*, and finally *GID*. That may seem no better than chance, but some principles are involved—the operators transform the stimulus word (the nonsense syllable) to similar words by changing one letter. The first time through might be an unintelligent search, but then search-control chunks would be built that draw on *BAJ* as the search-control context to select the way. Other sorts of search might be possible, such as generating a sequence from the nonsense syllable to a word to its referent or embedding the syllable in a self-generated semantic image. The details are not important here, only that a variety of schemes might be possible for shaping the generation. Which one would actually be useful would depend on the task context and the person.

A second possibility for exploiting search control is to *construct* the response object (*GID*) using the input response object itself as search control (Figure 6-11). For instance, since *GID* is composed of the three letters *G, I,* and *D*, then *GID* can be constructed by an operator that produces *G* for the first letter, then an operator that produces *I* for the second, and then an operator that produces *D* for the third. The problem of producing *G* for the first letter can be solved by proposing operators for all the letters and using the letter in the first place of the input response (to wit, *G*) to select the right operator (to wit, the one that produces *G*). It takes only three independent selections to construct *GID*, as opposed to the sequential generation of all triples. If this seems to be a basic lesson in how to beat the combinatorics in AI by the application of heuristics, that

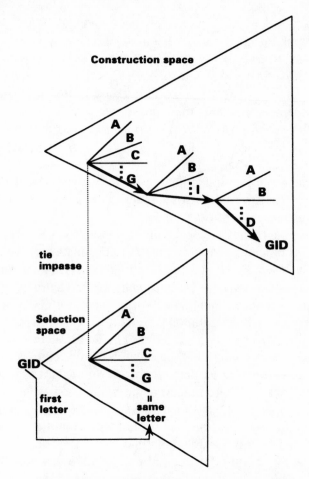

Figure 6-11. Constructing the response *GID*.

is exactly right. The case is isomorphic to one of the earliest examples of the use of heuristics, namely, how to open a combination safe if a slight click can be heard as each tumbler falls into place (Newell, Shaw, & Simon, 1958).

Let us examine this scheme in some detail (Rosenbloom, Laird, & Newell, 1988b). This will take us into the trenches, but the excursion will provide some appreciation of the details of Soar, a glimpse of an interesting technical problem, and an example of how the architecture tells us new things. The full solution will take three steps. First, we must build the recognition of the result (*GID*). Second, we must build a basic generator of what has been learned.

Task: recognize a compound item **(a b c (d e))**
Study trial: given item, become familiar
Test trial: given item, say if familiar
Recognize by internal name **(^name *n6*)**

Study trial: try to recognize (self-posed task)
Recognition problem space
• Operator: recognize-next-element
  Fails if subitem is not recognized; get an impasse
    Subgoal—Learn to recognize subitem
• Assign a name (now recognize item)
• Chunk is created to assign name if item is recognized

Test trial: given an item **(a b c (d e))**
If chunk fires, name is assigned and item is recognized
If chunk fails to fire, item is not recognized

Figure 6-12. Soar solution to recognition of data.

Third, we must build a way to use cues (from *BAJ*) to modulate that generator to obtain only the learned item associated with the cues.

Figure 6-12 shows building the recognition test. This is a simple recognition task in which some item, such as *(a b c (d e))*, is presented. We use an example that has some hierarchical structure, in contrast to *(BAJ, GID)*. On a study trial Soar is presented an item and is to learn it. On a test trial Soar is presented an item and is supposed to indicate whether the item has been presented earlier. There are many study and test trials with a population of data items, so that appropriate distractors can be presented as well as items actually presented on earlier trials. Recognition means that Soar has developed an internal name and is able to present the name as an indicator of the item's prior presentation. This name (*n6*, for example) was generated internally, not given to Soar as an externally presented associate to be recalled—that would change the task from recognition to recall.

On the study trial, Soar must evoke a self-imposed task. If there is no task, there is no learning, because there is no chunking. The self-imposed task is to try to recognize the item—that is, to go through the task that will be formed on the test trial. Soar goes into a recognition problem space, which has a single operator, *recognize-next-element*. It first asks whether the item already has an internal name, in which case it knows it has seen it before. If the item does not have a name, then the operator starts attending to each component of the data item, asking if it recognizes the item (recognition being the production of an internal name for the component item). Wherever a component is not recognized, Soar will recurse and build up a recognition of the subcomponent. The recursion happens because Soar gets an impasse when it cannot recognize a component, at which point it passes into a subgoal for which it evokes the problem space to recognize the substructure. When Soar gets finished with all this, it has finally recognized all the components. Then it can assign a new name (for example, *n137*) to the new structure that is made up of recognizable parts. When Soar succeeds and terminates this effort, a chunk will be created. The conditions of the chunk are the names of the components in the structured arrangement, and the action of the chunk is the newly assigned name. Thus, on a test trial, if the same item arrives, which is to say, an item consistent with this arrangement of components, each recognized as an already presented item, then this chunk will fire and the assigned name will be put in working memory, signaling that the total item is recognized. Thus a recognizer has now been built. The easiest part of the total recall task has been accomplished.

The second step, shown in Figure 6-13, is the construction job. This requires a free-recall task that is not quite the usual task posed in psychological research, for it is genuinely context free. The recognition task, on the other hand, is identical to the psychologist's recognition task—was this just-presented item presented earlier? In this new *free-recall task*, as we'll call it, there is a study trial, where an item is presented to be learned for recall later. On the test trial the person is to recall all items ever presented. This is a free recall with no limit on the context from which one should do the recall. Its purpose, of course, is to learn to construct the item from nothing, so that it is not dependent on some particular contextual features, which would limit the ability to evoke the generator at some future time.

The situation at the study trial is a presented item and the need to learn to recall it later. The self-posed task is to do the future task. Soar goes into a *recall problem space*, which has a single *recall operator*. This space contains *all* the known items. Each item is an instantiation of the recall operator. Thus, when in this space all these instantiations are proposed as the actual operator to be selected. Given the task of *recall what you know*, items literally rain down in this space.

Task: free recall (a special context-free recall task)
Study trial: given item, learn to recall it
Test trial: recall **all** items
Study trial: try to recall **this** item (self-posed task)
Recall problem space
• Operator: recall
Space contains all known items
Given item acts as search control to construct it
• Materials are the known items
• Construction operators are a fixed set
Try to recognize item: if so already can recall it
If cannot recognize item, get impasses and construct item in subgoal
Test trial: just reproduce all items

Figure 6-13. Soar solution to free recall of data.

The self-imposed task is to recall the item Soar has in hand at the moment. If the presented item arrives in the rain of items, then of course it can recall it and the task is attained. It knows it has recalled it, because it has the item in hand and can compare it with the item recalled. This verification takes place on the item itself, not on its internal name (not on *n6*). Although this name is part of the recalled item, no internal name is attached to the item in hand. So the comparison must be on the content of the item.

A study trial may introduce a new item. Then Soar will find itself in the recall space, with all the known items around, but the presented item will not be one of them. Its task now (one might think of this as the *real* study task) is to construct an item identical to the presented item. It does this in response to a no-change impasse that occurred when it attempted to apply the *recall operator*. The chunk that will be built from resolving this impasse will be a new instantiation of the *recall operator* that will produce the new item when applied. Next time, when the recall operator is selected, this instantiation will be proposed along with all the others.

Since Soar has in hand the presented item, the task of construction is actually a task of copying, analogous to that shown in Figure 6-11. The materials available for use in this copying are all the known items (which are all laying around in the current state). It will start out just with primitive items, *a, b, c, . . .* (just as in Figure 6-11). Pretty soon it gets small structures, such as *(a b c)*, then larger structures, such as *(a (a b) b (c d (a b)))*. Any item that has

Task: cued recall (given **a**, recall $((a\ b)_s\ (c\ d)_r)_p$)
Might be posed as, given **a**, recall **(c d)**
The task is subject-centered
To discriminate presented item **p** from other candidates
Distractors are internally generated

Study trial: try to recall item using cues (self-posed task)
Do free recall
If retrieve multiple items, apply discriminate operator
Discriminate operator discovers a cue and rejects alternatives
Chunk is created to reject alternative on basis of cue

Test trial: if chunks discriminate a single item, then recall succeeds
If chunks don't discriminate, then get a set of alternatives

Figure 6-14. Soar solution to cued recall of data.

already been built can be used for the copy. Soar also has construction operators, which are a small fixed set of actions that link items into structures. They are available from the beginning and are used throughout the growth of recallable items (only the operators corresponding to items grow). The presented item in hand is used as search control to select these construction operators (just as in Figure 6-11). The construction is terminated by the firing of the recognition chunk, which indicates the copy is complete.

Figure 6-14 shows the third and final step, which is to do a cued-recall task. The task is set up as a paired-associates task, in which the stimulus item $(a\ b)_s$ and the response item $(c\ d)_r$ are put together into a pair structure $((a\ b)_s\ (c\ d\ )_r)_p$. Thus, there is a single presented structure, just as in the first two steps. In the test trial, a part will be presented, to wit, the stimulus $(a\ b)_s$, and what should be recalled is another part of the structure in which this first part occurred, to wit, the response part $(c\ d)_r$. Soar is to attempt to recall the total structure (the pair) and then to extract the response part.

It's important to realize that the problem of cued recall is a subject-centered problem. The experimenter may say, "I hereby point out this cue, and when I present the cue to you again, then recall this response item." From the subject's point of view, however, the real problem is to distinguish what needs to be recalled from all the other items that might be recalled—from the internally generated *distractors*, to use the language of experimental psychology. Thus, from the subject's viewpoint, the problem is one of discrimination, and the subject must find the discriminators. The subject cannot get them from the experimenter, because the experimenter doesn't know what is in the subject's mind that might be confusing to the subject. Indeed, the subject doesn't know either, until the confusion occurs.

Again, there must be a self-posed task for the study trial. This is to try to recall the object using cues—not using prespecified cues, but whatever cues happen to be around, which of course includes what the experimenter has provided. Soar starts with a free recall, in order to obtain what arrives naturally. This is the previous task in which all the candidates rain down. The experiment assures that in the test trial the item will have the given cue, $((a\ b)_s\ .\ .\ .)$, so the candidates that arrive in the rain of candidates can be tested for having this cue. There are three possible outcomes. First, there may be no candidates that have the cue. Then Soar must do what it does in the free-recall study task in order to be able to generate the candidate. Second, there may be exactly one candidate that has the cue. Then Soar can do no better than to take it as the correct recollection and extract its response part, $(c\ d)_r$, to use for the response.

Third, there may be several candidates with the cue. Then the problem is how to distinguish the right one from all the other distractors. This shows up as a tie impasse (as always) and Soar goes into a problem space to resolve the tie. In this selection space (which is different from the look-ahead space used in the blocks-world task in Figure 4-10), it applies a *discrimination operator*. This operator takes one of the tied items and compares it to the input item to find something that discriminates the two of them on the basis of their cue parts. Remember, only the cue part of the correct item will be available at test. Having discovered a discriminating feature, Soar can use it to reject the alternative. That is, it executes an operator that puts in a rejection preference and that provides the solution to the self-posed task. Then Soar creates a chunk that automatically puts in a rejection when the stimulus cue is present and when a retrieved candidate has the given feature. There might be several distractor candidates; then the discrimination operator may have to be applied several times—though not necessarily once for each candidate, because a given feature may discriminate several candidates.

When a test trial occurs, Soar opens up and lets all the candidates rain down. All three results are still possible. First, no items at all arrive. Then Soar can fail the recall task or it can set up the task of guessing on other grounds. Second, a single candidate that fits arrives. Then Soar can extract the response part as the response. Third, multiple candidates arrive. But now the rejection chunks that have been learned also fire immediately and discriminate the true recollection from all the other distractor items that show up. This may be enough to let the single candidate emerge, and then this is just like the unique case above. Alternatively, there could still be a residual set, smaller than the original. Soar will then be faced with a tie impasse between these candidate items. It could just guess (now a more narrowly based guess), or it could seek some other knowledge to help it discriminate.

This scheme applies directly to the original paired-associates task, *(BAJ-GID)*. The stimulus is taken as a source of cues, and the whole structure is retrieved, with the response then being extracted out. At retrieval time the following sequence occurs: $BAJ \rightarrow B,J \rightarrow (BAJ\ GID) \rightarrow GID$. This scheme works and it provides a solution to the data-chunking problem.

Let us return from Soar's trenches and see what has been achieved. We found a genuine difficulty in functional capability, which we dubbed the data-chunking problem. We stayed with the architecture and found an interesting technical solution. This solution now works as advertised (Rosenbloom, Laird, & Newell, 1987, 1988b). The way is now clear for Soar to learn declarative data, at least in situations analogous to the recognition and recall tasks of the verbal-learning literature. Given that Soar is our candidate unified theory of cognition, we should expect that this solution will now exhibit many of the phenomena that arise in the human verbal-learning literature. These explorations have not yet been carrried to the point of detailed contact with experimental results on human memory. But a number of interesting properties can still be noted.

First, we have been led to a *reconstructive* view of declarative memory. The architecture has told us that when an item is recalled it is reconstructed. We didn't start out with any notion of reconstruction. In fact, we first looked for guessing strategies as generators. Reconstruction emerged as a technical solution for the generation of candidates routinely and efficiently. The case for reconstructive memory has a long history in psychology, of which Bartlett's *Remembering* (1932) is perhaps the best known. Although we have not run examples to show it, it should be clear from the structure of data chunking that the reconstructed memory is open to modulation, distortion, error, and default composition.

Second, the recognition test is reminiscent of the sort of immediate familiarity tests that show up in some dual-process psychological models of retrieval, epitomized by the model of Atkinson and Juola (1973). These models posit an immediate test of familiarity, which takes constant time no matter how many items have been presented from which the test item must be discriminated. If familiarity is strong enough, there is an immediate decision that the test item has been seen; if familiarity is weak enough, there is an immediate decision that the item has not previously been seen. Only if familiarity is in-between is a detailed search of memory done. (These models bear a strong similarity to the random-walk decision models we looked at briefly in Chapter 1; see Figure 1-11.) The recognition test in Soar, which always has to be there, is playing exactly this role. It is, of course, a nongraded version. The more interesting point is that it occurs here because it is part of the technical solution, not because it is posited for psychological purposes.

Third, the mechanisms that have emerged in Soar are exceedingly close to the mechanisms in the *Epam* theory of verbal learning (Feigenbaum & Simon, 1984; Simon & Feigenbaum, 1964), a theory embodied in a simulation program that goes back to the early years of the cognitive revolution (Feigenbaum, 1959). This similarity is important enough to explore in some detail. The top of Figure 6-15 shows the main features of Epam.[7] Epam learns verbal items by growing a network of discriminations—so an item (*BAJ*) can be discriminated from distractors. Each node has an associated test, which sorts the incoming item toward a terminal node. If an item is sorted down to a terminal node that contains other items, then it conflicts with them and the network is extended by creating some new test that discriminates the items. Epam handles paired associates by embedding the stimulus and response in a single structure (*BAJ-GID*), which is just the way Soar encodes the paired-associate task.

The Epam theory predicts a number of results in verbal learning, as listed in the figure, adapted from Feigenbaum and Simon (1984).

7. The version to be described is Epam III, the most mature version (Simon & Feigenbaum, 1964).

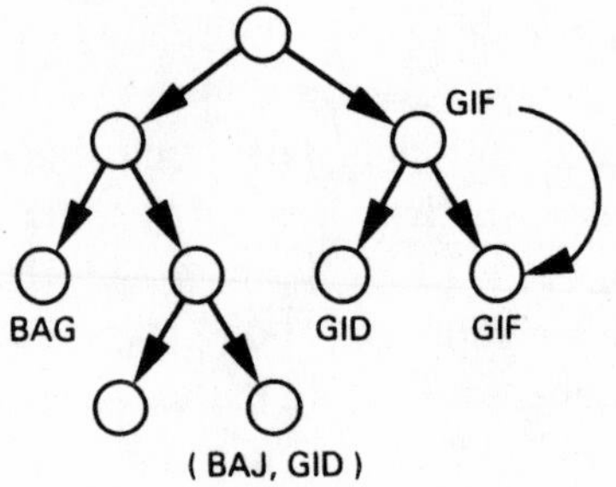

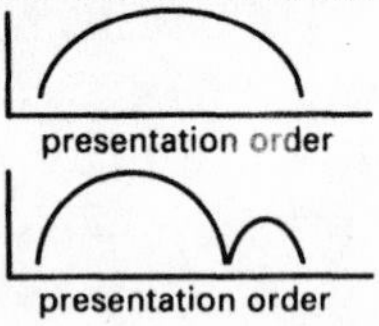

1. Bowed serial-position curve, relative curve constant

2. Von Restorff effect (sharp dip at salient item)

3. Fixation time is independent of presentation time

4. Single trial learning (Rock effect)

5. Retroactive inhibition (one forgets previously learned items)

6. Oscillation (forgotten items remembered again)

7. Effects of familiarity

8. Effects of meaningfulness, serial and paired-associates

   (three-to-one learning time for low vs. high trigrams)

9. Effects of similarity, serial and paired-associates

10. Letter-order effects in tip-of-tongue phenomena

Figure 6-15. The Epam theory of verbal learning.

It predicts the bowed serial-position curve, a classical result. If an ordered list of items is memorized by repeated trial, then the items at the ends of the list are learned before the items in the middle of the list. The little curve opposite result 1 in the figure shows the curve—number of trials needed to learn the item versus serial position of the item in the list. Likewise, Epam predicts the Von Restorff effect—if one item is colored red and the rest are black, the red item is learned before the others. The serial-position curve has a notch in it at the distinguished item. Epam has strategic control for how it distributes its attention on the different items, and both of these results arise from simple strategies for learning associations to *anchor points*, which are items with naturally available cues for retrieval. I won't bother to work through the whole list, but I include it as a reminder of the substantial number of known regularities about the cognitive behavior (like the Salthouse 29).

Soar is in the same position with Epam as it was with the GOMS theory of stimulus-response compatibility in Chapter 5. It will become a theory of verbal learning substantially identical with Epam. Soar will effectively incorporate the Epam theory, not provide an alternative to it. This is an aspect of unified theories of cognition that I have emphasized on earlier occasions, and I want to do so again here. Synthetic theories come to join together what is well understood, and hence already captured, in existing theories of restricted domains. They do not come either to tear asunder or to displace existing understanding. Of course, it is not possible always to join together radically contending theoretical interpretations. But more often than might be suspected, the appearance of radical difference masks analogous underlying mechanisms that *can* be captured in a unified theory.

Soar's version of verbal learning is not identical to the Epam theory in all particulars. Epam is a top-down discrimination net, with control at each node about what feature to test next. Unadorned, this structure implies that features are always taken in the same order and must always be available or the path down the net will be broken. Hence, Epam nets seem sensitive to environmental variability and noise, which has been a source of concern all along, though learning tests at multiple points in the tree might work. The Soar discrimination net, on the other hand, is essentially a bottom-up construction which is prepared to use features in whatever order they arise. Soar has this structure not because of the noise problem that arises in Epam, but because the entire discrimination process must happen within an elaboration phase, with its parallel productions, so that the whole process operates as a recognition system. The discrimination process must happen without deliberate control—even though the analog of such processes can be done in a deliberate way with operators. If the discrimination process is constrained in an appropriate way, then it can just run free as an automatic process.

The fourth lesson to be learned from Soar's data-chunking problem is an example of how a unified theory of cognition can tie disparate phenomena together. Figure 5-11 noted that the time the Soar model of stimulus-response compatibility took to recognize a word was proportional to the number of letters, at ~20 ms per letter, reflecting a substantial number of empirical results, both for word naming and reading. The Soar-Epam model determines what that time should be, namely (ignoring setup) the number of production cycles to do the identification (they run serially in the elaboration phase). We know from the current data-chunking programs that it takes two production cycles per discrimination. This is larger than the minimum of one production cycle assumed. The number of cycles is not the number of letters, however, but the number of cues needed to discriminate the items. This will be roughly proportional to, but somewhat less than, the number of letters in a word. Thus, the model of one part of the cognitive world connects with the model in another. The models are not yet good enough to provide a tight constraint on each other; but it is important that they are in the same ballpark.

Fifth, Soar automatically provides for extending the model. At two places in the above account, Soar would get tie impasses because of a lack of any further ability to discriminate. Soar must guess at these points, which is to say, Soar must seek other ways, if it can find them, to make selections. Guessing is, of course, a standard accoutrement of many models of retrieval and response. But it is always a deus ex machina, for it is never explained how it is that guessing can be a response of the person at the requisite point. With Soar, the context of guessing (here two separate ones), the ability of Soar to make a guess, and the way Soar will emerge with the resolution of a guess are all provided by the theory. Following this up goes beyond our concern here, but Soar as a unified theory provides the setting for integrating guessing behavior into the mainstream of recognition and recall behavior.

Finally, a broader point needs to be made. This solution for data chunking is a general learning mechanism that can be used to associate any two items. It might be thought that all learning should now be done this way. On the contrary, this should be viewed as a special mechanism well adapted to handle specific kinds of recognition and recall. It is a learning mechanism built by means of another learning mechanism, chunking. Chunking provides other ways of doing other learning tasks more directly than by using the apparatus of data chunking. The picture that emerges is of a cognitive system that develops particular modes of behavior for particular task domains. Far from being a system that is uniform at the level of behavior, it is one that is diverse. Far from being a system that has a single learning mechanism (chunking), Soar has many different learning mechanisms. This should not be surprising, for a lesson of all computational systems is that diversity emerges out of unity.

6.5. Skill Acquisition

Let us turn to the acquisition of skill. Currently the received taxonomy of psychology places procedural memory (skill or know-how) in a major category of its own, separate from episodic memory and semantic memory. In Soar, of course, all types of (long-term) memory are built up from chunking, which is basically procedural (though at the level of a content-addressed memory). One does not ask how Soar does skill acquisition per se—that comes with the territory, so to speak—but rather how Soar attains the other kinds of memory. That is what the investigation of data chunking has been all about, as well as the earlier discussion of episodic and semantic memory.

The human acquisition of skill exhibits many regularities. We could compile a list of thirty or forty regularities, just as we did for transcription typing or item recognition. Rather than give such a list, Figure 6-16 just shows the sorts of regularities we might expect. The first sort concerns the power law of practice, with which we've already become familiar. The main issues are its form (a power law) and its ubiquity. But there is also the question of what absolute rates of learning can be expected and what determines the asymptotes. The second sort of regularity concerns transfer effects. We have seen lots of transfer effects in the various Soar examples, but the question is what transfers in human skill. One broad regularity is that learning is in general highly specific, but if matters are arranged correctly there can be substantial transfer. A third sort concerns factors and regimes that affect the rate of learning. One classical result concerns the positive effect of immediate feedback of knowledge of results. Another robust generality is that spaced practice is more effective than massed practice. Regimes can affect transfer as well as rates and, if anything, transfer is more important.

The only regularity we'll discuss is the power law of practice,

1. Power law of practice and its ubiquity
   - Absolute rates of acquisitions
   - Limits and exceptions
2. Transfer effects
   - Skill learning is generally highly specific
3. Regimes that affect learning rate and transfer
   - Spaced vs. massed practice
   - Immediate feedback and knowledge of results

Figure 6-16. Types of regularities of skill acquisition.

which plays an interesting role in Soar as a unified theory of cognition. In discussing the data-chunking problem we reviewed the history of our research on chunking, how we developed the chunking theory of the practice law, and then we developed two different production-system architectures (Xaps2 and Xaps3) that exhibited the power law. However, when we developed Soar chunking out of these ideas, we left behind the three-production chunk and the parallel hierarchical structures of encoding and decoding. The latter, in particular, seemed strongly involved in obtaining the power law. Thus, an important question is whether Soar still provides an explanation of the power law of practice.

As Figure 6-17 demonstrates, Soar does indeed still exhibit the law. This task is the same 1,023-choice reaction task (Seibel, 1963) illustrated in Figure 1-3: the subject places ten fingers opposite ten lights, a pattern of lights is displayed, and the subject strikes the corresponding chord. Soar can be set to do that task by giving it an appropriate set of problem spaces and operators. The only important feature, besides chunking, is that it encodes regions of the stimulus and response as intervals and not just as individual lights and buttons. The version of Soar whose performance is plotted in Figure 6-17 split the fields in half, but an exact split does not make any difference. The figure shows the data for 125 trials of the Seibel task; the log of the number of decision cycles is plotted against the log of the number of trials. The decreasing straight line means that Soar skill acquisition follows the power law, in at least this one instance.

The bottom graph shows the behavior of a single person for 408 trials at the beginning, which corresponds to the Soar curve. What is immediately noticeable is that the slope of the human curve is very shallow ($-.17$) compared with Soar's ($-.80$). In general, the

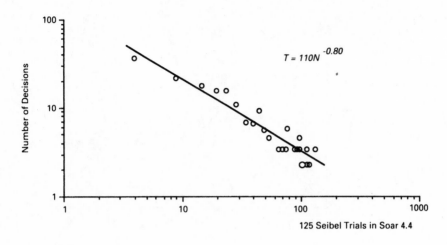

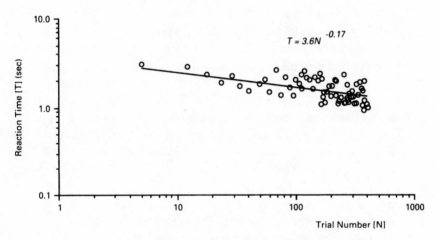

Figure 6-17. Soar on skill acquisition.

rate at which chunking occurs decreases with how much there is to learn. If there's not much to learn, there's not much variability in the situation and the learning curve is fairly steep. One can see from the Soar graph that it is sitting almost at the asymptote (observe how many points are exactly at two decision cycles). If there's lots of detail in the situation, then the curve is fairly shallow. At the moment it is unclear where all the variability of detail comes from in the human's learning experience. This simulation is not yet embed-

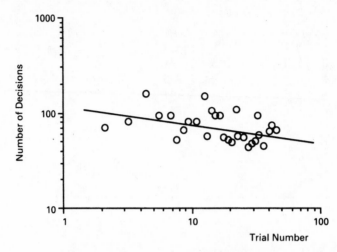

Figure 6-18. R1-Soar on skill acquisition.

ded in the Soar total cognitive system, and there are sources of variability in the interior milieu that haven't been accounted for, so it is premature to worry too strongly about the differences in learning rates. But it is an important gap in Soar as a unified theory of cognition that needs to be accounted for at the proper time.

The Seibel task of Figure 6-17 is artificial in several ways, not just because it is a laboratory task but because we simply posited the encoding for Soar. There is no easy way to avoid something like this, given that Soar lacks the perception and motor capabilities that a human has. However, we can look for a natural example of learning in Soar. Figure 6-18 was plotted from a set of 30 consecutive runs of R1-Soar on a collection of 15 tasks. It can be seen that again Soar exhibits a power law. It appears very noisy, but this is because each point is a single learning trial, whereas in Figure 6-17 the data are grouped in fives (and the human data in Figure 1-3 are grouped in sets of 1,024).

The Soar mechanisms that produce the power law are clear. Thus, we can apply the general scheme to a well-known series of studies by Paul Kolers (1975, 1976) on reading geometrically transformed text. Figure 6-19 shows at the top a sentence of inverted text. True to form, human practice in reading this type of text follows the power law, as we showed in Figure 3-12. People start out reading backward at a much slower rate than normal reading rates, and as they read more and more pages they get better and

The quick brown fox jumps over the lazy dog.
⊥ɥǝ dnᴉɔʞ pɹoʍu ɟox ɾnɯbƨ oʌǝɹ ʇɥǝ ʅɐzʎ qoƃˑ

Read word
Input string → word → access meaning

Input string
If character → read; else decompose string

Read inverted word
Input-inverted-string → word → access meaning

Input inverting string
If character → read → invert; else decompose string

Figure 6-19. The inverted reading task.

better, but they never read backward as quickly as they read normally.

The figure shows a simple version of how Soar might do the task of reading aloud. Soar has not actually been run on the Kolers inverted-text task; this example is used as another exercise in how to work with Soar at an abstract level of analysis. Soar has an operator for reading a normal word—input the string of letters, then get the word, and then access the meaning. Each of these is an operator in the implementation space of the read-word operator. We are interested only in the operator to input a string of letters—if what has been input is something recognizable, then read it; otherwise, decompose the string to find recognizable subparts. Soar would start out by decomposing until it reached individual recognizable elements, in essentially the same way it did the typing in Chapter 5. As chunks get built, sequences of letters will be recognized. The chunks build up a hierarchy.

Given this organization for normal reading aloud, an inverted word will be read as shown at the bottom of the figure. Exactly the same activities occur, except *input-inverted-string* reads the string, rather than *input-string*. Again, if the string is recognizable, then it is read; if it is not and it is composite, then it is decomposed. This new situation occurs when an inverted character is obtained. This inverted character must be recognized by reference to the normal character. What is required to recognize the character depends on the character—recognizing inverted c, d, k, and m all pose different problems. Several operations are available—hypothesizing characters, testing features, imaginal inversioning (either of the given inverted character or of a hypothesized upright character). This system will chunk and it will exhibit a power law, just as Kolers' data illustrate.

In a series of notable studies, Kolers established a number of interesting regularities about transfer and retention of the inverted-reading skill (comparing performance up to a year later). There was some general transfer—people got to be better readers of inverted text—but there was mostly highly specific transfer—they would read exactly the same line of inverted text faster one year later (with no known intervening relevant activity). It can be seen that Soar will show the same effects, at least qualitatively. Chunks are constructed at all parts of this task. Some parts are relatively context free, such as the skill of dealing with the individual inverted letters. These will transfer to reading any inverted text. But chunks are also built up for the specific words and even for sequences of words—for *quick* and for *quick brown*. How high these chunks go on a single reading cannot be determined at this level of analysis. But, because the task is difficult, some fragments of it are processed more than once (just as occurs in normal reading, as shown by regressive eye movements). Repeated processing provides additional opportunity for higher-level chunks to build up. Furthermore, the Soar model of long-term memory does not include any true forgetting, so it would exhibit these skills even a year later, as long as the higher context allowed the problem spaces to be invoked. (This latter qualification brings with it many interesting issues, but not ones that Soar is yet prepared to shed light on, one way or the other.)

Besides providing one more example of Soar's explanation of skill acquisition, the discussion of these studies is useful because Kolers interpreted them to support a view of skill that was very different from the one extant in psychology. He saw skill as embodied completely in the procedures people built up. Furthermore, he quite specifically concluded from this work that production systems and the physical symbol system hypothesis (which he took production systems to epitomize) were an inadequate formulation of human behavior—not just a little inadequate, but radically so (Kolers & Roediger, 1984; Kolers & Smythe, 1984). Hence, it is interesting that production systems, and learning systems that take them as the unit of learning, explain Kolers' results.

While there is a modicum of intellectual fun to be had in exhibiting the twist above, it contains a more serious point. One needs to have a relatively detailed cognitive architecture in hand to reason from. In his analysis, Kolers depended on inferences from a highly generalized view of the nature of production systems. When an actual architecture is considered, and the task performed with it, the general inferences may be found to be wide of the mark. The irony in this is that the explanation that Soar provides is not at variance with the basic ideas of Kolers. Soar puts procedural learning at the heart of all learning. It is an instance of exactly the sort of theory that I believe Paul Kolers wanted. It shows exactly how a thoroughgoing proceduralism is compatible—indeed, inextricably linked—with symbols and symbolic systems.

6.6. Short-Term Memory (STM)

So far we have attended exclusively to long-term memory—to seeing how Soar, with its uniform recognition memory, provides explanations for all sorts of memory—procedural and declarative, the latter including episodic and semantic. There is also short-term memory. In the classical cognitive formulation (from the fifties and sixties), the major divisions are between long-term memory, short-term memory, and sensory buffers. Little has been done with Soar concerning the latter two types of memory, in part because there is a strong interaction with perception (especially for the sensory buffers) and in part because the natural stance in using Soar as an AI system is to let the working memory last as long as necessary for the tasks being performed. Nevertheless, Soar must contain implicitly the outlines of a theory of these short-term memory effects. As an architecture, it is already sufficiently unified to constrain strongly how such phenomena would show up. As we phrased it earlier, it must be possible to read out of the Soar architecture a theory of short-term memory.

It is useful to start with a brief history of the conceptual development of short-term memory—so brief as to be labeled a nanohistory. Prehistory (prior to the mid-fifties) is a period without a notion of a distinct short-term memory. There has always been an awareness of short-term memory phenomena, such as the limited immediate memory for digits, called the *digit span* (Woodworth, 1938; Woodworth & Schlosberg, 1954). But the received theory, whose mature formulation came at the hands of Leo Postman (1961) and Benton Underwood (Underwood & Schulz, 1960), was of a single memory. Actually, the emphasis was not on memory at all, but on learning. The theory was of a single learning process (stimulus-response associations), which implied a single memory. The central explanatory mechanism was that of *interference* between associations, either with those that came before (*retroactive*) or with those that came after (*proactive*).

The notion of a distinct short-term memory system emerged in the mid-fifties (Broadbent, 1954; Miller, 1956). Following almost immediately came the evidence for a very short-term perceptual buffer for vision (Sperling, 1960), often called the *icon*. If a buffer existed for vision, there should also be one for other sensory modalities, and one was posited almost immediately for audition (the *echo box*), although good evidence for it didn't arrive until later (Darwin, Turvey, & Crowder, 1972). Each memory was defined by a collection of distinct phenomena that permitted its inferential identification. This plethora of memories can be taken as a sufficient cause for the shift of view from learning to memory, which occurred in this period. In fact, coincident with it is the conceptual impact of computers, in which memory plays a striking and obvious role. The causal arrow runs the other way to some extent—from the operationalization of memory in computers to using that conceptual structure to begin the characterization of human behavior in terms of its memory. In any event, this all coincides with the beginnings of the modern cognitive revolution—and constitutes psychology's unique response to it.

Throughout the sixties occurred the elaboration of memory structure and its functional characterization. The processing sequence was seen as from sensory buffers to STM to LTM, with information transferring between the memories. STM was seen as a device for limiting attention (Broadbent, 1958). It was of small capacity, 7 ± 2 *chunks*, not *bits*, the latter being at the time the coin of the realm for measuring information capacity (Miller, 1956). STM decayed rapidly, with a half-life of about 7 seconds without rehearsal (Brown, 1958; Peterson & Peterson, 1959). The code in STM was acoustic (or articulatory, it was hard to tell which), in contrast with the physical sensory code in sensory buffers and the semantic code in LTM (Conrad, 1964). Before the sixties were over, complete mathematical models of the memory structure had emerged (Atkinson &

Shiffrin, 1968). It was a very neat picture, a major experimental and theoretical achievement.

Good things don't last—or at least they seem not to in psychology. In the seventies came the erosion of this conceptual structure. It started with the enunciation of the *levels of processing* (Craik & Lockhart, 1972). This theory substitutes a continuous scale of elaboration for the set of separate memories with transfers between them. The more a memory is elaborated, the better it is remembered. But it is all in the processing and there is no separate memory structure. The psychologists approved of continuity in processing on general philosophic grounds, and as the Zeitgeist shifted, the earlier formulation was often referred to pejoratively as *boxology*.

By the early eighties, we get the "Demise of STM"—the title of an article by Robert Crowder. Crowder had produced one of the best integrated books on learning and memory (Crowder, 1976) and his book, along with that of Ben Murdock (1974), stands as the major record of these two decades of research into memory. As Crowder notes, it is not the phenomena of short-term memory that is in decline—the phenomena never go away, though they can sometimes be ignored. Rather, it is the demise of the notion that a separate short-term memory structure exists. Furthermore, it was not that there was a sharp Popperian refutation—a result that absolutely contradicted short-term memory of any kind. Rather, sufficiently dissonant and confusing experimental results made it no longer possible to believe there is anything in the brain called a short-term memory. Consider the recency effect in free recall (Glanzer & Cunitz, 1966), which is better recall of the last few items in a long sequence of items presented for recall in any order. This effect was long considered a signature of short-term memory, but then along came long-term recency effects that mimic a lot of the classical characteristics. Consider, also, the recall of an item after an interval filled with distractors (the Brown-Peterson effect; Peterson & Peterson, 1959), another signature of short-term memory. The two main explanations for this effect, one involving initial learning, the other involving retrieval, have little to do with the properties of a putative STM and much more to do with long-term memory issues. Consider a central tenet of the STM model, that storage in LTM occurs as a function of residence time in STM (Atkinson & Shiffrin, 1968). Here, data directly refute this mechanism. And on it goes.

As noted, Soar does not have a well-developed theory of short-term memory. There is a good reason for this. A persistent theme of the STM history just related is that STM's small capacity and short lifetime is a brute fact. It is assumed to be a *technological* limitation—as if neural technology and evolution could not have developed a large-capacity short-term memory to eliminate the STM effects that we assess as limitations. STM theories typically posit structural features, such as limited storage capacity, rapid decay, or interference, to account for the STM effects. Such technological assumptions are foreign to Soar at its current stage of development. Soar's mechanisms are dictated by the functions required of a general cognitive agent. We have not posited detailed technological limitations to Soar mechanisms.[8] There is nothing inappropriate or wrong with such constraints. They may well exist, and if they do, they must show up in any valid theory.

There is likely to be some difficulty in getting evidence for such technological limitations independent of the STM effects they are to explain, at least until direct neurophysiological indications emerge (I know of no attempts to ask the question empirically). The difficulty is that a feature can be dysfunctional for some class of tasks (such as remembering looked-up phone numbers) but still be functional for some other tasks, so that the dysfunction expresses not a technological limitation but a trade-off between multiple facets of behavior. Thus, given the starting point of Soar in functionalism, the obvious strategy is to attempt to extend its functional potential as far as possible, to provide as clear a picture as possible against which to detect technological limits.

We can attempt to read out of Soar the outlines of a functional theory of short-term memory—that is, what short-term phenomena might arise just because of how Soar must be designed in order to perform, learn, and interact with the external world. Insofar as design explains some STM regularities, then technological limitations need not be posited to do so. This is a worthwhile exercise, even if technological limitations exist. STM phenomena that arise for functional reasons will still arise (for the same reason) even when technological limitations are added to the theory.

8. We have posited that Soar can be built using neural technology (Chapter 3). However, this claim operates in a very global way to dictate the cognitive system levels; it is not a model for a detailed technological mechanism that constrains specific operations.

Functionally, working memory must be a short-term memory. It is used to hold the coded knowledge that is to be processed for the current task. It is necessary to replace that knowledge when the current task changes. That replacement can be achieved in many ways, by moving the data, by moving the processes, or by changing the access path. If new data must come to play the role that was played by the old data, this necessarily defines a change of memory. Time bounds can be put on such memory changes by the functional requirements. First, the shift must occur at the rate of simple-operator times, because it is operators that demand new operands. This would put the lower times at ~1 sec, except that we know from Chapter 5 that speeded simple operators can take less than ~100 ms. Second, the memory must last long enough for problems to be solved, to wit, problem-space residence times. That must be at least ~~10 sec, because that is the order of the first level at which goal solution occurs. There is no apparent upper limit to how long it might take to work in a problem space to resolve an impasse, given the ability to generate impasses within impasses, but we do know that a system can work satisfactorily through just having memory enough for the minimal-time processing. We know the lower limit from our experience with bottom-up chunking in Soar, in comparison with all-goals chunking. Given many learning occasions, bottom-up chunking leads to the same total set of chunks.

To meet the functional requirements, working memory changes with each new production cycle, which is very rapid. [9] Residence times of working-memory elements are tied directly to the duration of problem-space activity. As long as a problem space remains active (by occurring somewhere in the goal context), then the working-memory elements associated with it remain available. Thus, the requirement for problem-space residency is satisfied for all problem spaces, however many subspaces intervene. Working memory for cognition has no continued functional existence outside these limits, however, since elements that are no longer linked to the goal stack become unavailable. Furthermore, problem spaces themselves have no existence independent of the impasses they are

9. Actually, behind this rapid change is another memory, *instantiation memory*, which holds the bindings of variables in the productions just long enough to discover a match and communicate the binding information to the actions of the production that deposit new working-memory elements in working memory. This memory must be created and destroyed within each production cycle.

created to resolve. Thus, working-memory elements are locked in to the functions of resolving impasses and are not available in an independent way (as if written on an internal scratch pad).

Without going any further than this, Soar can be seen to be a classical organization of a short-term memory and a long-term memory. It would be hard to build a system that was more classically structured—there is the working memory and there is the production memory, and that's that. It fits the classical organization so well that if, per Crowder, we have witnessed the demise of STM, presumably Soar has suffered demise as well, just as it was about to be born.

The direct way to go further is to assess specific tasks that show STM effects (for humans), such as the digit-span task (the length of the sequence of digits, presented one per second, that can be repeated back verbatim). The issue is whether the short-term character of working memory, as described above, limits the size of the span. If no effective functional constraint exists, then the requirement for some technological limitation has been demonstrated (for example, the autonomous decay of working-memory elements). Certainly, the way we have been using states in problem spaces throughout the book would make this seem to be the case. One should just be to able attach an indefinite number of digits to an attribute of the current state (as we did in the item-recognition task in Chapter 5). And if, by some twist, it were not possible to do it in a subspace and have these elements stay around, then it could be done in the top space, which never disappears because it is not generated by an impasse. That we are not prepared here to add technological limitations to the architecture pretty much stymies progress along this route.

Some cautions can be raised about whether this is really the end of the story. First, by now some barrier should exist to thinking of arriving digits simply as symbols to be affixed to states. What about the Epam-like recognition system that data chunking has led us to establish? Externally presented digits have to be recognized through this net, and then they may need to be discriminated from other digits that show up earlier or later. Second, establishing the single-state principle (moving from Soar4 to Soar5) has changed when attributes persist or vanish, even in the top state, because a single data structure, representing the current state, is modified continuously. Finally, the research on the excessive power of the current (Ops5-based) recognition match points to the representation of a single attribute (digit) with multiple attributes (6, 5, 9, 1, . . .) being a major expression of the excessive power. It is likely that such representational power will not be available in an appropriately weakened match, in which case this obvious way of storing a digit sequence would no longer exist. All of these points are simply signals that the door may not be closed on the possibility that the central context stack exhibits functional STM limitations.

Some progress may be made in a different direction, however. An intriguing place to look is the multiplicity of short-term memories for which there is evidence. This variety was not one of Crowder's main complaints, but perhaps it should have been. Not only are there the classical STM's of acoustic/articulatory coding, plus the visual and auditory iconic memories, but good evidence also exists for a short-term visual memory that is not the visual icon (Kroll et al., 1970), an articulatory loop involved with vocal rehearsal, but not easily identified with classical STM (Baddeley & Hitch, 1974), motor short-term memory (Schmidt, 1982), and imaginal memory (Posner et al., 1979; Kosslyn, 1980). Other kinds of memories are there as well, though we don't usually include them, such as the use of fingers for counting, body orientation, coordinative rhythms, maybe even afterimages. There is evidence for a veritable zoo of short-term memories—enough to shake the confidence of a theorist imbued with the parsimony of the classical STM-LTM picture.

It is intrinsic to the Soar architecture that it can have multiple short-term memories. To see this, note that the total cognitive system for Soar consists of more than the working-memory elements that are tied to the context stack of central cognition. Working-memory elements have an independent existence when they are the products or objects of processing of the perceptual and encoding processes on the one hand or the decoding and motor processes on the other. The elements of working memory thus group into a set of regions or *fields*, each of which is associated with some characteristic type of processing—perceptual, cognitive, or motor. There could also be intermediate fields of some sort of elaborated, parsed structures, created by encoding productions from perceptual working-memory elements. On the motor side, analogously, there could be fields of elaborated motor programs or stages of dynamic-system construction, created by decoding productions from compact motor commands. In each such field, the elements have characteristic residence times, dictated by the temporal dynamics of the entities they deal with. These temporal dynamics are functional, that is, their time constants are dictated by the semantics of the date elements, not arbitrarily by the physical structure of the fields. This follows from the assumption that biological systems are adapted to their function.

On the short-duration side, that processing time is tied to function is fairly clear. The region of the brain that processes visual fixations doesn't hold information for an hour because the vision system is built around eye movements of about 200 ms. Hence there is a replacement of one visual content with another every 200 ms. A similar argument holds for audition, although the duration of temporal integration would increase the time constant to perhaps 1 sec. Again, the motor-system command region has its own characteristic times in which it must be replaceable by new commands, in order to permit appropriately dynamic action.

Given these functional time constants, Figure 6-20 shows how multiple STM's arise. It depicts the familiar total cognitive structure, with the left-hand vertical column being where attention is focused at time t_1; Soar is working on the element labeled X. Suppose, at t_2, Soar attends to something in the right-hand vertical column. The element X is now outside the central system and thus it proceeds to be replaced (hence removed) at some time constant. If at time t_3 attention is shifted back to the left-hand column, and if X is still there, then Soar has obtained a memory for X from t_2 to t_3. This region of working memory has become an autonomous short-term memory for as long as elements stay around. It will have whatever replacement rate is associated with the field of such working-memory elements.

These memories provide *extra* short-term memory, in addition to the one that automatically supports the normal operation of the system through the goal context stack. These memories are not created to be short-term memories per se. They are exploited as short-term memories by the central cognitive component. Their memorial characteristics derive from their being operand memory for specific kinds of processing, which therefore work at the time scale of the subsystems that use them. They are inherent in the structure of a system with controllable attention (the A operator) and variable replacement-time constants for separate fields. The ad

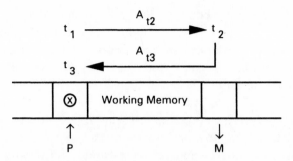

Figure 6-20. Soar on multiple short-term memories.

hoc exploitation of these short-term memories implies that their use is strategic—*metacognitive* is the term that has become familiar (Brown, 1978). Soar situates metacognition of short-term memory within the total processing context, which means that to discover what is true of STM metacognition we need only explore Soar without resorting to additional theory.[10] However, not all short-term memory is strategic—management of the goal context stack is built into the architecture. If it were not so, no way would exist to behave prior to learning the strategic use of short-term memory.

Soar will show interference effects in the use of these extra short-term memories. Interference follows from the nature of attention (*A*). When the decision is made to redirect attention to the to-be-remembered item (the act of STM retrieval), a search is required. The exact item cannot be known for Soar—indeed, if it were, Soar would have kept the item in its continuously accessible working memory. Thus, the attention operator must seek the item, and it must do so by simple criteria. This means it may not only recover the item (assuming that it is still there), but it may get several others as well. This will be especially true if, as in classical STM experimental paradigms, multiple items can be distinguished only by their class membership—all digits, for example, or all faces.

Soar STM will exhibit multiple codes, corresponding to the codes of the fields that are exploited for the short-term memory. Certain codes may be dominant (for example, acoustic/articulatory), simply because they are the predominant fields used, and this predominance may itself derive from ease of controlling such a memory or

---

10. This does not say anything about other forms of metacognition.

ease of learning how to do so. Certain fields may be little exploited as short-term memory, except under the press of experimenter-imposed tasks. Soar does not yet have these fields circumscribed sufficiently so that we can explore the ease or difficulty of using them to build up a more detailed theory.

This presentation of the Soar theory of short-term memory has been another exercise in reading off what follows from the existing characteristics of Soar's architecture. The most important result was the realization that Soar provides only a functional theory of STM, and that existing theories of STM all appear to rely on some underlying technological limitation. We were able to sketch some of the ways in which working memory had to be an STM to function, but we were frustrated in the attempt to confront directly the main phenomena of STM, such as the digit span. On the other hand, some features of the architecture permitted us to make a conjecture about one STM phenomena, namely, the plethora of separate short-term memories.

6.7. Summary

Soar, as a unified theory of cognition, must provide a theory of human memory and learning. This chapter has been devoted to exploring such a theory. Mostly we have treated matters qualitatively and shown how the Soar architecture has the right general shape. Qualitative exploration is important, for it is no good getting the microscopic details right if the general shape will not do. This is especially true for a unified theory, substantial discrepancies in the details of which can be tolerated if the theory can still be used to integrate the diverse phenomena of cognition.

The phenomenon of verbal learning provided a valuable lesson, namely, that the global shape of a theory could be right and yet the next level of detail could be wrong—not just wrong in some details, but wrong enough to demand substantial investigation. This was the problem of data chunking. It appeared that Soar was going to be unable to learn declarative data presented from the outside. As it turned out, we did not have to modify Soar—though that seemed a possibility when we first tripped over the phenomenon. The essence of the solution was separating the generation of the remembered item from the test. Another lesson is that, now that we have squeezed through the eye of the needle, so to speak, and found a

1. How humans are able to exhibit intelligence (Chapter 4)
2. Many global properties of human cognitive behavior (Chapter 4)
3. Human immediate behavior (~~1 sec) (Chapter 5)
4. Discrete perceptual-motor behavior (Chapter 5)
5. Verbal learning (recognition and recall) (Chapter 6)
6. Skill acquisition (Chapter 6)
7. Short-term memory (Chapter 6)

Figure 6-21. The coverage so far of Soar
as a unified theory of cognition.

solution, interesting features burst upon us. Memory for declarative material appears to be strongly reconstructive and the theory has many of the earmarks of an existing theory of human verbal learning, namely Epam.

Our treatment of other aspects of memory and learning was somewhat cursory. We showed that Soar got back the power law of practice, which it might have lost in modifying the original chunking scheme to incorporate it into Soar. This could be taken as something of a point of honor with the Soar project. With short-term memory, we focused on what short-term characteristics followed from functional requirements, and in doing so we managed an interesting hypothesis about how the zoo of short-term memories might arise.

Despite the cursory treatments, each topic discussed in the chapter adds to our running box score on the scope of Soar as a unified theory of cognition (see Figure 6-21).

Finally, we have provided several examples of our theme—that one should trust the architecture. Good architectures and good theories are alike. They contain within them nonobvious solutions to many problems. The right approach, more often than not, is to tease out the solution from the existing architecture, rather than modify the architecture according to some a priori notion. Indeed, as Soar (or any other unified theory of cognition) attains substantial coverage, changes in the architecture must be considered with great care and attention to detail. Changes can have widespread and unanticipated ramifications for those aspects that the architecture already deals with successfully.

Intendedly Rational Behavior

7

In this chapter we will explore how humans go about obtaining their goals—how they *intend* to be rational. Think of it as exploring the foothills of rationality. Ideally, given sufficient time, an intelligent system moves toward the knowledge level, where the signs of the internal struggle to think fade away and only the adaptive response to the task environment remains. At this point the system may be said to have gained the peaks of rationality. But getting there takes some doing. Indeed, an entire territory must first be traversed. Especially when the system has only modest time to think and problem-solve, its behavior must reflect the interaction of its basic cognitive capacities (the focus of Chapters 5 and 6), the structure of the task environment, and the body of knowledge it can bring to bear to filter through its partial and imperfect representation and accessing structure.

I cannot cover this whole territory in one chapter. Instead, I shall pick three particular tasks that will allow me to make several points. We will look at cryptarithmetic, then syllogisms, and finally simple sentence verification. The tasks are all quite simple, though not so simple as the immediate-response behaviors examined in Chapter 5 and the basic learning situations in Chapter 6. The points I wish to make are not how Soar does these tasks—they are simple enough to provide no challenge, given what we know about information processing and AI—but about the nature of intended rationality and how it arises.

In this chapter my secondary theme is the different uses of simulation. A unified theory of cognition, I have argued, is to be cast as an architecture. That is a major source of the communality that binds together the behavior on all the tasks that the organism faces. Thus the question arises of how to extract from the stipulated architecture its consequences for human behavior, both in the large and in the small.

The basic answer must be like the one about wrestling a gorilla— in any way you can and with no holds barred. Actually, we have already exhibited a fair variety of ways to reason from the architecture. We have argued from the architecture's general character to the shape of human cognition (Chapter 4). We have abstracted away from the details of the conditions of productions to an accounting of functionally necessary operators (Chapter 5). We have made detailed simulations from which learning curves could be plotted (Chapter 6). However, not all types of theory have surfaced. We have not produced any strong mathematical theories or proven any theorems about the architecture. The general reason lies in the complexity of the architecture. Only when strong simplifications are made, such as in the operator-accounting methods (Chapter 5) or the highly abstract general model of learning by chunking (Chapter 1), is mathematics potent enough to be useful.

Simulation is obviously an important technique for complex systems, but there are many ways to use simulation and it is useful to illustrate their variety, for it will be a staple analysis technique for any unified theory of cognition. In my own experience, psychologists generally treat their simulations fairly diffidently. They tend to keep them off stage and to use them primarily as confirmation that their theory is operational. Two examples may be cited, both from classic works in cognitive science, whose positive impact is beyond doubt. In both Anderson and Bower's *Human Associative Memory* (1973) and Kosslyn's *Image and Mind* (1980), simulation models operate as the guarantors of the functionality of the models, but they are allowed only a brief appearance to support the claim. Nothing is said about their details, and they never enter into any deductions, inferences, or demonstrations of the model. There are lots of other uses for simulations than just providing warranties.

Intendedly rational behavior implies that the system is approaching the knowledge level. To review (from Chapter 2), a knowledge-level system is determined completely from its goals, its actions, and the knowledge that it has to relate those two—operating, of course, within a circle of external constraints. As a system moves toward the knowledge level, behavior becomes more a function of the task environment and no longer a function of internal constraints. Gradually one leaves the cognitive band and moves up into the rational band (recall the time scale of human action in Figure 3-3). The movement is gradual, since it depends on the abilities of the organism to overcome, in each and every concrete case, the constraints of how knowledge is internally represented and distributed. Thus, the architecture remains visible in behavior and so does the symbolic processing to arrive at the appropriate responses.

Intelligence is a system's degree of approximation to being a knowledge-level system. It improves, presumably for most everybody, as more time becomes available. Soar is a model of a system with these properties. We spent some time in Section 4.6 examining the mechanisms of Soar to see how they contributed to being a good approximation of the knowledge-level system. Intelligence is affected by many aspects of internal organization, however, which means that, for fixed duration, some systems are more intelligent than others. We have hardly probed the ways intelligence might vary or, equivalently, what things might get in the way. As we look at human behavior, lots of questions arise. How does a system approach being rational? How fast does it approach? What other limits might exist besides the temporal one? This is the conceptual territory over which this chapter will travel.

7.1. Cryptarithmetic

Let us start with cryptarithmetic. This task was first analyzed by Bartlett (1958) and later by Herb Simon and myself (Newell & Simon, 1972). It plays an important role in the emergence of cognitive psychology—at least for me, and perhaps for others. It has been the strongest convincer that humans really do use problem spaces and do search in them, just as the AI theory of heuristic search says.

A cryptarithmetic task is just a small arithmetical puzzle (see Figure 7-1). The words *DONALD*, *GERALD*, and *ROBERT* represent three six-digit numbers. Each letter is to be replaced by a distinct digit (that is, *D* and *T* must each be a digit, say *D* = 5 and *T* = 0, but they cannot be the same digit). This replacement must lead to a correct sum, such that *DONALD* + *GERALD* = *ROBERT*. Mathematically viewed, the problem is one of satisfying multiple integer constraints involving equality, inequality, and unequality.

Humans can be set to solving cryptarithmetic tasks, and pro-

Assign each letter a unique digit to make a correct sum

$$
\begin{array}{r}
\text{DONALD} \\
+ \text{GERALD} \\
\hline
\text{ROBERT}
\end{array}
\qquad D = 5
$$

Figure 7-1. The cryptarithmetic task.

tocols can be obtained from transcripts of their verbalizations while they work (Newell & Simon, 1972). Analysis shows that people solve the task by searching in a problem space and that the search can be plotted explicitly.[1] Figure 7-2 shows the behavior of S3 on *DONALD + GERALD = ROBERT*.[2] The plot is called a *problem-behavior graph (PBG)*; it is just a way of spreading out the search so it can be examined (Figure 1-4 showed a PBG for chess). S3 begins in the upper left dot (state), and the search moves out horizontally. Each segment represents an operator application in the space, each application yielding a new state. There is no room in the figure to label each of these links with its operator. When the search line ends at the right of a horizontal line, S3 has stopped searching deeper and returns to some prior state he has already generated. This is indicated by the vertical line (all vertically connected dots represent the same state on successive returns). Then another horizontal line occurs representing another series of successively deeper states. The double lines indicate where S3 applies an operator already applied earlier, where, in other words, the same path in the space is being retrod (though without labels it is not always possible to tell which prior path is being repeated).

S3 wanders around in the space for about 30 minutes, which is ~2,000 sec. This is three orders of magnitude longer than immediate-response behavior, which is ~2 sec. So this is extended behavior, although 30 minutes is still short compared with other time scales humans operate on. The average residence time in each state is ~7 sec, which is in the ballpark of the ~~10 sec we have been using for operators that are constructed for a specific task, here the cryptarithmetic-space operators.

1. Not all people use the same problem space (Newell & Simon, 1972, chap. 7).
2. It comes as something of a shock to realize that S3, who was just a young college student when this protocol was taken in 1960, must be about fifty years old now. As I said, the cognitive revolution is getting on in years!

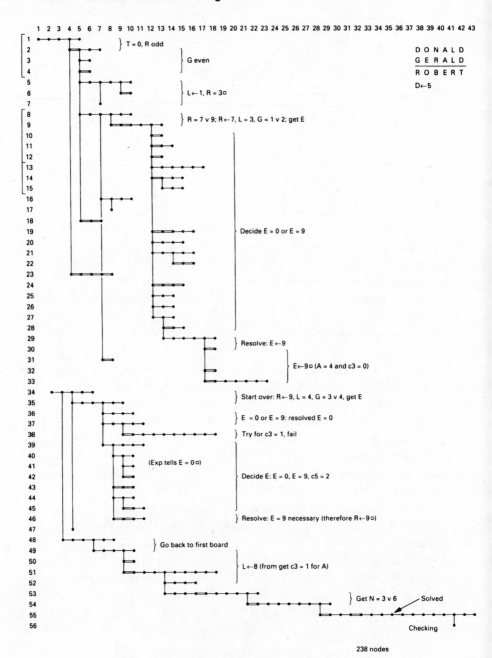

Figure 7-2. Problem-behavior graph of subject S3 on
DONALD + GERALD = ROBERT.

Figure 7-2 represents genuine cognitive behavior. Hence Soar should model it. It is that simple. A unified theory of cognition is to be the theory used for all such tasks—not theory *A* for task *A* and theory *B* for task *B*. Thus, some effort has been devoted to getting Soar to produce a detailed simulation of this protocol.[3] This may seem an odd thing to do. After all, this very protocol was analyzed over twenty years ago (Newell, 1967; Newell & Simon, 1972), in more detail than most psychologists would think interesting or perhaps even possible. A simulation was produced from a production system and, even though the whole analysis was manual (this being before production systems existed as real programming systems), it still seems odd to flog once more this poor dead horse. In fact, two good reasons exist to lay on the straps, a small one and a large one.

The small reason first. Soar, as a unified theory of cognition, should ultimately cover all of cognitive behavior—providing explanations or predictions (as the case may be) for all the phenomena that have been accumulated. There is an immense backlog of such phenomena, including worked-out analyses. Even though Soar can be seen to be the right sort of theory, it certainly cannot be taken on faith that it covers bodies of phenomena to which it hasn't been applied. Thus, we must continually test Soar (or any other unified theory of cognition) by taking old results from throughout the cognitive domain and applying Soar to them. We have already done some of this in the work on stimulus-response compatibility, transcription typing, and Epam. Here, we extend our tests to the problem-solving level, as represented by the cryptarithmetic analyses in *Human Problem Solving*.

The large reason responds to a basic issue in cognition. That the human has a cognitive architecture is tantamount to there actually being a mechanics of the mind. In principle, it should be possible to follow the actual trajectory of the mind as it zigs and zags its way through the forests of facts that cover the hillsides of a specific task. We all understand that the mind and the situations it inhabits are so complex and inaccessible that actually computing such a trajectory will seldom be possible. The temptation is all too easy to view cognitive theory as but a convenient sort of abstract fiction—useful to compute some molar phenomena, but not able to track the molecular zigs and zags. This view is easily reinforced by the spread-

---

3. This is work by Olin Shivers.

ing interest in chaos theory (Gleick, 1988), which shows that quite simple nonlinear dynamic systems can be essentially unpredictable. But human cognition, though undoubtedly nonlinear, is also shaped strongly to adapt behavior to attain the person's goals. A sufficiently developed theory of cognition should be able to follow a person's intendedly rational moves, if enough is known of the task environment and the person's goals and knowledge.

Thus, it is critically important to find some cases where cognitive theory can predict long stretches of behavior—long stretches that are relatively unconstrained, during which humans can be assumed to be freely thinking. Even one or two such instances would go a long way toward convincing us of the essential correctness of cognitive theory. Cryptarithmetic has always been a major candidate for a critical demonstration of this sort.[4]

This is not a project that would seem to have wide appeal in psychology, given the methodological paradigms that have occupied center stage for the last thirty years. Besides the assessment of technical difficulties, hinted at above, it runs too near deep-seated doubts about the possibility of a truly mechanistic psychology, not for chaotic reasons, but because of matters of free will versus determinism. Nevertheless, the project seems to me of absolutely first-rank importance. Thus, we've gone back to an old task and old data precisely because it is a relatively secure place to start. The goal is ultimately to get Soar to do detailed moment-by-moment simulations of behavior over many minutes.

The cryptarithmetic task, although done in a laboratory, and a puzzle by anyone's definition, is also, by all the usual canons, free and unconstrained. S3 was simply sitting at a table for 30 minutes working on this problem—just trying to find some way to solve the puzzle. What is going on in his head is feeding entirely upon the momentary state of the task that he has brought about and is con-

---

4. There are other candidates. A good one is the performance and learning of multidigit subtraction by young children (Brown & Burton, 1978; Burton, 1982; Brown & VanLehn, 1980; VanLehn, 1983; VanLehn & Garlick, 1987). Interestingly, the subtraction domain is not disjoint from cryptarithmetic, because of the latter's use of arithmetic reasoning. Another candidate is the area of skilled memory; Chase and Ericsson (1981) trained an undergraduate to recall a digit span of 87 digits presented at one per second and did a remarkable series of studies to reveal the cognitive structure of the skill. Additional work has confirmed the picture (Ericsson & Staszewski, 1989), and it now provides an elegant, detailed demonstration of the efficacy of the modern view of cognition.

templating. It is only remotely controlled by his being in a psychological laboratory—perhaps an aura of slight extra pressure or a feeling of self-exposure. But these feelings and considerations only float around the periphery of a situation where, second after second, he must think about these letters and these digits to solve the puzzle. There is no way that knowledge of the outer context can be brought to bear to affect most of the decisions.

7.1.1. Soar on Cryptarithmetic

Soar simulates two segments of the protocol, each about 100 seconds long, as marked in Figure 7-2. The behavior in the initial segment is fairly straightforward, the second quite complex. Our initial objective is to get Soar to provide a detailed simulation—in other words, a description—of the search that S3 carries out in the problem space. Thus, the simulation assumes the lower-level behavior of the system, that is, the operators of the basic space. Important questions may be asked about how these operators are carried out, especially the more complex ones, but the strategy of investigation here is to divide and conquer. The initial step is to assume the operators and to investigate the search control that determines the problem behavior graph of Figure 7-2. The implementation of this strategy involves an interesting style of simulation. Whenever Soar implements an operator, it comes out to an oracle (the investigator or an internal table), states the inputs and the situation, and requests the outputs. The oracle provides this information from the actual experimental data, thus assuring that the simulated operator at that point delivers exactly what the person did at the corresponding point in the protocol. The question being asked is what the system will do if the operators deliver exactly what the person's operators deliver, or what is the role of search-control knowledge?

Figure 7-3 shows the operators in the space. The four at the top are the ones that obtain new knowledge. The first one, *PC, processes a column* of the display and derives new knowledge from arithmetic knowledge and what is known about the letters and carries in a column. The second one, *AV, assigns* a digit to a letter. That is, it posits an assignment. This is not new knowledge, in the sense that it is derived from other data, but it produces a situation in which the person acts henceforth as if that assignment were correct—and does so until some evidence arises that invalidates the

Knowledge acquisition operators: main task space
PC   Process a column
AV   Assign a digit to a letter
GN   Generate the acceptable digits for a letter
TD   Test if an assignment is possible

Attentional focus operators: find-operator subspace
FC   Find a column
FL   Find a letter to attend to
GNC   Generate the columns
FA   Find the antecedent of an expression
FP   Find the production that produced an expression

Goal operators: main space (new in Soar)
GET   Letters, carry, expression
CHECK   Expression, column

Control attributes on expressions in a state
new
contradiction
unclear
unknown

Figure 7-3. Soar on cryptarithmetic (following Newell & Simon, 1972).

claim. The third one, *GN, generates* the acceptable assignments for a given letter. Every letter is hedged round with multiple constraints because of its participation in various columns of the sum. Hence at any point it will be able to take on only a subset of the full set of digits (0, 1, . . . , 9). *GN* generates this set. The fourth and final operator, *TD, tests* whether an assignment of a digit to a letter is permitted, given the values that are excluded by assignments of digits to other letters. A strong assertion about problem spaces is being made here—throughout the 30-minute problem-solving period, these and only these operators are being performed to gain new knowledge about the task.

Other operators are also required, however; they can be thought of as *focusing* operators. Their necessity stems from the need to instantiate the knowledge-gaining operators. These four operators are abstract. *PC* does not specify what column it is to apply to. *AV* does not specify what variable is to be assigned a value or what value it is to be assigned. *GN* does not specify what letter is to have its values generated. *TD* does not specify what assignment (a letter and a digit) is to be tested. Thus, additional operators are required that operate in a space of attentional foci—a letter, a column, a value—within the fixed context of the current state of the problem, what is known about the possible digits for each letter.

There is an operator, *Find-column*, which takes the current state and attentional focus as input and produces a column for *PC*. This has built into it the purpose of the focus—namely, that the resulting column is going to be processed and hence that a column should be found that will yield some new knowledge. The same is true of the *Find-letter* operator, although this is the high-level selection of a variable with which to pursue the total task and is thus not curtailed by the constraints of the current focus. *Generate-columns* is needed to systematically obtain the next column from right to left to check that a sum is right. It is an operator that is part of the basic repertoire for multidigit addition. The last two focusing operators, *Find-antecedent* and *Find-production*, permit access to earlier states. They do not enter into the behavior fragment simulated here, but I have listed their names anyway. They both raise interesting issues of memory and access and are realized somewhat differently in Soar than in the original system, because Soar has no access to the productions per se.

Finally, Soar has some *goal operators*—operators that establish that information of a specific type is desired. These were goals in the original architecture specified in Newell and Simon (1972). However, Soar generates its own subgoals from impasses. Thus, the original goals are cast as Soar operators to produce the desired information and are no different from other operators that Soar deliberately decides to apply.

The search control in S3's performance on this task resides in the space of the focusing operators. The result of these operators determines which of the main operators, *PC*, *AV*, *GN*, and *TD*, is applied next and, more particularly, which instantiation will be applied. This selection space takes as given the display and particular assignments and constraints known about the variables (letters and carries). It augments this representation with a small set of *control attributes*, which encode the knowledge to make the control decisions. These are just simple attributes of a state: whether a result is *new*, whether a *contradiction* has been produced, whether something is *unclear*, and whether something is *unknown* in a situation where it is desired to be known. Their semantics are given by the heuristics that are defined in their terms. For instance, the semantics of a result being labeled *new* is that its implications should be

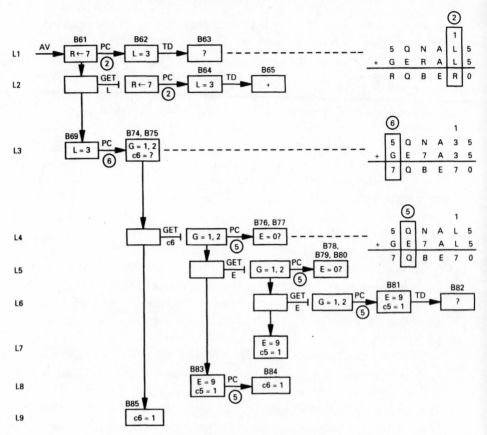

Figure 7-4. Problem-behavior graph during a complex
situation in cryptarithmetic.

sought. This is the weak method of constraint propagation, in which
obtaining new information from a constraint (a column or an assignment) sends the system to process other constraints involving that
information. The semantics of an item being labeled *unclear* or
unknown is to find out about the items.

Several scientific questions surround search control. What
search heuristics characterize a person's behavior? How much behavior do they control? Does a small set of such heuristics control
long stretches of behavior? Or does the body of knowledge (here,
search-control knowledge) grow continually with time?

Figure 7-4 shows the short fragment of the protocol simulation
between lines 8 and 12 on Figure 7-2. The action centers on the fifth

column, $O + E = O$, although it involves other columns as well. It is apparent from the total problem-behavior graph that S3 has a difficult time with this column. He continues to work on it from lines 9 through 29, about 10 minutes, and then again from lines 35 through 46, another approximately 7 minutes. The source of difficulty is clear enough. In $O + E = O$, the value of O does not make any difference (or, if the column is thought of as a constraint equation, then the O's cancel out). In fact, this just makes the value of E depend on the carries in and out: $c_{in} + E = 10c_{out}$. But if the carries are not always taken into account, it is easy to get confused and uncertain. Thus, ignoring the carries entirely leads to the conclusion that $E = 0$, which conflicts with the fact that $T = 0$ is already solidly concluded. If the conclusion were based on explicitly positing that $c_{in} = 0$ and $c_{out} = 0$, then it would be easy to consider changing one or the other to $c = 1$, but if the carries have been ignored, there seems to be no place to go. In any event, this is the mire S3 is in.

Thus, we have a good example of what a person does when he is puzzled and confused and is trying to reason out something at the limits of his ability. Figure 7-5 gives the protocol data for this period. There are clear indications that S3 is indeed uncertain of the situation (B62–65 and B80–82). For us—for Soar as a unified theory of cognition—the question is whether the control of such behavioral turbulence can be described. The problem-behavior graph in Figure 7-4 is that of Soar and it is indistinguishable from that of S3, given the limits of the protocol data to establish it. Over each state box of Soar's PBG are the B-numbers indicating the corresponding part of the protocol.

Let us go through the segment. It starts at line L1, where S3 has just assigned R to be 7 (through AV) and is focused on column 3. The prehistory to this step is such that $D \rightarrow 5$ and $T = 0$ with a carry of 1 into column 2, but its details can be safely ignored. S3 then processes (PC) column 3, getting that L equals 3, and follows this by testing (TD) the assignment. This sequence is tightly coupled. The search control first says, if a *new* result occurs ($R \rightarrow 7$) then see where it leads (to PC on column 3 and $L = 3$). Then it says, if there is a *new* value for a letter ($L = 3$), then check if it is okay (TD on $L = 3$). This sequence of PC followed by TD occurs repeatedly throughout the protocol by the application of these two bits of search-control knowledge. The result of TD is *unclear (?)*. From the

L1 B61. So we'll start back here and make it a 7.

B62. Now if the . . .

B63. Oh, I'm sorry, I said something incorrect here.

B64. I'm making . . .

L2 B65. No, no, I didn't either.

B66. R is going to be a 7,

B67. then this will be 7,

B68. and that will be 7,

B69. and it's the Ls that will have to be 3s,

B70. because 3 plus 3 is 6

L3 B71. plus 1 is 7.

B72. Now, it doesn't matter anywhere what the Ls are equal to . . .

B73. so I'm independent of L when I get past the second column here.

B74. But now I know that G has to be either 1

B75. or 2,

B76. depending on whether or not E plus O is greater than 10

B77. or greater than 9.

B78. Now I have this O repeating here in the second column from the left.

B79. That is, itself plus another number equal to itself.

L4 B80. This might indicate that E was zero . . ..

L5 B81. In fact, it might have to necessarily indicate that.

L6 B82. I'm not sure.

L7 B83. Or, E could be 9

B84. and I would be carrying 1,

L8 B85. which would mean that I was carrying 1 into the left-hand column.

L9 B86. (E: What are you thinking now?)

Figure 7-5. Protocol fragment during a complex situation.

point of view of this search-control-level simulation, this result simply emerges from the execution of an operator (*TD*) and we need not inquire about it. The bases in reality for the uncertainty, which have their effect inside *TD*, is that $L = 7$ would also be possible if R were not 7; there is thus an extra interaction between the two relations involving 7, with one of them ($R \to 7$) being posited, rather than derived, so it could be changed. This is apparently enough to induce *unclear*. To explore that requires models for the cognitive behavior in *AV*, *PC*, and *TD*.

Having decided that *TD*'s result is *unclear*, S3 (that is, our Soar simulation of S3) comes back (line L2) and executes the operator *GET L*. This operator leads the system (via a no-change impasse in the usual way) to its implementation space and goes down the same path again—repeating the processing. This time, having gone through it a second time, S3 is now clear about $L = 3$. (Again, our simulation sees this simply as the result of *TD*.) S3 returns from the impasse with a confirmed value of 7 for R (B66). This and the *new* item ($L = 3$) leads him over to column 6 (line L3). The PBG does not show the operation of the focusing operators, namely that *FC* went looking for columns containing L and did not find any, but the protocol makes it explicit (B72–73). So this search-control heuristic, which we have seen used before, does not yield anything. R is also still *new,* so this same search-control heuristic applied to R picks up that R occurs in columns 2, 4, and 6. Column 6 is a more constraining column (it has $D = 5$ and it is at the left edge, which determines the carry-out) than column 4 (which has two unique letters, N and B), so column 6 is selected and processed (*PC* on 6). The result is that G equals 1 or 2, with the carry into column 6 being *unknown (?)*.

This result is not a definite one, so *TD* does not get selected. Rather, that $c6$, the carry-in to column 6, is *unknown* selects the *GET* operator (L4) on $c6$. This leads again to an implementation subgoal, which leads S3 back to the source of $c6$, column 5, and hence to processing (*PC*) column 5. This search control is simply the upstream version of the constraint-propagation heuristic, namely, to find out about something go to a source that has knowledge about that thing. The first attempt to process column 5 does not do very well. S3 produces $E = 0$, but labels it as *unclear (?)*. As we noted above, it is not surprising that he is uncertain about $O + E = O$, although from the point of view of the simulation, this is just a given. Being *unclear* about E, S3 applies the operator to *GET E* (line L5). Note that he was not attempting to get E when he first processed column 5; he was attempting to get $c6$. The operator to get E leads once more to an implementation space and a repeat of *PC* on that column (just like the repeat of *PC* on column 3 at the beginning of the fragment).

Again S3 obtains $E = 0$, but he remains *unclear* (another given to the simulation). This leads him to apply *GET E* a second time (line L6) and to go down into one more implementation space. This time he considers that the carry-in from the prior column ($c5$) might be 1. Thus, the attempt to process column 5 produces $E = 9$. This is a certain result so he applies *TD* on $E = 9$ with a positive outcome (just like the application of *TD* to column 2 earlier). This confirmed result leads him to realize that he has the result of the first *GET E* (line L7) and then to return to getting $c6$ (line L8), which now can be produced by *PC* on column 5 to be $c6 = 1$. This finally brings him back to the original *PC* of column 6 (line 9).

The sequence of behaviors by Soar in Figure 7-4 is very close to the sequence that S3 goes through, but it shows only the beginning of his perseveration on column 5 (see Figure 7-2), so there is much more to unravel. More generally, this initial effort, done for the purposes of using Soar to illustrate a unified theory of cognition, still leaves much undone. There remains (as always) some discrepancies between Soar and S3, both of omission and commission. For example, the simulation does not exhibit the way S3 checks explicitly each of the three columns in which *R* occurs (B66–B68). More important, ultimately Soar should perform the concurrent task of thinking aloud. Not only is this part of the task that S3 performs, but without it there remains an irremediable gap between the data produced by the human and the data produced by the simulation. For instance, there is nothing in the protocol corresponding to line L7, where S3 is returning to the first *GET E*; it is plausible that this step does not generate any verbal behavior, but that needs to be addressed by the theory. Furthermore, a process theory of thinking aloud has already been developed by Ericsson and Simon (1984) in their study of using protocols as data. So this is a natural extension to expect from a unified theory.

We have here a variant use of simulation. The normal style is to program up a total system and to run it, once or many times, to generate traces of a system's behavior or to estimate parameters numerically. In our cryptarithmetic example, the entire bottom level of the system is left undefined. This allows us to test the upper levels without the lower levels, the conceptual advantage being to factor out the influences of the lower levels by design beforehand, rather than by analysis from the total simulation record. There is also a major gain in research efficiency in not having to create the simulation of the lower levels. The present case indicates how significant this can be. If a lower level is to be included, then it must be very accurate or else it will contaminate all attempts to understand the higher level. One error in *PC* (say) and the simulation will forever diverge from the person's behavior.[5] But some of the lower-level units, *PC* especially, are scientific puzzles in their own right. Thus, what is being avoided is not just the effort of programming up the operators, but putting another scientific problem on the critical path to the main scientific question, which is the nature of search control in complex problem solving.

Of course, the question of the operators and their problem spaces is of equal scientific importance, even if tactically it is useful to bypass it for a while. A major feature of a unified theory of cognition is vertical integration. Soar must be able to provide a theory of *PC, AV, GN,* and *TD.* But that is not the end of it. *PC* involves a mixture of arithmetic, inferencing, and selection of what result to obtain. All these elements are present in deriving *G* equals 1 or 2 when the carry-in is unknown (in column 5). The context in which *PC* is accomplished is the set of arithmetic procedures for adding up two multidigit numbers. The person's behavior here ties in with his behavior in other tasks, such as multidigit subtraction (VanLehn, 1983) and single-digit addition and subtraction (Siegler, 1987). These latter processes operate at the level of stimulus-response compatibility and choice-reaction times, as discussed in Chapter 5. Vertical integration links problem solving with immediate cognitive behavior. Unfortunately, these steps have not yet been taken for cryptarithmetic in Soar, so we cannot use it to illustrate this unification.

An interesting feature of this search-control system is the use of a small, fixed collection of control symbols, *new, contradiction, unknown,* and *unclear.* These symbols encode in declarative form the momentary state of knowledge about the problem solving in order to control behavior. A set of four discrete symbols seems like a highly artificial scheme, for we would expect a person to have a much more articulated and fine-grained sense of evaluation and control. This is belied to the extent that the actual behavior of the person can be seen to be determined by just such a simple control scheme. An interesting possibility is that a person creates a set of control signals for a specific situation and that these symbols are elaborated only as necessary for the task at hand.

---

5. If there is any doubt about this, think of an error as a hint; for example, suppose that S3 was told that $E = 9$ was correct.

All actors are bowlers
All bowlers are chefs
_____

All actors are chefs

Some B are not A
All B are C
_____

What follows necessarily?

19/20, 19/20, 19/20, 19/20 correct

~3 sec duration

0/20, 2/20, 12/20, 14/20 correct

~10 sec duration

Four forms	Four figures	Validity
A: All A are B	A B | B A	4 have 4 valid conclusions
I: Some A are B	B C | B C	2 have 3 valid conclusions
E: No A are B	A B | B A	5 have 2 valid conclusions
O: Some A are not B	C B | C B	16 have 1 valid conclusion
		37 have no valid conclusion
		64 total syllogisms

Figure 7-6. Categorical syllogisms.

7.2. Syllogisms

Syllogisms are probably familiar to most readers—for they go all the way back to Aristotle and they stood at the center of concern in logic for many centuries. Figure 7-6 gives some examples and defines the domain of *categorical syllogisms,* deductions about categories of things. The left-hand example is to be read *All actors are bowlers, all bowlers are chefs, therefore, necessarily, all actors are chefs.* This is a straightforward example, framed in concrete terms. In the right-hand one—*Some B are not A, all B are C*—the premises are abstract and the conclusion has been omitted, so you can derive it yourself. What necessarily follows? This one is not so easy.

Syllogisms are basic inference schemes involving three terms— *A, B,* and *C*—linked in a *major premise, (A, B),* and a *minor premise, (B, C).* Each premise is composed from the quantifier *all* or *some,* with the logical connective of *affirmation* or *negation* of attribution (also called the *sign*). *No A are B* is synonymous with *All A are not B.* Thus, there are four possible premise *forms* (or *moods,* to use the terminology of classical logic), which are listed at the left of Figure 7-6. Their abbreviations—*A, I, E, O*—date from the medieval scholars. The terms in a syllogism can be arranged in four different ways, which are called the four *figures,* as shown in the middle of Figure 7-6. Taking all the variations, there are four forms for first premises times four forms for second premises times four figures, which yields 64 distinct syllogisms. A conclusion of a syllogism is a valid inference in one of the four forms that relates the *end terms, A* and *C.* Nine different conclusions are possible for a given syllogism, namely, four different forms times two different orders *(AC* or *CA),* plus *no valid conclusion (NVC).* As shown at the right of Figure 7-6, the number of valid conclusions for a single syllogism can vary from none up to four. The *NVC* response is correct most of the time (37/64), and only 27/64 of the cases have some valid conclusion.

The syllogism task sits at the very beginnings of the range of intendedly rational behavior. A person familiar with syllogistic reasoning—for example, someone doing many of them in the course of an experiment—will take ~10 sec, the top of the cognitive band but hardly an extended task. The time will be substantially longer when the task is unfamiliar, but then much of the effort is involved in understanding the task.

The central psychological phenomena concerning syllogisms are their difficulty and the strong variation in difficulty as a function of the specific syllogism. Many people, even educated people, do not get the correct result. Consider the two examples in the figure. Four groups of 20 people tried these two syllogisms in the course of going through all the 64 different syllogisms (Johnson-Laird, 1983; Johnson-Laird & Bara, 1984). Almost everyone got the easy example (on the left), 19/20 in each group, but the syllogism on the right was an entirely different story, 0/20, 2/20, 12/20, and 14/20 for the four groups.[6] The first two groups are from an open-admissions Italian city university and the last two are from a relatively elite private university in the United States, so there are differences in the general intellectual level of the two populations even though both are made up of college students. These central results have been replicated repeatedly, so there is no doubt that some syllogisms are reliably difficult.

Although it could not be described as ever occupying the main-

---

6. Both syllogisms were phrased in concrete terms (as the example on the left) rather than abstract terms (as on the right).

stream, the study of syllogistic reasoning has a long active history (Evans, 1982; Falmagne, 1975; Johnson-Laird, 1983; Revlin & Mayer, 1978; Woodworth & Sells, 1935). The reason for the activity is not far to seek. It is the tension in Western civilization between reason and passion—between the mind and the heart. Can people be rational and logical? Or are they slaves to their passions? A necessary condition for the ascendancy of reason would seem to be that people be able to think straight. What could be a greater indicator of straight thinking than making logical inferences? Syllogisms, the epitome of logical reasoning from Aristotle onward, were a natural focus for anyone investigating the question. Although they seem somewhat arcane to us now, their recession into the background has occurred only with the rise of modern symbolic logic.

If the most elementary and certain forms of reasoning (syllogisms) are in fact difficult, then (it was often suggested) perhaps people are not logical at all, are not rational, or have severe limits on their reasoning powers. The notion arose that perhaps humans follow some sort of *psychologic*—that their reasoning is not faulty but rather follows laws of its own. Most such discussions were carried on in public and philosophical forums, but even so they have fueled a continual stream of experimental psychological work.

For us, as well, that they are difficult makes syllogisms interesting (though it is only one reason, as we shall see). The theory of cognition sees humans as gradually approximating the knowledge level. At the knowledge level it would seem (would it not?) that syllogisms would be performable. There could be difficulties, of course, in understanding the language—about the meaning of *All chipmunks are conserved* or *Some butterflies are not gardeners* or even the instructions, *What follows necessarily?* But having gotten over that hump, we should have clear sailing ahead. Difficulty could also be expected if time was short—time scale is always critical. But with unlimited time, and tasks that take only some few seconds when successful, difficulty should not be a factor. Thus, when substantial difficulties emerge and persist, as they do for syllogisms, then the task offers a useful case in probing how humans approach and approximate the intendedly rational level. Possibly we can discover other sorts of limits on rationality besides temporal ones.

In addition to the focus on untoward difficulty, which gives the task its scientific appeal, we also want to look at what regularities humans exhibit in syllogistic reasoning. In Chapter 5, I made a

1. Difficulty level: syllogisms can be extremely difficult to do correctly, though they are simple to state.
2. Difficulty variation: syllogisms vary widely in their difficulty.
3. Individual abilities: people vary in their ability to do syllogisms, in terms of the difficulty attainable.
4. Atmosphere effect: conclusions tend to agree with the premises on quantifier and sign.
5. Conversion effect: people behave as if they interpret *All A are B* as *All B are A.*
6. Figural effect: when either order of a conclusion is valid (AC or CA), the order is determined by the order of chaining:
   AB, BC $\Rightarrow$ AC rather than CA
   BA, CB $\Rightarrow$ CA rather than AC
   No prediction is made for the other two figures: BA, BC and AB, CB.
7. Concreteness effect: the content of syllogisms affects the difficulty relative to abstract syllogisms, sometimes easier, sometimes harder.

Figure 7-7. The regularities of syllogistic reasoning.

point of observing how many regularities are already known in psychology. For syllogisms, I must admit—somewhat contrary to my central tenet—that psychology seems to have discovered relatively few phenomena. The central question of difficulty seems to have dominated, probably because it has received unsatisfactory answers. Figure 7-7 gives a few regularities that have been found, but I would be hard pressed to produce thirty.

The first three regularities decompose the central conundrum into its independent constituents. (1) The individual premises are easy to comprehend and the task is easy to state. Yet, syllogisms can be extremely difficult. (2) The degree of difficulty depends strongly on the particular syllogism. Our two examples showed the extremes. Thus, it is not just that the task of syllogistic reasoning per se is surprisingly difficult. (3) The difficulty varies according to intellectual capability. The left-hand syllogism was so easy that everyone got it. The right-hand syllogism was hard, but for the first two test groups it was very hard whereas for the second two groups, half solved it.

(4) One of the earliest regularities discovered is the *atmosphere effect* (Woodworth & Sells, 1935). If either premise is particular (*some*), then universal conclusions (*all*) rarely occur (which of course agrees with valid reasoning). However, if both premises are

universal, the conclusions given tend to be universal, even in cases where the valid conclusion is particular (*some*). It is as if the person made the decision about the quantifier (*all* or *some*) of the conclusion just on the basis of the quantifiers of the premises. A similar situation exists with respect to positive and negative signs. Negative premises tend to lead to negative conclusions. Many errors are consonant with the atmosphere of the premises.

(5) The *conversion effect* (Chapman & Chapman, 1959) is the tendency to transpose premises: *All A are B* is interpreted as also meaning *All B are A*. That is (as with the atmosphere effect), a substantial number of errors can be explained by assuming such a change in the specifications of the syllogism. This effect has been interpreted as occurring at an encoding stage; the reasoning itself is not seen as the source of errors (Henle, 1962). The conversion effect reflects the general issue in reasoning tests that it is difficult to separate the effects of language comprehension from the effects of reasoning per se.

(6) The *figural effect* concerns which of several valid syllogisms a person will produce (Johnson-Laird, 1983). As Figure 7-6 indicates, many syllogisms have multiple solutions. Many of these are composed of pairs of the same form but whose terms are in a different order. For example, *Some A are C* and *Some C are A* always go together, both valid or both not. The figural effect predicts which order will be produced, as shown in Figure 7-7. The rule applies in two of the figures (*AB,BC* and *BA,CB*), but is silent in the other two (*AB,CB* and *BA,BC*). It is as if the reasoning constructs a chain through the premises: in the *AB,BC* case the chain goes *A* to *B* to *C*, thus linking *A* to *C*; in the *BA,CB* case it goes *C* to *B* to *A*, thus linking *C* to *A*.

(7) Whether syllogisms are *concrete* (*all actors are bowlers*) or *abstract* (*All A are B*) seems to have a pronounced effect (Wilkins, 1928; D'Andrade, 1989). However, the situation is more complicated than just a difference in difficulty (abstract syllogisms being harder). The content of the syllogism (not just its concreteness) has an effect. If the syllogism agrees or is consonant with the content, it is easier to do; but if the syllogism disagrees or is discordant with the content, then it is harder to do. Thus, concrete syllogisms that arise in natural situations tend to be easier relative to abstract ones, where the absence of content provides no help. But likewise, perverse concrete syllogisms, such as might occur in psychological

experiments, would be expected to be more difficult (though the experiments do not seem to have been done).

We now seem ready to examine how Soar, as a unified theory of cognition, applies to syllogistic reasoning. In the background is the idea that a unified theory should extend to any domain of cognitive behavior, hence (why not?) to syllogistic reasoning. In the foreground is the question that has been central to the field, namely, the nature of human rationality. However, the theories proffered by psychology for syllogistic reasoning provide us with yet another reason for considering the domain: the issue of whether humans think in terms of *propositions* or *mental models*. These two notions, especially mental models (Gentner & Stevens, 1983), play a strong role in other areas in cognitive science. Neither of these concepts is part of Soar, as described in the previous three chapters. The additional question, then, is how does Soar come to grips with major concepts that play strong roles in cognitive science but are foreign to Soar?

7.2.1. Propositions and Models

Let us focus on the hypothesis that humans reason by means of *mental models* rather than by means of *propositions*. This has been formulated most clearly by Philip Johnson-Laird (Johnson-Laird, 1983, 1988b).[7] The hypothesis is to be taken quite generally, but we will stay focused on syllogistic reasoning, which is also the task Johnson-Laird has explored in great detail.

Figure 7-8 gives an example of Johnson-Laird's mental models for syllogisms. When a human reads a syllogism, say *Some B are not A* and *All B are C*, he or she constructs an internal model of a concrete situation that the premises assert. For instance, Model 0 in the figure might be constructed for premise P1. Each line represents an individual with specific properties (*A, B, C, . . .*), where the prefixed *o* means optional. Thus, there is an individual who might be an *A*, another who is an *A* and might be a *B* and a third who is a *B*. The barrier in the model indicates that this latter individual defi-

---

7. Johnson-Laird has been one of the most active workers in the psychological study of syllogisms and other forms of logical reasoning for many years (Wason & Johnson-Laird, 1972). He and his colleagues are the only ones who have provided data in the literature on all possible syllogisms by the same set of people, so that other investigators can use the data for their own theories, as we have done. Making good data sets available is important for the enterprise of unified theories.

P1. Some B are not A
P2. All B are C
_____

P3. Some C are not A

Model 0
for P1
oA
A oB
_____
B

Model 1   ⇒   **Model 2**
for P1 and P2   **for P1 and P2**
A   oB = C   A   oB = C
oA   oA   oC
_____   _____
B = C   B = C
oC

- Examine a model directly for counterexamples
- The premises can be satisfied by multiple models
- Necessarily valid conclusions satisfy all possible models
- Difficulty depends on multiple models

Figure 7-8. Syllogistic reasoning by mental models
(after Johnson-Laird, 1983).

nitely cannot be an *A*; this is the way negation is encoded in the model.

When the second premise is read, it is added onto the original model to create a single model of the situation. This is Model 1, where each of the individuals in the model who were *B*'s are now also *C*'s. However, in addition another individual has been created, who is just a *C* optionally, that is, who might be a *C*. The equal signs (=) indicate that the properties so joined definitely go together. Thus, a person builds up a symbolic model of a concrete situation. Only one individual of each type is shown, but of course there could be any number of them—that depends on the encoding process.

New facts can be found simply by examining the model—they can simply be *read off*. The aim of syllogistic inference is to find some fact that involves both *A* and *C*—that links the two so-called end terms. For instance, the third individual is a *C* but is not an *A* (the barrier). Since there is another individual (the second) who is both a *C* and an *A*, then what is true is that *Some C are not A*, rather than *All C are not A* (equivalently *No C are A*). The presence of this second individual, by the way, does not lead to another conclusion, since he is optional (the *o*) and hence need not necessarily occur in the model.

What has been concluded by inspection holds only for this particular model, but this is not necessarily the only model that can be built to correspond to the premises. Indeed, following the standard model-theoretic view (Addison, Henkin, & Tarski, 1972), a conclusion is necessarily true only if it is true in *all possible* models. The Johnson-Laird theory posits that humans realize the logic of this view and attempt to generate alternative models that provide tests of the initial conclusion (namely, *Some C are not A*). For instance, Model 2 is also consistent with the premises, where there are three individuals, with one of them being a *C* and an *A*, but there are no individuals that are just *C*'s. It turns out that in this model, as well, there are some *C*'s that are not *A*'s, so the conclusion holds. These two models exhaust the possibilities, which means that the conclusion necessarily follows and can be produced as the final conclusion.

A theory of syllogism based on mental models must describe how the person generates the multiple models and how he or she knows that a sufficient (covering) set has been generated. It turns out that, because of the simplicity of syllogisms, only a few models are ever required, often only a single one.[8] Johnson-Laird's theory of difficulty is based on the number of models. The initial model that people will generate can be described by giving explicit encoding rules for each premise form. It is quite easy to determine the set of syllogisms for which this single initial model suffices. These are the easy problems. The theory does not describe the generation of the additional models when more than one model is required; this depends on many issues of internal representation, the types of psychological operations that the person uses, and how they are deployed. It turns out, however, that the split between single and multiple models suffices to give the theory a good deal of explanatory power.[9]

8. Though in general an infinite set of models is necessary to confirm the validity of a general quantified expression.

9. Johnson-Laird (1983) presents a stronger form of the theory that distinguishes between two-model and three-model syllogisms, but it has become clear in the intervening period that matters are more complicated than he envisioned at that time.

P1. Some B are not A	P1. (∃x) [B(x) ∧ ¬A(x)]
P2. All B are C	P2. (y) [B(y) ⊃ C(y)]

| P3. Some C are not A | P3. (∃x) [C(x) ∧ ¬A(x)] |

Given premises P1 and P2, prove P3

	Assumption	Conclusion	Justification
1.		(∃x) [B(x) ∧ ¬A(x)]	Premise P1
2.	B(a) ∧ ¬A(a)		Assume
3.	B(a) ∧ ¬A(a)	B(a)	Split
4.	B(a) ∧ ¬A(a)	¬A(a)	Split
5.		(y)[B(y) ⊃ C(y)]	Premise P2
6.		B(a) ⊃ C(a)	Specialize 5
7.	B(a) ∧ ¬A(a)	B(a) ⊃ C(a)	Add to 6
8.	B(a) ∧ ¬A(a)	C(a)	Modus ponens 3 and 7
9.	B(a) ∧ ¬A(a)	C(a) ∧ ¬A(a)	Join 4 and 8
10.	B(a) ∧ ¬A(a)	(∃x) [C(x) ∧ ¬A(x)]	Abstract conclusion 9
11.	(∃x) [B(x) ∧ ¬A(x)]	(∃x) [C(x) ∧ ¬A(x)]	Abstract assumption 10
12.		(∃x) [C(x) ∧ ¬A(x)]	Chain rule 1 and 11. QED.

Legend for justification
Premise: Conclude a premise
Assume: Assume anything
Split: Assume A ∧ B, conclude A, or conclude B
Specialize: Conclude any specialization of a universal
Add: Add assumptions to any step
Join: If A and B, conclude A ∧ B
Modus ponens: If A ⊃ B and A, conclude B
Abstract conclusion: If A(t), conclude (∃x) [A(x)]
Abstract assumption: If assume A(t), then assume (∃x) [A(x)]
Chain: If A and (if assume A then conclude B) conclude B

Figure 7-9. Syllogistic reasoning by propositional inference.

Model-theoretic reasoning is not the same as working with propositions and applying rules of inference to them to derive new propositions. The propositional reasoning required involves quantifiers, so it is not completely straightforward. Figure 7-9 gives an indication of what is involved. First, we translate the premises and desired conclusion into expressions in first-order predicate calculus. The categories *A*, *B*, and *C* become predicates *A(x)*, *B(x)*, and *C(x)*; for example, *A(x)* is true if *x* is a member of category *A*, false otherwise. Then, *Some B are not A* becomes *There exists an x such that B(x) and not A(x)*; in other words, there exists a person of whom *B(x)* is true and *A(x)* is false. Similarly, *All B are C* becomes *For all x, if B(x) is true, then C(x) is true*. Given these two premises, the task is to prove that the proposition corresponding to P3, *There exists an x such that C(x) and not A(x),* follows.

There are many variant (but equivalent) forms of the predicate calculus that differ in their rules of inference, axioms, and style of proof. We will follow Ebbinghaus, Flum, and Thomas (1984), which uses no axioms but embodies everything in rules of inference and permits the use of additional derived rules. Its style is to make assumptions, reason given these assumptions, and then remove the assumptions. Thus, in Figure 7-9 a proof has a column for what is being assumed and a column for what has been concluded, with a further column at the right to indicate the rule of inference that justifies the step. Let us simply talk our way through the proof, to give some flavor of what is required.

(1) Premise P1 is introduced as a conclusion. (2) Any assumption may be made, since what can be concluded will remain conditional upon it. The ease of finding a proof depends, of course, on making useful choices. This one is an instance of premise P1 with an arbitrary individual (a) from the domain of x. (3, 4) From an assumed conjunction either of its parts can be concluded, so both parts are brought over to the conclusion column. Their validity remains conditional upon the assumption. (5) Now premise P2 is introduced. (6) Universal quantification permits any instantiation to be concluded. Thus P2 can be specialized to the individual a. (7) The rules of inference only combine conclusions with identical assumptions. Arbitrary assumptions can be added (though assumptions cannot be arbitrarily dropped, of course). Thus the expression in step 6 is declared to be true with assumptions being used elsewhere. (8) Now steps 3 and 7 can be combined by modus ponens (from A and $A \supset B$, infer B) to get $C(a)$. (9) Next, this conclusion can be joined with step 4, since if two expressions are conclusions their conjunction is as well. (10) $C(x) \wedge \neg A(x)$ has been concluded in step 8 for the specific individual a, hence it is possible to make the weaker conclusion that there exists an x that makes $C(x) \wedge \neg A(x)$ true. (11) Inferencing has been proceeding under the assumption of $B(a) \wedge \neg A(a)$. It is now necessary to make the conclusion unconditional. The first step is to abstract the assumption away from the specific variable a. If the conclusion holds under the assumption of $B(a) \wedge \neg A(a)$, then it will hold under the assumption that there exists an x that makes $B(x) \wedge \neg A(x)$ true (since such an x exists, namely, a). This change of assumption is valid only if the conclu-

sion in step 10 doesn't depend on a. But step 9 accomplished exactly the removal of a from the expression. (12) Finally, since the assumption of step 11 is known to be valid (step 1), its conclusion is unconditional. This rule is another form of modus ponens, that from A and $A \supset B$ conclude B. Step 12 is P3, the desired conclusion.

It is possible to consider a theory of human syllogistic reasoning based on propositional methods. The sequence of steps in Figure 7-9 seems formidable and one would not expect a human to go through these in real time. In fact, one would not expect to use this as a process theory, but rather more as an indicator of difficulty. In this particular formulation, the proofs of easy and hard syllogisms take about the same number of steps, but other formulations might work out better. However, there are additional requirements for a theory based on propositions. The proof must be discovered, not just worked through. The proof in Figure 7-9 requires considerable invention. Also, the proof is just a verification procedure. The conclusions to attempt must be generated. These add to the difficulty of formulating a general propositional theory; however, our task is not to do so, but simply to illustrate the nature of propositional reasoning.

With these examples of model-based and proposition-based reasoning in hand, let us examine more closely the nature of models and propositions. Given the amount that has been written on the topic, we must be satisfied with a relatively superficial examination, but the essentials can be brought out. Even so, our main point will be one that is not often at the center of such discussions.

Models and propositions are both representations. As we saw in Chapter 2, a system has a representation of some object in the outside world when it can encode the object and encode its transformation into some internal object and activity (these being the representation proper), and then apply the encoded transformation to the encoded object to product an encoded result, and finally decode this result to some aspect in the outside world, in agreement with the external transformation. When the two paths end at the same point (for the purposes at hand), the internal path satisfies a representational law. Propositions and models are both representations in this sense. Both can be used to represent the external world. Furthermore, both propositions and models can be symbol structures, and both can be composed so as to satisfy a wide range of representational laws. (Models, however, need not be symbol structures, as in the analogue representation discussed in Chapter 2.)

Representations can be characterized along two dimensions—their *scope* (what they can represent) and their *processing cost* (how difficult is the processing required to use them). Propositions and models are distinguished along both dimensions. This is reflected in differences in their representational form and in the mappings between their forms and external objects. We can start with form. It might seem that the distinction in form should be categorical and central—propositions have one form and models have another—but the essential distinction is one of processing. Consequently, the concepts of proposition and model are more like prototypes and their forms cannot be categorically distinguished.

Figure 7-9 showed several small but prototypical propositions in the first-order predicate calculus. They form assertions by the use of various devices—terms, logical connectives (*and, or, . . .*), predicates and quantifiers (also functions, but none occurred in the example). Key is the phrase structuring that arises out of the recursive character of connectives, in which the arguments of connectives are truth values and the connectives in turn create propositions that yield truth values. The central mapping between a proposition and the external world is *truth*—each proposition must be true of the world it represents under the mapping of the terms, predicates, and functions. It is easy to see how the whole representational loop is there.

Propositional representations can be *universal* in scope and *hard* in the processing required. On the representational side, there is essentially nothing that cannot be represented. This is reflected in the ability to formulate set theory and all of mathematics in the first-order predicate calculus. Correspondingly, the processing to use such representations can be very hard. For instance, consider two propositions in the predicate calculus, each of which uniquely characterizes an object. To determine whether the two objects are actually the same object is a theorem-proving problem that in general can be arbitrarily difficult. Likewise, going from an internal propositional characterization of an object to some external manifestation of it, such as constructing it, is again a derivation or theorem-proving problem. This is not surprising. A propositional representation permits the expression of arbitrary bodies of knowledge, and the problems that arise in processing such knowledge must therefore be as hard as problems can get.

Model representations are *limited* in scope, but *easy* to process. Simplicity is obtained because models adhere to a *structure-correspondence principle*. The model representation (that is, the internal data structure) has parts and relations; each of these corresponds to a part and relation in what the model represents in the external world. Thus each individual part and relation of the internal model represents something. No completeness or exhaustiveness is implied. The external world can have many other parts, relations, and whatnots—the world is always indefinitely rich relative to any model. It might be thought that this is the way all representations work, but a glance at the predicate calculus expressions in Figure 7-9 will show this not to be the case. In P2, for example, nothing in the external world corresponds to the parts of the expression (the data structure that *is* the representation), namely, nothing corresponds to (y), $B(y)$, $\supset$, or the rest. One might think $B(y)$ should correspond to something, but it occurs on the antecedent side of the implication—if $B(y)$ holds, then $C(y)$ does also, but nothing of which $B(y)$ holds need be there. What P2 does is express a truth about the external world; that is where much of its representational power comes from. Not every aspect of a model (the data structure) represents, of course. A model is a physical object and thus contains an indefinite set of aspects and characteristics of its own. Thus, the principle takes as given some characterization of the model as a data structure, with its own distinguished parts and relations; and it is for these that each must have its correspondent in the referent.

The important consequence of this principle is that match-like and counting processes suffice for working with the model. Matching and counting are fundamentally inexpensive processes. To test whether two representations represent the same object requires only that their parts be put into correspondence and tested for identity, which itself is a match process. If an incompleteness occurs in matching, it is immediately apparent. If a failure occurs in matching, it is known that no further processing will reverse the result. To construct an object to the specifications of the representation is possible if the model is used as a template—again, a match-like process. Thus, the processing is not only inexpensive, it is bounded in strong ways.

Something must be paid in return for inexpensive processing. It is representational scope. Not everything can be represented in a model. What is difficult to represent, and where models show their limitations, is the various forms of incomplete knowledge about the environment. In particular, in a model it is hard to represent knowledge involving negation, disjunction (alternatives), optionality, conditionals, constraints, trade-offs, uncertainty, and so on.

The situation can be made clear by considering disjunctions. Suppose it is known that a man will come to your home to receive an answer to a question. It is easy to construct a model of that, with a model of the doorway and of the man. But suppose either the man or his valet may arrive. Now there are two different situations. However, since the man and his valet are fairly similar, and only their presence and their function of being a receiver of information are relevant, it is still possible to construct a single model with an abstract person at the door. But suppose either the man may arrive or he may call on the telephone? Or that he may arrive, but if he does not arrive before 8 o'clock, then you should go to his house? At some point, there is no way to combine the alternatives in a single composite model (without abstracting away from everything of interest). It seems relatively straightforward to represent in a model any of the actual situations that might eventuate. What produces difficulty is variation in the state of knowledge about these various situations.

When a single model fails (and one is unwilling to retreat to propositions), there is a general way out—to enumerate a collection of models, each of which corresponds to one of the alternatives. Processing now must proceed by iterating over the separate models and becomes thereby more expensive. If there is just a single dimension of variation, the increase in processing is only linear. As multiple optional and conditional situations arise, however, the increase easily becomes combinatorial. Thus, the key issue in the viability of enumeration is the processing required.

Propositional and model representations differ in another important way. Propositions suffer the *frame problem,* models do not. The frame problem (McCarthy & Hayes, 1969; Pylyshyn, 1987) refers to what background knowledge (the frame of reference) remains valid when some action is taken. The problem arises in applying an operator to a state to produce a new state in a search space (which is an action on representations). Let the states be represented propositionally, that is, by a collection of assertions that conjunctively hold true of the external situation. Let the application of the operator represent an actual change in the external situation. That is, the new situation is different from the old; it is not the case that the agent simply acquires additional knowledge about the original situation. It is often easy enough to associate with the operator a collection of new assertions that state the new, changed aspects of the resulting situation that are *directly* affected by the operator (that is, are named in its assertions). But what are the *indirect* consequences? In particular, what about all of the other assertions that held of the original situation? Which of them are true and which false, and what other assertions should now hold? The frame problem is how to compute the resulting representation, and the essential difficulty is that, with a propositional representation of the power of the first-order predicate calculus, there is no way to contain the consequences of an operator application. To answer the frame question in general is equivalent to proving an arbitrary theorem. This is a version of propositional representations being hard to process.

On the other hand, there is no frame problem for models. More correctly, the frame problem has a direct and satisfactory solution. The operators that are admissible in the model simply produce the new situation by modifying those aspects of the model that are appropriate. The unmodified aspects of the situation are simply that, unmodified. Of course, this works only because the internal operators represent the external ones, and hence represent their effects. The avoidance of the frame problem is in part the inability to represent complex situations (of knowledge), so it reflects restricted scope. In addition, there can certainly be hidden effects of the external-world transformation that are not captured in the internal-model operator. This is taken as a failure of the specific representation, not as a reflection of some special updating difficulty (the frame problem). Representational error is a mundane possibility that is always present with representations of whatever sort. There is no magic here, only the result of accepting limitations.

7.2.2. Annotated Models

Models, defined by the structure-correspondence mapping from the model to the external situation, are theoretically neat, with a solid underpinning in a branch of logic called model theory.[10] But for the purposes of an agent attempting to adapt to a real world, models are too restrictive. They give away too much in terms of representational scope. There is no reason not to consider richer representations. The ultimate criterion for whether they can be used is whether their processing can be kept within sufficient limits a priori, so that the agent can meet the real-time constraints it faces.[11]

It is possible to augment models with propositions in ways that still preserve the essentials of match-like processing. Models with such augmentations will be called *annotated models*. Where needed, we will refer to representations that strictly satisfy the structure-correspondence principle as *pure models*. A good example of an annotation can be seen in Johnson-Laird's model representation (Figure 7-8). It permits a tag that declares a given element of the model to be optional. The tag is affixed to the model at the individual to which it applies. The tag is a way of avoiding having two pure models, one which has the individual present and one which does not. These can be built into a single model with an *optionality annotation*, because the processing to deal with the option is localized to one part of the model. If multiple options exist in a model, each is independent. Thus, each model in Figure 7-8, having two options, represents four ground situations.

As the example in Figure 7-8 indicates, many representations that are thought of as models are not pure models (that is, they do not adhere strictly to the correspondence principle) but affix annotations of one sort or another to increase the representational scope. Besides *optional*, an object in a model might be labeled *not-exist*. That is, the model represents an external structure from which that

10. In model theory, however, terminology is turned around. One is given a propositional system and realizes its semantics in a model. Thus the model is playing the role of the external world (model theory tends to include the mapping into the semantic domain as part of the model). In our considerations, the model is a representation of an external world "out there" and this latter does not normally have another representation in the analysis.

11. Actual or expected processing costs of a representation are distinct from a priori guaranteed processing limits. The latter may be the more important.

specific object is absent. This clearly violates the correspondence principle, but it does so in a way that still permits the model to be put in one-to-one correspondence with local checking about the absence of the part. Another annotation is *many,* where the object in the model corresponds to many corresponding external objects; another is *pair,* which specifies the exact number of correspondents.

It is useful to think of an annotation as being any proposition, as long as it is attached to one part of the model and applies to that part. Thus, the essence of an annotation is that it requires processing only when its part is involved, hence its processing is local. It is not necessary to scan for all the annotations and treat them as if they were an arbitrary set of constraints. The simplest forms of annotations are propositions that refer just to their attached object, such as *optional* or *many.* However, the scope of annotations can be permitted to increase by letting them refer to other parts of the model, defined relative to the point of annotation. For example, an annotation *left(chair)* requires checking other parts related to the attached part; it also means that in processing any part the possibility of annotations on other parts must be taken into account. (The processing may still be limited to relatively local searches, however, so it may be kept under control.) As the annotations increase in scope they become indistinguishable from full propositional representations. Processing the representation then loses its match-like character; more and more, the consequences and implications of the multiple assertions dominate the processing and less and less do simple matching, scanning, and counting suffice. The important point of annotated models is the possibility of relaxing the stringent scope requirements of pure models for the payment of increased processing, not that there is any sharp dividing line between annotated models and full propositional representations.[12]

7.2.3. Soar and Mental Models
We are now ready for one of the questions with which we started. How do mental models, which have emerged as an important con-

---

12. The distinctions being made on the limitations of propositional form involve the numbers and types of variables and quantifiers. They do not involve whether the representation looks propositional, for example, by using notations such as (box *A*) or box(*A*). It is quite possible to investigate the issues of models entirely within predicate logics, by imposing limitations on the forms of logic expressions, right down to where the expressions are isomorphic with pure models. See the *vivid* representations of Levesque (1986).

struct in cognitive sciences, fit into Soar? This question is an instance of a question that needs to be answered repeatedly by any unified theory of cognition. How do schemas fit? How does activation fit? How do grammars, transformational, lexical-functional, and otherwise, fit? In sum, how does any construct fit that has proved to have strong explanatory power in cognitive science and is not a direct part of the Soar theory?

Taking such questions seriously may seem antithetical to the stance implied by paradigms in the sense of Kuhn (1962), namely, that a new paradigm presumably asks new questions, unasked by the old paradigm, and ignores the old questions. On the contrary, this serves to emphasize that a unified theory of cognition is not like a new paradigm. The function of a unified theory is to integrate and synthesize existing knowledge within the existing paradigm, not to propose new questions and radically different answers. Or, if one feels that cognitive psychology is not yet a paradigm science—seeming too scrappy perhaps—then the function of a unified theory is to precipitate and consolidate a paradigm from the saturated solution of empirical results and successful microtheories that currently exist.

The answer to the question is straightforward. Mental models are put forward as what are manipulated in solving a problem. Hence, they must just be the representation of the state in the problem space. They do not add any new entity to what is currently in Soar. However, they do specialize the nature of the state representation—namely, that it shall be an annotated model, rather than a propositional representation or some other type of representation. Along with this restriction comes corresponding specializations of the operators in problem spaces to respect the semantics of such representations.

Interestingly, this has not been the view in the mental-models world, where mental models have been considered an alternative to problem spaces. Actually, what the literature on mental models shows is that problem spaces and heuristic search are simply absent (Gentner & Stevens, 1983; Johnson-Laird, 1983). This is a little surprising, given the obvious relation between mental models and problem spaces just described. Much of the basic work in heuristic search in AI—the source of the notion of problem spaces—has always used models for state representations—toy tasks (Missionaries and Cannibals, Tower of Hanoi), chess programs, spatial layout programs (Pfefferkorn, 1971), and so on. They almost all used annotated models, decorating the basic pure-model structure with various flags and tags to expand the representational scope or to control processing.

There are two plausible reasons why mental models could be seen as conceptually distinct with respect to problem spaces. One is the growth of the use of logic as a representation language in AI, including its use for problem spaces (Fikes & Nilsson, 1971; Sacerdoti, 1974, 1977; Nilsson, 1980). Indeed, by now, a movement within AI that calls itself the *logicists* (Genesereth & Nilsson, 1987) takes as axiomatic that all systems should be described in logical form. Thus, the contrast between mental models and propositional representations could easily be taken to be the contrast between mental models and problem spaces, despite the massive work to the contrary. The other reason is the focus, in early AI work in mental models, on dynamical physical systems, such as reasoning about balls rolling down hills (Bobrow, 1985). In contrast, the early work on problem spaces was static; all changes were due to the thought (or action) of the problem solver. This made the two cases seem quite different, especially since work on the dynamical situation focused on the issues of mentally running models that were only qualitatively defined (envisionment) while pretty much ignoring the other types of operators of the problem space. Mental models soon expanded to include reasoning about light switches or temperature shifts, but the separation was probably pretty well fixed by then.

7.2.4. Soar on Syllogisms

Let us assume that humans use annotated models as their internal representation. This is an additional hypothesis beyond the Soar architecture as described in Chapter 4. The basic representational media of objects with attributes and values is neutral with respect to the use of propositional or model representations, or any other assumption about the way internal structure corresponds to the external world. We ignore the issue of what gives rise to this restriction. It could be genuinely architectural, or it could be due to the way encodings are developed, say, because of operating in real time. In any event, the emphasis here is not on the hypothesis per se, but on exploring its incorporation into Soar.

Thus, we can now turn to syllogisms to see how Soar would do them, given that it uses annotated models.[13] Since Soar is an exemplar unified theory of cognition, this will be a theory of how humans do syllogisms. Let us proceed (as usual) by asking what is the obvious way to do syllogisms within Soar. We can start with the constraints imposed by the syllogism task itself, then by annotated models, and finally by the Soar architecture.

At the very least, the task requires reading the premises and constructing some form of internal representation of them, and then constructing and uttering a conclusion that relates the end terms of the premises in a way that is believed to be true. This description leaves open exactly how the premises are represented and how the conclusion is inferred and constructed. The use of annotated models goes some way toward meeting these requirements. The premises are represented in a *situation model*—an annotated model of the situation described by the premises. As a model, the structure of this representation corresponds directly to the structure of the described situation (except where an alternative interpretation is indicated by an annotation). Thus, it will have symbols in it that correspond to persons and that have attributes that correspond to the properties stated in the premises—a person who is a bowler and perhaps also a canoeist.

There is a potential difficulty in this arrangement, because the premises may not describe a situation that can be directly captured in a single annotated model of people with properties. The premises may be ambiguous, so that any of several different (possibly mutually exclusive) situations could correspond to the premises. Then any process that constructed a single annotated model would end up with only one. Conceivably, the ambiguity might be detected, but that cannot be seen at this stage. Of course, this difficulty arises precisely because of the scope limitations of annotated models.

On the other hand, this limitation in scope allows for efficient match-like processing. Given a situation model, the properties of a person in the model, or whether there is a person with some property, can simply be read off by inspection from the model. The conclusion, of course, asks about a particular relation, namely

---

13. This is work by Thad Polk. The particular system described here is Syl-Soar/S88 (Polk & Newell, 1988), which has since moved toward a more general formulation to deal with immediate reasoning (Polk, Newell & Lewis, 1989).

about the people who have specific properties (namely, those given by the end terms of the premises). If these are in the model, they can be read off, but they might not be. Such a failure will be apparent from inspection. Then it may be necessary to augment or modify an initial model before a conclusion can be constructed. The source of knowledge for doing this is the premises, so they may need to be consulted again. If the premises are no longer perceptually available, some representation of the premises must remain available in the internal representation. Hence, in addition to a model of the situation described, it is necessary to have a model of the premises as well (an *utterance model*).

These constraints of the task and of annotated models dictate the qualitative features of syllogistic reasoning. Reading the premises leads to the construction of models of both the premises (the utterance model) and the situation they describe (the situation model). The situation model will not completely capture all the information available in the premises, either because models lack the necessary representational scope or because the comprehension process failed to extract all the available information. If a conclusion cannot be constructed from direct inspection of the model, more information is extracted from the premises until a conclusion can be read off.

This is enough structure to make contact with the third source of constraint—the Soar architecture. Mental models are just the states in problem spaces, and as such they are constructed and manipulated by operators in those problem spaces, but we can go further. Lack of knowledge leads to an impasse and therefore to recursive problem solving to resolve the impasse. An incomplete model of the premises is clearly a situation in which knowledge is lacking. Soar will then reach an impasse whenever a conclusion cannot be directly constructed and resort to problem solving in another problem space to try to resolve that impasse. In this subspace, it should go back to the premises and try to extract information that can be used to augment the situation model.

From these constraints we may determine the types of problem spaces needed to do syllogistic reasoning. There must be a problem space that can process incoming premises and construct annotated-model representations of their linguistic structure and of what they describe. There must be a problem space that can construct a conclusion about a situation based on a model of that situation. There must be problem spaces that can go back to the premises, extract more information, and refine the situation model.

These problem spaces provide arenas in which task-relevant processing can go on. The movement between these spaces depends on the impasses that occur. The processing that occurs within each of these spaces depends on the search-control knowledge available. Some of that knowledge flows directly from the task definition, such as inspecting the situation models for the end terms. But other choices may occur where it will not be clear which one of the possible things to do. In particular, there is no way to avoid putting together the conclusion part by part. The parts are known because it must be like a premise, with a subject, an object, a sign, and a quantifier. But which part should be obtained first? Perhaps it makes no difference, in which case the choice can be indifferent. But it might make a difference. The effect might be only how long it takes to find out the right choice; for example, some parts (say the sign) can't be determined before others (say the object), so choosing wrong causes a dead end. But the effect might be an error, because no knowledge exists to tell whether a particular part is correct or not. (After all this is the process of determining a valid conclusion; it cannot use knowledge of whether it gets a valid conclusion to check whether it is right!)

These effects are the consequences of choosing. The situation that faces the reasoner is one of multiple choices without the knowledge to select. This implies a Soar tie impasse, but an impasse only provides the opportunity to seek the knowledge. Given that the knowledge is actually unavailable, the reasoner is led to another choice situation but still lacks adequate knowledge to make the choice. Note that the situation is different from the blocks-world example in Chapter 4. There, responding to a tie impasse by looking ahead allowed Soar to contact some solid knowledge about the desired situation. Here, looking ahead is certainly possible and occurs, but no contact is made with a sure source of knowledge (what is a valid inference) because no such knowledge exists in the reasoner. The question is whether any knowledge could be available to the reasoner such that accessing that knowledge is better than choosing indifferently among various open options when they arrive. In fact, there is one plausible heuristic. The conclusion arises

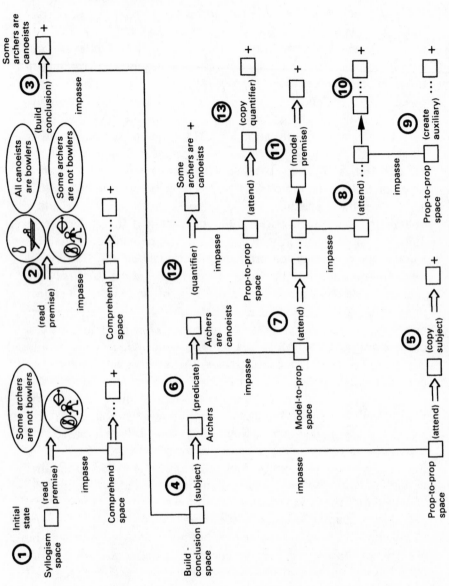

Figure 7-10. Soar's behavior on *Some archers are not bowlers, All canoeists are bowlers.*

from the premises and thus it must in some general way be determined by the nature of the premises. It is better, then, to restrict attention to things that are similar to the things already assembled. Thus, there are attention operators in these spaces that operate associatively to determine what to attend to next.

We implemented the structure described above in a specific Soar system for syllogistic reasoning. This system makes use of six problem spaces. Three of them, *comprehend, syllogism,* and *build-conclusion,* form the top-level path between the presented premises and the response. The knowledge to form them comes from the definition of the task, plus general skills in reading and writing. The comprehend space embodies the ability to deal with natural language, but the premises are sufficiently restricted in form that we could replace this general capability with specific encoding operators geared to the simple single-word character of the premises used in experiments. These encoding operators construct an initial (possibly incomplete) situation model in terms of *objects* with *properties,* and the annotation *not*; they also leave as a by-product a model of each premise as a proposition (the utterance model), with parts *subject, object* and *sign* (which constitute the predicate), and *quantifier.* The other three problem spaces, *prop-to-prop, model-to-prop,* and *prop-to-model,* have the basic operators required to refine situation models and proposition models, and also to guide attention. They extract information from a part of the representation (either the premises or the situation model) and use it to refine another part of the representation. For the task of syllogisms, which involves only understanding a static situation, no *model-to-model* space is needed.

Figure 7-10 illustrates the system's behavior on *Some archers are not bowlers, All canoeists are bowlers.* (This syllogism is different from the one in Figure 7-6; though it is not much easier to solve.) The steps are marked on the figure. (1) It starts in the syllogism problem space and applies a read-premise operator, implemented in the comprehend space, to the first and then the second premise. (2) This results in an initial situation model, plus the two internal propositions (the utterance models). This encoding only extracts information about the subject of the premise. (3) Since the overall task is to produce a conclusion, a build-conclusion operator is applied. Its space (build-conclusion) puts together legal propositions.

The knowledge of the task, which is to produce *what necessarily follows between the two end terms,* is in the form of search control in this space. The task is decomposed into discovering the subject, predicate, and quantifier of the conclusion—the components of the conclusion. The task knowledge permits determining some parts without other parts being specified. Incomplete or incorrect knowledge leads to composing conclusions that are invalid. (4) Generating the subject is tried first, which uses the prop-to-prop space because the propositions, not the model, distinguish between subjects and objects. (5) Attend-to-prop selects the first proposition and copy-subject creates the subject of the conclusion (*archers*). (6) Next, generate-predicate is selected; this occurs in the model-to-prop space, because the propositions probably contain no useful information about the predicate. (7) The attend-to-object operator applies, but no others, because the model is incomplete. Use of this operator leads to augmentation of the model in the prop-to-model space. (8) Attend-to-prop selects premises to extract more information, but neither premise yields anything. (9) The create-auxiliary operator produces a new proposition in the prop-to-prop space. It attends to the second premise and applies operators that convert it, creating the new premise *All bowlers are canoeists.* (10) The new premise allows solving in the prop-to-model space to resume, for Soar now focuses attention on this new proposition and uses it to augment the model. (11) The model now suggests a predicate, so solving is able to continue in the model-to-prop space to obtain the predicate for the conclusion (*are canoeists*). (12) All that remains to be done in the build-conclusion space is to generate the quantifier. The model does not contain the knowledge about quantifiers, since this is what cannot be represented in a single situation model. So the prop-to-prop space is used again. (13) Soar attends to the first premise and copies its quantifier (*some*), finally obtaining *Some archers are canoeists.* This is incorrect, but many humans fail this syllogism as well. Getting a valid conclusion depends on appropriate knowledge being available at many local choice points, as Soar shuttles about inspecting the situation model and the premises.

We now have a Soar system for doing syllogisms that reflects directly the constraints of the syllogism task, the use of annotated models, the Soar architecture, and the heuristic knowledge that would seem to be available. Let us consider the human data and see how well this theory explains human performance. Figure 7-11 presents data from Johnson-Laird and Bara (1984) on the performance by 20 University of Milan students of all 64 syllogisms (with unlimited time) and also on the performance of Soar. The four sections of the chart correspond to the four figures. Each row corresponds to one of the 9 legal responses. The top number in a cell indicates the number of persons giving that response to a particular syllogism. *Some archers are not bowlers* and *All canoeists are bowlers* is abbreviated *Oxy,Azy,* which occurs in the lower left quadrant, where we see that 8 people responded *Ixz* (*Some archers are canoeists*), 7 responded *Oxz* (*Some archers are not canoeists*), 3 responded *NVC* (*no valid conclusion*), and no one gave any other response. Valid responses are shaded. The average was only 38 percent correct and 7 syllogisms were solved by no one.

Individual humans behave differently from one another and from themselves on different occasions. Individuals differ in their knowledge, in their understanding of terms such as *some, necessarily,* and *follows,* and in their learning, which depends on the microsituations they have encountered. This situation is revealed in Figure 7-11 by the existence of multiple responses to the same syllogism. The clustering of responses on a few responses out of the nine possibilities shows both the existence of individual differences and the strong shaping of it by the features of the task situation.

The considerations we have used to determine the Soar syllogism system do not lead to a unique system, which means that variant Soar systems can exist within the same general structure. We constructed a family of 12 Soar variants comprising three parameters, with 3, 2, and 2 possible values, respectively (3 × 2 × 2 possibilities equals 12 variants). The first parameter concerns how premises augment objects that have *not* annotations (3 values); the second, whether premises that refer to *some* objects augment the objects in the situation with the same properties (2 values); the third, whether or not internal propositions will be created (2 values). The first and second parameters reflect how negation and existential quantification are interpreted. The third might be thought of as an indication whether a person will really engage in internal reasoning or will only stay with the propositions given, analogous perhaps to whether a person will do internal look-ahead searches. Other parameters than these three could be defined that

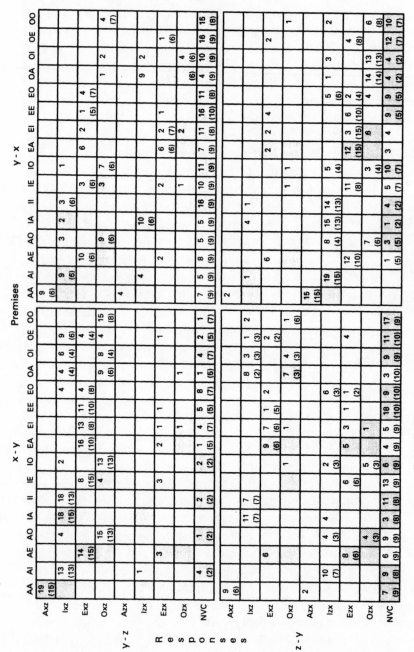

Figure 7-11. Data on human and Soar performance on syllogisms.

establish individual variation within the confines of the basic theory, which satisfies the constraints of the task, annotated-model representations, and the Soar architecture. Selecting these three may be interpreted as a form of data fitting. What is needed, in any event, is that the theory encompass some range of individual differences so that it can predict the feature of the data that not every individual behaves the same way.

This small family accounts for 980 out of 1,154 (85 percent) of the observed legal responses,[14] by covering 131 out of the 193 cells (68 percent) that contain 1 or more responses (all cells with more than 6 people are predicted, with one exception, $Oyx, Ayz = Izx$). Only one response is predicted that is not given by any person ($Oyx, Ayz = Ozx$). Frequencies were assigned to the different members of the family to produce the fit shown in parentheses in Figure 7-11 (15/20 of the people were assumed in the family because 25 percent of responses, which includes the 10 percent nonrecorded responses, were unpredicted). Notice that the cells containing the most and fewest people responses also contain the most and fewest program responses. Many additional micro-features of the way the Soar theory fits the data could be given; however, what is shown is enough to show that the theory does quite well.[15]

Having seen that the Soar theory accounts for the composite responses of a group of people, let us consider how it explains the major regularities listed in Figure 7-7. The extent to which it predicts most of the regularities is implicit in Figure 7-11—it is just a question of categorizing the responses and the syllogisms and looking at the totals for and against each regularity.

First, any syllogism whose solution requires an appreciation of an ambiguity in the premises should be more difficult than one that does not. This follows directly from the difficulty of representing ambiguity in annotated models. Furthermore, difficulty should vary among syllogisms since some are ambiguous while others are not. To take just one example, consider *all x are y, some y are z* (this appears as column AI in the *xy-yz* quadrant of Figure 7-11). A plausible model of these premises has *x*'s being *z*'s, but it is con-

---

14. Of the total of 20 × 64 = 1,280 responses, 126 were illegal responses or recording failures, and are not included in data, leaving 1,154 total. The illegal responses were such things as a conclusion about a middle term (*B*).

15. It would be preferable to have data for the 64 responses from each of the 20 individuals; however, the published data are given in this composite form.

ceivable (in another model) that none are (if none of the y's that are z's are x's). Getting the correct answer (that there is no valid conclusion) requires recognizing that either model could be correct and hence that it is not necessarily true that some x's are z's. Thus, we would expect this syllogism to be relatively difficult. We would also expect that *some x are z* would be a fairly common response. The data in Figure 7-11 bear out both these predictions. Only four subjects (and two Soar variants) gave the correct response (NVC), and 13 subjects (13 Soar variants) made the predicted error (Ixz). Similar predictions for the other syllogisms are also accurate (see Johnson-Laird & Bara, 1984, for a more detailed account).

We have also seen how the theory is tailored to account for individual differences by varying it along certain dimensions. The accuracy of this account can also be seen in Figure 7-11. Cells that contain people responses (have numbers in the top half) also tend to contain Soar responses (parenthesized numbers underneath). Also, responses that people did not give (no number in the top half) were virtually never given by any of the Soar variants (no number in bottom half). We were even able to fit the frequency of responses by varying the number of each Soar variant. Thus, there is a high correlation between the number of people responses in each cell (number in upper half) and the number of Soar-variant responses (number in lower half).

The theory also produces the atmosphere and figural effects. To see the atmosphere effect, consider the syllogisms in Figure 7-11 that have a *some* premise (the column heading contains either an I or an O). The most common responses for these syllogisms (both for subjects and Soar variants) tend to be *some* conclusions (Ixz, Oxz, Izx, or Ozx). Conversely, syllogisms that do not have a *some* premise tend toward universal conclusions (Axz, Exz, Azx, Ezx). Similarly, syllogisms that contain a negative premise (an E or O in the column heading) tend to lead to negative conclusions (Exz, Oxz, Ezx, Ozx), whereas syllogisms with only positive premises tend to lead to positive conclusions (Axz, Ixz, Azx, Izx). The figural effect shows up in the xy-yz and yx-zy figures of Figure 7-11 (the upper-left and lower-right quadrants). In the xy-yz figure (upper left), conclusions tend to have x as the subject rather than z, so there are many more responses (both for people and Soar variants) in the top four rows of that quadrant (Axz-Oxz) than in the next four rows (Azx-Ozx). In the yx-zy figure (lower right), the effect is reversed. Responses are much less common in the first four rows (Axz-Oxz) than in the next four rows (*Azx-Ozx*). The figural effect arises in the theory because selective attention biases the construction of conclusions toward conclusions that are similar to the premises. Thus, a conclusion whose subject is the same as one of the premises is tried before others, leading to the effect. Neither of these effects says anything about the frequency of *NVC* responses.

The conversion effect says that most responses (even errors) are valid under the assumption that both the premises *and their converses* are true. While *Some x are y* and *No x are y* entail their converses, this is not true for the other two premises. *All x are y, All z are y* (*Axy, Azy*), for example, has no valid conclusion. But if the converse of the second premise were true (*All y are z*), then *All x are z* would be a valid conclusion. And the data show that 9 people and 6 variants gave this response. This effect is probably mainly due to how people interpret premises. The theory produces it directly by varying the value of the first parameter corresponding to whether the interpretation of a premise should necessarily imply its converse.

The effects of concreteness do not show up in the data of Figure 7-11, because the experiment involved syllogisms only in concrete form. Moreover, the theory embodied in the system just described does not account for concreteness effects. The path to doing so, however, is rather clear. The locus of such effects will be the models that are constructed. Thus, it needs to make a difference someplace in the encoding whether the premise is *Archers that are bakers* or *A's that are B's*. Furthermore, if there are other facts known about archers, bakers, and their relationship, then these should, under some conditions, be retrieved and enter into encoding the situation model. These effects are localized in the language-comprehension components of the theory and cannot be approached until that is much more highly developed.

Let us now draw the lessons from this long excursion into syllogisms. First, mental models, as that term is used in cognitive science (Johnson-Laird, 1983; Gentner & Stevens, 1983), are just problem spaces, or more precisely the state representations of problem spaces. We have provided a clear demonstration of mental-model reasoning being done in problem spaces, from which it is manifest that the mental model is the state representation. It is a model, because that is the nature of the representation. From Soar's standpoint, the situation is perfectly standard.

What then happens to propositional representations under the assumption that a system uses annotated models? It is certainly possible to build problem spaces whose states are propositional representations and whose operators are logical inference rules. Are these simply banned in an organism that uses only mental models? The answer is a rather surprising one. No, these representations can be used. When they are, what the organism has is a *mental model of the proposition* (this is essentially the nature of the utterance model in syllogistic reasoning). When the organism manipulates that model by means of rules of inference, it is going from a model of one set of propositions to a model of a different set. But, of course, a model of a set of propositions is *not* a model of what those propositions are about. For a model-representing system to use propositional representations *directly* is for it to work *indirectly* with respect to the world those propositions represent. When the human does use propositions, the considerations always seem one off.[16]

Second, the central reason syllogisms are difficult is the inadequacy of the representation, namely, the use of (annotated) models. Models are adequate for many purposes, in particular, for dealing with the world as perceived. So there are good reasons why humans would use models routinely. But categorical syllogisms, with their quantifiers, are too complex to be represented by a single model with the sorts of annotations available to humans.

Representational inadequacy is not the sole reason for difficulty. Problems of the interpretation of the language used are possible, especially of *some* and *all*. Most important, the task situation is not one in which any corrective feedback occurs so that humans can discover how to reason correctly. Thus, a primary feature of human cognition, the ability to learn, is basically excluded. There seem to be no published studies on what learning occurs over the 64 syllogisms in an experiment, but some examination of the raw data from the study discussed here shows very little change in performance. As corroboration, Soar does learn in these syllogistic tasks, but only in terms of the speed, not of correctness. The effects of the

16. The use of propositional representations for the state is different from the use of annotations on a model, even though annotations are propositions. The annotations are processed as part of the match-like processing of the model itself; the propositions are processed by inference operators. Consequently, two forms of proposition-like operations can go on in the human, so that the identification of a proposition-like representation requires some care.

absence of feedback is evident in the reliance of the search on weak associational heuristics, with no opportunity for validation. Also, the errors of semantic interpretation would seem to be correctable to some extent with learning. Perhaps less obvious, the absence of feedback affects the possibility of finding a correct method. Reasoning with models can yield valid results if the conclusion is verified in all the models of a covering set. This is a more complicated method, but not one beyond the capabilities of many of the people in these experiments. But there is no opportunity to learn that simpler methods are inadequate and to discover and debug more complex methods. There are plenty of trials, but no knowledge of results.

Third, the small bow we made in the direction of individual differences can be used to make the point more generally. Unified theories of cognition must deal in a significant way with individual differences. Different humans use different representations and different methods, and the same human also does so on different occasions. Unless the variety of methods is considered, no close explanation of the detailed results can be expected. The single-method approach which is rampant throughout psychology can be viewed only as an initial iteration in obtaining an adequate theory for the field. What we did here in syllogisms was only a simple and inadequate step. For instance, we know there is at least one radically different method, namely, Venn diagrams, which a number of people use (especially those technically trained). This is a model representation of the sets involved, rather than the individuals. It is part of any complete theory of syllogistic reasoning.

Finally, there is a small methodological story here about simulation. The main use of simulation here is classical. We simulated all variations of the 12 synthetic individuals on all 64 syllogisms and accumulated a table of basic performance data (Figure 7-11), from which we read off the fit to the basic human data and to the various regularities. However, simulation played another role as well. We started out by building a high-level version of syllogistic reasoning in Soar, based directly on the view (in accord with Johnson-Laird) that syllogisms were to be done by inspecting models. We obtained a simulation system that did direct recognition by productions that we wrote. Then we reflected that these productions must have come from someplace. So we invented a space that would create these productions as chunks. This is how we obtained the spaces that go back to the premises and extract more information in order to refine the model. Thus, we used simulation to generate parts of the theory in Soar, by starting with a simulation and asking what its genesis was in a system that must obtain all of its immediate behavior by learning from experience. This use of simulation to aid theory construction is much less usual than its use to make predictions, but it does show the varied ways simulation can help.

7.3. Sentence Verification

We arrive at our third task on the foothills of rationality—elementary sentence verification. The paradigm for verification has its roots in the early 1970s. People read simple sentences such as *Plus is above star* (Figure 7-12). Then they look at simple pictures and make a simple indication of whether the sentence was *true* or *false* of the picture, such as by pushing one of two buttons. The entire business takes 2–3 sec. The task constitutes an elementary, but complete and quite natural, act of comprehending language, in a context where language is to be used in a natural and direct way. The research on these tasks was one step along a long path that cognitive psychology has been taking to work up from letters to words to sentences to paragraphs, exploring increasingly complex linguistic functioning.

To understand how sentences are comprehended, the researchers varied the tasks in systematic ways. For instance, the sentences can be as complex as *Star isn't below plus,* a false sentence in our example. The fundamental result is that the time people take to do such tasks varies in a highly regular way (there are essentially no errors with such simple tasks). The figure gives a typical result (Chase & Clark, 1972). The response time can be decomposed into a base amount of time (1,763 ms) that covers all the things that do not vary (perceiving the picture, reading the sentence, making the response movement); plus an amount of time (685 ms) if the sentence is negative; plus an amount of time (93 ms) if the sentence uses *below* rather than *above;* plus an amount of time (187 ms) if the sentence is false of the picture. These three factors (on top of the base time) account quite precisely for all eight combinations of positive/negative, above/below, and true/false (95–97 percent of the variance between the means). For the complex case shown in the figure's second sentence, the model predicts 2,728 ms versus an

Plus is above star	+ *
Star isn't below plus	+ *

$$RT = 1763_{rest} + 685_{neg} + 93_{below} + 187_{false} = \underset{2728}{\underline{predicted}} \quad \underset{2739 \text{ ms}}{\underline{observed}}$$

READ SENTENCE FIRST

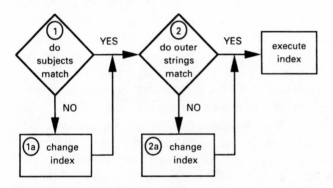

EXAMINE PICTURE FIRST

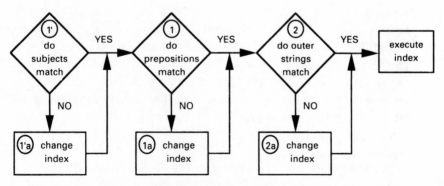

Figure 7-12. Elementary sentence verification
(after Chase & Clark, 1972).

observed 2,739 ms. The means conceal a fair amount of individual variation, but they reveal clearly the existence of orderly processing.

These experiments—and there was a small cottage industry in producing them in the 1970s (Clark & Clark, 1977)—provided an important part of the growing evidence that humans behave in highly lawful ways on truly cognitive tasks. The tasks that began the chronometric revolution in the 1960s were simple perceptual and memory-search tasks (Neisser, 1967). We examined one of these in Chapter 5, the Sternberg paradigm (Sternberg, 1966). The sentence-verification tasks moved up a ways in task complexity (as can be seen in going from ~1 sec to ~2–3 sec). More important, they engaged linguistic behavior, which occupies such a special role in our notion of higher mental processes. This paradigm thus played an important role in the early 1970s in building up the large body of regularities that have confirmed that humans are computational systems. It contributed its quota to our ~~3,000 regularities.

The style of theorizing about the information processing in these tasks was by means of *flowcharts* (as shown in the figure). Any psychologist can testify to the ubiquitous occurrence of such flowcharts throughout the cognitive literature. They provide the framework for analysis and discussion of the particular aspects that are being manipulated in an experiment. The interpretation of the upper flowchart goes like this. First (before entering the flowchart proper), the person reads the sentence and encodes it internally as a proposition. Then the person examines the picture and encodes the information from it as another internal proposition. This second encoding occurs because the two items of knowledge (from the sentence and from the picture) must be put in some common representational terms in order to permit comparison. Here the codes can be represented as *(plus (above star))* for the sentence and *(plus (above star))* for the picture. Before starting the actual comparison, an index is set for the expected answer (here, that the response will be *true,* because the default norm is for a sentence to be true). Given this setup, the flowchart in the figure shows the way the comparison proceeds. First, the subjects of the two codes are compared. If they match, processing simply proceeds. But if they fail to match, then the response index is changed (from *true* to *false*). Next, the "outer strings" are compared, which is the way the original article referred to the relation (*above* or *below*). Again, if the comparison holds, processing simply proceeds; but if the comparison fails, the index is changed again (from *true* to *false* or vice-versa). At the end, the response is made according to the index. This flowchart represents not just a way of doing the task, but the way humans do the task. The factors in the prediction equation correspond to the time taken by various component processes of the flowchart, and the independence between the times arises from the structural independence exhibited in the flowchart.

Clark and Chase proposed this flowchart to explain the particular sentence-verification task we have been using as an illustration, where the sentence is read first and then the picture is examined. They also considered a second task, namely, where the picture is examined first and then the sentence is read. They described the processing in this second task by the second flowchart in Figure 7-12. A little study will show that it is closely related to the first one, but it reflects the structure of the task of examining the picture first. In particular, when the person reads the sentence first, the picture can be examined according to what the sentence says. If it is about the star, attention can be directed at the star in the figure; if it is about the plus, attention can be directed at the plus. However, when the person examines the picture first, the sentence cannot be read differently, depending on what is seen in the picture. Linguistic expressions require that they be read as presented; otherwise their meaning cannot be extracted. Thus, an extra stage shows up in the picture-first case because the encoding can be different in one more way. This use of flowcharts to embody the theoretical processing framework is typical of their use in cognitive psychology. The example is a positive exemplar in terms of the beauty of their data, the historical significance of their work, and the sophistication with which they used the flowchart as simply one element in an analysis of the information processing that goes on during these tasks.

7.3.1. Soar on Sentence Verification
Where do the flowcharts come from? If this question does not immediately leap to mind, it should.[17] As they show up in the psycho-

---

17. The question leapt to my own mind some time ago (Newell, 1980c). This is my second attempt to answer this question; the answer has not changed, but Soar provides a much better way to demonstrate it.

logical literature, flowcharts stem from the experimenter's rational task analysis. As such, they constitute degrees of freedom for theory, even though there are no parameters to count. They are so obvious that they usually are not questioned. They represent a plausible and rational way to do the task. In fact, they reveal something about the person's response to the demands of the task. As such, the flowcharts ought to emerge from a unified cognitive theory. Indeed, if we come at flowcharts from the point of view of this chapter, which is to examine intendedly rational behavior, then we would naturally ask how humans organize themselves to behave according to such flowcharts. Thus, to repeat, the question is where flowcharts come from. It will not surprise you that Soar provides a theory of the origin of flowcharts. An exemplary unified theory of cognition could do no less.

The Soar theory is that flowcharts are nothing but composite, static images of wanderings through the problem space. A person accomplishes a task by working in a problem space—that is the general situation, according to Soar. If the person does variations of the task, then the paths in the space will vary depending on the detailed demands of the task and the knowledge available. Integrating over all the different paths that can be taken produces the flowchart. This integration, of course, is produced by the scientist, in order to represent how the person would behave in many situations.

Figure 7-13 illustrates this integration. The heavy line in the problem space is the actual path that the person takes: M1 corresponds to the first match, CI corresponds to changing index, M2 corresponds to the second match, and EI corresponds to executing the index. The other possible paths through the space are indicated by the light lines. The person is generating each path dynamically as he or she moves through the problem space for each task variation. The figures show no explorations off the main paths, because errors rarely occur by the time behavior has become routine enough to be characterizable by flowcharts.

No data structure exists within the person that is the flowchart that is being followed, as in an interpreter or plan implementor. As the person learns, the path may become quite reliable, because the search control will always say to do the same thing in the same situation, as shown. But the flowchart has no reality as a structure—it is the scientist's external representation of the behavior.

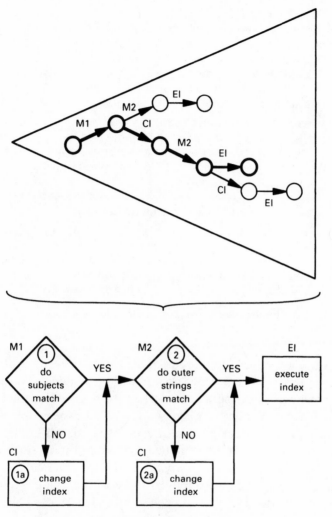

Figure 7-13. The Soar theory of flowcharts.

This does not imply that the person cannot ever operate interpretively according to a plan (people can obviously do this), only that in these skilled situations that is not what is going on.

Let us put some flesh on this example, by seeing how Soar would do the task of comprehending a sentence and verifying it.[18] The central features of Soar's method are laid out in Figure 7-14. Our

18. This is work by Gregg Yost.

Use P-E-A-C
Perception and encoding delivers words serially
A comprehension operator exists for each word
• Executes on each word as it arrives
• Determines the significance of a word in context
• Creates and reads expectations
• Builds up representation of the situation

Comprehension operators for the example

"plus"	Create an object with name plus
"is"	Expect a pre-object and a post-property
	Create predicate: the property of the object
"above"	Expect a post-object
	Create property: being above the object
"star"	Create an object with name star

Task organization

Problem space	Operators
Task space	acquire, compare, respond, done
Comprehension space	comprehension operators, read
Compare space	recode, change-index, done

Figure 7-14. Soar comprehension of a sentence.

tack, once again, is simply to ask of Soar what is the natural way for it to do the task—namely, to comprehend a sentence. In the background we have the operations of perception, encoding, and attending to the sentence on the display. We can take these operations as delivering the sentence as a sequence of words, in order. If Soar wants to comprehend the sentence, the natural thing for it to do is to execute a *comprehension operator* on the sentence. Since Soar acquires the sentence word by word, the natural thing is to execute a comprehension operator on each word as it arrives. This is just a version of the *immediacy of interpretation* principle of Just and Carpenter (1987).

The use of the term *natural* conceals an important point. There are many ways for Soar to implement the comprehension of sentences, or do any other task. Indeed, there are also many ways for a human to do so. A natural way is one that involves little additional knowledge and little computational apparatus and indirection. It is usually efficient, because it is straightforward, but it may not be the most efficient, because some intricate algorithm might be better—occasionally much better. The natural way is the place to begin analysis but is not the end of analysis. Its heuristic nature must be recognized and alternatives examined at some point. Ultimately, such a notion is to be replaced by theories of how ways of doing things are learned and improved or changed with experience— exactly what Soar chunking is supposed to provide. One of the general arguments for the importance of getting the architecture right, even though it appears to recede as the time scale increases, is that doing what is natural within the architecture will tend to be the way humans actually do a task.

Executing the word-comprehension operator is an attempt to determine the significance of the word in its total context (for the person). It is necessarily an expectation-based scheme, because language is such that the significance of a word often depends on words that are still to come. Hence, the action of a word-comprehension operator, while it can take into account the knowledge that prior words have provided (as processed by comprehension operators working on them), cannot take into account the knowledge that later words will provide (since they have not arrived yet). Therefore, the operator must create data structures that will be used by those later words (that is, by their comprehension operators) when they arrive. Functionally, these data structures are *expectations*. A comprehension operator need not always create further expectations. Sometimes it will have all the knowledge it needs to create a part of the meaning of the incoming utterance— indeed, ultimately some comprehension operators must be able to do so or the sentence will never be understood.

This scheme does the entire task of comprehension, taking into account syntactic and semantic knowledge. Thus, the scheme is not simply a parsing system, but its computational structure is analogous to an expectation-based parsing system. This case provides another opportunity to reinforce the notion that a unified theory of cognition (here Soar) does not primarily propose radically new theories for each of the phenomena that it attempts to cover. Soar does not provide a radically new theory of sentence comprehension. Expectation-based parsing is a well-explored path, closely related to case-based schemes. Many of the basic properties of the Soar scheme are familiar from these studies. Indeed, the scheme is very close in spirit to the *Word Expert* system of Steve Small (1979), which itself grew out of the approach to language analysis developed by Roger Schank and his colleagues and students at Yale (Schank & Riesbeck, 1981). The Soar system has some (important) wrinkles that appear to solve some of the problems with existing systems and permit extension in important ways (for example, to learning). But Soar is not implicitly making a claim about the novelty of these mechanisms. It is claiming—and this is no mean claim—that it is realizing these mechanisms within a total cognitive system in which the language mechanisms can be related to the mechanisms used for all other cognition and in which all these mechanisms mutually constrain one another.

Let's go through the words of the sentence, defining what each comprehension operator will do. We have indicated only the minimal knowledge needed to perform this specific comprehension. The word *plus* creates an object, with the name "plus." The word *is* creates an expectation for a pre-object (one determined by words occurring prior to the word in question) and an expectation for a post-property (one determined by words occurring after the word in question). These are expectations for objects in the semantic representation, not for words in the coming utterance. If these expectations are satisfied then the operator will create a predicate—that the object has the property. The word *above* creates an expectation for a post-object. If this expectation is satisfied, then the operator creates a property of being above the object. Finally, the word *star* creates an object with the name "star," analogously to *plus*.

We have not included any alternative meanings for these words. That might be thought just a question of expository or analytic simplicity. In fact, the laboratory task context of simple sentence verification is one in which persons do the task repeatedly after becoming familiarized with the task. Consequently, all linguistic ambiguities have disappeared, such as *plus* meaning addition. Of course, there remains the question of how the person becomes specialized, so as not to find any ambiguity in the task itself. Soar should certainly be expected to provide a theory of that as well. But for this task (and hence for this example) these issues are not in evidence.

Three problem spaces are required for this task. There is a task space, where the top-level task will be done. It has operators to *acquire* information, to *compare* representations, to *respond* by pushing a button, and to *recognize* when it is *done*. Some of these operators must be implemented in spaces of their own. The *comprehension space* is the space we have been describing that is full of comprehension operators. It also has a *read-word* operator to ac-

quire the next word from the environment. This space will sometimes be applied to the sentence and sometimes to the picture.
Comprehension is required more broadly than just for language. It
is a function that is required for any kind of contact with the external world. The *compare space* has the *recode* operator, the *change-
index* operator, and its own *done* operator. This space is in part
linguistic, in that some of the operators (recode) and their search
control come from knowledge of language—for example, what it
means to say that *plus* is *above star*.

This is a suitable example for showing a trace of Soar working on
a simple task (Figure 7-15). Soar starts out in the context of certain
trial-specific instructions, which are outside of this performance of
the verification task. The instructions are that, first, a warning light
will occur, then the sentence and the picture will arrive simultaneously in two separate panels of the display, then the sentence is
to be read, followed by the picture, and finally the appropriate
button is to be pushed. Each line of the figure is a decision cycle
(dc), numbered consecutively, followed by a description of the decision that was made, *p* (problem space), *s* (state), *o* (operator), or *g*
(goal), followed by the internal identifier of the object (*p194*), followed by a descriptive name (such as *comprehension,* for the comprehension problem space). The occurrence of an impasse is
marked by a right double arrow (as at dc 9) and the trace is then
indented until the impasse is resolved, at which point it is outdented
(at dc 43).

Soar starts in the base space, which is also the comprehension
problem space. This is where it reads in words by repeatedly executing a read-word operator. The first word is the warning light (at
dc 3) and it has to apply an install-node operator to link up the input
into the present state so it can access it. Soar needs to understand
what has come in, so it executes the comprehend operator on it
(dc 6). This leads it to execute an intend operator that says to
attempt the pending task (*do-c&c-sf*), which is the Chase and Clark
task that involves looking at the sentence first and then at the picture. This operator leads to a no-change impasse, which leads to a
subgoal to implement the intention (*g222* at dc 9). The problem
space for that is *do-c&c,* and the initial state is *s224.*

The first operator applied is get-input on the sentence channel (dc
12), since Soar knows to read the sentence first. All of the interaction between central cognition and the perceptual components (per-

Context from instructions: sentence-first condition
First, warning-light appears
Then, sentence appears: plus is above star
Then, picture appears: plus / star

dc 1 p: p194 comprehension
   2 s: s197
   3 o: o196 read-word
   4 o: o208 install-node(n209(warning-light *word))
   5 s: s210
   6 o: o213 comprehend(n209(warning-light *word))
   7 s: s219
   8 o: o215 intend(do-c&c-sf)
   9 ⇒g: g222   (intend(do-c&c-sf) operator no-change)
  10   p: p223 do-c&c
  11   s: s224
  12   o: o228 get-input(*predicate sentence-channel)
  13   ⇒g: g230 (get-input(*predicate sentence-channel)
                  operator no-change)
  14   p: p194 comprehension
  15   s: s225
  16   o: o231 attend(sentence-channel)
  17   o: o196 read-word
  18   o: o232 install-node(n233(plus *word))
  19   s: s234
  20   o: o237 comprehend(n233(plus *word))
  21   s: s241
  22   o: o196 read-word
  23   o: o244 install-node(n245(is *word))
  24   s: s246
  25   o: o249 comprehend(n245(is *word))
  26   s: s253
  27   o: o196 read-word
  28   o: o255 install-node(n256(above *word))
  29   s: s257
  30   o: o260 comprehend(n256(above *word))
  31   s: s263
  32   o: o196 read-word
  33   o: o264 install-node(n265(star *word))

Figure 7-15. Soar on the sentence-verification task.

```
34        s: s266
35        o: o269 comprehend(n265(star *word))
36        s: s273
37        o: o260 comprehend(n256(above *word))
38        s: s282
41        o: o249 comprehend(n245(is *word))
42        s: s299
43    s:    s304
44    o:    o308 get-input(*predicate picture-channel)
45      ⇒g: g309   (get-input(*predicate picture-channel)
                        operator no-change)
46        p: p194 comprehension
47        s: s299
48        o: o310 attend(picture-channel)
49        o: o196 read-word
50        o: o311 install-node(n312(plus *word))
51        s: s313
52        o: o316 comprehend(n312(plus *word))
53        s: s320
54        o: o196 read-word
55        o: o323 install-node(n324(/ *word))
56        s: s325
57        o: o328 comprehend(n324(/ *word))
58        s: s333
59        o: o196 read-word
60        o: o336 install-node(n337(star *word))
61        s: s338
64        o: o345 comprehend(n337(star *word))
65        s: s351
66        o: o328 comprehend(n324(/ *word))
67        s: s362
68    s:    s367
69    o:    o371 compare(w357(*predicate *is) w295(*predicate *is))
70      ⇒g: g372   (compare(w357(*predicate *is)
                      w295(*predicate *is)) operator no-change)
71        p: p373 do-compare
72        s: s379
73        o: o374 compare-done
74    o:    o381 respond(true)    Response: true
```

Figure 7-15 (continued).

ception and encoding) is hidden in this operator and leads Soar to re-enter the comprehension space, where it can attend to the sentence channel (dc 16) and begin to comprehend the stream of words using the read-word operator.

The first word read is *plus,* which is installed in the state (dc 18), and then the comprehend operator is applied to it. This pattern will be repeated throughout—read-word, install-node to new state, and then comprehend. Thus, we can spot the comprehension of *plus* (dc 20), *is* (dc 25), *above* (dc 30), *star* (dc 35). Although nothing shows in the trace, various expectations have been set and various objects created. We see the comprehension operator for *above* fire again (dc 37) and then also the comprehension operator for *is* (dc 41). Both of these are filling expectations satisfied by the comprehension of the word *star,* which has finally come along. Thus, there is some end-of-sentence processing. This completes the acquisition of information from the sentence channel, so Soar moves back to the base space.

Soar then gets the input from the picture channel, which again requires an attend operator to select the appropriate channel (dc 48). Soar goes through the read-word, install-node, and comprehend loop for each of the three pieces of information from the picture. We interpret this as if it were another sentence *plus/star,* because the pictorial display is so discrete and simple that a more elaborate perceptual model is not required. The comprehension operator on the geometric relation (/) executes again (dc 66), because its expectations become satisfied.

Finally (at dc 69 and back in the base space), the compare operator can execute; it will see if these two expressions designate the same situation. Comparison leads to an impasse (dc 70). In this particular case, the expressions are identical structures so there is no processing to speak of, except for actually doing do-compare and seeing that the comparison is done, compare-done (dc 73). This operator produces the attribute *true,* which the respond operator converts into an external response (dc 74).

We have just walked through a small bit of behavior by Soar that reads a simple sentence, reads a simple picture, compares them, and responds. This particular behavior generates one path through the flowchart, namely the heavy line in Figure 7-13. If we had given it other sentences Soar would have created traces through other parts of the space, and the whole would have added up to the

The experiment occurs

	Plus is above star

1. Light turns on.
2. Display shows.
3. Person reads, examines, and presses a button.

Prior trial-specific instructions
4. "Read the sentence."
5. "Then examine the picture."
6. "Press the T-button if the sentence is true of the picture."
7. "Press the F-button if the sentence is false of the picture."
8. "Then the task is done."

Prior general instructions
9. "At some moment the light will come on."
10. "After the light comes on, a display will occur."
11. "The left side of the display shows a sentence."
12. "The right side of the display shows a picture."

Introductory instructions
13. "Hello."
14. "This morning we will run an experiment."
15. "Here is the experimental apparatus."
16. . . .

Figure 7-16. Acquiring a task.

flowchart given by Chase and Clark. Thus, for one exceedingly simple but real case, we have produced the flowchart.

7.3.2. Soar on Acquiring a Task

The above demonstration shows how the flowchart comes from the problem space, but it leaves unanswered the next question. *Where does the problem space come from?* Let's step back and consider the larger experimental situation (Figure 7-16). The experiment occurs when the warning light turns on, a display shows up, the person reads the sentence, examines the picture, and presses the button. That could happen only if the person had some knowledge, which we can call *prior trial-specific instructions:* Read the sentence, then examine the picture, press the true-button if the sentence is true of the picture, press the false-button if the sentence is false of the picture, then the task is done. By itself, of course, that knowledge isn't enough to do the task. That requires in turn some other knowledge, which we can call *prior general instructions:* At some moment the light will come on, after the light comes on a display will occur, the left side of the display shows a sentence, and

Create an operator: Do-task
Create an operator-implementation problem space
The operators of this space come from the instructions

"Read the sentence."
Create an operator to read the sentence

"Then examine the picture."
Create an operator to examine the picture
Conditional upon having a result of prior operator

"Press the T-button if the sentence is true of the picture."
Create an operator to press T-button
Conditional upon truth-index having value true

"Press the F-button if the sentence is false of the picture."
Create an operator to press F-button
Conditional upon truth-index having value false

"Then the task is done."
Create an operator to recognize task as done

Figure 7-17. Prior trial-specific instructions.

so on. That isn't quite enough either, for this presupposes what can be called *introductory instructions:* Hello, this morning we'll run an experiment, . . . At some point, the outer context is sufficient to interpret what to do by what the person already knows and by being situated in the experimental room with the apparatus.

This is enough information to provide an answer to the question, at least in outline. Problem spaces come from whatever leads the person to set up the task—what we are calling *instructions.* As the figure shows, there is a succession of concentric layers of outer context (which ultimately terminate as a function of the initial knowledge). Let us take just the next layer out, the prior trial-specific instructions in Figure 7-16. Figure 7-17 shows how Soar does this task.[19] Its presuppositions include knowledge of the sort in the instructions lower down in Figure 7-16. In particular, Soar understands that it is to acquire a new task from reading the trial-specific instructions. (Actually, adding another sentence, such as *Here are the instructions for the task,* would have avoided this being a presupposition.)

Soar reads the sentences in the trial-specific instructions exactly

19. This is work by Gregg Yost. It has been continued and extended by Lewis, Newell, and Polk (1989).

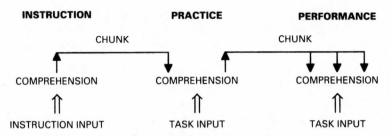

Figure 7-18. Stages of task acquisition.

as it reads the sentences in the task itself (as shown in Figure 7-15), only this time it is led to create a new operator *do-task,* with a new problem space to implement it, and then to comprehend in the context of this new implementation space to construct its operators from the instructions. The instruction sentences are quite simple and their comprehension does not occasion substantial difficulties. Each sentence gives the instruction for one operator. The knowledge for doing this is entirely embedded in the semantics of the words—that is, in the comprehension operators for *read, the, sentence, then, examine, . . . , done.* The new space it creates from these instructions is identical to the one coded by hand to give Soar the original capability to do the sentence-verification task.

Soar must do more than just comprehend the sentence instructions in Figure 7-17. It must organize itself to do the task. Hence, it must build the appropriate problem spaces and operators. To do that, it must build the appropriate ensemble of productions—that select the problem space at the appropriate impasses, that select the operators in the service of the goals, and that implement the operators. This means that Soar must pass from the instruction sentences to the appropriate productions. The only mechanism Soar has for acquiring new productions is chunking. Thus, Soar creates the appropriate productions by chunking. But this means, as we saw in the case of data chunking in Chapter 6, that Soar must perform tasks that lead to the right chunks.

Figure 7-18 shows, in outline, what is going on. Soar starts with the instructions being input in linguistic form, which is comprehended by the process we have seen. The result is a set of data structures in working memory that constitute this understanding. These data structures get stored in long-term memory for later use. Storage is done by chunking, naturally, since that is what long-term memory is. The task of accomplishing storage is a version of data chunking—there is a data structure that needs to show up as the actions of some to-be-created productions, such that it can be recalled at a later time as a function of some cues available then, but this data structure itself must not be part of the conditions of these productions or the productions can never be evoked. (More accurately, they can be evoked only when the data structure is already in working memory.) And indeed the mechanisms used to do this chunking are essentially the same ones used in data chunking.

When the first instance arises to perform the new task—here, the sentence-verification task—what Soar has available are these data chunks. Upon being evoked, the chunks produce in working memory a reconstructed version of the data structures. To perform the task the first time, though, Soar must *interpret* these data structures—by using problem spaces with operators (how else could it be done?). As a result, when the interpretation succeeds, new chunks are built that perform this task. On subsequent performances of the task of sentence verification, these productions directly implement the problem space and operators. Thus, Soar moves to acquire the task by passing through a stage of interpretation. In simple cases, such as the sentence-verification task used here, Soar acquires on a single pass exactly the productions that would have been (and were) produced by hand to do the task.[20] On more complex tasks, however, the single experience provides only a single swath through the possibilities of task performance, so later performances will be a mixture of chunked and interpreted behavior. The basic scheme works in Soar, in its present incarnation, in a collection of problem spaces called TAQ (Yost, 1988).

This form of skill acquisition, which passes from declarative structure to productions by means of interpretation, is a central tenet of the Act* theory of skill acquisition (Anderson, 1981, 1983). Thus, Soar uses the same acquisition scheme as Act* does. It does so, of course, entirely by means of the chunking mechanism and problem spaces, and this method integrates it into the rest of Soar. Thus, again, what we see arising in a unified theory of cognition is a convergence of mechanisms. Given that Act* is another candidate

20. Actually, the runs were made with chunking at all levels; if bottom-up chunking had been used, it would have taken several runs to learn all these productions.

universal theory of cognition, I take this convergence as positive evidence for Soar as well.

This example also emphasizes the way learning and problem solving mix together. It no longer makes much sense to keep them separate conceptually. The fundamental constructs of problem spaces, impasses, and chunking are well defined, because they are identifiable mechanisms in the Soar architecture. But the larger categorizations of behavior, such as learning as distinguished from problem solving—and, one suspects, cognition as distinguished from perception—will not be sharply definable, even in principle.

Thus, Soar really does embody the theory, laid out in Figure 7-13, that flowcharts are nothing but the reflection of problem spaces. The problem spaces are created dynamically in response to instructions, so they can be newly minted cognitive structures. Soar can take in information that gives it the instructions to create these problem spaces, at which point it then takes in the task and behaves in the appropriate fashion. Soar provides a genuine theory of how these task instructions get carried out. Furthermore, this theory is one with the theory of how the task is carried out, which is certainly something one would expect of a unified theory of cognition.

7.4. Summary

Let us summarize our explorations of how humans go about attaining their goals as they get a little temporal space within which to operate. We first looked at cryptarithmetic for clues to search control in problem solving over relatively long periods of time (~ 100 sec). Adequately modeling behavior at this level is important if Soar is to have enough scope as a unified theory of cognition. However, we have not yet pushed far enough to provide an example of the vertical integration that a unified theory should allow. We argued for the importance of devising detailed simulations of large stretches of complex behavior, especially relatively unconstrained naturalistic behavior, in order to build confidence that the cognitive theory is essentially correct. The use of simulation in cryptarithmetic illustrated that complexity could be controlled by providing the lower-level operators manually, so we could focus directly on the higher-level control issues. If we had got caught up in building the cryptarithmetic operators, it might have been a long time before we ever got to simulating the search-control behavior.

We used syllogisms to ask whether there were limits to rationality other than time. Syllogisms provide a good test of this question because, although they are relatively simple and short tasks, some instances turn out to be quite difficult, even for intelligent people. In general, the answer is that the difficulty lies in the formulation of the task. This is not primarily a question of encoding rules (though such effects exist, as the individual data showed). It comes from the use of a representation (models) that trades away representational power for speed of processing. Categorical syllogisms, for which quantifiers are used, reveal the limitations. Processing strategies exist that permit adequate performance even so, but these are complex (generating and examining multiple models) and, importantly, the tasks are presented without feedback or other instructions that would permit correct performance to be discovered. In terms of simulation, the interesting aspect of the syllogism story was having to build the theory practically on the fly. We essentially backed into our theory by simulating a version that was already direct, in the sense that it was done directly by productions, and then we backed into the spaces that were the deliberate spaces that would yield the chunked space with experience. This latter space was the one that turned out to have the interesting structure.

In the sentence-verification task, we tried to explain where executive-level flowcharts come from. We presented a theory that eliminated flowcharts as a structure with direct psychological validity and that showed them as static composite projections of dynamically generated behavior in problem spaces. The ultimate point— much more important, in fact—is that instructions and task performance need to be brought together in one theory. That is both an obligation of a unified theory of cognition and an opportunity for it. We were able to illustrate that Soar can approach this capability. From a simulation point of view, the lesson here is just the opposite of the usual one of trying to cope with complexity. The situations represented by sentence verification are quite simple. Consequently, the problem is how to be clear that the conclusions are being generated by the theory and not by the intuitive rationality of the analyst. The flowcharts that fill our psychological journals can stand as typical opportunities for smuggling in the implicit rational-

1. How humans are able to exhibit intelligence (Chapter 4)
2. Many global properties of human cognitive behavior (Chapter 4)
3. Human immediate behavior (~~1) (Chapter 5)
4. Discrete perceptual-motor behavior (Chapter 5)
5. Verbal learning (recognition and recall) (Chapter 6)
6. Skill acquisition (Chapter 6)
7. Short-term memory (Chapter 6)
8. Problem solving (Chapter 7)
9. Logical reasoning (Chapter 7)
10. Elementary sentence verification (Chapter 7)
11. Instructions and self-organization for tasks (Chapter 7)

Figure 7-19. The coverage so far of Soar
as a unified theory of cognition.

ity of the scientist. Simulation is used here to control theorizing in these simple situations.

Finally, these three topics make their contribution to our running box score on the scope of Soar as a unified theory of cognition. The expanded list is given in Figure 7-19. Our additions stand for the requirement that a unified theory of cognition operate over a wide temporal range.

Along the Frontiers

We arrive at the last chapter. Where do matters stand on the case for unified theories of cognition and what they promise for cognitive science? I have not argued the case abstractly but have chosen to exhibit a candidate unified theory, Soar. This seemed the only way to communicate what such a thing would be and how having one might make a difference. It needs repeating once more. In this book I am not proposing Soar as *the* unified theory of cognition. Soar is, of course, an interesting candidate. With a number of colleagues, I am intent on pushing Soar as hard as I can to make it into a viable unified theory. But my concern here is that cognitive scientists consider working with *some* unified theory of cognition. Work with Act*, with Caps, with Soar, with CUTC, a connectionist unified theory of cognition.[1] Just work with some UTC. That is the message of this book and the end toward which all its chapters are bent.

To continue restating basics, a unified theory of cognition is by definition a theory of mind. A theory of mind, however, is not by definition a theory of the computational and informational processes that constitute the mind. The psychological theories that preceded the cognitive revolution—behaviorism, Gestalt psychology, and psychoanalysis—establish the existence of multiple alternatives. In addition, a significant amount of current philosophic discourse seeks to challenge the computational view and to search for alternatives, although the field is not overloaded with specific well-developed candidates (see Costall & Still, 1987). The general presumption of the computational basis of mind is, however, the basic premise of cognitive science and it is adopted without ques-

---

1. I was going to propose a connectionist unified theory of everything, but that seemed a little cute.

tion by current candidates for unified theories of cognition. Soar shares this premise fully.

There is no alternative for a unified theory of cognition based on information processing but to be a theory of the architecture. The architecture is where the strong organismic invariants are, but it needs to be emphasized (one last time) that the architecture by itself does not determine behavior. Indeed, an architecture is precisely a device for making it possible for something else to determine behavior, to wit the knowledge encoded in its memories. Knowledge is about many different things; the system's goals, the system's bodily state, the local task environment, the social environment, the general nature of the physical world—all these are the burden of the knowledge level and the symbol level that supports it. However, it is the shape of the architecture that gives shape to the psychological regularities at the cognitive level. In agreement with this view, Soar is an architecture and was presented as one in Chapter 4.

The hallmark of a unified theory is the range of central cognition and its surround that it addresses. The number of regularities addressed is only a surrogate for the coverage provided. Thus, central to the case to be made for unified theories is that a single theory can have a broad range. Nothing is more important to illustrate, and once the architecture was out on the table, the remainder of the book, from the last of Chapter 4 through Chapter 7, was devoted to making plausible that a wide range was possible. Throughout this second half of the book, we have been accumulating a box score of the domains covered for our exemplar, Soar. Figure 7-19 provides the latest total. This may seem a little dramatic— or perhaps a little corny. Box scores don't belong to science, but to sports and politics. But some way was needed to emphasize how important coverage is. Once we have one or more unified theories, then what will count is whether a theory covers the particular collection of phenomena that some user of the theory needs. Until then, it is useful to be crass enough to emphasize sheer numbers—sheer coverage.

For Soar, what heads the list in Figure 7-19 is the prediction that humans can be intelligent. Soar's demonstration of this is as good as the state of the art in AI. Functionality, the explanation of how it is possible for humans to be intelligent, is a cornerstone of a theory of cognition. Next is the demonstration that Soar exhibits the qualitative shape of human cognition, though the particular list of global properties of cognitive behavior was ad hoc. Especially for a unified theory, it is important to attend to the in-the-large picture of the human that it presents, not just to how well it predicts detailed experimental results. For it should be possible to think generally and globally about human nature by means of the theory. That should be one of its important uses (Newell, 1990).

Next, we showed that Soar was a theory of immediate responses, those that take only about a second. Since Soar was originally developed to work at the problem-solving level, it was an important demonstration that Soar also applies at the micro level—that the details of its architecture are to be taken seriously. We extended Soar to simple discrete motor-perceptual skills, namely typing. This reinforced the work on immediate-response behavior. It was as close as we could get to motor-perceptual skills, since the total cognitive system (P-E-C-D-M) is still underdeveloped.

Soar provides a theory of acquisition of skills through practice. We showed that Soar still exhibited the power law of practice. Through a rather circuitous route, we described the Soar theory of recognition and recall of verbal material. This aspect of Soar, arising from the solution to the data-chunking problem, demonstrates how an architecture can be a source of unanticipated consequences. We touched on the Soar theory of short-term memory that was implicit in Soar, noting that it was necessarily a purely functional theory in contradistinction to most psychological theories of short-term memory, which posit technological limits. Although Soar's theory has not been well developed, we indicated how it provided a theory of the plethora of short-term memories. Finally, we showed how Soar provided a detailed theory of problem solving, a theory of logical reasoning, and a theory of how instructions are converted into the self-organization for doing new immediate-response tasks. These tasks were another temporal level or two above immediate responses and demonstrated the temporal reach of the theory.

These are the range of things this exemplar unified theory has addressed. Soar has addressed them with varying degrees of success, varying degrees of depth, and varying degrees of coverage. Mostly these limitations reflect where we have had time and energy to push Soar's development. Still, it is one system—one architecture—that does all of these tasks and does them in fair accord with human behavior on the same tasks.

It is important that Soar be seen to be a theory and not a framework of some kind. For instance, it is not a loose verbal framework, which guides the form of invented explanations but does not itself provide them. Nor is it the sort of computational harness system that has begun to appear in Human Factors, in which specific psychological theories can be plugged in as modules, with the framework providing some sort of integration based on task analysis. On the contrary, Soar is a specific theory by means of which one calculates, simulates, and reasons from its fixed structure. When it seems not to be that way—when it seems to be too underdetermined—the difficulty is almost invariably that the other determinants of behavior are not sufficiently known (goals, knowledge, the structure of the task environment). This is a genuine problem for all the human sciences, even more so than for science in general, just because humans, within their heads, bring into any situation so much knowledge of the rest of the world and its history. It is a genuine problem, but it does not make Soar a framework.

Soar is hardly perfect. No scientific theory is, of course. But with Soar just an exemplar, there is no need to conceal its vulnerability throughout. Moreover, we have spent no effort probing the limits of Soar's explanatory adequacy. Instead, we have been driven by the need to show that Soar has the earmarks of a unified theory of cognition. Certainly, the positive description of Soar does not gainsay what still needs to be done to analyze complete sets of regularities in detail and to find where Soar breaks down.

In particular, given the ~~3,000 regularities that have been discovered, there is a long way to go to obtain coverage of the aspects of human cognition about which much is already known. To help make this last point, Figure 8-1 lists a potpourri of areas that have not been addressed by Soar. It would be easy to generate twice as many. I have put them in alphabetical order—what other order is there for a potpourri?

Some of these items may seem peripheral, but some are exceedingly important in probing whether Soar has the right fundamental character. Consider a sampling (the starred items), to appreciate the variety of what is missing. Start with *consciousness*. Soar provides a theory of *awareness*. Soar is aware of something if its deliberate behavior can be made to depend on it. In this sense, awareness is operationally defined and fundamental, and it is a much-used notion throughout cognitive psychology. But consciousness can be

      Arithmetic (simple and multidigit)
      Cognitive styles
* Consciousness (as opposed to awareness)
* Contingencies of reinforcement (animal learning)
* Concept learning, prototypes
      Counting and comparing (also, subitizing and estimating)
      Daydreaming
* Decisions under risk and uncertainty
      Discourse comprehension
* Dreaming
      Dual tasks
      Emotion and affect
* Imagery
      Individual differences
      Intelligence testing
      Lexical access
      Memory for frequency of occurrence
      Memory for items versus memory for order
      Metaphor and analogy
      Motivation (intensity, not directionality)
      Phonemic restoration effect
      Play
* Perceptual decisions
* Priming
      Probability matching
      Same-difference judgments
      Story understanding
      Symbolic comparisons
      Values and morals

Figure 8-1. A potpourri of what Soar has not done.

taken to imply more than awareness in this sense, namely, the phenomenally subjective. It can mean the process, mechanism, state (or whatever) that establishes when and what an honest human would claim to be conscious of, both concurrently or retrospectively.[2] Soar does not touch the phenomena of consciousness, thus designated. Neither does much else in cognitive psychology. That it seems out of reach at the moment might justify pushing the

2. This claim, of course, is filtered through culturally established communication, with the meaning of the term *conscious* established by the same social process involved in any other linguistic term. This certainly complicates matters, but it doesn't get rid of the phenomena of consciousness.

issue into the future, until additional regularities and phenomena accumulate, but the challenge remains.

Contingencies of reinforcement is a term that can be made to stand for a large and well-established body of regularities that link human behavior and animal learning behavior. First, speaking specifically, Soar must explain why (and to what extent) humans obey the various laws established in operant conditioning about how the frequency of specific responses can be brought under the control of specific environmental events. That these regularities have been developed in an area outside cognitive psychology (and which mostly predate cognitive psychology) is not relevant to their status as regularities and to the need for Soar to cover them. Speaking more broadly about the psychology of animal behavior, unification is certainly required. It is already under way from the animal-behavior side (Rescorla, 1988), but the integration needs to be pursued from the human-cognitive side as well.

The areas of *concepts* and *concept learning* was originally defined in terms of categories defined by predicates (Bruner, Goodnow, & Austin, 1956). A person has a concept if he or she can determine whether the predicate was true of a presented object or situation. The area was enriched in the 1970s by being extended to prototypes, where membership was defined by the resemblance of an object to a central category (Rosch & Lloyd, 1978). Hence, an object was a better or worse exemplar of a concept. The extension to prototypes has been taken to imply a fundamental revision of our views of the nature of mind (Lakoff, 1987). At issue is whether the mental world of humans is constructed propositionally, hence with all concepts categorical, or whether in some other way—the same underlying concern that motivates the study of syllogisms. Soar must give an account of prototypes and show how they arise when the situations call for them, just as predicates arise when the situations call for them. Here is a place where it would occasion surprise (at least on my part) if additional architectural assumptions were needed to get these different types of concepts, and others as well. That a processing device that is designed, so to speak, to provide the ultimate flexibility in response functions is limited to computing only predicates would seem passing odd.

Decisions under risk and uncertainty (Pitz & Sachs, 1984) are the domain of behavioral decision theory, whose central concept is *subjective expected utility (SEU)*. Given a set of alternatives, indi-

viduals calculate the utility to be expected on taking each alternative according to their subjective probabilities of what will eventuate and then select the alternative with the highest expected
utility. This is an important area of cognition, which remains isolated in many ways from the rest of cognitive science and psychology, mostly because of its conceptual origins in game theory
and econometrics but also because its typical task situations
(choices among abstract gambles) are of little interest to the rest of
psychology. Ultimately, there must be an integration of this area
into the rest of cognition. Soar is a natural vehicle for bringing
decision theory into the fold because of its strong flavor of intendedly rational behavior, but how Soar will deal with probabil-
istic alternatives and expected outcomes, especially in the abstract
gambling tasks so dear to decision theory, is far from clear.

Both *dreaming* (Foulkes, 1985) and *imagery* (Kosslyn, 1980) are
phenomena that Soar, in its current form, does not deal with. Perhaps progress can be made simply by doing again what we have
now done several times, namely, asking what is the natural way to
generate the appropriate phenomena. But, equally, additions to the
architecture could be required. Indeed, the smart money would go
for the latter. In either case, there is an obligation for Soar to cover
the full range of cognitive phenomena. It is conventional nowadays
not to task a cognitive theory with dreaming, but it takes little
reflection to see that dreaming is a first-order phenomenon. The
capability of dreaming, at least, should be explainable by any
unified cognitive theory worth its salt. On the other hand, thanks to
the imagery debate and to the subsequent explorations and models,
such as Kosslyn's (1980), it may become the norm to include imagery as a standard cognitive phenomenon that must be covered. We
seem to have much further to go before we feel the same way about
dreaming.

In Chapter 1 we discussed research in *perceptual decisions* as a
special harbinger of the convergence of theoretical explanations
into a narrow family involving cumulation of evidence with cutoffs,
modeled by random walks (Figure 1-11). We haven't applied Soar
to this area, because the details of perception are not well enough in
place yet. Some aspects of how Soar would treat these phenomena
are clear. Perceptual decisions that are automatic occur within the
elaboration phase, which is indeed a mechanism for accumulation.
If the perceptual situations are more complex and require some

control, then sequences of minimal operators will be required, analogous to the SRC situations discussed in Chapter 5. But more is specified by the random-walk models. The accumulation is to be additive and the comparisons against the cutoffs are to be quantitative inequalities. Thus, this domain requires that we augment the Soar architecture to deal with primitive quantities. This can be called the problem of the *basic quantitative code*. It is easy to show that an architectural mechanism is required, since the issue is the transduction from perceptual signals, which are clearly quantitative (intensity, direction), to symbols in Soar's representation, and from such symbols to motor signals, which are again clearly quantitative (force, direction). This transduction must not only be built in, it must lead to a representation (code) that is built in. Coming to grips with these phenomena of perceptual decisions will force a significant addition to the Soar architecture. It will also move Soar into an issue that psychophysics should have dealt with long ago but managed mostly to avoid, namely, what are the internal representations of subjective magnitudes. Psychophysics simply assumes that people are able to represent subjective magnitude (such as brightness or degree of pain). For many purposes, this is all that seems necessary—one can characterize the psychophysical function without knowing the representation and one can even calculate it by working with the scientist's external representation of quantities, in radix and floating point. But much that is important about psychophysics may derive from the actual representation used by humans.

Priming provides a basic experimental paradigm for the concept of *activation* (Anderson, 1984). Currently, activation is taken almost entirely for granted in cognitive psychology and is used almost as a descriptive term for broad classes of phenomena. Soar does not have activation as a fundamental construct and undoubtedly this is one of the things that will make Soar unattractive as a theory to many cognitive scientists. Soar should not necessarily provide a construct analogous to activation, but it should be made to explain the priming experiments. Its success would provide strong indications of how the concept of activation is to be dealt with generally. Its failure would open up an important dissonance that could point to how the Soar architecture might be genuinely inadequate.

It is tempting at least to ask of Soar where its treatment of priming might naturally arise. The basic priming experiment (Meyer & Schvaneveldt, 1971) presents to a subject a sequence of independent letter strings, to which the subject responds yes or no whether the string is a word.

(1) . . . cacke—no, truck—yes, butter—yes, . . .
(2) . . . hope—yes, bread—yes, butter—yes, . . .

The response is faster if the string is a high associate of the *previous* word. The response of *yes* to *butter* in line (2), where it follows *bread*, is faster than in line (1), where it follows the neutral word *truck*. The standard interpretation is that the occurrence of *bread* produces a forward association (spreading activation) that makes *butter* more available for a short while. The independence of the actions on each word is important, so there is no task reason to produce any association; independence shows the effect to be automatic. Interestingly, for Soar two alternative paths seem indicated. On the one hand, the elaboration phase of Soar's decision cycle seems to be exactly the right mechanism for autonomous forward associations. The entry of *bread* in working memory provides the element that permits a production for *butter* to fire during that same decision cycle—a forward effect that happens automatically. Thus, *butter* is already in working memory as a known word when it arrives as the next presented stimulus, somehow saving a little time (a few tens of ms). It remains to be discovered how free-association productions might get built in the first place and why the pre-occurrence of some internal representation of *butter* aids in the word/nonword decision. Neither step can be simply posited; they require working out the details. On the other hand, our data-chunking analysis indicates that lexical recognition may proceed by a built-up discrimination mechanism. Perceived strings are words if they come through this process identified as words and are nonwords if they come through it with a failure of identification (they could of course be familiar nonwords). If that is the case, then the forward associational mechanism is located at a quite different place and engages different mechanisms, and the sources of slight speedup are quite different as well. Both of these paths require considerable investigation before an explanation of priming could be available.

The list of what is still to be done goes on and on. Figure 8-1 is a random selection, more or less, and the items we discussed a random subset within that. Though a sample, it could be taken as a way of defining the current frontier for the Soar unified theory of cognition. There is certainly a frontier somewhere out there, though a random list seems a pretty unsatisfactory way of locating it.[3]

A different possibility for describing the frontier is to go back to the list of multiple constraints on mind, which we used in Chapters 1 and 4 (see Figure 8-2). As I said before, a unified theory of cognition must account for how all these constraints are satisfied by the mind. Soar was designed explicitly to deal with the first five constraints plus learning, and it represents hypotheses about what is necessary to take them into account. Perception and motor control are anomalous, in that the design has been augmented to cover them, but the effort is not complete. For all the rest there has been no explicit design of Soar—for language, development, autonomy and socialization, self-awareness, and how to realize the cognitive system by means of neural technology, embryology, and evolution. These aspects can be taken to define the frontier. A unified theory of cognition must ultimately be extendible to provide explanations for how these other constraints are satisfied by the cognitive system.

These unattended items of Figure 8-2 can be used to construct a tour along the frontier. Touring the frontier is a proper way to conclude this book. We shall ask what Soar has to say about language, development, the social band, and the biological band. The frontier of a theory consists of more than just scientific domains. There is also a large frontier facing the applications of the theory. We need to consider at least one representative application to complete our considerations, though the frontier differs for different applications. We will let human-computer interaction be that representative. Along the frontier, we will be even more speculative than we have been in the earlier chapters. From the point of view of Soar as an exemplar, the following sections are exercises in how a unified theory copes with phenomena outside the domain of its design.

3. No two candidate unified theories will have anything like the same frontier. Certainly the other candidates mentioned in Chapter 1—Act*, the collective systems in *Induction* (Holland, Holyoak, Nisbett, & Thagard, 1987), MHP, or CAPS—focus on quite different domains. Not until deliberate efforts are made for all theories to attain the same coverage will there be a common frontier, which will then express the border of the scientifically unknown.

1. Behave flexibly as a function of the environment   yes

2. Exhibit adaptive (rational, goal-oriented) behavior   yes

3. Operate in real time   yes

4. Operate in a rich, complex, detailed environment
   - Perceive an immense amount of changing detail   interface only
   - Use vast amounts of knowledge   yes
   - Control a motor system of many degrees of freedom   interface only

5. Use symbols and abstractions   yes

6. Use language, both natural and artificial   no

7. Learn from environment and from experience   yes

8. Acquire capabilities through development   no

9. Operate autonomously, but within a social community   no

10. Be self-aware and have a sense of self   no

11. Be realizable as a neural system   no

12. Be constructable by an embryological growth process   no

13. Arise through evolution   no

Figure 8-2. The design of Soar and the multiple constraints on mind.

8.1. Language

Language is a central feature of human mind-like activity. As noted in the first chapter, I have stayed away from theorizing about language, because I find it formidable in terms of the collection of results that has accumulated and the degree of controversy that seems to attend competing views in linguistics. There seems no way to enter the fray with a little theory, even a highly approximate one. To do so is to invite the wrath of the linguistic gods. Full blown from the brow of Zeus or nothing! Clearly, though, any unified theory of cognition must include a theory of language and language acquisition. Indeed, we have sidled up to one already in the last chapter. So, in this more speculative chapter, let us see how Soar would approach linguistic phenomena.

In a fashion familiar from earlier chapters, we can read out the general outlines of the natural theory of language that Soar provides. At a high level, there is not much choice about what it should be. Language, in Soar, is handled by the cognitive architecture. Hence, it is a cognitive phenomenon. Language starts externally and ends externally. Consequently, it is a perceptual-motor phenomenon and so engages the whole *P-E-C-D-M* structure of perception to encoding to cognition to decoding to motor behavior. If one were to mark all the apparatus that was touched by language, it would be seen to course throughout the total cognitive system, not just central cognition.

Moreover, language is patently a skill. Hence, in Soar, it will be learned as other skills are learned, namely, through chunking. Language in Soar is a totally functional behavior—because Soar itself is a totally functional system (recall the discussion of short-term memory in Chapter 6). That is, Soar is a system in which everything is organized, not as independent subsystems of data and process but as elements that will work in problem spaces to resolve impasses. A fortiori, language will be dealt with from a functional standpoint. Those functions of course will be the functions of the human, and indeed of local circumstances as well as larger ones. It is easy enough to denote the overall function as communication, requiring comprehension of utterances on input and encoding and production of utterances on output, but it is not easy to discover what these functions amount to in detail, a problem that depends on the way they are decomposed into problem spaces.

This view of language, that it is embedded in cognition, is simply the *obvious* readout from Soar—it is how Soar would naturally deal with language. It contrasts with much work in linguistics and psycholinguistics, which posits special mechanisms for dealing with language. The contrast is hardly novel, but runs along familiar lines long drawn in discussions between linguistics and psychology. Still, some discussion of this issue is worthwhile, but I will put it off to the end of the section.

8.1.1. Language Comprehension
This readout I've just presented simply locates language within Soar to be dealt with by the usual apparatus of problem spaces and

Interpret the environment by comprehension operators
Comprehension operator
• Execute on any object that is not comprehended
• Produce data structures (the comprehensions)
   Interpreted by being used (by productions)
   Thereby becoming productions (by chunking)
Applies to all situations requiring comprehension
• Language, vision, . . . (terminals and nonterminals)
Operates within a context of expectations
• An expectation is a data structure of partial comprehension
• Required by the task, since comprehension-operators are local
   A word can have pre- and post-expectations

Figure 8-3. The comprehension-operator principle.

impasses. Figure 8-3 shows the next step for comprehension. In Chapter 7 we actually had an example of Soar comprehending a few very simple English sentences. The mechanisms used there constitute the natural theory of language for Soar. Its central principle is the *comprehension-operator principle*. Soar interprets the environment by applying *comprehension operators* to specific aspects of an environment that it wants to comprehend. A comprehension operator is simply an operator in the *comprehension problem space*, which is evoked to comprehend an environment where it is not known in advance exactly what aspects and arrangements of aspects yield the to-be-acquired knowledge. Comprehension operators are executed repeatedly on the various aspects of the environment that are recognized until the total comprehension emerges in terms of Soar's use of it. What gets produced by executing a comprehension operator is a data structure in the current state that is the comprehension, by virtue of its being interpretable by other parts of Soar in doing other tasks. As it is used by other productions (in operators or in search control) in other spaces, the temporarily held comprehension data structures become chunked, and thus get converted into productions, finally becoming assimilated into long-term memory.

That is the Soar theory of language in a nutshell. It seems so general as to be almost tautological, but it has exactly the generality necessary to be applicable in all situations and the degree of specificity, when embedded in the structure of the rest of the Soar architecture (problem spaces, operators, impasses, chunking), to be actually operational. We saw parts of it in action in Chapter 7 in

Figures 7-14 to 7-17. In the *Star is above plus* example, Soar executed a series of comprehension operators on the incoming sentence, one for each word. It then applied comprehension operators to the picture. The result was a structure that evoked operators to compare the encodings and to perform the task required (to judge whether the sentence was true of the picture).

This is a theory of how Soar deals with any uncomprehended aspect of an external environment, whether linguistic, auditory, visual, or whatever. Thus, it applies to both the sentence and picture. It applies to internal aspects as well, thus to partially constructed objects (such as what corresponds to nonterminals in a developing analysis of an utterance). What is specifically linguistic about the theory is the knowledge that the environment is producing linguistic utterances or text, and the knowledge of language.

A comprehension operator is not a highly general operator that knows nothing. On the contrary, a separate comprehension operator exists for every word. This individualized comprehension operator embodies the specific knowledge of what it means to have that word in that particular context. It embodies knowledge of the word senses, the syntax, the semantics, the discourse, and the larger context. Thus, the comprehension-operator principle is a hypothesis about the form in which linguistic knowledge is held, not about the content of that knowledge.

The theory implies that language action is entirely local, since an operator is fired for each object as it comes along (each word, for language). Sometimes the knowledge is available in the current state for the comprehension operator to produce a structure that represents the comprehension, but this need not be the case, and indeed language systematically exploits the occurrence of multiple words distributed over substantial stretches of an utterance to determine the intended meaning. In consequence, comprehension operators must be able to produce at execution time structures that hold what the operators do know, even though the remaining knowledge needed to produce comprehension has not yet arrived. Such structures are, in essence, *expectations*, since their only role is to be used later by other applications of comprehension operators. Thus, language interpretation operates within a context of expectations. This is not an added assumption but a necessary consequence of the comprehension-operator principle. Language is such that when a word in a sentence is heard, it gives knowledge about how to interpret the other parts of the utterance as well as knowledge about the reference domain of the utterance. Given this fact about language, given the decision for local operators, and given the Soar architecture, then expectation data structures follow.

For example, the word *hit* (designating an action) expects a *pre-object* (the hitter). This expectation is both about the semantics (what kinds of things can be hitters) and about the linguistic forms that can designate them (noun phrases). It expects knowledge about them to be around already (which is why we called it a pre-object). Likewise, *hit* expects a *post-object* (the thing that was hit), and again this expectation comprises both semantic knowledge and linguistic knowledge. Any other word, such as *Jim*, also has expectations, one of which can be the things that a *Jim* can do (to wit, hit). Thus, expectations are not exclusively associated with verbs, although, as the study of case grammars shows, fairly comprehensive schemes can be built by associating all expectations with verbs.[4]

The Soar scheme seems extraordinarily simple. Nothing has been added but the commitment to execute so-called comprehension operators one after the other. Yet, there is a fair yield from this simple assumption. First, we know from the Soar architecture and how it attains general problem solving that this scheme is indefinitely powerful (not *all-powerful*, only having no a priori fixed limit). An operator (here, a comprehension operator) can lead to problem spaces to implement it that can open up to any kind of problem solving whatsoever. The results of such problem solving can be brought back to bear on the difficulty (the impasse) that evoked the problem solving. Thus, the simplicity in the comprehension-operator scheme does not lie in any limitation of activity,

---

4. A side note: This paragraph exhibits in clear form how the knowledge level actually gets used in practice. The paragraph says (repeatedly) that a word *expects* something, for example "*hit* expects a *post-object*." This is short for saying that Soar expects something when it encounters the word in an utterance, and that this expectation is embodied in the comprehension operator of the word, which will thereby take appropriate action on the basis of its knowledge, the appropriateness deriving from the goals of Soar, via the occurrence of a nest of impasses. Thus, a symbol-level description of how Soar understands language is made in terms of knowledge-level descriptions of symbol-level mechanisms, which relate to the knowledge-level description of Soar, taken as a given. *Expectation* is a knowledge-level term, since it does not refer to how the expectation is represented or the processes that operationalize it. Indeed, what is being spun out here concerns these symbol-level matters. With this semantic background, saying that "*hit* expects a *post-object*" is a legitimate use of language.

but in not having elaborate machinery at the top level that is to be evoked willy-nilly. Elaboration comes in, when it does, in the act of attempting to comprehend.

That the comprehension operator combines knowledge of syntax, semantics, discourse, the task, and background context necessarily follows from the scheme. It is not an independent assumption. The comprehension operator is the only way that knowledge is brought to bear. To claim some knowledge is not in the comprehension operator, say some semantic or discourse knowledge, is to claim that the knowledge is not in fact brought to bear. This may be true in some cases, but that is an empirical assertion about a particular word, not an assertion about the computational scheme.

Grammatical constructions arise from the forms of the expectations—phrase structure, word order, complex constructions. To say it again, this is not a novel theory of language; it has much in common with other expectation-driven systems (Small, 1979) and even with systems that don't declare outright their expectational character (MacWhinney, 1987a). Soar tends to be like those theories that fit with the rest of the cognitive structure that Soar has. After all, the fundamental issue is what *knowledge* of language, communication, and task is to be brought to bear. Given that the expectations are in the direction expected—adjacent before it and adjacent after it, with due regard for the possibility of interposed words—then the usual dependency and phrase-structure diagrams describe what is going on. This scheme works not only for natural language but also for formal and artificial kinds of notations. In fact, the first place we used the comprehension-operator scheme was in acquiring tasks from notations typical of programming languages.

This theory of language is embedded in a unified theory of cognition. Thus, additional implications arise immediately. For instance, the approximate speed of reading is immediately determined, along with a number of additional chronometric aspects of the reading task. Without being very precise about it, because it is only a single, simple sample, we can look back at the comprehension trace in Figure 7-14. It executes a few operators per word (mostly, read-word, install-node, and comprehend). If we assume that these operators are well practiced (language is highly skilled behavior), then they would seem to be minimal operators, working at ~60 ms, in terms of what we used for the chronometric analysis of immediate-response behavior in Chapter 5. That yields ~180 ms per word or about 330 words/min.

Various factors could make reading speed faster or slower. There is extra time at the end of the sentence (inspecting the figure indicates a couple of operators' worth, for ~120 ms), arising from the refiring of comprehension operators as their expectations become satisfied. This is in agreement with much psychological analysis, which puts the time in the ballpark of ~100 ms (Just & Carpenter, 1987). The delay slows reading down, though not very much. Some comprehension operators take longer than minimal time, which would also slow reading down. On the other hand, we have not taken into account the issue of whether there would really have to be read-word or install-node operators in series with comprehend, or whether they can in part run along concurrently with comprehension operators. That depends on the details of the *P-E-C-D-M* structure. The *P-E-C* structure will make its own contribution to reading rate in the identification of words, and it could become the limiting factor with long words. We know from the human data that word length seems to be the strongest effect in reading rates. If we estimate the absolute upper bound for central speed it would be ~60 ms per word (one operator per word), or ~1,000 word/min. If we estimate the absolute upper bound for perceptual speed, using ~20 ms per letter (Figure 5-11), then we get ~100 ms per word or ~600 words/min. The situation is one of concurrent processes and hence critical-path analysis, analogous to the situation we examined in transcription typing (Figure 5-17). So the effective maximum lies somewhere between the two.

Without the perceptual embedding system in place and without a more extensive development of the language system, such an exercise in inferring psychological phenomena can be only a plausibility check. If the numbers were way out of line in some respect, it could signal an important difficulty with Soar. As it is, the various estimates are all comfortably within acceptable ranges. However, the exercise can operate as a reminder that all of the other psychological properties of a unified theory of cognition become relevant. No sooner is there a theory of language then there is also a theory of language performance, with all the implications that the experimental data bring. To mention one more, Marslen-Wilson and Tyler's (1980) results about information being available from language comprehension within ~50 ms imply that we should expect some sort of concurrency with the mechanics of moving through the words (the read-word and install-node operators), or else ~120 ms goes by before one gets any information from the comprehension. On the other hand, given that concurrency, then Soar is quite capable of delivering the sorts of information in these experiments within the time ranges indicated.

8.1.2. Language Learning

Language learning must happen by the chunking of comprehension operators. Words will arrive that are unknown to Soar or have unknown senses or cause the comprehension to go awry. These should lead at some point to Soar not knowing what to do, which is to say, getting an impasse of some sort. Impasses should evoke problem solving on the part of Soar, which when successful should lead to the chunking of new comprehension operators, or the chunking of new additions to old ones. Thus, language learning should occur gradually, chunk by chunk, filling out comprehension operators from experience by problem solving in the context of language use. This much is essentially given by the Soar architecture, plus the adoption of the comprehension-operator principle and the context of language use. One reason comprehension operators seem right is that they come with a theory about how they will be acquired.

In general, Soar can learn anything, but what, in fact, Soar learns depends on the tasks that are posed (whether by an external agent, the environment, or Soar itself). The nontrivial issues are what the tasks should be to learn a specific thing and how these tasks should be posed. The story in Chapter 6 on data chunking and its resolution provides one lesson about how Soar learns. Therefore, although the overall picture above can be taken as an initial sketch, we must reserve judgment until more details are available.

To push this claim a little, we can attempt once more to play our standard strategy of seeing whether we can get Soar to do some small bit of language acquisition, to see what the resulting structure looks like.[5] This task will at least take us beyond the general characterizations above and let us know whether some difficulties are hiding immediately beneath the surface.

Let us go back to the simple example we used in Chapter 7. Instead of the utterance *Plus is above star*, we will use a different word for the subject of the sentence—*Check is above star*—and

5. This is work by Gregg Yost.

Soar does not know the word *check* and hence (necessarily) does not know it refers to $\sqrt{}$. This is about the simplest sort of situation in which something is to be learned within the language structure itself. It is learning a lexical item rather than a bit of syntax, but it is a start.

It would seem, as noted above, that in processing this sentence with the unknown word Soar should get some sort of an impasse. But, in fact, it doesn't. The reason is not far to seek. Explicit expectations are a device for providing a form of loosely-coupled computational organization. Comprehension operators put expectations into working memory, at their pleasure, so to speak, and only if the appropriate information arrives from other comprehension operators (at *their* pleasure) will later evocations occur that finish the comprehension. When some information fails to become available, all that happens is that nothing gets evoked later on.[6] It might appear that we have stumbled upon another genuine difficulty, but the problem is only one of not using relevant available knowledge. Let us rephrase the difficulty. Because of the openness of expectations, the comprehension-operator strategy does not know whether things are going right or wrong, so the solution lies not in modifying the strategy but in making available the requisite knowledge. The system needs to know when it comprehends. There is no way to know this with absolute certainty, for the system does not already comprehend what it is attempting to comprehend and hence has no way of knowing whether the comprehension that it has manufactured is right. This is the existential situation of the language user in a real world, which nothing can change. The interesting question is what surrogate criteria are available. In an expectation-driven system the natural criterion is whether expectations are satisfied. To put the matter in an apparent tautology—what more can you expect than the fulfillment of all your expectations about the utterance?

Thus, Soar must not only have expectations for what is coming, it must also have expectations that its expectations will be satisfied. It cannot expect every expectation to be satisfied. Many expectations are alternatives to other expectations—for example, different word

6. This is typical of cooperative computation, in which global properties such as termination, success, and failure are system properties unknown to the individual processing elements.

senses, only one of which can be satisfied on a given occasion. Soar's expectations are structured as disjunctive sets of expectations, plus an expectation that at least one of the set must be satisfied. This latter expectation includes an expectation of when the other expectations will be satisfied—for instance, by the end of the sentence. It is these expectations about the satisfaction of other expectations that finally put bounds on the comprehension effort, so Soar doesn't go on forever, day after day, waiting for some final bit of information to arrive.

Figure 8-4 shows a high-level trace of Soar doing this elementary bit of language learning. Operators are in brackets, and the comprehension operators are italicized. Soar starts through the sentence. When it reads *check* nothing happens, because it doesn't know anything about *check*.[7] Then the comprehension operator for *is* fires, putting two expectations in working memory. Angle brackets indicate expectations. Then the comprehension operator *[above]* fires. It expects a post-object, and this expectation is placed in working memory. Finally comes *[star]*, which produces a particular bit of semantics that says there is an object called *star*. Objects in the task domain are in parentheses. This permits the *[above]* operator to fire a second time, producing the domain object *(above star)*. This is exactly what happened in the original sentence of *Plus is above star*. That ends the sentence; since no more words arrive, hence no more comprehension operators fire. If, per contra, Soar had known *check*, then an object corresponding to it would have been around and the *[is]* operator would then have been evoked a second time.

Soar is now in a situation where some unsatisfied expectations are lying around (two, actually). At the end of the sentence, the expectation that there shouldn't be unsatisfied expectations at the end of a sentence causes the [handle-incomprehension] operator to fire. This operator is not a comprehension operator, but one that recognizes unfulfilled expectations that demand to be satisfied. Soar descends into an implementation subspace. There, the first operator to fire generates interpretations. It examines the situation

---

7. Soar could have an expectation that it will know every word it receives. Most adults do, although children don't. An expectation of this sort would provide another path for evoking language learning, which would help for completely unknown words, as here, but not for words with missing word senses or for known words used inappropriately. In general, multiple paths for detecting error will exist.

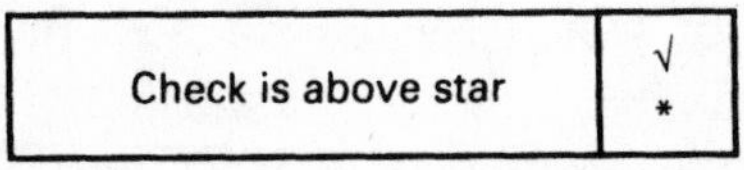

Check is above star	√ *

(Soar does not know what √ means)

1. *[check]*
2. *[is]* ⇒ <pre-obj> <post-property>
3. *[above]* ⇒ <post-obj>
4. *[star]* ⇒ (obj)
5. *[above]* ⇒ (above star)
6. [handle-incomprehension]
7.   [generate-interpretations] ⇒ [check → (obj)]_{data}
8.   [interpret]
9.   [check]
10.   [apply-operator]
11.   [match]
12.   [match]
13.   [install]
14.   {chunk [check]}
15.   *[is]* ⇒ (is check (above star))

Legend
[operator]
[comprehension operator]
<expectation>
(object structure)
{chunking}
⇒ the result of an operator
→ chunk (production)

Figure 8-4. Soar acquisition of language.

and asks what are the plausible hypotheses that could satisfy the unsatisfied expectations. This is a heuristic generator that produces plausible hypotheses for what could satisfy the unfulfilled expectations. It is not blind, of course, since it can examine these expectations as well as the surrounding context of sentence analysis. In the present case, it hypothesizes that if the word *check* would create a domain object, then this would satisfy the existing dangling expectations. [Generate-interpretations] produces a data structure that represents this comprehension operator for the word *check*. In the trace, this object is put in brackets like an operator but is labeled *data*, so its role is not mistaken.

In this simple example, only this one hypothesis gets generated. In more complicated situations than this, a collection of hypotheses would be generated. This would lead to a tie impasse and into a selection space to decide which one to attend to first. Immediate search control might tell right away which is the most likely hypothesis. Otherwise, the whole apparatus of problem solving for selection could be evoked to help choose which interpretation to pursue first.

In this case, with $[check \rightarrow (obj)]_{data}$ the only choice, Soar is able to move on to execute the [interpret] operator. This operator goes back into the comprehension space and proceeds to permit firing of whatever comprehension operators can fire. *Check* can fire immediately. It has an associated data structure, which *interpret* knows defines a comprehension operator that's supposed to be applied to the word *check*. Soar goes into a further subspace and fires an *apply-operator*. This operator actually interprets the data structure in terms of matching the requisite elements and producing instantiated results—in effect it simulates production matching and execution.

Execution of the operator by interpreting it leads to the creation of a chunk. This chunk is exactly what would have been in the comprehension operator for *check*, if that operator had been built by hand (the way the one for *plus* was in fact built). Thus, Soar has actually learned a new comprehension operator.

Soar continues after the execution of the apply-operator (the chunking being a side effect). The comprehension operator for *[is]* can now execute, since the (interpreted) operator for *check* put *(obj)* into working memory. Soar does not go back and reinterpret the whole sentence; it just proceeds to interpret what it doesn't comprehend again until it's satisfied. Thus the trace ends when Soar returns to the state it was in, prepared to comprehend the next sentence.

So far, all that has happened is that the definition of *check* as an object has been created. Soar hasn't linked *check* with the $\sqrt{}$ in the figure. That missing link would not be discovered in the midst of interpreting the sentence. Rather, it would be found in the context of attempting the rest of the task, that is, in comparing the comprehension structure from the sentence with the comprehension structure from picture. Then Soar would find two items being compared that were not just unequal, but disparate. It would then be in a position to generate a hypothesis that the object the word stands for is the mark in the picture. Once that was linked up, the result would gravitate back into the comprehension operator as well. These last steps haven't actually been attempted, but the part in Figure 8-4 works.

8.1.3. Reflections on Soar and Language

Where have we gotten to? We decided that Soar has to be able to move toward a theory of language. Once more, we've played our standard game. First, we read out of the Soar architecture the general features of a natural theory of language. Then we pushed Soar a little bit down this path, first for language comprehension and then for language acquisition.

Even at this preliminary stage, the theory can be seen to have some strong characteristics and attractive features. It shows comprehension to be a skilled activity that occurs in real time. It provides a way for semantic considerations of whatever depth to integrate with syntactic knowledge. It provides the outlines of a theory of language acquisition integrated with Soar's theory of linguistic performance. It places language acquisition in the context of performing tasks that use language. That is, it provides a theory of when the occasions of learning occur and how the knowledge from that occasion transfers back to the language system itself. All of these aspects come along because the theory is embedded within Soar as a preexisting unified theory; they do not have to be posited separately as part of the theory of language.

All the above is laid out only in outline form. The three examples, two of performance in Chapter 7 and one of learning in this chapter, serve as guarantors that there is reality behind the outline, but almost everything is still missing relative to the state of linguistics.

The biggest issue is grammar. There is no question that a grammar can be built with comprehension operators, given the scheme's family membership in the class of expectation-based grammars. There are by now a large variety of schemes for the syntactic structure of natural language, many with substantial linguistic success and some also reflecting psycholinguistic aspects (Sells, 1987; Mac-Whinney, 1987b). In fact, the situation in linguistics seems analogous to the situation described in Chapter 1 on the decision process (Figure 1-11). Theories are possible, they must be detailed to provide explanations and predictions, but any of a large family of theories, differing in details, is essentially equivalent to the others.

The issue for Soar is how grammatical regularities are going to show up. Linguistics has many well-established grammatical regularities that hold across a given language in terms of highly abstract classifications (and apply uniformly to all human languages). This seems to contrast with the word-centered comprehension-operator scheme, where each operator is a separate entity. How will this scheme be able to exhibit these regularities? No definitive answer can be given, of course, but certain things can be noted.

First, whether language-wide regularities emerge in the comprehension-operator scheme depends on how the operators are structured internally. If sets of operators corresponding to significant classes of words have common processes, then they will exhibit regularities. The form of comprehension operators does not preclude system-wide regularities.

Second, even granting this first point, the regularities will be embodied extremely redundantly, with structure duplicated in every operator. This may strike some as simply too improbable a way for it to be, for a single regularity would seem to imply a locus for that regularity within the system. Such a reaction is based on an architectural intuition, however, and one that is misplaced for experiential learning systems, such as Soar. If we view Soar as a living system, we assume it will acquire structure from each experience throughout its waking life, amounting to $\sim 10^6$ chunks per year. The architecture is technologically structured to accommodate this process of accumulation throughout the lifespan. Thus, very large amounts of structure can be expected to be devoted to any domain, such as language, that occupies substantial fractions of life. Further, this structure will be immensely redundant, because experience is immensely redundant. It is to be expected that the same knowledge will be encoded redundantly in many places, though with variations due to the variation of experience.

Third, the source of the regularity must be learning. Soar's chunking is like a pipe that transmits knowledge encoded in some problem spaces into other problem spaces. Suppose, to adopt one obvious arrangement, that whenever a comprehension operator impasses, a common space is used to engage in the problem-solving activities to successfully employ the operator. The common structure of this space, as embodied in its operators and state representation, will get transferred into the specific operators. If this space reflects the appropriate linguistic regularities, then these regularities will show up in the individual comprehension operators.

Fourth, the prior point drives the source of linguistic regularities back to the structure of this *basic-language space* and to the question of where this space comes from.[8] A key aspect of this space is its symbols, the symbols that are used for the states in this space and the operators. These symbols play the role of the primitive grammatical categories, such as noun phrase, verb phrase, determiner, and the like. As the variety of syntax systems show, there is some freedom in the formulation of an adequate category system for language. What is important is that a category system must exist. Categories can simply be posited as the given structure of the base space, analogously to the way they are posited in almost all grammars. However, the question of the origin of the categories will surely not be far away.

Assuming all the above to work out, there is little to indicate that the Soar comprehension-operator scheme will be radically different from existing schemes. Rather, I think that it can be safely assumed it will be consonant with the existing family of parsing schemes. All of these reflect the same basic regularities of language, and the Soar scheme must as well. In sum, although no strong answer can be provided to whether Soar and the comprehension-operator scheme can show language-wide regularities, the path toward exploring this question is fairly well marked.

We have enunciated what seems the obvious Soar theory of language. It could be different. The comprehension-operator principle is an added assumption beyond the Soar architecture, analogous to the assumption of annotated models. Like the latter, it does not seem to be an additional architectural assumption, but rather a way of organizing and representing specific task domains. Certainly, Soar can process language by other means. Indeed, early on we did construct Dypar-Soar, a version of Soar that parsed natural language according to the case-based scheme in the Dypar parser (Boggs & Carbonell, 1983). But humans, as well, can parse sentences by other means than their naturally acquired mode of comprehending. Linguists of different persuasions prove this every day by their practice in applying their own theories. Their behavior is deliberate, of course. With practice this behavior also becomes

---

8. Whether chunking can transmit the regularities to the comprehension operators is also a valid issue, though we don't pursue it.

skilled, though presumably it does not attain the degree of automation of the way that humans naturally process language.

Actually, it is not evident whether any real degrees of freedom exist for Soar language, whether one could adopt as the central mechanism in linguistic processing some other scheme, such as Lexical-Functional Grammar (Bresnan, 1982). There are many constraints from Soar that must be satisfied, other than just those of syntax. The comprehension-operator scheme must comprehend language, not just parse it. It must extend to the use of language, to discourse (for example, speech acts), and to language learning. Furthermore, it must be computationally realized by means of problem spaces, operators, and impasses. Most important of all, it must operate in close to real time, which forces linguistic processing to fit the architecture like a glove.

It is worth discussing one alternative to the operator-comprehension scheme, namely, *modularity* (Fodor, 1983). Modularity is an architectural assumption that language comprehension occurs in its own processing system that is separate from the processing system for general cognition. In particular, analysis of phonological, lexical, and syntactic aspects of the incoming utterance occurs without the dynamic participation of knowledge of semantics, discourse context, or task context. Modularity does not specify the actual language-analysis scheme, especially within the family of familiar grammars. It does exclude a large class of schemes, namely, those that integrate semantics and other more general sources of knowledge. Modularity is receiving substantial attention currently (Garfield, 1989), not only for language but for other specialized mental functions, such as perception.[9]

The Soar comprehension-operator scheme is certainly nonmodular as it stands, if we look at its structure vis-à-vis central cognition. It is the natural way to handle language in Soar precisely because it makes use of the processing facilities that are there. On the other hand, the Soar architectural structure would admit additional processing modules. In engineering terms, the total cognitive system (Figure 4-15) is a bus-oriented system, and additional modules besides *P, M,* and *C* (general cognition) could be hung on the bus.

---

9. Fodor (1983) casts the issue of modularity quite generally. For our purposes, we narrow the discussion to language, which was also a central concern of Fodor's.

Independent of anything concerned with language, such a module might be indicated for imagery (Kosslyn, 1980). Nothing says that a system (here Soar) should not have multiple processing modules. Positive reasons can come from considerations of processing or from how subsystems were created in the first place.

Fodor (1983, p. 37) characterized modules as systems that are domain specific, innately specified, hard-wired, autonomous, and not assembled. Most of these properties are not easily determined for systems known only through their behavior, such as language. So in arguing for language to be modular, he refined this list to be: domain specificity, mandatory operation, limited central access to intermediate states, fast operation, informationally encapsulated, shallow outputs, neural specificity, breakdown specificity, and fixed ontogeny. One way to explore the relation of Soar to modularity is to ask where the comprehension-operator scheme resides on these various dimensions. Unfortunately, the list is rather a long one. For some of the items, in particular the last three, no characterization of Soar seems possible. These seem to have relatively less weight in any event. For the other six something can be said, though even here we must be brief. The question is not to what extent modularity, as delineated by Fodor, characterizes human mental operations, but what Soar looks like if considered along the dimensions that characterize modular systems.

On *domain specificity*, Fodor notes that all language processors are domain specific in that they process language. This doesn't help much, so he points to the eccentricity of the domain (its special characteristics), to which the processor (the module) becomes highly tuned. For language, the eccentricity is universal grammar and the intricacy of current syntactic systems constitutes the tuning. Although, per above, we can't say much about universal grammar, chunking is precisely a system for constructing specific mechanisms tuned to the features of an environment. In Soar, the generality of cognition is not that every situation must be treated generally, but that generality is always possible when knowledge is missing (impasses) and that the construction of special-purpose mechanisms (chunks) works to avoid future breakout.

On *mandatory operation,* Fodor focuses on the fact that one must treat received speech as speech—that the option exists of turning away, but not of hearing it differently (as nonspeech). Soar's recognition memory is, of course, also mandatory in the same sense, the option for doing something different coming at the decision cycle. The key question is how Soar will process the speech signal as something else (as opposed to attending to something else). It has built up the skill for processing the speech signal as speech. It has no other built-up skill for processing speech as something else. If it turns its recognition system on it (the earlier encoding productions and finally comprehension operators), then it will produce speech comprehension. Fodor dismisses the evidence for making processes nonmandatory with large amounts of practice, but such large amounts of practice seem to be what is involved in the skills under discussion becoming mandatory.

On *limited central access,* the issue is the unavailability to other (more central) processes of presumed intermediate levels of representation, namely, acoustic, phonetic, lexical, and syntactic form. In general, in recognition-based systems, processes have access only to what they can recognize. They are blind to other encoded knowledge in the system. For there to be lots of cross-transfer of knowledge by multiple examination of it in working memory, the knowledge must have been put into a common code. The real problem for Soar may be how to get significant communality, not how to avoid it. One difficulty in addressing this issue is that our experience with systems such as Soar is mostly with human system-designers positing common representations, given their intelligent prevision of what they want to happen. Only as we move to more autonomous modes of operation, as hinted at by the attempt to get Soar to take task instructions, will we see these issues clearly.

On *fast operation,* Fodor discusses the fact that language comprehension is a real-time activity that presses close to the operation of the neural technology. This, of course, was the subject of Chapter 3, and Soar has been constructed to be a system that satisfies the real-time constraint. The trace in Figure 7-15 indicates how Soar may be able to run comprehension in real time, although a much more complete language system is required to verify this.

On *information encapsulation,* which is the limitation of the sources of knowledge available for language comprehension, Fodor brings forth two major considerations. First, relative autonomy of input from belief and desire is functional for the organism (so it sees what is there). Second, processing difficulties will arise if input processing is opened up to all the centrally held beliefs that could conceivably be relevant (for example, contemplating all that has been written about panthers as part of recognizing a panther in the path). Fodor's discussion on information encapsulation is extensive and convoluted, because there are many effects that superficially weigh in on each side of the argument, such as the resistance of illusions to modification by beliefs in their illusory nature, and the phoneme-restoration effect that people perceive phonemes that are not in the input signal under suitable masking. As to the first consideration, Soar's distinguishing belief from perceived reality would seem to be primarily a representational issue of being able to discriminate the sources of knowledge. We need a more definitive commitment on Soar's part to the way perceived information is encoded to assess the issue of confusion. As to the second consideration, Soar is certainly a system that is prepared to permit cognitive considerations to penetrate into perceptual processing. Whether Soar would ever be overwhelmed by a loss of control in a great rush of cogitations seems dubious. Comprehension is structured as a real-time process, by means of the comprehension operators. Arbitrary cognitions can be brought to bear through impasses, but these are relatively infrequent and carry no characteristic loss of control. Indeed, impasses occur from a lack of knowledge in the ongoing process (here, input comprehension) and their search for distal knowledge is driven by relevant knowledge that is obtained in the process.

On *shallow outputs,* which is the question of what knowledge the language input module delivers to general cognition, Fodor mostly discusses what is implied by the other properties of modularity (fast processing, encapsulation, and so on) for the content of the output of the language module. There do not seem to be additional independent considerations or evidence that can be brought to bear to help establish the nature of a modular system. The intent of the discussion is to make plausible that something like the linguistic and logical form of perceived utterances constitutes the content of the output. Likewise, we don't get useful new considerations from the examples we have of Soar comprehension. In our small examples, the output representation is clear enough (the models of the situation), but too simple to see whether so much knowledge can be delivered as to be dissonant with some criterion of shallowness of output. One difficulty is that we haven't gone far enough to discover what the inner structure of comprehension operators must be like—which is what governs what knowledge comprehension can encode into the output representation (except for additions from a few impasses). A second difficulty is that we haven't yet pursued revealing test cases, such as ironic statements (discussed by Fodor); it would be interesting to see whether (or when, or by what preparatory encodings) irony is delivered as part of the comprehension process.

The upshot of this iteration through the criteria for modularity is genuine ambiguity. Structurally, Soar is a nonmodular system for language comprehension, because it uses exactly the same mechanisms for comprehension as it does for general cognition. But the system will behave in strongly modular ways. Or so it seems—the story is hardly clear. However, the source of the ambiguity is not far to seek. Soar is a cognitive system that continually specializes itself on the basis of experience. This drives it to meet the fast-operation constraint and also drives it to have many of the other modularity properties for highly skilled activities.

One lesson in this for unified theories of cognition echoes the secondary theme of Chapter 6—there are more possibilities in architectures than might be imagined. The research on modularity consists mostly of high-level arguments that attempt to establish strong general properties of the class of architectures for the human mind. This research works with a sketchy characterization of the architecture for language processing and an almost null characterization of the architecture for general cognition. For the latter, it relies mostly on the functional requirement that any knowledge must be able to be brought to bear. This is essentially a knowledge-level characterization. It does not have a sharp enough characterization to discover that classes of architectures for general cognition can have the structure to appear modular under the appropriate conditions. This appearance is not a unique property of Soar, of course. It will tend to hold for systems that learn from experience in the general manner of chunking.

8.2. Development

Let us move on to another point along the frontier—the development of cognitive capabilities in children. It is not possible to talk about the psychology of development in the second half of the twentieth century without starting with Jean Piaget. It is he who has structured the whole field, establishing conceptually the notion that development occurs in *stages* and providing the field with an entire array of tasks by which to assess and analyze the growth of cognitive capabilities (Piaget, 1977). Conservation tasks, set-inclusion tasks, seriation tasks—on and on it goes. Each task is performed with different degrees of success and in remarkably different ways by children of different ages, these differences marking out stages of cognitive growth. The tasks are literally the woof through which we trace the warp of cognitive development. There are, of course, limits, even to genius and long life. Though Piaget provided us with the notion of stages, he did not provide us with any notion of the processes that take the child through the stages. He certainly talked about such processes in highly general terms— about *assimilation, accommodation*, and *equilibration*, to name the big three. But to modern ears, even just a few years after Piaget has died, it all sounds mostly like prolegomena, not like actual process models of what is going on.

With the cognitive revolution came the information-processing reformulation of Piagetian psychology. This stream of work accepts the framework of tasks as developed by Piaget and his collaborators and works within it. In an important sense it is neo-Piagetian, in that it attempts to extend and refine what Piaget brought to development rather than to replace it with a radically different approach. After all, Piaget's theories are not antithetical to processing notions, they simply attempt to make a structural analysis suffice. Some of the major people involved in this information-processing reformulation are Robbie Case, from the Ontario Institute (Case, 1985), Rochel Gelman, from the University of Pennsylvania (Gelman & Gallistel, 1978), and David Klahr (Klahr & Wallace, 1976) and Bob Siegler (Siegler, 1986), from Carnegie Mellon. The characteristic approach has been to study Piagetian tasks, for each of which there now exists a substantial experimental and theoretical history, and to produce detailed information-processing models of the performance at each of the stages (an example is coming presently). Thus, if a child is at stage A and behaves thisaway, then here is a detailed model of the processes that could produce this behavior. If a child is at stage B and behaves thataway, then here is a detailed model of the processes. And so on. Comparing the processing at one stage to the next leads to a partial understanding of what must happen for development to occur from stage to stage, but the processes that accomplish the transition from stage to stage are absent. In short, the analysis provides comparative statics, but no dynamics, no mechanisms of transition. Collectively this work constitutes a major accomplishment. It provides the necessary frame of psychologically relevant task analysis.

The central question in the current era for the psychology of cognitive development is what the transition mechanisms are.[10] There is an underlying dilemma associated with this question by now, at least in my own interpretation of the field. There appear to be two quite different alternatives, and the question is which alternative holds. It is a dilemma because each alternative has its own special difficulty.

One alternative is that there is some long-term mechanism that accounts for development. Development takes a long time, ~~years. Thus there could be some undiscovered long-term mechanisms with the appropriate time constants of the order of ~~months. If you take this horn of the dilemma, then your problem is what such a mechanism could be. Although there are a few ideas that seem plausible for the very young, such as the growth of myelination of nerve fibers (Case, 1985), there are no reasonable candidates for what might work after the child is a few years old. You can simply posit something, such as a mechanism for the autonomous growth of short-term memory, but the evidence is not with you (Chi, 1978). So, that is one alternative.

The other alternative is that development occurs via the acquisition mechanisms that we already know something about. There are two such mechanisms. One is long-term memory acquisition, which phenomenally occurs on the time scale of minutes or even as short as ~~10 sec. The other is skill acquisition, which phenomenally occurs on the time scale of days to weeks.[11] If you choose this horn of the dilemma, then the problem is why development takes so long. If development is just an issue of learning what to do, what is going on that takes months or years to happen? Although skill has a more commensurate time course, it seems to have exactly the

10. I have phrased the story in terms of Piagetian stages. Naturally enough, part of the field denies stages and saltatory transition mechanisms. The story could also have been told in terms of this other approach. The processes of change that take the cognitive four-year-old to the cognitive twelve-year-old remain unexplicated, no matter how you smooth out the transitions.

11. In Soar, both acquisitions occur by chunking with its own special time constants as a mechanism; but I wish to pose this dilemma from a more general perspective.

wrong character, namely, it seems to be a vehicle for tuning behavior rather than for substantially reorganizing intellectual operations.

In either case there is a problem—which is why choosing between them is a dilemma. I have asked some of my developmental friends where the issue stands on transitional mechanisms. Mostly, they say that developmental psychologists don't have good answers. Moreover, they haven't had the answer for so long now that they don't very often ask the question anymore—not daily, in terms of their research.

8.2.1. The Balance-Beam Task

Figure 8-5 examines the issue more concretely by considering a specific task, called the *balance-beam task*. It has its beginnings, as do all these tasks, in the work of Piaget and his colleagues, in this case Inhelder and Piaget (1958). The particular experiment was done by Bob Siegler a decade ago (Siegler, 1976), but there have been many other experiments using this task, both before and since. The child sits in front of a balance beam, which has four pegs on each side and some disk-like weights on the pegs, as shown. The beam is held in place by a support under each end (not shown). The child is asked whether, when the supports are removed, the balance beam will tilt down to the left, balance, or tilt down to the right. Even fairly young children do not have any trouble understanding what the task is and carrying it through.

A child does this task differently at different ages. The correct rule derived from elementary physics is to compute the total torque[12] on each arm, compare them, and predict accordingly. Siegler found that children's behavior could be described very cleanly by simple rules. There are four rules, which gradually increase in complexity and in adequacy for the task. In all cases, the children obtain some quantity from the figure that applies to each arm and permits comparison; then they behave accordingly—equals means balance and unequals means the greater goes down. This is already a lot of cognitive organization. The rules differ on the quantities and when a quantity is relevant. The simplest rule is to respond to weight only. Children whose behavior is described by this rule

---

12. The total torque is the sum of the torques of each part of the beam, where the torque of each part is the weight times the distance to the fulcrum. The parts include the disks, pegs, and the beam itself. The pegs and beam can be ignored since they are symmetrically placed, leaving only the contribution of the disks to be calculated.

Age	Rule					Definition of rules
(years)	1	2	3	4	None	
5–6	77	0	0	0	23	**1** Weight only
9–10	10	30	40	7	13	**2** Weight equal, then distance
13–14	10	23	57	3	7	**3** Weight and distance, if not conflict
16–17	0	20	63	17	0	**4** Compute torque

Correct rule

Compute the total torque on each arm

• Torque for each peg = weight of discs × distance of peg from fulcrum

• Total torque = sum of the torques

If torques equal, then beam balances

If torques unequal, arm with greater torque goes down

Figure 8-5. The balance-beam task (percent fitting each rule; Siegler, 1976).

know all about distance (as do all children at these ages). But they do not respond to the distance of the weights from the center, even if it is relevant to the balance. They just respond to the total weight on each side (the heavier side goes down, the same weight on both sides balances). The next rule is to respond by weight, if the total weights on each side are different; but if the weights on both sides are the same, then respond according to distance. Distance has become salient, but only when weight doesn't count. Thus, the child's behavior is really described by two rules, 1 and 2. The third rule is to take weight and distance both into account appropriately, as long as no conflict exists between weight and distance. As long as weight alone or distance alone determines the correct result, this rule gives the right answer. In case there is a conflict, various kinds of behavior occur. In Siegler's phrase, they just sort of muddle through. The fourth rule is to compute the torque, the correct physics rule.

The table shows the percentage of children of a given age that can be well described by these rules, according to stringent requirements. There were 120 children total, 30 in each age bracket. The *None* column gives the fraction that could not be described by any of the rules. This starts at 23 percent for the youngest group (5– 6 years) and diminishes to 0 percent for the oldest group (16–17 years). The small size of these residuals is the evidence that behavior is highly regular. As might be expected, regularity increases with age. It can be seen from the table that the youngest children use only the simplest rule and then, as age increases, the fractions of the more complex and adequate rules continually grow. Even with the oldest children, however, only a small fraction (17 percent) are using the fully adequate torque rule. Even most adults don't compare torques.

These data provide a particularly impressive example of the stage analysis provided by information-processing developmental psychology. These rules fit within a simple process model, so that simple simulations predict just how the bulk of the children behave. The rules themselves are clearly ordered from simple to complex. Indeed, they form a hierarchical tree of tests, such that each successive model has all the capabilities of the prior ones. Thus, we see clearly in evidence the comparative-statics analysis. Everything seems to be here—except how the children move from stage to stage.

There are two other important facts about the balance-beam situation (derived and supported from this and other related experiments by several investigators). First, there is a fair amount of evidence that encoding is important, namely, what children decide to encode in the situation and thus attend to. The rules are based on what information is actually attended to in the task, not on what we know the child must know in general. All the children know about distance and use this knowledge in various ways throughout their daily life. They do not all use it to encode the balance beam, however, and so it is not in fact available in the situation.

Second, children can be trained on this task to behave according to more advanced rules than they use of their own accord. Furthermore, they can actually move up some levels in the developmental sequence by such training, in that advanced behavior attained through training seems to be a relatively permanent acquisition. This is a result that has emerged in the last ten to fifteen years. Piaget himself believed that the stages of development were pretty much fixed. Children could not advance beyond their cognitive station, so to speak. Early experiments seemed to confirm that children could not be moved ahead in the developmental sequence.

By now, however, it is pretty clear that such movement can occur, if it is known exactly what a child needs to learn and if this is made the focus of an individual training regime. Then children can learn to move up to higher developmental stages and stay there. This shift from the early to the later experiments, with a complete turn-around in results, is understandable given the experimental manipulations. The early techniques were generally nonintensive manipulations that were not focused on the individual but were more like classroom demonstrations. The techniques that work involve much feedback and intensive learning activities with each individual. There is also here a nice instance of the difficulty of proving a negative—that something can't be done.

This last result about learnability provides evidence for one horn of the dilemma, namely, that standard learning mechanisms are the engine of development. Of course, it does not resolve the issue of why it takes so long. It only says on which horn to prefer impalement.

8.2.2. Soar on the Balance Beam: The Issues

Development is a point on the frontier. Soar is a theory of formed intelligence. Nothing in Soar is responsive to developmental concerns. As noted in Figure 8-2, such concerns did not enter into the design of Soar at all. If Soar is going to be a unified theory of cognition, however, it must ultimately extend to being a theory of development. At least it must be for those aspects of development that occur within the cognitive band. If mechanisms below the cognitive band drive development, they must have strong cognitive effects and Soar must provide the theory for these effects.

So let us explore Soar and the balance beam.[13] Soar can perform the balance-beam task—it is just another toy task. Also, Soar can do the task using each of the four rules. The basic simulation is hardly an issue. The experiment by Siegler is so clear that almost all the regularity in the behavior is captured by the rules, and simulation adds little. The important question is whether Soar can learn its way from rule to rule. If it does, then at least it generates a candidate transition mechanism. Soar can indeed do this, using chunking. Perhaps that seems like it could be taken for granted by this time. In fact, there are interesting and important issues at work

13. This is work by Rex Flynn.

here. Again, we will find ourselves listening to what the architecture says.

The real issue for Soar in this situation turns out to be an internal precondition for learning, rather than the scientifically more salient issues concerned with forming and acquiring new concepts. How does Soar recover from structural error? That is, given that Soar knows how to perform a task or solve a problem, and given that it transpires at some point that the knowledge Soar has available is wrong—what does Soar do then? Even to raise this issue is to reveal that there are two quite different learning situations. One occurs when a system does not know something and acquires that knowledge for the first time. The second occurs when it does know something, but has it wrong and must relearn it correctly. Much of the research on learning, both with humans and with computers, concerns only the acquisition of new information. Even when interference is the focus of concern, as in much verbal learning, there is no real conflict. The list given yesterday is not the list given today. It is not like knowing all your life that the first president of the United States was George Washington and then finding out one day (say it isn't true!) that it was Sam Adams instead.

The balance-beam developmental situation is that a child learns to predict the tilt of the balance beam according (say) to rule 1. It has behaved this way for a while. Then, one day it finds out that the rule is wrong (the experimenter arranges the world so that the conflicting facts cannot be ignored). The child's problem is to change its behavior.

Perhaps these still do not seem like two qualitatively different learning situations. Let us view it from Soar's standpoint. Adding new chunks seems a reasonable way for Soar to acquire new knowledge. In fact, it works just fine, as we have seen repeatedly throughout the book. Chunking adds productions permanently to Soar's long-term memory—it adds permanent structure. So now suppose that a bunch of these productions are wrong. What is Soar to do about it? This is the internal problem that Soar has. It must be solved before a Soar theory of development is possible, for development is a situation in which the child learns, is wrong and relearns, is wrong again and relearns yet again—and so on into old age or whenever the old-dog, no-new-tricks stage finally takes over, if indeed it ever does for most of us.

This problem bears some outward resemblance to the data-chunking difficulty we faced in Chapter 6. It is a real problem, not a

Search in problem spaces

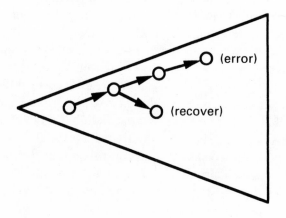

(error)

(recover)

Decision-time override

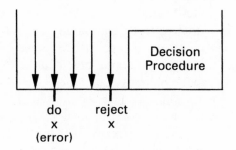

Decision
Procedure

do   reject
x   x
(error)

Figure 8-6. Basic mechanisms for error recovery in Soar.

pseudoproblem, and it is a problem where again we need to listen to the architecture. The architecture of Soar comes equipped with two error-recovery mechanisms (Figure 8-6). First, Soar does every-thing in problem spaces. Problem spaces are fundamentally error-recovery mechanisms, although that way of viewing them is per-haps not too common. To go down one path in a problem space is to be capable of backing off, for whatever reason, and going down an alternative path. That is an error-recovery procedure. If problem spaces were the only recovery mechanism that Soar had, it would in effect have to problem-solve its way through life, repeating life's early errors each time before finding a workable solution.

The second Soar mechanism for error recovery can be called

the *decision-time override*. In the decision cycle, during the elaboration phase, everything pours in from recognition memory (the production memory) until quiescence occurs, after which the decision procedure determines the choice that will occur (including impasses). Thus, productions propose, decide disposes. The nature of the preference system is always to permit anything proposed by one production to be rejected by another. Thus, even if there were a rogue production that says, *under all conditions the balance beam balances*, it is always possible to create another production that will spot a proposal of the rogue production and reject it. Consequently, no single production can ever grab control of Soar's behavior. With the override, later learning can annul earlier wrong learning. Furthermore, overriding occurs within the automatic level, so that the rejected behavior never surfaces externally as something being considered.

To make the override work requires that Soar be able to learn new productions that reject the bad learning. It also requires that it be able to learn new correct solutions even though the other old learning is around. Techniques to do this have been developed (Laird, 1988). They involve forcing an impasse following the feedback that some learning is incorrect, hence that all previous subspaces are suspect, and then learning new chunks to this new impasse. Even with these techniques, using the decision-time override cannot be the complete solution. The elaboration phase would keep building up. An organism that exists over a long period of time would steadily accumulate productions that propose actions along with the search control to negate their proposal. Each elaboration phase would have to recapitulate all of the bad learning that has ever been learned in that given context. Thus, these mechanisms do not seem sufficient, just by themselves, to solve the problem of recovery from bad structure.

There are several possible approaches to solving this problem. The first is to extirpate the bad structure. If it gets dug out and thrown away, then it won't be around any longer. Most artificial learning systems operate this way, in part because learned structure is just data structure in computer memory anyway. However, there are some problems with such an approach. Good stuff may get thrown away with bad stuff. More important, the learning occurred within a certain context and therefore exactly what should be extirpated may not be evident. This is not to say that the approach cannot work; only that it has deficiencies.

The second approach is to modulate learning by processes of strengthening and weakening. The viewpoint is that adding permanent structure is serious business, not only because it will be around for a long time but because whether it is in the organism's interest to have it or not cannot be determined quickly. Therefore, commitment should occur slowly and reflect the accumulation of experience. Weights associated with each production provide a natural mechanism for making this commitment. The weight governs the probability that the production will fire if satisfied. With every positive experience with the production the weight is increased; with every negative experience it is decreased. No structure is actually permanent, for its weight can be decreased so much that the production will never be evoked again. This solution has a lot to recommend it. It has a venerable history going all the way back to linear-operator stochastic learning theory (Bush & Mosteller, 1955). It is the solution that Act* adopts (Anderson, 1983). However, it does have some problems. It commits to slow acquisition, whereas fast acquisition may be what the situation demands. In effect, it treats learning as a distinct long-term process with a limited role to play in performance. It can also pose credit-assignment problems.

The third approach is to build a discrimination mechanism so that the bad structure is never (or hardly ever) evoked again. If the system never goes down that way again, then the productions never get a chance to fire. It always works in an environment where only the successful learning exists. It avoids the built-in slow adaptation of the strengthening approach, because once the discrimination mechanisms are in place, the bad past behavior in effect does not exist any more and hence doesn't take up any time or effort.

There is a hitch. This solution requires that there be a way to get upstream of the bad structure. If the system waits until it encounters the bad learning again, then it is already in error-recovery mode and wading through the decision-time override. It needs to avoid the bad learning, not recover from it. Thus, once it has been discovered that some productions are wrong in a certain situation, what the right actions are, and even how to discriminate the good from the bad, the discrimination mechanism must still be installed so the preferred situation is encountered before that contaminated situation. That is a problem, since we are not talking about getting upstream in some existing static structure but in the stream of behavior.

Of the several alternatives to approach this problem, the natural one for Soar is the third alternative, upstream discrimination. It is the natural path because it does not disturb the architecture. Both excision and production strengths would introduce major perturbations to the architecture. Excision, in particular, seems actually wrong for Soar, in which one of the justifications for chunking is that it replaces and shortcuts what is already there. Excision, by removing what was already there (which are chunks built from earlier activity) deranges this plan. Also, chunks are created within a context where enough is known about conditions and actions to construct it. None of that knowledge is available when it comes to excising the production, so it does not seem a very safe context for such action.

8.2.3. Avoiding Bad Structure by Discrimination

We wish to explore the discrimination path to error recovery to see how it can be made to work. As it turns out, it leads to some interesting mechanisms. The key is to exploit the higher-level organization that problem spaces impose on activity, namely, that almost all activity, including bad learning, is encased in a specific problem space. That is, the productions that generate the activity, whether operators or search control, are conditional on the problem space. Hence if new problem spaces can be created from contaminated ones so that only their good activity is saved, then the bad activity can be left behind. This solves the problem of discriminating the good from the bad. The problem of doing the discrimination upstream is solved because problem spaces are selected, just as are operators and states. Thus if the new, clean problem space is selected in preference to the old, contaminated one, the discrimination has been made once and for all. There is of course a cost to this arrangement—the preferences that select the right problem space—but this is a fixed, minuscule cost.

There is actually quite a bit more to the solution than the key idea sketched above. Figure 8-7 provides a bird's-eye view of the processing. Soar wanders around in a large number of distinct problem spaces, the interesting aspects of which pertain to what functions these spaces serve and how they relate to each other. It is too microscopic a view to look at Soar's behavior at the grain size of the production, the decision cycle, or even the operator. Now the

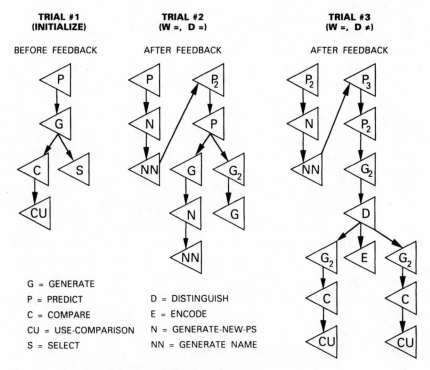

TRIAL #1
(INITIALIZE)

TRIAL #2
(W =, D =)

TRIAL #3
(W =, D ≠)

BEFORE FEEDBACK

AFTER FEEDBACK

AFTER FEEDBACK

G = GENERATE
P = PREDICT
C = COMPARE
CU = USE-COMPARISON
S = SELECT

D = DISTINGUISH
E = ENCODE
N = GENERATE-NEW-PS
NN = GENERATE NAME

Figure 8-7. Overview of how Soar develops.

unit of behavior is the use of a problem space, and the analysis is in terms of patterns of problem spaces.

Each triangle in the figure is a problem space, with the arrows indicating that one space is a subspace of the other, arising through an impasse in the space at the tail of the arrow. For instance, P is a prediction space. It contains *prediction operators*, which predict whether the balance beam will tilt down on the left, balance, or tilt down on the right. Soar performs the actual task of predicting the balance beam in the P space. All of the other spaces arise out of impasses that start in the P space. The figure shows three separate trials. On each trial, Soar is presented a specific balance beam and asked to make a prediction. Let's give an overview of what occurs in the sequence, and then come back and go through the detail.

The first trial, in the left-hand column, gets things started. To begin with, Soar does not even have a prediction operator for doing the task. Hence, it must build itself a prediction operator. It is not given feedback to know whether it is right or wrong, but it is able to get itself to do the task, that is, to make a prediction. Because it chunks what it does, Soar will thereby gain some permanent structure (which may then be wrong in later trials).

The second trial, in the middle column, follows immediately after the first. Soar is presented another balance beam, for which its prediction (produced by the operator built on the first trial) turns out to be wrong. It is provided with this information by a feedback operator in the P space in the upper left of the second column. It then has to correct itself and when it succeeds in doing this, it is operating at rule 1—which says look at weight only. It will apply this rule to any balance-beam arrangement.

The third trial, in the right-hand column, follows the second. Again, Soar is presented with a balance beam, for which its prediction (produced by the operator incorporating rule 1) turns out to be wrong. Again, it finds this out via a feedback operator in the P space (called P_2) at the upper left of the third column. Thus, Soar has to go through another cycle of dealing with prior learning that has turned out to be wrong. Success here leads it to operate at the level of rule 2—which says to respond according to weight (rule 1) unless weight happens to be the same on both sides, in which case use distance. It will apply this prediction scheme to any balance arrangement.

The fourth trial is not shown. It is like the third trial; the balancing task invalidates rule 2 and therefore provides the opportunity once more for Soar to deal with learned information that is wrong. Success at this task will lead Soar to learn rule 3. Soar takes this step, just like it takes the ones shown on the figure.

However, Soar does not take the final step of going to rule 4. There are good reasons why it shouldn't. The transition to rule 4 is not experimentally secure and indeed probably never occurs spontaneously by experiential learning. There are many ways to improve the adequacy on the balance-beam task, without moving directly to the computation of torque. Rule 3 stops short of making the reasoner have to cope with any trade-off between weight and distance. A number of qualitative and partial numerical schemes are available to deal with some aspects of compensation, and humans do show some of these other intermediate rules. This is especially true because the balance beam actually used is extremely simple, with four equally spaced pegs and all weights identical. Thus, in terms of an appropriate cognitive theory, Soar should not directly learn the computation of torques. It should invent various more elaborate (even Ptolemaic) schemes. It should certainly not invent the concept *torque* in over-the-board play with a balance beam.[14]

Given this overview, we can go through the figure again, this time focusing on two things—first, how Soar solves the problem of getting the right prediction and the right learning; and second, how Soar solves the problem of recovering from bad learning. The two problems intertwine so that the task that Soar performs may not seem much like development. We will try to disentangle all these activities at the end, but for now we will deal with the complete behavior.

Start again at the first (left-hand) trial. Soar gets the task and doesn't have an operator to do it, so it gets an impasse. This leads to the G space, in which it attempts to *generate* an operator. A prediction operator must encode the particular balance beam, then compare the encoding of the left side against the encoding of the right side of the beam, and then use that comparison to select one of three predictions: down to the left, balance, down to the right. This set of final, mutually exclusive actions is given by the definition of the task, and children from age 5 up understand it with a little instruction and interaction. Likewise, they understand that there is a comparison of the two arms, although that is less explicitly spelled out. Rather, the symmetry of the situation and the nature of the final selection alternatives (down-left, balance, down-right) would seem to account for the understanding children have of this aspect of the task. The encoding of the situation, of course, is simply part of the general way humans deal with their environment. Thus, the knowledge of encode → compare → select is built into the operators of the P space.

The attempt to generate an operator leads Soar down into a comparison space (C) to make the comparison of the two sides. The comparison space actually does the comparison; to get the chunk requires going into an implementation subspace for it, called CU. Making some comparison, on this initial trial, is straightforward; and there is no criteria to guide it other than completing the task. Once the comparison exists, the problem for Soar is to get it hooked up to one of the three alternatives, as an appropriate response. In

---

14. Most people who learn about torques do so because they are taught. There was, of course, an initial untaught learning event, but this had the character of scientific discovery—reflecting, observing, hypothesizing, experimenting.

fact, it gets a tie impasse between those three operators, which leads down into a selection subspace (S), where it picks one indifferently (since there is no knowledge to guide it). However, this at least gives it a response, which it then makes in P space. This is the end of the first trial. There is no feedback, so Soar doesn't know whether it is right or wrong, but Soar at least learns to respond in a legitimate way (with one of the three predictions) when given a balance-beam task.

The second trial occurs. Soar's interaction with the external experimental situation does not show. The task is projected entirely into P space in the actual Soar run. The presented balance-beam is received by the attend operator, Soar applies the prediction operator, which uses the operator created in trial 1 to produce a response; and the feedback from the experimenter is received (from a production). Soar's response is wrong (it was arranged to be that way). Soar then rejects the prediction operator, because of this external feedback. Soar now has a space in which the main operator has been rejected. This is one form that bad spaces can take. Soar still needs to respond, but the operator that is proposed to give the response has been rejected. Thus, it now needs to manufacture a new and more appropriate response. It also needs to be able to select that new response in preference to the original and it needs to do so without forever having to deal with the old response as a candidate. In short, we have a paradigm example of the need to discriminate upstream.

The essence of the solution is to construct a new problem space that will take over the functions of the old one that contains the bad learning, but without the bad learning. The process starts with an impasse in P space, caused by the feedback from the failure to respond correctly. This leads to a subspace (N) to generate a new prediction problem space. This will be called space P_2, but it is necessary to generate an appropriate name for it so that it can be accessed from P space. This is done in a generate-name space (NN).

The two problem spaces, P_2 and P, are related to each other in a way partly analogous to inheritance in AI frame systems, namely, P_2 is a P. Soar will enter P_2 and work in it as long as it can, but whenever it cannot proceed, it will use the knowledge in P. This will happen in P_2 anytime an impasse occurs. An impasse is exactly the signal that there is not sufficient knowledge to proceed within a given space. Thus, P space functions as the backup space for P_2. Hence, there is no issue of what must be known to create P_2—absolutely nothing except that P should be entered to find out what to do if P_2 does not have appropriate knowledge.

When created, P_2 is an empty problem space. As a result, all problem solving actually occurs initially in P space. But every time an impasse (from P_2) is resolved in P space, a chunk is built that transfers this solution up into P_2 space. This happens because P space is the subspace to resolve impasses in P_2 space. Next time in P_2 that particular impasse will not occur, and instead behavior will proceed in P_2 without reference to P space. Gradually, then, the knowledge in P space is transferred into P_2 space. Of course, only that knowledge transfers that is the solution to the problems that actually occur in P_2 space. Thus, the various proposals and rejections related to the bad learning in P do not get transferred. The rejections in P see to that.

The analogy of the relation of P_2 to P being like an inheritance hierarchy fits some aspects quite well—P_2 space is a P space with modifications. And, as we will see presently, an extended hierarchy can build up. However, the analogy also misleads. First, though mostly just an annoyance, the language of *up* and *down* is reversed. As an inheritance hierarchy, one moves from P_2 up to P; but as an impasse hierarchy one moves *down* from P_2 to P. (We will stick with saying *down* from P_2 to P.) Second, there is filtering—not everything is brought up into P_2 by chunking. Indeed, the whole purpose of the mechanism is to filter out some aspects of P space (the bad learning). The filtering is accomplished by the natural processes of problem solving and chunking, which make what is brought into P_2 space functional for the tasks for which P_2 was created. Third, there is automatic migration of information from the original elements in the hierarchy to the more recent elements, whereas in inheritance the knowledge remains with the original element. These differences reflect that the purpose of inheritance is to save space and centralized control by storing knowledge only in one place, at the expense of using a little more time; whereas the purpose of the P_2-P hierarchy is to save time and avoid processing bad elements, at the expense of using a little more space.

This entire inheritance-like mechanism happens by impasses and chunking. No additional mechanisms are involved. Impasses and chunks have exactly the right characteristics (the filtering) for this task. They are not being bent out of shape to perform it.

To return to the problem-space-level trace in Figure 8-7, the second trial comprises two columns (both shown in the middle of the figure). The left one (which is what we have just been through) constructs P_2. The right one uses P_2 to construct a new response by constructing a new prediction operator. At the top we see the P_2 space leading to P space by means of impasses. There is actually more than one trip between the two spaces. The task is to generate a new operator, which leads to the G space, just as happened in trial 1. However, the G space has learned to produce the original operator. Thus, although it is possible to reject this operator—that is, not to produce the inappropriate operator—it is necessary to obtain a new generate-operator space, G_2, which will bear the same relation to the G space as P_2 bears to P space. And, indeed, the entire pattern recurs of G space to N space to NN space, producing G_2 space, backed up by G space. Working now in G_2 space, an appropriate new operator is constructed that satisfies the task requirements. This is not difficult because the feedback provides the information about what response is appropriate. It is a question of hooking the comparison information up with the correct prediction response (the correct one of the three). At this point, Soar is now working essentially at the level of rule 1, of taking into account weight only.

Soar arrives at the third trial. The same situation repeats itself (because the experimenter arranges it so). The prediction operator (created on trial 2) produces the wrong response to the balance-beam task and this is noted by the feedback from the experimenter. Thus, the now-familiar pattern of P_2 to N to NN occurs to produce a new problem space, P_3, which is backed up by P_2. There is now a three-tiered hierarchy of prediction spaces. Starting in P_3 to get a new prediction operator leads Soar down to P_2, which in turn leads to G_2.[15] In G_2, a new difficulty arises, namely that there is no way to create a new operator that is satisfactory, just by changing the way

15. It might be thought the path should go from P_3 to P_2 to P in order to get to G_2, but it turns out that the direct link from P_2 to G_2 is created by one of the chunks created in trial 2. The story of why that direct bit of inheritance works, why Soar need not forever have to work all the way to the bottom of a growing hierarchy—$P_n, P_{n-1}, \ldots, P_1, P$—is too detailed for this exposition.

the comparison-description of the balance beam is hooked up with a response. Hence, a new operator cannot be constructed. This was not a problem in trial 2, where the difficulty was that the prior operator said less weight on the left side means left goes down. In trial 3, the experimenter has arranged it so that distance is the relevant dimension, but the concept still in use involves only weight. So nothing can be done at this level.

This impasse leads to the discrimination space (D). Both the comparison and the encoding process are sources of additional discrimination. Soar first tries to make a new comparison (the left subcolumn G_2 to C to CU). But this fails, because Soar's initial encoding includes only weight and the weights on both sides are the same but the distances are different. Soar then attempts to augment its encoding. The encoding space (E) has a collection of operators for taking measurements and noting features of the actual balance beam. It thus builds new descriptions of the balance beam. It does not build the description from scratch each time, but rather attempts to add features to the description that it has. In the case in hand, the children already know about distance (from many tasks at which they are facile). Thus, the issue is that distance has not been evoked as relevant to the current situation, although it is included in the set of operators available in the encoding space. Other operators are there as well, such as the ability to notice the specific pegs, or the color of the disks (they alternated black and white in Siegler's experiment, for ease of counting), or the number of disks (children are well aware of the small numbers, such as one, two, and three, that occur in the experiment).

In the case illustrated in the figure, distance gets selected right away as a relevant additional encoding. Given the encoding in terms of distance, another attempt at constructing a useful comparison operator works (the right-hand subcolumn, G_2-C-CU). This leads to an acceptable prediction operator (the result of G_2) and successful performance on this balance-beam task. Soar has now acquired the concept of rule 2, namely, if the weight is equal, then discriminate on distance. It gets the assignment of comparison-description to prediction right (the side with the greater distance goes down), because the feedback provides the appropriate information (which was not provided in the first trial).

The same basic strategy works again in the fourth trial which is not shown in Figure 8-7. Instead, Figure 8-8 shows one additional

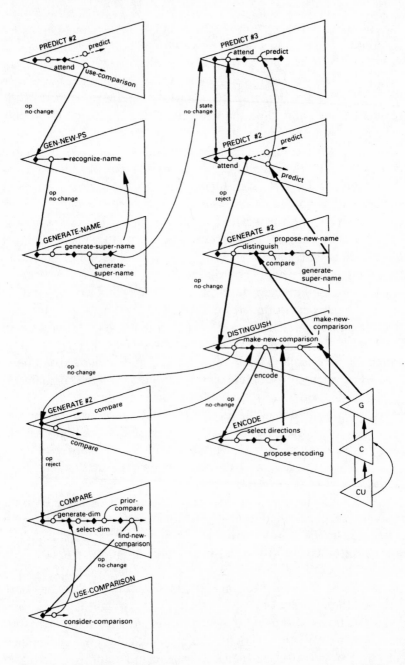

Figure 8-8. How Soar develops: detailed view (level 1 to level 2).

level of detail of the third trial, which moves from level 1 to level 2. The paths in most of the individual spaces are shown and the impasses are labeled. Some things can be seen more explicitly here, such as the multiple trips between P_3 space and P_2 space. Also the specific chunks are noted (the upward-sweeping double arrows). Actually, the situation turns out to be not quite identical to the prior trial. The space P_3 works fine, so there is no need to develop a new P_4 space. This is because the bad learning for both trial 2 and trial 3 remains in P_2. So P_3 remains clean, so to speak, and can be used to develop the next operator. Also, going from rule 2 to rule 3 does not require new additions to the encoding, only additional elaborations to the comparison.

For simplicity, the most direct successful case has been shown. If by chance some other addition has been made to the encoding (say, about the color of the pegs), then there would be another loop through the operator-creation column, G_2-C-CU, because no satisfactory concept could have been built. If, again by adventitious chance, a discriminating feature for this particular task had been found, then Soar would have gone with it, and another trial would have been required to reveal its inadequacy. Thus, what we have been doing is tracing through the mechanism of successful change, not tracing through a simulation of what a child does in an actual series of experimental trials.

This example lets us note the dynamic range of Soar as a unified theory of cognition. We have moved up many levels of abstraction from where we started in Chapter 3, at the bottom rungs of the cognitive band. Productions are at the basic symbol and memory-access level, the decision cycle is a level above that, and elementary operators a level above that. We applied Soar to this latter level, which was that of immediate response (Chapter 5). In the present analysis we have moved up not just to the level of the problem space, where we examine sequences of operator applications, but up to where we collapse all the operators in a space together and treat all of it simply as the activity in a space. In fact, we have begun to rise to yet one more level of abstraction, to where patterns of problem-space evocations are significant—the X-N-NN-X'-X pattern of failing in a space (X), creating and establishing a new version of that space (X'), for which the original (X) serves as a backup. This pattern occurred three times in Figure 8-7, twice for

P and once for *G*. It need not take an exceptionally long time—~50 operators in the present case—but it does impart a measure of higher-order regularity to behavior.

The presentation of Soar's behavior on this task has been highly abstract, but the actual analysis has not been abstract at all. All the details, down to the productions, are going on under the floor of Figure 8-7. Thus, the situation here differs from the technique introduced for immediate-response behavior, where we carried through the entire analysis at an abstract functional level. Here, no such abstract analytical technique is yet possible. Only by working with a full simulation can one have any confidence of what will happen. This may not always be the case, of course. As patterns develop it could become clear what evokes them and what their yield will be, and a way to abstract away from them might be found.

8.2.4. Reflections on Soar and Development

Let us reflect upon what has been attained in this analysis of development. Most important, Soar has demonstrated an actual transition mechanism. It actually makes the transition at two points, from the level of rule 1 to that of rule 2, and from the level of rule 2 to that of rule 3. This transition mechanism has several important characteristics. It does it all by chunking, so it is certainly an example of regular learning—of short-term learning, when viewed on the time scale of development. It learns both new encodings and new comparisons. The investigation was somewhat truncated with respect to both encoding and comparison, but the processes were there and they operated to produce new processes of the appropriate type.

Development is driven by feedback from an external source (here the experimenter) in response to bad predictions. Soar recovers from its errors by creating the ability to discriminate prior to evoking the old errors again. It does this by means of revision problem spaces. It is noteworthy that this solution has been achieved without modification of the Soar architecture. Just as with data chunking, we have been led to interesting mechanisms simply by listening to the existing architecture. The solution, as sketched out in Figures 8-7 and 8-8, seems complex, although this is partly in the eye of the beholder, because we're granted a bird's-eye view. From the system's viewpoint, it is simply responding to impasses with local considerations. For instance, when Soar is in a problem space, trying to produce a predict-operator and failing to have sufficient knowledge, going back to the prior analogous situation is a local response and a rational one at that. Furthermore, it seems natural to enter into that prior situation attempting to solve the present problem, not simply adopting the prior solution by rote. All this corresponds to what is going on with revision problem spaces.

Although we have not capitalized on it here, it is useful to remember, once again, that all this is occurring within Soar as a unified theory. Consequently, general psychological plausibility carries over into this situation and operates as general support for this theory of transition mechanisms. It also operates to provide many specific constraints with which to test the theory and confront it with evidence from quite distant parts of cognitive psychology.

Finally, let us come back to the dilemma and its horns. The solution that arises from Soar clearly opts for one horn—development occurs by learning. What, then, about the associated question of why development takes so long? It seems to me the answer is composed of three parts—three reasons that conjointly stretch out the time it takes for children to complete development.

First, children have only a limited time to spend on specific tasks. Kids have lots of things to do with their lives. They do not spend months and months doing the balance-beam task. The world of behavior requiring development occupies an immense volume, so to speak, and in consequence any one piece of it moves relatively slowly. Furthermore, development isn't deliberate on the part of children; they have no strategy for making it happen (though their parents and teachers sometimes do). Development is just something that happens. Undoubtedly, this is one reason for the apparently slow pace of development, even though it is independent of the detailed mechanisms of development as proposed by Soar (or any other theory). Second, the nature of the process, as revealed in Figure 8-7, is quite complex. Actually, learning doesn't take so long. As we noted earlier, Soar can move through its problem spaces quite rapidly. Rather, the compound character of the process—the number of different activities that enter into the whole—simply adds up to a long period of development. Even without a detailed theory of errors, it can be seen that there are manifold ways in which the transition sequence shown here can go astray on any particular trial. In general, just comparing mechanisms would imply that relearning is an order of magnitude slower than new learning. Development is a prototypical example of relearning, for prior modes of response must be seen to be inadequate and must be replaced by better behavior.

Third, chunks are, by their nature, specialized. If Soar uses representations that make it attend to odd details, then it will build chunks that incorporate these details in their conditions. These chunks will not be evoked, even in apparently equivalent situations. This is a version of the general point about the minimal transfer of skill learning. From the standpoint of development, specialization means that a system can be learning all the time but that most of the learning is encapsulated, so to speak, so that nothing happens developmentally. It takes a long time before a child stumbles across the right way of learning a particular competence and is finally able to transfer that knowledge to a new situation. This hypothesis is consistent with how experimenters finally attain success in making development occur deliberately, namely, by arranging learning situations very carefully and focusing them strongly.

This third reason also reinforces the first, namely, that if learning is relatively narrow in its transfer characteristics, then from the child's point of view, the world seems like a very large collection of places, each of which requires its own quota of learning time. If, on the other hand, transfer were generally high, then the world would be a much smaller place learning-wise, and more time would be available for learning each part of it.

These remarks are simply speculative hypotheses about why development might take a long time. Such speculation is suitable, given that our aspiration in this chapter along the frontier is only to make plausible that a unified theory of cognition (here Soar) will be able to approach realms of behavior that are far from the theory's core. This ability has been amply demonstrated here. In fact, we have actually gone somewhat further—suggesting a viable idea for a developmental transition mechanism—in an era when transition mechanisms are in short supply, despite the centrality of such mechanisms for developmental theory and the recognized need for them.

8.3. The Biological Band

For two points along Soar's frontier—language and development—we have been bold enough to indicate strong vectors for how Soar might approach them. For other points we must be satisfied with briefer discussions. We are indeed along the frontier, and the terrain ahead is unmapped.

With respect to the biological band, the frontier below, we have already taken one absolutely important step in this book. We pinned down the temporal scale of the information-processing level—symbolic access at ~~10 ms, smallest deliberation at ~~100 ms, simple operators at ~~1 sec (capable of providing the fastest commerce with the external environment), and fastest goal satisfaction at ~~10 sec. This mapping is independent of Soar. It was generated from extremely general considerations of the nature and time constants of neural technology, the nature of cognitive behavior, and what we called the real-time constraint on cognition, namely that behavior with the environment starts at ~~1 sec, only two system levels above the neural technology. Soar fits this mapping (Figure 4-23). All other information-processing theories of cognition must do so as well.

Throughout the history of information-processing psychology, an important element of its rhetoric has been that it is not anchored to the structure of the brain. Sometimes this claim reflected an agnostic viewpoint, adopted simply to provide theoretical breathing room; sometimes it was more an argument for functional autonomy. It was, I think, an important stance and the right one for its time—certainly, I participated in it as much as anyone. I think that period is about over and Chapter 3 represents my contribution to its demise. That demise, of course, does not result just from a single analysis. Information processing can no longer be divorced from brain structure because our knowledge of the biological band has begun to take on a scientific solidity that breeds confidence about the broad outlines of what is going on in the temporal space that reaches from milliseconds to behavior. Those ~~3,000 behavioral regularities—or at least the subset of them that press closest to the temporal limits of immediate behavior—have also contributed to the rejection of the old view. The demise seems evident to me. The great gain—and independent of any immediate success in fashioning unified theories—is that many additional constraints can be brought to bear as we examine information processing more deeply. But that puts it too abstractly. The great gain is that we finally bridge the chasm between biology and psychology with a ten-lane freeway.

One major expression of the increased connection between

neuroscience and cognitive psychology is *connectionism*. For all I know, Jerry Feldman, in using the term *new connectionism* (Feldman, 1979), had in mind a double meaning—not only the connectivity of neural networks, but a more intimate connection finally attained between brain and behavior. Let me, then, remark on what I think is the relationship between Soar and connectionism (McClelland, Rumelhart, & the PDP Research Group, 1986; Rumelhart, McClelland, & the PDP Research Group, 1986).

We need to distinguish three aspects of connectionism, which is, after all, not all of a piece. First, connectionism is a commitment to a particular neural-like computational technology. In a nutshell, this technology consists of excitatory-inhibitory summing networks with thresholds for behaving; and adjusting weights or thresholds by experience for learning. Such "neural networks," as they are called, are naturally parallel in operation and also consist of very large numbers of elements—hence the massive parallelism of which the connectionists always speak. It is unclear how realistic this is as a model of biological neural circuit technology. In fact, its idealizations and its mismatch in level (basically, a neuron-level model is stretched to cover neural-circuit-level systems) have given rise to a vocal subgroup within connectionism that wants to convert the endeavor into a study of general dynamic systems (Smolensky, 1988). Nevertheless, it is certainly a more realistic model of neural technology than many other underlying technologies that could be taken as the base for the cognitive band. In particular, it realizes massive parallelism, fixed connectivity networks, and a continuous medium, all of which seem important.

Second, connectionism is interested in a particular class of computations that it deems natural to carry out with that technology. Any even moderately general computational technology can be used to realize a wide range of algorithms. The focus in connectionism is on constraint-satisfaction systems with hill climbing as the major method for seeking equilibrium solutions. This focus persists even across the very substantial differences in how knowledge is encoded in the networks, namely, point representations, in which each node in the net corresponds to a semantically meaningful concept, and distributed representations, in which each node participates in many concepts and each concept is therefore spread across many nodes. There is more variation in the algorithms to be used for learning, such as the back-propagation model currently undergoing extensive development, but this is because the field is still searching for learning schemes with the right properties.

Third, connectionism sees neural networks as being the natural way to provide certain kinds of powers that are deemed to be significant for human cognition. There are several such powers and not every connectionist assigns the same significance to each one, since connectionism is a large enough social movement now to have subgroups with divergent opinions. Furthermore, there is no need for agreement on the nature of these significant powers, because it is possible to adopt a bottom-up stance that connectionist neural networks accomplish brainlike computations, hence automatically will provide whatever powers cognition exhibits. There is, nevertheless, a strong functionalist urge in connectionism, just as there is throughout AI. Humans exhibit incredibly flexible intellectual power, which must be achieved by computational organizations of some sort. Showing that the right sorts of power and flexibility are provided by a given computational technology (here, connectionist neural networks) is a major way to discover the nature of the brain and mind.

Perhaps the cognitive power most universally held to be provided by connectionist networks is the ability to become organized in task-relevant ways just by performing tasks, without requiring programming by an intelligent agent. Connectionist neural networks exhibit this through their continuous learning by adjustment of weights. Another cognitive power that seems significant is finding the solution to very large systems of weak or soft constraints. Thus, the multitude of influences that impinge on cognitive behavior all seem to be brought to bear at each instant of behavior. Connectionist neural networks exhibit this because activation simultaneously flows throughout the network until equilibrium is reached, with the final, stable state reflecting the entire network. Yet a third cognitive power is the ability for all processes to be graded rather than discrete. Connectionist neural networks exhibit this naturally because their medium of activation is continuous and quantitative. The significance of this last power is felt very strongly to be of the essence of human cognition. The reverse side of this is a deep doubt and suspicion of discrete, symbolic structures as a medium for human experience—amounting almost to a visceral aversion, it sometimes seems.

So how does Soar stand with respect to these three aspects? As to the first, Soar is obviously intended to be realizable in neural technology within the time constraints of Figure 3-9. This does not seem entirely implausible on the present account. Though widespread, the opinion that symbolic-systems models of cognition are somehow so serial that they cannot be made to jibe with the brain's organization and speed of operations is simply misguided. I have been rather careful in this book to worry about this constraint; an entire chapter was devoted to it. There are, of course, massively parallel aspects of Soar. Production systems form a massively parallel recognition-memory system. But production systems are no more parallel than they have always been, even though they also often seem to be taken as the epitome of symbolic systems and rule-based behavior. There is more than a little clash here between what production systems are technically and the role they have been cast in by the rhetoric of dissent against symbolic systems.

With respect to the second aspect, the central computations for Soar's performance are those of match and recognition. Matching bears a substantial relation to constraint satisfaction, but it seems much more specialized. In particular, there are strong structural constraints about how parts must correspond and what is to happen upon failure. The current match processes in Soar (derived from Ops5 assumptions about the power of the match) are computationally suspect, as we discussed at some length in Chapter 5. Thus, a little caution is in order about predicting what the computational character of the ultimate Soar match will be like. It does seem unlikely that the sort of constraint-satisfaction processes emphasized in connectionism will be the center of attention.

To be sure, other processes besides match are involved in Soar's performance, such as the decision procedure, but they do not seem to be of much computational moment (complexity-wise). Chunking, which is the processing specifically associated with learning, is a fairly homogeneous process, and it is not clear how complex or extensive it would be in a neural-technology implementation. More generally, the entire motor system is outside central cognition. Although we were unable to be definitive about the motor system, we leaned toward composable dynamic systems. This clearly has a computational character all its own, which need not have any particular relation to the recognition system. The processing in the perceptual system is somewhat more ambiguous. On the present account, the characteristic computational function to be performed by both perception and cognition is recognition. Thus, there might be many computational homologies and even common processing substrates. However, there are differences. In particular, cognition works in an interior milieu and perception specifically addresses the problem of how to transduce stimulus energies from an exterior world into this interior world. Thus the computational solutions in the interior may be specialized in ways we do not understand as yet.

With respect to the third aspect, the significant powers of human cognition that are naturally provided by a computational technology or scheme, Soar focuses on different aspects from those connectionism focuses on. It considers high-level cognition, such as problem solving and planning, to be important, as well as the breadth of cognitive activity. It takes unlimited qualitative adaptation (as we phrased it in Chapter 3) to be significant, and thus the need for the flexibility associated with universal computation. These characteristics are not beyond connectionist systems, but they represent items on its far-future agenda.

As to the human cognitive powers that have special appeal to connectionists, enumerated above, the Soar position is mixed. Soar, just as much as connectionism, takes automatic learning from experience as a key power of human cognition, as indicated by the pervasive role played by chunking. Soar also sees the ability to bring to bear what the human knows as a key power of cognition. It approaches this by using a recognition memory and making its iterative accessing the inner loop of cognition. But this is a more structured and limited computational scheme than the ability of connectionist networks to resolve huge networks of constraints. In fact, the real-time constraint on cognition seems to work against too powerful constraint satisfaction. Bluntly put, there isn't time in the short run to do much integration that isn't fairly well focused. Weak constraints would seem to imply that the information that is to determine the solution is well distributed throughout the set of constraints. In turn, that would seem to imply many iterations to extract the equilibrium state that satisfies all constraints, for not until some information was extracted from some constraints would the information in other constraints apply. The real-time constraint is simply that only a modest number of iterations are available. The iterative matching of recognition memory also must work within the real-time constraint, but its more structured processing is built to assure that. On the other hand, Soar has put off to its future agenda dealing with the continuous and quantitative nature of human cognition (the third human cognitive power that appeals to connectionists). The temporal grain of the Soar system, with recognitions occurring at ~~10 ms, is fine enough that it is unclear whether the behavioral continuity has to be lodged in the medium (although it is clear that at some level neural circuits are continuous). The basic representation of quantities is an important lacuna in Soar, which needs to be filled.

The temporal mapping induced by the real-time constraint has an interesting implication for the concept of a *subsymbolic level*, which has emerged in connectionism as a general way of describing a possible relation of symbol processing and neural nets (Smolensky, 1988). The root idea is that there exists a distinct neural-system level, which accomplishes certain functions normally assigned to symbolic computation. Prominent among these are recognition, immediate response, and learning (the functions that have received most attention in connectionist investigations). This level then implements[16] an approximation to symbolic processing as a higher system level, which will accomplish other cognitive functions, such as deliberate planning, problem solving, extended sequential rule following, and the like.

The temporal mapping implies there can't be any subsymbolic level—there isn't enough temporal space. The symbolic memory access is already at the ~~10 ms level, according to this mapping. There is no way that any substantial level could get in between this and the neural level. The real-time constraint on cognition turns out to make impossible a view of the world that posits a neural-circuit (subsymbolic) level that accomplishes lots of functions and then has a symbol level on top of it. However, it would be possible (attending to just this constraint) to posit that behavior up to ~~100 ms is a connectionist system, and that it produces a higher-level organization above it (~~1 sec and up). According to the mapping, this would have the connectionist system performing all the basic symbolic functions up to and including basic deliberate decision making (or whatever analogue to them is posited in the connectionist system).

16. A variant view takes the symbolic level as simply a weak approximation, which does not have any strong closure properties as a systems level.

The general relationship of a symbol architecture, such as Soar, to connectionism plays only a minor role in determining how the science of the mind should move forward. More pertinent is whether enough constraining information can cross the gap between the biological band and the cognitive band (in either direction) to help in winnowing theories on the other side. The temporal mapping only helps to establish the possibility of such information flow. It doesn't assure that it can or will happen. Life between the bands has been a continual oscillation of rising hope that *the* bridge has finally spanned the chasm, followed by the realization that the time has not yet arrived in fact.

This book has emphasized the real-time constraint on cognition, in part because we managed to extract some useful inferences from it, but this is surely an overemphasis. Even in terms of highly general constraints, there are others whose consequences might be of interest. There is an analogous spatial or volume constraint—the brain all fits into ~1,000 cubic centimeters, and systems are built up from components in space as well as time. Functionality requires volume and in a system that appears in general to assign regions of space to global functions, there is the possibility of doing much more functional accounting than we have yet attempted. One could even try to dig beneath the surface of the general allometric relations that show that over species the volume of the brain is roughly proportional to surface area (Jerison, 1973). There is also no doubt some sort of functional continuity constraint, arising from embryological considerations, that nearby micro-regions mostly accomplish similar computational functions. This constraint underlies an organization of spatial specialization with distal intermodule communication. There might even be energy-budget constraints that have an effect, and some of the new brain scans may make us aware of that. There are also the general effects of stochastic operation. These carry a general implication of asynchronous operation, but maybe much more. The brain is a product of evolution and is constructed embryologically. Some agreement exists on the principles of evolutionary construction, for example, that systems are additive and existing mechanisms are subverted to accomplish new functions. Attempts have been made to exploit some of these constraints, as in the hypothesis of the triune brain, in which the brain is layered in evolutionary stages (reptilian, paleomammalian, and neomammalian) and this layering has direct implications for behavior (MacLean, 1970). This hypothesis received a mixed reception, but that is only to be expected. In any event, all these possibilities attest to the potential of further scientific knowledge of the biological band, even of a global character, to guide a unified theory of cognition.

8.4 The Social Band

There is even less of a definitive nature to say about the social band—the frontier above. Still, some discussion of this point on the frontier is imperative. One important measure of success of a unified theory of cognition will be whether it extends into the social band and provides an improved base for the study of social psychology and other social sciences.

Recall from Chapter 3 that the social band was characterized as starting roughly around $\sim\sim 10^5$ sec ($\sim$days). That figure is derived from the length of time humans spend in isolated individual activity—often hours, rarely a whole day. Asking when the beginnings of social activity will occur pushes the time scale down. In our society, typical significant contained social interactions last about an hour—a conference, a game, a meal, a lecture. It is not without warrant that classroom sessions are not set at 10 minutes. In the structured workplace, where much context is preset and the goals of an interaction are often quite narrow, the interaction durations decrease. Market exchanges are often ~ 10 min ($\sim\sim 5 \times 10^2$ sec). Executive diaries place the rate at which middle-level managers shift from one task to an independent one at ~ 10 min (Mintzberg, 1973), though we were all surprised at the rapidity.

The functional characterization of a social level is interaction among multiple humans.[17] A social system, whether a small group or a large formal organization, ceases to act, even approximately, as a single rational agent. Both the knowledge and the goals are distributed and cannot be fully brought to bear in any substantial way on any particular decision. This failure is guaranteed by the very small communication bandwidth between humans compared with the large amount of knowledge available in each human's

17. This is not the social considerations engaged in mentally by the isolated but thinking individual. Such considerations show only that humans operate in a social context and that both their knowledge and their goals are socially conditioned.

head. This feature of social systems says nothing about whether the social group can make better decisions or arrive at better solutions than the individual. Manifestly it can, if the combined knowledge of the group contains specific facts that are in total possessed by no single individual. So what kind of model is appropriate for the social-system level? Modeling groups as if they had a group mind is too far from the truth to be a useful scientific approximation very often. It is, of course, much used in human discourse; we refer to even the largest social institutions (governments and corporations) as individuals and legitimize such use by legal fictions. People simultaneously retain awareness of the social character of such institutions, however, and do not treat them simply as individuals.

How can a unified theory of cognition contribute to the social-band—to social psychology and sociology? The obvious answer is that individual psychology contributes a model of the social person, which can then be used as a component within social psychology. This answer seems essentially correct, although it leaves undetermined how big a role a model of the individual social person plays or could play in social science. Even if the role were tiny, it is still probably the key to what a unified theory of cognition has to offer. A look around at the current scene in the social sciences reveals a great deal of emphasis on the individual, though taken in a social context. Studies of attribution, social perception, affiliation, and attachment—all these are primarily focused on the individual within the social context, not on the interacting groups, organizations, or institutions that make up the social band proper. Thus, the model of the social human to be used in social science is of more than minor import, and it should be a prime contribution of cognitive science.

Indeed, *social cognition* is exactly the area within social psychology that has attempted to take the stance of modern cognitive psychology and move it into the study of the social band. The roots of the social cognition movement go back fifteen years (Carroll & Payne, 1976),[18] and the area is by now fairly mature. My own as-

18. There is a much longer history of the intertwining of the social and the individual, of which the work of Soloman Asch (1956) can be taken as the emblem. But the roots of this earlier movement are in Gestalt psychology, and it was a distinct and notable event when social psychology moved, in the early 1970s, to pick up on the then-maturing information-processing psychology. A perusal of the edited symposium just referenced makes this clear.

sessment, which I do not wish to defend too strongly, is that its promise has not been realized. It has failed to extract very much of use from cognitive mechanisms and has remained with the standard methodological paradigm of social psychology, which is a form of comparative statics. Independent variables are defined sui generis, dependent variables are defined ad hoc, and the studies attempt to establish how the dependent variables differ given differences in the independent ones. It has indeed found liberation to freely consider cognitive variables, such as encodings and attitudes, and to refer to processes such as storage and retrieval, but the underlying models of the social human are a mere shadow of what they need to be. They need to engage the symbol-level mechanisms that give shape and constraint to the close-in dynamics of social actions.

Do unified theories of cognition offer interesting prospects? That is the question to be asked all along the frontier. It seems a harder question to deal with for the social band than for either language or development. That is not surprising, perhaps, given that the social band involves substantial integrations beyond the cognitive band, whereas both language and development are within the cognitive band itself. No strong case can be made yet that unified theories of cognition provide any special leverage—no stronger than the general faith that symbol-level models of the individual must ultimately provide the foundation for understanding much of social action. However, it may be useful to note how deeply some aspects of the lower band penetrate into the social band.

One feature of the social band is that all social action is embedded within nonsocial technologies—within nonsocial worlds. Without a theory of that world, the particular mechanisms that are the focus of social effects are thin, isolated strands. They are so disjointed and isolated that no coherent theory can be built up. At every stage the connections are dependent upon some support in terms of the physical environment or the task structure. As we noted in Chapter 3, there seem some reasons to doubt the strength of the systems levels above the intendedly rational level, that is, above the level where the components are individually intelligent. The disjointedness of the social band is real, a reflection of the essential openness of systems at that level to influences from below. "A horse, a horse, my kingdom for a horse!" implies that without a theory of horses there can be no theory of kingdoms. If such is the case (though it can hardly be argued conclusively from the stance of this book), then theorizing at the social level will always be a mixed affair. Then models of the individual as intelligent agents interacting with such real worlds would seem essential.

This does not mean that the individual in the social situation is just the isolated cognitive agent that we have been sketching out. It is an important task to sort out the different kinds of mechanisms or ingredients that need to be incorporated into a model of the individual human agent within a social context.[19] Think of an agent making a response in a social situation. What characteristics of the agent must we consider when we try to predict or explain his or her response? There are at least five types of ingredients that seem worth distinguishing (see Figure 8-9). They are not alternative characteristics; each one is an addition to the ones before it. In other words, the sequence advances from minimal assumptions for a social agent to more inclusive assumptions.

[N]. The response may be predictable simply on the basis of the agent being intendedly rational in terms of the *nonsocial* aspects of the situation—its task structure. This type of prediction is what Soar provides—think of the blocks world or designing algorithms. This basic model of a rational agent provides more than one might think. Besides the mechanisms of goal pursuit, such as goals, problem spaces, and impasses, Soar includes mechanisms for being interrupted and for learning. If this is all there is to social behavior, Soar in its present form would be a good initial approximation.

[M]. A social situation, of course, includes other agents, who have goals and knowledge and take actions in pursuit of their goals in the light of their knowledge, themselves taking into account that other agents know about them and consider them goal oriented. The situation becomes complicated in what seems to be an essentially social way. The response is still that of an intendedly rational agent, but the task environment is now quite different from that of the blocks world. We can refer to it as a *multiagent* situation. The knowledge that each agent has is the knowledge of the (nonsocial) task plus the knowledge of the other agents plus some knowledge of their goals and knowledge. This is just the situation for which game theory was created (with the type-[N] situation being the one-

19. This is work in progress with Kathleen Carley.

[N] Intendedly rational agent in **nonsocial** situations (Soar)
Goal-oriented behavior (bringing knowledge to bear)
Interruption
Learning

[M] Intendedly rational agent in **multiagent** situations
Task environment has agents that know, want, pretend, . . .

[G] Intendedly rational agent with specific concurrent **goals**
Perform the group task
Maintain the social group
Enhance and preserve self-esteem and personal payoff

[E] **Emotional** and affective agent
Basic emotions: joy, sadness, anger, fear, disgust
Multitude of cultural emotions: guilt, pride, shame, . . .

[S] **Socialized** agent with specific social knowledge
Historically contingent social knowledge
Socialization provides culture-specific norms, values, . . .

Figure 8-9. The social agent.

person game against nature). Game theory, of course, is an entirely knowledge-level analysis; it has no theoretical apparatus to deal with the symbol level, where most real games are won or lost.

[G]. Soar, as we have been considering it, has a single deliberate goal, which can be taken as an operator in the base-level space. This is T, the tasking operator, in the scheme of Chapter 5, although that chapter focused on immediate behavior. This top task gets expanded out into an indefinite goal stack because of the difficulties that are encountered, so there are multiple goals. But this goal hierarchy is entirely devoted to a single outcome (the top task, T). It is characteristic of social situations that there are multiple, somewhat independent goals around at all times. This multiple-goal situation may be an essential feature of a social situation. Moreover, it may not be the multiple-goal character per se that counts but the specific content of these goals. There are (at least) three of them. Each individual cares about the task the group is performing. The individual also cares about maintaining the social situation of the group. Finally, each individual cares about his or her own position in the group and the personal satisfactions to be obtained from membership in the group. These three goals interact in characteristic ways. It may be that we do not have social agents in social

situations unless these three goals are all operating simultaneously.[20]

[E]. A large number of studies of social behavior have to do with
affective behavior, no doubt because the affective dimension is
almost always significant in relationships between people. It is entirely possible that before one can define a model of a social agent of
any real use in studying social phenomena, substantial progress
must be made in welding affect and emotion into central cognitive
theories. We noted earlier the role (or lack thereof) of emotion in
Soar. We take emotion and affect to be in part like multiple specific
goals. Existence of an affective dimension to an interaction would
seem to imply a separate basis for guiding the interaction in addition
to whatever task orientation might exist. Furthermore, the specific
content may be important, not just that there exist multiple bases.

[S]. Beyond all the mechanisms listed above, social situations
involve specifically *social* knowledge—norms, values, morals,
myths, conventions, beliefs, and the like. The source of this knowledge is the specific culture with its specific beliefs and practices,
within which the agent has lived and been socialized. The transmission of this knowledge via experience over a lifetime presupposes
learning within a social context, but the basic learning capabilities
are already assumed in the basic intendedly rational model [N]. The
specific import of the social ingredient is that the content of social
knowledge is not given, nor derivable from, the basic mechanisms
and task features that are presupposed in the earlier ingredients.
There is an element of fundamental historical contingency in social
situations. The content of the knowledge might vary rather arbitrarily between social groups and cultures, but some such body of
mores is required. Again, [S] is an element that adds onto all the
prior elements. An agent has not only social knowledge, but some
knowledge of other agents' social knowledge, emotional responses,
and (perhaps) multiple goals. The simplest assumption, of course, is
that social knowledge is entirely shared in common, but in fact the
knowledge is distributed in complex and incomplete ways throughout a social population.

This set of analytic distinctions is aimed at an understanding of

---

20. That on occasion a given member may have essentially no investment in some of
these goals only serves to define special groups and special group members.

what is involved in a model of a social actor, and what a unified theory of human cognition might bring to such a model. All ingredients—[N], [M], [G], [E], and [S]—presume the intendedly rational individual—the cognitive and intendedly rational bands. What changes in the social band is the task situation, the goals, and the content of the knowledge. At issue is whether a theory of only some of these capabilities is required in order to have an effective model of a social agent. For instance, the complexities of reasoning in multiagent situations may be sufficiently complicated that just arriving, so to speak, with a good model of intendedly and approximate rational agents does not go very far. Similarly, the nature of social knowledge may be sufficiently distinctive and constraining that the behavior of agents that embrace such knowledge is radically different from the behavior of agents without such knowledge—not just that different actions get taken, but that most of the scientific effort must be directed at understanding the consequences of such knowledge.

To pursue this analysis, we looked at an old and familiar piece of social psychology, called *social comparison theory (SCT)*, set forth more than thirty years ago by Leon Festinger (1954). SCT addresses what sort of decisions a person makes in a social situation; in particular, it posits that the person bases his or her decision on a comparison with analogous decisions made by other persons. It remains a live theory, which continues to be used in analyzing many social situations and indeed continues to be developed theoretically (Suls & Miller, 1977). The question we wish to address is what role is played by the different aspects of the social agent we have teased out. In particular, would having had a unified theory of cognition available (say, Soar) have helped with the analysis?

A nice thing about Festinger's style of theorizing is his tendency to write down an explicit set of axioms. Thus, we can classify the axioms for SCT with respect to the type of agent being posited— which axioms refer simply to the agent being a rational decision maker [N], which to the multiagent nature of the situation [M], which to having multiple goals [G], which to emotions [E], and which to having specifically social knowledge [S]. Figure 8-10 lists the nine axioms, suitably classified. It is not necessary to go through the axioms in detail, but let's take a couple, just for illustration. Axiom 1 says every agent has a drive to evaluate. That is certainly a basic tenet of general cognitive behavior in support of

[N] 1. Every agent has a drive to evaluate its opinions and abilities

[M] 2. If the agent can't evaluate its opinions and abilities objectively, then it compares them against the opinions and abilities of others

[M] 3. Comparing against others decreases as the difference with others increases

[N] 4. Every agent has a drive to improve abilities, but not opinions

[N] 5. Improving abilities is objectively more difficult than improving opinions

[E] 6. Ceasing to compare with another is accompanied by hostility and derogation if continued comparison implies unpleasant consequences

[M] 7. The more important a group for comparison of an opinion or ability, the more pressure there is toward uniformity on that opinion or ability

[M] 8. A large divergence of opinion or ability with others that differ strongly on relevant attributes leads to a narrowing of the range within which comparison will occur

[M] 9. The pressure toward uniformity of opinion or ability is stronger for those close to the mode of opinion or ability than for those more distant

Figure 8-10. The axioms of social comparison theory (Festinger, 1954).

rational behavior. Soar evaluates all the time. Soar, of course, does it under the impress of a goal to be attained, whereas SCT ascribes the tendency to evaluate to a basic drive. But a review of the way Festinger uses the theory shows that this is a distinction without much difference—the effect of axiom 1 is to permit the analyst to posit an evaluation anywhere he finds it expedient. Thus, we classify axiom 1 as [N].

Axiom 2 specifies that if objective evaluation is not possible, then the agent compares against what others do. This is essentially a principle of cognitive operation in a multiagent situation. If evaluation is necessary, then others' evaluations are a source of relevant knowledge. Thus, it is classified as [M]. There is no specific social content involved.

Each of the axioms can be classified in this way. The interesting result is that only one, axiom 6, is other than [N] or [M]. This is the assumption that hostility and derogation will accompany the act of ceasing to compare. If an agent has been using someone as the basis of comparison, and then ceases to do so, then the agent dumps on the other person. That does not follow from any obvious rational considerations, even in the multiagent situation, and it is clearly emotional behavior, so it is labeled [E].

The interesting conclusion from this brief analysis is that, to get some theoretical action in the domain of social comparison, Festinger had to provide an entire structure that was mostly nonsocial. He had to spend most of his theoretical degrees of freedom building up the basic apparatus of choice behavior. The elements of a social situation that were necessary were primarily the existence of other social actors, not any strong assumptions about the contents of their beliefs. Many of the inferences of SCT do not follow from strongly social aspects. Mostly, they follow just from the objective character of the task environment, such as the reliability of decision criteria, and the mere extension to the existence of other rational agents. Possibly, with a general cognitive theory, such as Soar, more substantial progress can occur in the enterprise of which SCT is one part. Maybe an appropriate theory of the individual agent at the cognitive level—and not just at the knowledge level, which is what game theory and its psychological derivative, decision theory, basically provide—can provide the common ground for all such efforts. The pattern of pervasive limits to rationality revealed by behavioral decision theory already indicates some of the ingredients that need to be included (Kahneman, Slovic, & Tversky, 1982; Pitz & Sachs, 1984), though it does not integrate these results into a unified architecture.

8.5. The Role of Applications

Applications are an important part of the frontier of any theory. They are not quite the same as the scientific frontier, at least not in the usual way of describing the scientific enterprise, but they are equally diverse in character. Furthermore, the commerce across an application frontier goes in both directions, not just from the science to the application.

The first important point about applications was already touched on in Chapter 1. A unified theory of cognition is the key to successful applied cognitive science. Real tasks engage many aspects of cognition, not just a single aspect. Consequently, it is necessary for an applied cognitive psychology to be able to treat all the aspects

1. Stimulus-response compatibility (immediate response)
2. Typing and keying behavior
3. Routine cognitive skills to perform unit tasks
4. Immediate instruction
5. Acquisition of cognitive skill
6. Reading and comprehension

---

7. Visual search and inspection (regularities exist)
8. Use of external temporary memory (not studied)

Figure 8-11. Activities integral to interaction
at the human-computer interface.

involved—not just memory, not just decision making, not just perception, but all of them, in a way integrated enough to produce the answers in the applied domain. This proposition says that unified theories of cognition are exactly what are needed to make progress in building an applied cognitive psychology.

To illustrate this, consider human-computer interaction (HCI). Recall from Chapter 1 (Figures 1-9 and 1-10) that one of my own precursors of the current attempt at unified theories of cognition was the work with Stu Card and Tom Moran on what we called the Model Human Processor (MHP), an attempt at a rough-cut, broad-spectrum theory of the user (Card, Moran, & Newell, 1983). It was intended to cover all the activities that a user exhibits when working at a modern display-oriented interface, such as a personal computer or workstation, as listed in Figure 8-11.

During the course of this book, we've gotten Soar to cover a number of the activities in this figure (those above the line). Actually, we did not explicitly cover the performance of routine cognitive skills involved in using command languages, such as text editors, which occupied a central role in the earlier work as the GOMS model and the Keystroke-level model. But that sort of routine cognitive skill, consisting of a succession of short (~~10 sec) unit tasks, with clear task phases (get the next task, locate the place to modify, make the modification, verify if necessary) fits easily within the multiple problem spaces of Soar. An operator corresponds to a task, such as *edit-manuscript*, which requires implementation by subspaces of more specialized operators *(get-next-edit, make-edit, verify,* and *get-next-page)*, and so on. Indeed, the stimulus-response compatibility methods of Chapter 5 are the extension of the GOMS techniques down to a finer temporal grain. Thus, we can take Soar as the foundation for a second iteration of the Model Human Processor, which already moves well beyond the initial MHP, both in scope and in detail.

Other areas that are integral to interaction but that Soar has not yet covered are listed below the line in the figure. One is visual search and inspection. Lots of good regularities exist here, with not only very good data but also good quantitative models (Teichner & Krebs, 1974; Teichner & Mocharnuk, 1979). No attempt has yet been made to extend Soar to this domain, in part because it depends critically on the perceptual structure of Soar, which is not yet in sufficient shape for such an exploration. However, many of the existing visual-search models do not require any more of perception than transcription typing requires of the motor system. This is an excellent area in which to extend Soar with every expectation of success.

Another area is the use of external temporary (or scratch) memory in rapid feedback situations. Here there is not much data in the literature, and there may be interesting surprises. There are actually two areas here. One is the idea, currently termed *situatedness*, that the external environment is as much a source of knowledge for what the human does as is long-term memory (Suchman, 1988). The second is the external short-term temporary memory, in which the human builds a rapid ($\sim\sim 1$ sec) feedback loop between himself and an easily modified and accessed external medium. The former is beginning to receive a lot of attention; but this latter still has not evoked the experimental work necessary to lay out the basic regularities.

The collection listed in the figure is almost a complete set of activities that occur at the display interface in modern interactive computing. Soar does not quite cover the set, and even in those activities where some work has been done with Soar, there is still much to do. Yet, it is a reasonable research goal to set for Soar that it cover the entire collection. Such coverage would indeed create a new version of a Model Human Processor that would be able to deal in an integrated way with the tasks at the interface.

Actually, the most important thing about applications is their relation to science in the other direction—not what unified theories of cognition can do for applications, but what applications can do for cognitive theories. Applications provide crucial ingredients for the overall basic scientific enterprise. They provide the successes that convince the polity that the science is worth supporting—that goes without saying in the current era—but they provide much more than that. Applications are critical as well for the internal conduct of the science. They establish what is worth predicting. They establish what accuracy is sufficient. They establish when a regularity is worth remembering. They establish when a theory should not be discarded.

Perhaps all that seems like quite a bit. But if a theory is doing good things in terms of applications, then, even if it seems uninteresting for other reasons, it will be kept and used. Applications say it is worth remembering Fitts' law, but applications are silent on the phenomenon of the *release from PI*. The latter is certainly a regularity (Wickens, 1970).[21] It was quite interesting during the early 1970s, in connection with interference theories of short-term memory. Fitts' law is tied in deeply with many applications. Release from PI is not tied in with any applications, as far as I know. Without applications as a guide, there is only current theory to maintain interest in it. But current theory is fickle—it exists in the minds of scientists, not in the world of real effects. Thus, as the theory goes, so goes interest in its facts. There is a theme in current philosophy of science that emphasizes that facts are theory bound—which even goes so far as to deny the status of fact to a regularity if it is not part of a theoretical view. And so we tend to forget about release from PI when interference theory goes out of fashion. And we tend to ignore Fitts' law when motor behavior is not fashionable in current cognitive theory. But some of us don't forget Fitts' law, because applications keep us interested in it.

This is not an argument against basic science. Just in case it is not

21. Here is the basic phenomenon, for those not acquainted with it. A basic experimental paradigm to show short-term memory for verbal material is to present a verbal item (say three letters), then fill the next short interval (say 15 sec) with distracting activity (counting backwards by sevens) to prevent rehearsal, then ask for recall of the item. There is almost perfect recall in the first of an experimental sequence of trials, but then recall falls off with additional trials if they occur in a continuous sequence. It is said there has been a *buildup of proactive inhibition*. If a somewhat different item is given after a while, say three digits, it is remembered easily. However, if triplets of digits are then continued, they too become hard to remember after a few trials. It is said there has been a *release from proactive inhibition (PI)*. The standard explanations ascribe the phenomena to the need to discriminate the new items from the old ones, so that when a different item is given it is easily discriminated.

obvious from my discussion in Chapter 5, I hereby go on record as being in favor of the ~~3,000 regularities. Many, indeed most, of these are arcane and not related to application. They gain their significance only when theory finds them important. We can't just attend to all ~~3,000 regularities on the hope that they will have relevance for the future. Applications have a wisdom that the current fashions of theory do not have, and indeed probably should not.

An area of application provides an external reason for working with certain kinds of theories and therefore for grounding the theories. It creates sustained communities that nourish a theory for a right reason—because it serves them. Interestingly, pure concern for science doesn't have that character. The scientist is free to forget some phenomena and just go on to other phenomena. As individual scientists, we properly exercise that freedom all the time. But applications ground our work in the larger motivation for the application.

Let me draw the lesson for Soar, just to make the point concrete. I expect Soar to work for HCI and to be used, so to speak, every day in every way—at least eventually. I am working to make that happen, though the published indicators don't yet mention Soar (Newell & Card, 1985; John & Newell, 1989). Grant that for the moment. Now suppose, just for example, that some data from neuroscience on localization of function turn out to be radically different from the way Soar apparently is. Some strong disconfirming evidence shows up. Soar will survive that just fine, as long as there is a domain for which Soar is being used and for which the neuroscience data are not particularly relevant. For Soar that area is HCI applications. It will hold work on Soar in place, until someone finally comes up with a theory that takes into account both the functional neuroanatomy data and the higher-level phenomena about how humans interact with computers.[22] Without such an anchor, the discovery of a domain that clearly shows Soar to be wrong could lead cognitive scientists simply to walk away from Soar. In short, having domains of applications is extremely important to having good scientific theories. Unified theories of cognition are no exception.

22. Of course, if Soar also turns out to be no good for the applications, or less good than new theories that come along, then it simply fades away, as it should.

1. Have many unified theories of cognition
   - Unification cannot be forced
   - Theories can even be quite similar, such as Act* and Soar
   - Exploring the architecture requires owning it
2. Develop consortia and communities for working with a unified theory of cognition
   - Unified theories of cognition require many person-years
3. Be synthetic
   - Incorporate (not replace) local theories
4. Modify unified theories of cognition, even in apparently radical ways
   - Coupling between parts is loose (but nonzero)
5. Create data bases of results and adopt a benchmark philosophy
   - Each new version must run on the benchmarks
6. Make models easy to use, easy to make inferences from
7. Acquire one or more application domains to provide support

Figure 8-12. Recommendations for the development of unified theories of cognition.

8.6. How to Move toward Unified Theories of Cognition

We have finished our tour of the frontier, although we have hardly traveled it all. The remaining questions are not ones of science, but ones of strategy. How are we to evolve unified theories of cognition? How are we to get from *here*, where I have claimed they are in prospect, to *there*, where we will all be working within their firm and friendly confines? What we need are recommendations, and I record mine in Figure 8-12.

(1) There should be many unified theories of cognition—at least for a while. I've reiterated this theme many times throughout the book. It is worth doing so once more. You cannot force unification. We are a field not yet unified and we do not know what unification feels like. Everyone is king, or at least can think it so, as long as no one is. Any attempt to settle on a unified theory by any means other than open competition in the marketplace of ideas—to use the cliché—will only end in squabbling. If this book is seen simply as a literary device for my making the case for Soar, then it will surely meet cynical dismissal. I get my day in the sun, courtesy of the Harvard Psychology Department. Other days belong to others, from other petty principalities. I am, of course, intrigued by Soar; I

am even in favor of it. After all, if not I (and my co-creators), who else should be? But that is not the point.

Again, there must be many unified theories. They can even be quite similar, like Act* and Soar, which have an immense communality in their base. The case of Act* and Soar makes clear one important reason why there must be many unified theories. Anyone who wants to work with architectures must control one. He or she must be free to reformulate it. Ultimately, when a single unified theory of cognition takes its place as *the* theory of cognition, and its assimilation and acceptance is behind us, then architectural theorists will work differentially off of the base theory. And the rest of us can go about our business of using and developing the base theory—of working on puzzles within the paradigm, to use the Kuhnian way of speaking. But at the moment there is no accepted base theory with anything like the required coherence and coverage.

(2) We should develop consortia—substantial collections of cognitive scientists who are committed to putting together a particular unified theory. Unified theories of cognition are not the product of a single person. They take a lot of work. Remember all those ~~3,000 regularities! There is no critical subset of 7 ± 2 regularities, the rest of which can be ignored. Architectures are complex and somewhat loosely coupled, and so it takes a lot of regularities to hammer one into shape. This requires a lot of people engaging in a lot of work, more so than can be provided by any isolated, individual investigator. It may seem an odd way to express it, but hoping for a Newton Inc. to arrive seems a much better bet for cognitive science than hoping for a Newton. It should be evident, however, that consortia are cooperative efforts among free-standing scientists, so coordination is implied, not subordination. Even so, such team efforts would imply a shift of style for many cognitive psychologists.

The Soar effort provides an illustration of the scale and style that seems to me necessary. This effort is better viewed as a community than as a consortium. Originally (circa 1983) there was a typical informal research project at CMU consisting of two graduate students and a professor (John Laird, Paul Rosenbloom, and Allen Newell). This has grown into a geographically distributed project, as the investigators dispersed to separate institutions—the University of Michigan (John Laird), the University of Southern California

(Paul Rosenbloom), and CMU (Allen Newell). Each of these three sites has become the scene of a typical university research project, with graduate students, post-docs, research associates, and support staff, and responsibility for its own funding. But with the aid of the Internet and the telephone, the three groups manage to behave like a single project in terms of scientific direction and coordination, under the leadership of the three principal investigators. Circa 1988, the three project groups comprised perhaps 35 people.

Surrounding this rather well integrated center are a number of other investigators who are interested in Soar for their own scientific and technical purposes. Some are located geographically at the three universities, especially at CMU, the site that has been active for the longest time. But many are at other universities and research centers, some in the United States and some in Europe. Circa 1988 there were perhaps another 20 people involved from half a dozen institutions. These investigators have a wide range of interests and come from a wide range of fields—psychology, social science, engineering, computer science. Their investments in Soar and their commitment to it varies widely. This total collection of some 50 people forms a scientific community, with email communication among the members of the community. The central sites provide the single version of the Soar system that everyone uses, along with the usual software-system organizational apparatus of versions, bug reports, bug fixes, and the like. About every eight months everyone gets together for a two-day Soar Workshop to exchange results and (most important) to get to know each other face to face. There are no barriers of entry to the community except the serious intent to work with Soar and each independent group or individual works on its own scientific efforts.[23] This latter characteristic is what makes the organization more community-like than consortium-like.

(3) Be synthetic. Incorporate existing local theories. Indeed, incorporate other groups' unified theories! This is another theme I've been returning to throughout the book. It is not necessarily a good thing for Soar to propose theories that are radically different from those already floating in the literature. Better to see Soar as an

23. Anyone interested in making contact with this community can write to any of its members (see the preface for their names and locations) or send email to soar@cs.cmu.edu on the Internet.

attempt to express these other theories in a way that will allow them to combine with other parts of cognition. As we have noted, the same explanatory mechanisms can operate with theories or architectures that seem quite distinct. What holds for Soar holds for other unified theories as well. The aim is to bring theories together, so we should operate cooperatively, not competitively.

(4) Be prepared to modify unified theories of cognition, even strongly and in radical ways. They are not monolithic, though the whole does bring constraints to bear that make modification a stirring—even exciting—proposition, and one for the young and energetic. Let me illustrate. We have (circa 1989) essentially completed the move from Soar4 to Soar5, the latter incorporating the single-state principle (Chapter 5). This has required substantial reorganization of the basic structure of Soar—working memory, the processing of preferences, the actions of productions—although it does so in a way that leaves the picture in this book almost unchanged. Installing it has been like jacking up a house and moving a new foundation under it. It has taken us a couple of years to make it happen. The ripples will still be felt for another year—indeed, we expect the conceptual consequences of this change to become a ground swell.

The question of the fundamental power of the match (Chapter 5) provides another illustration, though one that is still in midflight. It reinforces both the possibility of radical change and the long time scales involved with extensive investigation and preparation. The story has several parts. One is a conversation I had during the William James lectures with Danny Hillis and Dave Waltz of Thinking Machines, makers of a massively parallel computer called the Connection Machine (Hillis, 1985). Was it possible to abandon the production system entirely and replace it with something like the memory-based reasoning scheme they have explored on the Connection Machine, which seems to fit its structure very well (Stanfill & Waltz, 1986)? We could identify clearly the role of the production system in Soar as an associative recognition memory with a certain modularity for chunking. Maybe, if we just preserved those two properties, we could wheel out the productions and wheel in a memory-based reasoning system, thus employing a much simpler nearest-neighbor match. We explored this path and discovered a number of difficulties (Flynn, 1988). A second part of the story is the discovery that the current match is definitely too powerful, since it gives rise to chunks that are extremely expensive to process (Tambe & Newell, 1988). Thus, we have been propelled into an extensive research effort to discover weaker matching schemes that avoid these expensive chunks (Tambe & Rosenbloom, 1989), although this search has not yet been crowned with complete success. A third part of the story is that connectionist systems lend themselves naturally to weaker forms of matching. Thus, this research effort has extended to exploring whether connectionist technology admits of matching schemes that could support Soar (Rosenbloom, 1989). All three efforts are parts of an extended and still unconcluded endeavor to discover what sort of recognition match fits all the constraints of Soar. We expect its final phase to be the modification of Soar to incorporate a new and perhaps radically different recognition scheme. But we also expect the great body of behaving Soar systems to survive this change in operational form—though they will all become somewhat different in ways that should be theoretically significant.

One lesson to be gained here is that we should view a unified theory of cognition as a research programme in the sense of Lakatos, a programme that is to be continually modified as long as the changes remain progressive.

(5) Create data bases of results. Develop a benchmark mentality—don't walk away from old data, but preserve them in accessible form. Then expect any new theory to run on the old benchmarks—that is, to provide postdictions and explanations of them. Simply disbelieve, or at least disown, the Kuhnian rhetoric that new paradigms speak past each other and that progress never happens at the paradigm level. Be an engineer in this regard, rather than a scientist. Establish data banks of the best of the ~~3,000 regularities.

Play a cooperative game of *anything you can do, I can do better*. Your attitude should be—I have this unified theory of cognition and I've got to try to make it work on all the phenomena that Sam's unified theory works on. Theory replication must be as important as experiment replication. In truth, we should try to make it a good deal more important, so that we will gradually build up to more and more integrated theories. In this respect, do not believe that to show a unified theory of cognition wrong in some particulars is immediately fatal. Big investments demand that abandonment be a deliberate business, done only when the preponderance of evidence shows it must be done.

(6) Unified theories of cognition must be made easy to use and easy to make inferences from. This becomes especially important for theories of very wide scope and for theories that are, in important ways, embedded in simulations. We have learned in computer science the immense effort required to produce a successful programming language or a new operating system or a new statistical package. It requires much more than the lone investigator with the good idea and the initial implementation—as many lone programmers have found out to their sorrow. It requires attention to the user interface, to user documentation, to training workshops, to system support. These tasks are especially important for building up a community around a unified theory and have become a significant component of the Soar community effort.

(7) Finally, I repeat the exhortation to acquire domains of application, which can support and invigorate a theory intellectually. Building application domains, by the way, creates a community with a large investment in ease of use, and hence with a willingness to expend the effort to create the tools to make it happen.

■

So we end where we began, but with understanding.

Psychology has arrived at the possibility of unified theories of cognition—theories that gain their power by positing a single system of mechanisms that operate together to produce the full range of human cognition.

I do not say they are here. But they are within reach and we should strive to attain them.

References

Indexes

References

Addison, J. W., L. Henkin, & A. Tarski. 1972. *The Theory of Models*. Amsterdam: North-Holland.

Allport, D. A. 1975. The state of cognitive psychology. *Quarterly Journal of Experimental Psychology, 27,* 141–152.

Anderson, J. R. 1976. *Language, Memory and Thought*. Hillsdale, N.J.: Erlbaum.

—— 1978. Argument concerning representations for mental imagery. *Psychological Review, 85,* 249–277.

—— (ed.). 1981. *Cognitive Skills and Their Acquisition*. Hillsdale, N.J.: Erlbaum.

—— 1983. *The Architecture of Cognition*. Cambridge, Mass.: Harvard University Press.

—— 1984. Spreading activation. In J. R. Anderson & S. M. Kosslyn (eds.), *Tutorials in Learning and Memory*. San Francisco: Freeman.

—— 1990. The place of cognitive architectures in a rational analysis. In K. VanLehn (ed.), *Architectures for Intelligence*. Hillsdale, N.J.: Erlbaum.

Anderson, J. R., & G. Bower. 1973. *Human Associative Memory*. Washington, D.C.: Winston.

Anderson, J. R., & R. Thompson. 1989. Use of analogy in a production system architecture. In S. Vosniadou & A. Ortony (eds.), *Similarity and Analogy*. New York: Cambridge University Press.

Asch, S. E. 1956. Studies of independence and conformity: I. A minority of one against an unanimous majority. *Psychological Monographs,* vol. 70(9), Whole No. 416.

Ashby, W. R. 1952. *Design for a Brain*. New York: Wiley.

Atkinson, R. C., & J. F. Juola. 1973. Factors influencing speed and accuracy of word recognition. In S. Kornblum (ed.), *Attention and Performance IV*. New York: Academic.

Atkinson, R. C., & R. M. Shiffrin. 1968. Human memory: A proposed system and its control processes. In K. W. Spence & J. T. Spence (eds.), *The Psychology of Learning and Motivation,* vol. 2. New York: Academic.

Baars, B. J. 1986. *The Cognitive Revolution in Psychology.* New York: Guilford Press.

Bachant, J. 1988. RIME: Preliminary work toward a knowledge acquisition tool. In S. Marcus (ed.), *Automating Knowledge Acquisition for Expert Systems.* Boston: Kluwer.

Bachant, J., & J. McDermott. 1984. R1 revisited: Four years in the trenches. *AI Magazine, 5,* 21–32.

Baddeley, A. D. 1978. *Memory.* New York: Basic Books.

Baddeley, A. D., & G. Hitch. 1974. Working memory. In G. H. Bower (ed.), *The Psychology of Learning and Motivation,* vol. 8. New York: Academic.

Barclay, J. R., J. D. Bransford, & J. J. Franks. 1972. Sentence memory: A constructive versus interpretive approach. *Cognitive Psychology, 3,* 193–209.

Bartlett, F. C. 1932. *Remembering: A Study in Experimental and Social Psychology.* Cambridge, England: Cambridge University Press.

———— 1958. *Thinking: The Development of a Skill.* Cambridge, England: Cambridge University Press.

Bell, C. G., & A. Newell. 1971. *Computer Structures: Readings and Examples.* New York: McGraw-Hill.

Berliner, H., & C. Ebeling. 1989. Pattern knowledge and search: The SUPREM architecture. *Artificial Intelligence, 38,* 161–198.

Bernstein, N. 1967. *The Co-ordination and Regulation of Movements.* Oxford: Pergamon.

Bobrow, D. G. (ed.). 1985. *Qualitative Reasoning about Physical Systems.* Cambridge, Mass.: MIT Press.

Boff, K. R., L. Kaufman, & J. P. Thomas (eds.). 1986. *Handbook of Perception and Human Performance,* vols. I and II. New York: Wiley.

Boggs, M., & J. Carbonell. 1983. *A Tutorial Introduction to DYPAR-1.* Computer Science Department, Carnegie-Mellon University, Pittsburgh, Penn.

Bower, G. H., & D. Winzenz. 1969. Group structure, coding and memory for digit series. *Journal of Experimental Psychology Monograph, 80* (May, part 2), 1–17.

Brentano, F. 1874. *Psychology from an Empirical Standpoint.* Leipzig: Duncker und Humbolt. (Reprint: New York: Humanities Press, 1973.)

Bresnan, J. (ed.). 1982. *The Mental Representation of Grammatical Relations.* Cambridge, Mass.: MIT Press.

Britton, B. K., & J. B. Black (eds.). 1985. *Understanding Expository Text.* Hillsdale, N.J.: Erlbaum.

Broadbent, D. E. 1954. A mechanical model for human attention and immediate memory. *Psychological Review, 64,* 205.

———— 1958. *Perception and Communication.* New York: Pergamon Press.

Brooks, V. B. 1986. *The Neural Basis of Motor Control.* New York: Oxford University Press.

Brown, A. L. 1978. Knowing when, where, and how to remember: A problem in metacognition. In R. Glaser (ed.), *Advances in Instructional Psychology.* Hillsdale, N.J.: Erlbaum.

Brown, J. 1958. Some tests of the decay theory of immediate memory. *Quarterly Journal of Experimental Psychology, 10,* 12–21.

Brown, J. S., & R. R. Burton. 1978. Diagnostic models for procedural bugs in basic mathematical skills. *Cognitive Science, 2,* 155–192.

Brown, J. S., & K. VanLehn. 1980. Repair theory: A generative theory of bugs in procedural skills. *Cognitive Science, 4,* 379–426.

Brownston, L., R. Farrell, E. Kant, & N. Martin. 1985. *Programming Expert Systems in Ops5.* Reading, Mass.: Addison-Wesley.

Bruner, J. S., J. J. Goodnow, & G. A. Austin. 1956. *A Study of Thinking.* New York: Wiley.

Burton, R. R. 1982. Diagnosing bugs in a simple procedural skill. In D. Sleeman & J. S. Brown (eds.), *Intelligent Tutoring Systems.* London: Academic.

Bush, R. R., & F. Mosteller. 1955. *Stochastic Models of Learning.* New York: Wiley.

Card, S. K., W. K. English, & B. J. Burr. 1978. Evaluation of mouse, rate-controlled isometric joystick, step keys, and text keys for text selection on a CRT. *Ergonomics, 21,* 601–613.

Card, S., T. P. Moran, & A. Newell. 1983. *The Psychology of Human-Computer Interaction.* Hillsdale, N.J.: Erlbaum.

Carroll, J. S., & J. W. Payne (eds.). 1976. *Cognition and Social Behavior.* Hillsdale, N.J.: Erlbaum.

Case, R. 1985. *Intellectual Development: A Systematic Reinterpretation.* New York: Academic.

Cattell, R. B. 1971. *Abilities: Their Structure, Growth, and Action.* Boston: Houghton Mifflin.

Chandrasekaran, B., & S. Mittal. 1983. Deep versus compiled knowledge approaches to diagnostic problem solving. *International Journal of Man-Machine Studies, 19,* 425–436.

Chapman, I. J., & J. P. Chapman. 1959. Atmosphere effects re-examined. *Journal of Experimental Psychology, 58,* 220–226.

Chase, W. G., & H. H. Clark. 1972. Mental operations in the comparison of sentences and pictures. In L. W. Gregg (ed.), *Cognition in Learning and Memory.* New York: Wiley.

Chase, W. G., & K. A. Ericsson. 1981. Skilled memory. In J. R. Anderson (ed.), *Cognitive Skills and Their Acquisition*. Hillsdale, N.J.: Erlbaum.

Chase, W. G., & H. A. Simon. 1973. Perception in chess. *Cognitive Psychology, 4,* 55–81.

Chi, M. T. H. 1978. Knowledge structures and memory development. In R. S. Siegler (ed.), *Children's Thinking: What Develops?* Hillsdale, N.J.: Erlbaum.

Clancey, W. J., & R. Letsinger. 1981. NEOMYCIN: Reconfiguring a rule-based expert system for application to teaching. *Proceedings of the IJCAI '81.* Menlo Park, Calif.: American Association for Artificial Intelligence.

Clark, H., & E. Clark. 1977. *The Psychology of Language: An Introduction to Psycholinguistics.* New York: Harcourt Brace Jovanovich.

Cole, M., & S. Scribner. 1974. *Culture and Thought.* New York: Wiley.

Collins, A. M., & M. R. Quillian. 1969. Retrieval time from semantic memory. *Journal of Verbal Learning and Verbal Behavior, 8,* 240–247.

Conrad, R. 1964. Acoustic confusions in immediate memory. *British Journal of Psychology, 55,* 75–83.

Cooper, W. E. (ed.). 1983. *Cognitive Aspects of Skilled Typewriting.* New York: Springer-Verlag.

Costall, A., & A. Still (eds.). 1987. *Cognitive Psychology in Question.* New York: St. Martin's.

Craik, F. I. M., & R. S. Lockhart. 1972. Levels of processing: A framework for memory research. *Journal of Verbal Learning and Verbal Behavior, 11,* 671–684.

Crossman, E. R. F. W., & P. J. Goodeve. 1963. Feedback control of hand movements and Fitts' law. Paper prepared for a meeting of the Experimental Psychology Society, Oxford.

Crowder, R. G. 1976. *Principles of Learning and Memory.* Hillsdale, N.J.: Erlbaum.

——— 1982. The demise of short-term memory. *Acta Psychologica, 50,* 291–323.

D'Andrade, R. G. 1989. Culturally based reasoning. In A. Gellatly, D. Rogers, & J. A. Sloboda (eds.), *Cognition in Social Worlds.* New York: Oxford University Press.

Darwin, C. J., M. T. Turvey, & R. G. Crowder. 1972. An auditory analogue of the Sperling partial report procedure: Evidence for brief auditory storage. *Cognitive Psychology, 3,* 255–267.

De Groot, A. 1965. *Thought and Choice in Chess.* The Hague: Mouton.

Dennett, D. C. 1978. *Brainstorms.* Cambridge, Mass.: MIT Press, Bradford Books.

—— 1988a. *The Intentional Stance.* Cambridge, Mass.: MIT Press, Bradford Books.

—— 1988b. Precis of *The Intentional Stance* [with commentaries by 25 authors and final response by Dennett]. *Behavioral and Brain Sciences, 11(3),* 495–546.

Dewey, J. 1910. *How We Think.* Boston, Mass.: Heath.

Duncan, J. 1977. Response selection rules in spatial choice reaction tasks. In S. Dornic (ed.), *Attention and Performance VI.* Hillsdale, N.J.: Erlbaum.

Duncker, K. 1945. On problem solving. *Psychological Monographs, 58(5),* Whole no. 270.

Ebbinghaus, H. D., J. Flum, & W. Thomas. 1984. *Mathematical Logic.* New York: Springer-Verlag.

Ericsson, K. A., & H. A. Simon. 1984. *Protocol Analysis: Verbal Reports as Data.* Cambridge, Mass.: MIT Press.

Ericsson, K. A., & J. J. Staszewski. 1989. Skilled memory and expertise: Mechanisms of exceptional performance. In D. Klahr & K. Kotovsky (eds.), *Complex Information Processing.* Hillsdale, N.J.: Erlbaum.

Evans, J. St. B. T. 1982. *The Psychology of Deductive Reasoning.* London: Routledge & Kegan Paul.

Falmagne, R. J. (ed.). 1975. *Reasoning: Representation and Process in Children and Adults.* Hillsdale, N.J.: Erlbaum.

Feigenbaum, E. A. 1959. *An Information-Processing Theory of Verbal Learning.* Ph.D. diss., Carnegie Institute of Technology, Pittsburgh, Penn.

Feigenbaum, E. A., & H. A. Simon. 1984. EPAM-like models of recognition and learning. *Cognitive Science, 8,* 305–336.

Feldman, J. A. 1979. *A Distributed Information Processing Model of Visual Memory.* Technical Report TR52 (December). Computer Science Department, University of Rochester, Rochester, N.Y.

Feldman, J. A., & D. Ballard. 1982. Connectionist models and their properties. *Cognitive Science, 6,* 205–254.

Festinger, L. 1954. A theory of social comparison processes. *Human Relations, 7,* 117–140.

Fikes, R., & N. Nilsson. 1971. STRIPS: A new approach to the application of theorem proving to problem solving. *Artificial Intelligence, 2,* 189–208.

Fillenbaum, S. 1966. Memory for gist: Some relevant variables. *Language and Speech, 9,* 217–227.

Fiske, D. W. 1986. Specificity of method and knowledge in social science. In D. W. Fiske & R. A. Shweder (eds.), *Metatheory in Social Science.* Chicago: University of Chicago Press.

Fiske, D. W., & R. A. Shweder (eds.). 1986. *Metatheory in Social Science*. Chicago: University of Chicago Press.

Fitts, P. M. 1954. The information capacity of the human motor system in controlling the amplitude of movement. *Journal of Experimental Psychology, 47,* 381–391.

Fitts, P. M., & C. M. Seeger. 1953. S-R compatibility: Spatial characteristics of stimulus and response codes. *Journal of Experimental Psychology, 46,* 199–210.

Flynn, R. 1988. Placing Soar on the Connection Machine. *How Can Slow Components Think So Fast? Proceedings of the AAAI Mini-Symposium.* Extended abstract (March). Menlo Park, Calif.: American Association for Artificial Intelligence.

Fodor, J. A. 1983. *Modularity of Mind: An Essay on Faculty Psychology*. Cambridge, Mass.: MIT Press.

Fodor, J. A., & Z. W. Pylyshyn. 1988. Connectionism and cognitive architecture: A critical analysis. *Cognition, 28,* 3–71.

Forgy, C. L. 1981. *OPS5 User's Manual*. Technical Report (July). Computer Science Department, Carnegie-Mellon University, Pittsburgh, Penn.

Foulkes, D. 1985. *Dreaming: A Cognitive-Psychological Analysis*. Hillsdale, N.J.: Erlbaum.

Frank, K. 1959. Identification and analysis of single unit activity in the central nervous system. In J. Field (ed.), *Handbook of Physiology*. Sec. 1: *Neurophysiology*, vol. 1. Washington, D.C.: American Physiological Association.

Garey, M. R., & D. S. Johnson. 1979. *Computers and Intractability*. San Francisco: Freeman.

Garfield, J. L. (ed.). 1989. *Modularity in Knowledge Representation and Natural-Language Understanding*. Cambridge, Mass.: MIT Press.

Gelman, R., & C. R. Gallistel. 1978. *The Child's Understanding of Number*. Cambridge, Mass.: Harvard University Press.

Genesereth, M. R., & N. J. Nilsson. 1987. *Logical Foundations of Artificial Intelligence*. Los Altos, Calif.: Morgan Kaufman.

Gentner, D. R. 1983. The acquisition of typewriting skill. *Acta Psychologica, 54,* 233–248.

Gentner, D., & A. L. Stevens (eds.). 1983. *Mental Models*. Hillsdale, N.J.: Erlbaum.

Geschwind, N. 1981. Neurological knowledge and complex behavior. In D. A. Norman (ed.), *Perspectives on Cognitive Science*. Norwood, N.J.: Ablex.

Gibson, J. J. 1979. *The Ecological Approach to Visual Perception*. Boston: Houghton Mifflin.

Gilmartin, K. J., A. Newell, & H. A. Simon. 1976. A program modeling short-term memory under strategy control. In C. N. Cofer (ed.), *The Structure of Human Memory*. San Francisco: Freeman.

Glanzer, M., & A. R. Cunitz. 1966. Two storage mechanisms in free recall. *Journal of Verbal Learning and Verbal Behavior, 5*, 351–360.

Gleick, J. 1988. *Chaos: Making a New Science*. New York: Penguin.

Golding, A., P. S. Rosenbloom, & J. E. Laird. 1987. Learning general search control from outside guidance. *Proceedings of the IJCAI '87*. Menlo Park, Calif.: American Association for Artificial Intelligence.

Goldman, A. I. 1986. *Epistemology and Cognition*. Cambridge, Mass.: Harvard University Press.

Gupta, A. 1986. *Parallelism in Production Systems*. Ph.D. diss., Computer Science Department, Carnegie-Mellon University, Pittsburgh, Penn.

Guthrie, E. R. 1953. *The Psychology of Learning*. New York: Harper and Row.

Haber, R. N., & M. Hershenson. 1973. *The Psychology of Visual Perception*. New York: Holt, Rinehart and Winston.

Hart, P. E. 1982. Directions for AI in the eighties. *SIGART Newsletter, 79*, 11–16.

Henderson, L. 1982. *Orthography and Word Recognition*. New York: Academic.

Henle, M. 1962. On the relation between logic and thinking. *Psychological Review, 69*, 366–378.

Hick, W. E. 1952. On the rate of gain of information. *Quarterly Journal of Experimental Psychology, 4*, 11–26.

Hillis, W. D. 1985. *The Connection Machine*. Cambridge, Mass.: MIT Press.

Holland, J. H., K. J. Holyoak, R. E. Nisbett, & P. R. Thagard. 1987. *Induction: Processes of Inference, Learning, and Discovery*. Cambridge, Mass.: MIT Press.

Hollerbach, J. M. 1980. *An Oscillation Theory of Handwriting*. Technical Report. Artificial Intelligence Laboratory, Massachusetts Institute of Technology, Cambridge, Mass.

Hull, C. L. 1943. *Principles of Behavior*. New York: Appleton-Century.

Inhelder, B., & J. Piaget. 1958. *The Growth of Logical Thinking from Childhood to Adolescence*. New York: Basic Books.

Jacob, F. 1973. *The Logic of Life: A History of Heredity*. New York: Random House, Pantheon Books.

———— 1982. *The Possible and the Actual*. Seattle: University of Washington Press.

Jerison, H. J. 1973. *Evolution of the Brain and Intelligence*. New York: Academic.

John, B. E. 1988. *Contributions to Engineering Models of Human-*

Computer Interaction. Ph.D. diss., Psychology Department, Carnegie-Mellon University, Pittsburgh, Penn.

John, B. E., & A. Newell. 1987. Predicting the time to recall computer command abbreviations. *Proceedings of CHI'87 Human Factors in Computing Systems* (April). New York: Association for Computing Machinery.

—— 1989. Cumulating the science of HCI: From S-R compatibility to transcription typing. *Proceedings of CHI'89 Human Factors in Computing Systems* (May). New York: Association for Computing Machinery.

John, B. E., P. S. Rosenbloom, & A. Newell. 1985. A theory of stimulus-response compatibility applied to human-computer interaction. *Proceedings of CHI'85 Human Factors in Computer Systems* (April). New York: Association for Computing Machinery.

Johnson, D. M. 1955. *The Psychology of Thought and Judgment.* New York: Harper.

Johnson-Laird, P. 1983. *Mental Models.* Cambridge, Mass.: Harvard University Press.

—— 1988a. *The Computer and the Mind: An Introduction to Cognitive Science.* Cambridge, Mass.: Harvard University Press.

—— 1988b. Reasoning by rule or model? *Proceedings, Cognitive Science Annual Conference—1988* (August), Montreal. Cognitive Science Society.

Johnson-Laird, P. N., & B. G. Bara. 1984. Syllogistic inference. *Cognition, 16,* 1–61.

Just, M. A., & P. A. Carpenter. 1987. *The Psychology of Reading and Language Comprehension.* Boston: Allyn and Bacon.

Kahneman, D., P. Slovic, & A. Tversky (eds.). 1982. *Judgment under Uncertainty: Heuristics and Biases.* Cambridge, England: Cambridge University Press.

Kant, E., & A. Newell. 1983. An automatic algorithm designer: An initial implementation. *Proceedings of the AAAI '83.* Menlo Park, Calif.: American Association for Artificial Intelligence.

Keele, S. W. 1968. Movement control in skilled motor performance. *Psychological Bulletin, 70,* 387–403.

—— 1986. Motor control. In K. R. Boff, L. Kaufman, & J. P. Thomas (eds.), *Handbook of Perception and Human Performance,* vol. 2. New York: Wiley.

Kelso, J. A. S. 1977. Motor control mechanisms underlying human movement reproduction. *Journal of Experimental Psychology: Human Perception and Performance, 3,* 529–543.

—— (ed.). 1982. *Human Motor Behavior: An Introduction.* Hillsdale, N.J.: Erlbaum.

Kendler, H. H. 1961. Problems in problem solving research. In *Current*

Trends in Psychological Theory: A Bicentennial Program. Pittsburgh, Penn.: University of Pittsburgh Press.

Kieras, D. E., & M. A. Just (eds.). 1984. *New Methods in Reading Comprehension Research.* Hillsdale, N.J.: Erlbaum.

Kintsch, W., & J. G. Greeno. 1982. *Understanding and Solving Word Arithmetic Problems.* Technical Report. Department of Psychology, University of Colorado, Boulder, Colo.

Klahr, D., & J. G. Wallace. 1976. *Cognitive Development: An Information Processing View.* Hillsdale, N.J.: Erlbaum.

Kolers, P. A. 1975. Memorial consequences of automatized encoding. *Journal of Experimental Psychology: Human Learning and Memory, 1,* 689–701.

———— 1976. Reading a year later. *Journal of Experimental Psychology: Human Learning and Memory, 2,* 554–565.

Kolers, P. A., & J. L. Roediger III. 1984. Procedures of mind. *Journal of Verbal Learning and Verbal Behavior, 23,* 425–449.

Kolers, P. A., & W. E. Smythe. 1984. Symbol manipulation: Alternatives to the computational view of mind. *Journal of Verbal Learning and Verbal Behavior, 23,* 289–314.

Kosslyn, S. M. 1980. *Image and Mind.* Cambridge, Mass.: Harvard University Press.

Kroll, N. E. A., T. Parks, S. R. Parkinson, S. L. Bieber, & A. L. Johnson. 1970. Short term memory while shadowing: Recall of visually and of aurally presented letters. *Journal of Experimental Psychology, 85,* 220–224.

Kuhn, T. 1962. *The Structure of Scientific Revolutions.* Chicago: University of Chicago Press.

Laberge, D., & S. J. Samuels. 1974. Toward a theory of automatic information processing in reading. *Cognitive Psychology, 6,* 293–323.

Laboratory of Comparative Human Cognition. 1982. Culture and intelligence. In R. J. Sternberg (ed.), *Handbook of Human Intelligence.* New York: Cambridge University Press.

Lachman, R., J. L. Lachman, & E. C. Butterfield. 1979. *Cognitive Psychology and Information Processing: An Introduction.* Hillsdale, N.J.: Erlbaum.

Laird, J. E. 1984. *Universal Subgoaling.* Ph.D. diss., Computer Science Department, Carnegie-Mellon University, Pittsburgh, Penn.

———— 1986. *Soar User's Manual: Version 4.0.* Intelligent Systems Laboratory, Xerox Palo Alto Research Center, Palo Alto, Calif.

———— 1988. Recovery from incorrect knowledge in Soar. *Proceedings of the AAAI '88: National Conference on Artificial Intelligence.* Menlo Park, Calif.: American Association for Artificial Intelligence.

Laird, J. E., A. Newell, & P. S. Rosenbloom. 1987. Soar: An architecture for general intelligence. *Artificial Intelligence, 33,* 1–64.

Laird, J. E., P. S. Rosenbloom, & A. Newell. 1984. Towards chunking as a general learning mechanism. *Proceedings of the AAAI '84: National Conference on Artificial Intelligence.* Menlo Park, Calif.: American Association for Artificial Intelligence.

——— 1986. *Universal Subgoaling and Chunking: The Automatic Generation and Learning of Goal Hierarchies.* Boston: Kluwer.

Laird, J. E., E. S. Yager, C. M. Tuck, & M. Hucka. 1989. Learning in tele-autonomous systems using Soar. *Proceedings of the NASA Conference on Space Telerobotics.* Pasadena, Calif.: Jet Propulsion Laboratory, California Institute of Technology.

Lakatos, I. 1970. Falsification and the methodology of scientific research programmes. In I. Lakatos & A. Musgrave (eds.), *Criticism and the Growth of Knowledge.* Cambridge, England: Cambridge University Press.

Lakoff, G. 1987. *Women, Fire, and Dangerous Things: What Categories Reveal about the Mind.* Chicago: University of Chicago Press.

Landauer, T. K. 1962. Rate of implicit speech. *Perceptual and Motor Skills, 15,* 696.

Levesque, H. J. 1986. Making believers out of computers. *Artificial Intelligence, 30,* 81–108.

Lewis, R. L., A. Newell, & T. A. Polk. 1989. Toward a Soar theory of taking instructions for immediate reasoning tasks. *Proceedings, Cognitive Science Annual Conference—1989* (August), University of Michigan, Ann Arbor. Cognitive Science Society.

Loveland, D. W. 1978. *Automated Theory Proving: A Logical Basis.* New York: North-Holland.

Luce, R. D. 1986. *Response Times: Their Role in Inferring Elementary Mental Organization.* New York: Oxford University Press.

Luchins, A. S. 1942. Mechanization in problem solving. *Psychological Monographs, 54(6),* no. 248.

MacKay, D. G. 1987. *The Organization of Perception and Action.* New York: Springer-Verlag.

MacLean, P. D. 1970. The triune brain. In F. O. Schmitt (ed.), *The Neurosciences: The Second Study Program.* New York: Rockefeller University Press.

MacWhinney, B. 1987a. The competition model. In B. MacWhinney (ed.), *Mechanisms of Language Acquisition.* Hillsdale, N.J.: Erlbaum.

——— (ed.). 1987b. *Mechanisms of Language Acquisition.* Hillsdale, N.J.: Erlbaum.

Maes, P., & D. Nardi (eds.). 1988. *Meta-Level Architectures and Reflection.* Amsterdam: Elsevier Science Publishers B.V. (North-Holland).

Mandler, G. 1985. *Cognitive Psychology.* Hillsdale, N.J.: Erlbaum.

Marslen-Wilson, W., & L. K. Tyler. 1980. The temporal structure of spoken language understanding. *Cognition, 8,* 1–71.

McCarthy, J., & P. J. Hayes. 1969. Some philosophical problems from the standpoint of artificial intelligence. In B. Meltzer & D. Michie (eds.), *Machine Intelligence,* vol. 4. Edinburgh: Edinburgh University Press.

McClelland, J. L., D. E. Rumelhart, & the PDP Research Group. 1986. *Parallel Distributed Processing: Explorations in the Microstructures of Cognition.* Vol. 2: *Psychological and Biological Models.* Cambridge, Mass.: MIT Press.

McCulloch, W. S. 1965. *Embodiments of Mind.* Cambridge, Mass.: MIT Press.

McDermott, J. 1982. R1: A rule based configurer of computer systems. *Artificial Intelligence, 19,* 39–88.

McLean, R. S., & L. W. Gregg. 1967. Effects of induced chunking on temporal aspects of serial recitation. *Journal of Experimental Psychology, 74,* 455–459.

Merton, R. K. 1973. *The Sociology of Science: Theoretical and Empirical Investigations.* Chicago: University of Chicago Press.

Meyer, D. E., & R. W. Schvaneveldt. 1971. Facilitation in recognizing pairs of words: Evidence of a dependence between retrieval operations. *Journal of Experimental Psychology, 90,* 227–234.

Miller, G. A. 1956. The magic number seven, plus or minus two: Some limits on our capacity for processing information. *Psychological Review, 63,* 81–97.

Minsky, M. 1967. *Computation: Finite and Infinite Machines.* Englewood Cliffs, N.J.: Prentice-Hall.

—— 1975. A framework for the representation of knowledge. In P. Winston (ed.), *The Psychology of Computer Vision.* New York: McGraw-Hill.

—— 1986. *The Society of Minds.* New York: Simon and Schuster.

Mintzberg, H. 1973. *The Nature of Managerial Work.* New York: Harper and Row.

Mitchell, T. M. 1978. *Version Spaces: An Approach to Concept Learning.* Ph.D. diss., Computer Science Department, Stanford University, Stanford, Calif.

Mitchell, T. M., R. M. Keller, & S. T. Kedar-Cabelli. 1986. Explanation-based generalization: A unifying view. *Machine Learning, 1,* 47–80.

Morehead, A. H., & G. Mott-Smith. 1959. *Hoyle Up-to-date.* New York: Grosset & Dunlap.

Morin, R. E., and B. Forrin. 1962. Mixing two types of S-R associations in a choice reaction time task. *Journal of Experimental Psychology, 64,* 137–141.

Murdock, B. 1974. *Human Memory: Theory and Data.* Hillsdale, N.J.: Erlbaum.

Neisser, U. 1967. *Cognitive Psychology.* New York: Appleton-Century-Crofts.

———— 1974. Review of *Visual Information Processing*, edited by W. G. Chase. *Science, 183,* 402–403.

———— 1979. The concept of intelligence. *Intelligence, 3,* 217–227.

Newell, A. 1962. Some problems of basic organization in problem-solving programs. In M. C. Yovits, G. T. Jacobi, & G. D. Goldstein (eds.), *Self Organizing Systems.* Washington, D.C.: Spartan.

———— 1967. *Studies in Problem Solving: Subject 3 on the Cryptarithmetic Task: DONALD + GERALD = ROBERT.* Technical Report. Computer Science Department, Carnegie Institute of Technology, Pittsburgh, Penn.

———— 1970. Remarks on the relationship between artificial intelligence and cognitive psychology. In R. Banerji & J. D. Mesarovic (eds.), *Theoretical Approaches to Non-Numerical Problem Solving.* New York: Springer-Verlag.

———— 1973a. You can't play 20 questions with nature and win: Projective comments on the papers of this symposium. In W. G. Chase (ed.), *Visual Information Processing.* New York: Academic.

———— 1973b. Production systems: Models of control structures. In W. C. Chase (ed.), *Visual Information Processing.* New York: Academic.

———— 1980a. Physical symbol systems. *Cognitive Science, 4,* 135–183.

———— 1980b. Harpy, production systems and human cognition. In R. Cole (ed.), *Perception and Production of Fluent Speech.* Hillsdale, N.J.: Erlbaum.

———— 1980c. Reasoning, problem solving and decision processes: The problem space as a fundamental category. In R. Nickerson (ed.), *Attention and Performance VIII.* Hillsdale, N.J.: Erlbaum.

———— 1982. The knowledge level. *Artificial Intelligence, 18,* 87–127.

———— 1983. The heuristic of George Polya and its relation to artificial intelligence. In R. Groner, M. Groner, & W. F. Bischof (eds.), *Methods of Heuristics.* Hillsdale, N.J.: Erlbaum.

———— 1988. The intentional stance and the knowledge level: Comments on Daniel Dennett, *The Intentional Stance. Behavioral and Brain Sciences, 11(3),* 520–522.

———— 1989. Putting it all together. In D. Klahr & K. Kotovsky (eds.), *Complex Information Processing.* Hillsdale, N.J.: Erlbaum.

———— 1990. Metaphor for mind, theories of mind, should the humanities mind? In J. Sheehan & M. Sosna (eds.), *Boundaries of Humanity: Humans, Animals and Machines.* Berkeley, Calif.: University of California Press.

Newell, A., & S. K. Card. 1985. The prospects for psychological science in human-computer interaction. *Human-Computer Interaction, 1,* 209–242.

Newell, A., & P. Rosenbloom. 1981. Mechanisms of skill acquisition and the law of practice. In J. R. Anderson (ed.), *Cognitive Skills and Their Acquisition.* Hillsdale, N.J.: Erlbaum.

Newell, A., P. Rosenbloom, & J. Laird. 1989. Symbolic architectures for cognition. In M. Posner (ed.), *Foundations of Cognitive Science.* Cambridge, Mass.: MIT Press, Bradford Books.

Newell, A., J. C. Shaw, & H. A. Simon. 1958. Elements of a theory of human problem solving. *Psychological Review, 65,* 151–166.

Newell, A., & H. A. Simon. 1963. GPS, a program that simulates human thought. In E. A. Feigenbaum & J. Feldman (eds.), *Computers and Thought.* New York: McGraw-Hill.

—— 1972. *Human Problem Solving.* Englewood Cliffs, N.J.: Prentice-Hall.

—— 1976. Computer science as empirical inquiry: Symbols and search. *Communications of the ACM, 19,* 113–126.

Nickerson, R. S. 1972. Binary-classification reaction time: A review of some studies of human information-processing capabilities. *Psychonomic Monograph Supplements, 4,* 275–318.

Nilsson, N. 1980. *Principles of Artificial Intelligence.* Palo Alto, Calif.: Tioga.

Osgood, C. E. 1949. The similarity paradox in human learning: A resolution. *Psychological Review, 56,* 132–143.

Peters, S., & R. Ritchie. 1973. On the generative power of transformational grammars. *Information and Control, 18,* 483–501.

Peterson, L. R., & M. J. Peterson. 1959. Short-term retention of individual verbal items. *Journal of Experimental Psychology, 58,* 193–198.

Pfefferkorn, C. E. 1971. *Computer Design of Equipment Layouts Using the Design Problem Solver DPS.* Ph.D. diss., Computer Science Department, Carnegie-Mellon University, Pittsburgh, Penn.

Piaget, J. 1977. *The Essential Piaget: An Interpretive Reference and Guide.* Edited by H. E. Gruber & J. J. Voneche. New York: Basic Books.

Pitz, G. F., & N. J. Sachs. 1984. Judgment and decisions: Theory and application. *Annual Review of Psychology, 35,* 139–163.

Polk, T. A., & R. L. Lewis. 1989. Toward a unified theory of immediate reasoning in SOAR. *Proceedings, Cognitive Science Annual Conference—1989* (August), Montreal. Cognitive Science Society.

Polk, T. A., & A. Newell. 1988. Modeling human syllogistic reasoning in Soar. *Proceedings, Cognitive Science Annual Conference—1988* (August), Montreal. Cognitive Science Society.

Polson, P. G., & D. E. Kieras. 1985. A quantitative model of learning and performance of text editing knowledge. *Proceedings of CHI '85 Human Factors in Computer Systems* (April). New York: Association for Computing Machinery.

Polson, P. G., E. Muncher, & G. Engelbeck. 1986. A test of a common elements theory of transfer. *Proceedings of CHI '86 Human Factors in Computer Systems* (April). New York: Association for Computing Machinery.

Polya, G. 1945. *How to Solve It*. Princeton, N.J.: Princeton University Press.

Polyani, M. 1958. *Personal Knowledge: Toward a Post-critical Philosophy*. Chicago: University of Chicago Press.

Popper, K. R. 1959. *The Logic of Scientific Discovery*. New York: Basic Books.

Posner, M. I. 1978. *Chronometric Explorations of Mind*. Hillsdale, N.J.: Erlbaum.

Posner, M. I., S. J. Boies, W. H. Eichelman, & R. L. Taylor. 1979. Retention of visual and name codes of single letters. *Journal of Experimental Psychology, 79*, 1–16.

Posner, M. I., & C. R. R. Snyder. 1975. Facilitation and inhibition in the processing of signals. In P. M. A. Rabitt & S. Dornic (eds.), *Attention and Performance V*. New York: Academic.

Postman, L. 1961. The present status of interference theory. In C. N. Cofer (ed.), *Verbal Learning and Verbal Behavior*. New York: McGraw-Hill.

Pylyshyn, Z. W. 1984. *Computation and Cognition: Toward a Foundation for Cognitive Science*. Cambridge, Mass.: MIT Press, Bradford Books.

———— (ed.). 1987. *The Robot's Dilemma: The Frame Problem in Artificial Intelligence*. Norwood, N.J.: Ablex.

Quillian, R. 1968. Semantic memory. In M. Minsky (ed.), *Semantic Information Processing*. Cambridge, Mass.: MIT Press.

Rall, W. 1977. Core conductor theory and cable properties of neurons. In E. Kandel (ed.), *Handbook of Neurophysiology: The Nervous System: Cellular Biology of Neurons*. Bethesda, Md.: American Physiological Society.

Ratcliff, R. 1985. Theoretical interpretations of the speed and accuracy of positive and negative responses. *Psychological Review, 92*, 212–225.

Reitman, W. 1965. *Cognition and Thought*. New York: Wiley.

Rescorla, R. A. 1988. Pavlovian conditioning: It's not what you think it is. *American Psychologist, 43*, 151–160.

Revlin, R., & R. E. Mayer (eds.). 1978. *Human Reasoning*. Washington, D.C.: Winston & Sons.

Rich, E. 1983. *Artificial Intelligence*. New York: McGraw-Hill.

Richman, H. B., & H. A. Simon. 1989. Context effects in letter perception: Comparison of two theories. *Psychological Review, 96*, 417–432.

Rosch, E., & B. B. Lloyd (eds.). 1978. *Cognition and Categorization*. Hillsdale, N.J.: Erlbaum.

Rosenbaum, D. A. 1988. Successive approximations to a model of human motor programming. In G. H. Bower (ed.), *The Psychology of Learning and Motivation,* vol. 21. New York: Academic.

Rosenbleuth, A., N. Weiner, & J. Bigelow. 1943. Behavior, purpose, and teleology. *Philosophy of Science, 10,* 18–24.

Rosenbloom, P. S. 1983. *The Chunking of Goal Hierarchies: A Model of Practice and Stimulus-Response Compatibility.* Ph.D. diss., Computer Science Department, Carnegie-Mellon University, Pittsburgh, Penn.

———— 1989. A symbolic goal-oriented perspective on connectionism and Soar. In R. Pfeifer, Z. Schreter, F. Fogelman-Souile, & L. Steels (eds.), *Connectionism in Perspective.* Amsterdam: Elsevier.

Rosenbloom, P. S., & J. E. Laird. 1986. Mapping explanation-based generalization onto Soar. *Proceedings of AAAI '86.* Los Altos, Calif.: Morgan Kaufman.

Rosenbloom, P. S., J. E. Laird, J. McDermott, A. Newell, & E. Orciuch. 1985. R1-Soar: An experiment in knowledge-intensive programming in a problem solving architecture. *Pattern Analysis and Machine Intelligence, 7,* 561–569.

Rosenbloom, P. S., J. E. Laird, & A. Newell. 1987. Knowledge-level learning in Soar. *Proceedings of AAAI '87.* Los Altos, Calif.: Morgan Kaufman.

———— 1988a. Meta-levels in Soar. In P. Maes & D. Nardi (eds.), *Meta-Level Architectures and Reflection.* Amsterdam: North-Holland.

———— 1988b. The chunking of skill and knowledge. In H. Bouma & B. A. G. Elsendoorn (eds.), *Working Models of Human Perception.* London: Academic.

Rosenbloom, P. S., & A. Newell. 1986. The chunking of goal hierarchies: A generalized model of practice. In R. S. Michalski, J. Carbonell, & T. Mitchell (eds.), *Machine Learning: An Artificial Intelligence Approach II.* Los Altos, Calif.: Morgan Kaufman.

———— 1987. Learning by chunking: A production-system model of practice. In D. Klahr, P. Langley, & R. Neches (eds.), *Production System Models of Learning and Development.* Cambridge, Mass.: MIT Press.

Rosenbloom, P. S., A. Newell, & J. E. Laird. 1990. Toward the knowledge level in Soar: The role of the architecture in the use of knowledge. In K. VanLehn (ed.), *Architectures for Intelligence.* Hillsdale, N.J.: Erlbaum.

Rumelhart, D. E., J. L. McClelland, & the PDP Research Group. 1986. *Parallel Distributed Processing: Explorations in the Microstructures of Cognition.* Vol. 1: *Foundations.* Cambridge, Mass.: MIT Press.

Sacerdoti, E. D. 1974. Planning in a hierarchy of abstraction spaces. *Artificial Intelligence, 5,* 115–135.

———— 1977. *A Structure for Plans and Behavior.* New York: Elsevier.

Salthouse, T. 1986. Perceptual, cognitive, and motoric aspects of transcription typing. *Psychological Bulletin, 99,* 303–319.

Saltzman, E. L., & J. A. S. Kelso. 1987. Skilled actions: A task-dynamic approach. *Psychological Review, 94,* 84–106.

Sauers, R., & R. Farrell. 1982. *GRAPES User's Manual.* Psychology Department, Carnegie-Mellon University, Pittsburgh, Penn.

Schank, R. C., & C. K. Riesbeck (eds.). 1981. *Inside Computer Understanding.* Hillsdale, N.J.: Erlbaum.

Schmidt, R. A. 1982. *Motor Control and Learning.* Champaign, Ill.: Human Kinetics Publishers.

Schneider, W., & R. M. Shiffrin. 1977. Controlled and automatic human information processing: I. Detection, search, and attention. *Psychological Review, 84,* 1–190.

Sedgewick, R. 1983. *Algorithms.* Reading, Mass.: Addison-Wesley.

Seibel, R. 1963. Discrimination reaction time for a 1023-alternative task. *Journal of Experimental Psychology, 66,* 215–226.

Sells, P. 1987. *Lectures on Contemporary Syntactic Theories: An Introduction to Government-Binding Theory, Generalized Phrase Structure Grammar, and Lexical-Functional Grammar.* Stanford, Calif.: Center for the Study of Language and Information.

Shannon, C. E. 1949. Communication in the presence of noise. *Proceedings of the Institute of Radio Engineers, 37,* 10–21.

Shaw, R., and J. Bransford (eds.). 1977. Introduction: Psychological approaches to the problem of knowledge. In R. Shaw and J. Bransford (eds.), *Perceiving, Acting, and Knowing: Toward an Ecological Psychology.* Hillsdale, N.J.: Erlbaum.

Shepard, R. N. 1987. Toward a universal law of generalization of psychological science. *Science, 237,* 1317–1323.

Shepard, R. N., & J. Metzler. 1971. Mental rotation of three-dimensional objects. *Science, 171,* 701–703.

Shepherd, G. M. 1979. *The Synaptic Organization of the Brain,* 2nd ed. New York: Oxford University Press.

Sherrington, C. S. 1906. *The Integrative Action of the Nervous System.* The Yale Silliman Lectures. New York: Charles Scribner & Sons.

Shiffrin, R. M., & W. Schneider. 1977. Controlled and automatic human information processing: II. Perceptual learning, automatic attending, and a general theory. *Psychological Review, 84,* 127–190.

Shortliffe, E. H. 1976. *Computer-based Medical Consultations: MYCIN.* New York: American Elsevier.

Siegler, R. S. 1976. Three aspects of cognitive development. *Cognitive Psychology, 8,* 481–520.

—— 1986. *Children's Thinking.* Englewood Cliffs, N.J.: Prentice-Hall.

———— 1987. The perils of averaging data over strategies: An example from children's addition. *Journal of Experimental Psychology: General, 116,* 250–264.

Simon, H. A. 1962. The architecture of complexity. *Proceedings of the American Philosophical Society, 26,* 467–482.

———— 1974. How big is a chunk? *Science, 183,* 482–488.

———— 1975. The functional equivalence of problem solving skills. *Cognitive Psychology, 8,* 268–288.

———— 1989. *Models of Thought,* vol. 2. New Haven: Yale University Press.

Simon, H. A., & E. A. Feigenbaum. 1964. An information-processing theory of some effects of similarity, familiarization, and meaningfulness in verbal learning. *Journal of Verbal Learning and Verbal Behavior, 3,* 385–396.

Simon, H. A., & K. Gilmartin. 1973. A simulation of memory for chess positions. *Cognitive Psychology, 5,* 29–46.

Singley, M. K., & J. R. Anderson. 1989. *The Transfer of Cognitive Skill.* Cambridge, Mass.: Harvard University Press.

Small, S. 1979. Word expert parsing. *Proceedings of the 17th Annual Meeting of the Association for Computational Linguistics* (August). Association of Computational Linguistics. La Jolla, Calif.: University of California at San Diego.

Smith, D. R. 1985. Top-down synthesis of divide-and-conquer algorithms. *Artificial Intelligence, 27,* 43–49.

Smolensky, P. 1988. On the proper treatment of connectionism [with commentaries]. *Brain and Behavioral Science, 11,* 1–74.

Snoddy, G. S. 1926. Learning and stability. *Journal of Applied Psychology, 10,* 1–36.

Spearman, C. 1927. *The Abilities of Man.* New York: Macmillan.

Sperling, G. 1960. The information available in brief visual presentations. *Psychological Monographs, 74(11),* no. 498.

Stanfill, C., & D. Waltz. 1986. Toward memory-based reasoning. *Communications of the ACM, 29,* 1213–1228.

Steele, G. L., Jr. 1980. *The Definition and Implementation of a Computer Programming Language Based on Constraints.* Ph.D. diss., Massachusetts Institute of Technology, Cambridge, Mass.

Steier, D. M. 1987. CYPRESS-Soar: A case study in search and learning in algorithm design. *Proceedings of the IJCAI '87,* 327–330. International Joint Conference on Artificial Intelligence, Milan, Italy.

———— 1989. *Automating Algorithm Design within an Architecture for General Intelligence.* Ph.D. diss., Computer Science Department, Carnegie-Mellon University, Pittsburgh, Penn.

Steier, D. M., & E. Kant. 1985. The roles of execution and analysis in algorithm design. *IEEE Transactions on Software Engineering, SE-11*, 1375–1386.

Steier, D. E., J. E. Laird, A. Newell, P. S. Rosenbloom, R. A. Flynn, A. Golding, T. A. Polk, O. G. Shivers, A. Unruh, & G. R. Yost. 1987. Varieties of learning in Soar: 1987. *Proceedings of the Fourth International Workshop on Machine Learning* (June). Los Altos, Calif.: Morgan Kaufman.

Steier, D., & A. Newell. 1988. Integrating multiple sources of knowledge into Designer-Soar, an automatic algorithm designer. *Proceedings of the AAAI '88* (August). Menlo Park, Calif.: American Association of Artificial Intelligence.

Stelmach, G. E. (ed.). 1976. *Motor Control: Issues and Trends.* New York: Academic.

――― (ed.). 1978. *Information Processing in Motor Control and Learning.* New York: Academic.

Stelmach, G. E., & J. Requin (eds.). 1980. *Tutorials in Motor Behavior.* Amsterdam: North-Holland.

Sternberg, R. J. 1985a. Human intelligence: The model is the message. *Science, 230*, 1111–1118.

――― 1985b. *Beyond IQ: A Triarchic Theory of Human Intelligence.* Cambridge, England: Cambridge University Press.

Sternberg, R. J., & D. K. Detterman (eds.). 1986. *What Is Intelligence?* Norwood, N.J.: Ablex.

Sternberg, S. 1966. High-speed scanning in human memory. *Science, 153*, 652–654.

――― 1969. The discovery of processing stages: Extensions of Donders' method. In W. G. Koster (ed.), *Attention and Performance II.* Amsterdam: North-Holland.

――― 1975. Memory scanning: New findings and current controversies. *Quarterly Journal of Experimental Psychology, 27*, 1–32.

Suchman, L. A. 1988. *Plans and Situated Action: The Problem of Human-Machine Communication.* New York: Cambridge University Press.

Suls, J. M., & R. L. Miller (eds.). 1977. *Social Comparison Processes: Theoretical and Empirical Perspectives.* New York: Washington Hemisphere.

Tambe, M., D. Kalp, A. Gupta, C. L. Forgy, B. Milnes, & A. Newell. 1988. Soar/PSM-E: Investigating match parallelism in learning production systems. *Proceedings of the ACM Conference on Parallel Processing.* New York: Association for Computing Machinery.

Tambe, M., & A. Newell. 1988. Some chunks are expensive. *Proceedings of the Fifth International Conference on Machine Learning.* Los Altos, Calif.: Morgan Freeman.

Tambe, M., & P. S. Rosenbloom. 1989. Eliminating expensive chunks by restricting expressiveness. *Proceedings of the IJCAI '89*. International Joint Conference on Artificial Intelligence, Detroit.

Tasaki, I. 1959. Conduction of the nerve impulse. In J. Field (ed.), *Handbook of Physiology*. Sec. 1: *Neurophysiology*, vol. 1. Washington, D.C.: American Physiological Association.

Teichner, W. H., & M. J. Krebs. 1974. Visual search for simple targets. *Psychological Bulletin, 81*, 15–28.

Teichner, W. H., & J. B. Mocharnuk. 1979. Visual search for complex targets. *Human Factors, 21*, 259–275.

Thorndike, E. L. 1903. *Educational Psychology*. New York: Lemke and Buechner.

Tinbergen, N. 1960. *The Herring Gull's World*. New York: Basic Books.

——— 1969. *The Study of Instinct*. New York: Oxford University Press.

Toews, J. E. 1987. Intellectual history after the linguistic turn: The autonomy of meaning and the irreducibility of experience. *American Historical Review, 92*, 879–907.

Townsend, J. T. 1974. Issues and models concerning the processing of a finite number of inputs. In B. H. Kantowitz (ed.), *Human Information Processing: Tutorials in Performance and Cognition*. Hillsdale, N.J.: Erlbaum.

Townsend, J. T., & F. G. Ashby. 1983. *Stochastic Modeling of Elementary Psychological Processes*. Cambridge, England: Cambridge University Press.

Treisman, A. 1986. Properties, parts and objects. In K. R. Boff, L. Kaufman, & J. P. Thomas (eds.), *Handbook of Perception and Human Performance*, vol. 2. New York: Wiley.

Tulving, E. 1969. Episodic and semantic memory. In E. Tulving & W. Donaldson (eds.), *Organization of Memory*. New York: Academic.

——— 1983. *Elements of Episodic Memory*. New York: Oxford University Press.

Underwood, B. J., & R. W. Schulz. 1960. *Meaningfulness and Verbal Learning*. New York: Lippincott.

Unruh, A., & P. S. Rosenbloom. 1989. Abstraction in problem solving and learning. *Proceedings of the IJCAI '89*. International Joint Conference on Artificial Intelligence, Detroit.

Unruh, A., P. S. Rosenbloom, & J. E. Laird. 1987. Dynamic abstraction problem solving in Soar. *Proceedings of the Third Annual Conference on Aerospace Applications of Artificial Intelligence*. Dayton, Ohio.

van de Brug, A., P. S. Rosenbloom, & A. Newell. 1986. *Some Experiments with R1-Soar*. Technical Report. Computer Science Department, Carnegie-Mellon University, Pittsburgh, Penn.

Van Dijk, T. A., & W. Kintsch. 1983. *Strategies of Discourse Comprehension*. Orlando, Fla.: Academic.

VanLehn, K. 1983. *Felicity Conditions for Human Skill Acquisition: Validating an AI-based Theory*. Unpublished. Xerox Palo Alto Research Center, Palo Alto, Calif.

VanLehn, K., & S. Garlick. 1987. Cirrus: An automated protocol analysis tool. In P. Langley (ed.), *Proceedings of the Fourth International Workshop on Machine Learning*. Los Altos, Calif.: Morgan Kaufman.

Vinacke, W. E. 1952. *The Psychology of Thinking*. New York: McGraw-Hill.

Ware, W. H. 1962. *Digital Computer Technology and Design*, 2 vols. New York: Wiley.

Washington, R., & P. S. Rosenbloom. 1988. *Neomycin-Soar: Applying Search and Learning to Diagnosis*. Technical Report. Knowledge-Systems Laboratory, Stanford University, Stanford, Calif.

Wason, P. C., & P. N. Johnson-Laird. 1972. *Psychology of Reasoning: Structure and Content*. Cambridge, Mass.: Harvard University Press.

Waterman, D. A., & F. Hayes-Roth (eds.). 1978. *Pattern Directed Inference Systems*. New York: Academic.

Watson, J. B. 1913. Psychology as a behaviorist views it. *Psychological Review, 20*, 158–177.

White, L. A. 1949. *The Science of Culture: A Study of Man and Civilization*. New York: Grove Press.

Wickens, C. D., & J. M. Flach. 1988. Information processing. In E. L. Wiener & D. C. Nagel (eds.), *Human Factors in Aviation*. San Diego, Calif.: Academic.

Wickens, D. D. 1970. Encoding categories of words: An empirical approach to meaning. *Psychological Review, 77*, 1–15.

Wilkins, M. C. 1928. The effect of changed material on the ability to do formal syllogistic reasoning. *Archives of Psychology, 16*, no. 102.

Wilson, E. O. 1975. *Sociobiology: The New Synthesis*. Cambridge, Mass.: Harvard University Press, Belknap Press.

Woodworth, R. S. 1938. *Experimental Psychology*. New York: Holt, Rinehart and Winston.

Woodworth, R. S., & H. Schlosberg. 1954. *Experimental Psychology*, rev. ed. New York: Holt, Rinehart and Winston.

Woodworth, R. S., & S. B. Sells. 1935. An atmosphere effect in formal syllogistic reasoning. *Journal of Experimental Psychology, 18*, 451–460.

Yost, G. 1988. *TAQ Reference Manual* (March). Soar Project, Computer Science Department, Carnegie-Mellon University, Pittsburgh, Penn.

Name Index

Subject Index